University Casebook Series

December, 1981

ACCOUNTING AND THE LAW, Fourth Edition (1978), with Problems Pamphlet (Successor to Dohr, Phillips, Thompson & Warren)

George C. Thompson, Professor, Columbia University Graduate School of Business.
Robert Whitman, Professor of Law, University of Connecticut.
Ellis L. Phillips, Jr., Member of the New York Bar.
William C. Warren, Professor of Law Emeritus, Columbia University.

ACCOUNTING FOR LAWYERS, MATERIALS ON (1980)

David R. Herwitz, Professor of Law, Harvard University.

ADMINISTRATIVE LAW, Seventh Edition (1979), with 1979 Problems Supplement (Supplement edited in association with Paul R. Verkuil, Dean and Professor of Law, Tulane University)

Walter Gellhorn, University Professor Emeritus, Columbia University.
Clark Byse, Professor of Law, Harvard University.
Peter L. Strauss, Professor of Law, Columbia University.

ADMIRALTY, Second Edition (1978), with Statute and Rule Supplement

Jo Desha Lucas, Professor of Law, University of Chicago.

ADVOCACY, see also Lawyering Process

ADVOCACY, INTRODUCTION TO, Third Edition (1981)

Board of Student Advisers, Harvard Law School.

AGENCY, see also Enterprise Organization

AGENCY–ASSOCIATIONS–EMPLOYMENT–PARTNERSHIPS, Second Edition (1977)

Abridgement from Conard, Knauss & Siegel's Enterprise Organization.

ANTITRUST AND REGULATORY ALTERNATIVES (1977), Fifth Edition

Louis B. Schwartz, Professor of Law, University of Pennsylvania.
John J. Flynn, Professor of Law, University of Utah.

ANTITRUST SUPPLEMENT—SELECTED STATUTES AND RELATED MATERIALS (1977)

John J. Flynn, Professor of Law, University of Utah.

BIOGRAPHY OF A LEGAL DISPUTE, THE: An Introduction to American Civil Procedure (1968)

Marc A. Franklin, Professor of Law, Stanford University.

BUSINESS ORGANIZATION, see also Enterprise Organization

BUSINESS PLANNING (1966), with 1981 Supplement

David R. Herwitz, Professor of Law, Harvard University.

BUSINESS TORTS (1972)

Milton Handler, Professor of Law Emeritus, Columbia University.

CIVIL PROCEDURE, see Procedure

CLINIC, see also Lawyering Process

COMMERCIAL AND CONSUMER TRANSACTIONS, Second Edition (1978)

William D. Warren, Dean of the School of Law, University of California, Los Angeles.
William E. Hogan, Professor of Law, Cornell University.
Robert L. Jordan, Professor of Law, University of California, Los Angeles.

COMMERCIAL LAW, CASES & MATERIALS ON, Third Edition (1976)

E. Allan Farnsworth, Professor of Law, Columbia University.
John Honnold, Professor of Law, University of Pennsylvania.

COMMERCIAL PAPER, Second Edition (1976)

E. Allan Farnsworth, Professor of Law, Columbia University.

COMMERCIAL PAPER AND BANK DEPOSITS AND COLLECTIONS (1967), with Statutory Supplement

William D. Hawkland, Professor of Law, University of Illinois.

COMMERCIAL TRANSACTIONS—Text, Cases and Problems, Fourth Edition (1968)

The late Robert Braucher, Professor of Law, Harvard University.
The late Arthur E. Sutherland, Jr., Professor of Law, Harvard University.

COMPARATIVE LAW, Fourth Edition (1980)

Rudolf B. Schlesinger, Professor of Law, Hastings College of the Law.

COMPETITIVE PROCESS, LEGAL REGULATION OF THE, Second Edition (1979), with Statutory Supplement and 1982 Case Supplement

Edmund W. Kitch, Professor of Law, University of Chicago.
Harvey S. Perlman, Professor of Law, University of Virginia.

CONFLICT OF LAWS, Seventh Edition (1978), with 1982 Supplement

Willis L. M. Reese, Professor of Law, Columbia University,
Maurice Rosenberg, Professor of Law, Columbia University.

CONSTITUTIONAL LAW, Sixth Edition (1981), with 1981 Supplement

Edward L. Barrett, Jr., Professor of Law, University of California, Davis.
William Cohen, Professor of Law, Stanford University.

CONSTITUTIONAL LAW: THE STRUCTURE OF GOVERNMENT (Reprinted from CONSTITUTIONAL LAW, Sixth Edition)

Edward L. Barrett, Jr., Professor of Law, University of California, Davis.
William Cohen, Professor of Law, Stanford University.

CONSTITUTIONAL LAW, Tenth Edition (1980), with 1981 Supplement

Gerald Gunther, Professor of Law, Stanford University.

CONSTITUTIONAL LAW, INDIVIDUAL RIGHTS IN, Third Edition (1981), with 1981 Supplement (Reprinted from CONSTITUTIONAL LAW, Tenth Edition)

Gerald Gunther, Professor of Law, Stanford University.

CONTRACT LAW AND ITS APPLICATION, Second Edition (1977)

The late Addison Mueller, Professor of Law, University of California, Los Angeles.
Arthur I. Rosett, Professor of Law, University of California, Los Angeles.

CONTRACT LAW, STUDIES IN, Second Edition (1977)

Edward J. Murphy, Professor of Law, University of Notre Dame.
Richard E. Speidel, Professor of Law, University of Virginia.

CONTRACTS, Fourth Edition (1982)

John P. Dawson, Professor of Law Emeritus, Harvard University.
William Burnett Harvey, Professor of Law and Political Science, Boston University.
Stanley D. Henderson, Professor of Law, University of Virginia.

CONTRACTS, Third Edition (1980), with Statutory Supplement

E. Allan Farnsworth, Professor of Law, Columbia University.
William F. Young, Professor of Law, Columbia University.

CONTRACTS, Second Edition (1978), with Statutory and Administrative Law Supplement (1978)

Ian R. Macneil, Professor of Law, Cornell University.

COPYRIGHT, PATENT, TRADEMARK AND RELATED STATE DOCTRINES, Second Edition (1981), with Problem Supplement and Statutory Supplement

Paul Goldstein, Professor of Law, Stanford University.

COPYRIGHT, Unfair Competition, and Other Topics Bearing on the Protection of Literary, Musical, and Artistic Works, Third Edition (1978)

Benjamin Kaplan, Professor of Law Emeritus, Harvard University,
Ralph S. Brown, Jr., Professor of Law, Yale University.

CORPORATE FINANCE, Second Edition (1979), with 1980 New Developments Supplement

Victor Brudney, Professor of Law, Harvard University.
Marvin A. Chirelstein, Professor of Law, Yale University.

CORPORATE READJUSTMENTS AND REORGANIZATIONS (1976)

Walter J. Blum, Professor of Law, University of Chicago.
Stanley A. Kaplan, Professor of Law, University of Chicago.

CORPORATION LAW, BASIC, Second Edition (1979), with Documentary Supplement

Detlev F. Vagts, Professor of Law, Harvard University.

CORPORATIONS, see also Enterprise Organization

CORPORATIONS, Fifth Edition—Unabridged (1980)

William L. Cary, Professor of Law, Columbia University.
Melvin Aron Eisenberg, Professor of Law, University of California, Berkeley.

CORPORATIONS, Fifth Edition—Abridged (1980)

William L. Cary, Professor of Law, Columbia University.
Melvin Aron Eisenberg, Professor of Law, University of California, Berkeley.

CORPORATIONS, THE LAW OF: WHAT CORPORATE LAWYERS DO (1976)

Jan G. Deutsch, Professor of Law, Yale University.
Joseph J. Bianco, Professor of Law, Yeshiva University.

CORPORATIONS COURSE GAME PLAN (1975)

David R. Herwitz, Professor of Law, Harvard University.

CORRECTIONS, SEE SENTENCING

CREDIT TRANSACTIONS AND CONSUMER PROTECTION (1976)

John Honnold, Professor of Law, University of Pennsylvania.

CREDITORS' RIGHTS, see also Debtor-Creditor Law

CRIMINAL JUSTICE, THE ADMINISTRATION OF, Second Edition (1969)

Francis C. Sullivan, Professor of Law, Louisiana State University.
Paul Hardin III, Professor of Law, Duke University.
John Huston, Professor of Law, University of Washington.
Frank R. Lacy, Professor of Law, University of Oregon.
Daniel E. Murray, Professor of Law, University of Miami.
George W. Pugh, Professor of Law, Louisiana State University.

CRIMINAL JUSTICE ADMINISTRATION AND RELATED PROCESSES, Successor Edition (1976), with 1981 Supplement

Frank W. Miller, Professor of Law, Washington University.
Robert O. Dawson, Professor of Law, University of Texas.
George E. Dix, Professor of Law, University of Texas.
Raymond I. Parnas, Professor of Law, University of California, Davis.

CRIMINAL JUSTICE, LEADING CONSTITUTIONAL CASES ON (1981)

Lloyd L. Weinreb, Professor of Law, Harvard University.

CRIMINAL LAW, Second Edition (1979)

Fred E. Inbau, Professor of Law Emeritus, Northwestern University.
James R. Thompson, Professor of Law Emeritus, Northwestern University.
Andre A. Moenssens, Professor of Law, University of Richmond.

CRIMINAL LAW, Third Edition (1980)

Lloyd L. Weinreb, Professor of Law, Harvard University.

CRIMINAL LAW AND ITS ADIMINSTRATION (1940), with 1956 Supplement

Jerome Michael, late Professor of Law, Columbia University.
Herbert Wechsler, Professor of Law, Columbia University.

CRIMINAL LAW AND PROCEDURE, Fifth Edition (1977)

Rollin M. Perkins, Professor of Law Emeritus, University of California, Hastings College of the Law.
Ronald N. Boyce, Professor of Law, University of Utah.

CRIMINAL PROCEDURE, Second Edition (1980), with 1981 Supplement

Fred E. Inbau, Professor of Law Emeritus, Northwestern University.
James R. Thompson, Professor of Law Emeritus, Northwestern University.
James B. Haddad, Professor of Law, Northwestern University.
James B. Zagel, Chief, Criminal Justice Division, Office of Attorney General of Illinois.
Gary L. Starkman, Assistant U. S. Attorney, Northern District of Illinois.

CRIMINAL PROCEDURE, CONSTITUTIONAL (1977), with 1980 Supplement

James E. Scarboro, Professor of Law, University of Colorado.
James B. White, Professor of Law, University of Chicago.

CRIMINAL PROCESS, Third Edition (1978), with 1981 Supplement

Lloyd L. Weinreb, Professor of Law, Harvard University.

DAMAGES, Second Edition (1952)

Charles T. McCormick, late Professor of Law, University of Texas.
William F. Fritz, late Professor of Law, University of Texas.

DEBTOR–CREDITOR LAW, Second Edition (1981), with Statutory Supplement

William D. Warren, Dean of the School of Law, University of California, Los Angeles.
William E. Hogan, Professor of Law, New York University.

DECEDENTS' ESTATES (1971)

Max Rheinstein, late Professor of Law Emeritus, University of Chicago.
Mary Ann Glendon, Professor of Law, Boston College.

DECEDENTS' ESTATES AND TRUSTS, Fifth Edition (1977)

John Ritchie, Professor of Law Emeritus, University of Virginia.
Neill H. Alford, Jr., Professor of Law, University of Virginia.
Richard W. Effland, Professor of Law, Arizona State University.

DECEDENTS' ESTATES AND TRUSTS (1968)

Howard R. Williams, Professor of Law, Stanford University.

DOMESTIC RELATIONS, see also Family Law

DOMESTIC RELATIONS, Third Edition (1978), with 1980 Supplement

Walter Wadlington, Professor of Law, University of Virginia.
Monrad G. Paulsen, Dean of the Law School, Yeshiva University.

DYNAMICS OF AMERICAN LAW, THE: Courts, the Legal Process and Freedom of Expression (1968)

Marc A. Franklin, Professor of Law, Stanford University.

ELECTRONIC MASS MEDIA, Second Edition (1979)

William K. Jones, Professor of Law, Columbia University.

ENTERPRISE ORGANIZATION, Second Edition (1977), with 1979 Statutory and Formulary Supplement

Alfred F. Conard, Professor of Law, University of Michigan.
Robert L. Knauss, Dean of the School of Law, Vanderbilt University.
Stanley Siegel, Professor of Law, University of California, Los Angeles.

EQUITY AND EQUITABLE REMEDIES (1975)

Edward D. Re, Adjunct Professor of Law, St. John's University.

EQUITY, RESTITUTION AND DAMAGES, Second Edition (1974)

Robert Childres, late Professor of Law, Northwestern University.
William F. Johnson, Jr., Professor of Law, New York University.

ESTATE PLANNING, Second Edition (1982), with Documentary Supplement

David Westfall, Professor of Law, Harvard University.

ETHICS, see Legal Profession, and Professional Responsibility

ETHICS AND PROFESSIONAL RESPONSIBILITY (1981) (Reprinted from THE LAWYERING PROCESS)

Gary Bellow, Professor of Law, Harvard University.
Bea Moulton, Legal Services Corporation.

EVIDENCE, Fourth Edition (1981)

David W. Louisell, late Professor of Law, University of California, Berkeley.
John Kaplan, Professor of Law, Stanford University.
Jon R. Waltz, Professor of Law, Northwestern University.

EVIDENCE, Sixth Edition (1973), with 1981 Supplement

John M. Maguire, late Professor of Law Emeritus, Harvard University.
Jack B. Weinstein, Professor of Law, Columbia University.
James H. Chadbourn, Professor of Law, Harvard University.
John H. Mansfield, Professor of Law, Harvard University.
(Supplement edited in association with Norman Abrams, Professor of Law, University of California, Los Angeles and Margaret Berger, Professor of Law, Brooklyn Law School).

EVIDENCE (1968)

Francis C. Sullivan, Professor of Law, Louisiana State University.
Paul Hardin, III, Professor of Law, Duke University.

FAMILY LAW, see also Domestic Relations

FAMILY LAW (1978), with 1981 Supplement

Judith C. Areen, Professor of Law, Georgetown University.

FAMILY LAW AND CHILDREN IN THE LEGAL SYSTEM, STATUTORY MATERIALS (1981)

Walter Wadlington, Professor of Law, University of Virginia.

FEDERAL COURTS, Sixth Edition (1976), with 1981 Supplement

Charles T. McCormick, late Professor of Law, University of Texas.
James H. Chadbourn, Professor of Law, Harvard University.
Charles Alan Wright, Professor of Law, University of Texas.

FEDERAL COURTS AND THE FEDERAL SYSTEM, Hart and Wechsler's Second Edition (1973), with 1981 Supplement

Paul M. Bator, Professor of Law, Harvard University.
Paul J. Mishkin, Professor of Law, University of California, Berkeley.
David L. Shapiro, Professor of Law, Harvard University.
Herbert Wechsler, Professor of Law, Columbia University.

FEDERAL PUBLIC LAND AND RESOURCES LAW (1981)

George C. Coggins, Professor of Law, University of Kansas.
Charles F. Wilkinson, Professor of Law, University of Oregon.

FEDERAL RULES OF CIVIL PROCEDURE, 1980 Edition

FEDERAL TAXATION, see Taxation

FOOD AND DRUG LAW (1980)

Richard A. Merrill, Dean of the School of Law, University of Virginia.
Peter Barton Hutt, Esq.

FUTURE INTERESTS (1958)

Philip Mechem, late Professor of Law Emeritus, University of Pennsylvania.

FUTURE INTERESTS (1970)

Howard R. Williams, Professor of Law, Stanford University.

FUTURE INTERESTS AND ESTATE PLANNING (1961), with 1962 Supplement

W. Barton Leach, late Professor of Law, Harvard University.
James K. Logan, formerly Dean of the Law School, University of Kansas.

GOVERNMENT CONTRACTS, FEDERAL (1975), with 1980 Supplement

John W. Whelan, Professor of Law, Hastings College of the Law.
Robert S. Pasley, Professor of Law Emeritus, Cornell University.

HOUSING—THE ILL–HOUSED (1971) (Reprinted from Levy, Lewis and Martin's SOCIAL WELFARE AND THE INDIVIDUAL)

Peter W. Martin, Professor of Law, Cornell University.

INJUNCTIONS (1972)

Owen M. Fiss, Professor of Law, Yale University.

INSTITUTIONAL INVESTORS, 1978

David L. Ratner, Professor of Law, Cornell University.

INSURANCE (1971)

William F. Young, Professor of Law, Columbia University.

INTERNATIONAL LAW, see also Transnational Legal Problems and United Nations Law

INTERNATIONAL LAW IN CONTEMPORARY PERSPECTIVE (1981), with Essay Supplement

Myres S. McDougal, Professor of Law, Yale University.
W. Michael Reisman, Professor of Law, Yale University.

INTERNATIONAL LEGAL SYSTEM, Second Edition (1981), with Documentary Supplement

Joseph Modeste Sweeney, Professor of Law, Tulane University.
Covey T. Oliver, Professor of Law, University of Pennsylvania.
Noyes E. Leech, Professor of Law, University of Pennsylvania.

INTERNATIONAL TRADE AND INVESTMENT, REGULATION OF (1970)

Carl H. Fulda, late Professor of Law, University of Texas.
Warren F. Schwartz, Professor of Law, University of Virginia.

INTERNATIONAL TRANSACTIONS AND RELATIONS (1960)

Milton Katz, Professor of Law, Harvard University.
Kingman Brewster, Jr., Professor of Law, Harvard University.

INTRODUCTION TO LAW, see also Legal Method, On Law in Courts, and Dynamics of American Law

INTRODUCTION TO THE STUDY OF LAW (1970)

E. Wayne Thode, late Professor of Law, University of Utah.
Leon Lebowitz, Professor of Law, University of Texas.
Lester J. Mazor, Professor of Law, University of Utah.

JUDICIAL CODE and Rules of Procedure in the Federal Courts with Excerpts from the Criminal Code, 1981 Edition

Henry M. Hart, Jr., late Professor of Law, Harvard University.
Herbert Wechsler, Professor of Law, Columbia University.

JURISPRUDENCE (Temporary Edition Hardbound) (1949)

Lon L. Fuller, Professor of Law Emeritus, Harvard University.

JUVENILE COURTS (1967)

Hon. Orman W. Ketcham, Juvenile Court of the District of Columbia.
Monrad G. Paulsen, Dean of the Law School, Yeshiva University.

JUVENILE JUSTICE PROCESS, Second Edition (1976), with 1980 Supplement

Frank W. Miller, Professor of Law, Washington University.
Robert O. Dawson, Professor of Law, University of Texas.
George E. Dix, Professor of Law, University of Texas.
Raymond I. Parnas, Professor of Law, University of California, Davis.

LABOR LAW, Ninth Edition (1981), with Statutory Supplement

Archibald Cox, Professor of Law, Harvard University.
Derek C. Bok, President, Harvard University.
Robert A. Gorman, Professor of Law, University of Pennsylvania.

LABOR LAW (1968), with Statutory Supplement and 1974 Case Supplement

Clyde W. Summers, Professor of Law, University of Pennsylvania.
Harry H. Wellington, Dean of the Law School, Yale University.

LAND FINANCING, Second Edition (1977)

Norman Penney, Professor of Law, Cornell University.
Richard F. Broude, Member of the California Bar.

LAW AND MEDICINE (1980)

Walter Wadlington, Professor of Law and Professor of Legal Medicine, University
of Virginia.
Jon R. Waltz, Professor of Law, Northwestern University.
Roger B. Dworkin, Professor of Law, Indiana University, and Professor of Bi-
omedical History, University of Washington.

LAW, LANGUAGE AND ETHICS (1972)

William R. Bishin, Professor of Law, University of Southern California.
Christopher D. Stone, Professor of Law, University of Southern California.

LAWYERING PROCESS (1978), with Civil Problem Supplement and Criminal Problem Supplement

Gary Bellow, Professor of Law, Harvard University.
Bea Moulton, Professor of Law, Arizona State University.

LEGAL METHOD

Harry W. Jones, Professor of Law Emeritus, Columbia University.
John M. Kernochan, Professor of Law, Columbia University.
Arthur W. Murphy, Professor of Law, Columbia University.

LEGAL METHODS (1969)

Robert N. Covington, Professor of Law, Vanderbilt University.
E. Blythe Stason, late Professor of Law, Vanderbilt University.
John W. Wade, Professor of Law, Vanderbilt University.
Elliott E. Cheatham, late Professor of Law, Vanderbilt University.
Theodore A. Smedley, Professor of Law, Vanderbilt University.

LEGAL PROFESSION (1970)

Samuel D. Thurman, Dean of the College of Law, University of Utah.
Ellis L. Phillips, Jr., Professor of Law, Columbia University.
Elliott E. Cheatham, late Professor of Law, Vanderbilt University.

LEGISLATION, Fourth Edition (1982) (by Fordham)

Horace E. Read, late Vice President, Dalhousie University.
John W. MacDonald, Professor of Law Emeritus, Cornell Law School.
Jefferson B. Fordham, Professor of Law, University of Utah.
William J. Pierce, Professor of Law, University of Michigan.

LEGISLATIVE AND ADMINISTRATIVE PROCESSES (1976), Second Edition (1981)

Hans A. Linde, Professor of Law, Judge, Supreme Court of Oregon.
George Bunn, Professor of Law, University of Wisconsin.
Fredericka Paff, Professor of Law, University of Wisconsin.
W. Lawrence Church, Professor of Law, University of Wisconsin.

LOCAL GOVERNMENT LAW, Revised Edition (1975)

Jefferson B. Fordham, Professor of Law, University of Utah.

MASS MEDIA LAW (1976), with 1979 Supplement

Marc A. Franklin, Professor of Law, Stanford University.

MENTAL HEALTH PROCESS, Second Edition (1976), with 1981 Supplement

Frank W. Miller, Professor of Law, Washington University.
Robert O. Dawson, Professor of Law, University of Texas.
George E. Dix, Professor of Law, University of Texas.
Raymond I. Parnas, Professor of Law, University of California, Davis.

MUNICIPAL CORPORATIONS, see Local Government Law

NEGOTIABLE INSTRUMENTS, see Commercial Paper

NEGOTIATION (1981) (Reprinted from THE LAWYERING PROCESS)

Gary Bellow, Professor of Law, Harvard Law School.
Bea Moulton, Legal Services Corporation.

NEW YORK PRACTICE, Fourth Edition (1978)

Herbert Peterfreund, Professor of Law, New York University.
Joseph M. McLaughlin, Dean of the Law School, Fordham University.

OIL AND GAS, Fourth Edition (1979)

Howard R. Williams, Professor of Law, Stanford University.
Richard C. Maxwell, Professor of Law, University of California, Los Angeles.
Charles J. Meyers, Dean of the Law School, Stanford University.

ON LAW IN COURTS (1965)

Paul J. Mishkin, Professor of Law, University of California, Berkeley.
Clarence Morris, Professor of Law Emeritus, University of Pennsylvania.

OWNERSHIP AND DEVELOPMENT OF LAND (1965)

Jan Krasnowiecki, Professor of Law, University of Pennsylvania.

PARTNERSHIP PLANNING (1970) (Pamphlet)

William L. Cary, Professor of Law, Columbia University.

PERSPECTIVES ON THE LAWYER AS PLANNER (Reprint of Chapters One through Five of Planning by Lawyers) (1978)

Louis M. Brown, Professor of Law, University of Southern California.
Edward A. Dauer, Professor of Law, Yale University.

PLANNING BY LAWYERS, MATERIALS ON A NONADVERSARIAL LEGAL PROCESS (1978)

Louis M. Brown, Professor of Law, University of Southern California.
Edward A. Dauer, Professor of Law, Yale University.

PLEADING AND PROCEDURE, see Procedure, Civil

POLICE FUNCTION (1976) (Pamphlet)

Chapters 1–11 of Miller, Dawson, Dix & Parnas' Criminal Justice Administration, Second Edition.

PREPARING AND PRESENTING THE CASE (1981) (Reprinted from THE LAWYERING PROCESS)

Gary Bellow, Professor of Law, Harvard Law School.
Bea Moulton, Legal Services Corporation.

PREVENTIVE LAW, see also Planning by Lawyers

PROCEDURE—Biography of a Legal Dispute (1968)

Marc A. Franklin, Professor of Law, Stanford University.

PROCEDURE—CIVIL PROCEDURE, Second Edition (1974), with 1979 Supplement

James H. Chadbourn, Professor of Law, Harvard University.
A. Leo Levin, Professor of Law, University of Pennsylvania.
Philip Shuchman, Professor of Law, University of Connecticut.

PROCEDURE—CIVIL PROCEDURE, Fourth Edition (1978), with 1981 Supplement

Richard H. Field, late Professor of Law, Harvard University.
Benjamin Kaplan, Professor of Law Emeritus, Harvard University.
Kevin M. Clermont, Professor of Law, Cornell University.

PROCEDURE—CIVIL PROCEDURE, Third Edition (1976), with 1978 Supplement

Maurice Rosenberg, Professor of Law, Columbia University.
Jack B. Weinstein, Professor of Law, Columbia University.
Hans Smit, Professor of Law, Columbia University.
Harold L. Korn, Professor of Law, Columbia University.

PROCEDURE—PLEADING AND PROCEDURE: State and Federal, Fourth Edition (1979)

David W. Louisell, late Professor of Law, University of California, Berkeley.
Geoffrey C. Hazard, Jr., Professor of Law, Yale University.

PROCEDURE—FEDERAL RULES OF CIVIL PROCEDURE, 1980 Edition

PROCEDURE PORTFOLIO (1962)

James H. Chadbourn, Professor of Law, Harvard University.
A. Leo Levin, Professor of Law, University of Pennsylvania.

PRODUCTS LIABILITY (1980)

Marshall S. Shapo, Professor of Law, Northwestern University.

PRODUCTS LIABILITY AND SAFETY (1980), with Statutory Supplement

W. Page Keeton, Professor of Law, University of Texas.
David G. Owen, Professor of Law, University of South Carolina.
John E. Montgomery, Professor of Law, University of South Carolina.

UNIVERSITY CASEBOOK SERIES—Continued

PROFESSIONAL RESPONSIBILITY, Second Edition (1981), with Selected National Standards Supplement

Thomas D. Morgan, Dean of Law, Emory University.
Ronald D. Rotunda, Professor of Law, University of Illinois.

PROPERTY, Fourth Edition (1978)

John E. Cribbet, Dean of the Law School, University of Illinois.
Corwin W. Johnson, Professor of Law, University of Texas.

PROPERTY—PERSONAL (1953)

S. Kenneth Skolfield, late Professor of Law Emeritus, Boston University.

PROPERTY—PERSONAL, Third Edition (1954)

Everett Fraser, late Dean of the Law School Emeritus, University of Minnesota.
Third Edition by Charles W. Taintor, late Professor of Law, University of Pittsburgh.

PROPERTY—INTRODUCTION, TO REAL PROPERTY, Third Edition (1954)

Everett Fraser, late Dean of the Law School Emeritus, University of Minnesota.

PROPERTY—REAL PROPERTY AND CONVEYANCING (1954)

Edward E. Bade, late Professor of Law, University of Minnesota.

PROPERTY—FUNDAMENTALS OF MODERN REAL PROPERTY (1974), with 1981 Supplement

Edward H. Rabin, Professor of Law, University of California, Davis.

PROPERTY—PROBLEMS IN REAL PROPERTY (Pamphlet) (1969)

Edward H. Rabin, Professor of Law, University of California, Davis.

PROSECUTION AND ADJUDICATION (1976) (Pamphlet)

Chapters 12–16 of Miller, Dawson, Dix & Parnas' Criminal Justice Administration, Successor Edition.

PUBLIC REGULATION OF DANGEROUS PRODUCTS (paperback) (1980)

Marshall S. Shapo, Professor of Law, Northwestern University.

PUBLIC UTILITY LAW, see Free Enterprise, also Regulated Industries

REAL ESTATE PLANNING (1980), with 1980 Problems, Statutes and New Materials Supplement

Norton L. Steuben, Professor of Law, University of Colorado.

REAL ESTATE TRANSACTIONS (1980), with Statute, Form and Problem Supplement

Paul Goldstein, Professor of Law, Stanford University.

RECEIVERSHIP AND CORPORATE REORGANIZATION, see Creditors' Rights

REGULATED INDUSTRIES, Second Edition, 1976

William K. Jones, Professor of Law, Columbia University.

REMEDIES (1982)

Edward D. Re, Chief Judge, U. S. Court of International Trade.

RESTITUTION, Second Edition (1966)

John W. Wade, Professor of Law, Vanderbilt University.

SALES (1980)

Marion W. Benfield, Jr., Professor of Law, University of Illinois.
William D. Hawkland, Chancellor, Louisiana State University Law Center.

SALES AND SALES FINANCING, Fourth Edition (1976)

John Honnold, Professor of Law, University of Pennsylvania.

SECURITY, Third Edition (1959)

John Hanna, late Professor of Law Emeritus, Columbia University.

SECURITIES REGULATION, Fourth Edition (1977), with 1981 Selected Statutes Supplement and 1981 Cases and Releases Supplement

Richard W. Jennings, Professor of Law, University of California, Berkeley.
Harold Marsh, Jr., Member of the California Bar.

SECURITIES REGULATION (1982)

Larry D. Soderquist, Professor of Law, Vanderbilt University.

SENTENCING AND CORRECTIONS, SANCTIONS (1981)

Nicholas N. Kittrie, Professor of Law, American University.
Elyce H. Zenoff, Professor of Law, George Washington University.

SENTENCING AND THE CORRECTIONAL PROCESS, Second Edition (1976)

Frank W. Miller, Professor of Law, Washington University.
Robert O. Dawson, Professor of Law, University of Texas.
George E. Dix, Professor of Law, University of Texas.
Raymond I. Parnas, Professor of Law, University of California, Davis.

SOCIAL WELFARE AND THE INDIVIDUAL (1971)

Robert J. Levy, Professor of Law, University of Minnesota.
Thomas P. Lewis, Dean of the College of Law, University of Kentucky.
Peter W. Martin, Professor of Law, Cornell University.

TAX, POLICY ANALYSIS OF THE FEDERAL INCOME (1976)

William A. Klein, Professor of Law, University of California, Los Angeles.

TAXATION, FEDERAL INCOME (1976), with 1980 Supplement

Erwin N. Griswold, Dean Emeritus, Harvard Law School.
Michael J. Graetz, Professor of Law, University of Virginia.

TAXATION, FEDERAL INCOME, Third Edition (1981)

James J. Freeland, Professor of Law, University of Florida.
Stephen A. Lind, Professor of Law, University of Florida.
Richard B. Stephens, Professor of Law Emeritus, University of Florida.

TAXATION, FEDERAL INCOME, Volume I, Personal Income Taxation (1972), with 1979 Supplement; Volume II, Taxation of Partnerships and Corporations, Second Edition (1980)

Stanley S. Surrey, Professor of Law, Harvard University.
William C. Warren, Professor of Law Emeritus, Columbia University.
Paul R. McDaniel, Professor of Law, Boston College Law School.
Hugh J. Ault, Professor of Law, Boston College Law School.

TAXATION, FEDERAL WEALTH TRANSFER (1977)

Stanley S. Surrey, Professor of Law, Harvard University.
William C. Warren, Professor of Law Emeritus, Columbia University.
Paul R. McDaniel, Professor of Law, Boston College Law School.
Harry L. Gutman, Instructor, Harvard Law School and Boston College Law School.

TAXATION OF INDIVIDUALS, PARTNERSHIPS AND CORPORATIONS, PROBLEMS in the (1978)

Norton L. Steuben, Professor of Law, University of Colorado.
William J. Turnier, Professor of Law, University of North Carolina.

TAXES AND FINANCE—STATE AND LOCAL (1974)

Oliver Oldman, Professor of Law, Harvard University.
Ferdinand P. Schoettle, Professor of Law, University of Minnesota.

TORT LAW AND ALTERNATIVES: INJURIES AND REMEDIES, Second Edition (1979)

Marc A. Franklin, Professor of Law, Stanford University.

TORTS, Sixth Edition (1976)

William L. Prosser, late Professor of Law, University of California, Hastings College.
John W. Wade, Professor of Law, Vanderbilt University.
Victor E. Schwartz, Professor of Law, American University.

TORTS, Third Edition (1976)

Harry Shulman, late Dean of the Law School, Yale University.
Fleming James, Jr., Professor of Law Emeritus, Yale University.
Oscar S. Gray, Professor of Law, University of Maryland.

TRADE REGULATION (1975), with 1979 Supplement

Milton Handler, Professor of Law Emeritus, Columbia University.
Harlan M. Blake, Professor of Law, Columbia University.
Robert Pitofsky, Professor of Law, Georgetown University.
Harvey J. Goldschmid, Professor of Law, Columbia University.

TRADE REGULATION, see Antitrust

TRANSNATIONAL LEGAL PROBLEMS, Second Edition (1976), with Documentary Supplement

Henry J. Steiner, Professor of Law, Harvard University.
Detlev F. Vagts, Professor of Law, Harvard University.

TRIAL, see also Lawyering Process and Preparing and Presenting the Case

TRIAL ADVOCACY (1968)

A. Leo Levin, Professor of Law, University of Pennsylvania.
Harold Cramer, of the Pennsylvania Bar.
Maurice Rosenberg, Professor of Law, Columbia University, Consultant.

TRUSTS, Fifth Edition (1978)

George G. Bogert, late Professor of Law Emeritus, University of Chicago.
Dallin H. Oaks, President, Brigham Young University.

TRUSTS AND SUCCESSION (Palmer's), Third Edition (1978)

Richard V. Wellman, Professor of Law, University of Georgia.
Lawrence W. Waggoner, Professor of Law, University of Michigan.
Olin L. Browder, Jr., Professor of Law, University of Michigan.

UNFAIR COMPETITION, see Competitive Process and Business Torts

UNITED NATIONS IN ACTION (1968)

Louis B. Sohn, Professor of Law, Harvard University.

UNITED NATIONS LAW, Second Edition (1967), with Documentary Supplement (1968)

Louis B. Sohn, Professor of Law, Harvard University.

WATER RESOURCE MANAGEMENT, Second Edition (1980)

Charles J. Meyers, Dean of the Law School, Stanford University.
A. Dan Tarlock, Professor of Law, Indiana Unversity.

WILLS AND ADMINISTRATION, Fifth Edition (1961)

Philip Mechem, late Professor of Law, University of Pennsylvania.
Thomas E. Atkinson, late Professor of Law, New York University.

WORLD LAW, see United Nations Law

University Casebook Series

ESTATE PLANNING

CASES AND TEXT

SECOND EDITION

By

DAVID WESTFALL

John H. Watson, Jr. Professor of Law, Harvard University

Mineola, New York

THE FOUNDATION PRESS, INC.

1982

Library of Congress Cataloging in Publication Data

Westfall, David, 1927–
  Estate planning.

  (University casebook series)
  Rev. ed. of: Estate planning problems. 1973.
  Includes index.
  1. Inheritance and transfer tax—Law and
legislation—United states. 2. Gifts—Taxation—
United States. 3. Estate planning—United
States. I. Title. II. Series.
KF6572.W38 1981   343.7305'3   81–17245
                    347.30353   AACR2

ISBN 0-88277-043-8

To Lisa, Bill, Tom, Katharine,
and most of all, Elizabeth

*

PREFACE

This second edition has been completely revised to reflect all of the extensive changes made by the Economic Recovery Tax Act of 1981, as well as other new developments since the first edition, Estate Planning Problems, was published in 1973. This book consists of cases, text, and administrative materials dealing with problems in the practice of estate planning. A Documentary Supplement contains hypothetical estate plans, instruments to carry them out, and relevant state statutes. Problems dealing with chapters of the text in the context of the hypothetical plans and instruments will be available in the Spring of 1982 in a separate pamphlet for teachers. Provisions of the Internal Revenue Code and Treasury Regulations are not included, as it is assumed that students will buy them separately.

The first edition combined all of these materials in a single volume. Inclusion of the estate plans, instruments, and statutes in a separate Documentary Supplement will permit more frequent updating. It also will allow teachers to use this book in conjunction with problems based on local statutes instead of the New York statutes in the Documentary Supplement, and to assign drafting problems instead of focusing on completed instruments.

Like the first edition, these materials reflect my conviction that the most effective way to teach Estate Planning is through problems based on hypothetical estate plans. The book is designed for students who have had a course in the Federal Income Tax but none in estate and gift taxation and no more than an introductory acquaintance with the law of decedents' estates, trusts, wills, and future interests. In a more leisurely era, there often were required courses in each of these last four subjects. Today, at the Harvard Law School, Trusts alone remains, but as an elective course. Students' only other exposure to these four areas is in Property, already heavily burdened with its own distinctive subject matter. This leaves Estate Planning with many responsibilities. It must deal not only with planning considerations but also must provide background in all of the substantive bodies of law (apart from income taxation) on which estate planning is based.

In seeking the best use of the available time, I have concentrated on federal tax problems in estate planning and have sharply limited the consideration of state law aspects. The infinity of local variations in property law discourages any attempt at comprehensive coverage. And concentration on the law of any single state may be a source of frustration for students who expect to practice in another.

Nevertheless, such concentration is inevitable to a degree because no hypothetical estate plan can be considered realistically apart from state law. The estate plans and instruments in the Documentary Supplement are for New York residents, and most of the state cases and statutes are from New York. From a pedagogic standpoint, New

York law is ideal because so much is codified, making possible the consideration of tax questions affected by state law without assigning burdensome numbers of cases as necessary background.

If students have an adequate background in estates, trusts, wills, and future interests, Part I may be omitted.

I teach Estate Planning in four semester hours. For students who do not expect to specialize in this area of practice, this is a heavy time commitment. A shorter course can deal with the estate planning problems of the great majority of clients, who do not make either substantial lifetime transfers or charitable gifts or bequests. For this purpose, chapters 10 and 20 may be omitted and the time spent on chapter 9 substantially reduced.

ACKNOWLEDGMENTS

Much of the material in this edition appears in a different format in Westfall, Estate Planning Law and Taxation, © Warren, Gorham & Lamont, 1981, and is used here with permission.

Waggoner, Future Interests in a Nutshell, © 1981 Lawrence W. Waggoner, provided much of Chapter 3, dealing with perpetuities and powers. I am indebted to the author and West Publishing Company for permission to reproduce this unusually lucid treatment of two intractable topics.

George P. Mair, of Bingham, Dana & Gould, Boston, Massachusetts, made many important suggestions for revisions required to reflect the Economic Recovery Tax Act of 1981.

Many students in my twenty five years of estate planning classes at the Harvard Law School have contributed to this book. The following research assistants made valuable contributions to this edition:

Elizabeth E. Ashcraft	Gerald E. Lunn, Jr.
Laurence D. Atlas	Sharon Oxborough
Paul Darmitzel	Mark J. Thompson
Cary Forrester	Victor Thuronyi
William Hay	Jeannette Winn
	Marshall Winn

Professor Mary Louise Fellows, of the University of Illinois College of Law, used a prior multilithed edition in her Estate Planning class and made helpful suggestions for the final revision.

My secretary, Esther Fenerjian, did her usual fine work in typing and assembling the manuscript.

During the four years this edition was in gestation, my wife, Elizabeth B. Westfall, was an indispensable source of encouragement and support.

DAVID WESTFALL

Cambridge, Massachusetts
November, 1981

*

EFFECTIVE DATES OF CODE PROVISIONS

Students who use this book will not begin the practice of estate planning until after January 1, 1982, the effective date for most of the amendments of the Internal Revenue Code contained in the Economic Recovery Tax Act of 1981. Therefore, unless otherwise indicated, the text reflects provisions of the Internal Revenue Code applicable to transfers made and decedents dying after 1981. The old rules continue to be important in dealing with prior transfers and with estates of decedents dying before 1982.

No systematic effort has been made to include statutory or administrative materials published after October 1, 1981.

EDITORIAL MATTERS

This book departs from convention (aside from the former Tax Court practice) in giving full names of taxpayer litigants in lower federal court cases to facilitate use of indices and citators. Thus, for Courts of Appeals and District Courts, Smith v. Commissioner is cited as Malcolm W. Smith v. Commissioner. In Tax Court cases, "Commissioner" is omitted.

"Him" is used to refer to either sex and in many examples the husband is assumed to be the employed spouse and to predecease his wife.

Sections of the Internal Revenue Code of 1954 are cited simply by section number. References to their current counterparts have been inserted in brackets in place of sections of the Internal Revenue Code of 1939 referred to in cases. Other editorial insertions are also indicated in brackets.

Footnotes have been freely omitted from cases and other materials. Those which have been retained have been renumbered.

ABBREVIATIONS

N.Y.EPTL *New York Estates. Powers and Trusts Law.*

Internal Revenue Service Publications

CB   *Internal Revenue Service Cumulative Bulletins*

IRB   *Internal Revenue Service Bulletin*

Tax Reporting Services

CCH E&GT *Federal Estate and Gift Tax Reporter* (Commerce Clearing House)

CCH SFTR *Standard Federal Tax Reporter*

TCM   *Tax Court Memorandum Decisions*

USTC   *U.S. Tax Cases.* Estate and gift tax cases not yet in bound volumes are in CCH E> income tax cases are in CCH SFTR.

SUMMARY OF CONTENTS

TABLE OF CONTENTS

CHAPTER 3.   DESCRIBING BENEFICIARIES' INTERESTS—Cont'd

PART II.   LIFETIME ARRANGEMENTS

PART III.   ARRANGEMENTS FOR BENEFICIARIES AND POWER HOLDERS

xlii

*

TABLE OF CASES

[The principal cases are in italic type. Cases cited or discussed are in roman type. References are to Pages.]

1

TABLE OF SECTIONS OF THE INTERNAL REVENUE CODE OF 1954

TABLE OF INTERNAL REVENUE CODE SECTIONS

TABLE OF INTERNAL REVENUE CODE SECTIONS

TABLE OF INTERNAL REVENUE CODE SECTIONS

TABLE OF INTERNAL REVENUE REGULATIONS

TABLE OF INTERNAL REVENUE REGULATIONS

TABLE OF INTERNAL REVENUE RULINGS

Italic type denotes Rulings that are reprinted

ESTATE PLANNING
CASES AND TEXT

*

Part I

STATE LAW IN ESTATE PLANNING

Chapter 1

STATE LAW AND CLIENTS' GOALS

¶ 1.01 COMMON ESTATE PLANNING GOALS OF CLIENTS

Few other areas of law affect as many lives as do those which are important in estate planning. Although many people do not realize it, almost everyone either owns or has the power to dispose of some property. If its value is very small, no formal plan may be needed, as the owner may be content to let the law (in the form of state intestacy statutes) take its course. But most owners of even moderate amounts of wealth want to choose the beneficiaries who will receive it, as well as to provide for its management until it reaches their hands. And, in varying degrees, clients share a common desire to minimize taxes for themselves and their beneficiaries as well.

In helping clients carry out these goals, a lawyer's opportunities to affect the private ordering of human affairs are greater than in almost any other area of practice. The few legal limits on a client's freedom of action remain relatively unchanged by the twentieth century, and often may easily be avoided.

Of course the federal income, gift and estate taxes were largely unknown before 1900 and inevitably restrict a client's ability to dispose of his wealth. But such taxes are only a challenge, not a roadblock, and often may be greatly reduced by effective use of the common tools of estate planning. The Tax Reform Act of 1976 introduced a tax on generation skipping transfers which limits use of trusts in particular to minimize taxes on the transfer of wealth. But the new tax leaves open many avenues of avoidance.

The Economic Recovery Tax Act of 1981 made two major changes in estate and gift taxes which will substantially reduce their impact for many clients. First, after 1981 there no longer is any limit on the amount of the deduction allowed for transfers to a spouse. If the form of the gift or bequest satisfies the statutory requirements, the full value will be deductible for gift or estate tax purposes. Second, the Act substantially increases the amount which can be transferred free of gift or estate taxes, in addition to unlimited marital deduction gifts.

These two changes alone (and the Act contains many other provisions which also reduce the impact of the estate and gift taxes) may reduce the importance of estate planning for some clients who expect that their wealth will not exceed the amount that may be transferred tax-free. Beginning in 1982, that amount will be $225,000, and it is presently scheduled to increase annually until the $600,000 level is reached in 1987.

1

For many clients, however, the new provisions will increase rather than diminish the importance of sound estate planning advice. During the years it has been in force, the gift tax often has deterred lifetime transfers which might otherwise have been made in order to save income taxes, by shifting taxable income from the donor to one or more individuals or trusts. The increased freedom from gift taxes under the new Act greatly reduces this deterrent effect and should stimulate greater use of this major income tax saving technique. The liberalized requirements for marital deduction gifts include an important additional option in qualifying for the deduction which must be evaluated in choosing the form of gift to a spouse.

Moreover, the new Act does not eliminate the importance of estate planning to minimize taxes for a client's beneficiaries. An elderly client may be prepared to assume that his own wealth will never be large enough to be subject to a gift or estate tax. But it is another matter to make the same assumption about a young descendant's wealth—as well as to predict the level of the unified credit over the period of his life. Thus, it continues to be desirable to minimize beneficiaries' exposure to estate and gift taxes.

Trusts have long been used for such preventive estate planning, as well as to save income taxes for beneficiaries. Indeed, present tax provisions continue to provide a powerful inducement for the creation of trusts to last the maximum period permitted by local law. Such trusts may allow a client to give his descendants substantial benefits from his property for a period of eighty years or more with a minimum of taxation. Thus the existing governmental attitude toward estate planning decisions, as reflected in relevant federal tax provisions, cannot properly be described as one of laissez-faire neutrality. On the contrary, it offers substantial inducements for the creation of long-term trusts and discourages dispositions which give beneficiaries outright ownership of wealth.

To draft a trust instrument to govern the enjoyment of property for eighty years or more, with all of the consequences that wealth (or the lack of it) may hold for the beneficiaries, is a major responsibility. Only the most imaginative and far-sighted drafting can deal adequately with the problems which may arise from unforseen developments during a period of such length. Indeed, a high degree of professional skill is required merely to express clearly the owner's desires, so that court proceedings will not be needed in order to determine what his words mean. This book contains many illustrations of cases in which that standard was not met.

¶ 1.02 CHARACTERISTIC STAGES IN ESTATE PLANNING

Five major stages of the lives of estate planning clients will illustrate the particular tools and techniques which may be most appropriate at each stage. Needless to say, not every client passes through each stage, and the descriptions are subject to a multitude of variations in individual cases.

[1] Young Singles (and Childless Couples)

Until the client reaches 18, he usually cannot make a will or trust agreement and his ability to vary the estate plan incorporated in the applicable intestacy statute is relatively limited. He can designate a beneficiary of life insurance he purchases or of certain kinds of United States

Government bonds he buys.   He can open a joint bank account which upon his death will belong to the survivor.   But such arrangements are generally the limit of his ability to engage in formal estate planning.

When a client does reach 18, in most states he acquires the ability to make a valid will or trust agreement but, if he is unmarried, he often has little interest in doing either.   Unless he has received substantial gifts or bequests, he usually is content to let the law take its course in disposing of his wealth in the unlikely event of his death.   Occasionally this willingness is overcome by the desire to disinherit a parent (or both parents) or a sibling who would otherwise take a share under the intestacy statute.   Imminent departure for foreign military service also may stimulate the young single's interest in an individually designed estate plan.

[2] Young Couples

Even though the near term probability of his death is low, the young married client often is interested in an estate plan to provide for his spouse and children, including any to be born.   His major assets are likely to include one or more of the following:

1. An equity in a home;

2. Life insurance;

3. Employee death benefits;

4. An interest in a small business or professional practice.

Typically when the young married client first sees a lawyer, his spouse already has been designated as beneficiary of life insurance and employee death benefits, and title to any home is held with her in a form of joint ownership with a right of survivorship.   Thus for these assets the beneficiary designation or form of joint ownership is itself a partial estate plan which will be effective if the spouse survives the client.   The same often is true of any securities or bank accounts.   Whether this plan is sound in a given case is another matter.

A will normally is needed to cover the possibility that the spouse will not survive—a major risk if both spouses are involved in a common accident—as well as to dispose of any other assets.   A revocable trust agreement also may be desirable if the client's situation and local law and practice make it more effective than a will in achieving given objectives, such as confidentiality and freedom from court supervision of trusts.   In addition, a will is needed to name guardians for any minor children, including any yet to be born.

Most young married clients are not primarily concerned with saving wealth transfer taxes, other than to qualify for the federal estate tax marital deduction for transfers to the spouse.   They are usually not in a position to make substantial lifetime gifts, and the needs of their families are too pressing to permit major gifts to charities when they die.

Income taxes are another matter, particularly on income that is saved for anticipated educational expenses of children.   Many young married clients are interested in making gifts for the benefit of their children to permit funds to be accumulated for this purpose at a lower effective income tax cost.

Young unmarried couples, if they have (or expect to have) children and anticipate a long-term relationship with each other, are often in a situation not unlike that of young married couples. However, assets are less likely to be held in a form of joint ownership which has a survivorship feature, and the estate tax marital deduction is unavailable. Thus there is a more compelling reason to make a will or revocable trust to insure that on the death of one, the other will be a beneficiary. The state intestacy statute cannot be relied on for this purpose.

[3] Middle-Aged Couples (See Estate plans for Don Stevens and Robert Rhodes in the Documentary Supplement)

To be middle-aged is not necessarily to be wealthy. It has been estimated that after 1986, when the increased unified credit provided by the Economic Recovery Tax Act of 1981 has been fully phased in, only .3% of decedent estates will be large enough to pay a federal estate tax. But clients whose income and wealth is large enough so that taxes become a major concern form a disproportionately large percentage of many lawyers' clienteles. More often than not, such clients are middle-aged or elderly because of the time required to accumulate substantial wealth.

Middle-aged clients with such wealth are likely to be owners of businesses, highly-compensated executives or professional practitioners. For such owners, a major problem is disposing of the business itself. For clients in all three groups, a major part of the estate often consists of employee benefits or individual retirement arrangements.

Middle-age has been defined as the time when an individual becomes more aware of the number of years he has left, rather than the number of years he has lived. This factor, together with his accumulation of wealth over the years, often leads to an active interest in tax savings and a willingness and ability to make substantial lifetime gifts. The medium for such gifts frequently is an irrevocable trust, with no reversionary interest retained by the client.

Middle-aged clients who are in high marginal income tax brackets also may use short term trusts to reallocate income temporarily, in order to save taxes during their high earning years. At the same time, they retain a reversionary interest so that they will get back the principal at a future date when their earnings may have been reduced by retirement.

Smaller lifetime gifts often are made by means of present interest trusts (or trust substitutes) for children or grandchildren, in order to minimize gift taxes.

In these situations, a battery of estate planning vehicles may be appropriate:

1. A will (a revocable trust also may be desirable for a variety of reasons, depending on the client's situation and local law and practice);

2. An irrevocable trust, to shift wealth to children and other descendants at appropriate times;

3. A short term trust, to reallocate income temporarily;

4. Present interest trusts (or trust substitutes) for children or grand-children.

[4] Single Parents (See Estate plan for Louise D. Rhodes in the Documentary Supplement)

Single parents of any age have a particular need for a will or revocable trust to provide for their children, as well as to name guardians for any who are minors.   Wealth transfer taxes are a greater concern because of the absence of any marital deduction.   In other respects, the situation of single parents often parallels that of young or middle-aged married couples or of the senior client with children, depending on the age of the single parent.

[5] Seniors or Elderly (See Estate plan for Louise D. Rhodes in the Documentary Supplement)

The estate planning needs of senior or elderly clients differ from their younger counterparts chiefly with respect to their present and prospective ability to manage wealth.   Often another manager is needed because the client is either unwilling or unable to act himself.   Even if there is no immediate need for managerial assistance, it may arise at any time as the result of some physical or mental deterioration of the client.   A so-called "durable" power of attorney, which is not revoked by the incompetence of the grantor, is authorized in some states and may meet this need for management.

Often a revocable trust is better suited for this purpose but only after it has been funded by a transfer of substantial assets to the trustee.   If the client does not have an immediate need for management of his wealth, a stand-by revocable trust may be created so as to be available whenever the need arises.

"There is nothing earthly that lasts so well, on the whole, as money.   A man's learning dies with him;   even his virtues fade out of remembrance;   but the dividends on the stocks he bequeaths to his children live and keep his memory green."

O. W. Holmes, Sr., The Professor at the Breakfast Table 6 (1860).

¶ 1.03   IMPORTANCE OF STATE LAW IN ESTATE PLANNING

State law has a profound effect on estate planning for four major reasons:

(1) Most wealth in the United States consists of money or other property whose ownership is determined by state law and which may be transferred only in accordance with that law.   Estate plans therefore consist chiefly of arrangements whose effectiveness depends on state law.

(2) Three major federal taxes that are important in estate planning depend on the nature of property interests under state law.   The estate tax provisions define the taxable estate largely in terms of

state-defined ownership and state-controlled transfers of property.[1] The gift tax is imposed on the transfer of property by gift;[2] whether such a transfer has occurred is generally determined by state law, although federal law determines which transfers constitute gifts.[3] The generation-skipping transfer tax applies to certain terminations of interests in or powers over property as determined under state law.[4] And deductions under all three taxes also are greatly influenced by state law.[5]

(3) State-created obligations to support dependents and to carry out the terms of court decrees also have important federal tax consequences.

(4) Finally, state tax consequences should not be ignored in developing an estate plan, although often the arrangement that produces favorable federal tax consequences is desirable from the standpoint of state taxes as well. For example, many states do not impose a gift tax, thus reducing the relative tax cost of lifetime transfers that are effective to remove the transferred property from the estate of the transferor in comparison to the tax cost of transfers at death.

The estate planning implications of the federal income tax are less dependent on state law than is true for the estate tax, gift tax, and generation-skipping transfer tax. For example, the assignment of income doctrine may cause income to be attributed for tax purposes to the person whose services or property produced it, even though as a matter of state law the right to receive such income had been transferred to someone else.[6] However, there are many income tax questions in which federal law refers to that of a state, so here, too, state law has substantial importance.[7]

1. The gross estate includes property owned at death, § 2033, and certain transfers during life. See §§ 2035–2038.

2. § 2501(a)(1).

3. See, e.g., Preston L. Spruance, 60 T.C. 141 (1973), aff'd without published opinion 505 F.2d 731 (3d Cir. 1974).

4. § 2613(b)(1).

5. See, e.g., § 2053(a), which provides an estate tax deduction for certain claims and expenses "as are allowable by the laws of the jurisdiction * * * under which the estate is being administered." This provision has particular importance in community property states, where state law determines whether a claim is a separate property debt and is thus wholly deductible, or is a community property debt, only half of which is deductible. See United States v. Stapf, ¶ 18.07 infra.

See also Estate of Wesley A. Steffke v. Commissioner, 538 F.2d 730, 76–2 USTC ¶ 13,145 (7th Cir. 1976), cert. denied, 429 U.S. 1022 (1976) and Estate of Leo J. Goldwater v. Commissioner, 539 F.2d 878, 76–2 USTC ¶ 13,146 (2d Cir. 1976), cert. denied 429

U.S. 1023 (1976), where the court held that the decedent's estate was not entitled to a marital deduction for property passing to a surviving "spouse" because the law of the state where the deceased's estate was being administered did not recognize the deceased's marriage as valid.

If the state where the estate is being administered recognizes a marriage as valid, it may be irrelevant that another state considered the marriage a nullity. See Estate of Amy A. M. Spalding v. Commissioner, 537 F.2d 666, 76–2 USTC ¶ 13,144 (2d Cir. 1976).

6. For a discussion, see ¶ 4.01[2][a] infra.

7. For example, eligibility to file a joint return may turn on the validity of a marriage as determined by state law. Compare Harold K. Lee, 64 T.C. 552 (1975), aff'd per curiam 550 F.2d 1201, 77–1 USTC ¶ 9349 (9th Cir. 1977) (joint return not allowed when marriage was invalid under California law) with Estate of Herman Borax v. Commissioner, 349 F.2d 666, 65–2 USTC ¶ 9592 (2d Cir. 1965), cert. denied 383 U.S. 935 (1966) (joint return permitted although marriage not valid under state law).

¶ 1.04　STATE COURT DECREES

Because state law determines both the effectiveness of transfers of property and the kinds of property interests created by a transfer, state court decrees can be an important tool in estate planning.

Where the effectiveness of an attempt to transfer property is in doubt (e.g., when a provision of a will is susceptible to several interpretations), the affected parties may seek a state court determination that fixes their rights. Even though federal tax consequences may flow from the decree, the Commissioner of Internal Revenue generally does not participate in litigation between private parties.[8] The private parties involved may all be seeking the same result: a state court decree that will fix rights in a manner most favorable from a federal tax standpoint. Although the state court decree does not specifically determine federal tax consequences, it may as a practical matter have that effect. Parties who are unwilling or unable to seek such a state court determination may rely on favorable state court decisions in similar cases to buttress their arguments with the Commissioner.

A body of doctrine, however, has limited the binding effect of state court decrees, most recently by the tests the Supreme Court laid down in the *Bosch* [9] case. In *Bosch*, the Court faced the question of the weight to be given determinations by state courts that, if recognized for federal tax purposes, would be favorable to the taxpayer and adverse to the Commissioner by causing an interest to qualify for the marital deduction or by increasing the amount deductible. The Court held that the federal tax authorities must apply state law to determine what property interests had been created, but also held that a decision of a state's trial court is not dispositive of the question of what state law is. On the other hand, a recent decision of a state's highest court is controlling. If there is no such decision, the Court said that the federal tax authorities "must apply what they find to be the state law after giving 'proper regard' to relevant rulings of other courts of the State." [10]

Although widely criticized,[11] the *Bosch* decision has major consequences in estate planning. It limits the importance of determinations of state trial courts and intermediate appellate courts because federal tax authorities (and federal courts, if tax litigation ensues) may disregard the decisions of those courts if they find them not to be the state law.[12] This is also true of older decisions of the state's highest court, if there is reason to believe that those decisions are no longer good law. But because controlling weight is given to recent decisions of a state's highest court, parties who are willing and able to pursue an issue through the entire state court system may

---

8. Mim. 6134 (April 3, 1947), 80–9 SFTR ¶ 5781.4192.

9. Commissioner v. Estate of Bosch, ¶ 18.04[2] infra.

10. 387 U.S. at 465, 87 S.Ct. at 1783, 18 L.Ed.2d at 894, 67–2 USTC at 85.552.

11. See, e.g., Wolfman, "Bosch, Its Implications and Aftermath: The Effect of State Court Adjudications on Federal Tax Litigation," 3 U.Miami Inst. on Est. Plan. ¶ 69.200 (1969).

12. This is most likely to occur when a trial court decision is inconsistent with an earlier decision of one of the state's higher courts, and the trial court decision has not been overturned because neither party has appealed.

prevail in a federal tax controversy. In these instances, the state court decree can be an important tool in revising an estate plan, and may achieve the substantial equivalent of a taxfree transfer of property interests.[13] For example, it may construe the will as relieving a bequest to the surviving spouse from liability otherwise imposed by state law for payment of a portion of the federal estate tax, thereby causing a larger part of the estate to pass to her and to qualify for the estate tax marital deduction.

¶ 1.05 SUPPORT OBLIGATIONS

A major state-created right and correlative obligation is that of one person to support from another. Usually, this obligation is owed by one spouse to the other spouse or to a former spouse,[14] or by a parent to a child.[15] Often, obligations to support parents [16] or other relatives are also imposed by state law, but these obligations are much less important in estate planning.

An obligation to support a spouse or a child may affect estate planning in several ways:

(1) For income tax purposes, transfers of appreciated property to discharge the obligation may cause the transferor to realize taxable income to the extent of such appreciation; [17]

(2) For gift tax purposes, a transfer that discharges the obligation is not a taxable gift; [18]

(3) For estate tax purposes, provisions for the use of income from transferred property to discharge a support obligation of the transferor may constitute retention of income by him and thus require inclusion of the transferred property in his gross estate; [19]

(4) For both gift and estate tax purposes, a person who has the power to use property, which was transferred by someone other than himself, to discharge his obligation to support his dependents, has a "general power of appointment." [20] The release of such a power may constitute a gift of the property by the power holder.[21] The donees are the persons who are named as takers in default of exercise of the power and whose taking is assured when the power is released. In addition, upon the death of the power holder, the property subject to the power of appointment may be included in the deceased's estate.[22]

13. See, e.g., Ray C. Imel v. United States, 523 F.2d 853, 75–2 USTC ¶ 9698 (10th Cir. 1975).

14. See, e.g., N.Y.Dom.Rel.L. §§ 32,236.

15. See, e.g., Cal.Civ.Code § 242 (West Supp. 1980).

16. Id.

17. See Rev.Rul. 57–507, 1957–2 CB 511; Rev.Rul. 59–47, 1959–1 CB 198.

18. See Rev.Rul. 68–379, 1968–2 CB 414; Estate of H. B. Hundley, 52 T.C. 495

(1969), aff'd per curiam 435 F.2d 1311, 71–1 USTC ¶ 12,736 (4th Cir. 1971).

19. Reg. § 20.2036–1(b)(2). For a discussion, see ¶ 5.02 [4][a][i] infra.

20. See Reg. §§ 25.2514–1(c)(1), 20.2041–1(c)(1). "General power of appointment" is defined identically for purposes of the estate tax (§ 2041(b)(1)) and gift tax (§ 2514(c)).

21. See § 2514(b).

22. See § 2041(a)(2).

(5) For generation-skipping transfer tax purposes, the possibility that trust income or principal may be used to discharge a support obligation may make the support obligor a beneficiary of the trust. Assignment of beneficiaries to generations younger than that of the grantor, distributions to them, and terminations of their interests are determinative in applying the tax. Thus the effect of this possible use of trust income or principal may be to increase the burden of the tax.

A sometimes overlooked factor in estate planning is the dilemma of the parent of a disabled child.[23] Although the legal obligation to support the child will end with the death of the parent, the moral obligation to make special provisions for the child will continue. In doing so, however, it is important to bear in mind that the beneficiary of such provisions may be the federal or state government, rather than the child himself, if resources provided by the parent have the effect of disqualifying the child for some form of public assistance. Giving a trustee discretion to provide supplementary assistance may for this reason be preferable to giving the child an absolute right to trust income or principal. Of course, some of the same considerations apply to a child who does not have the handicap of disability, but without the prospect that the period during which assistance is needed may continue throughout the child's life.

¶ 1.06   INTESTACY

No one is ever without an estate plan from the moment of his birth, even if he never sees a lawyer or makes a will. The state intestacy statutes provide such a plan for everyone who cannot or does not make one of his own. For clients who prefer an individually tailored plan of their own, the most common alternatives to the intestacy statutes are wills and revocable trusts, either of which may be used as the vehicle to dispose of substantially all that the client owns. Other common methods of choosing beneficiaries include joint ownership with a right of survivorship and beneficiary designations for life insurance, employee benefits, and individual retirement arrangements. If the client's desires are best carried out by dying intestate, he has no need of a lawyer's help in doing so. But the number of clients in this category is small. Even if the intestacy statute specifies the exact disposition which the client has in mind as to beneficiaries and their respective shares, his lawyer usually can make substantial improvements in arranging for management of his wealth. And the shares provided in the intestate statute often are not what the client would choose.

For example, young married clients with modest estates frequently wish to disinherit any children in favor of their spouses, on the assumption that the spouse will use whatever is needed for the benefit of the children without being legally obligated to do so as the children's guardian. Wealthier clients with a greater concern for tax savings wish to make qualifying marital deduction gifts in a size or form differing from the spouse's share on intestacy, or to make gifts to charitable beneficiaries. And if their

---

23. For a discussion, see Frolik, Estate Planning for Parents of Mentally Disabled Children, 40 U.Pitt.L.R. 305 (1979).

concern for taxes includes, as it should, the tax exposure of their beneficiaries, they may wish to give their children limited interests or bypass them altogether in favor of grandchildren or other descendants.

The intestacy statutes remain, however, an important starting point in the study of estate planning for several reasons. Many decedents die without a complete estate plan of their own choosing, so that the alternative plan provided by law in the intestacy statutes must control the disposition of some or even all of their wealth. For some decedents, there may have been no choice because they were minors or otherwise lacked the legal capacity to make a will or to create a trust.[24] Furthermore, in developing a client's plan, it is important to determine what assets he may receive by intestacy from others. And in disposing of his wealth, the fact that an intended beneficiary will lack the legal capacity to dispose of what the client gives him is an important factor in deciding whether, or in what form, to make the gift. Finally, many estate plans expressly incorporate an intestacy statute to control the disposition of wealth when the other provisions of the client's plan cannot be carried out because, for example, the beneficiaries have all died before the assets are fully distributed.

The intestacy statute referred to in this chapter is that of New York. The New York statute is, in broad outline, similar to those in effect in most non-community property states:

1. "Exempt property" is made available for the decedent's spouse and issue and is freed from creditor's claims;[25]

2. "Advancements" (gifts to descendants of the decedent made by him during his life) may under some circumstances be treated as part of his estate in determining the shares of beneficiaries;[26]

3. After exempt property has been set apart, the claims of creditors and tax collectors have been met, and the costs of administration of the estate have been deducted, the balance of the estate is divided in specified shares.[27]

---

[1] Exempt Property for Spouse and Descendants

Many states provide by statute that whether or not a decedent leaves a will, a portion of his estate shall be free from the claims of creditors and available for the surviving spouse and any minor children of the decedent. The New York statute refers to "exempt property";[28] elsewhere the local law may create a "homestead"[29] or provide an allowance for the support of the widow or widower and minor children[30] or may accord both types of

---

24. In some states, by statute or court decision, it is possible to obtain judicial approval of transfers on behalf of an incompetent individual based on tax and other estate planning considerations. See, e.g., Mass.Gen. Laws Ann. c. 201, § 38; In re Irénée duPont, 41 Del.Ch. 300, 194 A.2d 309 (1963).

25. N.Y. EPTL 5–3.1. This provision also applies to testate estates.

26. Id. 2–1.5.

27. Id. 4–1.1.

28. Id. 5–3.1.

29. See, e.g., Mass.Gen. Laws Ann. c. 188, §§ 1–10.

30. Id. c. 196, §§ 1–2.

protection. Ordinarily, the estate planning significance of these provisions is limited because of the relatively small amount of property affected, except for the so-called "widow's allowance."

_____

[2] Advancements to Descendants

When an individual has made gifts to his descendants during his lifetime, should these gifts be counted in dividing his estate if he dies without a will? Many states provide such gifts shall be counted in specified circumstances, as "advancements" in determining the donee's share of the estate.[31] These statutes are relatively unimportant in estate planning, however, because an effective plan ordinarily will exclude the operation of the local statute on advancements.[32]

_____

[3] Shares of the Residuary Estate

After exempt property has been set apart, creditors and tax collectors have been paid, and costs of administration have been deducted, what remains of the estate usually is divided into shares as follows:

1. The surviving spouse receives a share which may or may not be affected by the number of descendants who also survive the decedent;

2. The balance, after deducting the spouse's share, or the entire residue if there is no surviving spouse, is given to the descendants of the decedent;

3. If there are no descendants, the surviving spouse may be entitled to the entire residue or may divide it with more remote relatives of the decedent;

4. If there is no surviving spouse and there are no descendants, the estate goes to the closest surviving relative;

5. If no relative is able to establish his claim, the residue escheats to the state.

States vary as to the degree of relationship which will be recognized for purposes of inheritance. Some impose no limit, so that if all mankind has a common ancestor, escheats occur only as a result of a failure of proof of relationship. Other states seek to prevent the passage of property to "laughing heirs" and the depletion of estates to pay for the services of professional genealogists by limiting the number of degrees of relationship within which claimants are recognized.

_____

[a] Degrees of Blood Relationship

The civil law method of determining degrees of relationship illustrated in the following chart is used in New York and in many other states as

---

31. See, e.g., N.Y. EPTL 2–1.5.

The New York statute also applies to a gift in satisfaction of a legacy under an existing will. In many jurisdictions, such gifts may be subject to the doctrine of satisfaction of legacies. See Atkinson, Wills § 133 (2d ed. 1953).

32. Atkinson, supra at § 129.

well.[33]   It is based on the number of links connecting the decedent, the common ancestor, and the claimant.   For example, a decedent and his first

Degrees of Blood Relationship[34]
(Civil Law)

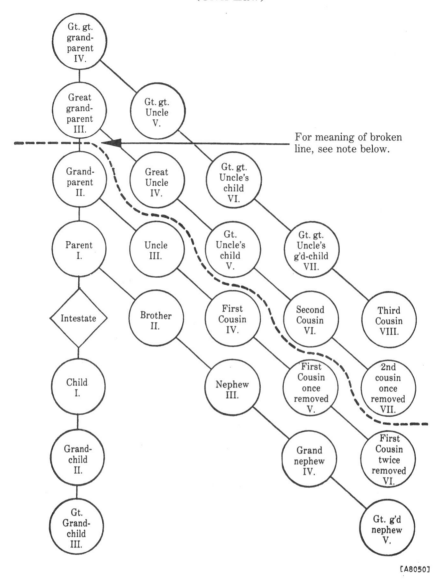

For meaning of broken line, see note below.

[A8050]

Where the distributee is a male, the female is included.   Thus with brothers read sisters, with uncles read aunts, etc.

Note: Meaning of broken line. The broken line indicates the limit of the right to inherit from an intestate under the EPTL where the decedent was an adult and competent at the time of death.   If the decedent was an infant or adjudged incompetent at the time of death, the limit would be extended to the great-grandparent and his issue * * * .

33. See 23 Am.Jur.2d Descent and Distri-
     bution § 48 (1965).

34. 29 Carmody-Wait, Cyclopedia of New
     York Practice with Forms § 169.42 (3d ed.

1981).   Copyright © 1981 The Lawyers Cooperative Publishing Company.   Reproduced with permission.

cousin are related in the fourth degree because there are two links between the decedent and the common ancestor, his grandparent, and two more links between the common ancestor and the first cousin.

[b] Per Capita and Per Stirpes Distribution

Innumerable litigated cases have dealt with the question whether distribution to the descendants of an individual is to be made "per capita" or "per stirpes." A *per capita* distribution gives an equal amount to each claimant, each taking in his own right.[35] For example, if A dies, leaving no children who survive him and six grandchildren who do survive him, a *per capita* distribution would give each grandchild one-sixth of A's estate.

A *per stirpes* distribution, on the other hand, would, in the absence of statutory modification, be based on an initial division of A's estate between those of his children who left descendants who survived him. So if four grandchildren were offspring of A's deceased daughter and two were offspring of A's deceased son, the initial division would be into halves. One half would then be divided among the daughter's children, each taking one eighth of the estate, and the other half would be divided between the son's children, giving each one-quarter of the estate. Under a *per stirpes* distribution, the claimants who are not in the first generation take the share their parent or more remote ancestor would have taken had he lived.[36] However, by statute this rule often is modified where all claimants are related to the common ancestor in the same degree.[37] Under the usual statutory modification, in the case just described there would be a *per capita* division, giving each grandchild one-sixth.

¶ 1.07 WILLS

Despite the widespread use of revocable trusts and joint ownership with a right of survivorship as will substitutes, wills remain an important estate planning tool. Although a revocable trust may serve many of the purposes which might otherwise be served by a will, it rarely eliminates the need for a will altogether. Few clients wish to transfer title to all of their assets to the trustee of a revocable trust, and even if they did, subsequent acquisitions would not be part of the trust unless further transfers were made whenever assets were acquired. Joint ownership with survivorship is an even less comprehensive alternative to a will, as it does not provide for the possibility that the other joint owner may not be the survivor.

Aside from controlling the disposition of at least the residual assets of a client which are not part of a revocable trust when he dies, wills serve other purposes which revocable trusts cannot perform:

(1) To exercise any powers of appointment which the client holds and wishes to exercise, and which are exercisable only by will.

(2) To appoint an executor. Even if all of a client's assets have been transferred to a revocable trust, an executor will be needed to perform various functions after the client's death, such as filing tax returns.

---

35. See, e.g., N.Y. EPTL 1–2.11.

36. Id. 1–2.14.

37. Id. 2–1.2.

(3) To appoint a guardian of the person or of the estate or both for any minor children of the client.

If a will is to be fully effective to carry out the client's choice of beneficiaries, it must:

1. Qualify for admission to probate;

2. Express the client's choices so clearly that court proceedings are not required to determine what it means;

3. Avoid disruption by the exercise by a surviving spouse or child of rights given by state law to a share of the estate;

4. Avoid violation of the Rule Against Perpetuities and related rules, discussed in chapter 3.

[1] Requirements for Admission to Probate

In order for an instrument to be entitled to admission to probate, the testator must have had the mental capacity required by state law to make a will, have attained some minimum age, usually 18, and must not have acted as a result of fraud or undue influence.   In addition, there are statutory formalities for its execution—chiefly the presence, and signatures, of witnesses who are not beneficiaries.

A will may be amended by a codicil,[38] which has the advantage of saving typing and proof-reading time when the testator wishes to make only minor changes in an existing will.   One important disadvantage of a codicil is that the will which it amends must also be offered for probate and thus its terms before amendment become a matter of public record.

Another major disadvantage of a codicil is that it may substantially increase the cost of the probate proceeding by requiring service of process upon persons whose interests are adversely, if minutely, affected by the codicil,[39] and who consequently may require representation by a guardian ad litem.[40]   Finally, if the codicil changes provisions of the will dealing with a long-term testamentary trust, a proper regard for the individuals who will have to refer to the governing provisions over the years suggests that they should be incorporated in one, rather than several, documents.

If the testator wishes to revoke his will, he may do so by another will, or by destroying the old will with intent to revoke it, in addition to less common methods which may be recognized in a particular state.[41]   Some states use partial revocation as a means of affording protection to omitted children born to the testator after the execution of his will, absent evidence that the omission was intentional.[42]

---

38. See N.Y. EPTL 1–2.1.

39. See N.Y.Surr.Ct.Proc.Act 1403(c).   In the absence of a codicil affecting their interests, such persons would be entitled to be personally served with process (as distinguished from mere notice by mail) only if they were distributees.   Id. 1403(a).

40. See ¶ 2.02 [1] infra.

41. See, e.g., N.Y. EPTL 3–4.1.

42. Id. 5–3.2.

In some states, marriage revokes a will,[43] and divorce revokes provisions in favor of the former spouse unless the will expressly provides otherwise, under some statutes.[44]

---

[2] Expressing the Client's Choice of Beneficiaries

Lawyers and clients find it relatively easy to think and write in precise terms about immediate gifts of specific items or amounts to named individuals—e.g., Greenacre to my daughter Mary or $10,000 to my son John. Even such simple gifts raise problems:

(1) If either Mary or John fails to survive the testator (see [a] below);

(2) If the testator transfers Greenacre before he dies, or does not leave enough property to pay debts, expenses, and taxes, and still give Greenacre to Mary and $10,000 to John (see [b] below).

Additional problems arise if the beneficiaries are described as members of a group or class, such as "children," "issue," or "heirs," rather than by name (see ¶ 3.01 infra).

---

[a] Beneficiaries Who Die Before or at the Same Time as the Testator

An obvious gap often is created in an estate plan if a beneficiary dies either before or simultaneously with the death of the testator. Of course a completely adequate plan would provide for that contingency, but many plans do not. In most states, legislation has been enacted which seeks to fill these gaps on the basis of the presumed intention of the testator.[45]

[b] Abatement and Ademption

Abatement and ademption are common law doctrines dealing with different aspects of a single problem: an insufficiency of assets to carry out the provisions of the testator's will. Abatement is concerned with a general insufficiency of assets to pay debts, expenses and legacies.[46] New York has, by statute, specified the order in which estate assets shall be used for this purpose.[47] Ademption, on the other hand, relates to the absence from the estate of the subject matter of a specific bequest or devise.[48] For example, the testator devises "my land in Rochester" to X but he sells or gives away the land before he dies. The devise of the land is adeemed and X takes nothing.

The sale or gift of the land is a clear-cut example of ademption. The borderline cases involve the exchange of bequeathed property for other property. For example, a partnership is incorporated. A bequest of an

43. See, e.g., Mass.Gen.Laws Ann. c. 191, § 9.

44. See, e.g., N.Y. EPTL 5–1.4.

45. See, e.g., N.Y. EPTL 2–1.6 (simultaneous death); 3–3.3 (lapse statute).

46. See Atkinson, Wills § 136 (2d ed. 1953).

47. See N.Y. EPTL 13–1.3.

48. See Atkinson, supra note 46 at § 134.

interest in the former partnership may not cover the stock the decedent received in exchange for that interest when the corporation acquired the partnership assets.[49]

[3] Rights of Spouses and Descendants

Protection of spouses from disinheritance is discussed in ¶ 1.08. Protection of children and other descendants from disinheritance is far more limited.

Unlike the civil law, with its concept of a legitime or forced share for the descendants of a decedent, the common law tradition has accorded only very limited protection to disinherited children. As a practical matter, the most important protection is provided by the willingness of juries to find that a disinheriting will reflected lack of testamentary capacity, fraud, or undue influence.

A number of states provide protection from unintentional disinheritance in the case of children born after the execution of the will,[50] and in many states the protection extends to children living at the time of execution as well.[51]

Disinheritance in favor of a charity is specifically restricted in a few states.[52]   However, the restrictions may be of limited effect for the well advised testator.   For example, if the gift to charity is followed by a proviso creating an alternative gift, if the charitable disposition is ineffective, in favor of a non-relative of the testator, there may be no member of the protected class with standing to invoke the restriction on charitable gifts.[53]

¶ 1.08   VARIATIONS IN STATE MARITAL PROPERTY LAW

Almost all states give widows some protection from disinheritance by their husbands, and many grant similar protection to widowers as well.[54] But the form of such protection differs from state to state, particularly between common-law and community-property states.

In the eight community-property states—Arizona, California, Idaho, Louisiana, Nevada, New Mexico, Texas and Washington—each spouse has a one-half interest, from the moment of acquisition, in certain property

---

49. See generally, Note, Ademption and the Testator's Intent, 74 Harv.L.Rev. 741 (1961).

50. See, e.g., N.Y. EPTL 5–3.2.

If the testator wishes to disinherit afterborn children, he need merely say so to overcome the statute. E.g., "This devise and bequest is made notwithstanding any children which may be hereafter born to us." See ● Matter of Meng, 201 Misc. 589, 590, 110 N.Y.S.2d 263, 264 (Surr.Ct.1952).

51. See, e.g., Mass.Gen.Laws Ann. c. 191, § 20.

52. See, e.g., Fla.Stat.Ann. § 732.803 (West 1976);   Ga.Code Ann. § 113–107 (1975); Ohio Rev.Code Ann. § 2107.06 (Page 1976).

53. See Central Nat'l Bank of Cleveland v. Morris, 9 Ohio Misc. 167, 222 N.E.2d 674 (1967), aff'd 10 Ohio App.2d 225, 227 N.E.2d 418 (1967).   See also the following cases decided under former N.Y. EPTL 5–3.3: Matter of Cairo, 35 A.D.2d 76, 312 N.Y.S.2d 925 (2d Dep't 1970), aff'd mem. 29 N.Y.2d 527, 272 N.E.2d 574, 324 N.Y.S.2d 81 (1971);   Matter of Norcross, 67 Misc.2d 932, 325 N.Y.S.2d 477 (Surr.Ct. 1971), aff'd 334 N.Y.S.2d 600 (1st Dep't 1972).

54. See generally, Report of Committee on Administration and Distribution of Decedents' Estates, Spouse's Elective Share, 12 Real Prop. & Tr.J. 323 (1977).

acquired by either spouse during marriage.[55]   Community property includes whatever is not classified as the separate property of a spouse.   Separate property is generally defined as property owned before marriage and property acquired during marriage by gift, bequest, devise, or descent.[56]   Under this definition, the earnings of either spouse during marriage are community property, as well as any income derived from investment of such earnings. In some states, the income received from separate property during marriage is also separate; [57]   others treat such income as community property.[58]

In the forty-two common-law states and the District of Columbia, protection of spouses from disinheritance usually consists of a statutory right to take an elective or forced share of the estate of the deceased spouse, without regard to the provisions of his will.[59]

Among both groups of states, there are significant variations in the property rights of spouses. In the community-property states, there are major differences in the extent to which the spouses may change the character of property from community to separate and vice versa.[60]

Within the common-law jurisdictions, the variations in the kind of protection given spouses against disinheritance include:

(1) Differences in the size of the share of a deceased spouse's estate that the surviving spouse takes if he or she elects against the will; [61]

(2) Differences in the extent to which one spouse may "disinherit" the other by disposing of property while both are still living,[62] and

(3) Differences in the extent to which one spouse is entitled to a share of the other's property upon divorce.[63]

---

55. See, e.g., Cal.Civ.Code §§ 5105, 5110 (West Supp.1980).

56. Id., §§ 5107 (wife), 5108 (husband).

57. Ariz.Rev.Stat.Ann. § 25–213 (West 1976); Cal.Civ.Code, §§ 5107 (wife), 5108 (husband) (West Supp.1980); Nev.Rev.Stat., § 123.130 (1979); N.M.Stat.Ann., § 40–3–8 (1978); Wash.Rev.Code Ann., §§ 26.16.010 (husband), 26.16.020 (wife) (1979).

58. Idaho Code § 32–906(1) (Supp.1980) (unless conveyance or written agreement states such income shall be separate property of one spouse): La.Civ.Code Ann., art. 2339 (West Supp.1980) (unless spouse follows statutory procedure to cause such income to be separate property); Tex.Const., Art. XVI, § 15, as construed in Arnold v. Leonard, 114 Tex. 535, 273 S.W. 799 (1925). See also Tex.Fam.Code Ann.tit. 1, § 5.01 (Vernon 1975).   An amendment approved by Texas voters November 4, 1980, permits spouses to agree in writing that income from separate property shall be separate and creates a presumption that if one spouse makes a gift to the other, the income from that property is presumed to be included in the gift.   For a discussion of recent changes in Louisiana law, see generally the "Community Property Symposium," 39 La.L.Rev. 323 (1979).

59. See, e.g., N.Y. EPTL 5–1.1.

60. E.g., compare Martin v. Pritchard, 52 Cal.App. 720, 199 P. 846 (1921) and Estate of Neilson, 57 Cal.2d 733, 22 Cal.Rptr. 1, 371 P.2d 745 (1962), allowing informal conversions of property from community to separate and vice versa, with Williams v. McKnight, 402 SW.2d 505 (Tex.1966), holding that a formal partition proceeding is required for spouses to change the character of community property.

61. See, e.g., 20 Pa.Cons.Stat.Ann. § 2203 (Purdon Supp.1979);   Ohio Rev.Code Ann. § 2107.39 (Page 1976).

62. E.g., compare Kerwin v. Donaghy, 317 Mass. 559, 59 N.E.2d 299 (1945) with N.Y. EPTL 5–1.1.

63. See ¶ 8.05 note 86 infra, with respect to joint ownership in some states of property acquired by joint efforts of the spouses during marriage, at least for purposes of division thereof on divorce, and recognition of such joint ownership for federal income tax purposes.

Generally, however, only the basic classifications of property as community or separate are recognized for federal tax purposes.[64] Thus, although the respective rights of spouses vary from state to state, the only relevant question for federal tax purposes is whether or not a given item is community property under the law of some state.

[1] Community Property

Community property differs from other common estate planning tools in four major ways:

(1) Clients often use it to control the disposition of all or a large part of their wealth, without having made any conscious choice in the matter other than having spent at least part of their married lives as residents of a community-property state.

(2) Usually, there is no formal written document to establish whether, or to what extent, a given asset is community property. Instead, its character must be determined by informal records (such as cancelled checks used to pay for it) or by presumptions which control in the absence of adequate records.[65]

(3) If a couple moves from a community-property state to a common-law state, it may be important to preserve evidence of the community-property character of particular assets in order to obtain federal tax advantages.[66]

(4) If a couple moves from a common-law state to a community-property state, evidence of the character of property acquired before the move may be important. In its absence, assets may be treated as community property which in the light of such evidence should be classified as separate under applicable state law. In some cases, this is not advantageous from a federal tax standpoint. There may also be substantial non-tax advantages for the owner of separate property in having the character of such property recognized. For example, community-property states generally do not divide separate property on divorce [67] and they deny a surviving spouse any forced share of a decedent's separate property.[68]

---

64. One esoteric exception is California community property acquired before July 29, 1927, for which state law is regarded as giving the wife an expectancy in her share of the community property while both spouses are alive. Since the wife's interest in the community property does not come into being until the husband dies, the full value, (rather than one-half) is included in his estate. United States v. Goodyear, 99 F.2d 523, 38-2 USTC ¶ 9532 (9th Cir. 1938).

65. See, e.g., Cal.Civ.Code §§ 5110, 5111 (West Supp.1980); Tex.Fam.Code Ann tit. 1, § 5.02 (Vernon 1975).

66. See Johanson, The Migrating Client: Estate Planning for the Couple From a Community Property State, 9 U.Miami Inst. on Est.Plan ¶¶ 800, 830 (1975).

67. See, e.g., Ariz.Rev.Stat.Ann. § 25–318 (West Supp. 1979–1980). But see Wash.Rev. Code § 26.09.080 (1979). Separate property may, however, be used to satisfy an award of alimony or support. See, e.g., Idaho Code § 32–708 (Supp.1980); Nev.Rev.Stat. § 125.150(3) (1979), as amended, 1979 Nev.Stat.Ch. 685; N.M.Stat.Ann. § 40–4–7(B)(1) (1978).

Some states recognize an additional category, commonly known as "quasi-community property," which is generally defined as property which would have been community property had it been acquired in the community-property state. Such "quasi-community property" may be divided at divorce. See, e.g., Cal.Civ.Code §§ 4800, 4803 (West Supp.1980).

68. A surviving spouse in California is entitled to a one-half share of the "quasi-com-

In a given client's case, it often is not possible to predict which classification of an asset will ultimately prove to be more advantageous. His tax position, and that of his wife, may change over the years and their rights on divorce may never become relevant. This has led some to suggest that detailed record keeping may prove to be more of a hindrance than a help, since the absence of records may facilitate a free choice of classification of property as community or separate when the issue actually arises. However, aside from the ethical problems this approach raises, it impedes intelligent estate planning for a client who may own community property, as a sound plan necessarily begins with a determination of how assets are held.

Although a client should have his estate plan reviewed upon any change of state residence, such a review is particularly desirable on a move between a community-property and a common-law state. Community property affects the transfers used to minimize taxes during life and at death, and has non-tax consequences as well.

[2] Election Against the Will in Non-community Property States

The *Clark* case which follows illustrates the contrasting effects of a spouse's election against the will in two noncommunity property states, New York and Virginia. The Virginia statute [69] is the more typical, giving the spouse the absolute right to a share of the decedent's estate. The New York statute,[70] on the other hand, is unusual in two important respects:

1. If the testator gives the spouse income for life from an amount equal to or greater than her elective share, she has the right to elect to withdraw $10,000 and no more.[71] In most states, the spouse's right to elect a statutory share cannot be cut off or curtailed by merely giving her income for life from that share.

2. The statute specifies a number of inter vivos transfers that are included in determining the size of the elective share.[72] Many state statutes are silent on the extent of inclusion of inter vivos transfers for this purpose, leaving the matter for judicial construction.[73]

Whether such legislative protection of spouses is needed is very much in doubt. No similar protection is afforded other dependents of a decedent even though in the case of young children their opportunities for immediate self-support usually are much less favorable than such opportunities are for a spouse. And it is far from clear that any significant number of husbands or wives would choose to leave an insufficient provision for a dependent spouse if they were free to do so.[74] Moreover, as the following case illustrates, the protection provided is wholly unrelated to amounts reasonably required for the survivor's support.

The previous discussion assumes that the legislative protection of spouses is for their support needs. Another possible rationale is that it

---

munity property," see note 67 supra, included in a deceased spouse's estate. See Cal.Prob. Code § 201.5 (West Supp.1980).

69. Va.Code § 64.1–13.

70. N.Y. EPTL 5–1.1.

71. Id. 5–1.1(c)(1)(D).

72. Id. 5–1.1(b).

73. See, e.g., Kerwin v. Donaghy, 317 Mass. 559, 59 N.E.2d 299 (1945).

74. See generally Plager, The Spouse's Non-barrable Share: A Solution in Search of a Problem, 33 U.Chi.L.Rev. 681 (1966).

represents a recognition of the contribution of the survivor to the earnings of the decedent. That rationale, however, does not support an elective right in favor of the surviving spouse with respect to property the decedent acquired before his marriage. It is much more in keeping with the community property concept, which confines the survivor's rights to post-marital acquisitions.[75]

MATTER OF CLARK

Court of Appeals of New York, 1968.
21 N.Y.2d 478, 288 N.Y.S.2d 993, 236 N.E.2d 152.

FULD, Chief Judge. This appeal poses an interesting and important question concerning a widow's right of election to take against her husband's will. More particularly, may her husband, domiciled in a foreign state, by selecting New York law to regulate his testamentary dispositions, cut off or otherwise affect the more favorable right given his widow to elect by the law of their domicile?

In the case before us, Robert V. Clark, Jr., died in October of 1964, domiciled in Virginia, and there his widow continues to reside. His estate, consisting of property in Virginia and in New York, had an aggregate value of more than $23,000,000—the bulk of which consisted of securities on deposit with a New York bank. His will, made in 1962, contained a provision that "this Will and the testamentary dispositions in it and the trusts set up shall be construed, regulated and determined by the laws of the State of New York." It devised the Clark residence in Virginia, together with its contents, to the widow and created for her benefit a preresiduary marital deduction trust—under which she would receive the income for life, with a general testamentary power of appointment over the principal of the trust. The residue of the estate, after payment of estate taxes, was placed in trust for the testator's mother. There has been a bi-state administration of the estate. The New York executors are administering the major portion of the estate—consisting, as noted, of securities held in New York during Mr. Clark's lifetime—and the Virginia executors are administering the balance, including the real and tangible personal property located in Virginia.

The testamentary trust for the widow's benefit would satisfy the requirements of section 18 of our Decedent Estate Law, Consol.Laws, c. 13. However, it is conceded that, under the statutes of Virginia, the widow has an absolute and unconditional right to renounce her husband's will and take her intestate share (in the absence of issue, one half) of his estate outright (Virginia Code, § 64–16).[76] Timely notice of the widow's election having been given, the New York executors initiated this special proceeding in the Surrogate's Court, pursuant to section 145–a of the New York Surrogate's Court Act. The petition requests a determination denying the widow any right of election on the grounds that the terms of the will barred her from

---

75. See ¶ 1.08 supra.

76. In contrast, the New York right of election statute, in effect at the time of this testator's death (Decedent Estate Law, § 18), permits a decedent to defeat his spouse's right by creating a trust of the requisite size for her benefit and giving her the net income therefrom for life.

recourse to Virginia law and that, under New York law, the testamentary provisions in her favor were sufficient.   The executors contend that, by declaring that his testamentary dispositions should be construed by the laws of New York, the testator meant to bar his widow from exercising her Virginia right of election and that section 47 of the Decedent Estate Law requires that we give effect to his purpose.   That section—replaced, since the testator's death, by a very similar provision (EPTL 3–5.1, subd. [h])—provided, in essence, that, when a nondomiciliary testator recites in his will that he elects that his *"testamentary dispositions"* shall be construed and regulated by the laws of New York, "the validity and effect of *such dispositions* shall be determined by such laws." [77]

The Surrogate upheld the executor's position.   On appeal, the Appellate Division reversed, deciding that the widow's right to take in opposition to the will must be determined by the law of the domicile of the parties. Section 47—which relates solely to the decedent's "testamentary dispositions" and their validity and effect—was inapplicable, the court concluded, because "the right of a widow to inherit despite the will is not a 'testamentary disposition' in any sense" but is, on the contrary, "a restriction on the right to make a testamentary disposition."   (28 A.D.2d 55, 57, 281 N.Y.S.2d 180, 183.)

We thoroughly agree with the Appellate Division's construction of the statute and with the conclusion it reached.

*   *   *

Unlike the expressions of intent which constitute testamentary dispositions, the right of election, both in Virginia and New York, is statutory in nature and exists wholly outside of, and in direct contravention to, the provisions of a will.   *   *   *   As the court noted in Matter of Greenberg, 261 N.Y. at p. 478, 185 N.E., at p. 705, section 18 of the Decedent Estate Law, when enacted in 1929, introduced into this State a "new public policy which no longer permit[ted] a testator to dispose of his property as he please[d]."   This being so, it necessarily follows that the widow's right of election—or, more precisely, its availability or nonavailability—is not a "testamentary disposition" whose validity and effect may be controlled by the provisions of a will under section 47.   In the words of the Appellate Division, the spouse's right of election, far from being a testamentary disposition, is a "restriction on the right [of the decedent] to make [such] a *   *   * disposition."

A moment's reflection is all that is necessary to establish the difference between statutes which have to do with restrictions placed on the decedent's

---

77. Section 47 read, in somewhat greater detail, as follows: "The validity and effect of a testamentary disposition of real property, situated within the state   *   *   *   are regulated by the laws of the state, without regard to the residence of the decedent. Except where special provision is otherwise made by law, the validity and effect of a testamentary disposition of any other property situated within the state, and the ownership and disposition of such property *   *   *   are regulated by the laws of the state or country, of which the decedent was a resident, at the time of his death. *When-ever a decedent, being a citizen of the United States or a citizen or a subject of a foreign country wherever resident, shall have declared in his will that he elects that such testamentary dispositions shall be construed and regulated by the laws of this state, the validity and effect of such dispositions shall be determined by such laws."* (Emphasis supplied.)

testamentary power—for instance, to disinherit his spouse or other members of his family—and those which bear on discerning and carrying out the testator's wishes and desires.   Section 47 is an example of the latter sort of legislation.   * * *

Moreover, consideration of general principles of choice of law serve to confirm the conclusion, at which we have arrived, that it is the law of Virginia as to the widow's right of election, not that of New York, which here controls.   As between two states, the law of that one which has the predominant, if not the sole, interest in the protection and regulation of the rights of the person or persons involved should, of course, be invoked. [Citations omitted.]

Matter of Crichton, 20 N.Y.2d 124, 281 N.Y.S.2d 811, 228 N.E.2d 799, supra, is illustrative.   A domiciliary of New York had placed his personal property in a state (Louisiana) which had a very different method of protecting a surviving spouse.   In deciding that the law of the domicile ought to be applied, our court noted that Louisiana had no "interest in protecting and regulating the rights of married persons residing and domiciled in New York."   On the contrary, we declared, "New York, as the domicile of Martha and Powell Crichton, has not only the dominant interest in the application of its law and policy but the only interest" (20 N.Y.2d at p. 134, 281 N.Y.S.2d, at p. 820, 228 N.E.2d, at p. 806).

Although a declaration contained in a will that its law was to control might give a foreign state an interest in the application of its law that it would otherwise lack, this interest would not extend to a matter, such as the right of election, which is completely unrelated to, and indeed in contravention of, the decedent's intent.   Thus, in the *Crichton* case, the court made it exceeding plain that such a declaration would not be given any effect, if to do so would be to "avoid the New York statutory provision for the protection of the surviving spouse" (20 N.Y.2d, at p. 137, n. 10).   But, urge the appellants before us, even if a testator domiciled in *New York* could not avoid his spouse's right of election in that way, this State's interest in encouraging nonresidents to invest their funds here ought to be given effect, even at the expense of the rights given to a surviving spouse by the law of the domicile of the decedent and his widow.   The authorities upon which they rely, however, fail to support such a proposition.

In Wyatt v. Fulrath, 16 N.Y.2d 169, 264 N.Y.S.2d 233, 211 N.E.2d 637, and Hutchison v. Ross, 262 N.Y. 381, 187 N.E. 65, 89 A.L.R. 1007, we permitted non-domiciliaries to make dispositions of property located here which would have violated the public policy of their domicile, and it is asserted that a similar result should be reached in this case.   *Hutchison* and *Wyatt*, however, are inapposite; both involved *inter vivos* transactions between husband and wife.   Such *inter vivos* dispositions, unlike the unilateral provisions of a will, have traditionally been upheld if permitted under the law of place where the property was located.   [Citations omitted.]

Indeed, in the Hutchison case, (262 N.Y. 381, 391, 187 N.E. 65, 69, supra), this court specifically referred to the distinction drawn between *inter vivos* and testamentary dispositions.   After noting that "The rules that both the capacity to make a valid conveyance of tangible chattels and securities and the essential validity of such conveyance are determined by the law of the state where chattel is situated   * * *   have been generally applied to conveyances *inter vivos*", the court went on to say that "[t]hey are not generally applied to passage of title by will or the intestacy of a decedent owner.   With possible limitations, not relevant to the question here presented [cases cited], the rule is well established that the essential validity of a testamentary trust must be determined by the law of the decedent's domicile" (p. 391, 187 N.E. p. 69).

In point of fact, recent legislative changes serve to confirm our conclusion that a widow of a nondomiciliary cannot be deprived of the right of election given to her by the law of the jurisdiction in which she and her husband were domiciled.   In 1965, the Legislature undertook a thorough re-evaluation of the law governing rights of election in this State and, as a result, adopted section 18–b of the Decedent Estate Law, to take effect September 1, 1966.   The new section explicitly provided (subd. 4) that the New York provisions "shall *not be available* to the spouse of a decedent who at the time of his death was not domiciled in this state."   In 1966, that same rule was restated as subdivision 6 of section 18–c and, again, as section 5–1.1 of the new Estates Powers and Trusts Law which was to go into effect the following year.   Thus, three successive legislative enactments had specifically provided that, regardless of any expression of intent, the spouse of a nondomiciliary was not entitled to exercise a right of election under New York law.   The purpose of the provision was undoubtedly to insure that the spouse's rights were to be determined by the law of the domicile (Fourth Report of Temporary State Commission on Estates, N.Y.Legis.Doc., 1965, No. 19, pp. 150–151).   This was considered necessary to achieve uniformity between the law which had been applied to real property and the existing law as to personal property which the commission found, "under established rules, is governed by the law of the decedent's domicile" (pp. 150–151).

However, effective September 1, 1967, the spouse of a nondomiciliary was given an additional right; section 5–1.1 (subd [d], par. [6]) of the new Estates Powers and Trusts Law was amended (L. 1967, ch. 686, § 39) to give to the surviving spouse the opportunity to elect against the will under New York law where the testator made an election to have his testamentary dispositions governed by New York law.   "The right of election granted by this section," the amended provision reads, "is not available to the spouse of a decedent who was not domiciled in this state at the time of death, unless such decedent elects, under paragraph (h) of 3–5.1 [formerly Decedent Estate Law, § 47], to have the disposition of his property governed by the laws of this state."

The effect of this provision, quite obviously, was to render the New York right of election *"available"*—that is, afford an opportunity—to a nondomiciliary to elect the New York right of election where, under prior law, she would have been limited to her rights under the law of the domicile. It was consistent with the policy of uniformity since, where a testator had declared that his will should be governed by the law of a foreign jurisdiction, no interest of the domicile would be prejudiced by extending to the surviving spouse the greatest protections which New York law might provide.   (See Scoles, Conflict of Laws and Elections in Administration of Decedents' Estates, 30 Ind.L.J. 293, 307.) Be that as it may, though, the statute was certainly not intended to *deprive* her of any rights afforded by the domicile in a case such as this, where it would provide her with a greater protection than the law of New York. On the contrary, as we have already observed, the amended statute extends an *additional* protection which she would not otherwise have had. In short, the statute manifests a strong legislative policy to limit the testator's power to deprive his spouse of support; it is designed to complement, not to frustrate, the policies of sister states directed toward the same end.

While Virginia, as well as New York, had demonstrated concern for surviving spouses, the two states have done so in substantially different ways. A right to the income of a trust, sufficient under our law (Decedent Estate Law, § 18), is by no means the equivalent of taking the principal outright as would be the widow's right upon her election under Virginia law. Whether the widow in the case before us would be adequately provided for under the will [78] or our own law is irrelevant, for the same principles must apply to an estate of $23,000 as to one of $23,000,000, and we reject the notion that New York ought to impose upon its sister states its own views as to the adequacy of a surviving spouse's share.

In sum, Virginia's overwhelming interest in the protection of surviving spouses domiciled there demands that we apply its law to give the widow in this case the right of election provided for her under that law. We find nothing in section 47 of the Decedent Estate Law or in the public policy of New York which would permit a decedent, by a mere expression of intent, to change this result.

* * *

QUESTIONS

1. What may have motivated Ms. Clark to elect a statutory share?
2. What is the effect on the remainders following the life estate for Ms. Clark under the terms of her husband's will? See N.Y. EPTL 5–1.1(d)(1), (3).
3. How could Mr. Clark have avoided the disruption of his estate plan which the widow's election caused?
4. What would have been the rights of Ms. Clark if New York law applied and the trust had given her the income only until remarriage?

NATIONAL SHAWMUT BANK OF BOSTON v. CUMMING

Supreme Judicial Court of Massachusetts, 1950.
325 Mass. 457, 91 N.E.2d 337.

WILKINS, Justice. The plaintiff bank is the surviving trustee under a declaration of trust, dated August 25, 1944, in which the bank and the settlor, William Gray Cumming, of Barre, Vermont, were named as trustees. The settlor died on August 19, 1947. The defendants are the settlor's

---

78. [The surrogate's opinion noted that the value of the assets of the trust which her husband had created for her was expected to exceed $11 million, with an annual income for her in excess of $400,000. See In re Estate of Clark, 276 N.Y.S.2d 507, 511, 52 Misc.2d 583, 588 (Surr.Ct.1966).—ed.]

widow, Cora Mann Cumming, and the mother, brother, and three sisters of the settlor, and constitute all the surviving life beneficiaries under the trust instrument.   This bill in equity seeks (1) the removal of a cloud upon the plaintiff's title as trustee of the trust property, as well as upon the beneficial interests of the defendants, the said cloud consisting of a claim asserted by the widow that the trust is invalid; and (2) a binding declaration of the rights of the parties under the trust instrument. G.L. (Ter.Ed.) c. 231A., inserted by St.1945, c. 582, § 1.   The answers of the defendants other than the widow admit the allegations of the bill and join in the prayers for relief.   The widow's answer sets up that the trust was created in bad faith with intent to defraud her of rights under Vermont law after waiver of the will, and that the validity of the trust is to be determined by the laws of the State of Vermont.   The widow (hereinafter called the defendant) appealed from a final decree adjudging that the trust is valid, and that she has no claim to the trust property except as a beneficiary under the trust instrument.   *   *   *

The trust agreement provided that the income, and such amounts of the principal as the settlor might direct in writing, should be paid to him for life; and that after his death the income should be paid equally to his widow, his mother, two brothers (one of whom predeceased him), and three sisters, the principal, if necessary, to be used to insure the receipt of $150 monthly by each beneficiary.   Upon the death of the settlor and the last survivor of the life beneficiaries, the trust was to terminate and distribution be made to the nieces and nephews of the settlor then living and to the living issue of each deceased niece or nephew by right of representation. The settlor reserved the power to amend, to revoke in whole or in part, and to withdraw principal.   The last paragraph reads, "This instrument shall be construed and the provisions thereof interpreted under and in accordance with the laws of the Commonwealth of Massachusetts."

*   *   *

In the summer of 1941 the settlor had accumulated a "sizable amount" of cash and government bonds, which he kept in Vermont.   He was solicited by an employee of the plaintiff, with which his company had an account, to use its facilities as trustee, and went to its offices in Boston, and made arrangements for the creation of the trust.   The attorney of the plaintiff drew the trust instrument, which the settlor signed in Vermont on August 25, 1944, and caused to be sent to the plaintiff in Boston, where it was executed by the plaintiff on August 26.   The annexed schedule of trust property listed a check for $50,000 of a Barre bank, drawn on a Boston bank and payable to the plaintiff, and $50,000 in Canadian government and United States Treasury bonds.   The check had been given to the plaintiff by the settlor on August 16, and the bonds had been sent by the Barre bank, and received by the plaintiff on August 19.   Later on five occasions between March 9, 1945, and August 29, 1945, the settlor delivered or sent, or caused to be sent, to the plaintiff bonds or checks in the total amount of $100,595.25, to be added to the principal.   These transfers to the trust were the greater part of his property.   *   *   *

The settlor and the defendant "had not gotten along well," and the "rupture became more pronounced in December, 1944, when being quite a sick man physically he made plans to go to Florida for his health, [and] he asked his wife to go with him, but her daughter was sick, and she remained home to take care of her." He returned from Florida on February 15, 1945, lived with her for a brief time in Barre, and about March 1, ceased to do so. In 1946 she brought a petition for a "divorce from bed and board forever," and in 1947 he asked her "to let him have a full divorce."

The judge stated: "I find that the settlor meticulously and designedly arranged his holdings and his business affairs so that his mother, wife, brothers and sisters would share the income, or principal, if necessary, equally after his death. That he knew that but for this arrangement his widow would have been entitled under the laws of Vermont to $4,000 and one half of his estate. But I do not find that in doing what he did * * * he was actuated by bad faith, or that he sought to accomplish something which he under all the circumstances considered to be unjust or unfair to his wife. I do not find that he set up the trust with the fraudulent intent of preventing his wife from obtaining her distributive share of his property. I find and rule that the trust is valid. * * * "

* * *

If the settlor had been domiciled in this Commonwealth and had transferred here personal property here to a trustee here for administration here, the transfer would have been valid even if his sole purpose had been to deprive his wife of any portion of it. Redman v. Churchill, 230 Mass. 415, 418, 119 N.E. 953; Eaton v. Eaton, 233 Mass. 351, 370, 124 N.E. 37, 5 A.L.R. 1426; Kerwin v. Donaghy, 317 Mass. 559, 571, 59 N.E.2d 299. The Vermont law we understand to be otherwise and to invalidate a transfer made there by one domiciled there of personal property there, if made with an actual, as distinguished from an implied, fraudulent intent to disinherit his spouse.

* * *

The plaintiff contends that the validity of the trust is to be determined by the law of this Commonwealth, and, in the alternative, that should the question be determined by Vermont law, the trust would still be valid on the judge's findings. The defendant, on the other hand, contends that the "trust is not valid under either Vermont or Massachusetts law." This argument is founded upon alleged illegality according to the law of Vermont and an assertion that our courts must look to the law of the State of domicil, which determines the right of succession to the settlor's personal property here. * * * The defendant's brief contains such statements as the "settlor was restricted or prevented by Vermont law from creating such a trust"; "the sole question is: Was the trust created to defraud the widow of the rights she has under Vermont law"; "capacity must be judged in the light of settlor's right to strip his wife of her dower rights, which in the last analysis is judged by Vermont law"; and the "trust property, all having come from Vermont, had its situs in Vermont."

One answer to the defendant's contention is that, wholly apart from what may be the law of Vermont, it was not shown that the trust was created to defraud the wife of statutory rights in Vermont. * * *

Another independent and insuperable difficulty is that before death the settlor had effectively disposed of the trust property, which had its situs in this Commonwealth and was not subject here to any equity in favor of a wife or to any similar limitation upon his power of disposition. He had expressed an intent in the trust instrument that it should be construed and interpreted according to the laws of this Commonwealth.

The elements entering into the decision as to the law of which State determines the validity of the trust are, on the one hand in Vermont, the settlor's domicil, and, on the other hand in Massachusetts, the presence of the property or its evidences, the completion of the trust agreement by final execution by the trustee, the domicil and the place of business of the trustee, and the settlor's intent that the trust should be administered by the trustee here. The general tendency of authorities elsewhere is away from the adoption of the law of the settlor's domicil where the property, the domicil and place of business of the trustee, and the place of administration intended by the settlor are in another State. The situation is unchanged by the fact that the one seeking to set aside the transaction is the widow of the settlor. * * * We are of opinion that the question of validity is to be determined by the law of this Commonwealth. There was no error under our law in adjudging the trust to be valid when created, or in omitting to adjudge it to be invalid at the time of the additions to principal made in 1945.

* * *

Chapter 2

PROVIDING MANAGEMENT FOR WEALTH

¶ 2.01 ALTERNATIVE WAYS TO PROVIDE MANAGEMENT FOR WEALTH

Just as the omnipresence of state intestacy statutes keeps clients from ever being without an estate plan, state-created arrangements for the management of wealth are equally omnipresent in theory, if not in practice. Legal machinery exists for the appointment of a manager of the property of anyone who lacks legal capacity to act himself. If the incapacity is due to minority, the manager is a court-appointed guardian of the minor's property or estate. If an adult is mentally incapacitated, the manager is again a court-appointed fiduciary variously known as guardian, conservator, or committee, depending upon state law.

Similarly, if an individual dies without having made an effective designation of a manager for his estate, state law provides for court appointment of an administrator. If he creates a trust, either during his life or by his will, without making effective provision for a trustee, one may be appointed by the court. And if any of his beneficiaries is a minor or otherwise legally incapacitated, an appropriately designated fiduciary may be appointed to receive and hold his share of the estate.

But these state-created arrangements for the management of wealth are usually even less well adapted to the needs of a particular client than is the estate plan provided for him by the state intestacy statute, for five reasons:

1. Unlike the intestacy statute, state provisions for wealth management usually are not self-executing. Someone must petition for appointment by the court. Often there is a significant delay, even after the petition has been filed, before the appointment becomes effective.

2. Many state provisions for wealth management give priority to close relatives of the owner, as in the appointment of administrators of decedents' estates, but others do not, as in appointment of trustees. In either situation, whether or not the court's discretion in making the appointment is governed by statutory priorities or is wholly unfettered, the court-selected manager may be far less satisfactory than one chosen by the client.

3. State provisions for wealth management often result in greater expense than privately tailored alternatives. For example, administration expenses for property in a revocable trust when the owner dies may be substantially less than such expenses for property which must be administered as part of his probate estate.

4. Privately tailored alternatives can give the manager a broader range of powers and greater flexibility in handling wealth than that provided by state law. For example, a trustee may be given powers by the grantor with respect to property held for the benefit of a

minor which a court-appointed guardian of the minor's estate could not exercise.

5. State wealth-management provisions are brought into play only in arbitrarily defined circumstances. Often such provisions are not available, in practice if not in theory, in situations in which provision is badly needed for management by someone other than the owner or a beneficiary. For example, the owner may be physically incapacitated to such an extent that he cannot manage his investments even though his mental capacity is not sufficiently impaired to require appointment of a guardian or conservator. Or a beneficiary may reach majority without automatically achieving the maturity required to handle wealth.

This chapter will focus on two alternatives for managment of a client's wealth upon his death:

1. Administration of a decedent's estate, either by an executor named in the client's will or by a court-appointed adminstrator, and distribution of shares in the estate to guardians or custodians for minor or incompetent adult beneficiaries;

2. Administration of a trust which is revocable during the client's life and which may or may not terminate upon his death.

In connection with the second, reference will also be made to other individually-chosen alternatives for management of wealth during the client's life, such as giving a manager a power of attorney to act on his behalf.

¶ 2.02   ADMINISTRATION OF PROBATE ESTATES

If the decedent left a valid will, it is admitted to probate and what follows is estate administration under a will, or testate administration. If the decedent left no valid will, there will be an intestate administration of his estate. In either case, the purpose of estate administration is to transfer wealth which was in the name of the decedent when he died into the names of the beneficiaries of his estate (or the name of a trustee for their benefit), after appropriate provision has been made for payment of death taxes, creditors, and funeral and administration expenses. The costs and delays of estate administration may be a significant factor in the choice of the vehicle to be used in carrying out a client's estate plan.

A great deal of wealth does not pass through estate administration because of the way title was held when the owner died. If he held title with a joint tenant who survived him, the property belongs to the cotenant without passing through estate administration. Similarly, insurance proceeds or employee death benefits payable to beneficiaries other than the executor or administrator of the insured or the employee bypass estate administration.

A more comprehensive arrangement to bypass estate administration and at the same time retain control of wealth is the transfer of property to a trust which is revocable by the transferor. Unlike the arrangements with respect to jointly owned property, insurance proceeds, and death benefits just described, a revocable trust can be used as the vehicle to dispose of a wide range of assets representing the bulk of a client's estate.

Although there are an infinity of local variations, the procedures often are largely prescribed by law, so that much is beyond the testator's control if he chooses to have his wealth go through estate administration.[1] One important difference, with tax consequences for the estate and its beneficiaries, is whether real estate vests immediately in the devisees under a will or is subject to administration by the executor or administrator.[2]

[1] Expense and Length of Administration

A variety of factors often combine to cause the process of estate administration to be lengthy. Some shortening may be achieved by the use of a revocable trust as the vehicle in disposing of the bulk of a client's wealth. But delays may be inevitable, whether or not assets pass through estate administration, if they are subject to death taxes when the client dies. Often the mechanics for federal and state estate and inheritance tax determinations are certain to cause substantial delays in any case.

The expense of administration is a product both of the professional skills and services that are required and the customary or statutory billing practices of fiduciaries and their attorneys. In New York, the statutory schedule of commissions for fiduciaries other than trustees is a sliding scale ranging from 5% on the first $100,000 to 2% on the excess over $5 million.[3] The sole executor of an estate of $250,000 would be entitled to $11,000. If there are two or more co-executors of an estate of this size, their total compensation would be twice that amount, or $22,000.[1] For estates of $300,000 or more, each fiduciary is entitled to full compensation unless there are more than three.

In addition to the executor's fee, the other major item of expense of administration is the fee of the executor's attorney, which is likely to be at least as large as the fee of a single executor. Whether his compensation will be reduced if substantial assets are transferred to a revocable trust and bypass estate administration depends on local practice. If the executor also performs services to the estate as an attorney, he is entitled to compensation in both capacities.[5]

A further item of expense in probate or accounting proceedings is compensation for the representatives appointed by the court to protect interested parties who are minors, incompetent, or unascertained at the time of the proceeding. In New York such representatives are called "guardians ad litem" [6] (formerly "special guardians").

The theory behind the appointment of the guardian ad litem is that a probate decree cannot bind a distributee, and an accounting decree cannot

---

1. Major reforms in this respect are embodied in the Uniform Probate Code. See generally Haviland, Shall We Rebuild Our House of Probate? The Uniform Probate Code, 19 Kan.L.Rev. 575 (1971); Wellman, The Uniform Probate Code: Blueprint for Reform in the 70's, 2 Conn.L.Rev. 453 (1970). Fourteen states have enacted the Code. See 8 Unif.Laws Ann. 106 (Supp.1981).

2. See ¶ 15.03[1] infra.

3. N.Y.Surr.Ct.Proc.Act 2307(1). Some corporate fiduciaries are unwilling to serve unless the will authorizes payment of a minimum commission of as much as $15,000.

4. Id.

5. Id. 2307(1).

6. Id. 403.

bind a beneficiary, unless such person's interest has been represented in the proceeding.   Since infant, incompetent, and unascertained persons cannot appear for themselves, someone must be appointed to represent them, unless "virtual representation" is provided by the presence of other parties with the same economic interests.[7]

The surviving spouse may well wonder why the estate should be put to the expense of compensating a strange attorney for what may often be a very cursory report and brief appearance, when the settlement of the estate is just a family affair.   The answer which her attorney must give to the client is that everyone who would take if there were no valid will must have independent representation in the proceeding for probate of the will. In an accounting there may be a conflict of interest between a parent who has a life interest and a child who is a remainderman as to whether an item should be treated as income or principal.

In certain cases the guardian ad litem does serve a valid function.   If a trustee or executor knows that at some future date his accounts may be reviewed by a stranger to the family, the guardian ad litem, the fiduciary is likely to be more careful, and perhaps more honest, in his management of the trust or estate.   And sometimes the beneficiaries will not all be closely bound by ties of family and affection.   In such cases the potential conflict between income beneficiary and remainderman may become very real.

Guardians ad litem have been much criticized for three reasons:

(1) Their fees are another expense to be borne by the estate, and, in the case of accounting proceedings for small estates, may represent a sizeable percentage of total estate assets.[8]

(2) The expense often appears to be unnecessary, particularly where the guardian is appointed to represent beneficiaries whose interests are extremely remote and contingent.

(3) Appointments are a form of political patronage.

In many cases, the need for appointment of a guardian ad litem may be eliminated if the court is willing to apply the common law doctrine of "virtual representation," which permits one party to a proceeding to represent, legally and conclusively, the interests of a person or class of persons who are not made parties.[9]   In New York, the common law rules have been codified and expanded.[10]   The theory underlying the doctrine is that the party to the proceeding and the represented persons have the same economic interests, and that in the pursuit of his own self-interest, the party will effectively protect the interests of the persons he represents.[11]

---

7. See text at notes 9–11 infra.

8. See, e.g., Matter of Becan, 26 A.D.2d 44, 270 N.Y.S.2d 923 (1st Dept.1966) (reduction from $250 to $100 of surrogate's award to guardian ad litem from estate of less than $2,500).

9. See 1 Amer.Law of Prop. § 4.85 et seq. (Casner ed. 1952).

10. See N.Y.Civ.Prac. 7703; N.Y.Surr.Ct. Proc. 315.

11. See L. B. Rodman and L. E. Rodman, Virtual Representation: Some Possible Extensions, 6 Real Prop., Prob. and Trust J. 281 (1971).

In many states, an effective means of short-cutting probate or reducing the expense which it entails is to create a revocable trust or to make other transfers during life which take assets out of the probate estate altogether. Another method is to facilitate the administration of the estate by providing in the will for flexible and liberal administration with as little court supervision as local law permits.[12] The extent to which such lifetime transfers in fact reduce costs varies greatly, however, depending on local billing practices.[13]

A will may facilitate the process of estate adminstration by (1) selecting one or more executors; (2) avoiding the expense of executors' bonds and encouraging them to act more aggressively and productively; and (3) naming guardians for minor children of the testator and providing a convenient means of distributing bequests to minor and incompetent adult beneficiaries. Naming guardians is, of course, important in providing for the care and custody of minor children quite apart from dealing with their shares of the estate.

---

[2] Selecting the Executor (and His Successors)

The practicalities involved in the choice of an executor will not be dealt with here,[14] except to note that some states disqualify non-resident individuals.[15]   New York, on the other hand, permits non-residents who are United States citizens to serve as executor, testamentary guardian, or trustee.[16]

---

12. A few states recognize a general waiver by will of court supervision of administration. See, Md.Est. & Trusts Code Ann. § 5–30 et seq. (1974) (administrative probate); Tex.Prob.Code Tit.Ann. § 145 (Vernon 1980) (independent administration); Wash.Rev.Code Ann. § 11.68.010 (West Supp.1981) (non-intervention will). The Uniform Probate Code makes judicial supervision of probate administration largely elective with the interested parties. See note 1 supra.

13. See ¶ 2.03[1] infra.

14. In many respects, the same considerations are relevant as in the choice of trustees. See § 2.03[2] infra.

15. See, e.g., Fla.Stat.Ann. § 733.304, (West Supp.1980), which disqualifies any person not domiciled in the state unless he is within a specified degree of relationship to the decedent by blood, adoption, or marriage. This section was held to deny the decedent "due process" under the Fourteenth Amendment. See Fain v. Hall, 463 F.Supp. 661 (M.D.Fla.1979). The court did not specify whether the unconstitutional deprivation was of "life, liberty, or property." The statute was upheld, however, in In re Estate of Greenberg, 390 So.2d 40 (Fla.1980), appeal dismissed sub nom. Estate of Pincus v. Greenberg, ____ U.S. ____ , 101 S.Ct. 1475, 67 L.Ed.2d 610 (1981).

A similar ban on foreign corporations in Fla.Stat.Ann. § 660.10 (amended and re-numbered as § 660.41 (West Supp.1980)) was invalidated in BT Inv. Managers, Inc. v. Lewis, 461 F.Supp. 1187 (N.D.Fla.1978), vacated and remanded on the ground, inter alia, that the constitutionality of the statute had not been fully determined by the District Court decision, 444 U.S. 822, 100 S.Ct. 41, 62 L.Ed.2d 28 (1980).

Unless the unconstitutionality of a statutory disqualification is well recognized, the testator who names a non-resident may expose his estate to time-consuming and expensive litigation, as well as to the risk that a public administrator may act for his estate. See In re Emery, 59 Ohio App.2d 7, 391 N.E.2d 746 (1978), upholding the probate court's refusal to appoint an out-of-state bank, licensed to do business in Ohio, as executor. The court rejected the argument that exclusion of non-residents violates the Federal Constitution.

16. N.Y.Surr.Ct.Proc.Act 707, 710.

Whether or not a foreign corporation qualifies in a given jurisdiction often is a more complex question because of reciprocity provisions in many state statutes, which condition the right of a corporation of another state to act locally on the right of local institutions to act in the other state.[17] If the testator does not make an effective designation of an executor, the fiduciary who will administer his estate is determined by local law by giving certain persons priority to apply for administration, or if all of them fail to qualify, a public administrator acts for the estate. There has been enough criticism of the work of some public adminstrators and of their fees and expenses to create a widespread preference for individually selected executors. It is thus essential that someone be named in the will who can and will qualify as executor and complete the administration of the estate.

If the testator's assets are located in more than one jurisdiction, it may be necessary or desirable for his executor to qualify as such both in the state of the testator's residence and in one or more others as well. If different residence requirements make it impossible for the domiciliary executor to qualify in other states, the will should designate qualified ancillary executors for each state other than the testator's residence in which he is likely to have assets requiring administration.

In addition to ascertaining that the executor of first choice is legally qualified, if he is an individual it ordinarily is desirable to name one or more alternate executors to cover the possibility that he may fail to qualify when the testator dies or may himself die or become incompetent before the process of administration is completed. These contingencies, of course, are inapplicable to a corporate executor, but it is desirable to find out in advance whether or not such an executor is willing to act for a given estate. In New York, such willingness may be conditioned on the inclusion in the will of a provision for commissions in excess of the statutory rates.[18]

Some testators seek to delegate the power to choose an executor. A provision of this type was upheld in Harnett v. Wandell,[19] and other cases generally are in accord.[20] Some state statutes, impose limits on the delegation of such power, however.[21]

Moreover, although the process of estate administration often is lengthy, it is short in comparison to the period of administration of a long-term trust. Thus the need to provide a mechanism for selection of successor executors (in addition to the alternates named in the will) is much less compelling than is the need to provide a similar mechanism for successor trustees.

---

17. See e.g., Mass.Gen.Laws Ann. c. 167, § 45A. (West 1977).

18. See note 3 supra.

19. 60 N.Y. 346, 19 Am.Rep. 194 (1875). Such a delegation is expressly recognized by N.Y.Surr.Ct.Proc.Act 1414(4): "A person named as an executor by a person other than the testator under a valid power contained in a will must appear and file an acknowledged selection of himself as executor."

20. See Annot., 11 A.L.R.2d 1284 (1950).

21. See, e.g., Calif.Prob.Code § 403; (West Supp.1980).

[3] Executors' Bonds, Powers and Liabilities to Beneficiaries

It is quite common to include in wills a waiver either of bond for the executor or of surety on his bond, depending on local practice, in order to save the expense to the estate of premiums for a professional surety. Although there are instances of misappropriation of estate assets by executors, many lawyers believe that if the testator has selected an executor who he believes needs to be bonded, he probably would be better off selecting someone else in whom he has more confidence instead of relying on the protection given by a surety bond.

It is also a common practice to include an extensive grant of powers to an executor. The extent to which such provisions will in fact encourage more aggressive action by executors without recourse to specific court authorization depends both on the breadth of the powers conferred by law [22] and the policy of the particular executor.

In addition, some wills seeks to reduce the executor's legal responsibility for his acts and omissions. The desirability of such so-called exculpatory clauses is questionable in many cases. They may provide deserved protection for the non-professional who acts with good intentions but unfortunate results, but the application of such provisions to professional fiduciaries is another matter. New York expressly limits the extent to which a will may free an executor from a duty of care, as well as the extent to which his power to value assets may be broadened.[23]

MATTER OF ESTATE OF ROTHKO

Court of Appeals of New York, 1977.
43 N.Y.2d 305, 401 N.Y.S.2d 449, 372 N.E.2d 291.

COOKE, Judge.

Mark Rothko, an abstract expressionist painter whose works through the years gained for him an international reputation of greatness, died testate on February 25, 1970. The principal asset of his estate consisted of 798 paintings of tremendous value, and the dispute underlying this appeal involves the conduct of his three executors in their disposition of these works of art. In sum, that conduct as portrayed in the record and sketched in the opinions was manifestly wrongful and indeed shocking.

Rothkos' will was admitted to probate on April 27, 1970 and letters testamentary were issued to Bernard J. Reis, Theodoros Stamos and Morton Levine. Hastily and within a period of only about three weeks and by virtue of two contracts each dated May 21, 1970, the executors dealt with all 798 paintings.

By a contract of sale, the estate executors agreed to sell to Marlborough A. G., a Liechtenstein corporation (hereinafter MAG), 100 Rothko paintings as listed for $1,800,000, $200,000 to be paid on execution of the agreement and the balance of $1,600,000 in 12 equal interest-free installments over a 12-year period. Under the second agreement, the executors consigned to Marlborough Gallery, Inc., a domestic corporation (hereinafter MNY), "approximately 700 paintings listed on a Schedule to be prepared," the consignee

---

22. See N.Y. EPTL 11–1.1.   23. Id. 11–1.7.

to be responsible for costs covering items such as insurance, storage, restoration and promotion.   By its provisos, MNY could sell up to 35 paintings a year from each of two groups, pre-1947 and post-1947, for 12 years at the best price obtainable but not less than the appraised estate value, and it would receive a 50% commission on each painting sold, except for a commission of 40% on those sold to or through other dealers.

Petitioner Kate Rothko, decedent's daughter and a person entitled to share in his estate by virtue of an election under EPTL 5–3.3, instituted this proceeding to remove the executors, to enjoin MNY and MAG from disposing of the paintings, to rescind the aforesaid agreements between the executors and said corporations, for a return of the paintings still in possession of those corporations, and for damages.   She was joined by the guardian of her brother Christopher Rothko, likewise interested in the estate, who answered by adopting the allegations of his sister's petition and by demanding the same relief.   The Attorney-General of the State, as the representative of the ultimate beneficiaries of the Mark Rothko Foundation, Inc., a charitable corporation and the residuary legatee under decedent's will, joined in requesting relief substantially similar to that prayed for by petitioner.   On June 26, 1972 the Surrogate issued a temporary restraining order and on September 26, 1972 a preliminary injunction enjoining MAG, MNY, and the three executors from selling or otherwise disposing of the paintings referred to in the agreements dated May 21, 1970, except for sales or dispositions made with court permission.   The Appellate Division modified the preliminary injunction order by increasing the amount of the bond and otherwise affirmed.   By a 1974 petition, the Attorney-General, on behalf of the ultimate charitable beneficiaries of the Mark Rothko Foundation, sought the punishment of MNY, MAG, Lloyd and Reis for contempt and other relief.

Following a nonjury trial covering 89 days and in a thorough opinion, the Surrogate found: that Reis was a director, secretary and treasurer of MNY, the consignee art gallery, in addition to being a coexecutor of the estate; that the testator had a 1969 *inter vivos* contract with MNY to sell Rothko's work at a commission of only 10% and whether that agreement survived testator's death was a problem that a fiduciary in a dual position could not have impartially faced; that Reis was in a position of serious conflict of interest with respect to the contracts of May 21, 1970 and that his dual role and planned purpose benefited the Marlborough interests to the detriment of the estate; that it was to the advantage of coexecutor Stamos as a "non-too-successful artist, financially," to curry favor with Marlborough and that the contract made by him with MNY within months after signing the estate contracts placed him in a position where his personal interests conflicted with those of the estate, especially leading to lax contract enforcement efforts by Stamos; that Stamos acted negligently and improvidently in view of his own knowledge of the conflict of interest of Reis; that the third coexecutor, Levine, while not acting in self-interest or with bad faith, nonetheless failed to exercise ordinary prudence in the performance of his assumed fiduciary obligations since he was aware of Reis' divided loyalty, believed that Stamos was also seeking personal advantage, possessed personal opinions as to the value of the paintings and yet followed the leadership of his coexecutors without investigation of essential facts or consultation with competent and disinterested appraisers, and that the business transactions of the two Marlborough corporations were admittedly controlled and directed by Francis K. Lloyd. It was concluded that the acts and failures of the three executors were clearly improper to such a substantial extent as to mandate their removal under SCPA 711 as estate fiduciaries. The Surrogate also found that MNY, MAG and Lloyd were guilty of contempt in shipping, disposing of and selling 57 paintings in violation of the temporary restraining order dated June 26, 1972 and of the injunction dated September 26, 1972; that the contracts for sale and consignment of paintings between the executors and MNY and MAG provided inadequate value to the estate, amounting to a lack of mutuality and fairness resulting from conflicts on the part of Reis and Stamos and improvidence on the part of all executors; that said contracts were voidable and were set aside by reason of violation of the duty of loyalty and improvidence of the executors, knowingly participated in and induced by MNY and MAG; that the fact that these agreements were voidable did not revive the 1969 *inter vivos* agreements since the parties by their conduct evinced an intent to abandon and abrogate these compacts. The Surrogate held that the present value at the time of trial of the paintings sold is the proper measure of damages as to MNY, MAG, Lloyd, Reis and Stamos. He imposed a civil fine of $3,332,000 upon MNY, MAG and Lloyd, same being the appreciated value at the time of trial of the 57 paintings sold in violation of the temporary restraining order and injunction.[24] It was held that Levine was liable for $6,464,880 in damages, as he was not in a dual position acting for his own interest and was thus liable only for the actual value of paintings sold MNY and MAG as of the dates of sale, and that Reis, Stamos, MNY and MAG, apart from being jointly and severally liable for the same damages as Levine for negligence, were liable for the greater sum of $9,252,000 "as appreciation damages less amounts previously paid to the estate with regard to sales of paintings." The cross petition of the Attorney-General to reopen the record for submission of newly discovered documentary evidence was denied. The liabilities were held to be congruent so that payment of the higest sum would satisfy all lesser liabilities including the civil fines and the liabilities for damages were to be reduced by payment of the fine levied or by return of any of the 57 paintings disposed of, the new fiduciary to have the option in the first instance to specify which paintings the fiduciary would accept.

The Appellate Division, in an opinion by Justice Lane, modified to the extent of deleting the option given the new fiduciary to specify which paintings he would accept. Except for this modification, the majority affirmed on the opinion of Surrogate Midonick, with additional comments.

In seeking a reversal, it is urged that an improper legal standard was applied in voiding the estate contracts of May, 1970, that the "no further inquiry" rule applies only to self-dealing and that in case of a conflict of interest, absent self-dealing, a challenged transaction must be shown to be unfair. The subject of fairness of the contracts is intertwined with the

---

24. The decree of the Surrogate's Court, New York County, dated January 15, 1976, was amended in this respect pursuant to an order filed April 28, 1976 by substituting "63" for "57" as the number of paintings sold and disposed of and "$3,872,000" as the amount of the fine instead of "$3,332,000."

issue of whether Reis and Stamos were guilty of conflicts of interest.[25] Scott is quoted to the effect that "[a] trustee does not necessarily incur liability merely because he has an individual interest in the transaction * * * In Bullivant v. First Nat. Bank [246 Mass. 324, 141 N.E. 41] it was held that * * * the fact that the bank was also a creditor of the corporation did not make its assent invalid, *if it acted in good faith and the plan was fair*" (2 Scott, Trusts, § 170.24, p. 1384 [emphasis added]). * * *

These contentions should be rejected. First, a review of the opinions of the Surrogate and the Appellate Division manifests that they did not rely solely on a "no further inquiry rule," and secondly, there is more than an adequate basis to conclude that the agreements between the Marlborough corporations and the estate were neither fair nor in the best interests of the estate. * * *

To be sure, the assertions that there were no conflicts of interest on the part of Reis or Stamos indulge in sheer fantasy. Besides being a director and officer of MNY, for which there was financial remuneration, however slight, Reis, as noted by the Surrogate, had different inducements to favor the Marlborough interests, including his own aggrandizement of status and financial advantage through sales of almost one million dollars for items from his own and his family's extensive private art collection by the Marlborough interests (see 84 Misc.2d, at pp. 843–844, 379 N.Y.S.2d at pp. 939–940). Similarly, Stamos benefited as an artist under contract with Malborough and, interestingly, Marlborough purchased a Stamos painting from a third party for $4,000 during the week in May, 1970 when the estate contract negotiations were pending (see 84 Misc.2d, at p. 845, 379 N.Y.S.2d at p. 941). The conflicts are manifest. Further, as noted in Bogert, Trusts and Trustees (2d ed.), "The duty of loyalty imposed on the fiduciary prevents him from accepting employment from a third party who is entering into a business transaction with the trust" (§ 543, subd. [S], p. 573). "While he [a trustee] is administering the trust he must refrain from placing himself in a position where his personal interest or that of a third person does or may conflict with the interest of the beneficiaries" (Bogert, Trusts [Hornbook Series–5th ed.], p. 343). Here, Reis was employed and Stamos benefited in a manner contemplated by Bogert (see, also, Meinhard v. Salmon, 249 N.Y. 458, 464, 466–467, 164 N.E. 545, 547–548; Schmidt v. Chambers, 265 Md. 9, 33–38, 288 A.2d 356). In short, one must strain the law rather than follow it to reach the result suggested on behalf of Reis and Stamos.

Levine contends that, having acted prudently and upon the advice of counsel, a complete defense was established. Suffice it to say, an executor who knows that his coexecutor is committing breaches of trust and not only fails to exert efforts directed towards prevention but accedes to them is legally accountable even though he was acting on the advice of counsel (Matter of Westefield, 32 App.Div. 324, 344, 53 N.Y.S. 25, 39; 3 Scott,

---

25. In New York, an executor, as such, takes a qualified legal title to all personalty specifically bequeathed and an unqualified legal title to that not so bequeathed; he holds not in his own right but as a trustee for the benefit of creditors, those entitled to receive under the will and, if all is not bequeathed, those entitled to distribution under the EPTL. [Citations omitted.]

Trusts [3d ed.], § 201, p. 1657). When confronted with the question of whether to enter into the Marlborough contracts, Levine was acting in a business capacity, not a legal one, in which he was required as an executor primarily to employ such diligence and prudence to the care and management of the estate assets and affairs as would prudent persons of discretion and intelligence (King v. Talbot, 40 N.Y. 76, 85–86), accented by "[n]ot honesty alone, but the punctilio of an honor the most sensitive" (Meinhard v. Salmon, 249 N.Y. 458, 464, 164 N.E. 545, 546, supra). Alleged good faith on the part of a fiduciary forgetful of his duty is not enough (Wendt v. Fischer, 243 N.Y. 439, 443, 154 N.E. 303, 304). He could not close his eyes, remain passive or move with unconcern in the face of the obvious loss to be visited upon the estate by participation in those business arrangements and then shelter himself behind the claimed counsel of an attorney (see Matter of Niles, 113 N.Y. 547, 558, 21 N.E. 687, 689; Matter of Huntley, 13 Misc. 375, 380, 35 N.Y.S. 113, 116; 3 Warren's Heaton, Surrogates' Courts [6th ed.], § 217, subd. 3, par. [b]).

Further, there is no merit to the argument that MNY and MAG lacked notice of the breach of trust. The record amply supports the determination that they are chargeable with notice of the executors' breach of duty.

The measure of damages was the issue that divided the Appellate Division (see 56 A.D.2d, at p. 500, 392 N.Y.S.2d at p. 872). The contention of Reis, Stamos, MNY and MAG, that the award of appreciation damages was legally erroneous and impermissible, is based on a principle that an executor authorized to sell is not liable for an increase in value if the breach consists only in selling for a figure less than that for which the executor should have sold. For example, Scott states:

> "The beneficiaries are not entitled to the value of the property at the time of the decree if it was not the duty of the trustee to retain the property in the trust and the breach of trust consisted *merely* in selling the property for too low a price" (3 Scott, Trusts [3d ed.], § 208.3, p. 1687 [emphasis added]).

> "If the trustee is guilty of a breach of trust in selling trust property for an inadequate price, he is liable for the difference between the amount he should have received and the amount which he did receive. He is not liable, however, for any subsequent rise in value of the property sold." (Id., § 208.6, pp. 1689–1690.)

A recitation of similar import appears in Comment *d* under Restatement, Trusts 2d (§ 205): "*d*. Sale for less than value. If the trustee is authorized to sell trust property, but in breach of trust he sells it for less than he should receive, he is liable for the value of the property at the time of the sale less the amount which he received. If the breach of trust consists *only* in selling it for too little, he is not chargeable with the amount of any subsequent increase in value of the property under the rule stated in Clause (c), as he would be if he were not authorized to sell the property. See § 208," (Emphasis added.) However, employment of "merely" and "only" as limiting words suggests that where the breach consists of some misfeasance, other than solely for selling "for too low a price" or "for too little," appreciation damages may be appropriate. Under Scott (§ 208.3, pp. 1686–1687) and the Restatement (§ 208), the trustee may be held liable for appreciation damages if it was his or her duty to retain the property, the theory being that the beneficiaries are entitled to be placed in the same position they would have been in had the breach not consisted of a sale of property that should have been retained. The same rule should apply where the breach of trust consists of a serious conflict of interest—which is more than merely selling for too little.

The reason for allowing appreciation damages, where there is a duty to retain, and only date of sale damages, where there is authorization to sell, is policy oriented. If a trustee authorized to sell were subjected to a greater measure of damages he might be reluctant to sell (in which event he might run a risk if depreciation ensued). On the other hand, if there is a duty to retain and the trustee sells there is no policy reason to protect the trustee; he has not simply acted imprudently, he has violated an integral condition of the trust.

"If a trustee in breach of trust transfers trust property to a person who takes with notice of the breach of trust, and the transferee has disposed of the property * * * [i]t seems proper to charge him with the value at the time of the decree, since if it had not been for the breach of trust the property would still have been a part of the trust estate" (4 Scott, Trusts [3d ed.], § 291.2; see, also, United States v. Dunn, 268 U.S. 121, 132, 45 S.Ct. 451, 69 L.Ed. 876). This rule of law which applies to the transferees MNY and MAG also supports the imposition of appreciation damages against Reis and Stamos, since if the Marlborough corporations are liable for such damages either as purchaser or consignees with notice, from one in breach of trust, it is only logical to hold that said executors, as sellers and consignors, are liable also *pro tanto*.

Contrary to assertions of appellants and the dissenters at the Appellate Division, Menzel v. List, 24 N.Y.2d 91, 298 N.Y.S.2d 979, 246 N.E.2d 742, is authority for the allowance of appreciation damages. There, the damages involved a breach of warranty of title to a painting which at one time had been stolen from plaintiff and her husband and ultimately sold to defendant. Here, the executors, though authorized to sell, did not merely err in the amount they accepted but sold to one with whom Reis and Stamos had a self-interest. To make the injured party whole, in both instances the quantum of damages should be the same. In other words, since the paintings cannot be returned, the estate is therefore entitled to their value at the time of the decree, i.e., appreciation damages. These are not punitive damages in a true sense, rather they are damages intended to make the estate whole. Of course, as to Reis, Stamos, MNY and MAG, these damages might be considered by some to be exemplary in a sense, in that they serve as a warning to others (see Reynolds v. Pegler, 123 F.Supp. 36, 38, D.C., affd. 223 F.2d 429, 2 Cir., cert. den. 350 U.S. 846, 76 S.Ct. 80, 100 L.Ed. 754), but their true character is ascertained when viewed in the light of overriding policy considerations and in the realization that the sale and consignment were not merely sales below value but inherently wrongful transfers which should allow the owner to be made whole. [Citations omitted.]

The decree of the Surrogate imposed appreciation damages against Reis, Stamos, MNY and MAG in the amount of $7,339,464.72—computed as $9,252,000 (86 works on canvas at $90,000 each and 54 works on paper at $28,000 each) less the aggregate amounts paid the estate under the two rescinded agreements and interest.   Appellants chose not to offer evidence of "present value" and the only proof furnished on the subject was that of the expert Heller whose appraisal as of January, 1974 (the month previous to that when trial commenced) on a painting-by-painting basis totaled $15,100,000.   There was also testimony as to bona fide sales of other Rothkos between 1971 and 1974.   Under the circumstances, it was impossible to appraise the value of the unreturned works of art with an absolute certainty and, so long as the figure arrived at had a reasonable basis of computation and was not merely speculative, possible or imaginery, the Surrogate had the right to resort to reasonable conjectures and probable estimates and to make the best approximation possible through the exercise of good judgment and common sense in arriving at the amount * * *.   This is particularly so where the conduct of wrongdoers has rendered it difficult to ascertain the damages suffered with the precision otherwise possible.   [Citations omitted.]   Significantly, the Surrogate's factual finding as to the present value of these unreturned paintings was affirmed by the Appellate Division and, since that finding had support in the record and was not legally erroneous, it should not now be subjected to our disturbance.

        * * *

The Marlborough corporations and Lloyd contend that there was no violation of either the temporary restraining order or the preliminary injunction by the delivery of paintings sold prior to the court's restraints and that, therefore, the finding of contempt was erroneous.   The Attorney-General in response contends that the "group" sales did not pass equitable ownership and that even if the invoices had been typed prior to said order and injunction no sale took place until after the injunction.   In support of the latter position, the Uniform Commercial Code (§ 2–106, subd. [1]; §§ 2–307, 2–401, subds. [2], [3]) is cited for the proposition that as a matter of law the questioned sales took place on delivery to the purchasers which in all instances occurred after the injunction, the latter of the two court restraints.   MNY, MAG and Lloyd counter with the argument that, under art market custom, invoices of paintings are sales and that the restraining order and preliminary injunction failed to clearly state what acts were prohibited.   In any event, the plain and simple import of both the order and the injunction—not to sell or otherwise dispose of the paintings (cf. Matter of Black, 138 App.Div. 562, 565, 123 N.Y.S. 371, 373)—was violated by dispositions of them.   Consequently, it is immaterial how the applicable Uniform Commercial Code provisions might be interpreted.   If MNY, MAG and Lloyd had invoiced paintings and were acting in good faith, they would have advised the court of their prior commitments.

We have considered the other alleged errors urged by the parties, and find those arguments to be without merit.   In short, we find no basis for disturbing the result reached below.

Accordingly, the order of the Appellate Division should be affirmed, with costs to the prevailing parties against appellants, and the question certified answered in the affirmative.[26]

* * *

[4] Guardians for Minors and Distributions to Minor and Incompetent Adult Beneficiaries

State law typically provides for appointment by the will of a parent of guardians of the person and property of minor children. Such appointment often must be followed by court confirmation or at least qualification of the guardian as a fiduciary. A provision appointing guardians normally is desirable in the will of each parent (or potential parent) who may have minor children at his death, in order to provide for the possibility that both parents may die in the same accident.

State law also deals with the management by guardians or other fiduciaries of the property of minors and of incompetent adults.[27] Often, however, such procedures are cumbersome, and privately-arranged alternatives may be more satisfactory.

Most state versions of the Uniform Gifts to Minors Act only authorize transfers by living donors to a custodian for a minor.[28] Some statutes, however, authorize distributions to custodians by executors or trustees as well, in the absence of a contrary provision in the will or trust instrument.[29] Where this is permissible, it may often be a satisfactory solution to the problem of bequests to minors.

¶ 2.03 ADMINISTRATION OF TRUSTS

Estates can and sometimes do remain in administration for what may appear to be inordinately long periods to impatient legatees—and to the Commissioner as well, who is not unmindful of the potential tax savings from continued treatment of an estate as a separate taxable entity. But a trust may continue for 80 or 100 years, while even 10 years is unusual for an estate, so the adminstrative provisions for a trust may be in effect for a much longer period. In order to anticipate intelligently the range of developments during a period of such length, such provisions should deal with everything considered in connection with estate administration and a good deal more.

Some of the most important aspects are (1) use of revocable ("living") trusts in estate planning; (2) selection and succession of trustees; and (3) trustees' powers, bonds, accounts, and liabilities to the beneficiaries.

---

26. [In subsequent proceedings reported at 98 Misc.2d 718, 414 N.Y.S.2d 444 (1979), the Surrogate approved legal fees to be paid from the estate in excess of $3 million. Of this amount, the largest portion was payable to the attorneys for the administratrix in the amount of $2.6 million, reduced from a requested $7.5 million)—ed.]

27. See, e.g., N.Y.Surr.Ct.Proc. 1710, 1711.

28. See, e.g., 20 Pa.Cons.Stat.Ann. § 5303(a) (Purdon 1975).

29. See, e.g., N.Y. EPTL 7–4.9.

[1] Use of Revocable ("Living") Trusts in Estate Planning

Trusts which are subject to the exercise of a power of revocation which will cause the trust assets to be returned to the settlor are an important means of carrying out estate plans.   Such trusts may be created with a minimal amount of principal, usually $5 or $10, with the balance to be added on the settlor's death, either in accordance with provisions of his will which pour over probate assets into the trust, or in accordance with the designation of the trustee as beneficiary of insurance on the settlor's life or a benefit payable on his death by his employer.   In other situations, such trusts may be funded by the transfer to the trustee of a substantial part of the settlor's wealth during his lifetime.   The estate planning objectives which the trust serves are greatly affected, of course, by the extent to which assets are transferred to the trustee before the death of the settlor.

The "living trust" in the literature of estate planning usually refers to a trust which is revocable by the settlor, acting alone.   This is the only kind of revocable trust discussed in this chapter.   As such, it ordinarily does not achieve any federal income tax advantage for him during his life or save estate taxes when he dies.

Once the settlor had died, the income tax situation changes because trust income no longer can be attributed to him.   At this point there may be very significant differences in the total income tax burden ultimately borne by his beneficiaries depending upon whether assets pass through administration as part of a client's estate or are already in a revocable trust at the time the client dies.[30]

The use of revocable trusts, whether or not substantial assets are transferred to the trust during the client's lifetime, usually is based on considerations having nothing to do with taxes.   One matter of importance is the total amount of the executor's commission and fees of guardians ad litem in accountings by the executor, both of which typically are based in large part on the size of the probate estate.   Thus to some extent, such expenses may be reduced by transferring assets to a revocable trust during the client's life.   The extent of the reduction, however, varies greatly.[31]   Some services are required after a client dies with respect to assets in a revocable trust at the time of his death, because such assets are includible in his gross estate and typically are subject to state death taxes as well.   Many professional fiduciaries make a charge with respect to such assets, but often that charge is lower than that which would be payable if the same assets were in the client's probate estate when he died, and the amount may be subject to negotiation, depending to local practice.

---

30. For a discussion, see ¶ 15.06.

31. Often a family member serves as trustee or executor without a fee.   However, this does not necessarily eliminate administration costs (apart from attorney's fees) for either trust or estate assets.   Some services still must be performed, unless the attorney does all of the work of the executor or trustee.   If the family member does the work himself, other uses of his time are blocked.   If he employs a professional fi-duciary as custodian of estate or trust assets, there will be a fee, although it may be less than the professional would charge as executor or trustee.

In other cases, the fact that a family member charges regular fees as trustee or executor produces a net tax saving because the income tax he pays on his fees is more than offset by the reduction in taxes for the estate or trust or its beneficiaries which results from the deduction of the fees paid.

Executors' commissions on probate assets, on the other hand, often are fixed by statute or by well-established practice and thus may be less readily negotiable.   Here, too, there are wide variations in local practices.   In some localities it is not easy to find a competent professional fiduciary or attorney who will undertake the administration of an estate at a fee which is below that set by statute or local practice.   In other areas such departures from established fee schedules are quite common for estates in which a fee determined under the local schedule is overly liberal in relation to the work required in a given estate.

Other non-tax reasons for the use of trusts created during life, both revocable and irrevocable, include:

(1) To avoid making the trust provisions a matter of public record in the local probate court, as would be necessary if it were created by the grantor's will;

(2) To anticipate and provide for the grantor's incapacity by transferring property while he is competent to act to a trustee whose powers will not be revoked by the grantor's subsequent incompetency:

(3) To avoid interruption and delays in the management of the trust assets at the time of the grantor's death;

(4) To choose as the governing state law for the trust, that of a state other than the grantor's domicile at his death;

(5) To avoid creation of a "court" trust.

The importance of any one of these possible reasons for a given client to create a revocable trust depends on many factors.

(a) *Secrecy.*   This is often cited as a reason but it does not inevitably follow from the use of a revocable trust as a vehicle to carry out the client's plan.   If the trust includes real estate, it may be necessary to record the trust agreement in order to have a clear record title to the property.   And even if it consists solely of intangible property, it is likely to be on file in a number of places—the trustee's office, the office of the trustee's counsel, the Internal Revenue Service, and perhaps the offices of various transfer agents as well.

(b) *Anticipating the grantor's incompetency.*   This probably is the most important single reason for using a revocable trust, outweighing even the possibility of saving probate expenses when the client dies.   It is an all too familiar fact of modern life that elderly individuals tend to experience a progressive decline in physical and mental faculties which leaves them increasingly unable to manage their own affairs or even to make the necessary arrangements for their personal care.   Clients who are willing to recognize that this may happen to them may anticipate this problem in stand-by provisions of an estate plan which will not restrict their freedom of action while they have the capacity to act but will be available immediately in case of incapacity.

Generally state law does not deal with the problems as satisfactorily as a revocable trust may.   Until recently, the major other way in which a clients could anticipate the problem was by giving a power of attorney to one or more trusted individuals.   But the power anticipated only the client's physical incapacity or absence, not loss of mental competence, as the latter event would automatically revoke the power.[32]   The so-called durable power of attorney authorized by many state statutes avoids this problem because it is not affected by the incompetence of the principal if the power so states.[33] However, the durable power, although often useful as an adjunct, does not serve the other four purposes noted above that may be served by a revocable trust.   And it does not provide for appointment of successors to act if the named holder of the power himself dies or becomes incapacitated himself.

In states which do not provide for a durable power of attorney, the only comprehensive way to deal with the legal problems created by a client's mental disability is to have him formally declared to be incompetent and a guardian, conservator, or committee appointed to handle his affairs.   Relatives, and often the individual concerned as well, are understandably uncomfortable about a public proceeding for this purpose, so that it tends to be postponed or avoided as long as possible to spare the feelings of all concerned.   And the objections to state procedures for the administration of the affairs of incompetents often are not based on sentiment alone. Residence requirements may eliminate children or other relatives of the incompetent, requiring the appointment, and compensation, of a local institution or unrelated individual.   And reports of the management of the incompetent's estate must be filed with the local probate court, so that there is a loss of secrecy as well.

A revocable trust, on the other hand, to which the client has transferred his wealth before incapacity sets in, can avoid all of these problems by eliminating the need for any public determination of incompetency and by permitting a gradual assumption of responsibility by the trustee rather than the total shift involved in a judicial determination of incompetency.

(c) *Avoiding interruption and delays at grantor's death.*   With the streamlining of state probate procedures, the period that must elapse between the decedent's death and the time when his executor is qualified to act in relation to his assets often is not as long as was formerly the case. But there may still be some delay, during which it is difficult except under emergency procedures to take any action in relation to the decedent's property.   Even after the executor is qualified and able to act, his permissible scope of action is far more circumscribed than that which a trustee with broad powers may have.   Executors are expected to conserve and liquidate, rather than to invest aggressively.   The result is that such investment normally must await distribution by the executor to estate beneficiaries who may invest in their personal capacity or to trustees to whom property is bequeathed.

(d) *Choosing governing state law for the trust.*   Two important reasons for choosing the law of a state other than that of the client's domicile are:

---

32. Restatement, Second, Agency §§ 120, 122 (1958).

33. See, e.g., N.Y.Gen.Oblig.Law § 5–1601. For a collection of similar statutes, see Lombard, Miller, Gother & Houghton, Le-

gal Problems of the Aged and Infirm—The Durable Power of Attorney—Planned Protective Services and the Living Will, Appendix A, 13 Real Prop., Prob. & Tr.J. 1 (1978).

(1) To permit a continuation of business relationships for a client who is moving away. If the client wants an institution with whom he has dealt over the years to continue to handle his property after he dies, it may be necessary to create a revocable trust if the institution will be unable to qualify as testamentary trustee under the law of his new state of residence.[34]

(2) To avoid the claims of a surviving spouse. States vary greatly in the degree of protection accorded a surviving spouse and in the recognition given to such claims under the law of another state.[35]

(e) *Avoiding creation of a "court" trust.* In many states a trust created by will is a so-called "court trust" with court appointment required for the trustees and accounts required to be filed. Not only is there a resulting loss of secrecy, but there may also be additional costs incurred as a result in connection with the allowance of the trustees' accounts. Inter vivos trusts, on the other hand, often are not treated as "court trusts" even with respect to amounts added ("poured over") by the grantor's will. Often the additional costs incurred for a "court trust" may outweigh any possible advantage from that status in affording easier or less expensive access to needed judicial action. In this situation, creation of at least a nominally funded inter vivos trust may be useful to avoid that status, even if the bulk of the trust assets will be added by the grantor's will.

[2] Selecting the Trustee (and Successor Trustees)

Of course the original trustee (or trustees) must be both legally qualified to serve and willing to do so. Corporate fiduciaries normally do not commit themselves before the death of the decedent to serve as trustee under his will and may refuse to accept a trust if it does not appear to be profitable under prevailing fee schedules. One New York Surrogate notes that the frequency of such refusals to accept testamentary trusts has accelerated in recent years and that it is "rare to see an institution qualify in matters not significantly in excess of $100,000." [36] If there is an individual trustee, it is desirable also to deal with the selection of his successor, unless a corporation will become sole trustee when he ceases to serve. If no successor is provided for, the trust will not fail—a court-appointed trustee will administer the trust—but there are obvious advantages in avoiding the necessity for court selection of the trustee. Even if the original trustee is a corporation, it may later wish to resign, so that again a provision for the selection of a successor is needed. Local practice may require that trustees thus selected also qualify in court, but this variation often may be of no practical effect.

All too often, a client's choice of original and successor trustees is hampered by a failure to analyze sufficiently the qualifications of potential trustees in relation to their duties and by an assumption that all of such

---

34. See, e.g., Cal.Fin.Code § 1751 (West Supp.1980).

35. See § 1.08[2] supra.

36. See Gelfand, Trusts Without Trustees— A Source of Avoidable Expense, 115 Tr.

& Est. 8, 45 (1976); a suggested safeguard is that an individual trustee be named as alternate. Id. at 45.

duties must be performed by the same trustee (or co-trustees). The major categories of services which may be required during the course of administration of a trust are:

(1) Custodial, accounting and tax services. Someone will have to hold trust securities, make deliveries when securities are sold, and accept deliveries when securities are purchased, as well as pay for them. Income items must be collected. Distributions to beneficiaries must be made, either in accordance with explicit directions in the trust instrument or pursuant to the exercise of discretionary powers by a trustee or the exercise of a power of appointment created by the instrument. Accounting records must be kept and tax returns prepared.

(2) Investment management services. The extent of investment decision-making required varies greatly in different trusts, depending on the nature of the trust assets and the investment objectives of the trust. Some trusts include interests in closely held businesses or real estate and require constant attention by the trustee. Other trusts consist of listed securities which require continuing supervision to determine when changes in investments should be made but involve no comparable degree of detailed attention. But no matter how the trust assets are invested, someone must decide when and at what price they shall be bought or sold.

(3) Discretionary powers with respect to distributions. Often a trust instrument does not provide explicit directions for distributions of income and principal, but instead authorizes one or more trustees to determine to whom and in what amounts such payments shall be made, or how receipts and expenditures shall be allocated between income and principal. In others, however, such services are not required because such discretionary powers are not given.

The foregoing description should make clear that there may be no single most satisfactory source for all three categories of service for a given trust, and that it is possible for one or more categories to be provided by someone who is not acting as trustee. Of course, the delegation by trustees of their duties requires explicit authorization,[37] either by statute [38] or by the terms of the trust instrument. Whether a single source or a combination of sources will be most effective in carrying out the objectives of a particular trust depends on many highly individualized factors, including cost of a "package deal" in relation to the total cost of services secured from separate sources.

With respect to the first category, custodial, accounting, and tax services, the choice usually is clear. In a trust of substantial size, these services should be secured from a professional fiduciary, either as trustee or co-trustee or as a custodian employed as agent for the trustee. In some

---

37. See 2 Scott, Trusts §§ 171–171.4 (3d ed. 1967); The Role of An Investment Adviser for Trust Investments in 2 Prentice-Hall, Successful Estate Planning Ideas and Methods ¶ 14,008.

38. See, e.g., N.Y. EPTL 11–1.1(b)(9), (employment of custodian).

localities, law firms are equipped to provide these and other fiduciary services. In most areas, the only important professional sources of custodial services for trustees are banks and trust companies. Few individual trustees can achieve the high caliber of custodial work which can be obtained from the better corporate fiduciaries without spending inordinate amounts of time in the process. Unless the trust is so small that the number of transactions during a year will be very few, or unless it is invested wholly in a few mutual funds which, in effect, provide the substantial equivalent of custodial and accounting services, most individual trustees should turn this work over to professionals.

Investment management services are another matter. Many clients fail to recognize that their choices of investment managers are among the most important financial decisions they will ever make and act on wholly inadequate information in the matter.[39] Here the choice between amateurs and professionals is less clear-cut, particularly in view of the fact that trustees who are not professional investors obtain investment advice from a variety of published sources at modest cost. And even without such advice, there undoubtedly are many individual investors who have made fortunes on their own, with a relatively small expenditure of time. For the trustee who does not want to manage trust investments, the major alternatives are:

(1) investment counsel;

(2) investment in mutual funds;

(3) professional fiduciaries who offer investment management as a separate service;

(4) brokerage firms who give advice as a part of their service to customers.

There are problems with all four alternatives.

If the investment results which would be obtained from a given source could be predicted in advance, the choice would be easy. Lacking the gift of second sight, clients and trustees are forced to turn to past performance records and hope that they will be reflected in future results. Obtaining information on the past investment performance of some professional investors is no easy matter. Published reports of mutual funds and of common trust funds of corporate fiduciaries offer some indication of the results obtained by their sponsors. From a given client's standpoint, the indications may be inconclusive, particularly if his trust will not be invested in the mutual fund or common trust fund but instead will be managed separately by the sponsoring counselling firm or corporate fiduciary. Because its results are publicized, the mutual fund or common trust fund may have been the showcase which benefited from the best investment thinking of its sponsor, and may not represent the results obtained in the average individual account.

In the case of brokerage firms, an analysis can be made of investment results which would have followed from the purchase of securities listed in the firm's published recommended lists over a period of time. However,

---

39. See generally, C. D. Ellis, Institutional Investing, ch. 16 (1971).

it is not unusual to find that the prices given in the published lists are more favorable than those at which most of the firm's customers were able to buy or sell.

Even if accurate information about past performance is obtained, whether it will be continued in the future is often unclear. Unusually favorable results may have been obtained only at the cost of assuming risks which are unacceptably high. Personnel changes may make past performance irrelevant, and even if there is continuity of personnel, marked variations in relative investment performance over different market cycles are the rule rather than the exception.

In comparison to the difficulties in evaluating and predicting comparative investment performance, fees are a relatively simple and straightforward matter. The range is from no charge (apart from regular brokerage commissions) in the case of brokers to an annual fee of 2% of principal or more, or even 20% of trading profits, in the case of higher-priced counselling professionals. The fact that many brokers make no charge for their investment management services does not, of course, mean that they necessarily are the most desirable sources. If the broker can only derive income from commissions on purchases and sales, that may create a predilection, whether conscious or otherwise, for excessive turnover of the account, with unfortunate results. On the other hand, some counselling professionals charge substantial fees for investment results which often are no better than the performance of representative stock averages, or not even as good.

With respect to discretionary powers over distributions, tax and other considerations often make it highly undesirable to give a beneficiary a discretionary power to make distributions to himself.[40] Depending on the particular family situation, however, the power may be given to another family member, either as trustee or as donee of a power of appointment, to make or direct distributions to others if he is not himself a beneficiary.

In view of the many uncertainties which surround the choice of a source of a given category of fiduciary services, the best course may be to avoid any long-term arrangement which cannot be changed if experience proves it to be unsatisfactory. Such flexibility can be obtained by naming family members as trustees, with authority to delegate many of their trust responsibilities to others. In this situation, the trustee in effect is acting primarily as a purchasing agent for trust services, with a maximum freedom to turn to other sources if the results obtained from one are unsatisfactory. Another approach is to name a professional trustee but to give one or more family members a power to remove the trustee and substitute another professional trustee. Although the flexibility offered by either of these approaches often is free from adverse tax consequences under present law,[41] this situation could change. To deal with that possibility, family trustees should be authorized to name successors and to resign, and family members

---

40. The tax problems are discussed in ¶¶ 11.01[1], 12.01[3] infra. In New York, a trustee cannot exercise a power to make discretionary distributions to himself. See N.Y. EPTL 10–10.1.

41. A power of removal held by the settlor himself, however, may produce adverse tax consequences. See ¶ 5.02[5][b] infra.

empowered to remove a trustee should be authorized to release the power of removal.

---

[3] Trustees' Powers, Bonds, Accounts and Liabilities to the Beneficiaries

The confused and unsatisfactory state of the law in many states with respect to trustees' implied powers [42] has led to the practice of including an extensive grant of express powers to trustees.   It is also common to waive bond, or surety, for the trustee, depending on local practice, if a surety bond would otherwise be required, just as in the case of executors.

The problem of trustees' accounts and liabilities to the beneficiaries may best be illustrated by assuming that Don Stevens, as trustee of a trust created by his mother, committed a breach of trust which caused a loss of $10,000 to the trust.   His liability to restore the $10,000 to the trust, with interest, might continue for a very long time.   Most statutes of limitations do not apply to equitable claims. [43]

In due course, Stevens' liability may be shared by a successor trustee as well, if Stevens ceases to serve as sole trustee.   One of the trust assets when Stevens ceased to serve as trustee was the trust's claim against him for $10,000.   If Stevens' successor fails to enforce that claim and it becomes uncollectable, the successor may also incur liability for breach of trust.

Family trustees, even those who are attorneys, often assume that they may ignore record-keeping and accounting formalities because "no one will sue."   Even though the beneficiaries abstain from litigation while the trustee is living, they may lose such inhibitions once he is dead.   In Matter of Crichton, [44] an attorney "with considerable experience in trust matters" became trustee of three trusts when his first wife died in 1923.   No formal accounting was ever made before he died in 1962.   Then the two children of his first marriage compelled his executor to file accounts for their father's service as trustee of all three trusts.   The children filed objections to the accounts, which were held to be barred by laches as to two of the trusts but were sustained in part as to the third.   The court pointed out that a surcharge based on such objections would come out of the father's estate and thus increase the shares of the children of his first marriage at the expense of the children of his second marriage.

Trustees are understandably reluctant to be required at a later date to defend their actions (and inaction) at some dim and distant time in the past, and successor trustees are even more reluctant to incur liability for the misdeeds of their predecessors.   If local practice provides a convenient procedure for judicial settlement of the trustee's accounts, so that his liability, if any, is finally determined, it may be used.   Such a procedure, however, ordinarily means that the accounts become a matter of public record, and often involves significant expense to the trust.   Thus it fre-

---

42. Some states, however, provide an extensive array of trustees' powers by statute, in the absence of a contrary provision in the trust instrument.   See, e.g., N.Y. EPTL 11–1.1.

43. See 3 Scott, Trusts §§ 223.2–3 (3d ed. 1967).

44. 160 N.Y.L.J. (Sur.Ct. Sept. 16, 1968) 18.

quently is desirable to provide for some alternative to judicial settlement of trustees' accounts.   In New York, however, the validity of a provision for binding approval of trustees' accounts by an income beneficiary on behalf of the remaindermen is in doubt.[45]   And an overly broad provision may raise federal tax problems as well.[46]

---

45. See In re Crane, 34 N.Y.S.2d 9 (Sup.Ct. 1942), aff'd mem. sub nom. Application of Central Hanover Bank & Trust Co., 266 App.Div. 726, 41 N.Y.S.2d 940 (1st Dep't 1943), appeal denied 266 App.Div. 846, 43 N.Y.S.2d 851 (1st Dep't 1943).

46. See generally, Westfall, Nonjudicial Settlement of Trustee's Accounts, 71 Harv.L.Rev. 40 (1957).

Chapter 3

DESCRIBING BENEFICIARIES' INTERESTS

¶ 3.01 CLASS GIFTS

Wills which describe beneficiaries as members of a group or class often are ambiguous, so that court proceedings are required to determine who is included and the size of their respective shares in the gift. The result has been a staggering amoung of litigation, costly both to the individuals affected and to society as well. Much valuable professional time and talent is diverted from more productive work; legatees' shares are diminished by substantial attorneys' fees; uncertainties as to the ownership and management of potentially productive assets may remain unresolved for years, inhibiting the use and development of the property.

To deal with such litigation, the courts long ago began to develop rules of construction to dispose of cases in which the language used was ambiguous. Whether such rules in fact operate to reduce litigation is not always clear, in view of the pronounced judicial willingness to recognize exceptions to such rules and to weigh the evidence in each case. However, neither drafting nor litigation can proceed intelligently without an understanding of the major problems which the rules of construction are used to resolve.

Volumes have been devoted to the topic which these materials must treat briefly. Accordingly, no effort is made to catalogue the major rules of construction. Rather, the goal here is to highlight those constructional problems which are most important to the draftsman who seeks to keep an instrument free from ambiguities in its use of class gift terms:

1. Who is included in the primary meaning of the term used;

2. How long are class members required to survive;

3. When does the class close to exclude additional members, usually those yet to be born;

4. What is the share of each class member.

Often, as in the first group of cases to be discussed, the solution to one problem is decisive as to others as well. Thus a determination as to who is included in a gift to "heirs" normally also settles the other three questions just mentioned. Each case in this chapter reached the courts because of the draftsman's failure to provide clear answers to one or more of the questions above.

[1] Gifts to "Heirs" or to "Issue"

One authority has identified six problems of construction which gifts to "heirs" are likely to raise:

> Is some statute dealing with the intestate succession of property to be employed to ascertain the devisees or legatees? If so, what statute? Are any of the persons described by the applicable statute to be excluded? As of what time is the appropriate statute to be applied? Is the ascertained group to survive to any future

date?   And finally, how much of the subject matter of the gift is each ascertained person to receive? [1]

N.Y. EPTL 1–2.10 defines "issue," and 2–1.2 deals with the question of whether they take per capita or per stirpes.   Often in other jurisdictions the matter is left wholly to case law.[2]

MATTER OF ESTATE OF SAYRE

Supreme Court of New York, Appellate Division, Fourth Department, 1956.
1 A.D.2d 475, 151 N.Y.S.2d 506, aff'd mem. 2 N.Y.2d 929,
161 N.Y.S.2d 890, 141 N.E.2d 920 (1957).

VAUGHN, Justice.   This is a proceeding for the construction of the will of James Sayre, deceased.   The serious question presented is whether the class of heirs of the testator, to whom the trust remainder is given upon certain contingencies, should be determined as of the testator's death or as of the time of distribution of the corpus.   The Surrogate has adopted the former construction, and a nephew of the testator appeals to this Court.

The testator's will, executed in 1905, provided as follows: "I give and devise all of my property, real and personal, unto my executors hereinafter named, in trust nevertheless, to wit: to receive the rents and income thereof, and to apply them to the use of my wife, Ida L. Sayre, during her life;   and, at her decease, I give and devise said property, real and personal, absolutely unto my children then living, in equal shares;   and the children of any predeceased child to take the share its parent would have received if living at my wife's decease.   And in event that no such child, or its descendants, shall be living at the decease of my wife;   then I give said real and personal property, absolutely to my sister, Anna L. Sayre, if she then be living at my wife's decease;   or, if said Anna L. Sayre, be then deceased, I give said real and personal property unto my heirs at law and next of kin, according to the provisions of the Statutes of the State of New York relating thereto."

The testator died in 1919 without issue.   His heirs at that time were four sisters (Anna, who died in 1927;   Caroline, died 1931;   Amelia, died 1935;   and Leonora, died 1938), one brother (George, who died in 1938) and one nephew (the present appellant, who is the son of a brother who predeceased the testator).   The testator's widow died in 1954.   His heirs, determined as of that time, would be his nephew (the appellant) and one niece (the daughter of George).   The present respondents are George Sayre's trustees and two charitable institutions named as remaindermen under his will.

We think that the following are the only two possible constructions of this will: (1) The heirs of the testator, to whom the ultimate remainder is granted, could be determined as of the time of his death.   Respondents urge this interpretation, under which appellant would receive only one sixth of the remainder.   This may be said to be the usual construction, in the

------

1.   Casner, Construction of Gifts to "Heirs"   2.   See Annot., 13 A.L.R.2d 1023 (1950).
and the Like, 53 Harv.L.Rev. 207, 208
(1939).

absence of an indication of contrary intent, Matter of Bump's Will, 234 N.Y. 60, 136 N.E. 295; Restatement of Property, § 308; (2) The heirs of the testator could be determined as of the death of the life tenant, i.e., at the time fixed for distribution of the corpus. Under this construction, appellant would receive one half of the remainder. For reasons to be discussed, we believe that is the correct result.

* * *

In the present case, there are sound reasons for determining the class of heirs of the testator, not at his death, but at the death of the life tenant. The will created three remainders. The first remainder was in fee "unto my children then living." As the testator never had issue, that remainder was contingent, not vested, because the remaindermen were uncertain and not in existence, Real Property Law, § 40. The second remainder, to testator's sister Anna, was likewise contingent because it was subject to the condition that Anna survive the life tenant, New York Life Ins. & Trust co. v. Winthrop, 237 N.Y. 93, 142 N.E. 431, 31 A.L.R. 791, which she did not do. If both of those remainders should fail, the testator granted the remainder "unto my heirs at law and next of kin, according to the provisions of the Statutes of the State of New York relating thereto." This ultimate remainder, dependent upon the failure of the first two, each of which was contingent, was itself contingent and substitutional. Until the death of Anna before the life tenant, it was uncertain whether the heirs would take at all. The remainder in their favor, being subject to a condition precedent, was contingent. Delaney v. McCormack, 88 N.Y. 174. Since the remainder to heirs was secondary, contingent, and substitutional, the class of remaindermen should be determined as of the death of the life tenant. * * * That construction seems particularly appropriate where, as here, survivorship is a condition of the prior remainders. The initial remainder was "unto my children then living." The second remainder was "to my sister, Anna L. Sayre, if she then be living at my wife's decease." Probably the testator intended that, if both of those remainders failed for lack of survivorship, the property should go to his heirs determined as of the time of distribution. Since he required survivorship as a condition of the first two remainders, it is unlikely that he intended his "heirs at law and next of kin" to be determined as of his death, so that persons who predeceased the life tenant might nevertheless qualify as heirs. If that were done, the remainder would not vest in his heirs, but in their heirs or residuary legatees. Such residuary legatees (for example, the present respondents) need not be the heirs or relatives of the testator at all. Such a result, we believe, conflicts with the testator's clear intent to benefit his closest blood relatives.

The remainder to Anna is dependent upon her surviving the life tenant. It is apparent that the testator wanted her to take all if she survived, and nothing if she did not. Yet by respondents' construction, although the specific remainder to her failed when she predeceased the life tenant, still she could qualify for a share as an heir. Indeed, for all the testator knew when he drew his will, she could have been his only heir at his death, in which case she would have received a vested remainder in fee, free from the requirement of survivorship which the testator specifically imposed upon the gift to her.   Such an incongruity is evidence that the testator did not intend his heirs to be determined at the time of his death.   [Citations omitted.]

Respondents' position is that the class should be determined as of the death of the testator in 1919, though it was then uncertain whether the heirs would ever take.   But even by that view the remainder would not vest in interest until 1927, when Anna predeceased the life tenant, because until then the remainder to heirs was still subject to a condition precedent. And that remainder did not vest in possession and enjoyment until the death of the life tenant in 1954.   By appellant's view, on the other hand, the remainder would continue contingent until the heirs were ascertained upon the death of the life tenant in 1954, and at the same time would vest in interest and possession.   This is the simpler and more natural construction. It fits in with the general testamentary scheme, particularly the requirement of survivorship.   It satisfies the testator's purpose to benefit his own heirs instead of their residuary legatees.   And it breathes meaning into the clause creating the remainder to heirs, rather than treating it simply as a pointless direction that the law take its course.

* * *

Respondents rely on Matter of White's Will, 213 App.Div. 82, 209 N.Y.S. 433, 434, in which the ultimate remainder was as follows: " 'I give * * * to the same persons who would have been entitled thereto * * * under the laws of the State of New York had I died seized and possessed thereof and intestate.' " Of course, if the testator had died seized of the property and intestate, it would descend to his heirs, determined as of his death.   He clearly expressed his desire that the law take its course. No such intention is to be found in the present case.

Respondents also cite Matter of Bump's Will, 234 N.Y. 60, 136 N.E. 295, supra.   The disposition in that case was such that, if the heirs of the testator were determined as of the death of his widow (the life tenant), then his sister, to whom he had granted only a life estate, would have taken the remainder as an "heir."   Such a result would have conflicted with the intention revealed by the specific grant of a life estate.   In the present case, on the other hand, such reasoning would seem to argue somewhat for a contrary result, else the testator's sister Anna, the primary devise to whom failed for want of survivorship, might nevertheless qualify as an "heir." It follows that the trust remainder, both principal and income, should be distributed to the testator's heirs at law and next of kin determined as of the death of the life tenant in 1954.

* * *

QUESTIONS

1. In the *Sayre* case, if the testator's heirs had been determined as of the time of his death, to whom would the property have been distributed?

2. What would have been the result in *Sayre* if when the life tenant died the only surviving issue of the testator had been a great-grandchild?

3. Why is it ordinarily desirable to provide in an instrument that "heirs" or "issue" shall be construed as referring to persons who are living when distribution is made?

[2] Gifts to Children

Gifts to a group described as the "children" of a given person might appear to present no significant constructional problems. In fact, however, they have been the subject of extensive litigation. State courts of last resort are called on to determine, for example, whether the term includes "grandchildren" in a particular context.[3] The status of adopted children under wills and trusts of persons who were not the adopting parent has been particularly troublesome. The New York statute includes adopted children in dispositions, in the absence of a contrary manifestation of intent.[4] This is in keeping with the general trend of modern legislation and decisions.[5]

Although the desire to end discrimination against adopted children is understandable, it should be borne in mind that in some cases their inclusion in dispositions could bring surprising results. In Minary v. Citizens Fidelity Bank & Trust Co.,[6] the court rejected the contention that adoption of a wife by her husband made the wife the husband's "heir" for purposes of his mother's will. In the more common situation of an intra-family adoption, it is conceivable that the adopted child could be entitled to shares in either or both of two capacities: as the child of his natural parents and as the child of his adoptive parents. Although it is possible to anticipate such problems in drafting instruments, the better course may be to forego intra-family adoptions if the effect on existing dispositive arrangements is uncertain or undesirable.

WILL OF HOFFMAN

Supreme Court of New York, Appellate Division, 1976.
53 A.D.2d 55, 385 N.Y.S.2d 49.

BIRNS, Justice. In this appeal from part of a decree entered in the Surrogate's Court, we are asked to decide whether the term "issue" in a will should be construed to include illegitimate grandchildren of an income beneficiary of a trust established under the terms of that will.

Mary Hoffman, the testatrix died in 1951. Her will established a trust for the benefit of her two cousins and provided that when the first of the two should die, his one-half share of the income should be paid for the remainder of the trust term "to his issue."

One cousin is still living; the other died in 1965, survived by a daughter and a son named Stephen. Stephen died in 1972 leaving two children, the infants represented by respondent-appellant herein. Stephen never married the mother of these children nor was an order of filiation entered. The Surrogate, however, determined that the two children were indeed the children of Stephen.

Relying on precedent, the Surrogate ruled that the two children, being illegitimate, could not inherit [Citations omitted.] because the term "issue"

---

3. See, e.g., Matter of Villalonga, 6 N.Y.2d 477, 190 N.Y.S.2d 372, 160 N.E.2d 850 (1959).

4. See N.Y. EPTL 2–1.3.

5. See generally, Halbach, The Rights of Adopted Children Under Class Gifts, 50

Iowa L.Rev. 971 (1965); Annot., 86 A.L.R.2d 12 (1962).

6. 419 S.W.2d 340 (Ky.1967).

as used in the will meant lawful issue only (Matter of Underhill, 176 Misc. 737, 28 N.Y.S.2d 984), and absent an intention to the contrary it could not be assumed that the testatrix intended illegitimate descendants as the object of her bounty. (Gelston et al. v. Shields et al., 78 N.Y. 275.)

In this court, as she did below, respondent-appellant asserted that inasmuch as the word "issue" in the provision of the will under consideration was not qualified by the word "lawful," the question of legitimacy was not in decedent's mind where she made her will. In addition, the change in conventional attitudes towards illegitimates, as reflected in statutes and decisions, would warrant a construction of the word "issue" as including illegitimates, in the absence of contrary intent to exclude them.

Petitioner-respondent emphasizes that under settled case law, where the word "issue" appears in a will it will be interpreted to mean only lawful descendants in the absence of clear evidence of a contrary intent of a testator.

We recognize that precedents do hold that in the absence of an express intent to the contrary by a testator, the word "issue" presumes lawful issue and not illegitimate offspring. This presumption had its roots in an earlier society where there was no sense of injustice in the teaching that the sins of the fathers were to be visited upon their children and succeeding generations. (Exodus, 20:4; Shakespeare, Merchant of Venice, Act III, Scene 5, Line 1.)

It is evident from these precedents that "presumed intent" on the part of a testator to include lawful descendants only in the use of the word "issue" was designed to harmonize testamentary language with the social mores of the times. The judicial policy to afford legitimate children a preferred status in society has placed upon illegitimates the burden of demonstrating an intent on the part of a testator to include such illegitimates in his testamentary use of the word "issue."

Because of changes in societal attitudes and recent developments in constitutional law, we are of the opinion that, to the extent that precedents require this burden to be placed upon illegitimate claimants under a will, the law is not only outmoded, but discriminatory and should be rejected. We would reverse.

Bottomed upon the ancient concept that an illegitimate child was indeed "filius nullius", i.e., a child of nobody, thus without legal status (New-Haven v. Newtown, 12 Conn. 164; Dickinson's Appeal from Probate, 42 Conn. 491), many jurisdictions, like New York, held the word "issue" to mean only legitimate issue. (Page v. Roddie, 92 Okl. 236, 218 P. 1092; King v. Thissell, 222 Mass. 140, 109 N.E. 880; Hardesty v. Mitchell, 302 Ill. 369, 134 N.E. 745.) Courts thus denied "illegitimate" claimants the right to share under provisions of wills not unlike the one before us.[7]

However, this archaic concept, with its moralistic overtones, was not accepted by all courts. Connecticut in 1914 first repudiated any common law principle which limited the words "child" or "children" to those only of legitimate status, observing that "by reason of our recognition of the relation of parent to child between a mother and her illegitimate offspring that no statute has been needed in this state to accomplish results which humanity

---

7. Most states have ruled that the word "children" in a will does not include illegitimates unless a contrary intent is shown. See C.J.S. Wills § 652.

and natural justice dictated, and which could be arrived at elsewhere only through statutory intervention." (Eaton v. Eaton, 88 Conn. 269, 91 A. 191.) And in a companion case the same court ruled that in the same will under consideration the words "issue of his or her body" did not reflect a limited use of those words, but included illegitimate issue, in the absence of anything to indicate the use of the words in any other than their prima facie signification. (Eaton v. Eaton, 88 Conn. 286, 91 A. 196.)

New York courts, in the main, have not subscribed to the Connecticut view but have clung to the rule that where such words are used in a will, the word "child" means "lawful child," and the word "issue" means "lawful issue," in the absence of a manifestation of contrary intent. (Central Trust Co. v. Skillin, 154 App.Div. 227, 138 N.Y.S. 884.)

Research has disclosed only six cases in which the courts of this state have actually construed "issue" or "children", not qualified by "lawful" or in any other way, and not otherwise explained, so as to exclude illegitimates. [Citations omitted.]

It is noted that the earliest of these decisions is over 100 years old, and the most recent is 35 years old. Two are by the same Surrogate. Only two are appellate decisions, the latest of which is 1894. Apparently the precise question before us has never been decided by the Court of Appeals or this court.

Illustrative of varied expressions of the New York rule is the recitation found in Matter of Underhill, supra: "The meaning to be ascribed to the word 'issue' depends upon the intention of the testator as derived from the context of the will or such extrinsic evidence as may be considered. * * * The test is what was included 'in the nomenclature or vocabulary of the testator.' * * * His intention is to be construed in the light of the statutes and decisions applicable at the time he executed his will and codicil. * * * "

* * *

Our statutes do provide continuing evidence of legislative concern for illegitimate children as reference to various sections of the Estates Powers and Trust Law will demonstrate.[8]

While nothing in the EPTL provides that illegitimate children are "issue" for purposes of taking under a will, rights of illegitimates to share in the estates of their kin are expanding. In fact, present attitudes appear to reject an inferior social or legal status for illegitimates.[9]

---

8. See EPTL:

Section 1–2.10 defines issue, unless a contrary intention is indicated, as the descendants in any degree from a common ancestor.

Section 3–3.3(b) dealing with anti-lapse clauses and limited thereto includes illegitimate children in the world "issue." An illegitimate child is the child of his father if he is entitled to inherit from his father under another section, i.e., section 4–1.2.

Section 4–1.2(a)(1), (2) dealing with descent and distribution through intestacy provides an illegitimate child is the legitimate child of his mother so that he can inherit from her and from his maternal kindred and is the legitimate child of his father so he can inherit from him if a valid order of filiation declaring paternity is entered timely.

* * *

9. Harry D. Krause, Illegitimacy: Law and Social Policy, (The Bobbs Merrill Co., Inc., Indianapolis, 1971).

Shirley Foster Hartley, Illegitimacy, (University of California Press, 1975).

The question raised is whether social and statutory changes require a reconsideration of the rule which presumed an intent by testatrix to exclude illegitimate descendants in sharing under her will.

Certainly, it cannot be said, as a matter of fact, that the testatrix was aware of these changes in societal attitudes as evidenced by the legislation referred to, or aware of community attitudes towards premarital sex or sex without marriage. Nor can it be said with any degrees of assurance that at the time she executed her will she was provided with an explanation of the word "issue" which appeared on the typewritten pages of that document. It is just as likely that the word "issue" in her mind had a meaning no different than "progeny" or "offspring." (Webster's New International Dictionary, 2d ed., G. & C. Merriam Co., 1947.)

The will itself supports the conclusion that the bequest to her cousins was of paramount concern in establishing the trust. It is most unlikely that she gave any more than passing thought to the children who now, 25 years after her death, claim under her will, particularly as to whether or not they would be legitimate.

The presumed intent of the testator with which all the precedents are concerned, although represented as rebuttable, is in fact, in most cases irrebuttable. The passage of time has made it impossible to establish that the testatrix did not intend to exclude illegitimate descendants from sharing under her will. This difficulty of proof was highlighted by a former Surrogate who said, "Indeed, a mere comparison of the material dates demonstrates the impossibility of presenting such evidence." (Matter of Underhill, supra, p. 740, 28 N.Y.S.2d p. 987.)

To continue to rely upon these precedents and then declare that in using the word "issue" in her will, testatrix intended only lawful issue and not illegitimates is to attribute to her a frame of mind not at all supported by the facts. We recognize that the testatrix should possess the broadest freedom of choice in making known the objects of her bounty, and that it is the duty of the court to ascertain the testatrix's intent. Nevertheless, the court should not under the guise of determining the testatrix's intent substitute its own preference as to the legatees who shall take under the will. There should be a demonstrable relation between judicial interpretation of a will and the testatrix's actual frame of mind.   *   *   *

*   *   * In the case before us, we are of the opinion that rigid adherence to precedent will produce a result not warranted by facts but rather by adherence to an anachronistic rule.

Therefore we reject the rule that where the word "issue," standing alone, appears in a will, it will be interpreted to include within its meaning only lawful descendants. We hold that the word "issue" should be construed to refer to legitimate and illegitimate descendants alike in the absence of an express qualification by the testatrix.

Further justification for our decision today can be found in expanding concepts of the Equal Protection Clause. (U.S Constitution, 14th Amendment.) To construe "issue" in a will as excluding illegitimate children otherwise entitled to inherit thereunder, is, as stated before, nothing more than the substitution of judicial preference for a testator's intent. Such preference, under the guise of judicial construction, we believe, is state action. (See Shelley v. Kraemer, 334 U.S. 1, 68 S.Ct. 836, 92 L.Ed. 1161.) State action is proscribed if it promotes discrimination based upon an unconstitutional classification [Citations omitted.] * * *

* * *

Because of the expanding concept of equal protection we should not adhere rigidly to the rules enunciated in the cases cited as precedents herein. To do so would require us to hold that illegitimates enjoyed a lesser status than legitimate children before the law in cases such as the one before us.

In rejecting archaism, we do no more in this appeal than hold that the word "issue" as used by testatrix in her will should have no meaning other than that ordinarily and customarily imputed to persons in its usage in the absence of any manifestation of an intent to the contrary. Thus, the test set forth in Matter of Underhill, supra, is still viable as long as it is not used to disguise judicial preferment. Accordingly, the law will not be required to discriminate against children labeled illegitimate through no fault of their own.

A remand in this case is not necessary inasmuch as the parties were before the Surrogate on an agreed statement of facts. Accordingly, the decree of the Surrogate should be reversed on the law and on the facts and upon a reading of the will, it is determined that the testatrix intended in her use of the word "issue" in her will legitimate and illegitimate descendants. The will is so construed with costs to all parties appearing and filing briefs payable from the trust estate.

* * *

All concur.

QUESTIONS

1. What problems does the *Hoffman* holding create for the corporate fiduciary of a trust under which income or principal is distributed to a class described as "issue" or "children"?

2. If you were counsel for a corporate fiduciary, what kind of provision would you recommend for inclusion in trust instruments and wills to deal with the problem just referred to?

[3] Rule of Convenience

A recurring problem in the construction of wills and trusts is determining how long distribution should be deferred in order to allow potential distributees to be born and otherwise qualify for their shares. For example, if T's will contains a bequest to "the children of A" and it means all children, whenever born, and A is living and is regarded as being capable of further reproduction, the executor faces a dilemma. If he makes distribution to the children of A who are living when T died, some of those whom T wanted to benefit may be excluded because they were not born in time. Of course it might be possible to require the living children to return part of their legacies to make up a share for an afterborn child, but this potential liability (if taken seriously by the legatees) might inhibit their enjoyment of the subject matter of the bequest as long as the liability continued.   On the other hand, if the executor made no distribution until A died and necessarily ceased to be capable of reproduction, the problem would not arise.   But such a delay in distribution would be inconsistent with T's desire to confer a present benefit on A's children.

To resolve this conflict, the courts developed the Rule of Convenience[10] as a rebuttable presumption that the testator would have preferred immediate distribution to the living class members, even if the effect is to exclude altogether any afterborn children of A.   In this situation, the Rule is concerned with the convenience of the living class members, and it may appear to ignore the interests of those yet unborn.   In fact, however, the unborn class members often may be no more than gleams in the judicial eye, if A is elderly and unlikely to acquire more children either by birth or by adoption (if adopted children are included in the disposition).   Thus the Rule may be harsher on paper than it is in practice.

A second aspect of the Rule is concerned with convenience of the taker of the residue.   For example, if T's will contains a bequest of $10,000 to "each child of A," and bequeaths the residue of his estate to B, and the meaning again is all children of A, whenever born, A's executor faces a dilemma of another sort.   If he distributes $10,000 apiece to the children of A now living and what remains to B, there is nothing to give afterborn children of A.   On the other hand, if the executor makes no distribution to B until A has died, T's intent to give B some present benefit is frustrated.

To resolve this conflict, the courts again applied the Rule of Convenience as a rebuttable presumption that the testator would prefer to exclude the unborn children of A in order to permit immediate distribution to be made to B.

Similarly, if T's will contains a bequest of $10,000 to "each child of A who attains, 21," the Rule of Convenience operates to exclude children who are unborn at the death of the testator.   With respect to children who are living at that time but who have not attained 21, a sufficient sum can be reserved to provide for the possibility that they will reach that age and become entitled to payment of their bequests.

The foregoing is no more than a brief introduction to a few basic aspects of the Rule as it applies to immediate gifts.

COLE v. COLE

Supreme Court of North Carolina, 1949.
229 N.C. 757, 51 S.E.2d 491, 5 A.L.R.2d 1335.

* * *

This action was brought by the plaintiff as administrator c. t. a. of the estate of A. B. Cole, and in his individual right, against various interested parties, to secure a declaratory judgment construing a part of the will as to which some doubt had arisen affecting the administration.   The item directly concerned reads as follows:

10.   See 5 American Law of Property §§
22.39–.46 (A. J. Casner ed. 1952).

"Item V.   I will devise and bequeath to my beloved nephews and any other children who may be born to Robert and Peg Cole, my house and lot at 301 Fayetteville together with the contents and the lot west of the home on Fayetteville Road."

The will was written April 27, 1945.   Cole died Jan. 10, 1948.   At the time the will was written and at his death the testator had three nephews: Robert L. Cole, Robert Leake Steele Cole (referred to in the will as Robert Cole and Robert S. Cole), and Walter F. Cole, Jr.   At the time the will was written, and at his death, the testator had three grand nephews, minor children of Robert Leake Steele Cole and wife, Mary Gregg (Peggy) Cole, and a fourth child of Robert and Peg was en ventre sa mere, and was born May 10, 1945.

At the time of testator's death there was in the house described in the above item of the will a metal safe containing choses in action, securities, and intangibles, including a trailer patent, in all worth approximately $47,000.   The residuary clause of the will left the remainder of the property, except that specifically given, to the eight nieces and nephews of the testator.

No other children have been born to Robert and Peggy Cole since testator's death.

*   *   * From the adverse judgment construing the devise in Item V to include only the children in esse at the death of the testator, the guardian ad litem for the unborn children appealed.

SEAWELL, Justice.   We have left for solution what seems to be the most troublesome problem dealt with by the court below: Whether the testator intended to include as beneficiaries under Item V of the will, above copied, only the children of Robert and Peggy Cole born, or to be born, prior to his death, or en ventre sa mere, or to include, as well, any and all children born to them at any future time before or after his death, and whether that intention may prevail over rules of construction contended for by appellees.

The directness of the issue depending upon the force and effect of the rule of construction invoked seems to demand a more specific, however brief, discussion of its nature and application than we find in our own decisions.

It is difficult to conceive how the testator could have used more comprehensive or all-inclusive language to express the intent that all the children born to Robert and Peggy Cole, regardless of his own span of life, should share in his bounty.   the rule widely accepted, however, is that when a testamentary gift is made to a class, with no preceding estate, only those of the class living or en ventre sa mere at the time of the death of the testator may take.   [Citations omitted.]   This is sometimes referred to as the "rule of convenience."   [Citations omitted.]   It is obviously based on the inconveniences of administration, distribution, or enjoyment of those presently let into possession by the immediacy of the gift, especially the uncertainties attending enjoyment and restriction on alienation, all of which might be obviated by a rule which closes membership in the class by calling the roll at the death of the testator, so that the owners, and the extent of their property rights, may then be ascertained without waiting for future members of the class, or cotenants who may never arrive. The "convenience" promoted by its application is that of the class members first taking and not that of the members excluded, or even of the testator who may have wished them to share.

The term "rule of convenience" aptly indicates its origin, its raison d'etre; but it argues little for its engraftment on the most fundamental canon of will construction—that of finding the intent of the testator from the will—since the inconveniences implied are objective and not necessarily connected with subjective intent.

Since these inconveniences are, as we have said, objective, and only by astute reasoning can be related to the intent, the assumptions which have been made to affiliate the rule with the intent of the testator have been challenged as unreal—as devices carrying only the camouflaged expression of a public policy modifying or destroying the intent. One of the assumptions involved in applying the rule is that the average man in making a will would hardly intend to leave his property in such an anomalous or unsatisfactory condition; or at least that propriety would not be offended by a presumption to the contrary. Page on Wills, § 4. Frankly there is no evidence that the average man ever made a will or ever will; and the standardization is open to the criticism that it ignores both the intelligentsia and those of humbler comprehension, just able to know their property, the objects of their bounty, and the effect of the disposition which they are making. And it is safe to say that the difficulties presented as a basis of the rule are the inconveniences to the members of the class earlier admitted and would appeal more strongly to the legalistic mind than that of the layman making the will. "In theory, at least, the determination of membership in a class is a matter of construction; that is if the testator clearly states his intent as to the time a maximum or minimum membership is to be determined, that statement controls. *Rules as to the determination of classes are simply rebuttable presumptions.* However, here, as in many other situations calling for constructions, it is improbable that the testator has thought of the problem which subsequently arises. Hence it is futile to talk of his intent. What we are doing is either determining what the testator would have done had he thought of the situation with which the Court was confronted, or else apply a rule of construction based on public policy." Simes on Future Interests, Part II, § 372 et seq.

Many of the terms used in cases following the rule, "administration," "distribution," "demand," are more appropriate to bequests of personalty than to devises of realty; and with such a testamentary disposition it may be said that the need of the rule is much more apparent than in case of a devise. "On the application of the rule to realty, the authority is slight." Simes on Future Interests, Part II, p. 146, sec. 382. But little discrimination is apparent in the use of the terms applied. It is worthwhile to note, however, that the majority of the older cases in our jurisdiction exemplifying the rule deal with bequests of personalty and not infrequently speak a language of necessity appropriate to that subject. This itself, by eliminating difficulties to administration and distribution, suggests a cleavage in treatment between bequests and devises. The most troublesome problem dealt with by the courts has been the question of the accumulation of profits or income ad interim. In this we might well follow the analogy of Shepherd v. Ingram, Amb. 448, holding, under comparable facts of that case, that those previously let into possession and enjoyment are not required to account for rents and profits accruing pending the birth of others entitled to share in the devise, the earlier takers being in the position of holding interests pro tanto defeasible. There is no necessity, therefore, of giving bond as suggested in the cited cases on bequests of money or personalty, or uncertainty as to the extent of the enjoyment.

These observations are not directed toward abrogation of the rule but toward its more considerate application, and the greater propriety of yielding to the contrary intent of the will, in particular cases, when clearly expressed. Restatement, Property, Future Interests, 3 and 4, sec. 294, p. 1574; Simes, Future Interests, supra, sec. 372 et seq. "The rule usually defeats the intent of the testator and the tendency of the courts is not to apply it unless it is necessary." Jarman, Wills, p. 1665. Nevertheless in the jurisdictions adopting it, the rule has been variously stated and applied with different degrees of strictness. We have to determine in the instant case whether in this jurisdiction the rule, however evolved, presents an insuperable barrier to the intent and in its strict application may have become a rule of property binding as stare decisis; and if not, then what effect it may have upon the present devise.

* * *

The determination of the maximum or minimum membership in the class to which the testator's bounty is directed is a substantial and important testamentary right, a property right, which ought not to be destroyed or abridged except through public necessity combining with clear authority.

We are led to the conclusion that we are dealing with a rebuttable presumption only; and that so long as the testator is within the rule against perpetuities and is not prevented by any statutory rule of construction, and when the intention to do so clearly appears, he may, without the creation of a preceding estate, make a class devise or bequest, of the character with which we are dealing, which may carry the gift beyond his death; and as in the instant case include all members of the class born to the persons specified as ancestors until the possibility of issue becomes extinct by the death of either of them. We think the language employed in this will, in its ordinary acceptation, is broad enough with respect to its futurity, nothing else appearing, to accomplish that purpose.

Introducing matter extraneous to the will on the question of intent, the appellees on the one hand argue that the language used by the testator is persuasively within the "rule of convenience," because he must have known the fact that Peg Cole was at the time enceinte, since she was a frequent visitor at his home, and that the provision for "any other children who may be born to Robert and Peg Cole" must have referred to this unborn child. And in favor of the opposite interpretation, the appellant points out that the devise was of the ancestral home of Robert and Peg, which had been acquired by the testator, and that he was in this devise giving the house back to the descendants of the original owner, amongst whom there was no reason to discriminate.

It is frequently said that in the judicial interpretation of a will every case must stand on its own bottom. We refrain from detailed discussion and comparison of the language used in the cited cases in making the devises and bequests, some of which are comparable and some disparate, although we have given them careful attention.

We are satisfied from the language of the will and the circumstances under which it was executed that it was the intention of the testator to extend his bounty to all the members of the described class which might at any subsequent period be born to Robert and Peg Cole and that the class membership may not be closed until the possibility of afterborn children is extinct through the death of one of these ancestors.

We do not know how long the inconveniences pointed out in the brief may be suffered by the devisees. The testator no doubt may have understood from the common experience of man that the period of gestation might be fixed at 10 lunar months; but he would hardly be supposed to have appreciated the naivete of the law, which still refuses to be advised, but contrary to human experience accepts the possibility of issue as long as there is life.

*   *   *

¶ 3.02   THE RULE AGAINST PERPETUITIES AND RELATED RULES

The most important restriction on the ability of a client to divide ownership of his wealth over time, so that successive beneficiaries may enjoy that wealth in the order and under the conditions determined by him, is the Rule Against Perpetuities. In its absence, it would be possible to create a perpetual trust for the client's descendants living from time to time. Such a trust would substantially increase the control of a deceased client over the enjoyment of his wealth, and would permit substantial tax savings as well, in comparison to the taxes paid by beneficiaries who receive outright ownership of wealth.[11]

In at least one state, Wisconsin, such a trust may be created. Its law does not restrict the duration of trusts if the trustee has the power to sell the trust property,[12] and the common law Rule Against Perpetuities is not in force.[13] Thus it is possible in Wisconsin to create a perpetual trust for the grantor's issue which is subject to termination by a court only in specified circumstances or under its general equitable powers.[14]

In almost every other state there is either a statutory or common law limitation on remoteness of vesting which applies both to legal interests and to equitable interests in a trust as well. It is appropriate to consider first the policy which the Rule reflects and then the mechanics of its application.

---

11. The generation-skipping transfer tax, imposed by chapter 13 of the code, has reduced but not eliminated such savings. See chapter 13 infra.

12. Wis.Stat. § 700.16 (3)(1969).

13. Id. § 700.16(5).

14. Id. § 701.13(6).

[1] Policies Involved

L. M. SIMES, FUTURE INTERESTS § 121 (2d ed. 1966)*

Purpose and Policy of the Rule

When future interests in specific land or other things are involved, the purpose and policy of the rule may properly be said to be the furtherance of marketability. But if the future interests are interests in a revolving fund, such as corporate shares or beneficial interests in trusts, a further rationale must be recognized, namely: the rule strikes a fair balance between the desires of the living generation to dispose of the property which it enjoys and the desires of future generations to dispose of the property which they will enjoy.

To say that the rule against perpetuities is a rule against remoteness of vesting does not tell us much about its underlying policy. In other words, this statement merely means that its underlying policy is carried out by striking down contingent future interests which may vest at too remote a time. Even Gray, who always insisted that the rule is one against remoteness of vesting and not against restraints on alienation, conceded that it was one of the "modes adopted by the common law for forwarding the circulation of property." [15] It would seem, however, that not only contingent interests, but also many vested future interests, tend to hamper alienability. Indeed, practically the only interests in real property which are readily marketable are the fee simple absolute and the lease for years. Yet the law does not go so far as to strike down all future interests other than the fee simple subject to a term of years. Indeed, it is assumed that vested future interests do not tend to take property out of commerce to the same extent as contingent interests. While, today, this assumption is not always completely accurate, the law does not apply the rule against perpetuities to vested future interests. Commonly, contingent future interests, even if they are alienable as a matter of law, are not readily marketable. No one is likely to be interested in buying except the owner of the interest which would be divested on the vesting of the contingent interest. Moreover, there is rarely any objective basis on which to evaluate the contingent interest. Besides, if the contingent interest is limited in favor of an unascertained or unborn person, it is truly inalienable, since there is no ascertainable person who can alienate it. Thus the American Law Institute Restatement of the Law of Property has appropriately described the rule against perpetuities as a rule against inconvenient fettering of property. [16]

This explanation of the policy of the rule against perpetuities appears to be satisfactory enough when we are considering the marketability of a specific piece of land. But the rule against perpetuities is not limited in its application to contingent legal interests in land. It applies also to equitable interest both in land and in things other than land. It applies to beneficial interests in trusts. It applies to shares of corporate stock. It applies to

---

15. Gray, The Rule against Perpetuities (4th ed. 1942) 4.

16. 4 Restatement, Property (1944) § 370, comment c.

contractual choses in action in the hands of the promisee.   If the rule against perpetuities were nothing more than a rule to further marketability, then we would find difficulty in explaining why it applies to a beneficial interest in a trust, or to a contingent future interest in shares of corporate stock. Undoubtedly the terms of most trusts give the trustee broad powers to alienate its subject matter.   Yet that does not make the contingent interest of the beneficiary valid under the rule.   One reason why this is true is because the power of any trustee to alienate is not absolute.   He cannot give the property away.   He cannot gamble it on the races.   In a sense the property is fettered or tied up while the trust lasts.   The subject matter of the trust may become what the economist calls "frozen assets."   This would seem to be socially undesirable, if it is to continue for too long a time.

A similar argument may be made with respect to contingent future interests in shares of corporate stock.   The tangible property of the corporation is not the property of the stockholder.   Yet that tangible property gives economic value to the shares of stock.   From an economic standpoint, the value of the share is, to a large extent, determined by the value of the property of the corporation.   Yet the property of the corporation is not tied up.   It may be said to be freely alienable.   However, the corporate directors are restricted to using the property for corporate purposes.   It is not as freely alienable as a piece of land which John Doe owns in fee simple absolute.   What the owner of a contingent future interest in a share of stock, or of a contingent equitable interest in a trust, really has, from an economic standpoint, is an interest in a revolving fund.

We may than ask this question: Is there any reason why a contingent future interest in a revolving fund should be subject to the rule against perpetuities?   It is believed that the answer is definitely in the affirmative.[17] If members of the present generation could tie up the property which they enjoy by the use of contingent future interests which would not vest for a very long time, then the property would come to succeeding generations in a fettered condition.   Thus later generations would be unable to do as they desire with the property which they enjoy.   Hence the rule against perpetuities may be said to be designed to strike a fair balance between the policy of allowing the present generation to do as it wishes with the property which it enjoys, and the policy of allowing succeeding generations to do as they wish with the property which they will enjoy.   That is to say, the rule offers a compromise between giving full scope to the desires of the present generation and to the desires of future generations.   Thus the rule against perpetuities is needed even though the marketability of specific property is not greatly impaired by the existence of contingent future interests.

* * *

[2] Vested and Contingent Interests

As the Rule is concerned with remoteness of vesting, it is appropriate to deal first with the distinction between vested and contingent remainders.[18] A remainder is contingent as long as there is any condition precedent (including the determination of who is to take) which must occur before the

---

17. See Simes, Public Policy and the Dead Hand (1955), c. 3.

18. See 1 American Law of Property §§ 4.32–.36 (A. J. Casner ed. 1952).

remainderman is entitled to possession of the property, in addition to the termination of preceding interests. For example: "to A for life, then if B survives A to B and his heirs," creates in B a remainder which is contingent upon B's surviving A. Similarly, "To A for life, then to A's children who survive A (and their heirs)," creates in A's children a remainder which is contingent upon their surviving A.

A remainder is vested if the remainderman is ascertained and there is no such condition precedent, other than the termination of preceding interests. For example, "To A for life, remainder to B and his heirs," creates in B a vested remainder, as does "To A for life, remainder to A's children and their heirs," if one or more children of A are living when the disposition becomes effective. In the latter case, each child of A takes on his birth an interest in a remainder which is vested, although it is subject to open to let in any other children who may be born to A.

---

[3] The Common Law Rule Against Perpetuities

WAGGONER, FUTURE INTERESTS IN A NUTSHELL*

§ 12.1   Statement of the Rule

As formulated by Professor John Chipman Gray   * * *   the Rule Against Perpetuities is that *"no interest is good unless it must vest, if at all, not later than twenty-one years after some life in being at the creation of the interest."* J. Gray, The Rule Against Perpetuities § 201 (2d ed. 1906).

No single-sentence formulation of so complex a body of law as the Rule Against Perpetuities could be entirely complete and accurate. And Gray's formulation is no exception, as he would have been the first to recognize. Nevertheless, his formulation is considered by the courts to be the classic statement of the Rule, and it does provide a good starting point for analysis.

* * *

The first step in considering the validity of an interest is to determine whether the interest is subject to the Rule. Only if it is subject to the Rule is the next step properly taken, which is of course to determine whether it violates the Rule.

§ 12.2   Interests Subject to the Rule

(a) Interests in Property. The sole concern of the Rule Against Perpetuities is whether an interest in *property* is certain to vest or fail to vest in due time. If a transaction creates a property interest, it makes no difference whether the interest is legal or equitable; nor does it make any difference whether the subject matter is real or personal property: the Rule is potentially applicable. But legal relationships which do not create property interests are not subject to the Rule. Thus contracts—even long term contracts—are generally exempt from the Rule. It has been held,

accordingly, that optional modes of settlement for the payment of life insurance proceeds cannot violate the Rule, nor can annuity contracts, even though future payments may be subject to uncertainties which might not be resolved within a life in being plus 21 years.   [Citation omitted.]

(b) Future Interests.   Even as to interests in property, not all are subject to the Rule.   The Rule is tied to the time of possible future *vesting*. This being so, property interests which are vested from the instant of their creation are exempt.   This narrows the scope of the Rule to *future* interests, since possessory interests are always vested, and it also exempts certain future interests as well.   Reversions are exempt because they too are by definition always vested.   *   *   *   Vested remainders are exempt for the same reason.   And this exemption includes remainders which are at their inception vested subject to defeasance, even when the event described in the condition subsequent or limitation might occur beyond the period of the Rule.   *   *   *

(c) Contingent Future Interests.   The scope of the Rule is thus narrowed to *contingent* future interests.   And even here, possibilities of reverter and rights of entry, which are by the better view classified as contingent   *   *   *, have not been subjected to the Rule, largely for historical reasons.   We are thus down to contingent remainders and executory interests (of the much more common type, i.e. those that are properly contingent) as the interests subject to the Rule.

(d) The Special Case of Class Gifts.   Class gifts are also subject to the Rule, and in fact are treated specially.   The early English decision of Leake v. Robinson [19] laid down the proposition that *if the interest of any potential class member might vest too remotely, the entire class gift is invalid.*   This is the so-called "all or nothing" rule, by which it is meant of course that a class gift is either *completely* valid or *completely* invalid.   It is not permissible to treat the interest of each class member separately, and say that the interest of certain class members is valid while the interest of other class members is invalid [unless the gift is a specified sum to each class member or is to a group of sub-classes (§ 13.3)—ed.]

*   *   *

The unborn members   *   *   *   of a class have executory interests which are contingent on their birth.   This explains why the interest of the unborn class members is subject to the Rule.   But the interests of the living class members may be *vested* subject to open, and if so the "all or nothing" rule not only subjects their interests to the Rule Against Perpetuities but also renders them invalid because of the invalidity of the interests of other class members.   *   *   *

§ 12.3   The Meaning of "Must Vest If At All"

Suppose we now have an interest which is subject to the Rule.   How do we determine whether it is valid?   As a preliminary matter, it should be made clear what the Rule requires.   Sometimes the Rule Against Perpetuities is depicted as requiring that an interest must vest within a certain period of time, the perpetuity period.   This is a loose and in fact an inaccurate statement of the Rule, as a moment's reflection reveals.   The Rule

---

19.   2 Mer. 363, 35 Eng.Rep. 979 (Ch. 1817).

does not and could not require a certainty that the interest will vest in due time; the certainty that the Rule does require, to use Gray's terminology, is that the interest will vest *if at all* in due time.   The phrase "if at all" means that what must be certain to happen within the perpetuity period is that there will be a resolution of the question whether the interest will ever vest.   Thus the interests prohibited by the Rule are those which might *remain* contingent for too long a time.   To satisfy the Rule, in other words, it must be certain that within the perpetuity period the interest will either vest or forever fail to vest.   Furthermore, this certainty must exist *as of the time of the commencement of the perpetuity period.*

§ 12.4   The Perpetuity Period

We can now state the Rule as follows.   To be valid, it must be certain as of the creation of an interest that the interest will vest or fail to vest no later than at the termination of the perpetuity period.   The perpetuity period is not a fixed number of years, but rather is, measured by a life in being plus 21 years.   Although Gray's formulation of the Rule does not mention this point, a period of gestation can be added either at the commencement of the period or at its termination or at both times, *but only when necessary.*

(a) *The Life in Being Part of the Period.*   The life in being, often called the *measuring life*, must be the life of a person "in being at the creation of the interest."   This means that the person whose life is the measuring life must have been alive or in gestation when the perpetuity period commences to run.   (For property law purposes generally, and for purposes of the Rule in particular, a child is deemed to commence his existence upon conception.   Thus a child in gestation at the commencement of the perpetuity period can be a measuring life because the child is considered then to be "in being."   This is what is meant when it is said that a period of gestation can be added *if necessary* at the commencement of the perpetuity period.)

The measuring life must also be a human life—the life of a corporation or of an animal cannot be used.   Simes & Smith § 1223.   There are no further restrictions, so that theoretically anyone in the world who was alive or in gestation when the interest was created can be the measuring life.   As a practical matter, though, it is not this simple, as we shall see in § 12.7, infra, when we get down to the problem of locating the measuring life in various hypothetical cases.

(b) *The 21-Year Part of the Period.*   The 21-year part of the perpetuity is described by Gray as coming *after* the death of the measuring life.   Thus a testamentary transfer "to such of my grandchildren as are living on the 21st anniversary of the death of *A*" would be valid.   The 21-year part need not, however, be preceded by a measuring life; it can stand on its own.   A testamentary transfer "to such of my grandchildren as are living on the 21st anniversary of my death" would therefore be valid without the necessity of locating a measuring life.   While authority on the question is scant, it seems to be agreed that the 21-year part cannot come first, followed by a life which is in being 21 years *after* the creation of the interest.   This is a consequence of the requirement that the measuring life be in being *at the* creation of the interest, and is not grounded on any reason of policy.   To give an example, suppose a testator bequeaths property in trust "to pay the income to the testator's children for 21 years, then to pay the income to such of the testator's grandchildren as may then be living for life, and on the death of the survivor to pay the corpus of the trust to the testator's lineal descendants then living per stirpes." If the testator is survived by one or more children, the remainder interest in the corpus of the trust violates the Rule and is invalid.

* * *

§ 12.5 Commencement of the Perpetuity Period, in General

The time when the perpetuity period commences to run is important because it fixes the time when the measuring life must be "in being." It is important for another reason, also. It demarks the facts that can be taken into account in determining the validity of an interest. Under the Rule, an interest is valid only if at the commencement of the perpetuity period, taking into account facts *then existing*, the interest is certain to vest or fail to vest within a life in being plus 21 years. The facts that *actually* occur from that time forward, with one exception concerning interests created by the exercise of certain powers of appointment, are irrelevant; all that counts thereafter is what *might* happen.

Generally speaking, the perpetuity period commences running when the questioned interest was created. (Some special cases where the commencement of the perpetuity period is postponed will be discussed later. See § 12.8, infra.)

(a) Testamentary Transfers. A will becomes effective as a dispositive instrument only upon death. An interest created by will is therefore created at the time of the testator's death, not at the time the will was executed. Thus the measuring life for testamentary transfers must be a person who was alive (or in gestation) when the testator died, and the facts that can be taken into account in determining the validity of an interest are those existing on the testator's death.

(b) Inter Vivos Transfers. An interest created by an inter vivos transfer is created at the time that the transfer becomes effective for purposes of property law generally. This would ordinarily be the date of delivery of the deed. Thus the measuring life for inter vivos transfers must be a person who was alive (or in gestation) when the transfer became effective, and the facts that can be taken into account in determining the validity of an interest are those existing at that time.

§ 12.6 Determining Validity Under the Rule

We now have the basic wherewithal to begin to develop a method of dealing with a perpetuities question. Dispositions of property, other than outright transfers in fee simple absolute, create more than one property interest. The first thing to do is to classify each of these interests.
* * *

If there are any interests which are subject to the Rule, then and only then do we properly go on to the next step, which is to determine whether there is a Rule violation. This process can be put thusly: Look at the situation at the time of the commencement of the perpetuity period, that is, take into account the facts then existing and the contingencies attached to the questioned interest. On the basis of these two items, ask yourself whether there is any possible chain of events that might arise after the commencement of the perpetuity period (no matter how unlikely it may be that this chain of events will actually occur) which would result in the questioned interest vesting or failing to vest too remotely? If the answer is yes, the interest is invalid. The facts that actually did occur after the commencement of the perpetuity period, even such facts as are known at the time of litigation, are irrelevant in almost all common law jurisdictions. Decisions in a very small number of states have taken into account the facts that were known at the time of litigation and declared valid an interest that might not have but in fact did actually vest within the perpetuity period.

* * *

How do you determine whether there is any possible chain of events that would allow the questioned interest to vest or fail to vest beyond the period of the Rule? Essentially this is a matter of identifying a measuring life. Of course, there are cases where an interest can be declared valid without the need of a measuring life—i.e., where the interest must vest or fail to vest within 21 years of its creation. See § 12.4(b), supra. But in most cases, a measuring life must be found if the interest is to be valid. In other words, if no measuring life can be found, the interest will not be valid because there will be a chain of possible post-creation events that will result in the interest's vesting or failing to vest too remotely.

Thus we come down to the mysterious matter of finding a measuring life. Before turning to that matter, though, one further point should be noted. Dispositions of property sometimes create more than one interest which is subject to the Rule. In such cases, the validity of each interest is treated as an individual matter. A measuring life which validates one interest might or might not validate the other interests. Since it is not necessary that the same measuring life be used for all interests created by a disposition, the search for a measuring life for each of the other interests must be undertaken.

§ 12.7   Locating the Measuring Life

(a) *When the Transferor Has Not Designated a Measuring Life.* Usually the measuring life is not stipulated in the transfer. In such cases, unless the questioned interest is certain to vest or fail to vest within the 21-year period following its creation, the validity of the interest turns on the discovery of a measuring life. If no measuring life can be located the interest violates the Rule and is invalid.

* * *

We can begin removing the mystery by setting forth a few guidelines. There are no formal restrictions on who can be selected as the measuring life, except that as noted in § 12.4 the life must be human and must be in being at the creation of the interest. This means that *theoretically* anyone in the world who was alive or in gestation when the questioned interest was created could be selected. It has long been established that the measuring life need not be a beneficiary or legatee.   Thellusson v. Woodford.[20]   The problem is that the life of a person unconnected to the transaction will not validate a questioned interest because any unconnected person who might be selected could have immediately died after the creation of the interest without having accelerated in any way the vesting of the questioned interest. Thus despite the absence of a formal restriction, there is nevertheless an implicit one: to validate the questioned interest, *the measuring life must be someone of whom it can be said that the interest is certain to vest within 21 years of such person's death.*   If this still seems mysterious, we will get to some examples soon.   But first, we can narrow down the possible candidates a bit further.   In most cases the measuring life will be the taker or takers of the questioned interest or a person related to them by blood or adoption.   Now we can go to some examples, and along the way gain some experience and some refinement of these principles.

Example 12–1.   *T* devised real property "to A for life, remainder to such of *A*'s children as attain 21."

The interest in question—the contingent remainder in favor of *A*'s children— is valid.   The measuring life is *A*.   It is impossible for any of *A*'s children to reach 21 (or die under 21) more than 21 years after the death of *A*.

Note the possibility of a child of *A*'s, though conceived during *A*'s lifetime, being born after *A*'s death.   If this were to happen, the child could not reach his 21st birthday within 21 years of *A*'s death.   The Rule is nevertheless satisfied because *if this were to occur* the length of the Rule would be extended to a life in being plus 21 years plus a period of gestation.   See § 12.4, supra.   Recall, however, that the period of gestation is not a formal part of the perpetuity period.   Thus if *T*'s devise had been "to *A* for life, remainder to such of *A*'s children as are living 21 years and 9 months after his death," the remainder would have been invalid.

In example *12–1*, *A* happened to be a legatee, but he is not the measuring life for that reason.   *A* would have been the measuring life even if the disposition had been "to *B* for life, remainder to such of *A*'s children as attain 21."   *A* is the measuring life because it is assumed that his or her death will terminate the possibility of any further children being born to him or her.   *   *   *

*   *   *

Indeed, the measuring life not only need not be a legatee; he need not even be mentioned in the instrument.   And, in appropriate cases the measuring life need not be individualized.   Rather, the measuring life can be an as yet (looking at the situation as of the date of the creation of the interests) unidentified member of a group of individuals.   It is common in such cases to say that the members of the group are the measuring *lives*.   It is acceptable to say it this way as long as it is recognized that the true meaning of the statement is that the measuring *life* is the member of the group who turns out to live the longest.   As the court said in Skatterwood v. Edge (K.B.1697), "for let the lives be never so many, there must be a survivor, and so it is but the length of that life; for Twisden used to say, the candles were all lighted at once."   The next example illustrates these points.

Example 12–2.   *T* devised real property "to such of my grandchildren as attain 21."   Some of *T*'s children are living at *T*'s death.

20.   11 Ves. 112, 32 Eng.Rep. 1030 (H.L.1805).

The interest in question—the grandchildren's springing executory interest—does not violate the Rule. *The* measuring life is that one of the testator's children who turns out to live the longest. It is impossible for any of *T*'s grandchildren to reach 21 or die under 21 more than 21 years after the death of *T*'s last surviving child.

Note the following points about this example: (1) It would commonly be said that *T*'s children are the measuring *lives;* (2) *T*'s children are not legatees; and (3) are not even mentioned in the instrument.

In the above two examples, the measuring life (or lives) was someone other than the legatees of the questioned contingent interest. But it is well established, though sometimes overlooked, that in appropriate cases the legatees of the questioned interest can be their own measuring lives. [Citation omitted.] This is an especially useful principle in cases where an interest is contingent on reaching an age in excess of 21 or is contingent on survivorship of a particular point in time which is or may be in excess of 21 years after the interest was created or after the death of a person in being at the date of creation.

Example 12–3. *T* devised real property "to such of *A*'s children as attain 25."

Or, *T* devised real property "to such of *A*'s children as are living on the 25th anniversary of my death."

A predeceased *T*. At *T*'s death, *A* had three living children, all of whom were under 25. (The ages of *A*'s children at *T*'s death are pertinent to the first case only.)

The questioned interest—the executory interest in favor of *A*'s children—does not violate the Rule. *A*'s children are their own measuring lives. Each one of *A*'s children will either reach the age of 25 (or survive the 25 year period in gross) or fail to do so within his own lifetime. To say this another way, we will know no later than at the time of the death of each child whether or not that child survived to the required age (or survived the required period in gross).

So far, we have looked at examples where a measuring life could be located, validating the questioned interest. We now turn to a few examples where the questioned interest is invalid.

*   *   *

Example 12–5. *T* devised property in trust, directing the trustee to pay the net income therefrom "to *A* for life, then to *A*'s children for the life of the survivor, and upon the death of *A*'s last surviving child to pay the corpus of the trust to *A*'s grandchildren." *T* was survived by *A* and by *A*'s two children, *X* and *Y*.

The remainder interest in the corpus in favor of *A*'s grandchildren is invalid. It is subject to the Rule because it is a class gift. See § 12.2(d), supra. (Note that the contingency attached to the interest is not the death of *A*'s last surviving child; that event is bound to occur, and consequently is not a contingency at all.) The class gift violates the Rule because it is possible that *A* will have a child (*Z*) who is conceived and born after *T*'s death and that that child will have a child (a grandchild of *A*) who is born (i.e., his contingent interest will vest) more than 21 years after the death of *A* and more than 21 years after the deaths of *X* and *Y*, the two children of *A* who were alive at *T*'s death. Since the interest of this grandchild might vest too remotely, the "all or nothing rule" dictates that the class gift in favor of *A*'s grandchildren is invalid in its entirety.

The remainder interest in the income in favor of A's children is also a class gift and consequently it, too, is subject to the Rule. As to this interest, however, a measuring life can be found—A. All of A's children will be born, or at least conceived, during A's lifetime. Thus this interest is valid. Note that the interest which each of A's children take on A's death is for the life of the survivor of A's children, not for their own respective lifetimes. Thus there are not cross remainders in the income in this case to worry about.

In § 12.6 an effort was made to emphasize the point that the facts existing at the creation of the questioned interest can be just as important in determining the validity of an interest as the contingencies attached thereto. Examples *12–3* and *12–5* are good illustrations of the point. By varying the facts existing on T's death in each of these examples, the remainder interest in favor of A's grandchildren could be made valid in *12–5*, and the executory interest in favor of A's children who reach 25 in *12–3* could be made invalid.

Example 12–6. The same disposition as in *12–5*. The facts are the same also, except that A predeceased T.

The grandchildren's remainder interest in the corpus is valid in these circumstances. Since A is dead at T's death, X and Y are the only children A will have. All of A's grandchildren will therefore be born or at least conceived during the lifetime of the survivor of X and Y. Thus X and Y constitute the measuring lives which validate the grandchildren's interest.

In applying the principle that the facts existing at the creation of the interest are to be taken into account, it is important to bear in mind that this refers not only to the facts as such but also to the rules of law or construction which those facts trigger. A rule of construction which figures prominently in many perpetuities cases is the rule of convenience * * *, as demonstrated by the next two examples.

Example 12–7. The same disposition as in the first case of *12–3*. The facts are the same also, except that A survived T.

In these circumstances the executory interest in favor of A's children who reach 25 is invalid. Before explaining why, it will be helpful to develop a little further the reason for their interest being valid under the facts as originally set forth. The key to the validity of the children's interest under the original facts was that, at T's death, it was impossible for any additional children of A to be born and become members of the class. The class was closed naturally upon A's prior death. The fact that the class was closed by the time of T's death allowed us to use A's children as their own measuring lives. It was certain that all of A's children were "in being" at the creation of their interest. Under the altered facts, however, additional children *can* be born to A after T's death. And, such after-born children can become class members, for the class of potential takers is not closed artificially at T's death by the rule of convenience. (The class is not then closed artificially because none of A's children is then entitled to possession; none has yet reached 25.) Thus more children can be born to A, and those conceived before the first child reaches 25 will be potential members of the class. This is what makes the entire class gift invalid: It is possible, looking at the situation as of T's death, for a child of A to be conceived and born after T's death but before the class closes (at the earlier of A's death or one of his children's reaching 25); and this after-born child might reach the age of 25 more than 21 years after the death of the survivor of the four people connected to the transfer who were "in being" at the creation of the interest—A and the three children of A who were living when T died.

Let us alter the facts a bit further. Suppose now that *A*'s eldest child had reached 25 by the time of *T*'s death. Under these circumstances, the interest is valid. Although it is possible for *A* to have additional children after *T*'s death, such after-born children will not be class members because under the rule of convenience the class closed artificially at *T*'s death. Thus the three children who were living at *T*'s death constitute their own measuring lives, just as they did under the original facts of *12–3*.

Example 12–8. *T* devised real property "to *A* for life, then to such of *A*'s children as reach 25." *A* survived *T*. By the time of *T*'s death, *A*'s eldest child had reached 25.

The interest in favor of *A*'s children who reach 25 is invalid. Unlike the last variation of example *12–7*, the rule of convenience does not close the class on *T*'s death despite the fact that one child has already reached 25. The reason is that *A*'s preceding life estate postpones distribution. Thus here the class will not close until *A* dies, leaving open the possibility of *A*'s having a child shortly before his death who will be a member of the class and who will reach 25 more than 21 years after the deaths of *A* and those of *A*'s children who were alive at *T*'s death. This possibility renders the entire class gift invalid under the "all or nothing" rule.

(b) When the Transferor Has Designated a Measuring Life. On occasion, transferors have designated their own measuring life. This statement needs some explanation. It means that transferors have on occasion geared the time when all interests must vest if at all to a designated measuring life, typically the last surviving member of a group of individuals. In such cases, the validity of the interests is assured as long as all members of the designated group are in being at the commencement of the perpetuity period and as long as proof of their deaths can reasonably be ascertained.

Example 12–9. *T* devised property in trust, directing the trustee to pay the net income therefrom "to my descendants from time to time living, per stirpes, until the 21st anniversary of the death of the last surviving descendant of mine who was living at my death, whereupon the corpus of the trust is to be divided among my then living descendants, per stirpes."

The above trust would probably be valid. Cf. Reagh v. Kelley.[21] The larger the designated group, the less connected the group is to the beneficiaries of the trust, and the more difficult it becomes to identify the members of the group initially and trace their deaths, however, the less likely it is that the trust would be upheld. The grounds for invalidity are likely to be put on the uncertainty involved rather than on a technical violation of Rule as such. Perhaps the widest group of designated measuring lives which has been upheld was the so-called royal lives clause of In re Villar.[22] In Villar, the testator provided for the vesting of all interests in a trust "at the expiration of 20 years from the day of the death of the last survivor of all lineal descendants of Her Late Majesty Queen Victoria who shall be living at the time of my death." Restatement of Property § 374, comment *l*, declares that a royal lives clause and specified similar periods such as "those persons whose names appear in the City Directory of the City of X" would be held invalid nowadays in an American court. Actual instances where a trust has been declared invalid by a court, however, are few.

* * *

21. 10 Cal.App.3d 1082, 89 Cal.Rptr. 425   22. 1. Ch.243 (C.A.) [1929].
    (1970).

(c) Savings Clauses. Transferors sometimes employ savings clauses in their instruments, though the frequency of their use is difficult to gauge. A typical savings clause might read: "The trust hereby created shall terminate in any event no later than twenty-one years after the death of the last survivor of all beneficiaries of this trust who are in being at the time this instrument becomes effective, and unless sooner terminated by the terms hereof, the trustee shall, at the termination of such period, make distribution to the persons then entitled to the income of this trust, and in the same shares and proportions as they are so entitled." This particular clause is a slightly modified version of the one found in Simes & Smith § 1295. Such clauses are a variation of the transferor's designating his own measuring life. But, unlike the situations described in *(b)*, above, savings clauses seldom actually become operational. Their main function, instead, is to serve as a back-stop to prevent inadvertent and merely technical perpetuity violations such as those described in § 12.13, infra.

§ 12.8 Postponement of the Commencement of the Perpetuity Period in Certain Cases

As pointed out in § 12.5, supra, the perpetuity period, generally speaking, commences to run when the transfer becomes effective for property law purposes—at the date of the testator's death for testamentary transfers and at the date of delivery of the deed for inter vivos transfers. A handful of decisions has held that, as to revocable inter vivos transfers, typically in trust, the perpetuity period does not commence running when the transfer becomes effective for property law purposes; rather, the commencement of the perpetuity period is postponed to the time when the power to revoke expires, which will be at the death of the settlor unless the power was released or fixed to expire earlier. In Cook v. Horn,[23] the court stated the principle to be based on the idea that "so long as the settlor of an inter vivos trust has the absolute right to revoke or terminate the trust for his own exclusive personal benefit, there is no tying up of property and no restraint upon the alienability of the property in the trust fund * * * ." While the authorities enunciating this principle are not numerous, there are no contrary decisions and the principle is widely regarded as a settled part of perpetuity law.

Example 12–10. *T* conveyed property to a trustee, directing the trustee to pay the net income therefrom to himself (*T*) for life, then to *T*'s son *A* for his life, then to *A*'s children for the life of the survivor of *A*'s children who are living at *T*'s death, and upon the death of such last surviving child, the corpus of the trust is to be distributed among *A*'s then living lineal descendants, per stirpes. *T* retained the power to revoke the trust.

The questioned interest—the remainder interest in the corpus in favor of *A*'s lineal descendants—is valid. The perpetuity period commences running at *T*'s death, not at the creation of the trust. The measuring lives are those of *A*'s children who are living at *T*'s death. If the perpetuity period had not been postponed, i.e., if it had commenced running when the transfer was effected for property law purposes generally, the questioned interest would have been invalid. A child of *A* might have been conceived and born between the date when the trust was created

---

23. 214 Ga. 289, 104 S.E.2d 461 (1958).

and *T*'s death, such after-born child might have turned out to be the last surviving child of *A* who was alive when *T* died, and such child might have lived more than 21 years beyond the death of all parties connected to the transfer who were "in being" when the trust was created—*T*, *A*, and *A*'s then living children. And the same can be said of every other person in the world who was "in being" when the trust was created.

Does this principle extend to any cases other than revocable trusts? Court authority on this question is sparse if not non-existent, but the commentators believe that it does. Simes & Smith § 1252.

§ 12.9   Constructional Preference for Validity

Gray declared that the will or deed is to be construed without regard to the Rule Against Perpetuities, and then the Rule is to be "remorselessly" applied to the provisions so construed. Gray § 629. Some courts still adhere to this proposition. [Citations omitted.] Most courts, it is believed, would today be inclined to adopt the proposition put by the Restatement of Property § 375, which is that where an instrument is ambiguous—that is, where it is fairly susceptible to two or more constructions, one of which causes a Rule violation and the other of which does not—the construction which does not result in a Rule violation should be adopted.   * * *

§ 12.10   The Consequences of Invalidity

When an interest is invalid because it violates the Rule Against Perpetuities, the invalid interest is stricken from the disposition. Unless the doctrine of infectious invalidity applies (§ 12.12), the other interests created by the disposition (assuming that none of them violates the Rule) take effect as if the invalid interest had never been created. Striking the invalid interest does not have the same consequences in all cases. The consequences depend on whether the invalid interest was a remainder or an executory interest and on whether the invalid interest was the last or an intermediate one.

When the invalid interest is a *remainder* or an *executory interest following a fee simple determinable*, a gap in the disposition will probably (though not necessarily) be created. If the transfer was inter vivos, the gap will be filled by a reversion or a possibility of reverter. In the case of a testamentary transfer, the gap will be filled by the residuary clause or, if the invalid interest was created in the residuary clause, by intestate succession.

Example 12–12. *T* devised real property "to *A* for life, then to *A*'s children for the life of the survivor, and upon the death of *A*'s last surviving child, to *A*'s grandchildren." *T* devised her residuary estate to her husband, *H*.

Due to the invalidity of the remainder in favor of *A*'s grandchildren, the disposition reads as if *that* remainder interest had never been created: "to *A* for life, then to *A*'s children for the life of the survivor." Since *T*'s devise did not validly dispose of all interests in the parcel of real property, the undisposed-of interest passes under *T*'s residuary clause to *H*. This testamentary transfer of the remainder interest to *H* is deemed to have occurred at *T*'s death. Thus when *A*'s last surviving child dies, the property goes to *H* (or *H*'s successor in interest).

Suppose *T*'s original devise had been in her residuary clause. In this case, the undisposed-of interest would have been intestate property and would have passed at *T*'s death to her heirs at law.

Example 12–13. *T* devised real property "to *A* for life, then for life to such of *A*'s children as reach 25, then to *B*."

The remainder for life in favor of *A*'s children is invalid. The effect of striking it is not to create a gap which must be filled by the residuary clause. Rather it is to accelerate *B*'s remainder: the devise now reads "to *A* for life, then to *B*."

* * *

When the invalid interest is an *executory interest* (other than one following a fee simple determinable), the effect will not be to create a gap. Rather, the invalidity of the executory interest will cause the condition subsequent to be stricken, too. * * * .

Example 12–15. *T* devised real property "to *A* for life, remainder to *A*'s children, but if none of *A*'s children reaches 25, to *B*." *T* was survived by *A*, who had two children, *X* and *Y*, neither of whom had reached 25.

B's executory interest is invalid. The remainder in favor of *A*'s children, as a result, is not subject to the condition of divestment in case all die under 25. Rather, while it still is subject to open, it no longer is subject to complete divestment.

* * *

§ 12.12 Infectious Invalidity

In appropriate cases, the invalidity of an interest may, under the *doctrine of infectious invalidity*, be held to invalidate one or more otherwise valid interests created by the disposition or even invalidate the entire will. The question turns on whether the general dispositive scheme of the transferor will be better carried out by eliminating only the invalid interest or by eliminating other interests as well. This is a question which must be answered on a case by case basis. Several items are relevant to the question, including who takes the stricken interests in place of those designated to take by the transferor. Some jurisdictions have become noted for a greater willingness to apply infectious invalidity than others. See Simes & Smith § 1262; 6 American Law of Property § 24.48 et seq.; Restatement of Property § 402.

§ 12.13 Three Classic Booby Traps

The required *certainty* that an interest will vest or fail to vest within the perpetuity period has caused some interests that do not violate the *policy* of the Rule to be invalid nevertheless. The policy of the Rule is not violated because, realistically speaking, the likelihood of the questioned interest's actually vesting beyond the perpetuity period is either zero or so remote as to be negligible. Such cases fall generally into three categories which received their names from Professor Leach's article, Perpetuities in a Nutshell, 51 Harv.L.Rev. 638 (1938): (1) the fertile octogenarian; (2) the administrative contingency; and (3) the unborn widow. For ways to avoid these booby traps at the drafting state, see McGovern, Perpetuities Pitfalls and How Best to Avoid Them, 6 Real Prop., Prob. & Trust J. 155 (1971).

(a) *Fertile Octogenarians: The Conclusive Presumption of Lifetime Fertility.*   In some of our previous examples, invalidity was predicated on the possibility of there being after-born children who would join a class. Let us reintroduce one of those examples, example *12–5*:

Example 12–18.   *T* devised property in trust, directing the trustee to pay the net income therefrom "to *A* for life, then to *A*'s children for the life of the survivor, and upon the death of *A*'s last surviving child to pay the corpus of the trust to *A*'s grandchildren." *T* was survived by *A* and by *A*'s two children, *X* and *Y*.

Under these circumstances, we concluded that the remainder interest in favor of *A*'s grandchildren was invalid because of the possibility that *A* would have a child (*Z*), conceived and born after *T*'s death, who would have a child conceived and born more than 21 years after the death of the survivor of *A*, *X*, and *Y*.

Would our previous conclusion change if at the time of *T*'s death *A* was infertile because she had passed the menopause?   Or, if *A* was then infertile for any other reason, such as he had undergone a vasectomy or she a complete hysterectomy or a tubal ligation?   We emphasized the point that the facts existing when the perpetuity period commences running are to be taken into account.   Are *these* facts to be taken into account also, so that the possibility of after-born children is to be regarded as extinct?   The answer which the courts have almost universally given is No.   For purposes of the Rule Against Perpetuities, early English decisions, of which Jee v. Audley [24] is the best-known, laid down the proposition that all persons are *conclusively* presumed to be capable of having children throughout their entire lifetime, regardless of their age or physical condition.   *   *   *

Only one American common law decision has squarely rejected Jee v. Audley and held in a perpetuities case that the presumption is rebuttable, not conclusive.   In that case, In re Lattouf's Will,[25] the presumption was rebutted because the person in question, a female—although apparently in her normal child-bearing years—had undergone a complete hysterectomy. *   *   *   The Restatement of Property § 377 squarely supports the conclusive presumption, and there are many perpetuities cases, recent as well as not so recent, which have adhered to it.   *   *   *   There is a different approach adopted by some courts that will provide relief in many though still not all cases.   It is the principle of construction discussed in § 12.9. The procedure is to hold that the possibility of future children being born to or adopted by the person in question was so remote that the transferor never contemplated it and so did not intend to include such children in the class gift language even if they were to materialize.   So construed, the perpetuity standard of absolute certainty *is* met, and the interest is valid. [Citations omitted.]   Since the relevant time for determining the intent of a testator is the time of *execution* of his will, not the time of his death (when the perpetuity period commences to run on testamentary transfers), this construction is ordinarily available to a court only if when the testator executed his will he knew that the person in question's age or physical condition realistically excluded further child-bearing.   Thus in example *12–18*, if *A* were a 25 year old female in normal physical condition when *T* executed his will, this method of avoiding a Rule violation would not be properly available even if when *T* died, *A* had gone through the menopause.

---

24.   1 Cox 324, 29 Eng.Rep. 1186 (Ch.1787).   25.   87 N.J.Super. 137, 208 A.2d 411 (1965).

Consequently, this approach is not a panacea, but it would alleviate the problem in many cases.   *   *   *

(b) *The Administrative Contingency.*   This refers to the performance by a fiduciary (an executor, a trustee) of some administrative function, the completion of which may, but is extremely unlikely to, take more than 21 years.   Typical examples are the completion of the probate of a will, the settlement of an estate, the payment of debts or taxes, the sale of estate assets, or the delivery of trust corpus on the termination of a trust.

Example 12–21.   T devised real property "to such of my grandchildren, born before or after my death, as may be living upon final distribution of my estate." T is survived by children and grandchildren.

The grandchildren's interest in invalid, by the majority view.   Though unlikely, there is a possibility that the final distribution of *T*'s estate will not occur within 21 years of *T*'s death.   [Citations omitted.]   This possibility eliminates validating the interest on the basis of the 21-year part of the period.   In addition, there are no measuring lives which can validate it.   Grandchildren may be conceived and born after *T*'s death, and such after-born grandchildren may survive the final distribution of *T*'s estate (or fail to do so) more than 21 years after the deaths of *T*'s children and grandchildren who were living at *T*'s death.

As the above example illustrates, the term "administrative contingency" is somewhat misleading.   It does not refer to the possibility that the administrative task will never be completed.   If it did, all interests to take effect in possession upon the completion of the task would be contingent. But in fact, such gifts are upheld.   Cases are collected in 6 American Law of Property § 24.23 n. 2.   Rather, it is accepted as certain that the task will be completed, presumably because of the fiduciary's legal obligation to do so; the uncertainty is that completion of the task might not occur within the perpetuity period.   Thus, as in example *12–21*, the adminstrative contingency problem commonly arises because of a contingency of survivorship of the administrative function.   In such cases the problem is really one of survivorship of a period of time which may be in excess of 21 years.   We have seen *this* problem before—in the second case of example *12–3*.   And, as exemplified by that case, interests which are contingent on survivorship of a period which may be in excess of 21 years are not always invalid.   They will, in fact, be valid if the legatees can themselves be the measuring lives, which requires that the questioned interest either be in favor of one or more individual takers or be in favor of a class which is closed at the testator's death.

Example 12–22.   T devised real property "to such of my children as may be living upon final distribution of my estate."   T is survived by children.

The children's interest is valid.   Since no children will be born to *T* after his death, his children are their own measuring lives.

When the questioned interest is in favor of a class which is not closed at the testator's death, the administrative contingency problem can also arise even if there is no condition of survivorship.   Let us take a variation of example *12–21* to illustrate this point.   Suppose that the gift were in favor of *T*'s great-grandchildren instead of his grandchildren.   The interest would be invalid even if the phrase "as may be living" were omitted.   A great-grandchild could be conceived and born before the completion of the probate of *T*'s estate and more than 21 years after the death of the survivor of *T*'s children and those of *T*'s grandchildren that were living at *T*'s death. Note, however, that the invalidity here is due to the fact that the class of great-grandchildren could not only increase after the testator's death but could also increase after the death of lives in being at his death.   If the class cannot increase after lives in being, the absence of a condition of survivorship will save a gift in favor of a class though it is not closed at the testator's death.   To illustrate this, let us return to the original facts of example *12–21*, where the gift was in favor of *T*'s grandchildren.   Now suppose that the phrase "as may be living" were omitted.   This would make the grandchildren's interest valid because no new members could join the class after the death of the survivor of *T*'s children, all of whom were of course "in being" at *T*'s death.

A minority of courts has devised an escape from the adminstrative contingency problem.   Since the adminstrative function is to be performed by a fiduciary, the procedure is to hold that the fiduciary's obligation is not only to complete the task, but to do so within a reasonable time, and that a reasonable time is less than 21 years.   [Citations omitted.]   The difficulty with this minority view is that, while there may be an obligation to complete fiduciary tasks expeditiously, it is a fiction to say that the settlement of an estate can *never* take more than 21 years without there being a violation of a fiduciary duty.   While rare, there can be cases where protracted and successive litigation over a multitude of issues legitimately ties up an estate for a very long time.   Even on a case by case basis it would seem to be impossible to conclude with the certainty required by the Rule and on the basis of the facts existing when the interest was created that no such delay will properly arise.

Depending on the language employed, the principle of construction described in § 12.9 may be available as a method of avoiding invalidity. For example, if a condition of survivorship is ambiguous on the point, it would probably be construed to relate to the death of the testator or of the life tenant rather than to the completion of the administrative task, such as the final distribution of his estate.   See Restatement of Property § 374, comment *f*.

* * *

(c) *The Unborn Widow.*   This refers to the fact that an unnamed "widow" (or "widower") of an individual who was himself alive at the commencement of the perpetuity period is excluded from serving as the measuring life.   She (or he) *might* turn out to be someone who was conceived and born after the creation of the interest, no matter how improbable that possibility is in the actual case.   Thus if no other measuring life can be located, the questioned interest if subject to the Rule is invalid.

Example 12–23.   *T* devised real property "to my son *A* for life, remainder to his widow for her life, remainder to *A*'s then living descendants."   *T* was survived by *A*, *A*'s wife *W*, and their adult children, *X* and *Y*.

The questioned interest—the remainder in favor of *A*'s descendants—is invalid. [Citations omitted.]   Though improbable, it is possible that *A*'s widow will not be *W*, but will instead be someone who was born after *T*'s death and who will outlive by more than 21 years *A* and any other person "in being" at *T*'s death.

Like the standard administrative contingency case, the possibility of an afterborn widow does not always create a perpetuity violation. The legatees of the remainder interest following the widow's death may be their own measuring lives. This would be the case if in example *12–23* the contingent remainder were in favor of named individuals (*X* and *Y* perhaps) or a class which was closed at *T*'s death (the children of *T*'s predeceased daughter, *B*). Furthermore, if the remainder was not contingent on survivorship, the fact that it was still subject to open at *T*'s death would not invalidate it if the class could not increase beyond lives in being. For example, in the absence of a condition precedent of survivorship, a remainder in favor of *T*'s grandchildren would be valid in example *12–23*.   *   *   * But one in favor of *T*'s great-grandchildren would be invalid.

Even when no other measuring lives can be located, as in the original facts of example *12–23*, the principle of construction outlined in § 12.9 can often be utilized to avoid the unborn widow problem. When the language of the instrument fairly allows, some courts have construed *T*'s reference to *A*'s "widow" as referring only to the person to whom *A* was married when the will was executed or when *T* died. [Citations omitted.] So construed, *A*'s widow could not be afterborn, and thus the measuring lives in example *12–23* would be *A* and *W*.

§ 12.14   Charitable Gifts

With one exception, future interests in favor of charities are subject to the Rule Against Perpetuities. And the Rule applies to such interests in the same way it applies to future interests in favor of private parties. Thus if there is a condition precedent attached to the interest, and if the condition precedent might not occur or fail to occur within the perpetuity period, the charitable interest fails.

Example 12–24. *T* devised real property "to *A* for life, then to such of *A*'s children as reach 25, but if none of *A*'s children reaches 25, to *X* Charity."

The remainder in favor of *X* Charity is invalid. So is the remainder in favor of *A*'s children.

*   *   *

As noted above, there is one formal exception to the principle that charitable future interests receive no preferential treatment under the Rule. Whether or not it is subject to a remote contingency, a future interest in favor of a charity is valid if the interest was preceded by an interest which is also in favor of a charity. The rationale for this exception is that, since the law allows a perpetual tying up of property for a single charity, it ought to do so when the transferor provides for a shift from one charity to another, even though the shift might take place beyond the perpetuity period.

Example 12–25. *T* devised real property "to the *X* School District so long as the premises are used for school purposes, and upon the cessation of such use, to *Y* City."

The executory interest in favor of *Y* City is valid.

LEACH, PERPETUITIES IN A NUTSHELL
51 Harv.L.Rev. 638, 671 (1938).

The competent drafting of wills is a difficult business which offers only austere rewards.   The monetary compensation in this type of practice is usually not adequate to the training and effort required.   Often enough the virtues or vices of a will do not appear until the draftman has long been under the sod.   No beneficiary of a well-drawn will is likely to strew orchids upon his grave, whereas defeated claimants under ill-drawn wills are sure to heap imprecations upon his memory.   But the counsellor who leaves behind him a will book which succeeds in placing property where his clients wished it without those uncertainties as to validity and ambiguities as to meaning which breed litigation, can sleep the eternal sleep in the comforting knowledge that he has upheld the finest traditions of his craft.

[4] Perpetuities in New York

The New York statutes [26] eliminate many of the absurdities noted by Professor Waggoner and codify the rules governing powers of appointment [27] but leave the basic period unchanged.   The New York statute also limits suspension of the absolute power of alienation.[28]

The New York statute provides:

"The absolute power of alienation is suspended when there are no persons in being by whom an absolute fee or estate in possession can be conveyed or transferred." [29]

Unlike the position taken in Wisconsin,[30] the New York courts early held that the existence of a power of sale in the trustee does not free a trust from the limit on the period of suspension, if the proceeds of sale remain subject to the trust.[31]   There is no suspension of the power of alienation if the settlor has "an unqualified power to revoke" [32] the trust or if a beneficiary has the power to demand the corpus.[33]   Similarly, if the trustees and beneficiaries can jointly convey the trust property, free of trust, the power of alienation is not suspended.[34]   But EPTL 7–1.5(1) generally bars assignments of rights to receive trust income, thus precluding effective assignments by income beneficiaries.   And some of the beneficiaries are likely to be unascertained, such as those who are to receive the principal when the trust terminates.

Thus for planning purposes the safe assumption is that every New York trust, in order to avoid violation of the suspension rule, must terminate either automatically or on demand by a beneficiary within the statutory period, measured either from its creation or from the expiration of any unqualified power of revocation in the settlor, whichever is later.

---

26. See generally N.Y. EPTL 9–1.1 – 9–1.3.

27. Id., 10–8.1 – 10–8.3.

28. Id., 9–1.1(a)(1)–(2).

29. Id., 9–1.1(a)(1).

30. See ¶ 3.02 at p. 64 supra.

31. Hawley v. James, 16 Wend. 61 (N.Y.1836).

32. N.Y. EPTL 10–8.1(2)(b).

33. See 5 R.R. Powell, Real Property ¶ 793[4] (P. Rohan rev.ed. 1979).

34. Id.

MATTER OF WOLFSOHN

Supreme Court of New York, Appellate Division, Fourth Department, 1973.
40 A.D.2d 273, 339 N.Y.S.2d 775.

MARSH, Justice.

This is an appeal from an order excising certain portions of a trust agreement, declaring valid the remaining provisions of the agreement, and settling the intermediate accounts of the trustees.

By instrument dated February 19, 1960,[35] Myer D. Wolfsohn, as grantor, conveyed irrevocably certain property to Robert S. Wolfsohn, Howard L. Wolfsohn, his sons, and Eugene M. Setel, as Trustees. Under the terms of the indenture, the following disposition of income and principal was directed:

"(a) During the life of the Grantor, the Trustees shall pay to him annually, or at more frequent intervals, or shall apply for his sustenance, maintenance, support, comfort or well-being the net income of and from the principal of this trust.

(b) Upon the death of the Grantor, the Trustees shall pay or apply to or for the sustenance, education, maintenance, support, comfort or well-being of Grantor's issue, in equal shares per stirpes and not per capita, the net income of and from the principal of this trust.

(c) Upon the death of the survivor of Robert S. Wolfsohn and Howard L. Wolfsohn, or upon the death or attainment by the youngest of the issue of Robert S. Wolfsohn or Howard L. Wolfsohn living at the time of the Grantor's death of the age of twenty-five (25) years, whichever shall occur last, the Trustees shall pay, transfer, convey and set over absolutely to Grantor's issue living at the time of such event the principal of this trust in equal shares per stirpes and not per capita to be his, hers or theirs, as the case may be, free of this trust absolutely and forever."

The grantor died on March 27, 1966, leaving a Last Will and Testament, which was admitted to probate by the Surrogate's Court of Erie County on February 7, 1967. Petitioners, Robert S. Wolfsohn and Howard L. Wolfsohn, are the executors of said will. Under the provisions of the will, one-third of the residuary estate was bequeathed in trust for the life of grantor's surviving spouse, Mae Kaplan Wolfsohn, with the remainder over to grantor's sons (outright to Howard, in trust for Robert).

At the time of the creation of the trust, the grantor had two children and two grandchildren. Of his three present grandchildren named in the petition, one was born subsequent to the execution of the trust agreement.

The trustees applied to the Supreme Court for an order judicially settling their intermediate account, allowing Robert S. Wolfsohn and Howard L. Wolfsohn to resign, and construing the trust agreement to determine whether there was a violation against the rule against perpetuities.

---

35. Provision for reduction of an age contingency in excess of 21 years, in order to avoid a violation of New York's rules, was made by former § 11–a of the Personal Property Law, added by 1960 N.Y.Laws, c. 452 § 2, effective 4/12/60.

The court held that the trust as written violated the rule against perpetuities, but that the offending language should be excised and that the remainder of the trust agreement was valid.   The court also granted fees to the trustees' attorneys and the guardian ad litem, but denied an allowance to the attorneys for the surviving spouse.

The parties all agree that the trust agreement as written violated the rule against perpetuities.   Under the trust the principal would have been paid to grantor's issue living at the time of either (1) the death of the survivor of the grantor's two sons, or (2) the death or attainment of the age of 25 by the youngest of grantor's sons' issue living at the time of grantor's death, whichever should occur last.   Under the trust as excised by the court, the trust principal would be paid to the grantor's issue living at the time of the death of the survivor of grantor's two sons.

Case law is explicit that the excision of an intermediate estate will not permit the acceleration of remainders unless such remainders are vested. That is to say, no contingent remainder will be permitted to accelerate.[36]

* * *

The gift by the grantor Myer D. Wolfsohn to his issue living at the date of the termination of the trust was a class gift the members of which were not to be determined until the happening of a specific event, hence, the makeup of that class could not be determined until the event happened. Such a gift to a class, the membership of which is to be fixed at a future date and conditioned upon survival to that date, is a contingent gift. * * * The estate measured by the life of the youngest grandson living at the date of the grantor's death is clearly an intermediate estate. * * *

Hence, if the trust provision which continues it until the grandson reaches 25 or sooner dies is excised, the remainders contingent upon it cannot be accelerated and the property must pass under the residuary clause of the grantor's will or by intestacy.

* * *

Prospective effect to the consideration of alternate contingencies was given in Matter of Kahn, (42 N.Y.S.2d 298) and in Matter of New Rochelle Trust Company (50 N.Y.S.2d 602).   In both cases neither the valid nor the invalid contingencies had occurred and the respective courts ruled that the determination as to the validity of the trust remainders should abide the event.   If the invalid contingency eventuated, then the invalid limitation and remainder thereon would be void and the property would pass by intestacy or under the residuary clause of the will as the case might be.

The instant trust is validly operating during the lives of the surviving sons and it is quite unlikely that the invalid life of the youngest grandchild living at the grantor's death will ever be used as a further measuring life since the trust terminates at the death of the two sons if the youngest grandchild is then 25 or deceased.   At the death of the survivor of the sons it can be determined whether the youngest grandchild living at the date of

36.   N.Y. EPTL 2–1.11 now provides generally for acceleration of subsequent interests upon renunciation of a prior interest.—ed.

the grantor's death is then 25 or deceased.   If such is the case, the trust will validly terminate with remainders to the grantor's issue then living per stirpes.   If the youngest grandchild is not 25, then the trust would not be permitted to continue for a life not in being at the creation of the instrument. It is unnecessary at this time to determine the validity of the trust upon the basis of an invalid contingency which might never eventuate (Matter of Mount, 185 N.Y. 162, 77 N.E. 999).

In view of the well-argued position by the attorneys for the surviving spouse of the grantor, there appears to be no reason to deny attorneys' fees and disbursements.

The order appealed from should be modified by deleting the provisions that excise that portion of the trust agreement which the court held violated the rule against perpetuities and that permit the vesting of the trust principal within the permissible period of lives in being, by providing that the validity of the trust provisions should not now be determined and by reversing that portion of the order which denied the surviving spouse's counsel fees and disbursements and remitting the case for such award, and as so modified, affirmed.

*   *   *

[5] Perpetuities in California

California has undertaken to modernize its codification of the rule in three ways:

(1) By authorizing judges, to whatever extent is feasible, to reform an interest void under the rule consistent with the evident intent of the creator.[37]   This *cy pres* doctrine provides an alternative to the "remorseless application" and strict blue-pencilling doctrines of the common law.

(2) By permitting an alternative period of 60 years in gross.[38]

(3) By resolving the problem of the unborn widow:

"In determining the validity of a future interest in real or personal property pursuant to Section 715.2 of this code, an individual described as the spouse of a person in being at the commencement of a perpetuities period shall be deemed a 'life in being' at such time whether or not the individual so described was then in being." [39]

[6] Time Restrictions on the Duration of Private Trusts

The combined effect in New York of restrictions on remoteness of vesting and suspension of the absolute power of alienation in limiting the permissible duration of trusts has already been discussed.[40]   In other jurisdictions, the effect of the attempted creation of a trust which may continue beyond the period of the Rule Against Perpetuities but under which all interests must vest, if at all, within the period is often unclear.

May the beneficiaries jointly secure the termination of the trust, even though such termination ordinarily would be refused if it would frustrate

37. Cal.Civ.Code § 715.5 (West Supp.1980).   39. Id., § 715.7.

38. Id., § 715.6.   40. See §3.02[4] supra.

a material purpose of the settlor? In many jurisdictions there is *no* clear answer;[41] California by statute allows such termination at the instance of a majority of the beneficiaries, after the perpetuities period has run.[42]

Assuming that all, or even a majority of the beneficiaries, may terminate a trust which has continued beyond the period of perpetuities, the situation nevertheless is quite different from that which exists in New York. There the interests which cause the trust to continue beyond the statutory period are void *ab initio*; elsewhere they are valid until the requisite proportion of beneficiaries agree otherwise. Securing such agreement may not be easy, as some may prefer to wait out the termination of the trust according to its terms.

¶ 3.03   POWERS OF APPOINTMENT AND THE RULE AGAINST PERPETUITIES

WAGGONER, FUTURE INTERESTS IN A NUTSHELL*

§ 14.1   General Introduction to the Nature and Theory of Powers of Appointment

This short introductory section is designed to acquaint the reader with sufficient background information about powers of appointment to facilitate an understanding of the way that the Rule Against Perpetuities applies to them. It is not intended to be even a brief description of the whole law of powers of appointment.

(*a*) *Power of Appointment Defined.* As defined in section 318 of the Restatement of Property, a power of appointment is a "power to designate, within such limits as the donor may prescribe, the transferees of the property or the shares in which it shall be received."

(*b*) *Parties.* The parties connected to a power of appointment are identified by a special terminology:

● *Donor.* The donor is the person who previously owned the appointive property and who created the power of appointment over it.

● *Donee.* The donee is the person upon whom the donor conferred the power.

● *Appointee.* The person whom the donee appoints (i.e., the person in whose favor the donee exercises the power) is the appointee. The appointee becomes the owner of the property interest appointed to him.

● *Objects.* These are the persons in whose favor the donee was authorized by the donor to exercise the power. They are, in other words, the permissible appointees. If the donor does not expressly designate objects, the donee is free to appoint in favor of anyone in the world including himself.

---

41. See 1 A. W. Scott, Trusts § 62.10, pp. 601–02 (3d ed. 1967); 4 id. § 337.1, pp. 2662–2663; 5 R. R. Powell, Real Property ¶ 772 (P. J. Rohan recomp. 1968).

42. See Cal.Civ.Code § 771 (West Supp.1980).

• *Takers in default.* These are the persons designated by the donor to take any property not effectively appointed.

The property subject to a power of appointment is called the *appointive property.* The property interest subject to appointment need not be one in fee simple absolute. In fact, most powers of appointment are over a remainder interest in property.

While there must of course be a donor and a donee, and there must be someone in favor of whom the donee can appoint, the other parties are not indispensable. Since the donee is under no duty to exercise his power, there will not always be appointees. Also, the donor need not expressly designate either objects or takers in default.

(c) *Powers of Appointment Differentiated.* Powers of appointment are differentiated in three ways: (1) on the basis of the donee's property interest, if any, in the appointive property; (2) on the basis of when and in what instrument the donee is authorized to make his appointment; and (3) on the basis of whether or not the donee himself (or his estate) is a permissible appointee.

(1) *Differentiation Based on the Donee's Property Interest, If Any, in the Appointive Property.*

* * *

(2) *Differentiation Based on the Type of Instrument In Which the Donee Is Authorized to Exercise his Power.*

• *Testamentary Powers.* Powers as to which the donor restricted the instrument in which they can be exercised to the donee's will are called testamentary powers.

• *Presently Exercisable Powers.* Powers as to which the donor imposed no restriction on the instrument in which they can be exercised are called presently exercisable powers. Such powers are exercisable either by an inter vivos instrument or by will.

• *Inter Vivos Only Powers.* It is possible for a donor to restrict the exercise of a power to appoint a remainder interest to an inter vivos instrument, but this is rarely done.

(3) *Differentiation Based on Whether or Not the Donee or his Estate is a Permissible Appointee.*

• *General Powers.* To be a general power, the donee must be authorized to appoint in his own favor or in favor of his estate. The authority to make such an appointment typically arises out of the donor's failure to restrict the objects of the power to any designated group of people. But it can arise in another way: where the designated objects include the donee, the power may properly be regarded as a general power, also. Cf. Restatement of Property § 320, comment *a.*

• *Special Powers (also called Limited Powers).* A special or limited power is one in which the objects do not include the donee or his estate and, according to the Restatement of Property § 320(2), do not constitute a group which is "unreasonably large."

• *Hybrid Powers (especially Non-general Powers).* According to the Restatement of Property § 320, comment *a,* a power which does not meet the definition of either a general or special power is classified as a "hybrid power." Hybrid powers are not invalid, and in fact there are several types of hybrid powers. The one type which is actually used in practice, however, is the power which contains no restrictions on the objects save for the exclusion of the donee and his estate. Hybrid powers of this type are sometimes called non-general powers. For purposes of the Rule Against Perpetuities, and for nearly all other purposes as well, non-general powers are treated the same way as special powers. Consequently, in the succeeding sections of this chapter, references to special powers should be understood to include non-general powers.

(4) *Examples.* A few examples illustrating the application of the above points follow.

Example 14–1. *T* transferred real property "to *A* for life, remainder to such person or persons as *A* shall appoint; in default of appointment, remainder to *B*."

A's power is in gross, presently exercisable, and general. It is in gross because the donee, *A*, has a life estate in the property in addition to his power of appointment over the remainder interest. It is presently exercisable because the donor, *T*, did not expressly restrict the exercise of the power either to a will or to an inter vivos instrument. The power is general because the donor did not forbid the donee from exercising the power in his own favor.

Suppose *A* decides to appoint to himself inter vivos. The ultimate effect of such an appointment would be that *A* would become the sole owner of the appointive property. The remainder interest held by *B* would be divested in favor of *A*. *B*'s interest, as the taker in default, was a vested remainder subject to divestment. * * * And as a consequence of *A*'s acquiring the remainder interest following his life estate a merger of the two interests would take place, causing *A* to own the property in fee simple absolute.

Suppose *A* decides to make an inter vivos appointment in favor of *C* rather than one in favor of himself. The consequence of such an appointment would be that *B*'s remainder would be divested in favor of *C*. *C* would not, however, become entitled to possession of the property. In other words, *A*'s life estate in not divested in favor of *C*. The reason is that *A*'s power of appointment was only over the remainder interest. The appointment would in effect alter *T*'s original disposition as if to read "to *A* for life, remainder to *C*."

Example 14–2. *T* transferred real property "to *A* for life, remainder to such of *A*'s descendants as *A* shall by will appoint; in default of appointment, remainder to *B*."

A's power is in gross, testamentary and special. It is in gross for the same reason it was in gross in example *14–1*: the donee, *A*, has a life estate in the property in addition to his power of appointment over the remainder interest. It is testamentary because of the donor's insertion of the phrase "by will." Thus any purported inter vivos exercise of this power by *A* would be invalid. *A*'s power is special because he is authorized to appoint only among his own descendants, a group which does not include him and which is not unreasonably large.

Example 14–3. *T* transferred real property "to *A* for life, remainder to such person or persons except *A*, his estate, his creditors, or the creditors of his estate, as *A* shall by will appoint; in default of appointment, remainder to B."

A's testamentary power in gross is a non-general power.

(d) *The General Theory of Powers of Appointment: The Doctrine of "Relation Back."*

* * *

The notion that, upon exercise of a power of appointment, the appointed interest passes directly from the donor to the appointee is called the doctrine of "relation back." That is to say, the donee's appointment is viewed as relating back to and becoming part of the donor's original instrument. In example *14–1*, for example, where we postulated *A*'s exercising his power in favor of *C*, we noted that the effect of *A*'s appointment is viewed as changing *T*'s original disposition to read: "to *A* for life, remainder to *C*." This was an application of the relation back doctrine.

The relation back doctrine is capable of providing a rather automatic answer to practically every legal question pertaining to powers of appointment. Unfortunately, however, the specific answers to which this doctrine would lead are in many cases undesirable and have not been adopted by the courts.

*   *   *

In many instances where relation back is not followed it is because the nature of the power itself is thought to put the donee's relationship to the appointive assets close enough in substance to that of an outright owner so that for the purposes of the particular question involved the assets should be treated as if owned by the donee. The Rule Against Perpetuities, as we shall see, follows or rejects relation back on this basis. That is, the relation back theory is followed in the case of certain types of powers but rejected in the case of other types of powers.

With the above background in mind, we can now turn to a consideration of the way that the Rule Against Perpetuities applies to powers. A power of appointment may violate the Rule Against Perpetuities. If so, the power is invalid, and the disposition takes effect as if the power had never been created. If the power itself is valid, some or all of the interests created by its exercise may violate the Rule and be invalid. We will in section 14.2 consider the validity of powers and then in section 14.3 move on to the validity of exercises of powers. Sections 14.4 and 14.5 explore some special applications of the principles developed in sections 14.2 and 14.3

§ 14.2   The Validity of the Power

The question to ask to determine the validity of a power under the Rule Against Perpetuities depends on what type of power is at issue. A *special power* (whether testamentary or presently exercisable) or a *general testamentary power* is invalid if it is *possible* for it to be *exercised* beyond the period of the Rule.

Example 14–4. *T* devised real property "to *A* for life, then to *A*'s first born child for life, then to such persons as *A*'s first born child shall by will appoint."

Or, *T* devised real property "to *A* for life, then to *A*'s first born child for life, then to such of *A*'s grandchildren as *A*'s first born child shall appoint."

T is survived by *A*, who is childless.

The power of appointment conferred on *A*'s first born child—a general testamentary power in the first case, a special power presently exercisable in the second—

is invalid.   The latest possible time of exercise is at the death of A's first born child, who cannot be the measuring life because he was not "in being" at the creation of the power.

*   *   *

Although a special or testamentary power cannot validly be conferred on an unborn person (unless some special restriction is imposed on it forbidding its exercise beyond the period of the Rule), an unborn person can be the recipient of a valid *general power presently exercisable*.   This is because a general power presently exercisable is not invalid simply because it might be exercised too remotely.   A general power presently exercisable is invalid only if its exercise is subject to a *condition precedent* which might occur beyond the period of the Rule.   This is consistent with the notion that such a power is equivalent to ownership of the property interests subject to the donee's appointment.

Example 14–6.   Suppose that in example *14–4* above, the power conferred on A's first born child had been a general power presently exercisable, which would have been the case if the relevant language had read "then to such persons as A's first born child shall appoint."   Now the power would be valid.   The power is indeed subject to a condition precedent—that A have a child—but this is a contingency which is certain to be resolved one way or the other within the perpetuity period, i.e., within A's lifetime.   If, however, the relevant language had been "then to such persons as A's first born child shall appoint after reaching the age of 25," the additional contingency of reaching 25 would have invalidated the general power presently exercisable.

§ 14.3   The Validity of the Exercise

If the power itself passes the appropriate test for validity as set forth above, it can validly be exercised.   Whether such a power has in fact been validly exercised is the question to which we now turn.   For the most part, the Rule Against Perpetuities applies to appointed interests in the same way it applies to interests created by an owner of property.   There are, though, as you might expect, some perpetuity questions and doctrines peculiar to appointments.

(a) *Time When the Rule Commences to Run.*   The first question is whether the appointed interests are considered to have been created by the donor of the power or by the donee thereof.   The answer to this question, which is really a facet of the relation-back puzzle, determines the time from which the perpetuity period is measured.   If the donee's appointment is deemed to relate back, then the donor is considered to be the one who created the appointed interests and as a consequence the perpetuity period is measured from the time that the power was created.   If on the other hand the donee's appointment is deemed not to relate back, then the donee is considered to have created the appointed interests and the period is measured from the time of exercise.   Whether the Rule runs from the time of the power's exercise or of its creation depends on the type of power which was exercised.

A *presently exercisable general power* is treated as the equivalent of ownership of the property subject to the power.   Accordingly, the donee is considered to have created the appointed interests.   The exercise is treated as if the donee first exercised the power in his own favor and then created the appointed interests out of the now owned property.   Consequently the perpetuity period starts running afresh when the exercise becomes effective.

*   *   *

At the pole opposite to a presently exercisable general power is a *special power*.   Since the donee of a special power (whether presently exercisable or testamentary) cannot appoint in his own favor, such a power is not treated as the equivalent of ownership of the property subject to the power.   Consequently the doctrine of relation back applies, and the starting point of the perpetuity period is the time when the special power itself was created for perpetuity purposes.   In other words, the appointed interests are deemed to have been created by the *donor* of the power, not by the donee.

Special powers and presently exercisable general powers present rather clear cases.   In between these two poles is the *general testamentary power*.   The issue whether the perpetuity period should begin when the power was created or when it was exercised was hotly debated in the law reviews in the earlier part of this century.   *   *   *   It appeared for a long time thereafter that the common law courts accepted Gray's position that the referent should be the date of creation.   A leading case so holding is Northern Trust Co. v. Porter.[43]   There was, to be sure, the English view enunciated in Rous v. Jackson [44] and now codified in the Perpetuities and Accumulations Act, § 7, along with legislation enacted in a very few American states, which declared the reference point for validity to be the date of exercise.   But the American common law courts unanimously used the date of creation as the referent.   This was true, at least, until 1966 when the Supreme Court of Rhode Island decided that the perpetuity period commences upon exercise.   Industrial Nat'l Bank v. Barrett.[45]   The Barrett court was convinced by the argument that at the death of the donee of a general testamentary power he can then "appoint to anyone of his choice including his own estate."   Thus "when the donee exercises his power, he is *at that time* the practical owner thereof, *for the purposes of the rule*." (Emphasis in original.)   The Restatement (Second) of Property § 1.2, comment *d*, illustration 12 rejects this reasoning on the ground that the "complete freedom of transfer by will that opens up momentarily on [the donee's] death is not enough to eliminate the interference with unqualified control of beneficial rights   *   *   *   that is caused   *   *   *   during [the donee's] lifetime."   The issue is more complicated than either of these statements suggests (and than can be explored here), and it remains to be seen whether other courts will join Barrett.   As it stands now, though, the vast majority view holds that the perpetuity period is measured from the date of creation of a general testamentary power.

(b) *The Second-Look Doctrine*.   Even though the validity of interests created by the exercise of special or testamentary powers is by the nearly unanimous view measured from the date of the power's creation, not from its exercise, the facts existing on the date of exercise can be taken into

---

43.   368 Ill. 256, 13 N.E.2d 487 (1938).

44.   L.R. 29 Ch. 521 (1885).

45.   101 R.I. 89, 220 A.2d 517 (1966).

account.　Taking this "second look" at the facts appears to be a well-established procedure.　[Citations omitted.]

Example 14–9.　*T* was the life income beneficiary of a trust and the donee of a special power over the succeeding remainder interest.　The trust was created by the will of his mother, *M*, who predeceased him.　*T* exercised his power by his will, directing the income to be paid after his death to his children for the life of the survivor, and upon the death of his last surviving child, to pay the corpus of the trust to his grandchildren.　At *M*'s death, *T* had two children, *X* and *Y*.　No further children were born to *T*, and at his death *X* and *Y* were still living.

T's appointment is valid.　The perpetuity period is measured from *M*'s death. If only the facts existing at *M*'s death could be taken into account, however, *T*'s appointment would partly fail because of the possibility of his having another child after *M*'s death who would turn out to have children more than 21 years after the deaths of *T*, *X*, and *Y*.　However, in considering the validity of *T*'s appointment, we are not restricted to the facts existing when the perpetuity period commences to run on *T*'s appointment.　The facts existing on *T*'s death can be taken into account under the second-look doctrine.　Taking these facts into account saves *T*'s appointment.　At *T*'s death, we know that no additional children were born to *T* after *M*'s death.　Thus *T*'s last surviving child will be either *X* or *Y*, both of whom were "in being" at *M*'s death and therefore constitute the measuring lives.

Suppose that after *M*'s death, a third child (*Z*) was born to *T*.　This would make the remainder in favor of *T*'s grandchildren invalid if *Z* survived *T*.　But if *Z* predeceased *T*, the grandchildren's remainder would be saved by the second-look doctrine.

Suppose *T*'s power had been a general testamentary power.　This would make no change in the above analysis.

Suppose *T*'s power had been a general power presently exercisable.　*T*'s appointment would now be valid whether *Z* was born and survived *T* or not because the perpetuity period would be measured from *T*'s death, not *M*'s.

The second-look doctrine is a departure from the fundamental principle that only the facts existing when the perpetuity period commences to run can be taken into account in determining validity.　See § 12.5, supra.　A persuasive justification put forward for this departure is that until the appointment is made the appointed interests cannot be known *and their validity cannot be litigated.*　Thus no useful purpose would be served by holding appointed interests to be invalid because of what might have happened after the power was created but which at the time of exercise can no longer happen.　See 6 American Law of Property § 24.35; Restatement of Property § 392, comment *a*.

*　　*　　*

Should this doctrine be extended to gifts-in-default?　That is, should a second look at the facts be taken at the time when the power expires (typically by the donee's having released the power or having died without exercising it)?

*　　*　　*

The treatise writers take opposite views on this question.　Section 24.36 of 6 American Law of Property, written by Leach and Tudor, supports a second look for gifts-in-default.　Shortly after this treatise was published, this position along with the reasoning there set forth was adopted in apparently the first American case to consider the question, Sears v.

Coolidge.[46]   Four years later, Simes & Smith § 1276 came out against the decision in Sears.   Not long after, however, a Canadian court upheld a gift-in-default by applying the second-look doctrine.   Re Edwards.[47]   Recently, the Pennsylvania court did the same thing, but did so without discussing the issue except to assert that it was "the better view." [48]   The authority of this decision is undercut by the fact that the Pennsylvania "wait and see" statute was applicable to the case and required the same result, and the court so noted.

Any analysis of this question must begin with the conceptual point that a default clause creates property interests no different from other property interests save one: they are subject to divestment upon the exercise of the power.   If T had not been granted a power of appointment in the above example, the interests created by the default clause would clearly be judged on the basis of the facts existing when M died.   No "second look" as of T's death would be permissible, at least not unless the jurisdiction had adopted the controversial "wait and see" proposal (advocated by Leach and opposed by Simes).   In an effort to justify the utilization of a second look, it is argued in American Law of Property that a donee's failure to exercise the power is the equivalent of his having exercised it in terms identical to the gift-in-default.   The Canadian court in Re Edwards relied squarely and primarily on this ground.   But there are grave difficulties with this theory. It is not only a fiction; it is a fiction that cannot always be indulged in. For one thing, there are cases where the permissible objects of the donee's power do not include all the takers-in-default.   (This was in fact the case in Re Edwards, but the court took no notice of it.)   For another, one or more of the takers-in-default may have predeceased the donee.   Even though as a taker-in-default such person's interest would not be defeated in the absence of an express or implied condition of survivorship, the donee could not have appointed in his favor.   (This would in fact be the case in example *14–10* if one of T's grandchildren had died during T's lifetime.) Finally, some jurisdictions (supported by the Restatement of Property § 369) follow the rule that an actual appointment in favor of the takers-in-default is a nullity.

The next point made in American Law of Property is that "the justification for [a second look when the validity of a gift-in-default is at issue] is the same as that for the 'Second Look' doctrine as applied to appointments (§ 24.35).   Until the power of appointment expires it cannot be known whether the gift-in-default of appointment is to control the disposition of the property or whether it is to be superseded by some appointment which the donee makes.   Therefore no possible delay in adjudging the validity of the remainder is involved in examining facts which exist at the date the power expires unexercised."   The justification for the second-look doctrine as applied to appointments, however, as noted above, was that the appointed interests were unknown (and consequently that it was *impossible* to adjudicate their validity) until the appointment was made, not that it was unlikely that anyone would want to adjudicate their validity until then.   The interests created by the default clause, unlike appointed interests, *are* known

---

46.   329 Mass. 340, 108 N.E.2d 563 (1952).

47.   20 D.L.R.2d 755 (Ont.1959).

48.   In re Frank, 480 Pa. 116, 389 A.2d 536 (1978).

and their validity *can* be litigated before the expiration of the power.   Thus the rationale for taking a second look in the case of appointed interests does not apply to interests created in the default clause.   And, as a practical matter, cases can be visualized where such an adjudication might be sought. Take example *14–10*, for instance.   Suppose that *T* during his lifetime became incompetent to exercise his power.   Suppose further that one of *T*'s grandchildren died while *T* was still living.   It might become important for estate tax purposes to get a judgment as to the validity of the grandchild's interest as a taker-in-default.

*   *   *

§ 14.4   The Validity of Appointed Powers and Exercises of Appointed Powers

The donee of a power of appointment might exercise it by creating another power of appointment.   When this occurs, the validity of the appointed power and the validity of its exercise are governed by a combination of the principles set forth in sections 14.2 and 14.3, above.

Example 14–11.   *T* devised real property to *A* for life, remainder to such of *A*'s descendants as *A* shall appoint.   At his death, *A* exercised his special power by appointing to his child *B* for life, remainder to such of *B*'s descendants as *B* shall appoint.   At his death, *B* exercised his special power by appointing to his child *C* for life, remainder to *C*'s children.

A and *B* were living at *T*'s death.   Thereafter, *C* was born.   *A* later died survived by *B* and *C*.   *B* then died survived by *C*.

B's power is valid.   Since it is a special power, its validity turns on whether it might be exercised too remotely.   This question is answered by measuring the perpetuity period from the time of *T*'s death, not *A*'s.   *A*'s power being a special power, *A*'s appointment relates back.   Since *B* was living at *T*'s death, *B*'s power cannot be exercised too remotely.   If *B* had been born after *T*'s death, however, *B*'s power would have been invalid; the fact that *B* was alive at *A*'s death would not have saved it.

Although *B*'s power is valid, his exercise is partly invalid.   The remainder in favor of *C*'s children violates the Rule because it is subject to increase too long. The perpetuity period runs from *T*'s death.   Since *B*'s power was a special power, *B*'s appointment under relation back is treated as having been made by *A*.   If *B*'s appointment related back no further than that, of course, it would have been valid because *C* was alive at *A*'s death.   However, *A*'s power was also a special power, so relation back goes another step.   *A*'s appointment (which now includes *B*'s appointment) is treated as having been made by *T*.   Since *C* was not alive at *T*'s death, he cannot be the measuring life.   And, since *C* might have more children more than 21 years after the deaths of *A* and *B* and any other person who was "in being" at *T*'s death, the remainder in favor of his children is invalid.

Note that if either *A*'s power or *B*'s power (or both) had been a general testamentary power rather than a special power, the above analysis would not change. However, if either *A*'s power or *B*'s power (or both) had been a general power presently exercisable, *B*'s appointment would have been valid.   (If *A* had the general power presently exercisable, the perpetuity period would be measured from *A*'s death, not *T*'s; and if the general power presently exercisable were held by *B*, the period would run from *B*'s death.)

§ 14.5 Fiduciary Powers

To return to the validity of powers for a moment, it should be noted that special powers are not conferred only on beneficiaries.   Often they are conferred on fiduciaries, making the power collateral rather than in gross. Examples of such powers are discretionary powers in the trustee of a trust to invade corpus, to accumulate income, or to spray income in various proportions among the members of a group.   Such powers are invalid if they might be exercised too remotely.

Example 14–12. T devised property in trust, directing the trustee to pay the income to A for life, then to A's children for the life of the survivor, and on the death of A's last surviving child to pay the corpus to B.   The trustee is granted the discretionary power to sell and to reinvest the trust assets and to invade the corpus on behalf of the income beneficiary or beneficiaries.

Although all of the property interests of the beneficiaries of the trust are valid, the trustee's power to invade corpus is invalid.   It might be exercised beyond 21 years after lives "in being" at T's death.   The trust can proceed to be carried out, but the trustee has no power to invade the corpus.   The trustee's power to sell and reinvest the trust assets, however, is valid even though it, too, might be exercised beyond the period of the Rule.   The reason is that purely administrative powers, as distinguished from discretionary powers to shift beneficial enjoyment, are not subject to the Rule.

Part II

LIFETIME ARRANGEMENTS

"Nothing is certain but death and taxes." [1]

This time-worn philosophy continues to hobble clients and their advisors by suggesting that taxes, like death, are beyond human control. On the contrary, for clients willing and able to give proper attention to tax considerations in arranging their affairs, estate planning may substantially reduce, or occasionally even eliminate altogether, federal income, gift, estate, and generation-skipping transfer taxes. And the price of these savings often is less than many clients realize. Frequently, tax-saving arrangements require no major change in the way the client would have disposed of his income and wealth if the taxes involved did not exist. And even if major changes are required to achieve savings, the amounts saved may be large enough to make it worthwhile for the client to modify some aspects of the plan which would best reflect his personal preferences.

Chapter 4

INCOME TAX ASPECTS

¶ 4.01 ARRANGEMENTS TO SAVE INCOME TAXES

It is the rare client who is not generally familiar with the federal income tax. What many do not realize is the extent to which estate planning may make the tax less burdensome for them and their beneficiaries. During a client's life, an analysis of the ways he handles his income and wealth often will reveal that estate planning techniques may allow him to make substantially the same use of his resources as he does now, but at greatly reduced income tax costs. After his death, present law offers a similar choice between high cost and low cost arrangements in using his resources to meet the needs and desires of his family and other beneficiaries.

This choice is offered because Congress has not undertaken in the Internal Revenue Code to tax all income at a uniform rate or to preclude postponement of its realization for tax purposes. Instead, any one of a variety of tax rates may apply to a given item of income, depending largely on the income, deductions, and marital status of the taxpayer to whom the item is attributed, as well as whether it is characterized as ordinary income, short- or long-term capital gain, or tax-exempt income. Clients often have a large measure of control over such factors and accordingly may influence the choice of the rate which will apply in any given case. Similarly, clients may often control the time at which income is realized for tax purposes. By postponing realization, the client or his beneficiaries may enjoy an in-

---

1. Benjamin Franklin used the phrase in a letter to M. Leroy in 1789. In context, it is apparent that Franklin was focusing on other matters:

"Our constitution is in actual operation; everything appears to promise that it will last; but in this world nothing is certain but death and taxes."

terest-free loan from the Treasury of the tax which would have been due if the income had been taxable earlier.

Many clients understandably place greater emphasis on saving income taxes while they live than on saving estate taxes, which will not be payable until they die. In addition to the psychological hurdles a person may encounter in thinking about his or her own death, an estate tax that is not due until that unpredictable date may be affected by many factors that cannot be forecast with any degree of confidence.

The income tax, on the other hand, impinges at least annually upon a client's consciousness. In addition, the potential benefits of income tax savings are more visible because a client can anticipate seeing them enjoyed while he lives and the relevant factors are more predictable, at least in the short run. A client may have some degree of confidence that his income for the next ten years will be more than he wishes to consume and that potential tax savings from shifting income to a taxpayer in a lower bracket will justify the costs and inconveniences that must be incurred in order to achieve them. He may lack the same degree of conviction that he can afford to give away permanently the wealth which produces that income in order to remove it from his taxable estate.

The estate-planning techniques used to save income taxes, unlike techniques to save taxes on wealth transfers (i.e., gift, estate, and generation-skipping (GST)), are based largely on the "common law" of income taxation that has been developed by the courts, rather than on express Code provisions. For example, after a transfer of property by gift, the income generally is taxable to the donee rather than to the donor, although no Code provision expressly requires this result.[2] At the same time, many techniques by which taxpayers have sought to shift income from one taxpayer to another have been frustrated by judicial decisions even though no Code section explicitly states such techniques shall be ineffective.[3]

However, there are many instances in which Code provisions are relevant in determining the income tax consequences of an attempt to shift the taxability of income from one taxpayer to another, most notably the Clifford sections of the Code (§§ 671–677), dealing with the use of trusts for this purpose. These sections delineate, with considerable precision, the circumstances under which a trust grantor will or will not be treated for income tax purposes as owner of all or a portion of the trust because of his dominion or control over it.

[1] Objectives

[a] To Shift Income to a Taxpayer in a Lower Bracket

With a highly progressive income tax rate schedule, it is obvious that shifting taxable income to a taxpayer in a lower bracket may double or even triple the amount remaining after federal taxes alone—to say nothing of applicable state and local levies. Income-shifting techniques include both formal transfers of income-producing property and a variety of informal

---

2. See, however, § 102(b)(1), under which the exclusion from income of property acquired by gift is inapplicable to the income from such property, implying that such income is taxable to the donee.

3. A prime illustration of this is the assignment of income doctrine, discussed at ¶ 4.01[2][a] infra.

arrangements that divert income from a client to his beneficiaries (or to trusts for their benefit). The latter includes gifts of services, interest-free or low-interest loans, and diversions of business or investment opportunities.[4]

[b] To Defer Payment of Income Tax (Without Interest)

Postponing the date at which income taxes must be paid is the substantial equivalent of obtaining an interest-free loan from the Treasury. When banks charge even prime loan customers high interest rates, an interest-free deferral of income tax is a particularly attractive way to borrow money.

Clients need sound advice to determine the value of deferral achieved through the use of estate-planning techniques, or, for that matter, through the variety of available tax shelters. Because of the widespread tendency to ignore the difference in the present value (apart from changes in purchasing power) of a dollar now and a dollar ten years from now, the value of deferral has at times been dismissed rather casually in public discussion of proposed Code amendments. The realities of the business world are otherwise; a deferral of income taxes represents an interest-free loan. Thus, an arrangement which achieves deferral of tax for ten years may have substantial value to a taxpayer.

Deferral is one of the most important concepts in tax planning. Because money not used to pay taxes can be invested until the tax is due, deferral of liability without interest can achieve a significant tax saving, depending on the after-tax rate of return that funds retained by the taxpayer as a result of his postponement of liability can produce and the length of time they remain in his hands. If taxes could be postponed indefinitely, deferral would be equivalent to complete forgiveness of liability. Instances of indefinite postponement are not common: The provisions for non-recognition of gain on like-kind exchanges under section 1031 are one example. But even a short term postponement may represent a significant reduction in the tax burden.

In estimating the value of deferral, we may assume for simplicity that the taxpayer has no preference as between paying a given amount now and paying that same amount with interest later. Of course, in a particular case, the taxpayer may be illiquid and unable to borrow at favorable rates, and may thus wish to postpone liability even though an arithmetic analysis indicates that there would be no advantage from doing so if the taxpayer had funds available.

The value of deferral depends first of all on the rate of return the client can obtain after tax on funds that would have been used to pay the liability deferred. Suppose, for example, that a client can obtain a 15% rate of return, and that he is in a 50% bracket, so that his after-tax rate of return is 7½%. If a $100 liability is deferred for one year, the client can invest the amount saved and obtain $107.50. On satisfaction of the tax liability in year 2, the client retains $7.50. If the purchasing power of money is declining, reflecting inflation, the value of the retained $7.50 will be reduced

---

4. For a discussion of such arrangements, see ¶ 8.01 infra.

accordingly, but he still retains the $7.50. He can never be a loser as a result of tax deferral because inflation diminishes the burden of his deferred tax liability just as it eats away at the purchasing power of the money saved. Postponement of liability for more than one year is even more favorable. For example, deferral for 5 years leaves the client with $43.56, and deferral for 20 years with $324.78.

This way of estimating the value of deferral must be qualified to take account of two factors:

(1) the client's marginal rate (or the marginal rate of the person who will be taxed, if the deferred income will be attributed to another taxpayer) upon future realization of taxable income may differ from his present rate. The value of deferral could either be offset by an increase in the tax rate, or be enhanced by a lower-than-expected tax rate. A realistic prediction of the likely rate change involves a consideration of the client's present and prospective future circumstances as well as the likelihood of statutory change.

(2) The amount subject to tax in the future as a result of deferral may also differ from the amount that would be taxed currently. An example of an increase in the amount subject to tax is provided by gain realized on sale of an asset. A decision may be made to defer liability for the tax by postponing the sale and this postponement will tend to save taxes because of the time value of money. At the same time, however, if the property appreciates in value the selling price also will increase. If the sale is to a family member or family trust and the benefit of price appreciation will inure to either the taxpayer or his family, no matter when the sale is made, deferral may be disadvantageous.

An intra-family sale of income-producing property for a price payable in installments or as a private annuity may result in both deferral of taxes and income-shifting. The Installment Sales Revision Act of 1980 [5] has substantially reduced the effectiveness of installment sales to achieve these goals but does not deal directly with sales for an annuity.[6]

Postponement combined with realization by another taxpayer also may occur when income-producing property is given to an intermediate recipient, such as an irrevocable trust, that is subject to tax at a lower rate. Although an additional tax may be imposed because of the throw-back rule [7] when the income is distributed to the trust beneficiary, this additional tax will have been deferred for the period between receipt of income by the trust and its distribution to the beneficiaries. This technique provides an interest-free [8] loan from the Treasury to the trust for this period.

5. Pub.L. 96–47, 96th Cong., 2d sess. (1980).

6. See H.R.Rep. 1042, 96th Cong., 2d sess. 10 n.12 (1980). Both kinds of sales are discussed in Chapter 8.

7. See § 667. For a discussion of the rule, see ¶ 11.02.

8. An interest charge is imposed only in the case of accumulation distributions by foreign trusts. See § 667(a)(3).

[c] To Recharacterize Income Items as Capital Gain or Tax-Exempt Receipts

Lifetime estate planning arrangements sometimes may be used to convert what would have been ordinary income, if realized by the client, into capital gain or tax-exempt receipts in the hands of a transferee. This may occur because:

(1) Property that is an ordinary income item in the hands of the transferor may be a capital asset in the hands of the transferee;

(2) The transfer may cause a step-up of basis of the property without resulting in a realization of income by the transferor; or

(3) The transferee is a charitable remainder annuity trust or unitrust.

The first situation is common; the activities of the transferor in relation to a given asset, or other similar assets, cause him to be deemed to hold it for sale to customers, so that it is not a capital asset in his hands.[9]   In the hands of the transferee, on the other hand, the asset may be free from any such taint.[10]

The second situation is illustrated by certain discretionary distributions of appreciated property by trustees or executors.[11]

In the third situation, the charitable remainder annuity trust or unitrust generally is exempt from income tax under § 664.[12]   This exemption includes income constituting unrealized appreciation at the time assets were transferred to the trust.[13]

[2] Non-Statutory Bars to Recognition

To be recognized for income tax purposes, income-shifting arrangements must successfully surmount two judicially developed principles:

(1) the assignment of income doctrine; and

(2) the requirement of substance, or economic reality.

In addition, the income tax consequences of any transfer are subject to the Secretary's authority, under § 482, to "distribute, apportion, or allocate gross income, deductions, credits, or allowances" among organizations "owned or controlled directly or indirectly by the same interests" if such authority is necessary "to prevent evasion of taxes or clearly to reflect the[ir] income * * *."   To date, the section has been applied almost exclusively to corporations, partnerships, and corporation-shareholder and partnership-partner relationships.   It expressly applies to unincorporated organizations, which the Regulations define as including "a sole proprietorship, a partnership, a trust, an estate * * *."[14]   It is not easy to contend that two individual taxpayers are "owned or controlled directly or indirectly by the same interests."   But the Commissioner has sought to apply this provision to a sale by an executor, who was also sole beneficiary of an estate,

---

9. See ¶ 6.04 note 112 infra.

10. But see ¶ 6.04 note 113 infra.

11. See Reg. § 1.661(a)–2(f)(3), discussed at ¶ 4.07 infra.

12. For a discussion, see ¶ 10.02 infra.

13. But see ¶ 6.01[2][c] infra with respect to realization of income on a transfer of property subject to liabilities in excess of the donor's basis.

14. Reg. § 1.482–1(a)(1).

to himself individually.[15] The section literally would apply to transactions between two trusts under common control, or between a trust and its grantor if the grantor were in control of the trust.

[a] Assignment of Income Doctrine

A transferor who seeks to shift the taxability of income faces a number of landmark judicial decisions which have frustrated similar efforts by other taxpayers. Some of the most important include Lucas v. Earl,[16] which held that a contract between husband and wife was ineffective to shift the taxability of income from one to the other; Helvering v. Clifford,[17] which taxed to the grantor the income payable to the beneficiaries of a short-term trust because of the grantor's dominion and control over the trust; Helvering v. Horst,[18] which held that a gift of unmatured interest coupons, detached from bonds by the taxpayer and given to his son, was ineffective to shift the taxability of the bond interest to the son; and Commissioner v. Court Holding Co.,[19] which attributed to a corporation the gain realized on a sale of corporate property by the stockholders following liquidation of the corporation. All four cases were decided under predecessors to § 61 and represent applications of the principle stated in *Earl*, in which the Court refused to find that "the fruits are attributed to a different tree from that on which they grew."[20] But it is not always clear whether the subject matter of a transfer is part of the tree, and hence effective to shift the taxability of income, or merely some of the fruit, and hence ineffective for this purpose.

For example, a life income beneficiary of a trust may assign a portion of his interest in the trust income. Does the assignment shift the taxability of that portion? The Supreme Court has held that if the portion assigned is for the duration of the beneficiary's interest, the assignment is effective for tax purposes,[21] but not if it is an assignment of income for only the following year.[22] The Commissioner has since held that the position of the assignor is analogous to that of a trust grantor.[23] Thus, the minimum term for an effective assignment of trust income is ten years or the life of the assignee, just as for a transfer in trust.[24] Furthermore, income which has already been "constructively received"[25] or accrued by the donor and hence taxable to him as "fruit" cannot be shifted to another taxpayer.

---

15. See James Davis, Jr. v. United States, 282 F.2d 623, 60–2 USTC ¶ 9715 (10th Cir. 1960).

16. 281 U.S. 111, 50 S.Ct. 241, 74 L.Ed. 731, 2 USTC ¶ 496 (1930).

17. 309 U.S. 331, 60 S.Ct. 554, 84 L.Ed. 788, 40–1 USTC ¶ 9265 (1940).

18. 311 U.S. 112, 61 S.Ct. 144, 85 L.Ed. 75, 40–2 USTC ¶ 9787 (1940).

19. 324 U.S. 331, 65 S.Ct. 707, 89 L.Ed. 981, 45–1 USTC ¶ 9215 (1945).

20. 281 U.S. at 115, 50 S.Ct. at 241, 74 L.Ed. at 733, 2 USTC at 2190. For a recent application, see Richard L. Wesenberg, 69 T.C. 1005 (1978), nonacq 1978–2 CB 4, in which a purported conveyance by the taxpayer of his lifetime services to a family trust was ineffective to shift the taxability of compensation for his services to the trust.

21. Blair v. Commissioner, 300 U.S. 5, 57 S.Ct. 330, 81 L.Ed. 465, 37–1 USTC ¶ 9083 (1937).

22. Harrison v. Schaffner, 312 U.S. 579, 61 S.Ct. 759, 85 L.Ed. 1055, 41–1 USTC ¶ 9355 (1941).

23. Rev.Rul. 55–38, 1955–1 CB 389.

24. Id.

25. See Reg. § 1.451–2, defining "constructive receipt."

[b] Requirement of Substance or "Economic Reality"

Some transfers are ineffective to shift taxable income because a court finds a lack of substance or "economic reality" in the arrangement.   For example, in C. James Mathews v. Commissioner,[26] a grantor transferred his business property in trust for the benefit of his dependents, with the property to be returned to him after ten years and one day, when the trust terminated.   The trustee, who was the grantor's attorney, then leased the property back to the grantor on a year-to-year basis.   The court denied the grantor a deduction for the lease payments made to the trust, finding that the arrangement lacked "economic reality" because the grantor had an interest in the trust property, and that the presence of a business purpose for the arrangement was not by itself sufficient to support the deduction.[27]

Another situation where courts have looked to the substance, rather than the form, of a transaction is where a grantor purports to sell property to a trust with nominal assets in exchange for an annuity payable by the trust to the sellor-grantor.[28]   If the grantor is considered instead to have made a gift in trust and retained the income from the trust property, such income is taxable to him rather than to the trust beneficiaries.[29]

[3] Saving Income Taxes by Using Trusts

Trusts are entities subject to income tax at rate brackets similar to those applicable to married individuals filing separate returns.[30]   By setting up a group of trusts so that no one of them receives very much income, a client can cause the trust to be in lower marginal tax brackets than the beneficiaries.   If income is accumulated in a trust one year and distributed to a beneficiary in a later year, there may be an additional tax due for the year in which the accumulated income is distributed.   The additional tax is intended to reflect the difference between the rates applied to the trust and to a beneficiary in a higher bracket.   This so-called "throwback tax" [31] is inapplicable to some distributions of accumulated income.[32]   Even if the

---

26. 520 F.2d 323, 75–2 USTC ¶ 9734 (5th Cir. 1975), cert. denied 424 U.S. 967 (1976).

27. Other trust leaseback cases have been decided in favor of the taxpayer. See, e.g., Richard R. Quinlivan v. Commissioner, 599 F.2d 269, 79–1 USTC ¶ 9396 (8th Cir. 1979), cert. denied 444 U.S. 996 (1979); Hobart A. Lerner, 71 T.C. 290 (1978). See also C. P. Brooke v. United States, 468 F.2d 1155, 72–2 USTC ¶ 9594 (9th Cir. 1972) (deduction allowed for rental payments where donor had transferred business property to himself as guardian for his minor children and paid rent for his continued use of the property).

For a different application by the Fifth Circuit of an economic reality test, see David M. Fender Trust No. 1 v. United States, 577 F.2d 934, 78–2 USTC ¶ 9617 (5th Cir. 1978).   The court disallowed a loss on a trust's sale of depreciated bonds to a bank in which the grantor-trustee had a substantial stock interest, followed by repurchase of the bonds 42 days later, finding no bona fide sale.

28. See Simon M. Lazarus v. Commissioner, 513 F.2d 824, 75–1 USTC ¶ 9387 (9th Cir. 1975), discussed at ¶ 5.02[4][a][v].

29. See § 677(a)(1).

30. See text at notes 44–46 infra.

31. Section 666 provides for allocation of an "accumulation distribution" to preceding years and § 667 imposes a tax on the amount so allocated.   For a discussion, see ¶ 11.02[2].

32. See, e.g., § 665(b), generally excluding from the definition of "accumulation distribution" for throwback purposes, amounts accumulated before the beneficiary attains 21 (or before his birth).

tax must be paid when such income is distributed, there is a saving from interest-free deferral of the throwback tax.[33]

If a trust pays out amounts to beneficiaries, the beneficiaries may be taxed on part or all of the income of the trust for the year in which such distributions are made.[34]   To that extent, there will be no tax savings from the trust's lower bracket, because for tax purposes the income of the trust flows through it and is taxed to beneficiaries.   But there remain tax saving possibilities.   For example, capital gain income of the trust is usually not considered to be distributed to beneficiaries, so that it is taxed at the trust's rates.[35]   And in some cases trusts can be used to achieve a tax free step-up in basis (regeneration of basis) of appreciated property distributed in kind to beneficiaries.[36]

Trust income thus is usually taxed to the trust or to one or more beneficiaries.   But a grantor or another person may be taxed on trust income even though it is not distributed to him.[37]   In addition, even if a trust qualifies as an entity separate from the grantor, gain recognized on the sale or exchange of appreciated property, contributed to the trust and disposed of within two years, is taxed at the grantor's rates, to the extent of appreciation when the property was contributed.[38]   Arrangements which cause trust income to be taxed to the grantor, or at the grantor's rates, usually offer no income tax savings.[39]

Charitable remainder trusts, which make distributions to noncharitable beneficiaries for life or a term of years with a remainder to charity, offer significant income tax savings because the trusts are generally exempt from tax on accumulated income.[40]   Charitable remainder trusts thus offer a way to realize gain on appreciated assets free of income tax.   In addition, if the trust is created during the grantor's life, he is entitled to an income tax deduction for the present value of the charitable remainder interest and a gift tax deduction for such value as well.[41]   If the trust is created upon his death, an estate tax charitable deduction is allowed.[42]

The taxable income of a trust generally is computed in the same manner as for individuals.[43]   The tax rates for trusts are similar to the rates for married individuals filing separately, except that the latter has an initial tax-free bracket of $1700 [44] and the deduction for the exemption amount is

33.   § 668, imposing a 6% interest charge on "throwback tax," applies only to accumulation distributions from foreign trusts.

34.   See § 652 (simple trusts); § 662 (complex trusts).

35.   Capital gains and losses generally are not included in the measuring rod of "distributable net income" which determines the amount includible by the beneficiary.   See § 643(a), discussed at ¶ 11.01[2].

36.   See ¶ 4.07 infra.

37.   See §§ 671–678, discussed at ¶ 9.01 (grantors) and ¶ 12.01[3] (non-grantors) infra.

38.   § 644, discussed at ¶ 9.02[2][a] infra.

39.   But see discussion of possible advantages at ¶ 9.01[1][b][ii] infra.

40.   See § 664.

41.   § 2522(c)(2)(A).

42.   § 2055(e)(2)(A).

43.   § 641(b).   The most important differrence is the deduction for distributions to beneficiaries.   See § 651 (simple trusts) and § 661 (complex trusts).   In effect, the distributions deduction allocates taxable income between the trust and the beneficiaries so that income which is distributed currently is taxed only once.

44.   § 1(d), (e).

$1000.[45] Trusts are allowed in lieu of a personal exemption a deduction of $300 for a trust required to distribute all of its income currently and $100 for all other trusts.[46] However, this deduction usually is of minor importance because the tax thereby saved is unlikely to be as large as the cost of professional preparation of the trust's income tax returns.

¶ 4.02 IMPORTANCE OF BASIS, CHARACTER, AND HOLDING PERIOD OF ASSETS

Three important income tax characteristics of any asset are:

(1) its basis,[47]

(2) its character as capital [48] or non-capital; and

(3) the owner's holding period.[49]

All three necessarily refer to the asset in a given owner's hands.

The general rule is that a taxpayer's basis is cost.[50] However, there are important exceptions for assets acquired from a decedent [51] or by gift,[52] so that a beneficiary's basis often is different from that of the testator or donor. A purchase of an asset usually causes the purchaser's basis to be his cost, rather than that of the seller, even though the sale was an intra-family transaction made in order to achieve estate-planning objectives.[53]

Basis should be taken into account in determining the total federal tax consequences of transferring an asset, as there may be trade-offs between different taxes. If the donor's basis is low in relation to the fair market value of property when it is transferred by gift, the transfer may be effective to shift the taxability of a large amount of gain from the donor to the donee. This follows from the fact that ordinarily a donor does not realize income as a result of making a gift of appreciated property.[54] Instead, unrealized appreciation when the gift is made is taxable only when the property is disposed of by the donee.[55]

Thus, from the standpoint of shifting income for tax purposes from a donor in a high bracket to a donee in a lower bracket, a gift of property

45. See § 151(a); § 151(f) (cost of living adjustment).

46. § 642(b).

47. General rules for determining basis are contained in §§ 1101–1017.

48. Section 1221 defines "capital asset" as "property held by the taxpayer," with specified exceptions. The exception of greatest significance for estate planning purposes is in § 1221(1), relating to property includible in inventory or held primarily for sale to customers in the ordinary course of the taxpayer's trade or business.

49. Long-term capital gains (and losses) are realized from the sale or exchange of capital assets held for more than one year. See § 1222.

50. § 1012. Adjustments to basis for capital expenditures, depreciation, etc., are provided in § 1016.

51. § 1014. For a discussion, see ¶ 4.03 infra.

52. § 1015. For a discussion, see ¶ 4.04 infra.

53. Sales are discussed in Chapter 8.

54. Realization of income as a result of a gift sometimes may be required by a specific Code provision. See, e.g., § 453B (realization of gain on disposition of installment obligation). Such realization may also be required by general rules developed to deal with transfers of property subject to a mortgage of lien. See ¶ 6.01[2][c] infra.

55. Under § 644, all or part of any gain recognized on a sale of property by a trust within two years of the gift may be taxable at the grantor's rates. See ¶ 9.02[2][a].

with a low basis is preferable to a gift of property with a high basis in relation to its fair market value. On the other hand, from the standpoint of the net amount the donee will retain after a sale of the asset, a gift of the latter is preferable.

For example, if a client owns assets *A* and *B*, each worth $100,000 but having bases of $20,000 for *A* and $100,000 for *B*, a gift of *A* followed by a sale of *A* by the donee may cause a substantial gain realized on the sale to be taxable to the donee, rather than to the donor.[56] This may mean a large saving in income taxes if the donee's bracket is lower than that of the donor. A gift of *B*, on the other hand, does not shift any taxable gain that may be realized on its sale unless it continues to appreciate in value after the gift is made (and before the donee sells it).

In the example just given, if the client is more concerned with minimizing gift taxes on the net proceeds that the donee will retain after a sale of the asset, a gift of *B* has more favorable tax consequences than a gift of *A*. After such a sale for $100,000, the donee will retain the entire amount undiminished by income taxes. The donor's gift tax is the same on a transfer of either *A* or *B* [57] but a gift of the former leaves less in the donee's hands after a sale of the property (and after the income tax he must pay as a result) than does a gift of the latter, also followed by its sale.

The character of an asset as capital or non-capital may be different in the hands of a transferee from that which it had in the hands of the transferor because its character is determined, in part, with reference to its owner's other dealings in similar assets. A transferor who has had extensive dealings in real estate, for example, is far more likely to be regarded as holding a given parcel for sale to customers than is a transferee who has sold little or no real estate.[58] Thus, the transferee may be able to treat his gain on a sale of the asset as a capital gain, even though such treatment would not have been available to the transferor if he had sold the same asset.

The transferee's holding period, which determines whether gain or loss from a sale of a capital asset is long term or short term, ordinarily starts with his acquisition of the asset. However, in specified instances § 1223 provides that his holding period includes that of the transferor. One such instance is a transfer by gift.[59] Such "tacking" of holding periods may be necessary to allow a donee to qualify for long term capital gains treatment when he sells the property.

¶ 4.03 PROPERTY ACQUIRED FROM A DECEDENT: THE NEW BASIS

The most important instance in estate planning in which property has a different basis in the hands of a transferee than that which it had in the

---

56. The donee's basis will be increased by a portion of any gift tax paid on the transfer which is attributable to the excess of fair market value over the donor's basis—here, $80,000. See § 1015(d).

57. The value of the property for gift tax purposes is not affected by the donor's basis. The general rule is that such value is "the price at which such property would change hands between a willing buyer and a willing seller * * * ." Reg. § 25.2512-1. A buyer would have no reason to offer a lower price because of the seller's low basis for the property.

58. See, e.g., Florence H. Ehrman v. Commissioner, 120 F.2d 607, 41-2 USTC ¶ 9537 (9th Cir. 1941), cert. denied 314 U.S. 668 (1941).

59. See § 1223(2).

hands of the transferor is property acquired from a decedent.   Under § 1014, property included in a decedent's gross estate generally has a basis in the recipient's hands equal to its value at the decedent's death (or on the alternate valuation date, if the executor elected to use that date for estate tax purposes).   The new basis often is referred to as a "stepped up" basis because the value of an asset when its owner dies frequently exceeds his basis.   It may also be "stepped down" if an asset has declined in value. A stepped down basis is not seen as often, however, because:

(1) the value of many assets has been pushed up by inflation and other causes;

(2) property owners have a tax incentive to realize losses while they are living by selling assets which have gone down in value. A new "stepped down" basis eliminates any deductible loss for such decline if the asset is retained until the owner dies; and

(3) property owners have a tax incentive not to realize gains before they die because gain that remains unrealized during the owner's life is forever free of income tax.

The new basis applies to the interest of a surviving spouse in community property held with the decedent,[60] even though the survivor's interest is *not* included in the decedent's gross estate.

For a time, following enactment of the Tax Reform Act of 1976, it appeared that the application of § 1014 to property received from decedents would be substantially restricted.   That Act added § 1023, which provided in many instances for a carryover of the decedent's basis, with various adjustments, for recipients of property of decedents dying after 1976.   The Revenue Act of 1978 postponed the effective date of the new provision, so that § 1023 would apply only to decedents dying after 1979.[61]   There was a great deal of dissatisfaction with carryover basis, and § 1023 was repealed retroactively by the Crude Oil Windfall Profit Tax Act of 1980.[62]   For decedents dying after 1976 and before November 7, 1978, the Windfall Profit Tax Act authorized an election by the executor to apply carryover basis determined in accordance with the repealed provision instead of in accordance with the new basis under § 1014.[63]

[1] Assets Denied New Basis

Section 425 of the Economic Recovery Tax Act of 1981 added § 1014(e) to the Code to make the new basis inapplicable to certain property which had appreciated at the time it was acquired by the decedent.   If the property was acquired by gift within one year of his death, and the property (or the proceeds of its sale) passes back to the donor (or the donor's spouse), its basis in the hands of the recipient is that of the decedent immediately before his death.

The purpose of the new provision is to prevent the use of gifts to dying donees for the purposes of obtaining a stepped-up basis in the hands of the donor or his spouse.   For example, assume that a wife gives property to her husband with a fair market value of $100,000 and a basis of $5,000 in

---

60. § 1014(b)(6), discussed at ¶ 18.03[1] infra.

61. Pub.L. 95–600, § 702(c)(1).

62. Pub.L. 96–223, § 401.

63. Pub.L. 96–223, § 401(d).   The election had to be made by July 31, 1980.

her hands and the husband dies within one year of the gift, bequeathing the property to his wife. Under the new provision, the wife's basis for the property will not be stepped up to $100,000, even though it is includible in her husband's gross estate.

The new provision has greatest significance for transfers between spouses, because of the unlimited marital deduction for gift and estate tax purposes. However, federal gift and estate taxes are no deterrent for transfers between individuals who are not married to each other, if each of them has an unused unified credit that is large enough to cover any anticipated gift or estate taxes. For such individuals § 1014(e) also will be important.

The new basis under 1014 does not apply to two other categories of assets included in the gross estate: annuities [64] and property representing income in respect of a decedent.[65] It also does not apply to those estate beneficiaries who receive property in satisfaction of cash bequests and therefore are treated, in effect, as purchasers with a cost basis equal to the amount of the bequest satisfied.[66] For example, if the executor satisfies a $10,000 legacy by delivering property worth that amount when it is delivered but having a value of $6,000 when the decedent died (the applicable valuation date), the legatee's basis is $10,000 and the estate realizes a gain of $4,000.

[2] Value Used to Determine New Basis

The income tax basis of an asset received from a decedent is deemed to be its value for estate tax purposes.[67] This presumption may be rebutted by the taxpayer, if he is not estopped to do so by his previous actions or statements, with clear and convincing evidence that the estate tax value was incorrect.[68] Thus, the executor's decisions in valuing assets and in determining whether to elect the alternate valuation date affect the income tax basis of estate beneficiaries.[69]

The alternate valuation date for estate tax purposes is six months after the decedent's death, except for property "distributed, sold, exchanged, or otherwise disposed of" within the six-month period.[70] Such property is valued as of the date of its disposition.[71] If the alternate valuation date is elected, an interest or estate whose value is "affected by mere lapse of

---

64. § 1014(b)(9)(A).

65. § 1014(c).

66. See Reg. § 1.1014–4(a)(3); see note 97 infra. In this situation, the estate gets a new basis and realizes gain only to the extent of post-death appreciation.

67. See Reg. § 1.1014–3(a).

68. Rev.Rul. 54–97, 1954–1 CB 113.

69. Some beneficiaries are treated, in effect, as purchasers and thus acquire a new basis for the estate assets they receive without regard to the value of the assets at the decedent's death. See note 66 supra.

In Estate of William W. Smith v. Commissioner, 77 T.C.No. 26 (1981), a widow sought to intervene in Tax Court proceedings initiated by the administrator of an estate, seeking a redetermination of a deficiency in estate tax because of alleged overvaluation of stock owned by the estate. The widow, who was entitled to a share of the proceeds of sale of the stock, contended that neither the Commissioner nor the administrator had any substantial interest in advocating her interest in securing a high valuation for the stock so as to minimize the income tax on gain on its sale. Her motion to intervene was denied.

70. § 2032(a)(2).

71. § 2032(a)(1).

time," such as a remainder, is valued as of the date of death, with adjustment for any difference in value, as of the alternate date, that is not due to mere lapse of time.[72]   For example, if the remainder is in a farm and the value of the farm changes during the period between the date of death and the alternate valuation date, an adjustment would be made in the date-of-death value to reflect the change in the value of the farm.

[3] Lifetime Transfers Includible in the Gross Estate

Property transferred during life may be included in the transferor's gross estate because he retained certain interests in or powers over the transferred property.[73]   Inclusion similarly is required if he transferred within three years of his death an interest or power which would have required inclusion of the property if the interest or power had been retained until he died, unless he received full consideration for the transfer.[74]   The basis determined under § 1014 applies to such property unless the transferee disposes of it before the transferor's death.[75]   For example, if land with a basis and fair market value of $100,000 is given to a donee and the donor retains the income from the land for his life, the land is included in his estate under § 2036 and its basis is adjusted to the fair market value at the date of death unless the donee has disposed of it.   Thus, if the land is worth $150,000 when the donor dies, the donee's basis will be increased to $150,000. On the other hand, if the donee had sold the land for $150,000 before the donor died, the donee would have realized a gain of $150,000, less his share of the donor's basis, and would get no benefit from § 1014.

The Regulations recognize an exception to this rule for gifts in trust, if the trust is required to be included in the donor's gross estate.   In that case, if the trustee sells the property given, what is included in the donor's estate is the fair market value of the trust property on the date of the donor's death (or alternate valuation date), rather than the property originally transferred in trust.   Thus, the trust will obtain a new basis for property representing a reinvestment of proceeds of sales of property given to the trust.[76]

[4] Uniform Basis Rule

The uniform basis rule provides that the basis of property acquired from a decedent is the same for every person possessing or enjoying the property.[77]   This rule determines the basis of assets included in a decedent's gross estate and also determines the basis of a life interest, remainder

---

72.   § 2032(a)(3); Reg. § 20.2032–1(f).

73.   §§ 2036–2038, 2041, 2042.

74.   See § 2035(d), added by § 424 of the Economic Recovery Tax Act of 1981, applicable to estates of decedents dying after 1981.   Previously, gifts within three years of the donor's death were includible in his taxable estate under the general rule of § 2035(a), unless the gift was not required to be reported on a gift tax return.   The exclusion from the taxable estate of gifts not reportable on a gift tax return is con-

tinued under the revised version of § 2035, unless the reason such reporting was not required is that the gift qualified for the gift tax marital deduction.   See § 2035(b)(2). In that case, the gift is includible if the decedent retained the requisite interest or power.

75.   Reg. § 1.1014–3(d).

76.   Id.

77.   Reg. § 1.1014–4(a).

interest, or other interest in property. For example, if a decedent (*D*) devises Blackacre, a piece of improved real estate worth $1 million on the date of *D*'s death, to *T* as trustee to pay the income to *L* for life, remainder on *L*'s death to *R* and his heirs, it may be necessary to determine both *T*'s basis in Blackacre and the bases of *L* and *R* in their respective interests in the trust. *T*'s basis is relevant in calculating depreciation on improvements to Blackacre and gain or loss on a sale of the property. The bases of *L* and *R* are relevant in determining the tax consequences of a sale of their respective interests in the trust. Such a sale has no effect on *T*'s basis in the property,[78] which continues to be determined under the uniform basis rule.

Under the uniform basis rule, *T*'s basis in Blackacre is controlled by its value as of *D*'s death (or on the alternate valuation date, if elected). The bases of *L* and *R* are the portions of *T*'s basis in the trust assets that are assignable to their respective interests, if both *L* and *R* transfer their interests in a single transaction.[79] Otherwise, no part of *T*'s basis is allocated to *L* for purposes of determining gain or loss on a disposition of his interest.[80]

Although the holder of a life, term, or income interest sold separately is denied any deduction for basis under § 1014 (or under § 1015 if the interest was acquired by gift), such sales may sometimes be a useful tool of estate planning, for four reasons: (1) The proceeds ordinarily will qualify for capital gain treatment; [81] (2) If the interest is acquired by bequest or devise, gain is treated as long-term without regard to the actual period the holder has held the interest; [82] (3) The purchaser will be entitled to an amortization deduction for the price paid,[83] and (4) the seller may be entitled to report the sale on the installment basis [84] or as a private annuity transaction,[85] thus deferring taxation of the gain.

---

78. Id.

79. Reg. § 1.1014–5(a).

80. See § 1001(e). As the provision states that the portion of basis of such interest shall be disregarded, it does not appear that it would be allocated to *R* if he sold his interest separately.

81. See, e.g., Beulah E. McAllister v. Commissioner, 157 F.2d 235, 46–2 USTC ¶ 9337 (2d Cir. 1946), cert. denied 330 U.S. 826, accepted in Rev.Rul. 72–243, 1972–1 CB 233. But see May T. Hrobon, 41 T.C. 476 (1964), in which a "sale" of an income interest by taxpayer in return for the purchaser's promise to pay her 60 percent of the net annual distributions of the trust was treated as merely an assignment of income, leaving her taxable on that portion of the trust income.

82. See § 1223(11).

83. § 273, denying an amortization deduction to the holder of "a life or terminable interest acquired by gift, bequest or inheritance," is inapplicable to a purchased interest. See Laird Bell v. Harrison, 212 F.2d 253, 54–1

USTC ¶ 9351 (7th Cir. 1954), accepted in Rev.Rul. 62–132, 1962–2 CB 73.

84. § 453. Installment reporting generally is not available on a sale of depreciable property to the seller's spouse or to an "80-percent owned entity," as defined. See § 453(g). The entities referred to are corporations, partnerships, and certain trusts. See § 453(g)(2). For a discussion of the installment basis for reporting gain, see ¶ 8.04[1] infra.

85. See Gladys C. Evans, 30 T.C. 798 (1958), acq. 1958–2 CB 5. In the *Evans* case, the seller was motivated by advice that retention of her life estate would require inclusion of the trust property in her gross estate. Even with such motivation, a sale of a life estate for annuity payments might be denied judicial recognition under an "economic reality" test. See ¶ 4.01[2][b] supra.

See also Rev.Rul. 79–94, 1979–1 CB 296, in which a retained right to income was transferred to the grantor's children in return for their agreement to make annuity payments equal to the trust income but not less than a specified amount, which was less than such income each year from the creation of the trust until the grantor's death.

For purposes of the uniform basis rule, "there is a common acquisition date for all titles to property acquired from a decedent within the meaning of section 1014 * * * ." [86] Thus, the actual date on which distribution is made to a legatee is irrelevant; value as of the date of death (or alternate valuation date) is controlling for purposes of the section.

[5] Use of Short Sales

In the case of a security for which a short sale is feasible, such a sale "against the box" (of stock already owned) may shift the risk of a decline in price [87] to the purchaser without loss of the new basis under § 1014.   In a short sale, the seller delivers borrowed stock, for example, rather than stock he already owns when the sale is made.   If the price declines, he can buy shares to repay the borrowing for less than the amount received from the short sale, and the difference is his profit.   If the price goes up, so that it costs him more to buy shares to repay the borrowing than the amount he received when he sold short, he will realize a loss.   But if the seller already owns as many shares as he sold short, subsequent changes in the price of the stock will not affect him.   Economically, he no longer has a position in the stock.   Any change in its price will affect the value of the shares he owns and of the shares he owes (and must eventually repay) in equal, offsetting amounts.

The reason for making a short sale, rather than a regular sale of the stock, is to retain ownership until the client's death.   At that time, his shares will have a new basis for gain under § 1014.   The Regulations under § 1233 treat a short sale as completed for income tax purposes only when stock is delivered to the lender to pay off the loan,[88] although § 1233 does prevent the use of this principle in various situations to convert short-term gains into long-term gains (or to convert long-term losses into short-term losses).   It appears that the suggested procedure would therefore be effective to shift taxability of the gain on the short sale from the decedent to the beneficiary who receives the stock from the client's estate and who would benefit from the new basis provided in § 1014.[89]   Of course the feasibility of this procedure depends upon how long the client lives after the sale and what costs are incurred in borrowing the stock sold short.   Normal brokerage procedures may require a short seller to deposit with the lender an amount equal to the proceeds of the short sale.   Thus he loses the use of the deposit, as well as being required to pay over to the lender any dividends paid on the borrowed stock.

It should be noted, however, that similar use of short sales to avoid the § 1091 "wash sales" provision, which disallows certain losses realized on a

The trust was held to be includible in the grantor's estate under § 2036(a) because of her retention of the right to income for her life.

86. Reg. § 1.1014–4(a)(2).

87. Purchase of a "put" option, which permits the option holder to sell stock at a set price during a specified time, would provide similar protection against price declines. However, the practical usefulness of puts for this purpose is limited.   Those publicly traded have a relatively limited maximum life.   And the cost of acquisition of a put at a "striking" or exercise price close to the current market is likely to be substantial.

88. See Reg. § 1.1233–1(a).

89. Rev. Rul. 73–523, 1973–2 CB 307, confirms that the short sale is consummated only when the sale is covered by delivery of the stock after the death of the decedent and that the stock delivered receives a new date of death or alternate valuation date basis as a result of the decedent's death.

sale if the same security is purchased by the seller within thirty days of the sale, has been barred by Reg. § 1.1091–1(g). These regulations were amended in response to William P. Doyle v. Commissioner,[90] in which the taxpayer purchased and sold short an equal number of shares of stock, using shares that he owned previously as collateral in the margin account with his broker. More than thirty days later, he instructed his broker to deliver the stock held as collateral to close the short sale. The taxpayer was allowed to deduct a loss on the transaction.

It is possible that other taxpayers may enjoy a similar success in using short sales to avoid a taxable realization of gain, but that course could be barred by an amendment of the regulations similar to the Commissioner's response to Doyle. There often is a premium in tax matters on being among the first to utilize any given avenue of relief. In Doyle, however, all that was required was the closing of the short sale after thirty days; a taxpayer who seeks to use a short sale to avoid realization during life must die in order to complete his use of this technique.

¶ 4.04 PROPERTY ACQUIRED BY GIFT

Unlike property acquired from a decedent, property acquired by gift generally has the same basis in the hands of the transferee that it had in the hands of the transferor,[91] increased (but not above fair market value) by a portion of any gift tax paid on the transfer that is attributable to the net appreciation in value of the gift (i.e., the excess of fair market value over the donor's adjusted basis).[92] For example, if the donor's adjusted basis when the gift was made was $10, the fair market value $40, and the gift tax attributable to the net appreciation of $30 was $5, the donee's basis would be the donor's basis plus the gift tax, or $15.

For purposes of loss, however, the donee's basis is limited to the fair market value of the property when the gift was made.[93] Thus, if the donor's adjusted basis at that time was $40 and the fair market value was $10, a sale by the donee for a price of $10 or $40, or any amount between the two, will give rise to neither a gain nor a loss.

The uniform basis rule discussed in connection with property received from a decedent also applies to property transferred by gift, with the donor's adjusted basis substituted for the value at the decedent's death.[94]

¶ 4.05 PROPERTY TRANSFERRED IN TRUST

The basis of property transferred in trust as a gift is governed by § 1015(a), discussed at ¶ 4.04. Transfers in trust that are not gifts come under § 1015(b). The general rule applicable to transfers without consideration—for example, a transfer to a trust revocable by the grantor—is that the basis of the trustee is that of the grantor. If consideration is received by the grantor, so that the transfer is in whole or in part a sale

---

90. 286 F.2d 654, 61–1 USTC ¶ 9237 (7th Cir. 1961).

rather than being limited by § 1015(d)(6) to the tax on net appreciation.

91. § 1015(a).

92. § 1015(d). For gifts made before 1977, the increase is for the entire gift tax paid,

93. § 1015(a).

94. See Reg. § 1.1015–1(b).

or exchange, the trustee's basis is that of the grantor, increased by any gain recognized on the transfer and decreased by any loss.

For example, if a trust grantor owns stock with a basis of $10 and sells it to an irrevocable trust for $30, he will recognize a gain of $20 on the sale. The basis of the trustee, therefore, is $30.

¶ 4.06 PROPERTY TRANSFERRED AS PART GIFT, PART SALE

Property acquired in a transfer that is part gift and part sale has a basis in the hands of the transferee equal to the amount paid or to the adjusted basis of the transferor, whichever is greater, increased by the transferor's gift tax attributable to the appreciation of such property over his basis.[95] For example, assume that a father's basis for property is $10 and he sells the property to his son for $15 when its fair market value is $40, incurring a gift tax of $5 on the difference between the value and the selling price. The son's basis is $20, the sum of the price he paid and the gift tax on the appreciation at the time of the sale. If the selling price had been $5 or any amount less than $10, the son's basis would have been the same as his father's ($10) increased by so much of the gift tax as is allocable to the $30 difference between the basis of $10 and the fair market value of $40.

¶ 4.07 PROPERTY DISTRIBUTED TO TRUST AND ESTATE BENEFICIARIES

A beneficiary's basis for property distributed by a trustee or personal representative of an estate may be determined in one or more of three different ways, depending upon the circumstances:

(1) If no part of the distribution is includible in income by the beneficiary and it is not in satisfaction of a cash legacy or other dollar obligation of the estate or trust, the general uniform basis rule applies.[96] The beneficiary's basis is the same as that of the trust or estate.

(2) If the distribution is in satisfaction of a cash legacy or other dollar obligation, the beneficiary has, in effect, purchased the distributed property by surrendering the claim that it satisfies. His basis is cost, without regard to the basis of the estate or trust.[97]

(3) If the distribution carries out "distributable net income" (DNI) of the estate or trust and thus is includible in income by the beneficiary, the basis of the trust or estate is adjusted in the manner described below.

Regulations Section 1.661(a)–2(f)(3) provides that the basis of property distributed in kind "is its fair market value at the time it was paid, credited, or required to be distributed, to the extent such value is included in the gross income of the beneficiary." The amount so included is determined by the beneficiary's share of the "distributable net income" (DNI)[98] of the

95. See Reg. § 1.1015-4(a).

96. See Reg. § 1.661(a)–2(f)(3), second sentence.

97. See Commissioner v. John H. Brinckerhoff, 168 F.2d 436, 48–1 USTC ¶ 9296 (2d Cir. 1948); Rev.Rul. 67–74, 1967–1 CB 194.

98. DNI is defined in § 643(a). For a discussion, see ¶ 15.05, infra.

trust or estate. DNI is a statutory measuring rod that limits both the amount of the deduction of the trust or estate for distributions to beneficiaries and the amounts includible in income by them. To the extent that property distributed in kind is not so included, the uniform basis rules of §§ 1014 and 1015 control.

If a beneficiary receives distributions of cash and property that together exceed his share of the DNI of the trust or estate, the Regulations allocate the DNI to the cash distribution first and "normally" treat only the DNI in excess thereof as requiring inclusion of property in income. In effect, the cash distribution absorbs an equivalent amount of DNI, so that it does not increase the basis of property distributed.

The resulting change in basis of distributed property from its basis in the hands of the fiduciary may be either up or down, depending upon whether such basis is lower or higher than the fair market value at the time of distribution.[99] Thus, it usually is undesirable for a fiduciary to distribute property in kind if its basis exceeds fair market value, and the property will be included in income by the beneficiary. The result will be a reduction in basis, so that the loss in value of the property will never be deductible. More favorable results from a tax standpoint could have been achieved if the fiduciary had sold the property, realizing a deductible loss, and distributed the cash.

* * *

REVENUE RULING 64–314
1964–2 CB 167

* * *

In accordance with the terms of the will of a decedent, who died in November 1960, a testamentary trust was established for named beneficiaries out of the residue of his estate. The estate terminated in 1962, and a final return, on Form 1041, U. S. Fiduciary Income Tax Return (For Estates and Trusts), was filed for the last taxable year of the estate reporting long term capital gain of $3x$ dollars realized from the sale of securities by the executor. Since the gain was realized in the year the adminstration of the estate was terminated, it was included in the distributable net income of the estate and gross income of the trust.

During the year in which the administration of the estate was completed, the trust required by the terms of the will was created and received the following property (values expressed in x dollars) from the estate:

Property	Basis to estate	Value at date of distribution
Real estate	25.0	25.0
Bond	1.0	1.1
A company stock	7.0	8.4
B company stock	10.0	9.0
C company stock	4.0	6.5
Cash	1.0	1.0
Total	48.0	51.0

99. See Rev. Rul. 64–314, infra.

A trust created under a decedent's will is a beneficiary of the decedent's estate (sec. 1.643(c)–1 of the Income Tax Regulations). The testamentary trust in this case was, therefore, a beneficiary of the estate for the purposes of sections 661 and 662 of the Internal Revenue Code of 1954.

Section 1.661(a)–2(f) of the regulations provides:

> If property is paid, credited, or required to be distributed in kind— * * * (3) The basis of the property in the hands of the beneficiary is its fair market value at the time it was paid, credited, or required to be distributed, to the extent such value is included in the gross income of the beneficiary. To the extent that the value of property distributed in kind is not included in the gross income of the beneficiary, its basis in the hands of the beneficiary is governed by the rules in sections 1014 and 1015 and the regulations thereunder. For this purpose, if the total value of cash and property distributed, credited, or required to be distributed in kind to a beneficiary in any taxable year exceeds the amount includible in his gross income for that year, the value of the property other than cash is normally considered as includible in his gross income only to the extent that the amount includible exceeds the cash paid, credited, or required to be distributed to the beneficiary in that year. Further, to the extent that the value of different items of property other than cash is includible in the gross income of a beneficiary in accordance with the proceding sentence, a pro rata portion of the total value of each item of property distributed, credited, or required to be distributed is normally considered as includible in the beneficiary's gross income.

Under the provisions of section 662(a) of the Code, and of section 1.662(a)–1 of the regulations, the extent to which the total value of cash and property distributed, credited or required to be distributed in kind is to be included in the gross income of the beneficiary is limited by the distributable net income of the estate or trust, as defined in section 643 of the Code and the applicable regulations thereunder.

In the application of the regulations quoted above, under circumstances where the amount includible in the beneficiary's (the trust's) gross income is $3x$ dollars and the amount which constitutes cash is $1x$ dollars, then the difference ($2x$ dollars) is the amount or portion of the property, at fair market value at the time of distribution, deemed to be included in the gross income of the trust. This portion of the distributed property takes, under the regulation, a basis in the beneficiary's hands equivalent to its fair market value, namely $2x$ dollars. A pro rata portion of each item distributed is considered as having been included in income at its fair market value. Therefore, if the fair market value of the property at the time of distribution differs from the uniform basis of the property in the hands of the estate, the beneficiary's basis will be the uniform basis adjusted (upward or downward) to reflect the difference between the uniform basis and the fair market value of that portion of the property deemed included in the gross income of the beneficiary.

In determining how much of the difference between the fair market value at the date of distribution and the uniform basis (adjusted to date of distribution) of property included in the beneficiary's gross income is to be allocated to, and will constitute an additional adjustment to, the uniform basis of the various items of property distributed, the adjustment to each item of property deemed included in part in the gross income of the beneficiary may be determined by multiplying the unrealized appreciation or depreciation in value of such item (measured from the uniform basis (adjusted to date of distribution)) by a fraction of which the amount (other than cash) includible in the gross income of the beneficiary is the numerator, and the total fair market value of the total property distributed to the beneficiary within the taxable year is the denominator. The common fraction may, of course, be reduced to a decimal fraction or factor (carried to a sufficient number of places to secure reasonable accuracy) which will serve the same purpose.

Using the values listed for the properties mentioned above, the applicable fraction would have a numerator of $2x$ dollars (distributable net income of $3x$ dollars less cash distributed of $1x$ dollars) and a denominator of $50x$ dollars (valuation at date of distribution of the property other than cash). The equivalent factor is .04.

Expressed in x dollars, the adjustments, and the adjusted basis in the hands of the trustee, of the properties distributed by the estate would be as follows:

Property	Unrealized appreciation or depreciation	Multiplied by .04	Adjusted basis
Real estate	0.0	0.000	25.000
Bond	.1	.004	1.004
A company stock	1.4	.056	7.056
B company stock	(1.0)	(.040)	9.960
C company stock	2.5	.100	4.100
Cash	0.0	.000	1.000
Total	3.0	.120	48.120

QUESTIONS

1. In the case dealt with by Revenue Ruling 64–314, how could the executor have made distributions in the manner which would produce more favorable income tax consequences for the trust under the decedent's will?

2. Under what circumstances may the trustee under a decedent's will be authorized to make distributions which will result in favorable adjustment of basis for the distributees?

3. Assume that the trustee in Revenue Ruling 64–314 had the requisite authority, that the values of the assets received from the decedent's executor remain unchanged, and that the trust's distributable net income for a given year was 8.0. Which item should be distributed in order to achieve the optimum consequences from a basis standpoint?

¶ 4.08   BASIS AFTER TRANSFER SUBJECT TO GENERATION-SKIPPING TRANSFER TAX

Section 2614 seeks to harmonize basis after a transfer subject to the generation-skipping transfer tax (GST)[100] with the basis rules for owned assets discussed above. Thus, a transfer subject to GST which occurs before the death of the deemed transferor results in a basis increase (up to fair market value) for the portion of GST attributable to the excess of the fair market value of the property over its basis, as in gifts of owned assets. A GST transfer at or after the death of the deemed transferor results in a new basis, as in other transfers by a decedent. The section refers to a new basis under either § 1014(a) or subsequently repealed § 1023, depending upon the date of the transfer.

Section 2614 was not amended by the Crude Oil Windfall Profit Tax Act of 1980, which repealed the carryover basis provisions of § 1023 and made § 1014 generally applicable in determining the basis of property received from decedents.[101] Presumably, this means that a GST transfer at or after the death of the deemed transferor will result in a new basis similar to that provided for owned assets, in the manner set forth in § 1014, and the reference to repealed § 1023 will be disregarded. Until clarified by legislation or regulations, however, the matter is not free from doubt.

---

100. The generation-skipping transfer tax is discussed in chapter 13.

101. Pub.L. 96–223, § 401.

Chapter 5

ESTATE TAX ASPECTS

The three federal wealth transfer taxes—the estate tax, gift tax, and generation-skipping transfer tax—are closely related to each other. The gift tax applies to lifetime transfers. The estate tax is based on the size of a decedent's taxable estate at death. The generation-skipping transfer tax applies to certain terminations of an interest in or power over wealth (or to distributions, which are similar in effect to termination of an interest).

Thus all three are based on changes in ownership of wealth, or in enjoyment of or control over wealth. A great deal of estate planning is directed toward determining which tax will apply to the client's wealth, and at what time.

The estate tax is discussed here, in a Part dealing with Lifetime Arrangements, because a major purpose of such arrangements often is to transfer property in such a way that it is not included in the transferor's gross estate when he dies. However, a description of the tax is in order first.

¶ 5.01 THE FEDERAL ESTATE TAX

The federal estate tax is imposed on the taxable estate of a decedent [1], which is defined to include certain transfers made during life [2] as well as property owned at death.[3] Other provisions require inclusion of certain annuities,[4] joint interests in property,[5] property over which the decedent had a general power of appointment,[6] insurance on the life of the decedent if either the policy is payable to the decedent's executor [7] or the decedent possessed incidents of ownership with respect to it,[8] and certain property for which a marital deduction was previously allowed.[9]

Deductions are allowed for certain transfers to a charity [10] or to the spouse of the decedent,[11] as well as for debts,[12] claims,[13] and administration expenses.[14] An exclusion is provided for certain employee death benefits [15] and individual retirement arrangements.[16]

Various credits against the tax are allowed. The most important is the unified credit [17] against gift and estate taxes. For estates of decedents

1. § 2001(a).

2. § 2035–38.

3. § 2033.

4. § 2039.

5. § 2040.

6. § 2041.

7. § 2042(1).

8. § 2042(2).

9. § 2044, added by § 403(d)(3)(A)(i) of the Economic Recovery Tax Act of 1981.

10. § 2055.

11. § 2056.

12. § 2053(a)(4).

13. § 2053(a)(3).

14. § 2053(a)(2).

15. § 2039(c), (d).

16. § 2039(e).

17. § 2505 (gift tax); § 2010 (estate tax).

dying in 1982, the credit is $62,800, equivalent to an exemption (applied against the bottom estate tax brackets) of $225,000. The credit (and equivalent exemption) increase annually for decedents dying after 1982, as follows:

Decedents dying in	Credit	Equivalent Exemption
1983	$ 79,300	$275,000
1984	96,300	325,000
1985	121,800	400,000
1986	155,800	500,000
1987	192,800	600,000
(and thereafter)		

Other credits are allowed for gift taxes on transfers required to be included in the taxable estate [18] and for all or part of the estate taxes paid on property transferred to the decedent by someone who died within 10 years before, or within 2 years after, the death of the decedent.[19] A limited credit also is allowed for certain state death taxes.[20]

The taxable estate is valued at the date of death [21] or, if the executor so elects, on the alternative valuation date, which is six months later except in the case of property sold or distributed during the six month period.[23] For such property, the value on the date of sale or distribution is used.[24]

The Regulations provide elaborate rules to determine when property is "distributed" for this purpose after the death of a decedent.[25] Such distribution may be made "either by the executor, or by a trustee of property included in the gross estate under sections 2035 through 2038, or section 2041." [26] The alternative valuation is available only if the gross estate is large enough to require a return to be filed,[27] and if it is filed on time.[28]

¶ 5.02 ARRANGEMENTS TO SAVE ESTATE TAXES

Ninety–eight percent of the adult population manages to avoid estate taxes altogether, often by one of two tax-saving techniques which may be used in most cases without formal professional advice: (1) they do not acquire enough wealth to leave a taxable estate; or (2) they spend whatever wealth they get their hands on. Spending for one's own gratification has been described as the ultimate form of wealth transfer tax avoidance.

Professional advice often is useful in helping a client, or his beneficiary, to avoid acquiring a taxable estate. Sophisticated techniques may be used

18. § 2012.

19. § 2013. The "two years after" provision is relevant in gifts made less than three years before the donor's death to a donee who predeceases him by less than two years, if the gift is includible in the donor's estate because of a retained interest or power. See § 2035(d)(2), added by § 424(a) of the Economic Recovery Tax Act of 1981, effective for estates of decedents dying after 1981.

20. § 2011.

21. § 2031(a).

23. § 2032.

24. § 2032(a)(1).

25. See Reg. § 20.2032–1(c).

26. See Reg. § 20.2032–1(c)(2). Rules are provided to deal with sales of such includible property. See Reg. 20.2032–1(c)(3).

27. See Reg. § 20.2032–1(b).

28. § 2032(c).

to allow either one of them to control or enjoy wealth without having the kind of interest in it which will cause it to be included in his taxable estate when he dies. An important goal of estate planning for a client is to protect the tax positions of his beneficiaries in these ways, a topic to be explored in Part III.

For clients who do accumulate wealth, lifetime arrangements to save estate taxes achieve this goal in three major ways:

(1) Estate freezing;

(2) Estate reduction;

(3) Minimizing asset values for estate tax purposes.

This paragraph will analyze in detail these basic techniques, and ways to carry them out.

One method of avoiding the estate tax which will not be explored here is to arrange to lose United States citizenship. A nonresident alien's gross estate is limited by § 2103 to that part of his gross estate which is "situated in the United States." The applicable rate schedule in § 2101(d) is lower than that provided in § 2001 for citizens and resident aliens. But the most tax-conscious client may balk at pursuing such an unpatriotic avenue of relief. Even if he is willing to do so, his estate will be taxed at the rates applicable to citizens and resident aliens if he dies within ten years after losing his citizenship, if avoidance of income or wealth transfer taxes was a principal purpose of such loss and it did not come within specified exceptions.[29]

[1] Objectives

[a] To Freeze the Estate

The most important single way to minimize the burden of estate taxes during a client's life is "estate freezing"—diverting future increases in wealth to beneficiaries. It is far easier and less expensive in taxes to keep wealth from piling up in a client's hands than to move wealth from the client to his or her beneficiaries. Estate-planning techniques that achieve such diversion include both formal transfers and a variety of informal arrangements to channel wealth to beneficiaries (or trusts for their benefit) instead of the client himself. The latter includes gifts of services, interest-free or low-interest loans, and diversions of business or investment opportunities.[30] Both kinds merit consideration and comparison.

A disposition of the client's entire interest in property means that its full value must be taken into account for gift tax purposes, if the transfer is by gift, or for income tax purposes, if it is sold or exchanged. A less costly but equally effective method of estate freezing is a disposition of an equity interest that gives the transferee the right to all or part of the future growth in value of the property.

For example, a client may own debt obligations or preferred stock, as well as common stock, in the family business. A gift or sale of the common stock by itself will give the transferee the benefit of any future growth in

---

29. See §§ 2107(a), (d).

30. For a discussion of such arrangements, see ¶ 8.01 infra.

value of the business without constituting as large a transfer for gift tax or income tax purposes as would a transfer of all of the client's securities in the business.   If the present capitalization consists only of common stock, a popular estate-planning technique is a recapitalization by which the common stock is exchanged for new issues of common and preferred stock in order to permit retention of preferred when the common shares are disposed of.[31]   Comparable arrangements may be made for family partnerships.[32]

[b] To Reduce the Estate

Moving the client's present wealth to his beneficiaries may appear to be a relatively unpromising avenue for saving estate taxes, in view of the unified credit provisions [33] and common rate schedule [34] for gift and estate taxes.   But the important tax objective that such a transfer serves is to insure against future increases in estate or gift tax rates or reduction in the unified credit.   Until the estate tax provisions of the Economic Recovery Tax Act of 1981 were enacted, the long-range trand had been toward higher estate tax rates, particularly considering the effect of inflation on the purchasing power of money.   Conservative clients may wish to guard against the possibility that the former trend toward higher rates may reappear in the future.   One way to secure a measure of protection from this risk is to make gifts equal to the amounts covered by the unified credit, as it increases annually between 1982 and 1987.[35]   On the other hand, taking advantage of the unified credit and current rates may mean foregoing opportunities to minimize gift and estate taxes by means of gifts in the future.   The present interest exclusion, which exempts from the gift tax [36] gifts to a donee up to $10,000 per year, favors a pattern of small annual gifts over a period of years rather than bunching of transfers to take advantage of current rates.

[c] To Minimize Asset Values for Estate Tax Purposes

Valuation of assets transferred during life is one area in which the taxpayer's position is often more favorable than the Commissioner's.   Assets may be chosen and their transfer timed in a manner designed to reduce gift taxes.   For example, assets expected to increase substantially in value may be transferred before such appreciation occurs.

In addition, a client may take steps during his lifetime that will minimize, for estate tax purposes, the value of assets he retains until death. For example, a client who owns a majority interest in the stock of a close corporation may find that reducing his ownership to a minority interest through lifetime gifts of some of the shares will save estate taxes.   If a majority interest is included in the client's estate at death, the stock may be assigned a higher per-share value because of the element of control that

31. See Cooper, "A Voluntary Tax? New Perspectives on Sophisticated Estate Tax Avoidance," 11 Colum.L.Rev. 161, 171–77 (1977); Ehrlich, "Corporate Recapitalizations as an Estate Planning Business Retention Tool," 34 N.Y.U.Inst.Fed.Tax 1661 (1976).

32. See Cooper, note 31 supra.

33. See §§ 2010, 2505.

34. See §§ 2001(c), 2502(a).

35. See ¶ 5.01 supra.

36. § 2503, as amended by § 441 of the Economic Recovery Tax Act of 1981, applicable to gifts made after 1981.   Prior to amendment, the exclusion was $3,000.   For a discussion, see ¶ 6.03[1][a] infra.

accompanies a majority interest.[37] This may be the case even if the shares pass to two or more beneficiaries, with no one of them receiving a controlling interest.

If what remains at the client's death is only a minority interest, there may be a valuation discount due to the fact that the client did not own a controlling interest.[38] However, the Commissioner may refuse to treat such a division as being effective to secure a minority interest discount. In Letter Ruling 8010017,[39] he denied such a discount for gift tax purposes for simultaneous gifts to each of three family trusts of one-third of the stock of a wholly owned corporation. Similar reasoning could be applied in valuing a minority interest remaining at death as a result of intra-family transfers during life.

[2] Statutory Requirements

Specific Code provisions limit the effectiveness of formal transfers in removing property from the transferor's taxable estate. Transferred property over which he retained or possessed at death specified interests or powers is included,[40] as well as certain transfers made (and all gift taxes paid) within the three years preceding the death of the transferor.[41] In addition, if the transfer is of an annuity or employee benefit [42] or if it is of insurance on the life of the transferor,[43] specific provisions for inclusion of such wealth must be avoided.

However, these estate tax provisions are applied on a relatively formal basis, without as much gloss from judicial interpretation as has been developed in testing the effectiveness of techniques to shift the taxability of income. The emphasis has been on ownership of property interests and possession of legal powers of control over transferred property rather than on fluid principles similar to the assignment of income doctrine, under which even a formal legal transfer of the right to receive income may be insufficient to keep the transferor from being taxed on that income. The Supreme Court has rejected, for estate tax purposes, the concept of substantial ownership,[44] which is embodied in the present statutory rules governing income-

---

37. See Reg. §20.2031–2(f), referring to "the degree of control of the business represented by the block of stock to be valued."

38. See, e.g., Estate of Louis Zaiger, 64 T.C. 927 (1975), acq. 1976–2 CB 3; Estate of Maurice G. Heckscher, 63 T.C. 485 (1975), acq. 1976–2 CB 2. However, if shares were transferred during life but within three years of the donor's death so as to be included in his gross estate under the former version of § 2035, they are treated as one block with the shares owned at death. If that block represents a controlling interest, that factor is taken into account in valuing it. See Rev.Rul. 79–7, 1979–1 CB 294. The principle reflected in the Ruling could be applied as well to transfers includible under §§ 2036–2038.

If a decedent's estate includes a one-half interest in a controlling block of stock held as community property with his surviving spouse, there is a division of authority as to whether the valuation of the stock should reflect a control premium. For a discussion, see ¶ 18.03[2] infra.

39. CCH E&GT ¶ 12,376, Dec. 6, 1979.

40. See §§ 2036–2037, referring to retention of specified interests or powers, and §§ 2038, 2041, and 2042, referring to powers possessed at the transferor's death. For the effect of relinquishment of an interest within the three years preceding his death, see ¶ 5.02[3][b][i] infra.

41. See § 2035(d)(2), discussed at ¶ 5.02[3] infra.

42. § 2039.

43. § 2042.

44. See United States v. Byrum, ¶ 5.02[5][b] infra; Helvering v. Safe Dep. & Trust Co., 316 U.S. 56, 62 S.Ct. 925, 86 L.Ed. 1266, 42–1 USTC ¶ 10,167 (1942). For a discus-

shifting to trusts and trust beneficiaries.[45]   As a result, formal transfers may be more reliable as a means of removing property from a transferor's estate than as a means of shifting the income from that property from the transferor to someone else.

[3] Inclusion of Transfers Made, or Gift Taxes Paid, Within Three Years of the Transferor's Death

Few estate tax provisions can match the complexity of § 2035.   Section 2035(a) states the general rule that transfers within three years of the transferor's death are includible in his gross estate but §§ 2035(b) and (d) proceed to gut it with exceptions.   The first is an exception for "any bona fide sale for an adequate and full consideration in money or money's worth." [46] It is entirely consistent with the obvious purpose of the rule: to prevent depletion of prospective taxable estates by transfers shortly before death. This exception applies to decedents generally.

Other exceptions cover gifts within the annual exclusion (except life insurance) and appreciation in the value of donated property after the gift is made.   The former applies to decedents dying after 1976; the latter to decedents dying after 1981.   Their combined effect is to leave the general rule with only a limited area of operation.

[a] Gifts Covered by Annual Exclusion

For decedents dying after 1976, the general rule does not apply to gifts (other than of life insurance) for which no gift tax return was required,[47] unless the reason no return is required is that the gifts qualified for the gift tax marital deduction.[48]   This means that if all gifts to a given donee in a given year are covered by the present interest exclusion, the gift is not includible in the donor's estate unless the subject matter is life insurance.

[b] Appreciation After Gift Is Made

For decedents dying after 1981, gifts made within three years of the donor's death generally are *not* includible in his gross estate,[49] although taken into account as "adjusted taxable gifts" [49a] in computing the estate tax due.

In two situations, gifts are includible if made within three years of the donor's death:

(1) transfers of interests included under §§ 2036–2038, 2041, or 2042, or which would have been so included if retained by the decedent; [50]

(2) for specified purposes, the three year rule is retained.[51]

Both exceptions merit further analysis.

---

sion, see Stephens, "The *Clifford* Shadow Over the Federal Estate Tax," 4 Ga.L.Rev. 233 (1970).

45.   §§ 671–78.

46.   See § 2035(b)(1).

47.   See § 2035(b)(2).

48.   Such gifts are not required to be reported on a return.   See § 6019(a)(2).

49.   See § 2035(d)(1).

49a.   See § 2001(b).

50.   See § 2035(d)(2).

51.   See § 2035(d)(3).

(i) Retained interest. This exception might be described as creating a "one transfer rule" if it is understood that two or more transfers with respect to the same property may be effective to remove the property from the transferor's estate as long as all are made more than three years before his death.

For example, if a decedent created a trust more than three years before he died, retaining the right to terminate the trust, the trust property is includible in his gross estate under § 2038, unless the retained right was released more than three years before he died (or for full consideration, if it occured within that period). On the other hand, if the decedent created the trust the day he died without retaining any offending interest or power, the transferred property is not includible even though as owner of the property he enjoyed complete control over it until that day.

If the original transfer was not required to be reported in a gift tax return because the present interest exclusion covered all of the donor's gifts to the donee for the year involved, it is within the exception discussed at [a] above. Although the question is debatable, the exception should prevail over the requirement elsewhere in the Code [52] or Regulations [53] that transfers be included under §§ 2036–2038 if the power or interest which would otherwise have required such inclusion was disposed of within the three years preceding death.

For example, assume that less than three years before he died, the decedent created a minor's present interest trust,[54] naming himself trustee. As such, he had the power to terminate the trust. That power, if possessed by him at his death, would require inclusion of the trust property in his gross estate under § 2038(a)(1). If he resigned as trustee the day he died, it should not be includible in his gross estate if the creation of the trust was within the gift tax present interest exclusion and hence not required to be reported on a return. Although § 2035(d)(2) makes the exception in § 2035(d)(1) inapplicable, the creation of the trust is covered by the exception in § 2035(b)(2). This should remove the trust altogether from the operation of the three year rule.

(ii) Three year rule retained for specified purposes. Certain Code provisions offer favorable treatment for estates if specified assets constitute a given percentage of the adjusted gross estate. The three year rule is retained in determining whether an estate qualifies for such favorable treatment with respect to redemption of stock,[55] special use valuation of real estate,[56] and extension of time for payment of the estate tax.[57]

The three year rule also is applied in determining what property is subject to estate tax liens.[58]

[c] Inclusion of Gift Taxes Paid

Even though gifts within the three years preceding the donor's death generally are not includible in his gross estate, all gift taxes paid by the

---

52. See § 2038(a)(1).

53. See Reg. § 20.2035–1(b).

54. For a discussion of such trusts, see ¶ 9.03[2].

55. § 2035(d)(3)(A).

56. § 2035(d)(3)(C).

57. § 2035(d)(3)(D).

58. § 2035(d)(3)(B).

decedent or his estate on any post-1976 gifts made within three years of his death are includible.[59] Inclusion of the gift tax is in no way dependent on inclusion of the gift which caused the tax to be due.

[d] Valuation of Transferred Property

The general valuation rule is that all property included in the gross estate is valued at the time of the decedent's death [60] unless the alternate valuation date is elected.[61] Since a transfer of a retained interest or power within three years of the donor's death generally does not remove the property from his gross estate if the property would otherwise be includible,[62] the general valuation rule applies.[63]

[e] Transfers of Insurance Policies and Payment of Premiums

Gifts of insurance policies on the life of the donor may appear to offer an easy way to reduce the prospective taxable estate of the donor. The value of such a gift for gift tax purposes often is small in relation to the policy proceeds included for estate tax purposes if the insured retains ownership of the policy until he dies. However, a gift of a policy within the three years preceding his death leaves it includible in his estate under § 2035.[64]

Although a sale of the policy may be effective in removing insurance proceeds from the insured's gross estate, such proceeds may then be subject to the transferee-for-value rule. Unless an exception applies, the rule requires the purchaser to include the policy proceeds in income, with a deduction for consideration and premiums paid.[65] This loss of the income tax exemption otherwise applicable to insurance proceeds payable by reason of the death of the insured [66] may outweigh the advantage of removing the policy from the insured's gross estate.

Payment of premiums by the insured on a transferred policy does not cause any part of the policy proceeds to be included in the insured's gross estate, if the policy was not purchased within the three years preceding his

---

59. See § 2035(c).

The Ninth Circuit has allowed a deduction for unpaid state gift taxes on such gifts, even though creditable against state inheritance taxes and includible in determining the federal estate tax credit for such taxes. See Estate of Grace E. Lang v. Commissioner, 613 F.2d 770, 80–1 USTC ¶ 13,340 (9th Cir. 1980). Where the state gift tax had been paid before the decedent died, the Tax Court refused to require inclusion of the amount paid as property owned at death under § 2033, even though it was allowed as a credit against state inheritance taxes. See Estate of George E. P. Gamble, 69 T.C. 942 (1978). But see Rev.Rul. 75–63, 1975–1 CB 294, requiring such inclusion.

60. § 2031(a).

61. § 2032. The alternate valuation date is six months after the date of death except in the case of property sold or distributed during the six-month period. For such property, the value on the date of sale or distribution is used. § 2032(a)(1).

62. § 2035(d)(2).

63. Cf. Rev.Rul. 72–282, 72–1 CB 306, dealing with former 3-year rule.

64. Although § 2035(d)(1), added by § 424 of the Economic Recovery Tax Act of 1981, provides generally that gifts within three years of the donor's death are not includible in the estate of a decedent dying after 1981, § 2035(d)(2) makes the rule inapplicable to a transfer of an interest in property which would have been included under § 2042 "if such interest had been retained by the decedent." Section 2042 requires, inter alia, inclusion of a policy of insurance on the life of the decedent if he "possessed at his death any of the incidents of ownership."

65. § 101(a)(2).

66. § 101(a)(1).

death.[67]   A more ambiguous situation is presented if the beneficiary purchases the policy within the three-year period.   He may pay the premiums with money given to him by the insured.   If the gift is viewed as being money, rather than insurance on the donor's life, the general rules governing transfers included under § 2035 would suggest that the money would not be includible in the insured's estate.[68]   However, if the insured directly paid the premiums on a policy purchased by the beneficiary within the three-year period, the proceeds are includible in his or her estate.[69]

[4] Inclusion of Transfers Because of Retained Beneficial Interests in Transferred Property

Several Code sections require that the value of transferred property be included in the transferor's estate if he has retained an interest in or control over the property.

Section 2036(a)(1) requires such inclusion if the transferor retained income from the property for life.   Section 2037 requires inclusion of certain transfers in which the transferor retained a reversionary interest.   Neither section applies if the transfer was "a bona fide sale for an adequate and full consideration in money or money's worth"—i.e., not a gift.   Both sections require inclusion of transferred property even when the transferor has disposed of the life interest or reversionary interest in the transferred property, if he did so within three years of his death, unless he received adequate and full consideration for the interest.[70]

Section 2038 requires inclusion, *inter alia*, of revocable transfers, under which the decedent had the power to cause the property to be returned to him.   But the section is much broader than that in its scope and covers powers to control the enjoyment of property by others as well.   Its estate-planning implications are discussed in connection with powers to control enjoyment.[71]

The planning implications of §§ 2036(a)(1) and 2037 include:

(1) Avoiding retention of income for life;

(2) Avoiding retention of a reversionary interest, which may cause inclusion of a transfer in the taxable estate; and

(3) Disposing of a retained interest so as to avoid inclusion of the transfer if the decedent dies within three years of such disposition.

[a] Avoiding Retention of Income for Life

After almost five decades in which § 2036(a)(1) and its predecessor provisions have been part of the tax law,[72] well-advised clients who wish to remove transferred property from their taxable estates avoid any explicit retention of rights to income.   The informal or implicit retention of such rights, however, is a continuing problem arising in five major areas:

---

67. See Rev.Rul. 71–497, 1971–2 CB 329.

68. § 2035(d)(1).

69. First Nat'l Bank of Oregon v. United States, 488 F.2d 575, 74–1 USTC ¶ 12,966 (9th Cir. 1973); Detroit Bank & Trust Co. v. United States, 467 F.2d 964, 72–2 USTC ¶ 12,883 (6th Cir. 1972), cert. denied 410 U.S. 929 (1973).

70. See Reg. § 20.2035–1.

71. See ¶ 5.02[5] infra.

72. The original provision was enacted by the Joint Resolution of March 3, 1931, H.R.J. Res. 529, Ch. 454, 71st Cong., 3d Sess., 46 Stat. 1516 (1931).

(1) Use of income to support the transferor's legal dependents;

(2) Use of income to pay the transferor's debts;

(3) Enjoyment of income or possession of transferred property by the transferor, without express provision therefor;

(4) Rights to income arising under state community property laws; and

(5) Recharacterization of purported sales or leases as transfers with a retained interest in income.

ESTATE OF IDA J. PYLE v. COMMISSIONER

United States Court of Appeals, Third Circuit, 1963.
313 F.2d 328, 63–1 USTC ¶ 12,132.

HASTIE, Circuit Judge.

The Tax Court has held that the proceeds of an insurance policy on the life of Wallace Pyle are includible in the gross estate of his widow, Ida Pyle, who has since died, as property which she transferred, reserving a life estate, within the meaning of section 2036 of the 1954 Internal Revenue Code. This ruling resulted in a determination of an estate tax deficiency. The executor of Mrs. Pyle's estate has brought the case here for review.

Mrs. Pyle applied for and obtained a $30,000 insurance policy on her husband's life, payable on his death to her. The policy granted Mrs. Pyle all the rights accorded the "insured" under the policy and she was the named beneficiary. Thus, it is clear that when the policy was issued Mrs. Pyle alone enjoyed the various incidents of ownership, including the rights of borrowing, assignment and cash surrender. She also had the right to change the beneficiary and to elect among settlement alternatives.

At Mrs. Pyle's request, during the life of her husband, a rider was attached to the policy providing that, upon the death of the insured husband, the proceeds would be retained by the company which would pay Mrs. Pyle 3% interest thereon, plus dividends, for the remainer of her life. Thereafter, the earnings, and ultimately the proceeds of the policy, were to be paid to her children. Mrs. Pyle reserved the right to revoke and change this revised method of settlement until the death of her husband, but did not do so. Upon the husband's death, the revised scheme of settlement became irrevocable.

Section 2036 of the 1954 Code requires that there shall be included in the gross estate of a decedent the value of "any interest [in property] * * * of which the decedent has at any time made a transfer * * * under which he has retained for his life * * * the right to income from, the property * * * ." The Tax Court concluded that, in the circumstances outlined above, Mrs. Pyle's action during the lifetime of her husband in changing the disposition to be made of the proceeds of the life insurance policy upon maturity constituted a transfer of property under which she retained a life estate.

Challenging this conclusion, the petitioner argues that it was the death of the insured husband rather than the earlier action of Mrs. Pyle which in legal contemplation effected the transfer of property. The fact that Mrs. Pyle's election as to the disposition of proceeds at maturity was revocable until her husband died and that interests in such proceeds were contingent or inchoate until her husband's death are thought to support this contention.

We think petitioner's argument is unsound.   The only transfer of property with which we are concerned is the transfer of the right to receive proceeds upon maturity.   That transfer could be accomplished only through the exercise of ownership rights created by the terms of the policy and vested exclusively in Mrs. Pyle from the date of issuance until her husband's death.   The fact that the husband's death was the event which caused the policy to mature and made Mrs. Pyle's election as to changes in the disposition of the proceeds irrevocable did not make him a transferor.   For he had no power over the disposition of the proceeds during his lifetime and no interest in them which could pass to another at his death.   An instructive analogy is provided by Goodnow v. United States, Ct.Cl., 1962, 302 F.2d 516, where a wife was held not to have been the transferor of the proceeds of a policy on her husband's life because he was the legal owner of the policy, with a vested right to elect among optional dispositions of the proceeds. As concerns the proceeds, the position of the husband there was essentially the position of the wife here.

Petitioner also points out that some of the premiums on the policy were paid by the husband.   But certainly this gave him no interest in and no power over the disposition to be made of the proceeds upon his death.   That is the only transfer which is relevant here.   There are other cases, notably Estate of Susie C. Haggett, 1950, 14 T.C. 325, acq., 1950–2 Cum.Bull. 2, upon which petitioner relies, in which the original purchase of insurance or an annuity was a transaction constituting a transfer of property which was to become effective in some degree only upon the purchaser's death.   The present case is different because it was neither the original purchase of insurance nor the payment of premiums which in fact or in law accomplished the decisive shifting of the right to proceeds.   Those transactions are simply irrelevant.

Here again, Goodnow v. United States, supra, is helpful.   For in that case the wife paid certain premiums on policies on her husband's life, but the husband was vested with ownership rights in the policies, including control over the disposition of proceeds.   In these circumstances, the wife's payment of premiums did not make her a transferor of any property interest in the policies.

It remains only to consider whether Mrs. Pyle's election of an alternative disposition of the proceeds was such a transaction as amounts to a transfer of property with a retained life estate, within the meaning of section 2036.   Mrs. Pyle was the beneficiary originally named in the policy and as such was entitled to receive the entire proceeds of the policy on her husband's death.   Then, as was her right under the terms of the policy, she caused the dispositive provisions of the policy to be changed so that she would receive only interest on the proceeds during her life, with ownership and enjoyment of this property passing to other designated persons upon her death.   If it had been after maturity that Mrs. Pyle gave up her absolute right to the proceeds of the policy and elected instead to receive income for life with remainder to others, the transaction would clearly have been a transfer of property within section 2036.   Estate of John Joseph Tuohy, Jr., 1950, 14 T.C. 245; Estate of Mabel E. Morton, 1949, 12 T.C. 380.   This case is different only in two respects.   Mrs. Pyle acted while enjoyment of her right to the proceeds was still prospective and contingent upon her husband's death.   Thereafter, so long as her husband lived, she could have revoked her action.   While such circumstances may affect the time when in legal contemplation the transfer is accomplished, they do not make the actor any less a transferor of an interest in property.   *   *   *

*   *   *

The decision of the Tax Court will be affirmed.

[i] Use of Income to Support the Transferor's Legal Dependents. The Regulations treat a decedent as having retained income from transferred property within the meaning of § 2036(a)(1) if that income "is to be applied toward the discharge of a legal obligation of the decedent." [73]   The term "legal obligation" includes an obligation under state law to support a dependent during the decedent's lifetime. [74]   The troublesome question is when income from transferred property "is to be applied" to the discharge of that obligation, thus requiring the property to be included in the decedent's estate.   This question is most likely to arise with respect to trust income, although the scope of the quoted Regulations is not limited to trusts.

When the terms of the trust instrument require use of income for this purpose, the transferred property is includible. [75]   But use therefor in the discretion of a trustee other than the decedent has not been sufficient to cause it to be included in the decedent's estate. [76]   Nor has a dependent's use for his support of income distributed to him been sufficient. [77]

From a planning standpoint, the estate tax consequences of the use of income from transferred property to discharge the transferor's support obligations are less certain than the income tax consequences.   For income tax purposes, a transferor is taxed on trust income only if his or her support obligations, under state laws, are not affected by the dependent's own resources—i.e., only if support is owed regardless of the magnitude of the dependent's wealth. [78]   The estate tax regulations, however, do not contain this limitation.   Thus, it is arguable that if trust income is applied to support someone whom the transferor would be legally obligated to support if that person were indigent, the transferor has retained income for his life within the meaning of § 2036(a)(1) even though such income would not be taxable to the transferor for income tax purposes.

Additional uncertainty arises because § 2036(a)(1) requires inclusion of transfers even though the transferor's retention of income was informal. [79]   Although to date that concept has not been applied to voluntary use of

73.   Reg. § 20.2036–1(b)(2).

74.   Id.

75.   See, e.g., Lynn S. Richards v. Commissioner, 375 F.2d 997, 67–1 USTC ¶ 12,463 (10th Cir. 1967); Estate of Joseph G. Gokey, 72 T.C. 721 (1979).

76.   See e.g., Estate of Abner W. Mitchell, 55 T.C. 576 (1970), acq. 1971–1 CB 2.

77.   See Estate of John H. Scheide, 6 TCM 1271 (1947); Estate of Alexander K. Ses-

soms, 8 TCM 1056 (1949).   See also cases cited in 9.01[9][b] note 117 infra, dealing with income tax consequences of a trust beneficiary's use of income to discharge the grantor's legal obligations.

78.   See ¶ 9.01[9][a].

79.   See ¶ 5.02[4][a][iii].

income by a dependent for his or her own support, it could be contended that such use is encompassed by the reference to income which "is to be applied" for support.

At least two approaches may be followed in dealing with the planning risk present where a trust that the transferor wishes to have excluded from his gross estate includes as a beneficiary someone whom the transferor is legally obligated to support. The first is to include a "support preclusion clause," such as: "Nothing herein contained shall authorize use of trust income or principal to discharge any legal obligation of the grantor hereunder, including an obligation to support or maintain any person." Such a clause is appropriate if the greater concern of the client is to prevent inclusion of the transfer in his estate and if he is willing to forego use of the trust as a source of funds in meeting support obligations.[80]

A second approach is to say nothing about the grantor's support obligations, on the assumption that either the support obligation will terminate during the grantor's life, as his children reach majority, or that the Commissioner will be unsuccessful in seeking to bring within the scope of § 2036(a)(1) a transfer which does not refer to support of dependents. This approach involves greater risks that the transfer will be included but leaves open the possibility that trust income will be available for a dependent's support if it turns out that it is needed for that purpose.

[ii] Use of Income to Pay the Client's Debts and Taxes; Transfers Subject to Liabilities. The estate tax consequences of gifts that require the donee to pay the donor's gift tax ("net gifts") or of a mortgage or lien on the donated property have not been litigated as extensively as have the income tax consequences of such gifts.[81] In Estate of Mary H. Hays v. Commissioner,[82] the decedent had transferred property into trust subject to a mortgage securing notes for which she was personally liable. As trustee she was authorized to use trust income to pay off the notes. Nevertheless, the trust property was not included in her taxable estate. The Fifth Circuit reasoned that the primary liability for the debt was on the decedent as trustee, so that the obligation being discharged was no longer hers individually.[83]

Such reasoning may be wholly consistent with the business realities of mortgaged property, in which the lender is often more concerned with the

---

80. It may be desirable to broaden the clause to preclude use of the trust to discharge support obligations of trustees to keep them from being deemed to possess a general power of appointment for gift tax and estate tax purposes. See Reg. §§ 25.2514–1(c)(1), 20.2041–1(c)(1). A support obligor may also be a beneficiary for purposes of the generation-skipping transfer tax, so that the clause might be further broadened to prohibit use of the trust to discharge support obligations whenever such use would cause the obligor to become a beneficiary for such purposes. For a discussion of the tax, see Chapter 13.

81. For a discussion, see ¶ 6.01[2][c] infra.

82. 181 F.2d 169, 50–1 USTC ¶ 10,762 (5th Cir. 1950).

83. This part of the court's holding has not been overruled or disapproved. Another part, dealing with the estate tax consequences of discretionary powers of the grantor as trustee, is inconsistent with Lober v. United States, ¶ 5.02[5] infra. In *Lober*, the Court's grant of certiorari was based on a conflict between *Estate of Hays* and the Court of Claims decision in Lober v. United States, 108 F.Supp. 731, 52–2 USTC ¶ 10,882 (Ct.Cl.1952). The Supreme Court affirmed the latter.

security than with the borrower's personal liability. At the same time it should be recognized that for transfers of mortgaged property, future payments of the debt to be made by the transferee expose the client to the risk that the *Estate of Hays* rationale will not be followed and that the property will be included in the transferor's estate under § 2036.[84]

It is difficult to apply the reasoning of *Estate of Hays* to the use of trust income to pay the transferor's gift tax under the terms of a "net gift." In this situation, the transferor is the primary obligor [85] and provisions for such use of income would provide a ground for including the transfer in his taxable estate. As soon as the tax has been paid, however, this ground arguably no longer is present.[86] Thus, the risk that the terms of a "net gift" will require inclusion of the transfer in the transferor's estate may exist for only a relatively short period—i.e., until the gift tax has been paid by the transferee.

[iii] Enjoyment of Income or Possession Without Express Agreement. It is clear that an informal agreement that the transferor shall retain the income from or possession of property is as effective as a formal reservation of such rights to require inclusion of the property in the transferor's estate under § 2036(a)(1). What is less clear are the circumstances under which an agreement will be inferred in the classic case: a transfer of residential property that the transferor continues to occupy. The issue commonly arises either after a transfer by a husband to his wife or by a parent to one of his children.

According to Revenue Ruling 70–155,[87] co-occupancy of a residence does not support an inference of an agreement for retained possession by the donor if the spouses are donor and donee but does support such an inference if the donor and donee are not spouses. This is generally consistent with the courts' treatment of this issue, which has made it more difficult for parental transfers than for spousal transfers to remove property from the transferor's estate.[88] The result is that it may be possible to remove the marital home from one spouse's gross estate by a lifetime gift to the other spouse.

---

84. See generally Report of Committee on Income Taxation of Estates and Trusts, "Tax Consequences of Gifts of Encumbered Property in Trust," 8 Real Prop., Prob. & Tr.J. 371, 384 (1973), suggesting "mandatory payment directions to the trustee and * * * provisions assuring that primary liability on the debt shifts from the settlor to the trustee."

85. § 2502(c).

86. Compare Victor W. Krause, 56 T.C. 1242 (1971), reaching a comparable result for trust income tax purposes. For a discussion, see ¶ 9.01[9][c] infra.

87. 1970–1 CB 189.

88. See, e.g., the following cases, in which spousal transfers were not included in the transferor's estate: Estate of Allen D. Gutchess, 46 T.C. 554 (1966), acq. 1967–1 CB 2; Estate of Gordon A. Binkley v. United States, 358 F.2d 639, 66–1 USTC ¶ 12,389 (3d Cir. 1966). But compare Estate of Francis M. Hendry, 62 T.C. 861 (1974) (agricultural land conveyed by decedent to his wife included because of implied understanding that decedent would continue to control and manage the property and the income therefrom). See also note 92 infra.

89. For decedents dying after 1981, §403(a) of the Economic Recovery Tax Act of 1981 generally removes the limitation on the maximum allowable marital deduction provided by former § 2056(c). But see ¶ 16.01[1] infra as to the effect of state death taxes.

Whether it makes sense to do so is another question.   For example, if the husband owns the marital residence, the estate tax marital deduction may allow him to transfer it free of tax to his wife, anyway, if he dies first.[89] Moreover, the fact that the wife received the residence in a lifetime transfer, rather than on her husband's death, will mean that there will be no new basis for it when he dies.   In addition, a lifetime gift of the residence to her creates the risk, if the couple is divorced or becomes estranged, that the wife will transfer the residence to someone else.

If the husband is willing to assume this risk and the wife in fact is the first to die, a lifetime transfer of the residence may prove to be advantageous from a tax standpoint because of the resulting new basis on her death.   But the practical value of any resulting increase in basis may be minor.   If the husband retains the residence until he dies, its basis will be relevant only if it is used for non-residential purposes and thus qualifies for a depreciation deduction.   And if the husband sells the residence, gain may be avoided by reinvestment of the sale proceeds in another residence.[90]   Absent such reinvestment, $125,000 of the gain can be excluded from income, if he has not previously elected such an exclusion for gain on sale of his principal residence.[91]

Transfers of residential property by parents to their children, followed by rent-free occupancy by the parent, have not fared well under § 2036(a)(1).[92] But in Estate of Roy D. Barlow,[93] the Tax Court held that a parental transfer of a farm to children, with a contemporaneous leaseback from the transferees to the parents at a "fair, customary rental," [94] did not bring the property into the father's estate, under § 2036(a)(1), despite the fact that the rent was not paid in full because of the father's financial difficulties.   However, the Tax Court later described *Barlow* as having "turned upon its special facts" [95] and in addition the court treated the rental as "fair."

[iv] Rights to Income Arising Under State Community Property Laws.   Rights created by state community property laws are relevant to § 2036(a)(1) both in determining who is the transferor [96] and in determining whether an interest has been retained by him or her.   The latter problem arises in the three community property states—Idaho, Louisiana, and Texas—that generally treat income from the separate property of either spouse as community property, unless specified procedures are followed.[97]

The result in those states is that the donor who makes a gift to his spouse arguably has retained an interest in income by operation of law, requiring inclusion of a portion of the transferred property in his taxable estate, although the Commissioner has ruled otherwise as to Texas.[98]

90. See § 1034.

91. See § 121(b)(1), as amended by § 123 of the Economic Recovery Tax Act of 1981.

92. See, e.g., the following cases in which parental tranfers were included in the transferor's estate: Estate of Florence Honigman, 66 T.C. 1080 (1976); Estate of Ethel R. Kerdolff, 57 T.C. 643 (1972); Estate of Emil Linderme, Sr., 52 T.C. 305 (1969). But compare Charles I. Diehl v. United States, 68-1 USTC ¶ 12,506 (W.D.Tenn.1967).

93. 55 T.C. 666 (1971), acq. 1972 CB 1, 3.

94. Id. at 671.

95. Estate of William du Pont, Jr., 63 T.C. 746, 766 n.3 (1975).

96. See ¶ 5.03 infra.

97. See ¶ 6.06[1] infra.

98. See ¶ 6.06[1] note 175, infra.

[v] Recharacterization of Transactions as Transfers With Income Retained. Sometimes transactions that are cast in another form are recharacterized as transfers of property with a retained life interest in income, requiring inclusion of the transferred property in the transferor's gross estate. A recent case in which this occurred is Simon M. Lazarus v. Commissioner,[99] where a trust with initial assets of $1,000 was created. During the same year that the trust was established, the grantors entered into an "Annuity Agreement" with the trustee, under which they transferred stock with a fair market value of $1,575,000 in exchange for the trustee's promise to pay an annuity to them of $75,000 for their joint lives. The actuarial value of the annuity was $864,533—approximately 55% of the value of the transferred property. The Ninth Circuit held that the transaction constituted a gift in trust, with a life estate retained by the grantors, rather than a sale of the stock to the trust.

The most striking taxpayer victory against such an attempt at recharacterization is Fidelity-Philadelphia Trust Co. v. Smith.[100] The decedent's simultaneous purchase of a single premium life insurance policy, which he then gave away, and an annuity, which he retained, was held not to be a transfer retaining a life estate. The court reasoned that two separate property interests were involved, even though it was clear that the insurance company would not have sold the insurance except for the concurrent purchase of the annuity by the insured. This case may have been superseded by § 2039 with respect to insurance-annuity combinations,[101] but for transfers that do not involve such a combination, it stands as a precedent against recharacterization to require inclusion of the value of the transferred property in the transferor's estate under § 2036.

If the Commissioner had prevailed in *Fidelity-Philadelphia Trust*, many common estate-planning techniques would be vulnerable under § 2036. For example, it is not unusual for a taxpayer to retain a right to income from a family corporation in the form of debt instruments or preferred stock and to give to his descendants the common stock, to which will inure the benefit of the future growth of the company.[102] Such a transfer could be viewed as coming within § 2036 if the taxpayer's various interests in the corporation are viewed as a single asset rather than separate property interests.

[b] Avoiding Retention of a Reversionary Interest That Will Require Inclusion of a Transfer in the Transferor's Estate

Often a transferor retains an interest that may cause the property to revert to him or to his estate. Such a reversionary interest may arise under the express terms of the instrument. It also may be implied by operation of law from the fact that the transferor did not dispose of all of the interests in the property that he owned before the transfer was made.

---

99. 513 F.2d 824, 75–1 USTC ¶ 9387 (9th Cir. 1975).

100. 356 U.S. 874, 78 S.Ct. 730, 2 L.Ed.2d 765, 58–1 USTC ¶ 11,761 (1958).

101. See Estate of Lafayette Montgomery v. Commissioner, 458 F.2d 616 n.1, 72–1 USTC

¶ 12,840 at 84,735 n.1 (5th Cir. 1972), cert. denied 409 U.S. 849 (1972).

102. See ¶ 5.02[1][a] infra which outlines the technique in more detail.

[i] Effect of Section 2037.   A reversionary interest, like any other property, is includible in a client's estate if it does not expire as a result of the client's death.   Whether or not it so expires, however, § 2037 may require inclusion of not only the reversionary interest but also the transferred property in which the reversionary interest was retained.   This follows from the fact that § 2037 deals with the situation not at the moment of the transferor's death but at the moment before he dies.   If at that earlier point in time, the transferor's reversionary interest was worth more than 5 percent of the value of the transferred property on the basis of the actuarial rules in the Regulations,[103] § 2037 will apply if there are interests which are subject to the requisite requirement of survival.

The result is to require inclusion in the gross estate of all interests in the tranferred property that are subject to a requirement that the beneficiary survive the transferor in order to obtain "possession or enjoyment of the property   *   *   *   through ownership of such interest.   *   *   *."[104]   Thus, the section makes it highly undesirable to retain a reversionary interest if the transferor wishes to exclude the entire value of the transfer from his taxable estate when he dies.

For purposes of § 2037, a reversionary interest includes not only the possibility that the property may revert to the grantor but also the possibility that it may be subject to a power of disposition by him.   The section applies to interests arising by operation of law [105] as well as by the express language of the instrument.

[ii] Effect of Doctrine of Worthier Title.   In determining whether or not a reversionary interest has been retained, the effect of the Doctrine of Worthier Title [106] must be taken into account.   A majority of states recognize the Doctrine as a rule of construction.   Its effect is to treat what purports to be a remainder in the grantor's heirs or next of kin as in fact creating a reversionary interest in the grantor.[107]   Thus, the Doctrine may cause a transfer to be included under § 2037 even though the grantor purports to dispose of his entire interest in the property.

Example 5.1.   G transfers property in trust to accumulate the income for the life of G, then to L if L survives G, or if not, to G's heirs.

103. See Reg. §20.2037–1(c)(1), (3).   The Commissioner has ruled that the value of the decedent's retained reversionary interest, if it is subject to valuation according to the actuarial rules set forth in Reg. § 20.2031–7, is to be determined solely thereunder and not on the basis of the facts surrounding his death.   Rev. Rul. 66–307, 1966–2 CB 429, last paragraph.   The courts are generally in accord.   See, e.g., Kent Robinson v. United States, 632 F.2d 822, 80–2 USTC ¶ 13,380 (9th Cir. 1980); Estate of Dwight B. Roy, Jr., 54 T.C. 1317 (1970).   For a contrary result requiring consideration of the decedent's actual life expectancy, see William S. Hall v. United States, 353 F.2d 500, 65–2 USTC ¶ 12,359 (7th Cir. 1965).

104. § 2037(a)(1).

105. If the transfer was made before October

8, 1949, the section is applicable only if the reversionary interest "arose by the express terms of the instrument   *   *   *."   See § 2037(a)(2).   For transfers made after that date, the section applies even though the reversionary interest arose by operation of law.   See Reg. § 20.2037–1(c)(2).

106. See 1 American Law of Property §§ 4.19–4.23 (Casner, ed. 1952); Restatement of Property § 314 (1940).   In some states, the doctrine has been abolished by statute.   See, e.g., N.Y. EPTL 6—5.9.

107. A reversionary interest arising under the Doctrine of Worthier Title is deemed, for purposes of the exception described in note 105 supra relating to pre-October 8, 1949, transfers, to arise by the express terms of the instrument.   See Reg. § 20.2037–1(f).

When G dies, more than three years after the transfer, L is living, so the trust property is distributed to L. Nothing is includible in G's estate under § 2033 because that interest has no value as of G's death. The Doctrine of Worthier Title could, where it is in force as a rule of construction applicable to such dispositions, cause the remainder to G's heirs to be construed as a reversionary interest in G. If the value of G's reversionary interest was more than 5 percent of the value of the property as of the moment before G's death, the entire value of the trust property would be included in G's estate under § 2037.

[iii] **Planning Implications.** To avoid unintended retention of a reversionary interest by the grantor of a trust, it is common practice to include an ultimate gift to one or more charities, in the event that all of the noncharitable beneficaries fail to take. Such failure may result because beneficiaries are required by the terms of the trust to survive until its termination, and none of them does so.

The grantor of a short term (Clifford) trust [108] does not expect to get the reversionary interest out of his estate. If he dies before the trust terminates, that interest will be includible in his taxable estate under § 2033 as property owned at death. Section 2037 will not be relevant in that case.

[c] Disposing of a Retained Interest

What can be done to help a client who has made a transfer under which he or she has retained a right to income or a reversionary interest in principal that may be expected to require inclusion of the transfer in his taxable estate at death? The obvious answer is to give away the offending interest. If the client lives more than three years after the interest has been given away, it will no longer require inclusion of the transferred property in his or her estate at death.

Of course, when that three-year period starts to run is necessarily uncertain until after it has become too late for the client to act. What can be done to guard against the risk that time has already run out?

If the retained interest is not disposed of or does not terminate until less than three years before the transferor dies, § 2035(d)(2) requires inclusion of interests subject to a requirement of survival if such interests would have been included under § 2037 if the reversionary interest had been retained by the decedent until his death. The result is that a disposition of the retained interest within the three-year period must be for the requisite "adequate and full consideration" of § 2035 is not to apply.[108a]

UNITED STATES v. CURTIS ALLEN

United States Court of Appeals, Tenth Circuit, 1961.
293 F.2d 916, 61–2 USTC ¶ 12,032.
Cert. denied 368 U.S. 944, 82 S.Ct. 378, 7 L.Ed.2d 340 (1961).

MURRAH, Chief Judge.

*   *   *

The pertinent facts are that the decedent, Maria McKean Allen, created an irrevocable trust in which she reserved ⅗ths of the income for life, the remainder to pass to her two children, who are the beneficiaries of the other

---

108. See ¶ 6.05[3] infra.   108a. See ¶ 5.02[3][b][i].

⅔ths interest in the income.   When she was approximately seventy-eight years old, the trustor-decedent was advised that her retention of the life estate would result in her attributable share of the corpus being included in her gross estate, for estate tax purposes.   With her sanction, counsel began searching for a competent means of divesture, and learned that decedent's son, Wharton Allen, would consider purchasing his mother's interest in the trust.   At that time, the actuarial value of the retained life estate based upon decedent's life expectancy, was approximately $135,000 and her attributable shares of the corpus, i.e., ⅗ths, was valued at some $900,000.   Upon consultation with his business advisors, Allen agreed to pay $140,000 for the interest, believing that decedent's actual life span would be sufficient to return a profit to him on the investment.   For all intents and purposes, he was a bona fide third party purchaser—not being in a position to benefit by any reduction in his mother's estate taxes.   The sale was consummated and, upon paying the purchase price, Allen began receiving the income from the trust.

At the time of the transfer, decedent enjoyed relatively good health and was expected to live her normal life span.   A short time thereafter, however, it was discovered that she had an incurable disease, which soon resulted in her untimely death.   As a result of the death, Allen ceased receiving any trust income and suffered a considerable loss on his investment.

The Internal Revenue Commissioner determined that ⅗ths of the corpus, less the $140,000 purchase money, should be included in decedent's gross estate because (1) the transfer was invalid because made in contemplation of death, and (2) the sale was not for an adequate and full consideration.

Plaintiff-executors paid the taxes in accord with the Commissioner's valuation of the estate, and brought this action for refund, alleging that the sale of the life interest was for an adequate consideration; and that, therefore, no part of the trust corpus was properly includible in the gross estate.

The trial court held for plaintiffs, finding that the transfer was in contemplation of death, but regardless of that fact, the consideration paid for the life estate was adequate and full, thereby serving to divest decedent of any interest in the trust, with the result that no part of the corpus is subject to estate taxes.

Our narrow question is thus whether the corpus of a reserved life estate is removed for federal estate tax purposes, from a decedent's gross estate by a transfer at the value of such reserved life estate.   In other words, must the consideration be paid for the interest transferred or for the interest which would otherwise be included in the gross estate?

In one sense, the answer comes quite simply—decedent owned no more than a life estate, could not transfer any part of the corpus, and Allen received no more than the interest transferred.   And, a taxpayer is, of course, entitled to use all proper means to reduce his tax liability.   See Cravens v. C. I. R., 10 Cir., 272 F.2d 895, 898.   It would thus seem to follow that the consideration was adequate, for it was in fact more than the value of the life estate.   And, as a practical matter, it would have been virtually impossible to sell the life estate for an amount equal to her share in the corpus.   Cf. Sullivan's Estate v. C. I. R., 9 Cir., 175 F.2d 657.

* * *

It does not seem plausible, however, that Congress intended to allow such an easy avoidance of the taxable incidence befalling reserved life estates.   This result would allow a taxpayer to reap the benefits of property for his lifetime and, in contemplation of death, sell only the interest entitling him to the income, thereby removing all of the property which he has enjoyed from his gross estate.   Giving the statute a reasonable interpretation, we cannot believe this to be its intendment.   It seems certain that in a situation like this, Congress meant the estate to include the corpus of the trust or, in its stead, an amount equal to value. * * *

* * *

BREITENSTEIN, Circuit Judge (concurring in result).

* * *

Trustor-decedent in 1932 created an irrevocable trust and received no consideration therefor.   She retained for life the right to income from ⅗ths of the property which she placed in the trust.   By the plain language of the statute that portion of the property held in the trust and devoted to the payment to her of income for life is includible within her gross estate.   Such property is an "interest" of which she made a transfer with the retention of income for life.

The fact that the transfer of the life estate left her without any retained right to income from the trust property does not alter the result.   As I read the statute the tax liability arises at the time of the inter vivos transfer under which there was a retention of the right to income for life.   The disposition thereafter of that retained right does not eliminate the tax liability.   The fact that full and adequate consideration was paid for the transfer of the retained life estate is immaterial.   To remove the trust property from inclusion in decedent's estate there must be full and adequate consideration paid for the interest which would be taxed.   That interest is not the right to income for life but the right to the property which was placed in the trust and from which the income is produced.

* * *

QUESTIONS

1. What should the decedent have done in Allen in order to remove the trust from her taxable estate?

2. Within what time period should she have acted in order to achieve this result?

[5] Inclusion of Transfers Because of a Power to Control Enjoyment of Transferred Property

A client who has transferred property but has retained a right to control that property may find that its entire value must be included in his estate under either of two Code provisions:

(1) § 2036(a)(2), referring to "the right, either alone or in conjunction with any person, to designate the persons who shall possess or enjoy the property or the income therefrom"; and

(2) § 2038, referring to a right, either alone or with another, "to alter, amend, revoke or terminate" the transfer.

As a result, many transfers that are subject to § 2038 are also includible in the transferor's gross estate under § 2036(a)(2) because of his power over the distribution of income. In some circumstances, there may be differences in the amounts includible under each section,[109] but such differences are largely academic from an estate-planning standpoint. If the goal is removal of the transferred property from the client's gross estate, care should be taken to prevent its inclusion under either section. For transfers in trust, ideally the transferor should not be named as trustee or co-trustee; if he is so named, the terms of the trust should grant the trustees no objectionable powers or the exercise of such powers should be restricted to one or more trustees other than the transferor.

Application of §§ 2036(a) and 2038 has raised problems in three major areas:

(1) Whether a transferor's powers as trustee or co-trustee are so limited as to be ministerial and hence do not require inclusion of the trust property under either section;

(2) Whether powers held by someone else as trustee should be attributed to the transferor because of his possession of a power to appoint a successor trustee; and

(3) Whether powers to control the voting of trust stock require inclusion of such stock under § 2036(a)(2).

Unlike Code provisions dealing with taxation of trust income to the grantor,[110] these estate tax sections contain no exception for powers held by the decedent jointly with an adverse party.[111] They also differ from the income tax provisions in not requiring inclusion of transfers in the estate of the transferor because of a power held by someone else,[112] except for instances in which his power to appoint a sucessor trustee may cause the trustee's powers to be attributed to the tranferor.[113]

The power to add to a class of beneficiaries by having children does not make a transfer includible in the estate of the transferor under §§ 2036(a)(2) and 2038 (a)(1).[114]

---

109. Compare Reg. § 20.2036–1(a)(ii) (inclusion of "value of the entire property, less only the value of any outstanding income interest   *   *   * ") with Reg. § 20.2038–1(a) (inclusion of "the value of any interest   *   *   * ").

110. See, e.g., § 674(a).

111. Both § 2036(a)(2) and § 2038 explicitly refer to powers held by the decedent with any person. Thus, there is no exception for co-holders who are adverse parties.

112. See, e.g., § 674(c), defining permissible powers for income tax purposes of "independent" trustees. For a discussion, see ¶ 9.01[5] infra.

113. See ¶ 5.02[5][b] infra.

114. See Rev.Rul. 80–255, 1980–2 CB 272. Letter Ruling 7820002, 3 CCH E&GT ¶ 12,258, Dec. 23, 1977, had reached a contrary result.

LOBER v. UNITED STATES

Supreme Court of the United States, 1953.
346 U.S. 335, 74 S.Ct. 98, 98 L.Ed. 15, 53–2 USTC ¶ 10,922.

Mr. Justice BLACK delivered the opinion of the Court.

This is an action for an estate tax refund brought by the executors of the estate of Morris Lober.   In 1924 he signed an instrument conveying to himself as trustee money and stocks for the benefit of his young son.   In 1929 he executed two other instruments, one for the benefit of a daughter, the other for a second son.   The terms of these three instruments were the same.   Lober was to handle the funds, invest and reinvest them as he deemed proper.   He could accumulate and reinvest the income with the same freedom until his children reached twenty-one years of age.   When twenty-one they were to be paid the accumulated income.   Lober could hold the principal of each trust until the beneficiary reached twenty-five. In case he died his wife was to be trustee with the same broad powers Lober had conveyed to himself.   The trusts were declared to be irrevocable, and as the case reaches us we may assume that the trust instruments gave Lober's children a "vested interest" under state law, so that if they had died after creation of the trusts their interests would have passed to their estates. A crucial term of the trust instruments was that Lober could at any time he saw fit turn all or any part of the principal of the trusts over to his children.   Thus he could at will reduce the principal or pay it all to the beneficiaries, thereby terminating any trusteeship over it.

Lober died in 1942.   By that time the trust property was valued at more than $125,000.   The Internal Revenue Commissioner treated this as Lober's property and included it in his gross estate.   That inclusion brought this lawsuit.   The Commissioner relied on § 811(d)(2) of the Internal Revenue Code, 26 U.S.C. § 811 (1946 ed.), 26 U.S.C.A. § 811.   That section, so far as material here, required inclusion in a decedent's gross estate of the value of all property that the decedent had previously transferred by trust "where the enjoyment thereof was subject at the date of his death to any change through the exercise of a power   *   *   *   to alter, amend, or revoke   *   *   *."   In Commissioner v. Holmes, 326 U.S. 480, 66 S.Ct. 257, 90 L.Ed. 228, we held that power to terminate was the equivalent of power to "alter, amend, or revoke" it, and we approved taxation of the Holmes estate on that basis.   Relying on the *Holmes* case, the Court of Claims upheld inclusion of these trust properties in Lober's estate.   124 Ct.Cl. 44, 108 F.Supp. 731.   This was done despite the assumption that the trust conveyances gave the Lober children an indefeasible "vested interest" in the properties conveyed.   The Fifth Circuit Court of Appeals had reached a contrary result where the circumstances were substantially the same, in Hays' Estate v. Commissioner, 181 F.2d 169, 172–174.   Because of this conflict, we granted certiorari.   345 U.S. 969, 73 S.Ct. 1111.

Petitioners stress a factual difference between this and the *Holmes* case.   The *Holmes* trust instrument provided that if a beneficiary died before expiration of the trust his children succeeded to his interest, but if he died without children, his interest would pass to his brothers or their children.   Thus the trustee had power to eliminate a contingency that might have prevented passage of a beneficiary's interest to his heirs.   Here we assume that upon death of the Lober beneficiaries their part in the trust estate would, under New York law, pass to their heirs. But we cannot agree that this difference should change the *Holmes* result.

We pointed out in the *Holmes* case that § 811(d)(2) was more concerned with "present economic benefit" than with "technical vesting of title or estates." And the Lober beneficiaries, like the Holmes beneficiaries, were granted no "present right to immediate enjoyment of either income or principal." The trust instrument here gave none of Lober's children full "enjoyment" of the trust property, whether it "vested" in them or not. To get this full enjoyment they had to wait until they reached the age of twenty-five unless their father sooner gave them the money and stocks by terminating the trust under the power of change he kept to the very date of his death. This father could have given property to his children without reserving in himself any power to change the terms as to the date his gift would be wholly effective, but he did not. What we said in the *Holmes* case fits this situation too: "A donor who keeps so strong a hold over the actual and immediate enjoyment of what he puts beyond his own power to retake has not divested himself of that degree of control which § 811(d)(2) requires in order to avoid the tax." Commissioner v. Holmes, supra, at page 487, 66 S.Ct. at page 260.

Affirmed.

Mr. Justice DOUGLAS and Mr. Justice JACKSON dissent.

[a] Limiting the Client's Powers as Trustee

It is well-settled that trust property is not included in the grantor's estate merely because he or she is a trustee or co-trustee.[115] But there have been enough cases in which the courts have given broad readings to §§ 2036(a)(2), 2038, and their predecessors to give pause to the cautious client or the estate-planning advisor. If the client is to be a trustee, it may be possible to limit his powers so that they are merely ministrial and will not require inclusion of the property under these sections.[116] For example, a trustee's power to invade principal for a beneficiary may be limited by an ascertainable standard. In the absence of such a standard, the power would cause inclusion of the property in the grantor-trustee's estate.

But administrative and judicial interpretations are subject to revision. In making arrangements to remove property from a client's taxable estate, the estate planner should seek to anticipate more than merely the application of presently prevailing tests. He should also take into account the prospective evolution of such tests during the decades that may elapse before the client dies and his estate tax is determined. With that goal in mind, the part of prudence is to refrain from making the transferor a trustee. For some clients, however, such abstinence represents a substantial sacrifice. Often a client's emotional involvement with his wealth is very great. For such a client, to surrender beneficial ownership of wealth in the pursuit

115. The leading case is B. Brewster Jennings v. Smith, 161 F.2d 74, 47–1 USTC ¶ 10,551 (2d Cir. 1947).

116. For a comparison of powers that require inclusion of a trust under § 2038 with those that do not, see Rev.Rul. 73–143, 1973–1 CB 407.

of tax savings is difficult enough without also surrendering any direct control over that wealth.

If that is the case, it may be appropriate to run whatever risks may be involved in naming the client as trustee or co-trustee. However, if there are co-trustees, the trust instrument should minimize such risks by excluding the client from the exercise of discretionary powers over distribution of income or principal.

ESTATE OF ARTHUR J. O'CONNOR

United States Tax Court, 1970.
54 T.C. 969.

RAUM, Judge.   *   *   *   On January 25, 1955, the decedent and his wife executed a single trust indenture creating four substantially identical trusts for the benefit of their four children.[117]   Arthur Joseph O'Connor, Jr. (then age 11), Mary Ellen O'Connor (age 10), Kathleen O'Connor (age 8), and Robert Paul O'Connor (then 10 days old), and naming O'Connor as the trustee.   By the terms of the indenture, O'Connor and his wife, as grantors, delivered, assigned, and conveyed to O'Connor as trustee and his successor trustees the sum of $79,000.   He actually contributed all the principal of the trusts, however, and served as trustee until his death in 1962.

Article FIRST of the trust indenture provided as follows:

Trust No. 1

FIRST: The Trustee shall hold, manage, invest and reinvest nineteen-seventy ninths (19/79) of the total trust funds in the manner hereinafter provided, collect and receive the income therefrom, pay therefrom all proper expenses, taxes and charges, in his discretion expend for the benefit of said Arthur Joseph O'Conor, Jr. (born May 4, 1943) any balance of income or any principal thereof, and accumulate and add to principal any income remaining until said Arthur Joseph O'Connor, Jr. shall attain the age of twenty-one (21) years.   When said Arthur Joseph O'Connor, Jr. shall attain the age of twenty-one (21) years, the Trustee shall thereupon pay over and distribute to him outright as his absolute property, any principal and income, including accumulated income, then held hereunder.   If said Arthur Joseph O'Connor, Jr. shall die before attaining the age of twenty-one (21) years, the Trustee shall on his death pay over and distribute to his estate any principal or income, including accumulated income, then held hereunder.

The following three articles of the trust indenture were substantially identical to Article FIRST, except that each named a different child as beneficiary, and in one instance the trust corpus consisted of 22/79 of the total trust funds.

The remaining provisions of the trust indenture governed all four trusts. They provided as follows:

*   *   *

117. [The trust provisions appear to reflect an attempt to qualify for the gift tax present interest exclusion for transfers to minors under § 2503(c), added by the 1954 Code shortly before the trust was created.   See ¶ 6.03[1][a] infra.—ed.]

SEVENTH: The trusts hereby created are irrevocable and under no circumstances shall any part of the principal or income therefrom revert to the Grantors or to their estates or be used or applied directly or indirectly for the benefit of the Grantors or be used or applied to meet or relieve the Grantors' legal obligations to support their dependents.

* * *

* * * None of the trust beneficiaries had attained the age of 21 at the time of their father's death. The four trusts were not included in O'Connor's gross estate reported on his estate tax return, although their existence was disclosed in a schedule attached to the return. The estate tax return reported a gross estate of $3,594,783.03 and a taxable estate of $1,473,000.

* * *

The Commissioner contends that the trustee's powers under the trust indenture were so extensive as to require inclusion of the principal of each trust in O'Connor's gross estate pursuant to the provisions of section 2036(a)(2) and section 2038(a)(1), I.R.C. 1954. In response, the taxpayer argues that the provisions of Article SEVENTH of the indenture restricted O'Connor's powers sufficiently to place the trust properties beyond the reach of those sections.

The parties agree that were it not for Article SEVENTH the principal of each trust would be includable in O'Connor's gross estate, and the case law makes this abundantly clear. It is well settled that section 2036(a)(2) requires inclusion of both the original principal and the accumulated income of an irrevocable trust in the settlor's gross estate where at the time of his death the settlor retains the discretionary power either to distribute trust income to income beneficiaries or to accumulate such income and add it to principal; the power to deny to the trust beneficiaries the privilege of immediate enjoyment and to condition their enjoyment upon their surviving the termination of the trust has been considered to be of sufficient substance to qualify as a power to "designate" within the meaning of section 2036(a)(2). * * * Similarly, it is also established that section 2038(a)(1) requires inclusion of the principal of an irrevocable trust in the settlor's gross estate where at the time of his death he retains the discretionary power to terminate the trust and distribute the principal and accumulated income to the trust beneficiaries; the settlor's power to terminate contingencies upon which the beneficiaries' rights to enjoyment of the trust principal depend has been considered a power to "alter, amend, revoke, or terminate" within the meaning of section 2038(a)(1). Lober v. United States, 346 U.S. 335, 74 S.Ct. 98, 98 L.Ed. 15 * * * .

Each of the first four articles of the O'Connor trust indenture gave O'Connor, as trustee, the discretion to expend trust principal and income for the benefit of the trust beneficiary or to accumulate trust income and add it to principal until the beneficiary attained the age of 21. Thus, unless modified by subsequent provisions in the indenture, the powers conferred by the first four articles require the trusts to be included in O'Connor's gross estate pursuant to sections 2036(a)(2) and 2038(a)(1). However, the taxpayer contends that Article SEVENTH of the trust indenture rendered "illusory" O'Connor's power—purportedly conferred by the first four articles of the indenture—to expend trust income and principal for the benefit of each beneficiary, and that therefore neither section 2036(a)(2) nor section 2038(a)(1) requires inclusion of the trusts in O'Connor's gross estate. This the Commissioner disputes, and the controversy between the parties thus concerns only the tax consequences of Article SEVENTH of the trust indenture.

The taxpayer argues first that by prohibiting the use of any part of the principal or income of the trusts to relieve O'Connor's support obligations, Article SEVENTH effectively neutralized the powers purportedly conferred upon him by the first four Articles of the indenture. The taxpayer reasons that since New York law measures the extent of a parent's support obligation with reference to his "station in life," and since O'Connor was a "very wealthy" man, any payments made for the benefit of his children while he was still alive would necessarily have relieved his support obligations and were therefore proscribed by Article SEVENTH. In essence, the taxpayer's argument is that for a father in O'Connor's financial position, no expenditure for the monetary benefit of one of his children could exceed his obligation to support that child, and that therefore Article SEVENTH prohibited any payments by O'Connor under the trust indenture. We disagree.

To be sure, since New York law provides that a father's support obligation is measured by his "station in life," O'Connor's support obligations were extensive. See New York Domestic Relations Law section 32(2); DeBrauwere v. DeBrauwere, 203 N.Y. 460, 464, 96 N.E. 722; Garlock v. Garlock, 279 N.Y. 337, 340, 18 N.E.2d 521, 522. However, the New York courts have consistently held that the authority to make expenditures of trust property for the "benefit" of an individual is far more extensive than the authority to make expenditures for his support.   *   *   *

The first four articles of the trust indenture authorized O'Connor, as trustee, to expend the income and principal of the trusts "for the benefit of" the child beneficiaries, and we think it clear under New York law that the authority thereby conferred permitted him to make payments in excess of his support obligations. As extensive as his support obligations may have been, they did not comprehend every payment that could possibly have benefitted his children. We conclude that the provision prohibiting the use of any part of the principal or income of the trusts to relieve O'Connor's support obligations left him with authority to make substantial payments of income and principal to the trust beneficiaries and that this authority was significant enough to render the trusts includable in his gross estate pursuant to sections 2036(a)(2) and 2038(a)(1).

However, the taxpayer argues that even if expenditures could be made for something other than the beneficiaries' support, any such expenditure would be barred by Article SEVENTH's provision that no part of the principal or income "be used or applied directly or indirectly for the benefit of the Grantors." The taxpayer urges that since all of the trust beneficiaries were O'Connor's children and since he, as trustee, decided how the trust funds were to be applied, any expenditure made for the benefit of the children would inevitably have redounded to his benefit as well—by satisfying his parental desire to please his children. In making this argument, the taxpayer places great emphasis on the fact that "direct or indirect" benefits were proscribed by the trust provision and urges that the receipt of subjective as well as material benefits were thus forbidden to O'Connor by the indenture.

The construction proposed by the taxpayer seems inconsistent with the context of Article SEVENTH. The other provisions of the Article declare the trusts irrevocable and prohibit trust income and principal from reverting to the grantors and from being applied to meet or relieve the grantors' "legal obligations to support their dependents." Plainly, these provisions attempt to prevent the grantors from deriving real economic advantages from the trusts, and there is no suggestion anywhere in the trust indenture that the "benefit" provision has a broader purpose. To be sure, as indicated above, the New York courts have customarily defined the word "benefit" in broad terms. But that definition has not to our knowledge been extended to include subjective satisfactions.

* * *

In arguing for a broader construction of "benefit" in this case, the taxpayer has attempted to explain the O'Connors' intentions in establishing the trusts. The taxpayer suggests that O'Connor and his wife deliberately designed the trust indenture so that Article SEVENTH would render "illusory" the powers otherwise conferred upon O'Connor by the indenture. The taxpayer theorizes that O'Connor and his wife wanted all of the trust income to be accumulated and added to principal while the two of them were alive (and presumably had sufficient resources to care for their children), that they also wished to ensure that if they both died before their children turned 21, the successor trustees would have the power to expend income and principal for the benefit of the children, and that since Article SEVENTH would limit the trustee's powers only as long as either O'Connor or his wife were alive, it was introduced into the indenture to achieve the foregoing purposes.

This explanation seems to us to be farfetched. Apart from the parties' stipulation that O'Connor was a "very wealthy" man, and the trust indenture itself, there is absolutely no evidence in the record to support it. Furthermore, the taxpayer would have us conclude that the O'Connors deliberately created an "illusion." But this theory fails to explain *why* they implemented their plan in such a circuitous and deceptive manner. The taxpayer's speculation as to the O'Connor's possible intentions is simply not enough to justify such an unusual and unlikely reading of Article SEVENTH.

The problem is merely one of construing the language of Article SEVENTH and the meaning of the word "benefit" as used therein. The fact that a taxpayer may derive "benefits" or personal "satisfaction" for certain purposes in respect of the income tax law (cf. Burnet v. Wells, 289 U.S. 670, 678, 53 S.Ct. 761, 77 L.Ed. 1439; Corliss v. Bowers, 281 U.S. 376, 378, 50 S.Ct. 336, 74 L.Ed. 916; and Helvering v. Horst, 311 U.S. 112, 116–117, 61 S.Ct. 144, 85 L.Ed. 75), does not warrant a construction of Article SEVENTH in such manner as to render illusory, during the lifetime of the grantors, powers conferred on the trustee in Article FIRST. We think that no such unusual construction was intended here. Had the

O'Connors intended that result it seems plain to us that they would simply have stated in Article FIRST itself that the powers in question were exercisable only by successor trustees after the deaths of the grantors. We do not accept the unnatural reading of the instrument which the taxpayer urges upon us.

Decisions will be entered under Rule 50.

[b] Avoiding Attribution to the Client of the Powers of Another Trustee

The Regulations make the obvious point that "if the decedent had the unrestricted power to remove or discharge a trustee at any time and appoint himself trustee, the decedent is considered as having the powers of the trustee." [118]   Revenue Ruling 79–353 [119] goes further and treats the decedent as having such powers if he may remove the trustee at will and appoint another trustee, even if he cannot substitute himself. The Ruling does not refer to Marian A. Byrum v. United States, [120] in which the Sixth Circuit held that such a power to replace the trustee with another corporate trustee did not make the trust property includible, a holding impliedly approved by the Supreme Court in the opinion below.

Clients who wish to avoid the risk that Revenue Ruling 79–353 will be sustained despite the *Byrum* decision should give the removal power to someone else.

UNITED STATES v. BYRUM

Supreme Court of the United States, 1972.
408 U.S. 125, 92 S.Ct. 2382, 33 L.Ed.2d 238, 72–2 USTC ¶ 12,859

Mr. Justice POWELL delivered the opinion of the Court.

Decedent, Milliken C. Byrum, created in 1958 an irrevocable trust to which he transferred shares of stock in three closely held corporations. Prior to transfer, he owned at least 71% of the outstanding stock of each corporation. The beneficiaries were his children or, in the event of their death before the termination of the trust, their surviving children. The trust instrument specified that there be a corporate trustee. Byrum designated as sole trustee an independent corporation, Huntington National

---

118. Reg. § 20.2038–1(a)(3); see § 2038(b), last sentence. See Warren H. Corning, 24 T.C. 907, 915 (1955), aff'd per curiam 239 F.2d 646 (6th Cir. 1956). Compare Rev. Rul. 77–182, 1977–1 CB 273, holding that a power to appoint a successor corporate trustee which was exercisable only if the original trustee resigns or is removed by judicial process does not cause the trustee's powers to be attributed to the grantor.

119. 1979–1 CB 265. The Ruling will not be applied to irrevocable transfers in trust made on or before the date of its publication, October 28, 1979. See Rev.Rul. 81–51, IRB 1981–7, 14, 3 CCH E&GT ¶ 12,441D.

120. 440 F.2d 949, 71–1 USTC ¶ 12,763 (6th Cir. 1971), aff'd 408 U.S. 125 72–2 USTC ¶ 12,859 (1972). The ground relied on by the Court of Appeals appears to be that the removal power did not permit the decedent to substitute himself as trustee, rather than that the trustee's powers were so restricted as not to require inclusion of the trust property even if the decedent were viewed as having such powers. The Court of Appeals cited in support of its conclusion, Estate of Ralph Budd, 49 T.C. 468 (1968), acq. 1973–2 CB 1 and Reg. § 20.2036–1(b)(3). In the *Budd* case, the decedent had the power to remove the trustee and appoint himself but the court held that the powers of the trustee were not such as to require inclusion of the trust property even if the decedent were viewed as having such powers.

Bank. The trust agreement vested in the trustee broad and detailed powers with respect to the control and management of the trust property. These powers were exercisable in the trustee's sole discretion, subject to certain rights reserved by Byrum: (i) to vote the shares of unlisted stock held in the trust estate; (ii) to disapprove the sale or transfer of any trust assets, including the shares transferred to the trust; (iii) to approve investments and reinvestments; and (iv) to remove the trustee and "designate another corporate Trustee to serve as successor." Until the youngest living child reached age 21, the trustee was authorized in its "absolute and sole discretion" to pay the income and principal of the trust to or for the benefit of the beneficiaries, "with due regard to their individual needs for education, care, maintenance and support." After the youngest child reached 21, the trust was to be divided into separate trusts for each child, to terminate when the beneficiaries reached 35. The trustee was authorized in its discretion to pay income and principal from these trusts to the beneficiaries for emergency or other "worthy needs," including education.

When he died in 1964, Byrum owned less than 50% of the common stock in two corporations and 59% in the third. The trust had retained the shares transferred to it, with the result that Byrum had continued to have the right to vote not less than 71% of the common stock in each of the three corporations. There were minority stockholders, unrelated to Byrum, in each corporation.

Following Byrum's death, the Commissioner of Internal Revenue determined that the transferred stock was properly included within Byrum's gross estate under § 2036(a) of the Internal Revenue Code of 1954, 26 U.S.C.A. § 2036(a). * * * The Commissioner determined that the stock transferred into the trust should be included in Byrum's gross estate because of the rights reserved by him in the trust agreement. It was asserted that his right to vote the transferred shares and to veto any sale thereof by the trustee, together with the ownership of other shares, enabled Byrum to retain the "enjoyment of * * * the property," and also allowed him to determine the flow of income to the trust and thereby "designate the persons who shall * * * enjoy * * * the income."

* * *

I

The Government relies primarily on its claim, made under § 2036(a)(2), that Byrum retained the right to designate the persons who shall enjoy the income from the transferred property. The argument is a complicated one. By retaining voting control over the corporations whose stock was transferred, Byrum was in a position to select the corporate directors. He could retain this position by not selling the shares he owned and by vetoing any sale by the trustee of the transferred shares. These rights, it is said, gave him control over corporate dividend policy. By increasing, decreasing, or stopping dividends completely, it is argued that Byrum could "regulate the flow of income to the trust" and thereby shift or defer the beneficial enjoyment of trust income between the present beneficiaries and the remaindermen. The sum of this retained power is said to be tantamount to a grantor-trustee's power to accumulate income in the trust, which this Court has recognized constitutes the power to designate the persons who shall enjoy the income from transferred property.

At the outset we observe that this Court has never held that trust property must be included in a settlor's gross estate solely because the settlor retained the power to manage trust assets.   On the contrary, since our decision in Reinecke v. Northern Trust Co., 278 U.S. 339, 49 S.Ct. 123, 73 L.Ed. 410 (1929), it has been recognized that a settlor's retention of broad powers of management does not necessarily subject an *inter vivos* trust to the federal estate tax.   Although there was no statutory analogue to § 2036(a)(2) when *Northern Trust* was decided, several lower court decisions decided after the enactment of the predecessor of § 2036(a)(2) have upheld the settlor's right to exercise managerial powers without incurring estate tax liability.   In Estate of King v. Commissioner, 37 T.C. 973 (1962), a settlor reserved the power to direct the trustee in the management and investment of trust assets.   The Government argued that the settlor was thereby empowered to cause investments to be made in such a manner as to control significantly the flow of income into the trust.   The Tax Court rejected this argument, and held for the taxpayer.   Although the court recognized that the settlor had reserved "wide latitude in the exercise of his discretion as to the types of investments to be made," it did not find this control over the flow of income to be equivalent to the power to designate who shall enjoy the income from the transferred property.

Essentially the power retained by Byrum is the same managerial power retained by the settlors in *Northern Trust* and in *King*.   Although neither case controls this one—*Northern Trust*, because it was not decided under § 2036(a)(2) or a predecessor; and *King*, because it is a lower court opinion—the existence of such precedents carries weight.   The holding of *Northern Trust*, that the settlor of a trust may retain broad powers of management without adverse estate tax consequences, may have been relied upon in the drafting of hundreds of *inter vivos* trusts.   The modification of this principle now sought by the Government could have a seriously adverse impact, especially upon settlors (and their estates) who happen to have been "controlling" stockholders of a closely held corporation.   Courts properly have been reluctant to depart from an interpretation of tax law which has been generally accepted when the departure could have potentially far-reaching consequences.   When a principle of taxation requires reexamination, Congress is better equipped than a court to define precisely the type of conduct which results in tax consequences.   When courts readily undertake such tasks, taxpayers may not rely with assurance on what appear to be established rules lest they be subsequently overturned.   Legislative enactments, on the other hand, although not always free from ambiguity, at least afford the taxpayers advance warning.

The Government argues, however, that our opinion in United States v. O'Malley, 383 U.S. 627, 86 S.Ct. 1123, 16 L.Ed.2d 145 (1966), compels the inclusion in Byrum's estate of the stock owned by the trust.   In *O'Malley*, the settlor of an *inter vivos* trust named himself as one of the three trustees.   The trust agreement authorized the trustees to pay income to the life beneficiary or to accumulate it as a part of the principal of the trust in their "sole discretion."   The agreement further provided that net income retained by the trustees, and not distributed in any calendar year, "shall become a part of the principal of the trust estate." The Court characterized the effect of the trust as follows:

> Here Fabrice [the settlor] was empowered, with the other trustees, to distribute the trust income to the income beneficiaries or to accumulate it and add it to the principal, thereby denying to the beneficiaries the privilege of immediate enjoyment and conditioning their eventual enjoyment upon surviving the termination of the trust. 383 U.S., at 631, 86 S.Ct., at 1126.

As the retention of this legal right by the settlor, acting as a trustee "in conjunction" with the other trustees, came squarely within the language and intent of the predecessor of § 2036(a)(2), the taxpayer conceded that the original assets transferred into the trust were includable in the decedent's gross estate. 383 U.S., at 632, 86 S.Ct., at 1126. The issue before the Court was whether the accumulated income, which had been added to the principal pursuant to the reservation of right in that respect, was also includable in decedent's estate for tax purposes. The Court held that it was.

In our view, and for the purposes of this case, *O'Malley* adds nothing to the statute itself. The facts in that case were clearly within the ambit of what is now § 2036(a)(2). That section requires that the settlor must have "retained for his life * * * the *right* * * * to designate the persons who shall possess or enjoy the property or the income therefrom." O'Malley was covered precisely by the statute for two reasons: (1) there the settlor had reserved a legal right, set forth in the trust instrument; and (2) this right expressly authorized the settler, "in conjunction" with others, to accumulate income and thereby "to designate" the persons to enjoy it.

It must be conceded that Byrum reserved no such "right" in the trust instrument or otherwise. The term "right," certainly when used in a tax statute, must be given its normal and customary meaning. It connotes an ascertainable and legally enforceable power, such as that involved in *O'Malley*. Here, the right ascribed to Byrum was the power to use his majority position and influence over the corporate directors to "regulate the flow of dividends" to the trust. That "right" was neither ascertainable nor legally enforceable and hence was not a right in any normal sense of that term.

Byrum did retain the legal right to vote shares held by the trust and to veto investments and reinvestments. But the corporate trustee alone, not Byrum, had the right to pay out or withhold income and thereby to designate who among the beneficiaries enjoyed such income. Whatever power Byrum may have possessed, with respect to the flow of income into the trust, was derived not from an enforceable legal right specified in the trust instrument, but from the fact that he could elect a majority of the directors of the three corporations. The power to elect the directors conferred no legal right to command them to pay or not to pay dividends. A majority shareholder has a fiduciary duty not to misuse his power by promoting his personal interests at the expense of corporate interests. Moreover, the directors also have a fiduciary duty to promote the interests of the corporation. However great Byrum's influence may have been with the corporate directors, their responsibilities were to all stockholders and were enforceable according to legal standards entirely unrelated to the needs of the trust or to Byrum's desires with respect thereto.

The Government seeks to equate the *de facto* position of a controlling stockholder with the legally enforceable "right" specified by the statute. Retention of corporate control (through the right to vote the shares) is said to be "tantamount to the power to accumulate income" in the trust which resulted in estate tax consequences in *O'Malley*. The Government goes on to assert that "through exercise of that retained power [Byrum] could increase or decrease corporate dividends, and thereby shift or defer the beneficial enjoyment of the trust. This approach seems to us not only to depart from the specific statutory language, but also to misconceive the realities of corporate life.

There is no reason to suppose that the three corporations controlled by Byrum were other than typical small businesses. The customary vicissitudes of such enterprises—bad years; product obsolescence; new competition; disastrous litigation; new, inhibiting Government regulations; even bankruptcy—prevent any certainty or predictability as to earnings or dividends. There is no assurance that a small corporation will have a flow of net earnings or that income earned will in fact be available for dividends. Thus, Byrum's alleged *de facto* "power to control the flow of dividends" to the trust was subject to business and economic variables over which he had little or no control.

    *   *   *

These various economic considerations are ignored at the directors' peril. Although vested with broad discretion in determining whether, when, and what amount of dividends shall be paid, that discretion is subject to legal restraints. If, in obedience to the will of the majority stockholder, corporate directors disregard the interests of shareholders by accumulating earnings to an unreasonable extent, they are vulnerable to a derivative suit. They are similarly vulnerable if they make an unlawful payment of dividends in the absence of net earnings or available surplus, or if they fail to exercise the requisite degree of care in discharging their duty to act only in the best interest of the corporation and its stockholders.

Byrum was similarly inhibited by a fiduciary duty from abusing his position as majority shareholder for personal or family advantage to the detriment of the corporation or other stockholders. There were a substantial number of minority stockholders in these corporations who were unrelated to Byrum. Had Byrum and the directors violated their duties, the minority shareholders would have had a cause of action under Ohio Law. The Huntington National Bank, as trustee, was one of the minority stockholders, and it had both the right and the duty to hold Byrum responsible for any wrongful or negligent action as a controlling stockholder or as a director of the corporations. Although Byrum had reserved the right to remove the trustee, he would have been imprudent to do this when confronted by the trustee's complaint against his conduct. A successor trustee would succeed to the rights of the one removed.

We conclude that Byrum did not have an unconstrained *de facto* power to regulate the flow of dividends to the trust, much less the "right" to designate who was to enjoy the income from trust property. His ability to affect, but not control trust income, was a qualitatively different power from that of the settlor in *O'Malley*, who had a specific and enforceable right to control the income paid to the beneficiaries.   Even had Byrum managed to flood the trust with income, he had no way of compelling the trustee to pay it out rather than accumulate it.   Nor could he prevent the trustee from making payments from other trust assets, although admittedly there were few of these at the time of Byrum's death.   We cannot assume, however, that no other assets would come into the trust from reinvestments or other gifts.

We find no merit to the Government's contention that Byrum's *de facto* "control," subject as it was to the economic and legal constraints set forth above, was tantamount to the right to designate the persons who shall enjoy trust income, specified by § 2036(a)(2).

II

The Government asserts an alternative ground for including the shares transferred to the trust within Byrum's gross estate.   It argues that by retaining control, Byrum guaranteed himself continued employment and remuneration, as well as the right to determine whether and when the corporations would be liquidated or merged.   Byrum is thus said to have retained "the enjoyment of * * * the property" making it includable within his gross estate under § 2036(e)(1).   The Government concedes that the retention of the voting rights of an "unimportant minority interest" would not require inclusion of the transferred shares under § 2036(a)(1).   It argues, however, "where the cumulative effect of the retained powers and the rights flowing from the shares not placed in trust leaves the grantor in control of a close corporation and assures control for his lifetime, he has retained the 'enjoyment' of the transferred stock."

It is well settled that the terms "enjoy" and "enjoyment," as used in various estate tax statutes, "are not terms of art, but connote substantial present economic benefit rather than technical vesting of title or estates." Commissioner of Internal Revenue v. Estate of Holmes, 326 U.S. 480, 486, 66 S.Ct. 257, 260, 90 L.Ed. 228 (1946).   For example, in Reinecke v. Northern Trust Co., 278 U.S. 339, 49 S.Ct. 123, 73 L.Ed. 410 (1929), in which the critical inquiry was whether the decedent had created a trust "intended to take effect in possession or enjoyment at or after his death," the Court held that reserved powers of management of trust assets, similar to Byrum's power over the three corporations, did not subject an *inter vivos* trust to the federal estate tax.   In determining whether the settlor had retained the enjoyment of the transferred property, the Court said:

> Nor did the reserved powers of management of the trusts save to decedent any control over the economic benefits or the enjoyment of the property.   He would equally have reserved all these powers and others had he made himself the trustee, but the transfer would not for that reason have been incomplete.   The shifting of the economic interest in the trust property which was the subject of the tax was thus complete as soon as the trust was made.   His power to recall the property and of control over it for his own benefit then ceased and as the trusts were not made in contem-

plation of death, the reserved powers do not serve to distinguish them from any other gift *inter vivos* not subject to the tax. 278 U.S., at 346–347, 49 S.Ct. at 125.

* * *

As the Government concedes, the mere retention of the right-to-vote shares does not constitute the type of "enjoyment" in the property itself contemplated by § 2036(a)(1). In addition to being against the weight of precedent, the Government's argument that Byrum *retained* "enjoyment" within the meaning of § 2036(a)(1) is conceptually unsound. This argument implies, as it must under the express language of § 2036(a)(1), that Byrum "retained for his life * * * the possession or enjoyment" of the "*property*" transferred to the trust or the "*income*" therefrom. The only property he transferred was corporate stock. He did not transfer "control" (in the sense used by the Government) as the trust never owned as much as 50% of the stock of any corporation. Byrum never divested himself of control, as he was able to vote a majority of the shares by virtue of what he owned and the right to vote those placed in the trust. Indeed, at the time of his death he still owned a majority of the shares in the largest of the corporations and probably would have exercised control of the other two by virtue of being a large stockholder in each. The statutory language plainly contemplates retention of an attribute of the property transferred—such as a right to income, use of the property itself, or a power of appointment with respect either to income or principal.

Even if Byrum had transferred a majority of the stock, but had retained voting control, he would not have retained "substantial present economic benefits." The Government points to the retention of two "benefits." The first of these, the power to liquidate or merge, is not a *present* benefit; rather, it is a speculative and contingent benefit which may or may not be realized. Nor is the probability of continued employment and compensation the substantial "enjoyment of * * * [the transferred] property" within the meaning of the statute. The dominant stockholder in a closely held corporation, if he is active and productive, is likely to hold a senior position and to enjoy the advantage of a significant voice in his own compensation. These are inevitable facts of the free enterprise system, but the influence and capability of a controlling stockholder to favor himself are not without constraints. Where there are minority stockholders, as in this case, directors may be held accountable if their employment, compensation and retention of officers violates their duty to act reasonably in the best interest of the corporation and all of its stockholders. Moreover, this duty is policed, *albeit* indirectly, by the Internal Revenue Service, which disallows the deduction of unreasonable compensation paid to a corporate executive as a business expense. We conclude that Byrum's retention of voting control was not the retention of the enjoyment of the transferred property within the meaning of the statute.

* * *

Judgment affirmed.

Mr. Justice WHITE, with whom Mr. Justice BRENNAN and Mr. Justice BLACKMUN join, dissenting.

I think the majority is wrong in all substantial respects.

*　*　*

Byrum's lifelong enjoyment of the voting power of the trust shares contravenes § 2036(a)(2) as well as § 2036(a)(1) because it afforded him control over which trust beneficiaries—the life tenants or the remaindermen—would receive the benefit of the income earned by these shares. He secured this power by making the trust for all intents and purposes exclusively dependent on shares it could not sell in corporations he controlled. Thus by instructing the directors he elected in the controlled corporations that he thought dividends should or should not be declared Byrum was able to open or close the spigot through which income flowed to the trust's life tenants. When Byrum closed the spigot by deferring dividends of the controlled corporations, thereby perpetuating his own "enjoyment" of these funds, he also in effect transferred income from the life tenants to the remaindermen whose share values were swollen by the retained income. The extent to which such income transfers can be effected is suggested by the pay-out record of the corporations here in question, as reflected in the trust's accounts. Over the first five years of its existence on shares later valued by the Internal Revenue Service at $89,000, the trust received only a *total* of $339 in dividends. In the sixth year, Byrum died. The corporations raised their dividend rate from 10¢ a share of $2.00 per share and paid $1,498 into the trust.　*　*　*

Byrum's control over the flow of trust income renders his estate scheme repugnant to § 2036(a)(2) as well as § 2036(a)(1).

To me it is thus clear that Byrum's shares were not truly, totally, "absolutely, unequivocally" alienated during his life. When it is apparent that if tolerated Byrum's scheme will open a gaping hole in the estate tax laws, on what basis does the majority nonetheless conclude that Byrum should have his enjoyment, his control, and his estate free from taxes?

II

I can find nothing in the majority's three arguments purporting to deal with § 2036(a)(1), which might justify the conclusion that Byrum did not "enjoy" a benefit from the shares his estate now asserts are immune from taxation.

1. The majority says that in Reinecke v. Northern Trust, 278 U.S. 339, 49 S.Ct. 123, 73 L.Ed. 410 (1929), "the Court held that reserved powers of management of trust assets, similar to Byrum's power over the three corporations, did not subject an *inter vivos* trust to the federal estate tax." This reading of *Northern Trust* is not warranted by the one paragraph in that antique opinion on the point for which it is now cited, see 278 U.S. 339, 346–347, 49 S.Ct. 123, 125, nor by the circumstances of that case. No one has ever suggested that Adolphus Bartlett, the settlor in *Northern Trust*, used or could have used the voting power of the shares he transferred to a trust to control or indeed exercise any significant influence in any company. A mere glance at the nature of these securities transferred by Mr. Bartlett (1,000 shares of the Northern Trust Co., 784 shares of the Commonwealth Edison Co., 300 shares of the Illinois Central R. Co., 300 shares of the

Illinois R. Co., 200 shares of the Chicago and North Western R. Co., etc.) shatters any theory which might lead one to believe that the Court in *Northern Trust* was concerned with anything like the transactions in this case.   On what basis then does the majority say that *Northern Trust* involved a decision on facts "similar to Byrum's power over the three corporations"?   And on what basis does it say that the Government's position that Byrum's use of trust shares to retain control renders those shares taxable is "against the weight of precedent"?

2.   The majority implies that trust securities are taxable only if the testator retained title or the right to income from the securities until death. But this ignores the plain language of the statute which proscribes "enjoyment" as well as "possession or * * * the right to income."

3.   The majority concludes with the assertion that Byrum secured no "substantial present economic benefits" from his retention of control.   It is suggested that control isn't important, that it either cannot be held by a private shareholder or that it is of so little use and relevance the taxpayer can hardly be said to have "enjoyed" it.   This view of corporate life is refuted by the case law; by the commentators; and by every day transactions on the stock exchange where tender offers and other trades repeatedly demonstrate that the power to "control" a corporation will fetch a substantial premium.   Moreover, the majority's view is belied by Byrum's own conduct.   He obviously valued control because he forbade the bank which served as trustee to sell the trust shares in these corporations without his—Byrum's approval, whatever their return, their prospects, their value, or the trust's needs.   * * *

In sum, the majority's discourse on § 2036(a)(1) is an unconvincing rationalization for allowing Byrum the tax free "enjoyment" of the control privileges he retained through the voting power of shares he supposedly "absolutely" and "unequivocally" gave up.

III

I find no greater substance in the greater length of the majority's discussion of § 2036(a)(2).

A

Approaching the § 2036(a)(2) problem afresh one would think United States v. O'Malley, 383 U.S. 627, 86 S.Ct. 1123, 16 L.Ed.2d 145 (1966), would control this case.   In *O'Malley* the settlor "[had] relinquished all of his rights" to stock, but he appointed himself one of three trustees for each of the five trusts he created, and he drafted the trust agreement so that the trustees had the freedom to allocate trust income to the life tenant or to accumulate it for the remainderman "in their sole discretion."   The District Court held that the value of securities transferred was includable in the settlor's gross estate under § 811(d) of the Internal Revenue Code of 1939, the identically worded predecessor of § 2036(a)(2), because the settlor had retained the power to allocate income between the beneficiaries without being constrained by a "definite ascertainable standard" according to which the trust would be administered.   O'Malley v. United States, D.C., 220

F.Supp. 30, 33 (1963). The court noted "plaintiff's contention that the required external standard is imposed generally by the law of Illinois," but found this point to be "without merit."

> The cases cited by plaintiff clearly set out fundamental principles of trust law: that a trust requires a named beneficiary; that the legal and equitable estates be separated; and, that the trustees owe a fiduciary duty to the beneficiaries. These statements of the law are not particular to Illinois. Nor do these requirements so circumscribe the trustee's powers in an otherwise unrestricted trust so as to hold such a trust governed by an external standard and thus excludable from the application of § 811(c) and (d). 220 F.Supp. 30, at 33–34.

It was another aspect of that case which brought the matter to the Court of Appeals, 340 F.2d 930 (C.A.7th 1964), and then here. We were asked to decide whether the lower court's holding should be extended and the accumulated income as well as the principal of the trust included in the settlor's taxable estate because the settlor had retained excessive power to designate the income beneficiaries of the shares transferred. We held that though capable of exercise only in conjunction with one other trustee, the power to allocate income without greater constaint than that imposed "is a significant power * * * of sufficient substance to be deemed the power to 'designate' within the meaning of [the predecessor of § 2036(a)(2)]." 383 U.S., at 631, 86 S.Ct., at 1126.

O'Malley makes the majority's position in this case untenable. *O'Malley* establishes that a settlor serving as a trustee is barred from retaining the power to allocate trust income between a life tenant and a remainderman if he is not constrained by more than general fiduciary requirements. See also Commissioner of Internal Revenue v. Estate of Holmes, 326 U.S. 480, 66 S.Ct. 257, 90 L.Ed. 228 (1946) and Lober v. United States, 346 U.S. 335, 74 S.Ct. 98, 98 L.Ed. 15 (1953). Now the majority would have us accept the incompatible position that a settlor seeking tax exemption may keep the power of income allocation by rendering the trust dependent on an income flow he controls because the general fiduciary obligations of a director are sufficient to eliminate the power to designate within the meaning of § 2036(a)(2).

B

The majority would prop up its untenable position by suggesting that a controlling shareholder is constrained in his distribution or retention of dividends by fear of derivative suits, accumulated earnings taxes, and "various economic considerations * * * ignored at the directors' peril." I do not deny the existence of such contstraints, but their restraining effect on an otherwise tempting gross abuse of the corporate dividend power hardly guts the great power of a controlling director to accelerate or retard, enlarge or diminish, most dividends. The penalty taxes only take effect when accumulations exceed $100,000, 26 U.S.C.A. § 535(c); Byrum was free to accumulate up to that ceiling. The threat of a derivative suit is hardly a greater deterrent to accumulation. * * *

The ease with which excess taxes, derivative suits and economic vicissitudes alike may be circumvented or hurdled if a controlling shareholder chooses to so arrange his affairs is suggested by the payout record of Byrum's corporations noted above.

C

The majority proposes one other method of distinguishing *O'Malley*. Section 2036(a)(2), it is said, speaks of the *right* to designate income beneficiaries. *O'Malley* involved the effort of a settlor to maintain a legal right to allocate income. In the instant case only the *power* to allocate income is at stake. The Government's argument is thus said to depart from "the specific statutory language" and to stretch the statute beyond endurance by allocating tax according to the realities of the situation rather than by the more rigid yardstick of formal control.

This argument conjures up an image of congressional care in the articulation of § 2036(a)(2) which is entirely at odds with the circumstances of its passage. The 1931 Revenue Act which first enacted § 2036(a)(2) in language unamended since that date, passed both houses of Congress in one day—the last day of the session. There was no printed committee report. Substantial references to the bill appear in only two brief sections of the Congressional Record. Under the circumstances I see no warrant for reading the words in a niggardly way.

* * *

IV

Apparently sensing that considerations of logic, policy and recent case law point to the inclusion of Byrum's trust in his estate, the majority would blunt these considerations by invoking the principle that courts should refrain from decision detrimental to litigants who have taken a position in legitimate reliance on possibly outdated, but once established, case law. This principle is said to bring great weight to bear in Byrum's favor.

I need not quarrel with the principle. I think, however, that its application in this context is inappropriate.

The majority recites these facts: This Court has never held that retention of power to manage trust assets compels inclusion of a trust in a settlor's estate. In fact, Reinecke v. Northern Trust, 278 U.S. 339, 49 S.Ct. 123, 73 L.Ed. 410 (1929), specifically held a trust arrangement immune from taxation though the settlor retained power to decide how the trust assets were to be invested. Though *Northern Trust* was decided before the passage of § 2036(a)(2), it has been followed by "several" more recent lower court decisions. Though most of the lower court decisions provide only the most oblique reference to circumstances like those of this case, a 1962 unappealed Tax Court decision, Estate of King v. Commissioner, 37 T.C. 973 (1962), is squarely on point.

On the basis of these two authorities, a 1929 Supreme Court decision and an unreviewed 1962 Tax Court decision, the majority concludes that there exists a "generally accepted" rule that Byrum might do what he had done here. It is said that the hypothesized rule, "may" have been relied upon by "hundreds" of others; if so, its modification "could" have a serious impact, especially upon settlors who "happen" to have been controlling shareholders in closely held corporations and who "happen" to have transferred shares in those corporations to trusts while forbidding the trustee to sell the shares without approval and while retaining voting rights in those shares.   Therefore the rule ought not to be "modified" by this Court.

A

The argument, apparently, is that what "appear[s] to be established" should become established because it has appeared.   Judges can and will properly differ on the questions of what deference to accord reliance on a well-established rule, but I doubt that we are prejudiced from reaching what would otherwise be a right result simply because in the minds of some litigants a contrary rule had heretofore "appeared to be established."   If the majority's approach were widely accepted, artful claims of past under-standing would consistently suffice to frustrate judicial as well as admin-istrative efforts at present rationalization of the law and every precedent—even at the tax court level—might lay claim to such authority that the Government and the tax bar could afford to leave no case unappealed.

B

Of course, the reliance argument is doubly infirm if the majority's rule cannot be said to have "appeared to be established."   Did Byrum have a sound basis for calculating that there was no substantial risk of taxation when he persisted in retaining the powers and privileges described above?

1.   Again the majority turns to Reinecke v. Northern Trust, but it is no more credible to use *Northern Trust* as a foundation for Byrum's § 2036(a)(2) position than it was to use it as a basis for the Court's § 2036(a)(1) argument.   *Northern Trust* was decided on January 2, 1929, two years and three months before Congress passed the first version of § 2036(a)(2).   Sec-tion 402(c) of the Act of 1921, the provision under which *Northern Trust* was decided, proscribed only transfers in which the settlor attempted to retain "possession or enjoyment" until his death.   It is thus not surprising that *Northern Trust* focused on the question of the settlor's "power to recall the property and of control over it *for his own benefit*," 278 U.S., at 347, 49 S.Ct., at 125 (emphasis added), and made no mention of possible tax liability because of a retained power to designate which beneficiaries would enjoy the trust income.   A holding in this context cannot be precedent of "weight" for a decision as to the efficacy of a trust agreement made—as this trust was—27 years after § 2036(a)(2) was enacted.

I note also that *Northern Trust* rests on a conceptual framework now rejected in modern law.   The case is the elder sibling of May v. Heiner, 281 U.S. 238, 50 S.Ct. 286, 74 L.Ed. 826 (1930), a three-page 1930 decision which quotes *Northern Trust*, at length.   *May* in effect held that under § 402(c) a settlor may be considered to have fully alienated property from himself even if he retains the very substantial string of the right to income from the property so long as he survives.   The logic of May v. Heiner is the logic of *Northern Trust*.   As one authority has written:

"When retention of a life estate was not taxable under the rule of May v. Heiner, it followed that mere retention of a right to des-ignate the persons to receive the income during the life of the

settlor was not taxable   * * * ."   I Beveridge, Law of Federal
Estate Taxation, § 8.06, p. 324.

That logic no longer survives.   When three Supreme Court *per curiams*
affirmed *May* on March 2, 1931, and thus indicated that this view would not
be confined to its facts, the treasury, on the next morning, wrote Congress
imploring it to promptly and finally reject the Court's lenient view of the
Estate Tax system.   Congress responded by enacting § 2036(a)(2) that very
day.   The President signed the law that evening.   Thus the holding of
May and the underlying approach of *Northern Trust* has no present life.
I note further that though Congress has refused to permit pre-1931 trusts
to be liable to a rule other than that of *May*, in 1949 this Court itself came
to the conclusion that *May* was wrong, and effected "a complete rejection"
of its reasoning.   Commissioner of Internal Revenue v. Estate of Church,
335 U.S. 632, 645, 69 S.Ct. 322, 329, 93 L.Ed. 288 (1949).

I seriously doubt that one could confidently rely on Reinecke v. Northern Trust when Byrum drafted his trust agreement in 1958.   This Court
is certainly not bound by its logic in 1972.   I do not mean any disrespect,
but as Mr. Justice Cardozo said about another case, *Northern Trust* is a
decision "as mouldy as the grave from which counsel   * * *   brought
it forth to face the light of a new age."   Cardozo, The Growth of the Law,
p. 132 (1924); Collected Writings, p. 244.

2.   The majority argues that there were several lower court cases
decided after the enactment of § 2036(a)(2) upon which Byrum was entitled
to rely and it is quite true that cases exist holding that a settlor's retention
of the power to invest the assets of a trust does not by itself render the
trust taxable under § 2036(a)(2).   But the majority's emphasis of these
cases as a proper foundation, for Byrum's reliance is doubly wrong.   First,
it could not have evaded Byrum's attention and should not escape the majority that all cited prior cases—save *King* (the tax court case written four
years *after* Byrum structured his trust)—involved retention of power to
invest by the settlor's appointment of himself as a trustee;   that is, they
posed instances in which the settlor's retained power was constrained by
a fiduciary obligation to treat the life tenant beneficiaries and remainderman
beneficiaries exactly as specified in the trust instrument.   Thus the "freedom" to reallocate income between life tenants and remaindermen by, e.g.,
investing in wasting assets with a high present return and no long-term
value, was limited by a judicially enforceable strict standard capable of
invocation by the trust beneficiaries by reference to the terms of the trust
agreement.   See Jennings v. Smith, 161 F.2d 74 (C.A.2d, 1947), the leading
case.   Byrum must have realized that the situation he was structuring was
quite different.   By according himself power of control over the trust income
by an indirect means, he kept himself quite free of a fiduciary obligation
measured by an ascertainable standard in the trust agreement.   Putting
aside the question of whether the situation described *should* be distinguished
from Byrum's scheme, surely it must be acknowledged that there was an
apparent risk that these situations *could* be distinguished by reviewing
courts.

Second, the majority's analysis of the case law skips over the uncertainty at the time Byrum was drafting his trust agreement about even the

general rule that a settlor could retain control over a trust's investments if he bound himself as a trustee to an ascertainable method of income distribution.   *   *   *

The point is not simply that Byrum was on notice that he risked taxability by retaining the powers he retained when he created his trust— though that is true.   It is also that within a month of the trust's creation it should have been crystal-clear that Byrum ran a substantial risk of taxation by continued retention of control over the trust's stock.   Any retained right can be resigned.   That Byrum persisted in holding these rights can only be viewed as an indication of the value he placed upon their enjoyment, and of the tax risk he was willing to assume in order to retain control.

The perception that a settlor ran substantial risk of estate tax if he insisted on retaining power over the flow of trust income is hardly some subtle divination of a latter-day observor of the 1958–1959 tax landscape. Contemporary observers saw the same thing.   *   *   *

More could be said, but I think it is clear that the majority should find no solace in its reliance argument.

V

The majority, I repeat, has erred in every substantial respect.   It remains only to note that if it is wrong in *any* substantial respect—i.e., either in its § 2036(a)(1) or (a)(2) arguments—Byrum's trust is by law liable to taxation.

[c] Limiting the Client's Powers to Vote Stock

Section 2036(b) defines retention of the right to vote stock in a controlled corporation as constituting retention of income.   For this purpose, a corporation is "controlled" if the decedent owned 20 percent of the stock, after application of the attribution of ownership rules of § 318, or had the right (either alone or in conjunction with any person) to vote stock possessing 20 percent of the combined voting power of all classes.[121]

If at *any* time within the three-year period preceding the decedent's death he or she had such a right, the stock will be included in the decedent's estate regardless of whether the right was held at death.[122]   Retention of voting rights is not material for estate tax purposes if the corporation is not "controlled" within this definition at any time during the three-year period.

The mechanical test contained in § 2036(b) facilitates planning by providing greater certainty as to the estate tax consequences of a retention of voting rights than that provided by the more general trust income tax provisions with respect thereto.[123]   However, the latter apply only to powers exercisable in a nonfiduciary capacity.   Section 2036(b) is not so limited.

121. See § 2036(b)(2).

122. Id.   For this purpose, "an agreement or arrangement with a trustee to vote the stock in accordance with the directions of the decedent" constitutes indirect retention of voting rights, requiring inclusion of the stock in the decedent's estate.   See Rev. Rul. 80–346, 1980–2 CB 271.

123. § 675(4).   For a discussion, see ¶ 9.01[7] infra.

It thus represents an additional reason for caution in naming the grantor as trustee or co-trustee, if the trust property includes stock in a close corporation. If he is so named, the grantor should be excluded from participation in the voting of such stock by the trustees.

¶ 5.03   WHO IS THE TRANSFEROR: RECIPROCAL TRUSTS

Taxpayers sometimes seek to avoid §§ 2036 and 2038, which require inclusion of transferred property in the transferor's estate if he retains an interest in or power over the property, by creating trusts on a reciprocal basis. The trustee may also be selected with a view to qualifying under § 674(c) so that the grantor will not be treated for income tax purposes as owner of the trust because of the trustee's discretionary powers.[124]

> *Example 5.2.* A husband (*H*) transfers property into *Trust #1*, naming his wife (*W*) and son-in-law (*S*) as trustees. The trustees may, in their discretion, distribute trust income to such descendants of the grantor (here, *H*) as they may determine, until the termination of the trust. *W* in turn transfers property into *Trust #2*, naming *H* and *S* as trustees. The provisions for distribution of income are the same as for *Trust #1*. Neither *H* nor *W* has an interest in or control over the property that he or she transferred into trust, although each has control over an equal amount of the other's property in his or her capacity as trustee. This arrangement nominally avoids the provisions of §§ 2036 and 2038. In addition, each fits within the provisions of § 674(c) so as to avoid income taxation of the grantor as owner of the trust.

In transfers of this general type, the courts apply the "reciprocal trust doctrine," so as to include in *H*'s estate the trust created by *W* to the extent of the value of the smaller trust, if *H*'s powers as trustee would have required such inclusion (as in *Example 5.2*) had he created the trust himself.[125] Similarly, *W*'s estate would include a comparable portion of the trust created by *H* if her powers as trustee would have required such inclusion were she the grantor of *H*'s trust.

From a planning standpoint, the significant question is when the creation of each trust is sufficiently related to creation of the other trust for the doctrine to apply. The Supreme Court has held merely that the trusts must be "inter-related." [126] In view of this uncertainty, the cautious advisor may prefer to avoid creating trusts under which family members are trustees of each other's trusts, unless there is a substantial time lag between creation of each trust. Of course this caution is unnecessary if the powers of the family trustee are sufficiently limited so as to avoid inclusion of property in the family trustee's estate if he were treated as the transferor.

124. For a discussion, see ¶ 9.01[5] infra.

125. See e.g., United States v. Estate of Grace, 395 U.S. 316, 89 S.Ct. 1730, 23 L.Ed.2d 332, 69–1 USTC ¶ 12,609 (1969).

126. Id. note 112, 395 U.S. at 324, 89 S.Ct. at 1735, 23 L.Ed.2d at 338, 69–1 USTC at 84,980.

ESTATE OF BRUNO BISCHOFF v. COMMISSIONER

United States Tax Court, 1977.
69 T.C. 32.

FAY, Judge:

OPINION

* * *

The second issue for decision is whether the trust corpora of certain trusts created by Bertha and Bruno for the benefit of their grandchildren are includable in their gross estates under either section 2036(a)(2) or section 2038(a)(1).

On December 31, 1957, Bruno created four trusts for the benefit of his and Bertha's grandchildren. He funded each trust with a 0.75-percent limited partnership interest in Frank Brunckhorst Co. and appointed Bertha trustee of each of the trusts. On January 1, 1958, Bertha created four identical trusts for the same beneficiaries and appointed Bruno trustee of these four trusts. In their respective roles as trustee, Bruno and Bertha had the power to accumulate trust income or to distribute trust income or corpus in their sole discretion for the benefit of the trust beneficiaries.

Sections 2036(a)(2) and 2038(a)(1) reach the value of property transferred by a decedent in which he died possessing the power to affect the enjoyment of its income.[127] It is undisputed that the powers held by Bruno and Bertha are within both sections. Thus, the sole question we must decide is whether each decedent should be treated as the "transferor" of the respective properties covered by their powers so as to require inclusion of such property in their respective gross estates.

At the outset, we note that it is clear Bruno and Bertha each nominally were not the transferors of the corpora which they trusteed. Bruno's powers extended over the property placed into trust by Bertha, and vice versa.

Respondent seeks to "uncross" these trusts, thereby making each decedent, in reality, the settlor of the trusts which, in form, were created by the other. In support of his position, he, in essence, argues the reciprocal trust doctrine as enunciated in United States v. Estate of Grace, 395 U.S. 316 (1969), and Lehman v. Commissioner, 109 F.2d 99 (2d Cir. 1940), cert. denied 310 U.S. 637 (1940).

Petitioners, on the other hand, contend that the reciprocal trust doctrine as espoused by the Supreme Court in *Grace* requires, as a condition precedent to its application, a finding that a decedent died possessing an economic interest in the property he allegedly transferred. In the present case, petitioners maintain the powers held by each decedent could not be used for their economic benefit and that fact operates as a bar to invocation of the doctrine.

Despite the excellence of petitioners' brief, we are not persuaded that the Supreme Court in *Grace* intended to delimit the doctrine's role to sit-

---

127. Sec. 2036(a)(2), in addition, requires that the decedent have "retained" the power.

uations where a decedent at his death possessed an economic interest in the property transferred.

The reciprocal trust doctrine, which dates back to 1940, was formulated to deal with estate tax abuse situations where grantors created trusts that, in form, accomplished completed transfers of their property, but under which they exchanged crossed gifts which might consist of a life income interest and a power to invade corpus, to change the beneficiaries, or to change the amount each would receive. In reality, therefore, each grantor had the same lifetime enjoyment of his property, albeit the property was in the other grantor's trust, that he would have enjoyed had he simply reserved the same entitlements in his own trust. The doctrine was developed to deal with this situation by "uncrossing" the trusts and treating each grantor as if he had created his own trust. As a result, a decedent was treated as the "transferor" of the property, which the other party had in form transferred, causing the trust corpus to be taxed in his estate at his death. The doctrine was first expounded in Lehman v. Commissioner, supra. In *Lehman* the Court uncrossed trusts created by two brothers for each other's benefit on the theory that they had been made in consideration of each other. Each brother had given the other a general power to withdraw corpus with respect to the trust created for his benefit. Once the trusts were uncrossed, the decedent was found to be the transferor of the corpus of his trust and, under the predecessor of section 2038, the amount of corpus subject to his power of withdrawal was included in his estate. Thereafter, in the majority of cases where the doctrine was litigated, the issue was whether the creation of one trust had been induced by, and represented a quid pro quo for, the creation of the other. Resolution of this issue produced two divergent points of view as to what set of circumstances was necessary to a finding of a quid pro quo. Both lines of cases made a factual determination as to whether the decedent had "paid for and brought about" the transfer. One line of cases decided the question by making a subjective inquiry into the decedent's motives for the transfer. See McLain v. Jarecki, 232 F.2d 211 (7th Cir. 1956); Newberry's Estate v. Commissioner, 201 F.2d 874 (3d Cir. 1953); Tobin v. Commissioner, 183 F.2d 919 (5th Cir. 1950), cert. denied 340 U.S. 904 (1950). The other line of cases resolved the issue of reciprocity basically by looking at the objective evidence. See Hanauer's Estate v. Commissioner, 149 F.2d 857 (2d Cir. 1945), cert. denied 326 U.S. 770 (1945); Cole's Estate v. Commissioner, 140 F.2d 636 (8th Cir. 1944). It is this backdrop of cases that set the stage for the Supreme Court's decision in United States v. Estate of Grace, supra.

In *Grace* the issue was whether the test of reciprocity between two trusts should be subjective, requiring proof of an actual bargaining between the grantors to show that the trusts were created "in consideration of" each other, or whether there should be an objective test of reciprocity not requiring such proof. The Court of Claims, with two judges dissenting, was unable to find the requisite consideration under either test, even though the two trusts involved were substantially identical in terms and created as part of a single transaction at approximately the same time.

The Supreme Court reversed and determined that in the area of intrafamily transfers, the traditional concept of "consideration" as a bargained-for exchange was unrealistic. As a basis for developing a different test of reciprocity, it found the subjective intent of the decedent difficult, if not impossible, to determine. Thus, it concluded:

> For these reasons, we hold that application of the reciprocal trust doctrine is not dependent upon a finding that each trust was created as a *quid pro quo* for the other. Such a "consideration" requirement necessarily involves a difficult inquiry into the subjective intent of the settlors. Nor do we think it necessary to prove the existence of a tax-avoidance motive. As we have said above, standards of this sort, which rely on subjective factors, are rarely workable under the federal estate tax laws. Rather, we hold that application of the reciprocal trust doctrine requires only that the trusts be interrelated, and that the arrangement, to the extent of mutual value, leave the settlors in approximately the same economic position as they would have been in had they created trusts naming themselves as life beneficiaries. [United States v. Estate of Grace, 395 U.S. at 324. Fn. ref. omitted.]

Petitioners contend that the Court in its usage of the words "leaves the settlors in approximately the same economic position as they would have been in had they created trusts naming themselves as life beneficiaries" meant to limit the application of the doctrine to situations where there exists the crossing of substantial economic interests and not where there are merely crossed powers. In support of their theory, petitioners make much of the fact that every one of the cases where the reciprocal arrangements were challenged involved the crossing between grantors of very substantial economic interest.

We simply cannot agree. First of all, petitioners' theory demonstrates a basic misconception of the doctrine's function. The purpose of the docrine is merely to identify the transferor of property. Standing alone, its application does not impose a tax; rather, the incidence of taxation depends upon the operation of a Code section when the shroud of form is lifted and the true transferor revealed. In other words, the doctrine's application is only part of a two-step process of taxation, i.e., it is not enough merely to "uncross" the trusts, there must also exist a basis for their taxation. In *Grace*, the two trusts were uncrossed because they were "interrelated" *and not*, as petitioners urge, because the decedent therein held a direct economic interest in the property. The basis of taxation which led to the inclusion of the value of the trust corpus in the decedent's estate was crossed life estates under section 811(c)(1)(B)(i) of the 1939 Internal Revenue Code (the predecessor of section 2036(a)(1)). Thus, in our opinion, the Court's reference to the "same economic position * * * as life beneficiaries" was merely its formulation of the basis of taxation on the facts before it.

Secondly, petitioners' contention that the sine qua non to the doctrine's application is crossed economic interests overlooks the fact that the case before the Supreme Court in *Grace*, as previously noted, involved section 811(c)(1)(B)(i). That section covered situations where the decedent retained "the possession or enjoyment of, or the right to the income from" transferred property—concepts clearly associated with a direct economic benefit. Because *Grace* involved crossed life estates and, consequently, fell within the reach of section 811(c)(1)(B)(i), any reference in the Supreme Court's opinion to retained economic interests cannot properly be interpreted to mean anything more than its expression of what would be necessary to a finding of taxation under that section.   In short, adoption of petitioners' interpretation of *Grace* would be tantamount to ignoring the fact that Congress had decided that the power to use property for one's own personal benefit will not be the only basis for taxation under sections 2036 and 2038.   Indeed, the mere power to affect the timing of the enjoyment of property is sufficient to attract a tax under sections 2036(a)(2) and 2038(a)(1).   United States v. O'Malley, 383 U.S. 627 (1966); Lober v. United States, 346 U.S. 335 (1953).   We simply are not convinced that the Supreme Court intended to close a perceived loophole under section 2036(a)(1) and, at the same time, permit one to flourish under sections 2036(a)(2) and 2038(a)(1).

* * *

The facts in this case clearly indicate that the trusts created by Bruno and Bertha were interrelated.   All that remains is finding a basis of taxation.   Here the powers involved are within those forbidden by sections 2036(a)(2) and 2038(a)(1).   Accordingly, we hold that the value of the trust corpora of the trusts created by Bruno and Bertha is includable in their respective estates.

* * *

TANNENWALD, J., concurring: While I agree with the result reached herein, I am concerned that the majority opinion may be interpreted as applying United States v. Estate of Grace, 395 U.S. 316 (1969), beyond its intended scope.   By the same token, I disagree with the narrow interpretation accorded to *Grace* by Judge Hall in her dissent.

In its opinion in *Grace*, the Supreme Court stated that the reciprocal trust doctrine does not depend upon a finding of a quid pro quo and that all that is required is an interrelationship between the trusts which leaves the settlors in the same economic position.

I read *Grace* neither to lay down a rule (as Judge Hall suggests) that, even where there is an interrelationship, the absence of an economic interest in the settlor precludes the use of that doctrine, nor to imply (as the majority opinion may be read to do) that the mere simultaneity of the establishment of the trusts is enough to produce the necessary interrelationship.

In short, I read *Grace* to require a determination that the trusts were in fact interrelated.   Thus, in instances where it is demonstrated that the trusts were established independently, the reciprocal trust doctrine would be inapplicable whether or not there was an economic interest in the settlor. Estate of Grace v. United States, 393 F.2d 939 (Ct.Cl.1968) (Davis, J., dissenting).   See also Note, "United States v. Estate of Grace: The Reincarnation of the Reciprocal Trust Doctrine," 17 U.C.L.A. L.Rev. 436 (1969). Such objective factors as a significant separation of time in the establishment of the trusts, the occurrence of intervening events, differing amounts placed in the trusts, or differing powers granted to each trustee may indicate that the trusts were created independently.

I believe that this interpretation is a reasonable one, founded in both logic and a knowledge of human affairs.   It is also consistent with footnote 10 of the opinion in *Grace* (see 395 U.S. at 324), which provides:

> We do not mean to say that the existence of "consideration," in the traditional legal sense of a bargained-for exchange, can never be relevant.   In certain cases, inquiries into the settlor's reasons for creating the trusts may be helpful in establishing the requisite link between the two trusts.   We only hold that a finding of bargained-for consideration is not necessary to establish reciprocity.

Under the circumstances of this case, I would hold that the reciprocal trust doctrine should apply.   The only evidence of record herein is that the trusts were established at or about the same time.   Such being the case, it cannot be said that the petitioners have carried their burden of proof that each trust was not bargained for by the establishment of the other trust.

STERRETT and WILES, JJ., agree with this concurring opinion.

HALL, J., dissenting in part: In every one of the cases in which the reciprocal trust doctrine has ultimately been applied, including United States v. Estate of Grace, 395 U.S. 316 (1969), the arrangements that were challenged involved the crossing between grantors of very substantial economic interests.   All but one of the cases involved the exchange of life estates or beneficial powers exercisable by the holders for their own benefit. The one exception, a decision of this Court, subsequently reversed by the Court of Appeals for the Third Circuit, involved the exchange of significant powers to shift economic interests as between beneficiaries, i.e., a spray power.   Estate of Newberry v. Commissioner, 17 T.C. 597 (1951), revd. 201 F.2d 874 (3d Cir. 1953).   However, even if our holding in *Newberry's Estate* could have survived the Third Circuit reversal, it could not survive the enunciation of the retained economic benefit test by the Supreme Court in *Grace*.

Applying the *Grace* approach to the present case, it seems clear that powers to use principal and interest for minor grandchildren's needs, deemed by respondent to be exchanged by Bruno and Bertha, were not powers having "economic value" to the decedents.   The majority, in applying *Grace*, in effect, reads the word "economic" out of the Supreme Court's formulation, saying it was not essential to the principle of the case.   Certainly these trusts did not reflect the thinly disguised retention of an "economic interest" which the Supreme Court found determinative.   Rather, in each case, the settlor made a completed gift in trust of his or her own property to their minor grandchildren, the natural objects of their bounty, not retaining any power which would include the corpus of the trusts in the settlor's estate. The trust conferred economic interests only on the beneficiary; they conferred no economic interest on the trustee whose only power was to accelerate the receipt of the economic interest by the beneficiary during his minority.   Not even a "spray" power was retained, so that the "retention" on uncrossing the trusts fell short of even the retention in *Newberry's Estate*, the previous high water mark of this Court's application of the reciprocal trust doctrine.   Neither settlor would have been economically worse off had the other not elected to make a concurrent gift to the objects of his natural bounty.   It is therefore also most difficult to perceive the "interrelation" between the trusts called for in *Estate of Grace*.   In my view, they were concurrent and similar, but not interrelated in any meaningful sense.   Had the property in question all happened to belong to one grandparent, there is no reason to believe that grandparent would not have wished to put it in trust, naming the other as trustee, and there would be no question of includability.   I see insufficient reason why essentially the same result cannot properly be achieved where each grandparent happens to own part of the property sought to be entrusted.   This is not the kind of situation the reciprocal trust doctrine was intended to cover or, at least since *Grace*, ever has been extended to cover.   I recognize the majority's argument that Congress has decided the question of retained powers which suffice for includability and that indirect retention of the equivalent of such powers through reciprocal arrangements should produce the same result.   However, I believe this would carry a good and necessary principle too far— certainly further than the language of *Grace* would warrant.   I conclude that such an extension of the doctrine is unwarranted under these circumstances.   While it is true that each settlor gave the other powers, retention of which would have frustrated the estate plan, Congress permits a grantor, and it is common planning, to put such powers in the hands of one's spouse. The mere fact that both spouses had similar property and one spouse concurrently does the same with his or her own trusts does not improve the economic position of the power-holding spouse or make the other spouse the "transferor."   Congress chose to allow the entrusting to a spouse of the power to accumulate trust income or to distribute trust income or corpus, which power could not be retained personally.   It seems to me that until Congress provides to the contrary, it is not for us to say that where spouses happen to own similar property they are barred from each doing concurrently what either could safely do alone.   Unlike the cases of illusory relinquishment of economic interests where the reciprocal trust doctrine has been applied, there has here been the real relinquishment of economic value which the statute contemplates for exclusion from the estate.

DRENNEN, SCOTT, and GOFFE, JJ., agree with this dissenting opinion.

¶ 5.04   GIFT TAX AND INCOME TAX CONSEQUENCES FOR THE TRANSFEROR

[1] Relation Between Gift Tax and Estate Tax

Any transfer without consideration that is effective to remove property from the client's gross estate is a completed gift for purposes of the gift tax. If it is a sale or exchange for a full and adequate consideration, the gift tax is avoided, but the transaction is subject to the income tax if the consideration received exceeds the transferor's basis in the property.   Even without such full and adequate consideration, the transfer may escape the gift tax because of available exclusions or deductions or the donor's unified credit.   However, transfers that fail to remove property from the client's gross estate may nevertheless be completed gifts for purposes of the gift tax.[128]   For example, if the transferor retains income from transferred

---

128. If a transfer is subject to both gift tax and estate tax, the gift tax payable ordinarily is credited against the estate tax otherwise due.   § 2001(b)(2) (post-1976 gifts); § 2012 (pre-1977 gifts).

property for his life, a gift of the remainder after his death is a completed gift for purposes of the gift tax even though the transferred property will be included in his estate under § 2036.

[2] Transfers for Insufficient Consideration

A transfer for insufficient consideration is a gift for purposes of the gift tax and may also be included in the gross estate under §§ 2035–2038. For gift tax purposes, the value of the gift is the difference between the value of what was transferred and the value of what was received in exchange.[129] For estate tax purposes, the consequences may be far more serious: a minor insufficiency of consideration may cause a substantial amount to be included in the transferor's estate. This follows from the manner in which the property transferred and the consideration received in exchange are valued.

Section 2043 requires inclusion of transfers described in §§ 2035–2038, that are made for an insufficient consideration. Like other property included in the gross estate, that which is transferred is valued as of the date of death [130] (or alternate valuation date).[131] That which is received in exchange is valued when it is received.[132] A common example of such a transfer in estate planning is the community-property widow's election.[133]

[3] Relation Between Income Tax and Estate Tax

The Code provisions taxing a trust grantor as owner for income tax purposes [134] are not coordinated with the provisions including lifetime transfers in the gross estate. A transfer may succeed in removing property from the client's gross estate without shifting the taxability of the income from the transferred property during his lifetime. It is also possible for trust income not to be taxable to the grantor and yet for the property to be included in his gross estate. These results flow from major differences in the structure of the two taxes, including the following:

(1) For estate tax purposes, powers may require inclusion of property if held by the grantor jointly with any person; [135] for income tax purposes, powers held jointly with an adverse party do not cause the grantor to be taxed as owner; [136] and

(2) A trust grantor may be taxed on trust income because of powers held by others,[137] but such powers do not require trust property to be included in the grantor's estate.[138]

129. Reg. § 25.2512–8.

130. § 2031(a).

131. § 2032(a). The alternative valuation date is six months after the date of death, except that property, sold, exchanged, or otherwise disposed of is valued as of the date of disposition. § 2032(a)(1). Such a disposition may be made by a donee to whom the decedent transferred property during his life. See Reg. § 20.2032–1(c)(3).

132. See, e.g., United States v. Howard Past, 347 F.2d 7, 14 n.6, 65–1 USTC ¶ 12,317 at 95,737 n.6 (9th Cir. 1965); Estate of Lela B. Vardell v. Commissioner, 307 F.2d 688, 62–2 USTC ¶ 12,089 (5th Cir. 1962).

133. See ¶ 18.03[3] infra.

134. §§ 671–77. For a discussion, see ¶ 9.01 infra.

135. See §§ 2036(a)(2), 2038(a). For a discussion, see ¶ 5.02[5] supra.

136. See, e.g., § 674(a).

137. Id.

138. Both § 2036(a)(2) and § 2038 refer to powers held by the decedent either alone or in conjunction with any person. Unless the decedent is a power holder, the sections literally are inapplicable. But see ¶ 5.02[5][b] supra.

Chapter 6

GIFTS AND GIFT TAXES

¶ 6.01 GIFTS IN ESTATE PLANNING

Lifetime gifts have long offered important savings in estate and income taxes. The potential estate tax savings were curtailed by the Tax Reform Act of 1976, and the importance of the estate tax was generally reduced by the Economic Recovery Tax Act of 1981. At the same time, the 1981 Act reduced effective gift tax rates and thereby cut the gift tax cost of transfers made to save either income taxes or estate taxes, or both.

[1] Estate Tax Consequences

[a] Advantages

Before the Tax Reform Act of 1976, gifts could be used to achieve estate tax savings in part [1] for four reasons:

(1) Gift tax rates were 25 percent less than estate tax rates; [2]

(2) A separate lifetime exemption of $30,000 was available for gift tax purposes; [3]

(3) Lifetime gifts were not taken into account in determining the donor's estate tax bracket unless the gift was includible in his gross estate for some reason; [4] and

(4) Gift taxes on lifetime gifts were not included in his gross estate, even if the gift itself was so included. [5]

The 1976 Act did away with the first three reasons for making lifetime gifts and curtailed the fourth, because:

(1) Gift tax rates are now the same as estate tax rates; [6]

(2) The separate gift tax and estate tax exemptions have been replaced by a unified credit, [7] which is applied against gift taxes on post-1976 gifts during the donor's life and then against his estate tax when he dies: [8]

---

1. Other reasons of major importance, which are unaffected by the 1976 Act, are discussed in ¶ 5.02[1] supra.

2. See former § 2502(a) (gift tax); former § 2001 (estate tax).

3. See former § 2521.

4. See §§ 2035–38, requiring inclusion of certain lifetime transfers in a decedent's estate. See also text at note 13 infra.

5. Gift taxes that have not been paid before the decedent's death are deductible as a claim under § 2053(a)(3). See Rev. Rul. 55-334, 1955-1 CB 449.

6. § 2502(a) (gift tax): § 2001(c) (estate tax).

7. § 2505 (gift tax): § 2010 (estate tax). The credit is reduced for both gift tax and estate tax purposes by 20 percent of the amount allowed as a specific exemption under prior law, former § 2521, with respect to gifts made between September 8, 1976, and December 31, 1976. See § 2505(c) (gift tax): § 2010(c) (estate tax). The unified credit is $62,800 in 1982. It is scheduled to increase until it reaches $192,800 in 1987. See ¶ 5.01.

8. When the donor dies, a tentative estate tax is computed by first applying the estate tax rates to the combined amounts of his taxable estate and his "adjusted taxable gifts." The total gift tax payable on all post-1976 gifts is then subtracted. See § 2001(b). The amount remaining is then

(3) Post-1976 lifetime gifts are taken into account in determining the donor's estate tax bracket even though the gift is not included in his gross estate; [9] and

(4) Gift taxes paid by the donor or his estate are includible in his gross estate if the tax is on a gift made within three years of death. [10]

The 1981 Act reduced the importance of gift and estate taxes for clients by reducing rates, increasing the amount of the unified credit, and providing an unlimited marital deduction for qualifying gifts to the donor's spouse. The effect of these changes is to increase the relative importance of using gifts to save income taxes and to decrease the relative importance of using gifts to save estate taxes. Nevertheless, gifts continue to offer savings in estate taxes for some clients for four major reasons:

(1) The base on which the gift tax is computed often is smaller than the base for the estate tax. The gift tax is computed on the value of the property given without including the gift tax paid by the donor. [11] The estate tax, on the other hand, is based on the size of the taxable estate, [12] before deduction of the tax itself. This difference disappears if the client dies within three years after making the gift. In that case, any gift tax paid by the donor or his estate is included in his taxable estate. [13] Thus, although the gift tax is not included in the amount of the gift for purposes of the gift tax, it enters into the computation of the estate tax.

(2) Section 2503(b) provides an annual exclusion of $10,000 per donee for gifts of present interests. The exclusion, which is offered on a "use it or lose it" basis, allows property that would otherwise be includible in the transferor's estate to be transferred free of estate taxes as well. If all of a donor's gifts to a donee during a given year are covered by the exclusion, none are includible in the donor's taxable estate, even if he dies within three years, as long as the gift is not "with respect to a life insurance policy." [14]

(3) Gifts not covered by the present interest exclusion are also removed from the donor's estate if he dies after 1981, unless he retains until

---

further reduced by the unified credit. See § 2010(a).

For example, if the decedent made no taxable gifts before 1977 and his post-1976 taxable gifts amounted to $500,000, all made in 1982, the gift tax payable would be $93,000 (tax of $155,800 would be reduced by a credit of $62,800). If he died in 1986 with a taxable estate of $250,000 and the gifts were not includible in his estate, his estate tax before any state death tax credit would be computed as follows:

Estate tax on $750,000 ($250,000 + $500,000 gifts)		$248,300
Less Gift Tax Paid	$ 93,000	
Unified Credit	155,800	248,800
Estate Tax Payable		$500,000

9. § 2001(b), last sentence.

10. § 2035(c).

11. § 2501(a). See ¶ 6.03[1][e] infra.

12. § 2001(a).

13. §§ 2035(c). Treatment of state gift taxes on such gifts is discussed at ¶ 5.02[3][c] note 59 supra.

14. See § 2035(b). Gifts not covered by the exclusion are included in "adjusted taxable gifts" under § 2001(b) and thus enter into the computation of estate tax.

within three years of his death an interest which requires inclusion of the transfer under §§ 2036–2038, 2041, or 2042.[15]

(4) The gift tax is based on the value of the property when the gift is made. If the donor retains the property until he dies, its value may go up and thus cause a larger amount to be included in his taxable estate than would have been subject to gift tax if the property had been transferred by gift instead.

[b] Disadvantages

There may be tax disadvantages from making lifetime gifts, including the following:

(1) If any gift tax is payable as a result of making a gift, the donor loses the use of the money for the rest of his life (and his estate loses its use until the estate tax is due, nine months after his death, when a larger estate tax would be payable if no gift had been made.) Loss of the use of the amount of the gift tax may mean loss of not merely interest or dividend income but foregoing as well the opportunity to acquire appreciating assets. However, if the unified credit and annual per-donee exclusion eliminate any gift tax, this factor need not be taken into account.

(2) The estate tax may be paid with Treasury bonds purchased at a discount and redeemable for this purpose at par.[16] No such option is available for the gift tax.

(3) Appreciation is not universal, as many investors learned from personal experience during the 1970s. Donated assets may decline in value; a smaller combined gift and estate tax might have been paid had the donor kept the property until death, even after taking into account the exclusion of the gift tax itself from the tax base.

(4) "Qualified real property", as defined in § 2032A, may be eligible for a reduction in estate tax value of as much as $700,000.[17] No such reduction is available for purposes of the gift tax. On the other hand, in order for property to qualify under the section, percentage tests provided in § 2032A(b)(1) must be satisfied. Gifts of other assets may increase the possibility that these requirements will be met.

As in other areas of estate planning, one must weigh conflicting considerations in order to judge whether significant transfer tax savings are likely to result from a particular gift.

[2] Income Tax Consequences

[a] Advantages

The potential income tax savings from gifts remain largely intact after the 1976 and 1981 Acts, except that the rate reductions diminish the amounts that may be saved. A gift that shifts the taxability of income produced by the property given from the donor to another individual or to a trust may

---

15. See § 2035(d)(2), discussed at ¶ 5.02 [3][b][i] infra.

16. See ¶ 16.03 infra.

17. See § 2032A(a)(2). The figure is scheduled to increase to $750,000 for decedents dying after 1982.

have the effect of moving income from the top income tax bracket to the bottom bracket or may even cause such income to be tax-free because the donee's income is too low to be subject to the income tax. Although income which is taxable to a trust when received may, under the throwback rule, be subject to an additional tax [18] when it is distributed, income accumulated for a beneficiary who is unborn or under age 21 is exempt from additional tax unless the beneficiary receives distributions of income from three or more trusts and the multiple trust rule applies.[19]

[b] Disadvantages

Gifts ordinarily have no adverse income tax consequences to the donee because § 102(a) expressly excludes gifts from gross income. The exclusion, however, is inapplicable to the income from property given or to gifts of income.[20]

A gift may have adverse income tax consequences to the donor either because the transfer causes him to realize income or because income from the transferred property will continue to be taxed to him despite his having given it away. Realization of income as a result of the transfer sometimes may be required by a specific Code provision [21] or by general rules developed to deal with transfers of property subject to liabilities. Income from the transferred property also may continue to be taxed to the transferor under the assignment of income doctrine.[22]

[c] "Net Gifts" and Other Transfers Subject to Liabilities

The income tax consequences of gifts subject to payment by the donee of the donor's gift tax ("net gifts") or of a mortgage or lien on the donated property have been extensively litigated, but some uncertainties remain. In a "net gift," the gift tax is deductible in computing the value of the gift if payment of the tax is a condition of the gift.[23] What remains unclear are the income tax consequences to the donor if the gift tax exceeds his basis. The courts are divided as to whether or not the donor realizes income to the extent of such excess.[24]

---

18. §§ 665–667. For a discussion of the rule, see ¶ 11.02 infra.

19. See ¶ 11.02[2] infra.

20. § 102(b).

21. See, e.g., § 453B (realization of gain on disposition of installment obligation).

22. For discussion, see ¶ 4.01[2][a] supra.

23. See Rev.Rul. 75–72, 1975–1 CB 310. Other rulings illustrate the gift tax computation for donors in states that also impose a state gift tax which the donee is to pay. See Rev.Rul. 76–49, 1976–1 CB 294 (New York); Rev.Rul. 76–57, 1976–1 CB 297 (North Carolina); Rev.Rul. 76–104, 1976–1 CB–301 (California); Rev.Rel. 76–105, 1976–1 CB 304 (Virginia).

24. Donor taxable: See Victor P. Diedrich v. Commissioner, 643 F.2d 499, 81–1 USTC

¶ 9249 (8th Cir. 1981); Estate of Aaron Levine v. Commissioner, infra; Joseph W. Johnson, Jr. v. Commissioner, 495 F.2d 1079, 74–1 USTC ¶ 9355 (6th Cir. 1974), cert. denied 419 U.S. 1040 (1974). But see Ralph Owen v. Commissioner, 652 F.2d 1271, 81–2 USTC ¶ 9509 (6th Cir. 1981), in which the Sixth Circuit declined to follow Johnson in a case involving a transaction which antedated the Johnson decision, stating " * * * we conclude that principles of stare decisis would be served by this panel's preservation of the coexistence of Johnson and Turner." 652 F.2d at 1271, 81–2 USTC ¶ 9509 at p. 87,659. In Turner v. Commissioner, 410 F.2d 752, 69–1 USTC ¶ 9416 (6th Cir. 1969), the Sixth Circuit's per curiam affirmance of a Tax Court decision had favored the taxpayer in a net gift case. These holdings leave the question unsettled in the Sixth Circuit.

Contra: See Edna B. Hirst v. Commissioner, 572 F.2d 427, 78–1 USTC ¶ 9166 (4th Cir.

Generally, a donor who gives property which secures a liability realizes for income tax purposes the amount of the liability [25] if either (1) the liability is non-recourse,[26] i.e., may not be enforced against him personally; or (2) the liability is recourse but the donee agrees to pay it.[27] If the liability exceeds the fair market value of the property transferred, the Commissioner includes the excess in the amount realized but the courts are divided.[28] Some courts apply a special treatment to "net gifts" and allow the donor to avoid realization of the excess of gift tax over his basis.[29] As the donee's basis becomes the amount of gift tax paid, a portion of the unrealized appreciation when the gift is made escapes income taxation. This tax-free portion is the excess of the gift tax over the donor's basis for the transferred property. For example, if the basis is $1,000, the fair market value is $100,000, and the donor's federal gift tax is $25,000 (resulting in a net gift of $75,000), the donee's basis would be $25,750.[30] The gain realized on a later sale by the donee would be only $74,250. If the donor had made the sale, he would have realized a gain of $99,000. The difference, $24,750, is never subjected to income tax.

"Net gifts" may be so arranged that trust income is not taxed to the donor because of its use to pay his gift tax. Direct use of such income for that purpose would subject the donor to tax under § 677 as a use of income for his benefit.[31] But if the tax is paid with funds borrowed by the donee

---

1978), *aff'g* 63 T.C. 307 (1974). See also Estate of Kenneth W. Davis v. Commissioner, 30 TCM 1363 (1971), aff'd per curiam 469 F.2d 694, 73–1 USTC ¶ 9124 (5th Cir. 1972).

25. The Regulations generally treat liabilities discharged as being included in "the amount realized from a sale or other disposition of property," see Reg. § 1.1001–2(a), and include gifts in "dispositions." See Reg. § 1.1001–2(a)(4)(iii). Exceptions are made for discharge of indebtedness excepted by § 108 or Reg. § 1.61–12, and for liabilities incurred by reason of the acquisition of property but not included in basis. See Reg. § 1.1001–2(a)(2), (3).

The general rule of the Regulations reflects the Supreme Court's holding in Crane v. Commissioner, 331 U.S. 1, 67 S.Ct. 1047, 91 L.Ed. 1301, 47–1 USTC ¶ 9217 (1947). Before the Regulations were promulgated, the Crane principle had been applied to a transfer in trust where the trustee assumed a mortgage on the transferred property, even though the transferor was not personally liable. See Estate of Aaron Levine, infra. See also Malone v. United States, 326 F.Supp. 106, 71–1 USTC ¶ 9475 (N.D.Miss.1971), aff'd per curiam 455 F.2d 502, 72–1 USTC ¶ 9417 (5th Cir. 1972) (transferor personally liable). But see Glenn E. Edgar, 56 T.C. 717 (1971), in which trust grantors borrowed sums secured by liens on stock that was transferred to their trusts shortly after the borrowing. The trusts in turn sold the stock to a third party with the understanding that the loans

would be repaid only out of the security. The Tax Court held that the trusts, rather than the grantors, realized the gain on the sale, which included the difference between the amount of the loans and their bases in the stock. 56 T.C. at 745. However, the holding is obscured by the fact that the Commissioner had determined that the grantors realized income when the third party "assumed their liabilities" rather than when the stock was transferred to the trusts. Id. at 744.

26. See Reg. § 1.1001–2(a)(4)(i).

27. See Reg. § 1.1001–2(a)(4)(ii).

28. See Reg. § 1.1001–2(b); Gavin S. Miller v. Commissioner, 577 F.2d 212, 78–2 USTC ¶ 9514 (3d Cir. 1978), cert. denied, 439 U.S. 1046 (1978); Winston F. C. Guest, 77 T.C. No. 2 (1981). Contra: John F. Tufts v. Commissioner, 651 F.2d 1058, 81–2 USTC ¶ 9574 (5th Cir. 1981).

29. See note 24 supra.

30. The donee's basis is that of the donor, increased by 99% of the gift tax, or $24,750. Basis is determined under Reg. § 1.1015–4, dealing with transfers which are part gifts and part sales. See IRS Letter Rul. 7752001, 3 CCH E&GT ¶ 12,105, Aug. 25, 1977; ¶ 4.06 supra.

31. See Victor W. Krause, 56 T.C. 1242 (1971).

trust and trust income is then used to repay the loan, the donor is not taxed on such income.[32]

The disadvantage of "net gifts" is that the donee may be unable to tack the donor's holding period.[33]　Thus, to qualify for long term capital gain treatment, if the property is to be sold, it must be held by the donee for more than one year [34] after the gift is made.　However, if the donee is a trust, a holding period of more than two years is required to avoid application of § 644, under which tax on the gain (to the extent of appreciation at the time of the transfer) would be computed at the rates applicable to the donor. In that situation, the inability to tack the donor's holding period for capital gain purposes is of no significance, as the two-year holding period required to avoid § 644 will necessarily satisfy the long term capital gain requirement.

The "net gift" technique is available only if the donor either had already exhausted his unified credit or does so with the transfer in question.　Under § 2505(a), any previously unused portion of the credit must be applied to reduce the gift tax otherwise due.　Failure to claim the credit will not preserve it for use in connection with later gifts, or to apply against the donor's estate tax when he dies.

ESTATE OF AARON LEVINE v. COMMISSIONER

United States Court of Appeals, Second Circuit, 1980.
634 F.2d 12, 80–2 USTC ¶ 9549.

FRIENDLY, Circuit Judge:

The estate of Aaron Levine and his widow Anna appeal from a part of a decision of the Tax Court, 72 T.C. No. 68 (1979), which found a deficiency of $130,428.42 in Aaron Levine's 1970 income tax.　The deficiency resulted from a determination by the Commissioner that the taxpayer had realized gain upon his gift, on January 1, 1970, of income producing property consisting of land and a building at 20–24 Vesey Street in New York City (the property) to a previously created trust for the benefit of three grandchildren.

The property was originally purchased on November 1, 1944, by a corporation wholly owned by Levine.　On August 22, 1957, the corporation, which was in the course of dissolution, made a liquidating distribution of the property to the taxpayer.　Thereafter Levine obtained two non-recourse mortgages secured by the property.　One of these, for $500,000, was obtained on March 17, 1966, from the Bowery Savings Bank and represented the consolidation of numerous earlier mortgages.　The other, for $300,000, was obtained from the Commercial Trading Company on November 21, 1968;　this was later amortized to $280,000.

Levine filed a gift tax return for 1970 reporting the transaction as follows:

32.　Id.　See Abbin, "Green Stamp Giving— the Net Gift," 8 U.Miami Inst.Est. Planning § 74,1800 (1974).　However, there is a planning risk in relying on the distinction. See ¶ 9.01[9][c] infra.

33.　See IRS Letter Rul. 7752001, 3 CCH E&GT ¶ 12,105, Aug. 25, 1977, declining to follow the contrary result reached in Citizen's Nat'l Bank of Waco v. United States, 417 F.2d 675, 69–2 USTC ¶ 9655 (5th Cir. 1969).

34.　See § 1222(3).

20–24 Vesey Street, City, County and State of New York—Appraisal value $925,000.00

Mortgages

Bowery Savings Bank $500,000.00
    Interest accrued
    12/1/69 to 12/31/69 .... 2,291.67
Commercial Trading* 280,000.00
    Interest accrued
    12/1/69 to 12/31/69 .... 3,616.67
                                $785,908.34

Expenses incurred by donor in 1969 and assumed and paid by donee:

Improvements $117,716.53
Supplies 387.83
Repairs 1,253.93
Paint 63.60
Electricity 1,827.56
Steam 3,324.13
Total expenses $124.573.58

Total mortgages, interest and expenses $910,481.92
Equity .... $ 14,518.08

*Between November 1968 and January 1970, $20,000 of the $300,000 principal was amortized.

and paid a gift tax on the equity of $14,518.08. The propriety of this was not challenged. However, the Commissioner assessed a deficiency in income tax on the ground that Levine had realized a gain in the amount of the excess of the total mortgages, interest and expenses aggregating $910,481.34, all of which were assumed by the donee, over Levine's adjusted basis, which, as increased by stipulation between the parties, was $485,429.55. The result was an excess of $425,051.79 and, upon application of capital gains rates, a deficiency of $130,428.42 in income tax. The Tax Court upheld the Commissioner largely on the authority of Crane v. C.I.R., 331 U.S. 1 (1947), which had affirmed this court's decision, 153 F.2d 504 (1945) (L. Hand, J.). This appeal followed.

At first blush the layman and even the lawyer or judge not conditioned by exposure to tax law would find it difficult to understand how a taxpayer can realize $910,484.91 in gain by giving away property in which he possessed an equity of $14,518.08. Doubtless Mrs. Crane experienced a similar difficulty when she was held to have realized $275,500 (for a net taxable gain of $23,031.45), after she netted a mere $2,500 on the sale of an apartment building that she had inherited subject to a $255,000 mortgage and $7,042.50 in overdue interest payments, and had sold, under threat of foreclosure, subject to the same mortgage principal and $15,857,71 in defaulted interest payments.   *   *   *

Instead of addressing himself directly to the ultimately dispositive question, what did Mrs. Crane receive, Chief Justice Vinson stated in his *Crane* opinion, 331 U.S. at 6, that "Logically, the first step   *   *   *   is to determine the unadjusted basis of the property   *   *   *." This must have struck Mrs. Crane as peculiar since she had claimed what would normally be the most favorable stance for the Commissioner in the determination of gain, namely, that her basis was zero. The answer to the Chief Justice's question lay in then § 113(a)(5), incorporated as modified in I.R.C. § 1014(a), which says that if property is acquired from a decedent the unadjusted basis is "the fair market value of such property at the time of such acquisition." On Mr. Crane's death the property had been appraised—somewhat unscientifically one might guess—as having exactly the value of the encumbrances, $262,042.50. If "property" as used in § 113(a) meant simply what the property was worth to Mrs. Crane, i.e., her "equity," her basis was zero, as she contended. However, *Crane* accepted the Commissioner's theory that since the term referred to "the land and buildings themselves, or the owner's rights in them, undiminished by the mortgage, the basis was the appraised value of $262,042.50."

The next step was to determine whether the unadjusted basis should be adjusted by deducting depreciation "to the extent allowed (but less than the amount allowable)" as required by § 113(b)(1)(B), now incorporated as modified in I.R.C. § 1016(a)(2). Here again the parties took unconventional positions. Proceeding from her zero basis theory, Mrs. Crane maintained that no depreciation could be taken, although she had in fact taken depreciation deductions totalling $25,500, 331 U.S. at 3 n. 2. The Commissioner, true to his theory of basis, see §§ 23(n) and 114(a) of the 1938 Act, now I.R.C. § 167(g), thought that depreciation deductions of $28,045.10 should have been taken, and the Court agreed.

"At last," said the Chief Justice, 331 U.S. at 12, "we come to the problem of determining the 'amount realized' on the 1938 sale." In fact the Court's answers to the two earlier questions had predetermined the answer to the dispositive one. If nonrecourse mortgages contribute to the basis of property, then they must be included in the amount realized on its sale. Any other course would render the concept of basis nonsensical by permitting sellers of mortgaged property to register large tax losses stemming from an inflated basis and a diminished realization of gain. It would also permit depreciation deductions in excess of a property holder's real investment which could never subsequently be recaptured. * * *

Taxpayer argues that, be all this as it may *Crane* is inapplicable because the transaction here was a gift and not a sale.

Apart from the general incongruity in finding that a gift yields a realized gain to the donor, petitioner argues that it is by no means clear how the Code's gross income, realization and recognition provisions apply to a donor's "gain" realized as incidental to a gift. Section 61(a)(3) defines gross income to include "[g]ains derived from dealings in property"—a term seemingly broad enough to include gains from gifts. The same is true with respect to § 1001(a), which provides that "[t]he gain from the sale *or other disposition of property* shall be the excess of the amount realized therefrom over the adjusted basis provided in section 1011 for determining gain * * * ." (emphasis supplied). Apparent difficulty is encountered, however, when we come to the critical provision, § 1001(c), entitled "[r]ecognition of gain or loss," which states that "[e]xcept as otherwise provided in this subtitle, the entire amount of the gain or loss, determined under this section, on *the sale or exchange* of property shall be recognized." (emphasis supplied).

Taxpayer suggests that the change in language from "other disposition of property" in § 1001(a), which seems broad enough to encompass a gift, but see United States v. Davis, 370 U.S. 65, 68–69 and n. 5 (1962), to "sale or exchange" in § 1001(c), which would appear not to be so, postpones recognition of any "gain" realized in the instant transaction. This, he argues, is appropriate because while a sale or exchange results in the transferee's acquisition of a new basis, see § 1012, a gift ordinarily transfers the donor's basis plus any gift tax paid to the donee, § 1015, and tax on any gain can thus fairly be postponed until the donee engages in a taxable disposition. However, this argument overlooks

> [t]he general rule * * * that when property is sold or otherwise disposed of, any gain realized must also be recognized, absent an appropriate nonrecognition provision in the Internal Revenue Code.

[Footnote omitted.] King Enterprises v. United States, 418 F.2d 511, 514 (Ct.Cl.1969). See 3 Mertens, Federal Income Taxation, § 20.13 at 50 n. 4 (1980). A comparison of the present § 1001(c) with its pre-1976 predecessors, which, of course, are here controlling, suggests that § 1001(c) merely limits nonrecognition to certain transactions described in detail elsewhere in the Code and does not confer it on all dispositions other than sales or exchanges. However, we need not decide this question in view of our disposition of the case.

Levine relies also on the established principle that a gift of appreciated unmortgaged property does not give rise to gain, even when deductions have been taken for business expenses which were necessary to the appreciation of the property. [Citations omitted.] However, the transaction here in question was not a "pure" gift. The donee assumed not only the $785,908,34 in mortgages and accrued interest for which Levine was not personally liable but also the $124,573.58 of 1969 expenses, not constituting a lien, for which he was. If the donee had paid the latter sum directly to Levine, this case would clearly be governed by *Crane* since the donor would have received "boot." However, the assumption of another's legal obligation or debt is considered income under Old Colony Trust Co. v. C.I.R., 279 U.S. 716, 729 (1929), and United States v. Hendler, supra, 303 U.S. at 566. We can thus see no sound reason for reaching a result differing from that in *Crane* on the facts of this case. We need not decide what the result should be if Levine had merely donated the property subject to non-recourse mortgages without an explicit "sale" element—in this case, the donee's assumption of his 1969 personal liabilities. Compare Johnson v. C.I.R., 495 F.2d 1079, 1083 & n. 8 (6 Cir.), cert. denied, 419 U.S. 1040 (1974).

In opposition to this the taxpayer relies on the "net gift" cases, notably Turner v. C.I.R., 49 T.C. 356 (1968), aff'd per curiam, 410 F.2d 752 (6 Cir. 1969), and Hirst v. C.I.R., 63 T.C. 307 (1974), aff'd, 572 F.2d 427 (4 Cir. 1978) (en banc). These cases involved intrafamily gifts of low-basis property conditioned on the donee's paying the donor's gift tax liability. Although the donor may subtract any gift tax liability assumed by the donee from the market value of the gift in computing gift tax, Rev. Ruling 71–232, 1971–1 C.B. 275, the Commissioner has long asserted that gift tax paid by the donee may constitute capital gains to the donor insofar as it exceeds the latter's basis on the donated property. The Commissioner's views did not prevail in *Turner* and *Hirst*.   Yet in Johnson v. C.I.R., supra, they subsequently triumphed in the same circuit that had decided *Turner*.   While the facts in *Johnson* were peculiarly favorable to the Commissioner, we consider that it effectively overruled *Turner* as a precedent.   With respect to *Hirst*, we join the commentators in believing that District Judge Thomsen's opinion written for the panel in *Hirst*, 572 F.2d at 434, which was adopted by two members of the *en banc* court, is far more persuasive than the contrary view of the prevailing opinions of that court. [Citations omitted.]

Although the Commissioner's position in the net gift cases goes further, the holding of *Johnson* and the reasoning of the dissent in *Hirst* are consistent with the narrow ground on which we rest our decision here, since the gift tax, like Levine's 1969 expenses, is a personal liability of the donor. See Hirst v. C.I.R., supra, 572 F.2d at 436 (Thomsen, J., panel opinion). This is not to say that we reject the broader analysis urged by the Commissioner and adopted by the Tax Court in this case, to wit, that *Crane* mandates that the transfer of property encumbered by any debt, nonrecourse or personal, results in potentially taxable benefits even in the case of a "pure" gift.   We simply leave this benefit orientation and the other arguments advanced to another day.   It is comforting to note, however, that an analysis of Levine's tax returns indicates his successful conversion of the appreciated value of the Vesey Street property into "benefits" at least as tangible as those in *Crane*.   The calculation of Levine's taxable gain, as found by the Tax Court, may be presented as follows:

(1) Amount realized

    (a) Expenses assumed
        by donee $124,573.00
    (b) Mortgages 780,000.00
    (c) Interest payments
        assumed by donee 5,908,34
    (d) Total $910,481.34

(2) Less: Adjusted basis

    (a) Unadjusted basis $385,485.02
    (b) Plus: Capital
        Improvements 334,542.00
    (c) Improvements paid for
        by donee 117,716.53
    (d) Subtotal 837,743.55
    (e) Less: Depreciation 352,314.00
    (f) Adjusted basis $485,429.55

(3) Gain $425,051.79

Of the total taxable gain of $425,051.59, the sum of $124,573.00 may be allocated directly to the 1969 expenses which Levine shifted to the donee-trust.   As was previously noted, these expenses are closely akin to the "boot" of $2,500 received by Mrs. Crane.   In addition Levine's mortgage schedule   *   *   *   indicates that of the $780,000 in mortgages on the Vesey Street property at the time of its transfer, at least $235,044.22 derived from an outstanding mortgage which Levine acquired with the property in

1957, while the remaining $564,955.77 represents the net non-recourse indebtedness incurred during the period of Levine's ownership.　As the table above indicates $334,452 of the later amount was reinvested in capital improvements.　Since the original mortgage of $235,044.22 must be assumed to have contributed toward Levine's unadjusted basis in the property,[35] and the subsequent capital improvements adjusted Levine's basis upward by the extent of their value, $569,496.23 (or $235,044.22 + $334,452.00) in basis credit derives solely from the non-recourse mortgages.　Yet, upon disposition of the property in 1970 Levine's stipulated basis was merely $485,429.55.　The shortfall between this and the aggregate contribution of the non-recourse mortgages, i.e., $84,066.68, can only be explained by depreciation deductions that Levine could not have taken *but for* the mortgages.　Finally, there are two additional sources of "benefit" in this case with no analogue in *Crane*.　One is the sum of $210,503.77 out of Levine's net borrowings of $544,955.77, see discussion supra, which was apparently not reinvested in capital improvements on the property, and which the taxpayer may thus be considered to have "pocketed."　The second is the $5,908.34 in interest payments owed by the taxpayer but assumed by the donee.[36]　Together, these four varieties of "benefit" sum exactly to what was found to be the taxpayer's total taxable income:

 (a) expenses assumed
   by donee $124,573.00

 (b) depreciation resulting
   from nonrecourse
   mortgages ....　84,066.68

 (c) pocketed mortgage
   funds ....　210,503.77

 (d) interest assumed by donee　　　　　　5,908.34
 TOTAL......................................$425,051.79

To tax these "benefits" upon a disposition, at capital gains rates and without interest, is scarcely harsh.　Failure to do so would mean, so far as we can see, that the $210,503.77 which the taxpayer obtained for his personal use by non-recourse loans against the appreciation of the property would never be taxed either as ordinary income or as gain (although, unless paid off by the donee, it would diminish any realization on the property), and that the benefits obtained by the depreciation deductions would remain untaxed unless and until the donee sold the property, when they would operate as a reduction of the donee's adjusted basis which was passed on to the donee. In light of the seeming equity of the result reached, an otherwise similar case lacking the element of personal debt assumed by the donee might lead us to look with sympathy on the scant case-law suggesting that the *Crane*

35.　Levine acquired his encumbered property at a basis equal to its market value, I.R.C. § 334(a).　Since any subsequent payments on the principal of the original mortgage would not have increased Levine's basis, see Ford v. United States, 311 F.2d 951, 953–55 (Ct.Cl.1963), this mortgage must be deemed to be included in the original basis of the property.

36.　The Commissioner in *Crane* did not include a similar sum of $15,857.71 in interest payments assumed by the buyer of the mortgaged property, see 331 U.S. at 4 n. 6, apparently because interest due was a deductible item.　This issue has not been raised before us.

principle may apply even to "pure" gifts, see Malone v. United States, 326 F.Supp. 106 (N.D.Miss.1971), aff'd, 455 F.2d 502 (5 Cir. 1972), even though a taxpayer could avoid application of *Crane* by withholding his beneficence until death. For reasons we have indicated, we simply do not find it necessary to decide that broader question on the facts here before us.

The judgment of the Tax Court is affirmed.

¶ 6.02 THE FEDERAL GIFT TAX

Unlike the estate tax provisions, which explicitly define the "estate" to be taxed,[37] the gift tax sections contain no definition of "gift." Section 2501(a)(1) imposes the tax on "the transfer of property by gift * * * by an individual" and § 2511 reiterates that various kinds of transfers are included, but neither section defines the term "gift." Although Congress has undertaken, in §§ 2514–2517, to categorize a limited number of transactions for gift tax purposes and the Commissioner has explicitly labelled others,[38] many definitional problems remain.

Unlike the income tax, the gift tax is cumulative throughout the life of the taxpayer. Beginning in 1982, there is an annual exclusion of $10,000 per donee for gifts of present interests; [39] there also is an unlimited marital deduction for qualifying transfers to the spouse of the transferor [40] and a deduction for certain transfers to charity; [41] and there is a unified credit of $62,800 against gift tax, under § 2505, that is equivalent to an exemption (applied against the bottom gift tax brackets) of $225,000. The credit (and equivalent exemption) are scheduled to increase annually until 1987, when they will be $192,800 and $600,000, respectively.[42]

Gifts that are not covered by the annual exclusion must be reported on an annual basis.[43] Each gift tax return carries forward the total of prior gifts in excess of the annual exclusion in order to determine the tax rate on gifts for the current period.

¶ 6.03 ARRANGEMENTS TO SAVE GIFT TAXES

Literally, the gift tax is the easiest kind of levy to avoid. Gifts are voluntary transfers of property, and a client who makes no such transfers incurs no gift taxes. Even though he wishes to move wealth into the hands of other people, he may be able to do so without making a gift. Sales and informal arrangements discussed in Chapter 8 often are used for this purpose. But these alternatives are not always available as a practical matter,

---

37. §§ 2031, 2051.

38. See Reg. § 25.2511–1(h).

39. § 2503(b), as amended by § 441(a) of the Economic Recovery Tax Act of 1981. Before the amendment, the exclusion was $3,000.

40. § 2523.

41. § 2522.

42. The credit is reduced for both gift tax and estate tax purposes by 20 percent of the amount allowed as a specific exemption under prior law, former § 2521, with respect to gifts made after September 8, 1976, and before January 1, 1977. See § 2505(c).

43. § 6075(b). Quarterly reporting for all taxable gifts was the rule between 1970 and 1981. Prior to 1971, annual returns were required.

and clients frequently do make transfers which constitute gifts for purposes of the tax. Their motives may be to save income taxes or estate taxes, or the myriad non-tax reasons for moving wealth into other hands. Arrangements to save gift taxes seek to allow clients to do what they want with their wealth at minimum cost.

The two major ways to achieve this goal with gifts are:

(1) Using statutory exclusions and deductions;

(2) Minimizing asset valuations.

[1] Using Statutory Exclusions and Deductions

Estate planning to minimize gift tax burdens is largely based upon specific statutory exclusions and deductions. The major possibilities for saving gift taxes by using these statutory provisions may be grouped under seven headings:

(1) The present interest exclusion;

(2) Gift-splitting by married persons;

(3) The gift tax marital deduction;

(4) The exclusion of qualified transfers for tuition and medical care;

(5) The gift tax charitable deduction;

(6) Exclusion of the donor's gift tax; and

(7) Other statutory exclusions.

[a] The Present Interest Exclusion

"An unrestricted right to the immediate use, possession, or enjoyment of property or the income from property (such as a life estate or term certain) is a present interest in property." [44] Transfers of such interests, as well as transfers to certain trusts and trust substitutes for minors, are freed from both gift taxes [45] and estate taxes [46] if the value of the donee's gift does not exceed $10,000 in a calendar year. If such value exceeds $10,000, an exclusion of that amount is still allowed. The excess, to whatever extent it exceeds the amount covered by the donor's unified credit, is a taxable transfer for gift tax purposes. Whether the gift is included in the donor's taxable estate depends on what interests in, or powers over, the property the donor retains or possesses at his death or during the three preceding years.[47]

Many clients who would like to qualify for the exclusion are not aware of the full range of possibilities to use it to transfer a maximum amount of their wealth with a minimum degree of control by the donee for whom the transfer is made. For example, some clients want a trustee to be able to determine the extent to which a beneficiary receives income and principal

44. See Reg. § 25.2503–3(b).

45. § 2503.

46. § 2035(b)(2). The exclusion is inapplicable to "any transfer with respect to a life insurance policy."

47. § 2035(d)(2), discussed at ¶ 5.02[3][b][i] supra. All such gifts after 1976 and within three years of the donor's death are includible in the donor's estate if he died before 1982, unless the present interest exclusion covers all gifts to the particular donee. See § 2035 prior to its amendment by § 424(a) of the Economic Recovery Tax Act of 1981.

until the beneficiary is mature enough to handle substantial sums himself. This can be achieved under the provision for present interest gifts for minors without losing the present interest exclusion. A trust may qualify under § 2503(c) even though it provides that distributions are discretionary with the trustee until the beneficiary reaches age 21.[48] Under Revenue Ruling 74–43,[49] the trust may even continue beyond that time, as long as upon attaining age 21, the beneficiary has the power to withdraw principal at any time within some specified period, such as the next 90 days; if he fails to do so, the principal may continue to be held by the trustee, with income and principal payable only in accordance with the donor's directions as set forth in the trust instrument (which may give the trustee discretion to determine when distributions shall be made, and in what amounts).

An even more aggressive planning technique is to make the exercise of the right of withdrawal available only in the year in which transfers are made in trust. For example, such transfers may be made when the beneficiary is six years old, subject to his (or his guardian's) right to withdraw the amount transferred within 30 days of notice to him that the transfer has been made. It is unlikely that the withdrawal right will be exercised but its existence creates a present interest in the full amount transferred.[50]

If the client is willing to give the beneficiary full control over trust income, it is possible to get the present interest exclusion for the major portion of the gift even though the beneficiary is never entitled to withdraw the principal. For example, if the beneficiary is a twenty-year-old female, the actuarial value of an interest in income for her life is over 94 percent of the total amount transferred [51] in trust. A transfer of $10,000 to a trust giving her such income would produce a present interest exclusion of over $9,400, leaving less than $600 as a future interest ineligible for the exclusion and hence required to be included in taxable gifts.

If a trust of $10,000 (or $20,000 if the donor's spouse consents to treat half the gift as made by her) is regarded as too much trouble to justify the income and gift tax savings it may produce, even with anticipated additions in future years, a less formal alternative is a gift to a custodian for a minor beneficiary under the Uniform Gifts to Minors Act.[52] The Act authorizes gifts to a custodian for a minor as a simplified alternative to gifts to guardians. The custodianship generally terminates at the age of majority under state law and the principal and any accumulated income must be paid to the beneficiary at that time. Until then, it is in the control of the custodian without the tax reporting formalities of a trust. As majority under state law is usually age 18, use of the custodianship instead of a § 2503(c) trust often means that the beneficiary will be entitled to the property three years earlier and without the opportunity that may be provided to extend the trust.

---

48. See Reg. § 25.2503–4(b)(1).

49. 1974–1 CB 285.

50. See D. Clifford Crummey v. Commissioner, ¶ 9.03[4] infra; Rev.Rul. 73–405, 1973–2 CB 321, which also discusses the requirement of notice and a reasonable period in which to exercise the withdrawal right.

51. Reg. § 25.2512–9(f), Table A(2).

52. See, e.g., N.Y. EPTL 7–4.1 et seq.

A list of the state statutes adopting the Uniform Gifts to Minors Act can be found at 2 CCH E&GT ¶ 8500.08.

LEONARD ROSEN v. COMMISSIONER [53]

United States Court of Appeals, Fourth Circuit, 1968.
397 F.2d 245, 68–2 USTC ¶ 12,539.

CRAVEN, Circuit Judge:

These consolidated appeals are taken from a decision of the Tax Court adverse to the taxpayers/appellants Leonard Rosen, Dorothy Rosen, Julius J. Rosen and Claire A. Rosen.   The only issue presented for review is their entitlement to annual exclusions of up to $3,000 per donee in the computation of gift taxes.   We hold that the taxpayers are entitled to the exclusions for the years in question, 1961, 1962 and 1963, in respect to the "income interests" of shares of Gulf American Land Corporation donated by the taxpayers to trusts created by them in 1961.   We further hold that valuation of the donated income interests may be accomplished by reference to actuarial tables published by the Commissioner and we remand the case to the Tax Court for a (1) determination as to which of the tables is most appropriate to value the donated income interests and (2) determination of the precise dollar amount of exclusion to which the taxpayers are entitled for each year.

Leonard Rosen and his brother Julius J. Rosen are in substantial control of Gulf American Land Corporation (Gulf American), a business incorporated in Florida in 1957 and devoted to the acquisition and development of large tracts of unimproved real estate into a planned community in which homesites, multiple dwelling sites and commercial and industrial lots are offered for sale.   Through subsidiaries, the company has also engaged in the construction of houses, in land drainage, the construction of roads and waterways, etc.   The company's major project during the years 1961–1963 was the development of a large tract of land on the southwest coast of Florida.   The company's basic policy has been to increase its raw land inventory for development and subdivision purposes.

Although Gulf American stock is held by public shareholders as well as the Rosens, the company has never paid a dividend on its common stock but has retained all of its earnings for growth purposes.   It is the failure of the company to pay dividends which has created the problem presented on appeal.

On September 14, 1961, Leonard Rosen transferred 21,000 shares of Gulf American common stock in trust, naming his three children as beneficiaries.   On the same date Julius J. Rosen transferred 24,000 shares of Gulf American in trust for the benefit of his four children.   The trust agreements, executed in 1961, were identical in all material respects, except for the number of shares constituting the *res*, the beneficiaries named therein, and except for the periods during which income was to be paid to each beneficiary prior to the distribution of the corpus.   The entire income interest of each trust was payable to the beneficiaries no less frequently than annually and the corpus of the trust was payable to the beneficiaries when they reached specified ages.   In the Leonard Rosen trust the corpus

---

53. For results contrary to Rosen, see Lera H. Stark v. United States, 477 F.2d 131 (8th Cir. 1973), cert. denied 414 U.S. 975 (1973), in which the district court distinguished Rosen on the ground that it was not suggested there that the income interest was valueless; and Fred A. Berzon v. Commissioner, 534 F.2d 528 (2d Cir. 1976). See Horvitz, How the Nature of Trust Property Can Kill the Gift Tax Exclusion, 113 Tr. & Est. 490 (Aug. 1974).

was distributable to each beneficiary in two installments, upon the beneficiaries reaching the ages of 25 and 30. The corpus of the Julius J. Rosen trust was distributable in three installments, at the ages of 25, 30, and 35. Provisions were made for gifts over in the event of the death of a beneficiary.

The trustees named in each trust were either members of the Rosen family or persons closely associated with the Rosens or with Gulf American. Significant to the disposition of this case the trustees were given the power to sell and reinvest the corpus of the trust (the donated Gulf American shares), and the power to hold and invest in non-income producing property.

In 1962 and 1963 Leonard and Julius J. Rosen made further gifts of Gulf American shares to the trust established by them. (Dorothy and Claire A. Rosen have filed consents to have the gifts of their husbands, Leonard and Julius, treated as if made one-half by each spouse.)

The claimed exclusions are based on Section 2503(b) of the Internal Revenue Code, 26 U.S.C.A. § 2503(b), which permits exclusion from the taxpayer's annual gross gifts of $3,000 per donee. The claimed exclusions relate only to the "income interests" of the donated shares. It is conceded that the corpus of each of the Rosen trusts is to be treated as a future interest, "limited to commence in use, possession, or enjoyment at some future date or time," C. I. R. v. Disston, 325 U.S. 442, 446, 65 S.Ct. 1328, 1330, 89 L.Ed. 1720 (1945), for which the Section 2503(b) exclusion is expressly not available. Since the Gulf American shares do not have, and have never had, a specific yield (no dividends have been paid), valuation of the "income interests" was made by the taxpayers by applying the actuarial factors taken from Table I, Column 3 of Section 25.2512(f) of the I.R.S. Gift Tax Regulations. The actuarial factors assume an income yield of 3½ percent [currently 6 percent–ed.] and are intended to reflect, for tax purposes, the present worth of a life estate and a remainder interest. Resort to the tables is justified in cases where valuation necessarily presents an element of speculation and where use of the tables is actuarially sound. Bowden v. C. I. R., 234 F.2d 937 (5th Cir. 1956), McMurtry v. C. I. R., 203 F.2d 659 (4th Cir. 1953). The factors "seldom accurately predict the value in a particular situation but prove to be accurate when used in a great number of cases." Hipp v. United States, 215 F.Supp. 222 (W.D.S.C.1962).

Use of the tables is prohibited to the taxpayer only in cases where such usage would result in an "unrealistic and unreasonable" valuation. Weller v. C. I. R., 38 T.C. 790, 803 (1962). Contrary to the government's contention we think it unreasonably unrealistic to deny value to the present interest concededly possessed by the donees. Only the most unsophisticated investor, certainly not the purchaser of growth stocks, looks to currently established dividend yield to value his *present* interest. Although it is hope for the future that accounts for the investment irony of *present* value inversely proportioned to yield, such hopes are not always long postponed in an era of conglomerate merger. To deny to the taxpayers here the use of the tables is to treat, for tax purposes, the donated income interests as having no value at all.

Moveover, the trust instruments vested the trustees with the power to sell the donated shares and to reinvest the proceeds in income producing property. The Tax Court, erroneously we think, considered that the power was "illusory" because the trustees were possessed of a present intention not to exercise it. True, the taxpayers have stipulated that: "In the view of the Trustees the probability of future dividends in substantial amounts was sufficient to warrant retention of stock, notwithstanding the absence of a current income   *   *   * . It was the specific belief of the Trustees that retention of Gulf American stock would furnish greater overall benefits to the beneficiaries than would an immediate sale and investment of the proceeds in then currently income-producing property." It does not seem to us that a business decision not presently to change an investment voids the power to do so.

It is important to note that it has not been suggested to us that the "income interest" was valueless. Rather the government concedes that a *present* income interest (rather than a future interest, C. I. R. v. Disston, supra) was in fact donated. The concession seems to us near fatal. The government entertains two inconsistent positions—on one hand conceding that a valuable right was donated and on the other contending that for tax purposes the right is valueless. The cases cited to us by the government generally stand for the proposition that the "ascertainable value" test is not met (and hence the exclusion not available) where some impediment, power or contingency stands in the way of actual realization of income. See 5 Mertens, Federal Gift and Estate Taxation § 38.08 (1959). This is not a case involving discretion to withhold income, C. I. R. v. Disston, supra, nor one where the trustee may destroy the right to receive income by exercise of a power to invade the corpus, Funkhouser's Trusts v. C. I. R., 275 F.2d 245 (4th Cir. 1959), or by exercise of a power to terminate the trust, La Fortune v. C. I. R., 263 F.2d 186 (10th Cir. 1958). Nor is the power to sell the Gulf American shares and reinvest in income producing property truly illusory in the sense that substantial impediments exist to its exercise, e.g., the nature of the underlying property causes conversion to be improbable. Hamm v. C. I. R., 20 T.C. 1814 (1961), aff'd 325 F.2d 934 (8th Cir. 1963). On the contrary, Gulf American shares appear to be freely marketable—the stock is held publicly and is listed on the American Stock Exchange.

In Estate of Irma Green, 22 T.C. 728 (1954), the specific yield of the income interest was ignored by the Commissioner in favor of an application of an actuarial table producing less income than actually realized. It is a difference without a distinction that in *Irma Green* use of the tables benefited the government and here their use benefits the taxpayers. [Citations omitted.]

There is, of course, no justification for a double standard. Neutral principles forbid that the Commissioner be allowed to apply the tables where to do so produces greater revenue and to refuse application where it does not. It is conceded that a valuable right to receive income has been donated. The right is incapable of precise valuation by reference to a specific yield. Absent extraordinary circumstances, and without regard to the amount of revenue produced, we think the taxpayers are entitled to resort to the actuary tables promulgated by the Commissioner himself. Hipp v. United States, 215 F.Supp. 222 (W.D.S.C.1962). "The United States is in business with enough different taxpayers so that the law of averages has ample opportunity to work." Gelb v. C. I. R., 298 F.2d 544, 552 (2d Cir. 1962). Reversed.

REVENUE RULING 69–344,
1969–1 CB 225

* * *

Advice has been requested whether the gift tax exclusion authorized by section 2503(b) of the Internal Revenue Code of 1954 is allowable under the circumstances set forth below.

The grantor executed an indenture and declaration of trust in favor of his grandchild. The trust provides that all of the income must be paid to the beneficiary. During the life of the beneficiary, the trustees are given liberal authority to invade principal for the benefit of the beneficiary. No income or principal, however, can be paid to anyone other than the income beneficiary during his lifetime.

The indenture of trust provides in part, as follows:

"The Grantor hereby authorizes the Trustees to invest, from time to time, in such securities and property as the Trustees may think most advantageous to any trust created hereunder, without responsibility for the exercise of their discretion in so doing. The Trustees are not to be limited in the selection of securities and property, but may, in their discretion, invest, reinvest and change investments in such stocks, bonds, shares, securities and obligations of any corporations, governmental bodies or agencies, unincorporated associations or partnerships, trusts, investment companies, investment trusts, or in a common trust fund without giving notice to any beneficiary, or in any other kind of real or personal property, domestic or foreign, wasting or non-wasting, productive or non-productive, as may, in their opinion, result in a future increase in the value or yield of any trust, notwithstanding the fact that any or all of the investments made or retained are of a character or size which but for this express authority would not be considered proper for Trustees.

"The Trustees are hereby authorized to exercise any and all options, rights, and privileges contained in any life insurance policy, or endowment contract or contracts which may become an asset owned by any trust created hereunder, including by way of illustration and not by way of limitation, the right to leave any sum on deposit with any life insurance company at interest for any length of time, to revoke any optional mode of settlement, to obtain the cash surrender value, or to convert any such policy to paid-up insurance, or extended term insurance, and the Grantor further hereby authorizes the Trustees to take out and/or continue in force and to pay the premiums on any life insurance, annuity (regardless of whether such annuity may be wholly wasting asset) or endowment contract or contracts which they may deem desirable to purchase upon the life of any beneficiary of any trust created hereunder or upon the life of any parent or spouse or issue or spouse of any issue of such beneficiary, for any purpose whatsoever, including, by way of illustration but not by way of limitation, the purpose of providing cash for the payment of taxes upon the death of such beneficiary. All details of any such contract shall be within the direction of the Trustees."

* * *

The decision in Jesse S. Phillips v. Commissioner, 12 T.C. 216 (1949), stands for the proposition that a gift in trust of the right to income from nonincome-producing property is a gift of a future interest, for which no annual exclusion is allowable. It was specifically held in that case that a gift in trust of life insurance policies is a gift of a future interest for which no annual exclusion is allowable.

The entire value of any gift of a future interest must be included in the total amount of gifts for the calendar year in which the gift is made.

The above-quoted language from the indenture of trust indicates an intention of the grantor that the trustees pursue an investment policy that results in a future increase in the value of the trust, rather than an investment policy to provide current income to the trust beneficiaries. Thus, the gift of the income interest does not create an unrestricted right to the income from property within the meaning of section 25.2503–3(b) of the regulations.

The purchase of life insurance policies authorized by the indenture further indicates an intention that future rather than present interests be created for life insurance policies are generally purchased for future rather than immediate use and enjoyment.

Accordingly, it is held that the gift in trust on the terms and conditions stated does not qualify as a gift of a present interest under section 2503(b) of the Code. Therefore, an annual exclusion may not be allowed in respect thereto.

The Internal Revenue Service will not follow the decision in Rosen v. Commissioner, 397 F.2d 245 (1968) in the disposition of similar cases.

[b] Gift-Splitting by Married Persons

Present law includes two related tax concessions for lifetime gifts by married persons:

(1) Gift-splitting allows half of the gifts by either spouse to third persons to be treated for gift tax purposes as having been made by the other (non-donor) spouse; and

(2) The gift tax marital deduction allows all qualifying gifts made after 1981 to a spouse to be free of gift tax.

Both are primarily important in minimizing taxes on wealth ultimately passing from spouses to third persons, although in form the gift tax marital deduction relates to wealth passing to a spouse instead.

Gift-splitting under § 2513 causes gifts to any third person by either spouse to be treated as being made one-half by the other spouse, if she consents to such treatment. Gift-splitting may result in a lower total tax because it divides the gift between the progressive rate brackets applicable to two donors instead of only one and uses all or part of any unused portion of the non-donor spouse's unified credit. If the gift is of a present interest, an exclusion will be allowed for each spouse under § 2503(b) for the total attributed to that spouse.

For example, a husband may wish to give his child $15,000. Without gift-splitting, only $10,000 of this amount would qualify for the present interest exclusion under § 2503(b). However, if his wife consents to treat the gift (and any other gifts to third persons made by the husband during the same calendar year) as having been made one-half by her, the entire amount will be exempt from gift tax because each spouse's $10,000 present interest exclusion exceeds one-half the amount of the gift.

As gift-splitting causes liability for the combined taxes of both spouses to be joint and several [54]—i.e., both are liable for the full amount of the tax—either may pay the entire amount due from both without thereby making a taxable gift to the other spouse.[55] However, for gifts made after 1981, the unlimited gift tax marital deduction eliminates the significance of this rule.

Of course, if the non-donor spouse had already made enough post-1976 gifts of her own, no saving would result from splitting gifts in excess of the spouse's annual exclusions. Such splitting could even produce a higher total tax on the split gift and on future gifts of the non-donor spouse.

Splitting also may lead to unfavorable estate tax results if the gift is included in the donor's estate.[56] If such inclusion is caused under § 2035 by the donor's retention of an interest or power until less than three years before his death, the portion attributed to the non-donor spouse as a result of gift-splitting is not included in her adjusted taxable gifts for estate tax purposes.[57] But if such inclusion is under another Code section, such as § 2037, dealing with reversionary interests, the portion attributed to the non-donor spouse remains includible in her adjusted taxable gifts even though such portion is also included and taxed in full in the donor's estate.[58]

[c] The Gift Tax Marital Deduction

The gift tax marital deduction, like gift-splitting by married persons (discussed in the preceding paragraph), is primarily important in minimizing taxes on wealth ultimately passing from spouses to third persons. In form, the gift tax marital deduction relates to wealth passing to a spouse instead.

In order to qualify for the gift tax marital deduction, an interest in property must be:

---

54. § 2513(d).

55. Reg. § 25.2511–1(d). For a discussion, see ¶ 6.03[1][f] infra.

56. Decisions under the pre-1976 Code provisions denied restoration to the non-donor spouse of the portion of her specific exemption which was applied against such gifts. See, e.g., Rachel H. Ingalls, 40 T.C. 751 (1963), aff'd per curiam 336 F.2d 874, 64–2 USTC ¶ 12,266 (4th cir. 1964). This result was endorsed by the Ways & Means Committee Report on the Tax Reform Act of 1976 with respect to the unified credit which replaced the specific exemption. See H.R. Rep.No. 1380, 94th Cong., 2d Sess. 13, re-

printed in [1976] U.S. Code Cong. & Ad. News 3356, 3357.

57. § 2001(e). For gift tax purposes it is included § 2502(a). § 2001(e) deals only with gifts includible under § 2035.

58. If inclusion in the donor's estate is caused by his retention until within 3 years of his death of an interest or power which he then transferred or released, whether or not such portion attributable to the non-donor spouse continues to be includible in her adjusted taxable gifts depends on whether inclusion in the donor's estate is under § 2035(d)(2) or under another Code section. See § 2038(a)(1).

(1) transferred by gift "to a donee who at the time of the gift is the donor's spouse"; [59] and

(2) not disqualified as a terminable interest.

The effect of the terminable interest rule is to disqualify certain interests given to a spouse that may terminate or fail and allow the property to pass to someone other than her or her estate. The rule applies to estate tax marital deduction gifts as well and is considered at length in connection with such gifts. [60]

The kinds of interests that qualify for the gift tax marital deduction are generally the same as their estate tax counterparts, and for gifts made after 1981 there is no longer any limitation on the maximum amount deductible. [61] Until the Tax Reform Act of 1976, the gift tax marital deduction was limited to one-half the value of qualifying gifts to the spouse, whatever their size. [62] For gifts made after 1976 and before 1982, the limit on the gift tax marital deduction was increased to the full amount of qualifying gifts to the spouse up to $100,000 plus one-half of such gifts in excess of $200,000. [63]

The Economic Recovery Tax Act of 1981, in addition to removing the previous limits on the amount of the deduction, allowed the deduction for lifetime gifts of "qualified terminable interest property," [64] similar to the new estate marital deduction provision for such interests at death. [65]

Qualifying gifts generally no longer need be reported on a gift tax return. [66] Such reporting is required, however, for gifts of "qualified terminable interest property," for which an election on a return is required. [67]

The gift tax marital deduction has sometimes been oversold. Its use rarely achieves any immediate income tax benefit, as ordinarily the donor and donee spouse file a joint return and the income of both will be taxable in the same marginal bracket. Clients do not need to make gifts to a spouse that qualify for the gift tax marital deduction because the federal estate tax marital deduction generally allows them to transfer as much as they wish tax-free to a surviving spouse when they die. [67a]

From the standpoint of state death taxes, however, such gifts may be advantageous, depending on the relative wealth of the spouses and the order in which they die.

If such transfers are made during life instead, the client necessarily assumes the risk that his wife may cease to be his spouse before he dies. The rising incidence of divorce underscores the magnitude of that risk. Nevertheless, there are clients who wish to make substantial gifts to a spouse. For them, the gift tax marital deduction may be important.

59. § 2523(a).

60. § 2056(b). For a discussion, see ¶ 18.02, 18.04 infra.

61. See § 2523(a), as amended by § 403(b)(1) of the Economic Recovery Tax Act of 1981.

62. § 2523(a) (before 1976 amendment).

63. § 2523(a).

64. See § 2523(f), added by § 403(d)(2) of the Act.

65. See § 2056(b)(7), discussed at ¶ 18.04[4].

66. See § 6019(a)(2), applying to gifts made after 1981.

67. See § 2523(f)(4).

67a. See ¶ 16.01[1] infra.

Some clients make marital gifts in order to insure that gifts to third persons will be split between the spouses for wealth transfer tax purposes. For example, a wealthy husband may bequeath half of his estate to his wife and half to his children. The wife's half, which qualifies for the marital deduction in the husband's estate, may in turn be given by her to the children. Thus, the effect for tax purposes is to split the transfer of the husband's wealth to the children between him and the wife. However, use of the estate tax marital deduction for this purpose necessarily depends on the spouse who wishes to achieve such splitting—typically the wealthier spouse—dying first.

Lifetime transfers to the poorer spouse, which qualify for the gift tax marital deduction, insure against the risk that she will not survive. Her death during the life of the wealthier spouse will end the opportunity to achieve gift-splitting either by transfers to descendants that the poorer spouse consents to treat as made half by her or by transfers to her that in due course will pass from her to the descendants. Gifts to the descendants while both spouses are living may qualify for gift-splitting but do not give the poorer spouse any benefit from the transferred property. Thus, lifetime marital deduction gifts may play a unique role in combining a benefit for her with insurance against the risk that she may not be the survivor. Of course, many factors may influence the combined taxes on the estates of *H* and *W* and non-tax factors should also be taken into account in determining whether to make such gifts.[68]

[d] The Exclusion of Qualified Transfers for Tuition or Medical Care

Section 2503(e), added by § 441(b) of the Economic Recovery Tax Act of 1981, provides an exclusion for any "qualified transfer," defined as "an amount paid on behalf of an individual—

(A) as tuition to an educational institution described in section 170(b)(1)(A)(ii) for the education or training of such individual, or

(B) to any person who provides medical care (as defined in § 213(e)) with respect to such individual for such medical care."

The provision is effective for payments made after 1981. It does not apply to educational expenses other than tuition, does not cover reimbursement of the donee (as distinguished from amounts paid on his behalf), and "does not change the income tax consequences otherwise applicable to such payments." [69]

From an estate planning standpoint, § 2503(e) will be helpful in allowing full use to be made of the $10,000 present interest exclusion for gifts to an individual in addition to payment by the donor of his tuition and medical expenses.

[e] The Gift Tax Charitable Deduction

Transfers to an eligible charity [70] are a way to save gift taxes by qualifying for the gift tax charitable deduction, as such transfers are not subject to the gift tax. But for the average client, who usually wishes to make the

---

68. For a discussion, see ¶ 16.01[1].

69. See H.R.Rep.No. 97–201, 97th Cong., 1st Sess., 194 (1981).

70. Categories of eligible charities are set forth in § 2522(a).

bulk of his or her wealth available for noncharitable beneficiaries, gifts that are not solely for charity are likely to be far more useful. In order for such transfers to qualify for the gift tax charitable deduction, the charitable interest must be in one of three forms:

(1) A remainder interest in a charitable remainder unitrust or annuity trust or pooled income fund.[71]

(2) An income or lead interest in a trust in the form of a guaranteed annuity or fixed percentage of the fair market value of the property (to be determined and distributed yearly);[72]

(3) An interest described in § 170(f)(3)(B),[73] which allows "a remainder interest in a personal residence or farm," as well as other less common varieties of partial interests in property, to qualify for an income tax charitable deduction.

In a charitable remainder trust, an annuity or unitrust amount is payable to one or more individuals, with the remainder on the termination of their interests going to one or more charities. Charitable remainder trusts are primarily useful as vehicles for income tax savings.[74] The gift tax charitable deduction is another tax advantage for such trusts, but is secondary in importance if the client's main concern is the welfare of his noncharitable beneficiaries.

In a charitable lead trust, the annuity or unitrust amount is payable to a charity, with the remainder on the termination of the charity's interest going to one or more individuals. Charitable lead trusts are usually useful only if the client, or his beneficiaries, has substantial wealth, so that they will not be adversely affected by failing to receive an amount set aside for current enjoyment by a charity.[75]

Gifts to charities of remainder interests in personal residences or farms are primarily useful as a source of income tax deductions. They allow the benefit of tax deductions for both income and gift tax purposes to be combined with present enjoyment of the property by a family member or other non-charitable beneficiary.

[f] Exclusion of Donor's Gift Tax

As an incentive to encourage the making of lifetime gifts, present law allows the donor to exclude the gift tax paid in computing the amount of the taxable gift.[76] Thus, for gift tax purposes, a gift of $50,000 on which a gift tax of $10,000 is paid is a gift of only $50,000 and not $60,000. The estate tax, on the other hand, is based on the size of the taxable estate, with no deduction for the estate tax itself. This difference in treatment of the gift tax disappears if the donor dies within three years after making the gift. In such a case, any federal gift tax paid by the donor or his estate is included in his taxable estate.[77]

---

71. § 2522(c)(2)(A).

72. § 2522(c)(2)(B). The statutory language is a more convuluted form of that given above.

73. § 2522(c)(2).

74. For a discussion, see ¶ 10.02 infra.

75. For a discussion, see ¶ 10.03 infra.

76. See H.R.Rep.No. 1380, 94th Cong., 2d Sess. 1, 12, reprinted in [1976] U.S. Code Cong. & Ad. News 3356, 3366.

77. § 2035(c), discussed at ¶ 5.02[3](c) supra.

A dramatic illustration of the potential savings from this exclusion is provided by In re Irénée duPont.[78]   The case was governed by the former version of § 2035, under which the client did not have to live three years in order to achieve the saving sought.   That saving continues to be available under the present § 2035, as long as the client lives 3 years after making the gift.

Before the former president of the duPont Company died at the age of 86, he had become incompetent, and a Delaware court had appointed two guardians to manage his $176 million estate.   On October 16, 1963, the court approved the guardian's request for authority to transfer on his behalf, to a trust for his children and grandchildren, securities he owned which were valued at $36 million.   As the terms of the trust were substantially the same as the terms of his will, the gift would not change the recipients of his property.   But by disposing of the $36 million during his life rather than as part of his estate when he died, the guardians expected to save his descendants over $16 million in estate taxes.

This saving could come about because duPont's estate would be reduced by both the $36 million given away and by the gift tax of about $21 million. A reduction of about $57 million in his taxable estate would reduce his tax by 77% [79] of that amount, or about $44 million.   Even if the gift were included in his taxable estate under the former version of § 2035, the $21 million gift tax would not be added back.   If the tax in fact had been paid when he died, the money would not be part of his estate, and if the tax had not been paid, it would be deductible under § 2053 as a claim against the estate.   In either case, the credit against the estate tax arising from the $21 million gift tax and allowed by § 2012 would not be treated as an estate asset because it does not constitute "property owned at death" within the meaning of § 2033.   Thus the estate would be reduced by some $21 million, cutting the estate tax in duPont's 77% bracket by over $16 million.

In fact, duPont died December 19, 1963, only a little over two months after the Delaware court approved the guardians' request for authority to make the gift.   Under present law, the fact that he did not live for three years after making the gift would cause the gift tax thereon to be included in his gross estate and would not permit the anticipated savings of over $16 million to be achieved.

[g] Other Statutory Exclusions

[i] Employee Death Benefits and Individual Retirement Arrangements (IRAs).   The only forms of wealth that the Code explicitly exempts from both estate tax and gift tax are employee death benefits and individual retirement arrangements described in §§ 2039 and 2517 and discussed in Chapter 21.   These two forms provide as nearly ideal a shelter from income and wealth transfer taxes as the Code offers because the transfer tax exemption is combined with opportunities for income shifting and deferral.[80] Not surprisingly, the exclusion is hedged about with restrictive require-

---

78. 41 Del.Ch. 300, 194 A.2d 309 (1963).

79. Under the law in effect when duPont died, the top estate tax bracket was 77% and applied to the portion of the taxable estate in excess of $10 million.   See former § 2001.

80. For a discussion, see ¶ 21.02[2], ¶ 21.05 infra.

ments, and clients require careful guidance if the value of the shelter is to be maximized.

[ii] **Disclaimers.**   In some instances, property may be transferred from one person to another without gift tax by the use of a disclaimer.   A disclaimer, or renunciation, is the refusal of a beneficiary or heir to accept ownership of a transferor's property.   Under § 2518, added by the Tax Reform Act of 1976, a "qualified disclaimer" is defined as "an irrevocable and unqualified refusal by a person to accept an interest in property," made within nine months after the transfer, which also meets other requirements therein specified.   Section 426(a) of the Economic Recovery Tax Act of 1981 added § 2518(c)(3), providing treatment of certain transfers as disclaimers.

The disclaimer provisions may create important opportunities for revision of an estate plan after the decedent's death by rearranging beneficial interests in his estate without incurring gift taxes as a result.[81]   For example, a father who has just inherited wealth may decide to make a disclaimer if the effect will be to cause property to pass to his children, if his own resources are adequate for his needs and if he would like to make a tax-free transfer to his children.

[iii] **Transfers in Connection With Divorce; Payment of Income Taxes on Joint Returns.**   Another express exclusion from taxable gifts that is of importance in estate planning is the exemption of certain transfers in connection with divorce.[82]   Payments of income taxes by either spouse filing a joint return also are excluded.[83]

[2] Minimizing Asset Valuations

For purposes of this discussion, ways to minimize asset valuations in order to reduce gift taxes may be analyzed under two headings:

(1) Asset selection; and

(2) Corporate ownership, partial interests, and other valuation reducers.

Gifts are better suited to the pursuit of such discounts than transfers at death because of the client's greater control over timing and asset selection in the case of gifts.   A series of well-timed gifts of portions of an asset, spaced over a period of years, may be valued for significantly less in total amount than a single transfer of the asset.

[a] Asset Selection

Valuation of assets transferred during life is one area in which the taxpayer's position is often more favorable than the Commissioner's.   Taxpayers can control the time at which a gift is made and, thus, the date on which it will be valued.   In addition, taxpayers may choose from their available assets those which are likely to be undervalued for gift tax purposes.   To deal with the mass of valuation questions which arise in tax

---

81. For a discussion, see ¶ 17.02 infra.

82. § 2516.   For a discussion, see ¶ 8.05 infra.

83. Both spouses generally are liable for the full amount of the tax.   See § 6013(d)(3)

(general rule); § 6013(e) (cases in which spouse is relieved of liability).   Thus, payment by one spouse of more than his pro rata share is not a gift to the other spouse. Reg. § 25.2511–1(d).

cases, the Commissioner is forced by considerations of administrative convenience and efficiency to rely upon generalized rules and mechanical formulae. It is inevitable that such rules and formulae will understate the intrinsic economic worth of particular assets owned by individual clients, making these assets prime candidates for lifetime transfers.

Striking example of such undervaluation are gifts of certain group term life insurance policies. The Commissioner's values fail to take into account the reasonable expectation that an employer will continue to pay premiums on the policy after it is transferred. Thus, the Commissioner treats such a policy as having value for gift tax purposes only to the extent that premiums have been paid for future coverage, because of the possibility that the employer may discontinue premium payments in the future.[84] The result is that it may be possible to transfer, free of gift tax, a policy that may be of substantial value when the insured dies. And each subsequent premium payment by the employer constitutes a separate gift by the employee to the insured, and may be covered by the present interest exclusion.[85]

[b] Corporate Ownership, Partial Interests, and Other Valuation Reducers

The gift tax is assessed on the "value" [86] of property transferred by gift, but the concept of "value" is elusive at best. It is most readily applied to a transfer of full, direct ownership of an asset to a single donee, although even here there is room for differences of opinion among experts if the value cannot be determined on the basis of market quotations. Value is far more difficult to determine if an asset is owned indirectly (as through ownership of shares in a closely-held corporation), especially if the transferred shares represent only a minority interest.

One commentator asserts that "it appears possible, with a bit of advance planning, to have transfer taxes apply to as little as one-third of the real value of property transferred by gift or bequest" [87] as a result of valuation discounts obtained chiefly through use of the closely-held corporation. He lists the major factors in such undervaluation as:

(1) blockage, or a discount reflecting the fact that a sale of a large block of stock may depress the market price;

(2) unmarketability;

(3) minority interest;

(4) selling costs, including underwriting an offering;

(5) restrictions on disposition; and

(6) capital gains and tax liabilities.

[i] **Minority Stock Interests.** As another commentator has pointed out, "minority interests in closely-held corporations are difficult to sell and, therefore, are generally worth less per share than the value otherwise determined.[88] In order to qualify for such a lower valuation, a majority

84. See Rev.Rul. 76–490, 1976–2 CB 300, discussed at ¶ 6.04[2][b] infra.

85. For a discussion, see ¶ 6.03[1][a] infra.

86. § 2512(a).

87. See Cooper, "A Voluntary Tax? New Perspectives on Sophisticated Estate Tax Avoidance," 77 Colum.L.Rev. 161, 195 (1977).

88. See Lewis, The Estate Tax at 482–483 (4th ed. 1979).

stock interest may be divided, by means of a lifetime gift, into two minority interests without affecting in any way the underlying corporate structure.

Such a division may, however, be ineffective to secure a minority interest discount on transfers of interests in family-controlled businesses. In Letter Ruling 8010017,[89] the Commissioner denied such a discount for gift tax purposes for simultaneous gifts to each of three family trusts of one-third of the stock of a wholly owned corporation. The Ruling relies in part on a Congressional goal, in the Tax Reform Act of 1976, to achieve equal tax bases for lifetime or deathtime transfers of the same amounts of wealth, subject to identified incentives for lifetime giving that do not include a discount for minority interests in intra-family transfers of family-controlled businesses.

[ii] Division Between Charitable and Non-Charitable Interests.
Another source of valuation discounts is the division of ownership between charitable and non-charitable interests. For example, a father owning waterfront property may wish to give the back lots to his children. He makes such a gift, retaining land between such lots and the water, and thus secures a reduced gift tax valuation based on the possibility that his children's water view will be blocked by construction on his retained land. A subsequent gift of a conservation easement prohibiting such construction is a deductible charitable transfer for both income and gift tax [90] purposes. At the same time, it may provide a tax-free enhancement in value for the children's land, which is no longer subject to loss of view.[91]

[iii] Recognition of Discounts. Clients relying on valuation discounts should be warned that such discounts rest on administrative and judicial views that are not reflected in any explicit Code provision and have yet to receive the imprimatur of the Supreme Court. Furthermore, the Commissioner is seeking to eliminate the use of unjustified discounts.[92] But at the present time, the discounts discussed here are recognized often enough to be rewarding for many taxpayers.

---

89. 3 CCH E&GT ¶ 12,376, Dec. 6, 1979.

90. § 170(f)(3)(B)(iii) (income tax); § 2522(c)(2) (gift tax). Valuation of the easement for income and gift tax purposes is determined by a comparison of the value of the donor's property before and after the granting of the easement. See Rev.Rul. 1973–2 CB 68. A later ruling requires that such comparison be based on the "total property" of the taxpayer even though only part is subject to the easement. See Rev. Rul. 76–376, 1976–2 CB 53. Thus if the grant of the easement increases the value of the donor's retained land (by eliminating the possibility that the landowner's view will be blocked by construction), such increase must be taken into account in the before and after comparison.

91. If an owner of adjoining land is closely related to the donor of the easement, the argument could be made that enhancement in value of such land constitutes a gift to such owner. See Report of Committee on Charitable Gifts, Trusts and Foundations,

"Tax Incentives for Sensible Land Use Through Gifts of Conservation Easements," 15 Real Prop., Prob. & Tr.J. 1, 13 (1980), suggesting that the Service should not act on this basis, "absent the most egregious circumstances," to avoid discouraging gifts of conservation easements.

92. See Internal Revenue Service, Examination Technique Handbook for Estate Tax Examiners, IRM 4350 at 6(11)(3) (1980). For recent judicial rejection of a donor's claim that the value of stock should be discounted to reflect restrictions on sale and the transfer of a minority interest, see James O. Driver v. United States, 76–2 USTC ¶ 13,155 (W.D.Wis.1976). In that case, however, the gift of a minority interest on December 31, 1968, was followed by an additional gift on January 2, 1969, which together gave the donor's nephew and his family a majority interest and control.

[3] Determining When a Gift Is Complete

The date on which a gift is complete is critical for the use of statutory exclusions and deductions as well as in determining the date on which the gift will be valued.[93] Until the transfer is complete, it will not be effective to shift taxable income from the donor to the donee or to remove the property from the donor's prospective taxable estate. The converse, however, is not true; transfers that are completed gifts and subject to the gift tax may fail to achieve either income or estate tax savings.[94]

Gifts are incomplete because control over the property has been retained by the donor.[95] Whether or not the donee had received possession of the property is not determinative.[96] Nor does it matter that the donor cannot get the property back himself [97] or that his power to choose the recipients can be exercised only with one or more co-trustees.[98] For example, in Frederic E. Camp v. Commissioner [99] the court held that a gift was incomplete in 1932, when a trust was created, because the donor reserved the power to alter, amend, or revoke the trust with the consent of his mother or his half-brother, who had no substantial adverse interest in the trust property. In 1937, however, the trust instrument was amended to give the power of further amendment or revocation to the donor in conjunction with his wife, who had a life interest in income. The amendment made the gift complete in 1937 because the interest of the person whose consent was required, the donor's wife, was substantial and adverse. When the trust was created in 1932, prior to enactment of the current gift tax, the person whose consent was required (the donor's mother or his half-brother) did not have such an interest, so the gift was still incomplete.

In other situations, the parties' roles may be reversed. The Commissioner may contend that a gift is complete and the taxpayer may insist otherwise. For example, in Estate of J. W. Kelley,[100] the taxpayers sold property to their children for a price payable in annual installments, which the sellers forgave each year as they came due. The Commissioner contended that the absence of intent to collect the installments meant that the buyer's obligation to pay the price was lacking in "economic substance," so that there was a gift of the entire value of the property "sold" when the sale was made. The Tax Court held instead that gifts were made only as annual installments were forgiven by the sellers.

---

93. § 2512(a).

94. For example, the power of a trust grantor to designate who shall enjoy the trust income during his life may cause him to be treated under § 674 as owner of the trust for income tax purposes and to require inclusion of the trust property in his gross estate when he dies under § 2036(a)(2). But that power would not cause the gift of the remainder interest in principal to be incomplete for gift tax purposes.

95. See Reg. § 25.2511–2(c).

96. See Reg. § 25.2511–2(a).

97. See Reg. § 25.2511–2(c).

98. See Reg. § 25.2511–2(e).

99. 195 F.2d 999, 52–1 USTC ¶ 10,849 (1st Cir. 1952).

100. 63 T.C. 321 (1974), nonacq. 1977–2 CB 2, acq. on other issues 1977–2 CB 1. Compare Rev.Rul. 77–299, 1977–2 CB 343.

BARBARA M. LOCKARD v. COMMISSIONER

United States Court of Appeals, First Circuit, 1948.
166 F.2d 409, 48–1 USTC ¶ 10,604.

MAGRUDER, Circuit Judge.

Barbara M. Lockard petitions for review of a decision of the Tax Court of the United States determining that "there is a deficiency in gift tax of $5,517.39 for the year 1941." 7 T.C. 1151.

Petitioner undoubtedly made a taxable gift in 1941. In her return she claimed the full $40,000 specific exemption. Internal Revenue Code, § 1004, 26 U.S.C.A.Int.Rev.Code, § 1004. The Commissioner disallowed this exemption to the extent of $22,595.95 on the ground that petitioner had claimed and been allowed an exemption of $19,363.93 in respect of a taxable gift made in 1938 and an exemption of $3,232.02 in respect of a taxable gift made in 1939. Petitioner now contends that she erroneously reported taxable gifts in 1938 and 1939, and therefore that no part of the specific exemption was properly consumed in either year. It is conceded by the Commissioner that the amounts which were claimed as exemptions in 1938 and 1939 were "allowed" within the meaning of I.R.C. § 1004(a)(1)—and thus pro tanto exhausted the $40,000 specific exemption—only if the taxpayer made taxable gifts in those years. Kathrine Schuhmacher v. Commissioner, 8 T.C. 453, 464 (1947); Carl J. Schmidlapp v. Commissioner, 1941, 43 B.T.A. 829. On this branch of the case the question is whether the beneficiary's irrevocable right to receive the income from the corpus of a short term trust constitutes a taxable gift in the year in which the property is transferred to the trust, notwithstanding the fact that the settlor may remain taxable on such income under the doctrine of Helvering v. Clifford, 1940, 309 U.S. 331, 60 S.Ct. 554, 88 L.Ed. 788.

There is also a question as to the valuation for gift tax purposes of the gift in 1941 of a right to income for life, with discretionary power in the trustee to distribute corpus up to a certain amount in each year if he deemed it necessary for the life tenant's comfortable maintenance and support.

On March 30, 1938, the petitioner created an irrevocable trust, with herself and another as cotrustees, under the terms of which the entire net income was directed to be paid to Derwood W. Lockard, her husband, for a term of six years; and upon April 1, 1944, or if the husband should die earlier, then on the date of his death, the principal was to revert to the settlor, free of trust. On March 30, 1939, the petitioner transferred additional property to the trust.

The Tax Court held that the transfers in trust in 1938 and 1939 constituted taxable gifts to Mr. Lockard, in those years, of the right to receive the income for a term of years; and therefore that the amounts of specific exemption claimed by petitioner in her gift tax returns for those two years, and allowed by the Commissioner, must be deducted from the $40,000 specific exemption claimed by her in her return of the 1941 gift. We agree with this conclusion. Valuation of these gifts in 1938 and 1939 is covered by stipulation and is not in dispute.

Section 501(b) of the Revenue Act of 1932, 47 Stat. 245, 26 U.S.C.A.Int.Rev.Acts, page 580, which is applicable to the transfers in 1938 and 1939, provides, that the gift tax is applicable "whether the transfer is in trust or otherwise, whether the gift is direct or indirect, and whether the property is real or personal, tangible or intangible." That the broad sweep of this language was not inadvertent is emphasized in the committee reports. H.R.Rep.No.708, 72d Cong., 1st Sess., at p. 27, stated: "The terms 'property,' 'transfer,' 'gift,' and 'indirectly' are used in the broadest and most comprehensive sense; the term 'property' reaching every species of right or interest protected by law and having an exchangeable value." See to the same effect Sen.Rep.No.665, 72nd Cong., 1st Sess., p. 39. See also Smith v. Shaughnessy, 1943, 318 U.S. 176, 180, 63 S.Ct. 545, 547, 87 L.Ed. 690, in which the court states that the amplitude of legislative purpose, thus expressed, "is broad enough to include property, however conceptual or contingent."

By the transfer in trust in 1938, Mr. Lockard acquired an equitable right to the income from the property for a period of six years, subject only to his earlier death. He then received a legally protected interest "having an exchangeable value"; and the commuted value of this right to future income is readily calculable. Helvering v. McCormack, 2 Cir., 1943, 135 F.2d 294, 296. See art. 19(7) of Regulations 79 (1936 Ed.). To the extent of this interest, the settlor abandoned control of the property upon its transfer in trust. Not only did the settlor reserve no power to revoke, and revest in herself, the beneficial interest thus donated; she could not even modify the donee's interest or shift the benefit, in whole or in part, to another. The transfer, therefore, meets every test of taxability under the language of the Act and under the criteria laid down in Smith v. Shaughnessy, supra. The same may be said of the additional transfer to the trust made in 1939.

The foregoing conclusion would have seemed inevitable and inescapable if one had never heard of Helvering v. Clifford, 1940, 309 U.S. 331, 60 S.Ct. 554, 84 L.Ed. 788, a case involving income tax liability. It is recited in the stipulation in the case at bar that the distributable trust income for the years 1938–1941, inclusive, was included by the Commissioner in the income of Mrs. Lockard under I.R.C. § 22(a), 26 U.S.C.A.Int.Rev.Code, § 22(a), as interpreted in the Clifford case. Exegesis of Helvering v. Clifford has proceeded apace, and not without difficulty, in a large volume of subsequent litigation in the lower federal courts. See United States v. Morss, 1 Cir., 1947, 159 F.2d 142. No doubt there would be many judicial sighs if the great body of Clifford learning had to be imported into gift tax litigation. But as this court held in Commissioner v. Prouty, 1 Cir., 1940, 115 F.2d 331, 337, 133 A.L.R. 977, "the gift tax does not seem to be so closely integrated with the income tax that decisions like the Clifford case extending the applicability of Section 22(a) to the grantor of a trust, must necessarily be read as holding that no gift tax was payable upon the creation of the trust." We tried to point out again, at considerable length, in Higgins v. Commissioner, 1 Cir., 1942, 129 F.2d 237, certiorari denied 1942, 317 U.S. 658, 63 S.Ct. 57, 87 L.Ed. 529, that under existing provisions of law respecting income, gift and estate taxes, it is quite impossible for the courts to achieve a complete integration of these three taxes. Chief Justice Stone made an apparent effort in Estate of Sanford v. Commissioner, 1939, 308 U.S. 39, 60 S.Ct. 51, 84 L.Ed. 20, to bring about a measure of correlation between the gift tax and the estate tax, by his statement page 44 of 308 U.S., page 56 of 60 S.Ct., 84 L.Ed. 20, that the test of completeness of a transfer for purposes of the gift tax is no different "from that to be applied in determining whether the donor has retained an interest such that it becomes subject to the estate tax upon its extinguishment at death." Cf. Higgins v. Commissioner, supra, 1 Cir., 129 F.2d at page 240–242. But in Smith v. Shaughnessy, 1943, 318 U.S. 176, 63 S.Ct. 545, 87 L.Ed. 690, the Supreme Court disavowed any intention to intimate in the Sanford case that there was "a general policy against allowing the same property to be taxed both as an estate and as a gift" page 178 of 318 U.S., page 546 of 63 S.Ct., 87 L.Ed. 690; and pointed out that the plan of Congress for integrating the estate and gift taxes is to be found in the provision of law granting a credit on estate taxes by reason of previous payment of gift taxes on the same property—a "system of secured payment on gifts which will later be subject to the estate tax" page 179 of 318 U.S., page 547 of 63 S.Ct., 87 L.Ed. 690. Aside from this, it seems that for the most part any correlation that may exist between the three taxes is "purely coincidental."

Petitioner does not contend that there is a complete integration between the income tax and gift tax, so that the mere fact that a transfer leaves the transferor still liable to income tax on the property always negatives a gift tax liability; but she does argue that the same question of fact underlies both liability for income tax under the Clifford rule, and liability for gift tax—namely, whether the settlor, after the transfer in trust, remains in substance the owner of the corpus. If, notwithstanding the transfer, the settlor is deemed to remain in substance the owner of the corpus, the income therefrom—the fruit of the tree—is, for income tax purposes, attributable to the settlor, and the settlor does not escape an income tax thereon "by any kind of anticipatory arrangement, however skillfully devised, by which he procures payment of it to another, since, by the exercise of his power to command the income, he enjoys the benefit of the income on which the tax is laid." Harrison v. Schaffner, 1941, 312 U.S. 579, 582, 61 S.Ct. 759, 761, 85 L.Ed. 406. See Commissioner v. Bateman, 1 Cir., 1942, 127 F.2d 266, 271–274. Petitioner argues from this that, for income tax purposes, the result is the same as if the settlor of the short term trust had continued to receive the income yearly and had made a series of assignments of such income. It is contended, further, that similar treatment for gift tax purposes is appropriate, so that no gift tax should be payable when the trust is created, but actual payments of income to the beneficiary should be taxable as gifts when such payments are made from year to year. This suggested mode of treatment may be appropriate and reasonable; the only trouble with it is that it is not sanctioned by the statutory scheme. As we have already pointed out, the income tax and gift tax each has its own independent criteria of taxability. In the trust now before us it may be true, under Helvering v. Clifford, that for income tax purposes the result is the same as if Mrs. Lockard had herself received the income each year and had made a series of assignments of it to her husband. But the fact is that she did not receive the income and then give it away by successive assignments. Upon creating the trust she made a single transfer whereby her husband then and there acquired an irrevocable right to the income for a period of years.　Under the plain language of the gift tax, and under the authorities above cited, this intangible right to future income must be valued as of the date of the transfer in trust, and taxed to the donor.　Accord, 2 Paul, Federal Estate and Gift Taxation, § 17.17 (1942).

We come now to the remaining question in the case, as to the valuation of the gift made by petitioner in 1941.

On December 31, 1941, petitioner, having meanwhile resigned as co-trustee, executed an instrument in which she undertook to assign to the remaining trustee all her reversionary interest in the trust and directed the trustee to continue from and after April 1, 1944, if Mr. Lockard should then be living, to hold the trust property in trust for the following purposes:

"2.　Until the death of my said husband, Derwood W. Lockard, to pay the entire net income thereof to him, and to pay to him such amounts from principal, not in excess of $3,000 in any calendar year, as the trustee in his uncontrolled discretion shall think necessary for the comfortable mainte-nance and support of the said Derwood W. Lockard.

"3.　Upon the death of said Derwood W. Lockard to transfer the prin-cipal then held to me if I shall then be living, and if I shall not then be living, to my executors, administrators or assigns free of trust."

Since petitioner had reserved no power to amend the terms of the original trust, this instrument of December 31, 1941, was perhaps technically the creation of a new trust rather than an extension of the term of the old one.　In any case, the instrument constituted a new taxable gift to Mr. Lockard.　Since he already had the irrevocable right to receive the income up to March 31, 1944, the new gift was of the right to receive the income from and after April 1, 1944, for the remainder of his life, plus the right to receive such amounts from principal, not in excess of $3,000 in any calendar year, as the trustee might in his uncontrolled discretion think necessary for the life beneficiary's comfortable maintenance and support.

In her gift tax return for 1941, petitioner valued this new gift to Mr. Lockard at $55,000.　The Commissioner ruled that this valuation should be increased to the amount of $99,459.37, which amount, according to the stipulation, is the "value as of December 31, 1941, of the right of the ben-eficiary to receive each year after March 30, 1944, the amount of $3,000 from the principal of the trust together with the income of the diminishing trust fund, for the remainder of his life."　Part of the deficiency determined by the Commissioner was attributable to this increase in the valuation of the gift.　The Tax Court upheld the Commissioner.

Petitioner challenges this ruling on the ground that it treats the dis-cretionary power in the trustee to make payments out of principal up to a maximum of $3,000 a year as a completed gift to the beneficiary of the absolute right to receive such payments, disregarding the limitations im-posed on the trustee's power to invade the principal.　It is argued that, since the corpus may never be invaded, the gift in 1941 should be valued at the sum of $84,535.90, which is the stipulated "value as of December 31, 1941, of the right of the beneficiary to receive the trust income after March 30, 1944, for the remainder of his life"; and that, if and when invasion of the corpus may become necessary, gifts of principal will then become complete and subject to the gift tax in the years in which principal is actually distributed.   This argument of petitioner, as the Tax Court conceded, "is an impressive one and has a strong practical appeal."   Nevertheless, we feel obliged to sustain the Tax Court in rejecting it.

By the transfer in 1941, there was a gift of something more than a right to future income; there was also a gift of another intangible interest of a contingent nature, a right to receive payments out of principal, to a maximum of $3,000 in any calendar year, to the extent that the trustee should deem such payments necessary for the confortable maintenance and support of the beneficiary.   This interest, which will be protected by a court of equity, is certainly worth something, despite its contingent nature; in fact the donee could hardly fail to regard its existence as a valuable assurance against future adversity, and it certainly is a property interest within the broad terms of the gift tax law.   The gift in its entirety must be valued as of the date of the gift.   I.R.C. § 1005, 26 U.S.C.A.Int.Rev.Code, § 1005.   If it be objected that the valuation fixed by the Commissioner ignores the limitations upon the trustee's power to invade corpus, it is equally true that petitioner's suggested valuation of the 1941 gift ignores the beneficiary's contingent interest in the principal conferred upon him by the transfer in trust executed by petitioner on December 31, 1941.

The government argues that, by the transfer of December 31, 1941, "the taxpayer relinquished completely her right to have the corpus to the extent of $3,000 annually returned to her"; that she "parted completely with the reversion to, and dominion over corpus to this extent"; and that, since so much of the corpus as will be necessary to pay such annuity of $3,000 per year for the remainder of the beneficiary's life "cannot be returned to her except because of contingencies beyond her control," she must be deemed to have made a taxable gift of corpus to this extent under the authority of Robinette v. Helvering, 1943, 318 U.S. 184, 62 S.Ct. 540, 87 L.Ed. 700, and Smith v. Shaughnessy, 1943, 318 U.S. 176, 63 S.Ct. 545, 87 L.Ed. 690.   We would not put the matter quite this way.   The taxpayer did not relinquish completely the right to have the corpus returned to her intact at the termination of the trust.   She retained the right to have the corpus so returned to her, except in so far as the trustee might find it necessary, within the limits of his discretionary power, to invade the corpus. It is true, as the government says, that the corpus cannot be returned to her intact "except because of contingencies beyond her control"; but that is not the test of her taxability for a gift in 1941 of an interest in corpus. This is apparent from Smith v. Shaughnessy, supra, where there was an irrevocable transfer of property in trust, the income to be paid to the settlor's wife for life, and upon her death the corpus to go to the settlor if living, or, if not, to the wife's heirs.   The government conceded "that the right of reversion to the donor in case he outlives his wife is an interest having value which can be calculated by an actuarial device, and that it is immune from the gift tax."   318 U.S. at page 178, page 546 of 63 S.Ct., 87 L.Ed. 690. This concession was made notwithstanding the fact that the corpus could not be returned to the donor except upon a contingency beyond the donor's control, namely, the predecease of the donor's wife.

The real difficulty with the petitioner's case here is that the Commissioner's determination is presumptively correct; and petitioner has not suggested, and cannot suggest, any reliable actuarial method of computing the value of her reserved right to receive the corpus back intact in case the trustee should not find it necessary to invade the corpus, to the extent permitted, for the comfortable maintenance and support of Mr. Lockard during the remainder of his life.   Robinette v. Helvering, supra.   See Rheinstrom v. Commissioner, 8 Cir., 1939, 105 F.2d 642, 648, 124 A.L.R. 861; Herzog v. Commissioner, 2 Cir., 1941, 116 F.2d 591.   Indeed, the stipulation of facts does not even furnish a sufficient basis for an informed guess, as of December 31, 1941, with respect to the likelihood of an invasion of corpus.   No facts appear as to Mr. Lockard's accustomed scale of living, nor as to his other sources of income, if any.   Considering Mr. Lockard's age (thirty-four, in 1941), the trust might well last for twenty or thirty years; and on the facts of record it could not be assumed to be unlikely that the trustee would find it necessary to invade the corpus for the beneficiary's "comfortable maintenance and support," in view of the modest income that might be expected from a trust estate of not over $140,000.   It appears from the stipulation that, up to October 1, 1945, the trustee had in fact not made any payment to Mr. Lockard from the principal of the trust.   But events subsequent to the date of the transfer have no bearing on the value of the gift as of the date it was made.   Cf. Ithaca Trust Co. v. United States, 1929, 279 U.S. 151, 49 S.Ct. 291, 73 L.Ed. 647.

A judgment will be entered affirming the decision of the Tax Court.

---

[4] Identifying the Donor and the Donee of a Gift

It is obvious that a determination of the identity of the donor is essential in order to know the tax consequences of a gift.   Liability for the gift tax is imposed on the donor,[101] and the rate of tax and availability of the unified credit depend upon his or her prior gifts.[102]   The identity of the donee is necessary to determine whether a present interest exclusion [103] or a marital [104] or charitable [105] deduction is available.   In addition, the availability of gift-splitting is conditioned on the gift being to a donee other than the donor's spouse.[106]   What may be less apparent is how any doubt could exist as to the identities of the donor and donee.

The question of the identity of the donee generally arises where an indirect gift is made.   For example, a father may make a gift to his son in consideration of the son's promise to render services to a third person. Although the gift is nominally from father to son, it may be recharacterized as an indirect gift from the father to the third party.[107]

Questions as to the identity of the donor may arise when two donors attempt to "trade" gifts in order to double the present interest exclusion.

101.   § 2502(c).

102.   § 2502(a).

103.   § 2503(b).

104.   § 2523.

105.   § 2522.

106.   § 2513(a)(1).

107.   See Reg. § 25.2511–1(h)(3).

For example, two sisters may wish to make gifts to their respective children. If each sister gave her own child $20,000, only half of that amount would qualify for the present interest exclusion, with the remainder being a taxable gift. If, instead, each sister gave her own child only $10,000 and gave the other $10,000 to the other sister's child, each child would get $20,000 in total but all four gifts would appear to qualify for the present interest exclusion. However, such gifts have been recharacterized by the courts to reflect their substance rather than their form—i.e., each sister would be deemed to have made a gift of $20,000 to her own child.[108]

A gift in trust is a gift to the trust beneficiaries and not to the trustee (except to whatever extent the trustee is also a beneficiary).[109] A gift to a corporation is a gift to its stockholders.[110]

¶ 6.04 NON-TRUST GIFTS

Gifts that are not in trust are a traditional estate-planning tool to shift the taxability of income as well as to save estate taxes. As used here, such gifts include any gift which is not made by a transfer of property to a trustee. Such non-trust gifts include outright transfers of full ownership of an asset as well as transfers of partial interests, such as legal life estates, remainders, and other present and future interests. A further possibility is a transfer by a beneficiary of a similar interest in an existing trust, such as an assignment of an equitable life estate or remainder.

A non-trust gift is the most appropriate vehicle if the donor or testator wants the donee to have maximum freedom in dealing with the property. For example, the donor may want the donee to be able to invest money in his individual business or to sell or remodel donated residential property. Another advantage of such gifts is that a sale of the property by an individual donee will not cause any gain realized to be taxed at the donor's rates. Under § 644, all or part of any gain realized by a trust on a sale of property within two years of the gift may be taxable at the donor's rates.[111]

In some situations, a gift may be used to convert what would be ordinary income to a client into capital gain for the donee. The determination that an asset is not a capital asset often is influenced by the fact that the client holds or has held other similar assets for sale to customers.[112] The gift of the same asset to an individual donee who neither has such assets nor has a past record of such holdings may be sufficient to eliminate the taint of

108.   See John A. Schultz v. United States, 493 F.2d 1225, 74–1 USTC ¶ 12,997 (4th Cir. 1974).

109.   Helvering v. Hutchings, 312 U.S. 393, 61 S.Ct. 653, 85 L.Ed. 909, 41–1 USTC ¶ 10,026 (1941).

110.   Irwin S. Chanin v. United States, 393 F.2d 972, 68–1 USTC ¶ 12,522 (Ct.Cl.1968). Such a gift is a future interest and does not qualify for the present interest exclusion. Stephen F. Heringer v. Commissioner, 235 F.2d 149, 56–2 USTC ¶ 11,622 (9th Cir. 1956), cert. denied 352 U.S. 927; Rev.Rul. 71–443, 1971–2 CB 337.

111.   For a discussion, see ¶ 9.02[2][a] infra.

112.   See e.g., Florence H. Ehrman v. Commissioner, 120 F.2d 607, 41-2 USTC ¶ 9537 (9th Cir. 1941), cert. denied 314 U.S. 668 (1941).   In Suburban Realty Co. v. United States, 615 F.2d 171, 80–1 USTC ¶ 9351 (5th Cir. 1980), the court characterized "the frequency and substantiality of sales" as the most important factor in determining whether a given asset was held for sale to customers in the ordinary course of business and thus not entitled to capital gains treatment.

ordinary income treatment from gains to be realized on its sale.[113]   If the gift is to a trust, on the other hand, any gain which is taxable at the transferor's rates under § 644, is characterized in the same manner as if the sale had been made by the transferor, taking into account any activities of the trust with respect to the property sold.[114]

For most substantial gifts, a trust is a better vehicle.   Without a trust, the gift must either give the donee absolute ownership of the donor's interest in the property, which ordinarily means it will be included in the donee's estate when she dies, or it must involve the creation of a succession of legal future interests.[115]   Such interests rarely provide suitable means for ownership and management of intangibles such as securities, in part because there usually is little law defining the relative rights and obligations of successive owners of legal interests.[116]

For real or tangible personal property, the rights of successive owners are better defined [117] but often do not facilitate effective management of investment property.   For example, the holder of a life estate in real estate used for business purposes may be unable to make any substantial changes in the buildings or other improvements, and its most profitable use may be precluded as a result.

Legal future interests are most appropriate as a means of providing for the successive enjoyment of residential real estate or valuable tangibles, such as paintings.   Even for such property, a trust often would provide greater flexibility in case the first beneficiary no longer wishes to use the property or becomes incapacitated.

There is no need for examples to illustrate outright gifts of absolute ownership of such assets as real estate, life insurance policies, securities, or cash.   But the range of possible subject matter is much broader and is limited only by the kinds of property interests whose transfer is recognized under applicable state (or sometimes federal) law.   Sometimes the most favorable tax results may flow from a gift of less traditional subject matter, such as the following:

> *Example 6.1.*   Income of a trust is payable to *B* for life, remainder to *R*.   The trust contains no spendthrift clause.   The value of the trust property is $100,000.   When *B*, a male, is 64, he gives his income interest to his daughter, *D*.   For gift tax purposes, *B*'s gift is valued at $49,585 [118] —less than one-half the value of the trust.   But it may be effective to shift the taxability of as much income (not including

---

113.   This conclusion assumes, of course, that the family member is not regarded for tax purposes as joint venturer in the client's real estate business, see Beverly B. Bistline v. United States, 260 F.2d 77, 58–2 USTC ¶ 9640 (9th Cir. 1958) (donee of lots), or as the conduit through which the client makes sales, cf. Philip W. Wrenn, 67 T.C. 576 (1976).

114.   See § 644 (c).

115.   The termination of such interests may be subject to the generation-skipping trans-

fer tax.   See § 2613(b)(1), discussed at ¶ 13.10 infra.

116.   See 1 American Law of Property § 2.27 (Casner, ed. 1952).

117.   Id. at §§ 2.17–2.24.

118.   See Reg. § 25.2512–9(f), Table A(1).

capital gains) [119] during the rest of *B*'s life as a gift of $100,000 in cash or property.

　　Example 6.2.　　*A*, an author, has completed the manuscript for a book.　If *A* has not published anything previously, the value of the manuscript for gift tax purposes may be quite modest.　A gift of the manuscript prior to publication may shift the taxability of substantial royalties if the book proves to be a success in the market.

[1] Choosing the Property—Relationship of Basis to Fair Market Value

Many tax considerations affect the choice of property to be transferred by outright gift.　For example, real property that would qualify for reduced valuation for estate tax purposes under the special valuation role of § 2032A,[120] if retained until the client's death is, other things being equal, a less desirable candidate for transfer by gift during life.　Similarly, a gift of depreciable property may destroy its "first user" status and thus limit the depreciation methods available to the donee.[121]

To attempt an exhaustive catalog of the various factors relevant in choosing the property is impractical because of the wide variety of assets clients may hold and the different tax factors relevant for each asset and each client.　Nevertheless, one characteristic relevant for any asset a client may have is the relationship between its basis and the current fair market value.　The new basis under § 1014,[122] if the donor holds property until he dies, may also be relevant.　If the property is given during the donor's life in such fashion as not to be included in his estate when he dies, the new basis under § 1014 will be lost.　Thus, if that basis is likely to exceed the current basis of the property, he should consider not giving it away while he lives.　On the other hand, if the donor expects the property to be sold before his death whether or not he gives it away, the prospective loss of a new basis may not be a factor in deciding what to give.

　　[a] Effect of Basis Equal to Current Fair Market Value.　The obvious example of property with a basis equal to its current fair market value is cash, but the client may own other assets which also fit the description. The net value to the donee of such property, if he sells it, will be greater because any taxable gain will not be increased by unrealized appreciation at the time of the gift.　On the other hand, the gift will not achieve any shift of income for tax purposes from donor to donee except with respect to future income from the property.　Since an increase in basis is allowed only for gift tax on appreciation at the time of gift,[123] the absence of appreciation means that, from the standpoint of a possible increase in the donee's basis, any gift tax paid is wasted.

　　[b] Effect of Basis Above Current Fair Market Value.　If the current fair market value of particular property is below the donor's basis, the

119.　Capital gains ordinarily would be taxable to the trust rather than to the beneficiary because they usually are not included in "distributable net income."　See § 643(a), discussed at ¶ 11.01[2] infra.

120.　For a discussion of § 2032A, see ¶ 16.02 infra.

121.　§ 167(c).

122.　For a discussion of § 1014, see ¶ 4.03 supra.

123.　§ 1015(d).

property is less desirable as a gift. The donee's basis for purposes of loss is limited to the fair market value when the gift is made,[124] so that part of the potential loss deduction which might otherwise be realized on a subsequent sale of the property will never become available. In addition, no increase in basis for gift tax paid will be available because such increase is only allowed for the part of the gift tax attributable to appreciation at the time of the gift.[125]

On the other hand, these factors do not justify a categorical refusal to consider making gifts of property with a current fair market value below the donor's basis. If all the donor's property has a basis in excess of its current fair market value, the potential advantages from making gifts may outweigh these factors. In such a case, the prime candidate from a tax standpoint is the asset whose basis is closest to fair market value; thus the amount of potential loss deduction eliminated by the transfer will be minimized.

As an alternative to giving property with a basis above its current fair market value, the donor may sell the property, realize a deductible loss, and give the proceeds to the donee. This option may be less attractive in practice than in theory, especially if the decline in value is regarded as temporary, if the property is not readily salable without significant selling expenses, or if the donor does not expect to be able to make effective use of any resulting deductible loss. Although losses may be carried forward without any time limit during the taxpayer's life,[126] the ability to carry forward additional losses may never produce a tax benefit because of the presence of other losses.

[c] Effect of Basis Below Current Fair Market Value. If the donor's basis is below the current fair market value, the net value of the gift to the donee if the property is sold will be less if he has to pay an income tax on unrealized appreciation at the time of the gift. On the other hand, this factor means that the gift is achieving a shift of such appreciation for tax purposes from donor to donee and, thus, may produce an additional saving in income taxes, aside from such taxes on future income from the property. In addition, the gift tax on such appreciation is added to the donee's basis.[127] The effects of these conflicting considerations must be balanced to determine the over-all income tax consequences of the gift.

[2] Life Insurance Policies

Gifts of life insurance policies are particularly useful estate-planning tools because few other assets embody such a wide spread between the donor's cost and the potential economic advantage to the donee.

The rules that determine whether or not the policy proceeds will be included in the taxable estate of the insured if he dies within three years of making the gift are discussed in ¶ 5.02[3][e]. If such proceeds are not includible and the donor's health is such that he is unlikely to live for his actuarial life expectancy, a gift of a policy on his life may achieve significant estate reduction at little or no gift tax cost.

---

124. § 1015(a). For a discussion, see ¶ 4.04 supra.

125. § 1015(d).

126. § 1212(b).

127. § 1015(d).

[a] **Valuation.** The Regulations state a general rule of valuation based on cost for life insurance policies and annuity contracts, but recognize that cost "is not readily ascertainable when the gift is of a contract which has been in force for some time and on which further premium payments are to be made * * *." [128]   For such contracts, value is based on the "interpolated terminal reserve at the date of the gift", increased by a proportionate part of the most recent premium payment covering the period extending beyond the date of the gift.   This reserve value normally exceeds the cash-surrender value, if the policy has one, but ordinarily is only a fraction of the face amount payable on the death of the insured.

The Regulations do state that if "because of the unusual nature of the contract such approximation is not reasonably close to the full value," it may not be used. [129]   They do not deal with the situation in which the valuation method described above departs from economic reality because the insured is terminally ill.

[b] **Group Term Policies.**   Gifts by employees of group term insurance provided by employers are unusually attractive in the light of Revenue Ruling 76–490, [130] which deals with an assignment of a group policy by an employee (*D*) to an irrevocable trust.   The Ruling does not depend in any way on the fact that the assignment was to a trust and appears to be equally applicable to an outright assignment.   However, it notes that under the terms of the trust the beneficiary or his estate "was to receive the full proceeds of the policy immediately" on the death of the insured.

Premiums were payable monthly in advance by the employer on the first day of each month.   The policy provided insurance coverage until *D* reached 65 or ceased employment with the employer, whichever happened first, but the employer was not contractually obligated to continue to pay the premiums.   The Ruling states:

(1) No taxable gift occurred when the employee assigned the policy on January 31 because the employer might have failed to make further premium payments;

(2) Each payment of a premium by the employer was an indirect transfer by *D*, subject to gift tax; and

(3) The gift qualifies for the present interest exclusion.

It is unclear why (1) is correct.   Of course the employee could have quite his job or, the employer could have stopped paying premiums even though the employee continued on the job.   But there may have been a substantial degree of probability that neither of these eventualities would materialize, and that coverage would continue even though the health of the employee was (or became) such that he could not obtain other insurance. Although it is not easy to assign a precise dollar value to these expectations, it is difficult to see why that value can be treated as nonexistent for gift tax purposes.   Thus the Ruling provides a favorable valuation rule for gifts of group term life insurance policies.

In this situation, however, if the policy is given to a trust, availability of the present interest exclusion depends on trust provisions for payment

128. Reg. § 25.2512–6(a).   130. 1976–2 CB 300.

129. Id.

of the policy proceeds immediately on the death of the insured.   Thus in Revenue Ruling 79–47,[131] the proceeds were to be retained in trust to pay the income to the beneficiaries, and the exclusion was denied.

From the standpoint of removal of the policy from the estate of the insured, it is essential that he survive for three years after he assigns his rights under the policy in order to avoid its inclusion under § 2035.[132]   If during that period there is a change in the master plan insurance carrier of the employer, an assignment by the insured of his rights under the new policy, in accordance with the agreement made when he assigned his rights under the former policy, is not a transfer requiring inclusion of the policy proceeds in the insured's estate under § 2035.[133]

[c] Present Interest Exclusions.   It is not easy to understand how a gift of a life insurance policy may be viewed other than as a gift of a future interest, except for the cash surrender value of the policy, if any.   The economic benefits the policy provides in excess of that value are not available until the death of the insured.   Nevertheless, the exclusion is not so limited by the Regulations, which state that payment of premiums by the insured constitutes a gift of a present interest if all incidents of ownership (including the right to surrender the policy) are vested in the donee.[134]

[3] Interests in Pre-Existing Trusts

Donors generally have been unsuccessful in securing a present interest exclusion for transfers of interests (other than a present income interest) in a pre-existing trust.   The Regulations understandably take the position that any remainder is a future interest.[135]   No exception is made for transfers of remainder interests in pre-existing trusts even though the donor may have given all that he has.   The same is true of the extension of an income interest in a pre-existing trust.[136]   The practical consequence is that

131.   1979–1 CB 312.

132.   See Estate of Ross H. Compton v. Commissioner, 532 F.2d 1086, 76–1 USTC ¶ 13,137 (6th Cir. 1976).

133.   Rev. Rul. 80–289, 1980–2 CB 270.   The Ruling notes that the new master policy and the individual employees' certificates of insurance were identical with the old policy and certificates with the employer's former insurance carrier.

134.   Reg. § 25.2503–3(c), *Example (6)*.   See also Letter Ruling 8006109, Nov. 20, 1979, 3 CCH E&GT ¶ 12,378, dealing with a transfer of a group-term policy to an irrevocable trust, where the beneficiary had a right to withdraw $3,000 annually from the trust.

135.   Reg. § 25.2503–3(a).   The principle is applicable even though the donor did not create the remainder interest but merely transferred all that he had received from another trust grantor.   See Rev. Rul. 54–401, 1954–2 CB 320.

In Arthur W. Clark, 65 T.C. 126 (1975), acq. 1977–1 CB 1, the donor had surprising success in getting the exclusion for a transfer to the income beneficiaries of his reversionary interests after a ten-year trust.   On the termination of the trust, the principal was payable to the donor if living or if not to other beneficiaries.   The Tax Court held that the gift resulted in a merger of income and reversionary interests which, under Wisconsin law, destroyed the interests of other beneficiaries and caused a partial termination of the trust.   The donees accordingly were entitled to immediate delivery of the trust property, and the gift qualified for the present interest exclusion.   Whether a similar result would be reached in a case from another jurisdiction depends, of course, on the effect of the doctrine of merger on interests similar to those created in other beneficiaries in the Clark case.   See 1 Amer. Law of Prop. §§ 4.60–4.61 (Casner, ed. 1952).

136.   Rev. Rul. 76–179, 1976–1 CB 290.

the grantor of a short-term trust who extends the term of the trust in favor of the same income beneficiaries cannot get a present interest exclusion for the value of the income interest for the extended term. Had he waited until the principal reverted to him when the original term expired, and then created a new trust, income interests therein could qualify.

¶ 6.05 GIFTS IN TRUST

Transfers in trust offer many advantages over outright gifts. Irrevocable trusts are important tax-saving tools. Revocable trusts—the so-called "living trusts" of estate planning—are primarily useful for non-tax reasons. As long as a trust is revocable, it ordinarily is not a tax-saving tool. When it ceases to be revocable, because the grantor has died or released his power to revoke (or it has expired), the trust may serve the same tax objectives as a trust that was irrevocable when it was created.

[1] Revocable Trusts

The most important reasons for using revocable trusts are:

(1) To save expenses of administration by avoiding probate;

(2) To avoid making the trust provisions a matter of public record in the local probate court, as would be necessary if it were created by the grantor's will;

(3) To anticipate and provide for the grantor's incapacity by transferring property while he is competent to act to a trustee whose powers will not be revoked by the grantor's subsequent incompetency;

(4) To avoid interruption and delays in the management of the trust assets at the time of the grantor's death; and

(5) To choose as the governing state law for the trust that of a state other than the grantor's domicile at his death.

The importance of any of these reasons for a particular client depends upon his individual situation. For example, the first is relevant only if the trust is to be funded with substantial assets before the client dies. The effect of such funding on administration expenses for his estate depends on whether the executor and the attorney for the estate will be paid professionals or uncompensated family members. If the work is done by paid professionals, the effectiveness of the funding of a revocable trust during the client's life in reducing expenses may be limited if under local practice the fees for probate administration are based in part on the value of assets in a revocable trust.

[2] Irrevocable Trusts

An irrevocable trust may permit the grantor to do the same things with part of his wealth, and the income it produces, that he would have done with it anyway had he not created the trust, but at a much lower federal tax cost. If he would have used that wealth to control actions of others, the trustee may exert similar control on his behalf. If he prefers to accumulate the income that his wealth produces, that likewise may be done by the trustee, and his beneficiaries need not be spoiled by a sudden flood of money.

The tax-saving opportunities for the beneficiaries are even greater than for the grantor himself. A trust may give beneficiaries a large measure of control or enjoyment or both, of wealth, without causing them to be taxed as heavily as they would be if they became the outright owners of that wealth. In addition, trusts offer a convenient and flexible mechanism for the management of property if the beneficiaries are not able to discharge that responsibility effectively.

Despite the impressive case that can be made for the use of trusts for almost every substantial lifetime transfer, large amounts of wealth continue to be given outright. In some instances, the donors may be unaware of the advantage of trusts. Others consciously reject such advantages because they believe the outright ownership of wealth builds character and enables a beneficiary to do what he pleases with his money. Better-advised donors, however, are aware that these objectives can be reconciled in large measure with important tax advantages under a well-drafted trust. Beneficiaries may be given substantial control over the trust in various ways, and thus enjoy many of the character-building and practical advantages of such control without incurring the full tax cost of ownership.

The major kinds of inter vivos trusts (and trust substitutes), which are important tax-saving tools, are:

(1) Short-term (Clifford) trusts;

(2) Long-term (non-reversionary) trusts;

(3) Present interest trusts (and trust substitutes) for minors; and

(4) Charitable split-interest trusts.

[3] Short-Term (Clifford) Trusts

Short-term (Clifford) trusts are created primarily to save income taxes and for no other important reason. They allow income to be shifted from the grantor to a lower-bracket taxpayer—either one or more beneficiaries or the trust itself. Such trusts may also reduce estate taxes by keeping income from the trust property from increasing the grantor's taxable estate, but this factor is ordinarily of lesser importance. The term of the trust usually is short and may be no more than the minimum required to shift taxable income away from the grantor to the trust or beneficiary.[137] At the end of the term, the principal is returned to the grantor.

The creation of a Clifford trust is a completed gift for gift tax purposes, as is any transfer without consideration that saves income taxes for the transferor. But if income during the trust term is required to be distributed to one or more beneficiaries in specified shares, the amount of the taxable gift will be reduced because their interests will qualify for the gift tax present interest exclusion.[138] If the grantor does not retain or possess at his death, (or within the three years preceding his death) the kind of interest or power requiring inclusion of property under §§ 2036–2038, only the ac-

---

137. The minimum period is ten years or the death of the income beneficiary, whichever occurs first. See § 673; Reg. § 1.673(a)–1(b). For a discussion, see ¶ 9.01[3] infra.

138. § 2503(b).

tuarial value of his reversionary interest in principal at the time of his death will be included in his taxable estate.[139]

Clients should be reminded that Clifford trusts are designed to shift taxability of the ordinary income of the trust and not to provide relief with respect to capital gains. Such gains will remain taxable to the grantor because his retained reversionary interest, which will be augmented by such gains when the trust terminates, causes him to be treated as owner for income tax purposes of the portion of the trust that generates capital gains (and capital losses as well).[140] In addition, Clifford trusts should not be used as vehicles for minimizing taxes on appreciated assets by means of discretionary distributions of property.[141] Giving such discretionary powers to the grantor often causes both income [142] and estate tax [143] problems. When a trustee other than the grantor has the discretionary power to distribute principal, the existence of such a power will make it difficult to value the gift, and this difficulty may be resolved by treating the entire property as having been transferred for gift tax purposes.[144]

In order to achieve the major advantage offered by such trusts—the ability to shift the taxability of ordinary income—the Code's rules must be followed with respect to:

(1) Providing a minimum period, which must be at least ten years or the life of the beneficiary, whichever ends first, during which the trust principal cannot be returned to the grantor; [145]

(2) Limiting the extent to which enjoyment of the trust property is subject to the control of the grantor or someone else; [146]

(3) Limiting the extent to which the trust may be administered in a manner that may divert income or principal from the designated beneficiaries; [147] and

(4) Avoiding the possibility that income or principal may be paid to the grantor or his spouse or used for this benefit.[148]

These rules are explored at greater length in Chapter 9.

If community property is transferred in trust with the consent of both spouses, both are grantors for purposes of applying the above rules.[149]

139. The reversionary interest is includible under § 2033 as property owned at death. In addition, to whatever extent there was a taxable gift of the income interest, it will be included in "adjusted taxable gifts" for purposes of the estate tax computation. See § 2001(b). Retention or possession of an interest or power may cause inclusion of the income interest in the grantor's estate under §§ 2036–2038. Similarly disposition of such an interest or power within three years of his death may cause such inclusion under § 2035(d)(2), discussed at ¶ 5.02[3][b][i].

140. See § 677(a)(1).

141. See ¶ 4.07 supra.

142. The grantor will be taxed as owner of the trust because of his power to affect ben-

eficial enjoyment of the trust property, unless the power fits within one of the exceptions to this rule in ¶ 674(b).

143. Such a power is likely to require inclusion of the property in the grantor's estate as a power to "alter, amend, revoke or terminate" within the meaning of § 2038.

144. See Rev. Rul. 77–99, 1977–1 CB 295.

145. See note 137 supra.

146. § 674.

147. § 675.

148. §§ 676a, 677.

149. See ¶ 6.06[3] infra.

[4] Long-Term (Non-Reversionary) Trusts

The long-term trust usually is used to combine income and wealth transfer tax savings by shifting the taxability of the income from the trust property to the beneficiaries or the trust itself and by removing the trust property from the grantor's taxable estate.[150]　"Long-term" is used to distinguish from short-term trusts, in which the grantor retains a significant reversionary interest and which are used primarily to achieve income tax savings. In order to remove the value of a "long-term" trust (except for such reversionary interest, which will remain includible if it does not expire on his death) from the grantor's taxable estate, it is not necessary that the term of the trust be any minimum length, as long as the value of grantor's reversionary interest at his death does not exceed 5 percent of the value of the trust property.[151]　If the trust term is short, the risk is greater that it will expire before the grantor dies, so that the full value of the trust will be includible in his taxable estate.　In that situation, use of the trust may appear to have increased total wealth transfer taxes, as the grantor's transfers will also include the gift made when the trust was created of the then value of the trust property, except for his reversionary interest.[152]　However, such an increase may be more than offset by the removal of the income from the trust property from the grantor's estate.　Had he created no trust, such income (after income taxes) would have been in his estate if he did not spend it or give it away during his life.

Non-reversionary trusts (or trusts in which the grantor retains a reversionary interest which does not exceed the limits set forth in § 2037—and the best way to insure that result is to retain no such interest) may or may not include provisions giving the trustee discretionary power over distributions of income and principal during the trust term.　Such a power may make possible the use of the trust to minimize taxable gains from appreciated assets.[153]　The presence of such a power may make it impossible to value any retained reversionary interest, with the result that the entire transfer in trust will be a completed gift for gift tax purposes without any reduction for such interest.[154]　But this usually is not objectionable from the client's standpoint because there either is no reversionary interest or it is of minor importance.

In order to combine income and wealth transfer tax savings, non-reversionary trusts must comply with the income tax rules for short-term trusts.[155]　In addition, if the non-reversionary trust is intended to shift the

---

150.　If the trust property has appreciated substantially at the time of the settlor's death, such removal carries the disadvantage, from an income tax standpoint, of loss of the new basis generally provided by § 1014 for property included in the gross estate.　See ¶ 4.03.

151.　See ¶ 2037, discussed at ¶ 5.02[4][b] supra.

152.　For example, if the trust term is fifteen years, the gift when it is created is valued at 58.2735 percent of the property transferred.　See Reg. § 25.2512–5(9)(f), Table

B.　If the grantor lives for ten years after the trust is created, when he dies his reversionary interest will be valued at 74.7258 percent of the value of the trust property at the date of his death.　See Reg. § 20.2031–10(f), Table B.　As a result, his total transfers (ignoring any present interest exclusion) will include 132.9993 percent of the trust property.

153.　See ¶ 4.07 supra.

154.　See Rev.Rul. 77–99, 1977–1 CB 295.

155.　See ¶ 9.01 infra.

taxability of capital gains from the grantor to the trust or its beneficiaries, § 644, which deals with the taxation of gains realized on a sale of property within two years of its transfer to the trust, must be taken into account. That provision causes the tax on gains from such sales (to the extent of appreciation when the property was transferred) to be computed at the rates applicable to the grantor, if the gain is realized during his life.

Trust provisions drawn to comply with such income tax requirements should also be viewed in the light of code sections which require inclusion of lifetime transfers in the grantor's estate.[156]

[5] Present Interest Trusts for Minors (and Trust Substitutes)

Present interest trusts for minors qualify for the gift-tax present-interest exclusion, usually by satisfying the requirements of § 2503(c). They are an attractive tool of estate planning that may combine income and estate tax savings without causing any gift tax to be incurred by the transferor. Custodianships and guardianships are useful alternative vehicles for transferring property to minor beneficiaries where the client is more concerned with the simplicity provided by these trust substitutes than with the greater flexibility that is possible with a transfer in trust for the minor's benefit.

In order to combine income and wealth transfer tax savings with qualification for the exclusion, present interest trusts for minors (and trust substitutes) must avoid the rules that require inclusion of trust income in the grantor's return (or taxation of gain at the grantor's rates under § 644) and the rules that require inclusion of lifetime transfers in the grantor's estate. The major problem, however, is likely to be the satisfaction of the requirements for the gift tax present interest exclusion.[157] If the gift tax requirements are met, as long as the grantor is not the trustee or custodian and gain on a sale of appreciated property is not taxed at the grantor's rates under § 644, there usually is no serious income or estate tax problem for him. There may estate tax problems for the trustee or custodian, however, if he is legally obligated to support the minor and has the power to use the trust or custodianship property to provide such support.[157a]

The custodianship is essentially a simplified version of the guardianship traditionally provided by state law for the management of property owned by minors.[158] The guardianship, and usually the custodianship as well, have the disadvantage of requiring that the property (and any accumulated income) be distributed to the minor when he or she attains the age of majority under state law—usually age 18. Many clients fear that their beneficiaries at that age may lack the maturity and judgment required for sound management of any significant amount of wealth. Thus, for many clients, the custodianship or guardianship is best suited to relatively small gifts.

---

156. See § 2035–2038, discussed at ¶ 5.02 supra.

157. § 2503(b). For a discussion, see ¶ 9.03 infra.

157a. See Reg. § 20.2041–1(c), discussed at ¶ 9.03[2]. Use of trust or custodianship property to discharge a support obligation of anyone, whether or not he is trustee or custodian, also may have generation-skipping transfer tax consequences. See Prop. Reg. § 26.2613–4(d), fourth sentence.

158. See, e.g., N.Y. EPTL 7–4.1 et seq. The Uniform Gifts to Minors Act statutes are collected at 2 CCH E&GT ¶ 8500.08.

A second characteristic of both forms of holding wealth for the benefit of the minor is that, unlike a transfer in trust for the minor's benefit, no separate taxable entity is created.   All income and gains (or losses) realized by the custodian or guardian are reported on the minor's income tax return,[159] whereas trust income may be taxed to the trust if it is not distributed currently.   Whether this is advantageous depends upon several factors. Eliminating the need for a trust income tax return avoids complexity and saves accountants' fees if the return would be prepared by a paid professional.   The fee for an individual return for a minor often will be lower than for a return for a trust.

Whether income taxes will be higher or lower if the income is individually reportable by the minor instead of in the form of a trust for his benefit depends upon a comparison of his tax brackets (including any otherwise unused exemption or allowance) [160] with that of a trust.[161]   Often the minor's brackets will be lower.

[6] Charitable Split Interest Trusts

The income tax and wealth transfer tax advantages of gifts in trust or outright for the benefit of one or more qualified charities are obvious,[162] but the deduction they provide is limited to the value of what in fact passes to the charity.   Although the circumstances under which that value is determined may cause it to be on the high side of fair market value, the Commissioner is well aware of this tendency and has undertaken to prevent the inflated valuation of gifts to charity, such as works of art.[163]

More impressive advantages are offered by charitable split interest trusts, which may allow a deduction for a larger amount than the actual value of what passes to charity.   Such trusts may take the form of either a charitable "lead" trust, in which an annuity or unitrust amount is payable to a charity, with the remainder on the termination of the charity's interest going to one or more individuals,[164] or a charitable remainder trust, in which the annuity or unitrust amount is payable to one or more individuals, with

159.   See Reg. § 1.641(b)–2(b) (estates of persons under a disability); Joseph Anatasio, 67 T.C. 814 (1977) (custodianship).   If the income from custodianship property is used to discharge the transferor's legal obligation to support the minor, such income is taxable to the transferor.   See Rev.Rul. 59–357, 1959–2 CB 212.

160.   The minor's "exemption amount" is $1,000, with a cost-of-living adjustment beginning in 1985.   See §§ 151(a), (f).   If he is under age 19 or a student, his parent may also be entitled to a dependency exemption for him.   See § 151(e)(1)(B).   However, if a dependency exemption is allowable with respect to the minor, his zero bracket amount is not available for unearned income in excess of itemized deductions.   See §§ 63(e)(1)(D), (e)(2).

161.   The trust's deduction for personal exemption, if it is not required to distribute all of its income currently, is $100.   § 642(b).

The applicable rate schedule provided in § 1(e) is the same as that for income in excess of $1700 of a married individual filing a separate return.   See § 1(d).   The rates in this schedule are higher than those for unmarried individuals in § 1(c), which apply to most minors.

162.   See Mangum, "Charitable Transfers and Estate Planning," 38 N.Y.U.Inst. on Fed.Tax.   §§ 40.00, 40.03[1] (1980).

163.   See, e.g., Philip K. Kaplan v. Commissioner, 43 T.C. 663 (1965), acq. 1965–2 CB 5 (claimed deduction of $5,500 for gift of personal property reduced to $500).

164.   See Callahan, "Charitable 'Lead' Trusts—The Forgotten Member of the Trilogy," 11 U.Miami Inst. on Est.Planning 500 (1977); Ashby, "Use of Charitable Income Interests in Estate Planning," 115 Tr. & Estates 12 (1976).

the remainder payable to a charity.[165]   In the case of the charitable lead trust, the rules for valuing the charity's interest could produce an unrealistically high value, so that a gift tax or estate tax charitable deduction may be allowed for elements of value which in fact are passing to individual beneficiaries.[166]   In the case of the charitable remainder trust, on the other hand, the most important source of tax savings is the trust's income tax exemption.[167]   The exemption is allowed because income and capital gains that are not distributed to the noncharitable beneficiary as payments of an annuity or unitrust amount will be paid to the charitable remainderman when the trust terminates.   In the meantime, however, such income and gains may be invested for the benefit of the noncharitable beneficiary, but the trust's income tax exemption remains unaffected.

¶ 6.06   GIFTS IN COMMUNITY-PROPERTY STATES

Gifts of community property to third parties present no special problems if both spouses join in making the gift.   As each spouse owns a one-half interest in the property, each reports one-half of its value for gift tax purposes.   However, if one spouse undertakes to make such a gift without the consent of the other, the gift may be voidable by the nonconsenting spouse, both during the joint lives of the spouses and after the death of the donor spouse, if that spouse dies first.[168]

The federal tax consequences of gifts from one spouse to the other of either community property or separate property, making the subject matter the separate property of the donee, depend on whether the income from separate property is also separate property under state law, or is community property.[169]   Additional problems are presented by a gift of either kind of property in trust.[170]

[1] Texas Rule: Income from Separate Property Is Community Property Unless Spouses Agree Otherwise

In Texas the income from both community property and each spouse's separate property is community property, unless, pursuant to a recent constitutional amendment, the spouses agree in writing that all or part of such income from separate property shall also be the separate property of the owner.[171]   Idaho and Louisiana have basically similar rules.[172]   The result

165. See Teitell, "Tax Exempt Charitable Remainder Trusts—Mission Untaxable," 116 Tr. & Est. 182 (1977).

166. See ¶ 10.03 infra.

167. § 664(c). For a discussion, see ¶ 10.02[2] infra.

168. See, e.g., Cal.Civ.Code § 5115 (West Supp. 1980). As construed, the section allows the nonconsenting spouse to treat the gift as being voidable during the joint lives of the spouses, and voidable as to her one-half interest after the death of the donor spouse, if she survives him. See Bank of California v. Connolly, 36 Cal.App.3d 350, 111 Cal.Rptr. 468 (1973); Harris v. Harris, 57 Cal.2d 367, 19 Cal.Rptr. 793, 369 P.2d 481 (1962).

169. See ¶ 1.08 notes 57, 58 supra.

170. See ¶ 6.06 [3] infra.

171. Tex.Const.Art. XVI, § 15, as amended by Amendment 9, approved by the voters November 4, 1980. For a discussion, see Vaughan, Texas Amends Its Constitution and Its Community Property System, 8 Community Prop.J. 59 (Winter 1981). The general rule that income from separate property during marriage is community property was established in Arnold v. Leonard, 114 Tex. 535, 273 S.W. 799 (1925).

172. See note 174 infra.

in all three states is that a gift of either community or separate property by one spouse to the other may leave the donor with a retained interest in one-half of the income from the transferred property by operation of law. In Texas, the donor is presumed not to intend to retain such an interest.[173] By following specified procedures, such retention may likewise be avoided in Idaho and Louisiana.[174]

If income were retained by the transferor, the results would be disadvantageous from a tax standpoint. Although the transfer from one spouse to the other is a completed gift for gift tax purposes, the Commissioner has contended that retention of income from the transferred property causes a portion to be included in the transferor's estate under § 2036, even though such retention is by operation of state community property laws.[175]

The constitutional amendment in Texas was in response to Estate of Charles J. Wyly, in which the Tax Court had sustained the Commissioner's contention by applying the reciprocal trust doctrine, but was reversed by the Court of Appeals.[176]

[2] California Rule: Income From Separate Property Also Separate

In states such as California, in which the income from separate property is the separate property of the owner spouse,[177] gifts of either community property or separate property from one spouse to the other present no special problem. A gift of community property may take the form of either an unequal division thereof between the spouses, so that each spouse then owns a portion of the asset as his or her separate property, or a transfer by one spouse of his entire interest in specific community assets to the other. In either case, there is a completed gift for purposes of the gift tax. Whether or not the transfer will be included in the taxable estate of the donor turns on application of the principles that govern inclusion of non-community property.

[3] Gifts in Trust of Community Property

Gifts in trust raise special problems if the subject matter of the gift is community property. Unless the property retains its community character for federal income tax purposes, there will be no new basis under § 1014 on

---

173. See note 171 supra.

174. See Idaho Code § 21–906(1) (income is community property unless conveyance or written agreement states such income shall be separate property of one spouse); La.Civ.Code Ann.Art. 2339 (West. Supp.1980) (income is community property unless spouse follows statutory procedure to cause such income to be separate property).

175. See Rev.Rul. 75–504, 1975–2 CB 305, revoked by Revenue Ruling 81–221, IRB 1981–39, 5, 3 CCH E&GT ¶ 12,445 C, on the basis of the construction of Texas law in Estate of Charles W. Wyly v. Commissioner, note 176 infra.

176. Estate of Charles W. Wyly, 69 T.C. 227 (1977), rev'd Estate of Charles W. Wyly v. Commissioner, 610 F.2d 1282, 80–1 USTC ¶ 13,332 (5th Cir. 1980). See also Estate of Winston C. Castleberry, 68 T.C. 682 (1977), nonacq. 1978–2 CB 3, reversed sub nom. Estate of Charles W. Wyly v. Commissioner, supra, in which the reciprocal trust doctrine was inapplicable and the Tax Court held one-fourth of the community property includible.

177. Cal.Civ.Code §§ 5107 (wife), 5108 (husband) (West Supp.1980).

the death of a spouse.[178]   There may also be complications for gift tax and estate tax purposes if the trust is subject to a power of revocation exercisable by either or both of the spouses.[179]   The fact that the subject matter is community property makes each spouse a grantor of the trust, and consideration of its tax consequences must take this into account.

178. See Vinnie A. Murphy v. Commissioner, 342 F.2d 356, 65–1 USTC ¶ 9246 (9th Cir. 1965), denying a basis step-up under § 1014 where such character had been lost, and Rev.Rul. 66–283, 1966–2 CB 297, recognizing a basis step-up where such character had been retained.

Some states provide statutory procedures to maintain such character for property transferred to revocable trusts.   See Cal.Civ.Code § 5113.5; Idaho Code § 32–906A (1979).   Otherwise, whether there has been a change in character of such property is a question of fact.   For example, in California such transmutation is authorized by Cal.Civ.Code § 5013 (West Supp.1980), and occurs when there is an agreement to change the character of property.   See Somps v. Somps, 250 Cal.App.2d 328, 58 Cal.Rptr. 304 (1967).   The agreement may be oral or written, see Woods v. Security First Nat'l Bank, 46 Cal.2d 697, 299 P.2d 657 (1956), expressed or implied, see Long v. Long, 88 Cal.App.2d 544, 199 P.2d 47 (1948), and the intent of the parties may be shown by circumstantial as well as direct evidence.   See Frymire v. Brown, 94 Cal.App.2d 334, 210 P.2d 707 (1949).

179. See Johanson, "Revocable Trusts, Widow's Election Wills and Community Property: The Tax Problems," 47 Tex.L.Rev. 1247 (1969); Phillips, "The Revocable Trust and the New California Community Property Laws," 4 Comm. Prop.J. 105 (1977).

Chapter 7

JOINTLY OWNED PROPERTY

¶ 7.01 USE OF JOINT OWNERSHIP WITH A SURVIVORSHIP FEATURE IN ESTATE PLANNING

Joint ownership with a survivorship feature is widely used, but its desirability from a federal tax standpoint is limited. Lay persons often mistakenly assume that such ownership saves federal estate taxes—an assumption which may cause people to pay higher taxes than would have been incurred with better advice and planning.

For purposes of this discussion, "joint ownership" refers only to those forms that include a right of survivorship:

(1) joint tenancy; and

(2) tenancy by the entirety (recognized only in some states, and there only between husband and wife).

The survivorship feature means that, upon the death of the other joint owner (or owners, if there are more than two), the survivor will become the sole owner.

Like joint tenancy, tenancy in common is not limited to husband and wife.   However, it is not "joint ownership" as that term is used here because it does not carry with it any right of survivorship.   If A and B own property as tenants in common, on the death of B his interest will be disposed of as part of his estate and may pass by will or intestacy to someone other than A.   If A does acquire B's interest on B's death, it will be because B devised that interest to A in his will or because A takes the property under the applicable state intestacy statute.

Community property is also not "joint ownership" as used here.   A deceased spouse may devise his or her share of community property to someone other than the surviving spouse.   If the surviving spouse does receive the deceased spouse's share, it will be because of an express provision in the will or by application of a state intestacy statute.[1]

¶ 7.02 JOINT TENANCY UNDER STATE LAW

Joint tenancy is recognized in almost all states either as a matter of common law or under express statutory provisions.[2]   Although joint tenancy is most often used by married couples, any two or more persons, related or not, may own property as joint tenants.

Property held in joint tenancy is not part of the probate estate of the first joint tenant to die, since full ownership of the property passes to the survivor by operation of law immediately upon the death of the first joint tenant.   The property is often, however, included in the decedent's estate for federal estate tax purposes.

---

1. See, e.g., Cal.Prob.Code § 201 (West Supp.1980).

2. See Powell, Real Property ¶ 602, ns. 3–6 (Rohan, Ed.; 1968).   Some statutes have expressly abolished joint tenancy.   See, e.g., Or.Rev.Stat. § 93.180 (1979).

Joint bank accounts pose a special problem because of wide variations in state law as to whether a surviving joint owner is automatically entitled to the funds in an account.   In some states, a survivorship right in a joint bank account is absolute in the absence of fraud, undue influence, mental incapacity, or mistake.[3]   In other states, a jointly-owned account only creates a rebuttable presumption that a right of survivorship was intended.[4] In addition, the rights of a noncontributing party during the lives of the joint owners vary from state to state.[5]

The right of survivorship in a joint tenancy cannot be destroyed by will; [6] e.g., if *A* and *B* own a home as joint tenants, *A* will be the sole owner on *B*'s death even if *B*, in his will, attempts to devise his interest in the home to someone other than *A*.

However, the right of survivorship may be destroyed by the affirmative action of one or both joint tenants while both are alive.   This can be accomplished in one of four ways:

(1) Both joint tenants may transfer the property to a third person, which will terminate all their rights to the property.

(2) One of the joint tenants, with or without the permission of the other, can transfer his or her interest in the property to a third person. The result is to convert the joint tenancy into a tenancy in common and thus to destroy the survivorship feature.   The third party and the other joint tenant then own the property as tenants in common, with no survivorship rights to the other's share.[7]

(3) The joint tenants may partition, or divide, the property.[8]   Such a division may be made physically, if the property is susceptible to an equal division without prejudice to either party.[9]   This often may be feasible for intangible personal property, such as shares of stock, but usually is not in the case of real property.   If an equal division of the property is not feasible, a sale, followed by division of the proceeds, is required.

Partition by sale can be accomplished by the parties themselves, or it can be accomplished pursuant to a court decree if one joint tenant refuses to partition voluntarily.   However, a judicially-

---

3. See, e.g., In re Estate of LaGarce, 487 S.W.2d 493 (Mo.1972).

4. See, e.g., Erickson v. Kalman, 291 Minn. 41, 189 N.W.2d 381 (1971).

5. Compare, e.g., In re Estate of Taggart, 15 Ill.App.3d 1079, 305 N.E.2d 301 (1973) (presumption that non-contributing joint owner is authorized to withdraw funds from a joint account) with New Hampshire Sav. Bank v. McMullen, 88 N.H. 123, 185 A. 158 (1936) (similar statutory presumption construed as being solely for the bank's protection, and not to affect rights as between depositors).

6. See, e.g., In re Estate of Barret, 137 So.2d 587 (Fla.App.1962).

7. See, e.g., In re Estate of Adams, 228 Cal.App.2d 264, 39 Cal.Rptr. 522 (1964) (joint tenancy destroyed by conveyance of joint tenant's interest to his son, followed by reconveyance by son); In re Polizzo's Estate, 308 N.Y. 517, 127 N.E.2d 316 (1955), cert. denied 350 U.S. 911 (1955) (joint tenant's assignment of his interest in mortgage terminated joint tenancy).   See Powell, Real Property ¶ 618 ns. 1, 2 (Rohan, Ed., 1968).

8. See Powell, Real Property, supra note 7 at ¶ 609.   The right to partition is subject to reasonable restriction by the creator of the joint interests.   See 1 Restatement of Property § 173 (1936).

9. Powell, Real Property, supra note 7 at ¶ 612.

ordered sale is likely to be more expensive than one informally agreed to, and also is likely to bring a lower price.

After partition, each former joint tenant is the sole owner of his or her portion of the partitioned property (or its proceeds), and no survivorship right to the other person's share exists.

(4) The joint tenants may, by mutual agreement, convert the joint tenancy into a tenancy in common or convey all rights to the property to one of them.

¶ 7.03 TENANCY BY THE ENTIRETY UNDER STATE LAW

Tenancy by the entirety is a form of joint ownership by married couples that is recognized in a number of states.   It differs from joint tenancy in that the ability of one spouse to destroy the other's survivorship right usually is limited.   As a general rule, neither spouse may terminate the other's survivorship right by conveying his or her interest in the property, and neither spouse may compel a partition of the property.[10]

There are significant variations among the states as to rights of spouses and of third parties, such as creditors.   For example, some states recognize equal rights to possession and income in both spouses, with each spouse being able to mortgage or encumber his or her interest and with such interest being capable of being reached by creditors.[11]

¶ 7.04 ESTATE TAX TREATMENT OF JOINT INTERESTS

The most significant potential disadvantage of joint ownership is the "consideration" test.   Under this test, the extent to which the property is included in a deceased joint owner's estate is determined by the portion of the consideration to acquire it that he furnished.   Where jointly owned property was paid for or otherwise acquired by only one of the joint owners, generally the *full* value of the property must be included in that owner's estate if he or she dies first.[12]   Thus, not only is the full value of the property taxed when that owner dies, but again when the survivor dies (assuming, of course, that each owner's estate is large enough to be subject to the estate tax).   Credit for all or part of the estate tax paid with respect to the joint property when the first joint owner dies is allowed against the survivor's estate tax, if he dies within ten years.[13]

If the joint owner who did not pay for the property dies first, the property is technically not includible in that owner's estate.   However, § 2040(a) creates a presumption that the property originated with the first joint owner to die, and places the burden upon the survivor to prove that the property originated with him or her rather than with the decedent. If the survivor cannot meet this burden of proof, then part or all of the value of the property may be included (albeit erroneously) in the decedent's estate.

For property that was acquired with contributions from both joint owners, or where the joint ownership was created when the owners acquired

10. See, e.g., Naurison v. Naurison, 132 So.2d 623 (Fla.App.1961).

11. See, e.g., Hiles v. Fisher, 144 N.Y. 306, 39 N.E. 337 (1895).   Compare Rev.Rul. 75–8, 1975–1 CB 309 (husband has sole

right to income in North Carolina tenancy by the entirety).

12. See § 2040(a).

13. See § 2013.

the property by gift, bequest, or devise, the estate of the first joint owner to die will include that part of the value of the property that is proportionate to the decedent's contribution to the acquisition of the property.   For example, if the first joint owner to die contributed 75 percent of the purchase price of the property, then his or her estate will include 75 percent of the value of the property at death.   Or, if the property was jointly acquired by gift, bequest, or devise, the estate of the first joint owner to die will include 50 percent of the value of the property.

If both joint tenants assume liability on a mortgage in connection with the purchase of the property, such assumption is a contribution by each of one-half of the mortgage liability.   However, subsequent payments to the mortgagee by one cotenant constitute contributions by that cotenant for purposes of § 2040.[14]

For married joint owners dying after 1981, § 403(c)(1) of the Economic Recovery Tax Act of 1981 has largely eliminated the consideration test for federal (but not necessarily state) death tax purposes.   One-half of the value of a "qualified joint interest" is includible in the gross estate of the decedent without regard to who paid for the interest or how it was acquired.[15]   The definition in § 2040(b)(2) includes:

> "any interest in property held by the decedent and the decedent's spouse as—
>
>   (A) tenants by the entirety, or
>
>   (B) joint tenants with right of survivorship, but only if the decedent and the spouse of the decedent are the only joint tenants."

However, this apparent legislative largesse is not an unmixed boon to taxpayers.   The 1981 Act also repealed the former limits on the amount allowable as an estate tax marital deduction, so inclusion of the full value of joint interests passing to a surviving spouse generally does not increase the taxable estate of a decedent.[16]   Limiting the amount includible to one-half the value of the property means that only one-half will qualify for a new basis under § 1014 on the death of the joint owner who dies first.   If the joint property has appreciated substantially, the failure to obtain a new basis for all interests in the property a serious disadvantage.

ESTATE OF MARCIA P. GOLDSBOROUGH

United States Tax Court, 1978.
70 T.C. 1077.

OPINION

Section 2040 provides in general that the decedent's gross estate includes the entire value of jointly held property but that section "except[s]

---

14.   See Estate of Fletcher E. Awrey, 5 T.C. 222 (1945).   Rev.Rul. 79–302, 1979–2 CB 328, illustrates the manner in which the survivor's contribution is computed where the survivor and the decedent's estate are jointly and severally liable for the mortgage debt.

15.   § 2040(b)(1).   The new version replaces prior Code provisions for "qualified" and "eligible" joint interests.   See former §§ 2040(b)(2), 2040(c)(3).

16.   See ¶ 16.01[1].

such part thereof as may be shown to have originally belonged to
* * * [the surviving joint tenant(s)] and never to have been received
or acquired by the latter from the decedent for less than an adequate and
full consideration in money or money's worth." Section 2040 further provides that if the decedent owned property jointly with another, the amount
to be excluded from the decedent's gross estate is "only such part of the
value of such property as is proportionate to the consideration furnished by
* * * [the surviving joint tenant(s)]." Mathematically this "consideration furnished" exclusion can be expressed as follows:

$$\frac{\text{Amount}}{\text{excluded}} = \frac{\text{Entire value of property}}{\text{(on the date of death or alternate valuation date)}} \times \frac{\text{Survivor's consideration}}{\text{Entire consideration paid}}$$

In the instant case, the decedent (Goldsborough) acquired on May 12,
1937, real property (St. Dunstans) in her individual name. On April 4,
1946, decedent transferred St. Dunstans, valued at $25,000 on that date,
to her two daughters (Eppler and O'Donoghue) as a gift. On July 17, 1949,
the daughters sold St. Dunstans to H. W. Ford and his wife for $32,500.
Sometime in that same year, each daughter invested her share of the proceeds from the sale of St. Dunstans in various stocks and securities; each
daughter took title to her respective stocks and securities in joint tenancy
with decedent. These stocks and securities remained in joint tenancy until
December 21, 1972, the date of decedent's death, and during the period of
joint tenancy the stocks and securities appreciated in value to $160,383.19,
the value on the alternate valuation date.

Thus, the section 2040 exclusion depends on the amount, if any, of the
consideration Eppler and O'Donoghue, the surviving joint tenants, furnished
toward the $32,500 purchase price of the jointly held stocks and securities.

Respondent contends that all the funds used to purchase the stocks and
securities in question were derived from decedent and thus the entire value
of the jointly held property ($160,383.19) is includable in her gross estate.

Petitioners Buppert and Eppler argue that only the value of St. Dunstans at the time the gift was made to decedent's two daughters (i.e.,
$25,000) is includable in decedent's gross estate. In the alternative, pe-
titioner Eppler contends that the gain of $7,500, measured by the appre-
ciation in value from the time St. Dunstans was given to the two daughters
in 1946 until that property was sold by them in 1949, constitutes consideration furnished by the daughters toward the $32,500 purchase price of the
jointly held stocks and securities. Thus Eppler argues that $37,011.50
($7,500/$32,500 of $160,383.19), the value of the jointly held property on the
alternate valuation date, should be excluded from decedent's gross estate.
We agree with this alternative argument.

To be sure, section 2040 is not a paragon of clarity, and the courts and
Internal Revenue Service have wrestled with the question of whether a
contribution made out of gain representing appreciation in value of property
received gratuitously from decedent is attributable to the decedent or, instead, is to be treated as income from the property and thus separate funds

of the surviving tenant.[17]   The law, as we perceive it, recognizes two distinct situations and treats the two differently.   In one situation, the surviving joint tenant receives property gratuitously from the decedent; the property thereafter appreciates, and the property itself is contributed in an exchange for jointly held property.   In this circumstance section 20.2040–1(c)(4), Estate Tax Regs., treats all the property as having been paid for by the decedent, and the entire value of the property is included in the decedent's gross estate.   See Estate of Kelley v. Commissioner, 22 B.T.A. 421, 425 (1931).

In the second situation, the surviving joint tenant receives property gratuitously from the decedent; the property thereafter appreciates or produces income and is sold, and the income or the sales proceeds are used as consideration for the acquisition of the jointly held property.   In this situation, the income or the gain, measured by the appreciation from the time of receipt of the gift to the time of sale, has been held to be the surviving joint tenant's income and a part of that joint tenant's contribution to the purchase price.   [Citations omitted].   Thus, in the words of the statute, "such part of the value of such property as is proportionate to the consideration furnished by [the surviving joint tenant]" is excluded. [Citations omitted.]

The facts of the instant case fall precisely within this second situation. In Harvey v. United States, supra at 465, the court characterized the facts and framed the issue as follows:

> The jointly held property is not the gift property itself, in either its original or transmuted form, but property traceable to (1) the profits made through sales of the original gift property and successive reinvestments of the proceeds of such sales or (2) the rents, interest and dividends produced by such property in its original or converted form, while title thereto was in the wife.   The question presented by this appeal, then, is whether such profits and income, realized from property originally received by the wife as a gift from her husband and traceable into property which was held by them as joint tenants at the time of the husband's death, came within the exception to the requirement of Section 811(e) [predecessor to sec. 2040] that the entire value of property held in joint tenancy shall be included in the decedent's gross estate.

The Government in *Harvey* argued that the full value of the jointly held property should be included in the decedent's gross estate, and the court dealt with that argument in the following manner (185 F.2d at 467):

> It seems clear that none of the cases cited contains any support for the novel proposition that income produced by gift property, after the gift has been completed, belongs to the donor and is property received or acquired from him by the donee; nor is there, in these cases, anything to impeach the conclusion of the trial court,

---

17.   It is clear that income from property acquired gratuitously from the decedent constitutes a contribution from a surviving joint tenant's separate funds.   Sec. 20.2040–1(c)(5), Estate Tax Regs.

or that of the Tax Court in the *Howard* case,[18] that the income produced by property of any kind belongs to the person who owns the property at the time it produces such income and does not originate with a donor who has made a completed gift of that property prior to its production of the income.   * * *

* * * Moreover, no reason is suggested for holding that one form of income, i.e., "profit gained through a sale or conversion of capital assets," * * * is outside the exception, whereas other forms of income, such as dividends, rentals and interest, fall within its terms.   It follows that the government's contention that the full value of the property held in joint tenancy by decedent and his wife at the time of his death should have been included in decedent's gross estate must be rejected.   [Citations omitted.]

Thus we conclude that Eppler and O'Donoghue furnished $7,500 toward the $32,500 purchase price paid for the stocks and securities they held in joint tenancy with decedent until her death on December 21, 1972.   Under the terms of the statute, such part of the value of the property, i.e., $160,383.19 on the alternate valuation date, as is proportionate to the $7,500 of consideration Eppler and O'Donoghue furnished is excluded from decedent's gross estate.   Under the mathematical formula, set out above, the amount of the exclusion is $37,011.50.

* * *

¶ 7.05   GIFT TAX TREATMENT OF THE CREATION AND TERMINATION OF JOINT INTERESTS

Both the creation and the termination of a joint interest may be a completed gift for gift tax purposes.   Creation between spouses of such an interest after 1981 is freed from gift tax consequences by § 2523(a), allowing an unlimited marital deduction for qualifying gifts to the donor's spouse. If the joint owners are not married to each other, the creation of the interest generally is a completed gift for gift tax purposes unless they furnish the consideration for its acquisition in proportion to the values of their respective interests.[19]   Thus, if *A* and *B* buy stock for $10,000 as joint tenants and *A* pays $6,000 and *B* $4,000, *A* thereby makes a gift to *B* of $1,000 (the difference between *B*'s one-half interest and the amount he paid for the stock).

The termination of any joint interest is treated as a gift if the proceeds of termination are not divided in proportions corresponding to the relative interests of the parties when such termination occurs.[20] Again, if the donee is the donor's spouse, the unlimited marital deduction eliminates any federal gift tax consequences.

¶ 7.06   WHEN TERMINATION OF JOINT OWNERSHIP MAY BE DESIRABLE

The most important tax reason for termination of joint ownership by owners who are not husband and wife is to avoid application of the "con-

---

18. Estate of Howard v. Commissioner, 9 T.C. 1192, 1202–1203 (1947).

19. See Reg. 25.2515–2(b).

20. See Reg. § 25.2515–4(b).

sideration" test, which requires inclusion of the property in the estate of the joint owner who paid for it.[21]   Married joint owners may wish to terminate joint ownership of appreciated property and to make the spouse who is expected to be the first to die the sole owner, in order to obtain a new basis for the entire property under § 1014 on his death.   Unfortunately, it is not always clear which spouse will die first.   If the spouses wait until their relative life expectancies have become more predictable, the survivor's interest may be denied a new basis under§ 1014(e).   This misfortune will follow if the decedent acquires that interest within a year of his death and either it (or the proceeds of its sale) [22] passes to the survivor.

Joint owners who are not married to each other have the same income tax inducement to transfer ownership of appreciated property to the owner who is expected to be the first to die.   But the gift tax may be a deterrent, as no marital deduction is available.

Conversion of joint ownership into a tenancy in common often may be effected without constituting a gift for gift tax purposes.   Such conversion does not lead to a new basis under § 1014 for the entire property, but may offer estate tax savings.   For example, if A and B own stock worth $10,000 as joint tenants and A paid for it, division of the stock so that A and B each own $5,000 worth is not a gift for gift tax purposes.   The result of such division will be that only $5,000 is includible in A's estate.

Another possible advantage of converting joint ownership into a tenancy in common is that it allows each co-tenant to dispose of his interest during life or by will to other persons, rather than having the property automatically become solely owned by the surviving joint tenant.   This may be desirable for married joint owners to avoid "over maritalizing" the estate of one of them.

For example, if other interests that will pass from H to W if she survives him can be expected to equal or exceed the optimal amount for tax purposes,[23] it may be desirable to convert such joint ownership between H and W into a tenancy in common.   Such conversion will leave H free to dispose of his interest, either during his life or upon his death, to someone else (or to give W an interest which will not be taxable in her estate when she dies).

It may also be desirable for joint owners who are not spouses to convert such ownership to a tenancy in common, in order to permit the share of the first person to die to pass to someone other than the other joint owner.   For example, assume that a father (F) and daughter (D) own stock worth $500,000 as joint tenants, and each contributed one-half of the purchase price.   If F and D want the stock ultimately to go to D's children, they may find that converting the ownership of the stock into a tenancy in common will reduce the total estate taxes that must be paid on the deaths of F and D, leaving a larger portion of the stock for the children. F, during his life or at death, will be able to give his one-half interest in the stock directly to the children or he will be able to transfer it in trust, giving the income from the trust to D for her life.   By terminating joint ownership, F and D

---

21. See § 2040(a).

22. See § 1014(e)(2)(B), discussed at ¶ 4.03[1] supra.

23. For a discussion, see ¶ 16.01[1].

will be able to keep *F*'s $250,000 share of the stock out of *D*'s estate.[24]　This alternative would not be available if the stock remained jointly owned, as *D* would be the sole owner of the stock on *F*'s death, by operation of law.

¶ 7.07　NON-TAX REASONS TO CREATE JOINT OWNERSHIP WITH SURVIVORSHIP

As was noted in the preceding section, joint ownership often does not save estate taxes, and may well result in a higher tax if the joint owner are not husband and wife and whoever paid for the property dies first.

However, some clients may prefer to own property jointly for a variety of non-tax reasons.　The non-tax factors of most importance to clients include:

(1) Expressing a couple's sense that the property is "ours."　This is the least debatable of the commonly assumed advantages.　It is most often referred to in connection with joint ownership by spouses, but may also apply to other couples as well.　The sense of "our" property is present with joint ownership in greater degree than with a tenancy in common, at least if both parties understand the legal significance of the difference.　This is an important reason for use of this form in the ownership of a residence.

(2) Avoiding probate or minimizing probate expenses.　Property which is jointly owned is not part of the probate estate of the first joint owner to die and, thus, some clients may wish to own their property jointly so that the survivor is not faced with probate proceedings at a time of emotional trauma.　In addition, excluding part or all of a decedent's property from the probate estate may affect the lawyer's fee and executor's commission for adminstering the estate. It is difficult to generalize about fees and the manner in which different forms of ownership may affect them.[25]　For a given estate, holding property jointly may or may not reduce lawyers' fees and executors' commissions.　Many factors enter into the determination of both fees and commissions, so that it is often impossible to say what they would have been if the assets had been held in another form.　One situation in which joint ownership may well reduce expenses is where the property is located in a state other than that in which the joint owners reside.　In this case, joint ownership will avoid ancillary probate proceedings in the state where the property is located, at least on the death of the first joint owner.

(3) Providing, in a joint bank account, funds that in some states will be immediately available to the survivor without the delays of probate.　A careful practitioner will advise his or her client to indicate, either on a bank form or in a separate document, that the surviving joint tenant is to have all rights to the bank account.　This should satisfy the requirements for a right of survivorship under state law,

---

24.　If *D* received a life estate or other limited interest, its termination may be subject to the tax on generation-skipping transfers. See § 2613(b)(1).

25.　See generally, Report of Subcommittee of Committee on Adminstration Expenses, "Fiduciary Compensation and Legal Fees with Respect to Nonprobate Assets," 8 Real Prop., Probl. & Trust J. 1 (1973).

and should avoid any claim that a survivorship right in the account was not intended.[26]

Even where it is clear that a survivorship right in a bank account is intended, some delay may occur before a survivor can obtain funds from an account. For savings accounts represented by a passbook, a bank may refuse to release funds if the passbook is not presented. If the book cannot be found, or is in a safe deposit box, the survivor may find that gaining access to the funds can be a time-consuming process. In addition, in some states a bank account is frozen until a state death tax waiver is obtained.

(4) Avoiding dower, curtesy, and the elective rights of a surviving spouse. Undoubtedly, some clients who take title as joint tenants with someone other than the spouse seek to avoid statutes which allow the surviving spouse to take a certain portion of a deceased spouse's estate regardless of the decedent's wishes. Whether this avoidance technique succeeds depends largely on state law, as some states give a surviving spouse a limited right to a share of property owned jointly by the deceased spouse and a third person.[27]

(5) Avoiding claims of creditors. Since jointly owned property is not part of the probate estate, it is not subject to the claims of estate creditors. It may also be free from creditors' claims during the lives of the joint owners as well.

The practical significance of the last-mentioned reason is limited by the fact that creditors often insist at the time credit is extended that both joint owners assume liability for the debt, so that it can be satisfied out of the joint property. Tort creditors and others who become creditors involuntarily do not have this opportunity, and the jointly owned property may be effectively insulated from their claims.

Although all of the above considerations are commonly discussed in connection with the purchase of property, they are also relevant when property is transferred by gift or will. For example, a client may choose to transfer property to a married child individually or to the child and his or her spouse as joint tenants, tenants in common, or tenants by the entirety. The same alternatives are available when transferring property to unmarried persons, except for tenancy by the entirety.

---

26. The majority view, absent a contrary statutory provision, is that a deposit in joint names (other than husband and wife) does not show an intent to create joint ownership. See notes 3–5 supra.

27. Sometimes the provision for elective rights of a surviving spouse expressly includes joint tenancies between the decedent and a third party. See, e.g., N.Y. EPTL 5–1.1(b)(1)(D) (applies if joint tenancy was created after August 31, 1966); Uniform Probate Code §§ 2–201, 2–202(1)(iii).

Chapter 8

SALES AND OTHER NON-GIFTS

¶ 8.01 INFORMAL ARRANGEMENTS

Clients often use informal arrangements, almost instinctively, to shift income from both property and services to their children and other beneficiaries. Some of the most important ways to achieve such a shift are gifts of services, interest-free or low-interest loans, and diversions of business or investment opportunities.

[1] Gifts of Services

Gifts of services are illustrated by the father who devotes his time and attention to managing his children's business interests or investments (or those of trusts for their benefit) without a fee, so as to increase their income and wealth without becoming taxable on such increase himself. As yet, there are few instances in which allocation of appropriate compensation for such services is required for income tax purposes, either by court decisions [1] or by explicit Code provisions.[2]

---

1. In Glenn E. Edgar, 56 T.C. 717, 746–48 (1971), the taxpayer was held to have received taxable compensation for his services in promoting the sale of stock through an arrangement by which a trust he had created was permitted to buy stock at a bargain price. The assignment of income doctrine was applied here and could be invoked in other situations in which a taxpayer diverts what would otherwise have been his income to either an individual or a trust he has created or wishes to benefit.

In James A. Hogle v. Commissioner, 132 F.2d 66, 42–2 USTC ¶ 9811 (10th Cir. 1942), a father was held taxable on profits realized by a securities trading account which was part of a trust for his children. No funds were transferred by the father to the trust and any net losses were to be made good by him, subject to repayment from future profits from the account. However, in a later decision involving the same taxpayer, the court described the first Hogle decision as an extreme application of the Clifford doctrine. (Under the current codification of the doctrine (§§ 671–677), trust income may be taxed to the grantor because of his dominion or control over it). See Commissioner v. James A. Hogle, 165 F.2d 352, 48–1 USTC ¶ 10,592 (10th Cir. 1947).

A parent's managerial control over income-producing property he had given to his child was held insufficient to make the parent taxable on such income in two cases involv-

ing related taxpayers. See Nella B. Alexander v. Commissioner, 190 F.2d 753, 51–2 USTC ¶ 9418 (5th Cir. 1951) and Harley Alexander v. Commissioner, 194 F.2d 921, 52–1 USTC ¶ 9232 (5th Cir. 1952).

2. The general rule of § 704 (e)(2) is that the distributive share of the donee of a partnership interest is includible in gross income by the donee. An exception is made "to the extent that such share is determined without allowance of reasonable compensation for services rendered to the partnership by the donor * * *."

Allocation of appropriate compensation for services has also been required under the general provisions of § 482 in the case of services performed for corporations by controlling shareholders. See Richard Rubin v. Commissioner, 429 F.2d 650, 72–1 USTC ¶ 9440 (2d Cir. 1970) (payments to corporation for management services rendered by taxpayer, its controlling shareholder, allocated in part to him); Victor Borge v. Commissioner, 405 F.2d 673, 69–1 USTC ¶ 9131 (2d Cir. 1968), cert. denied 395 U.S. 933 (1969).

See also § 1375(c), under which the Secretary may reallocate dividends received by members of a family who are shareholders of an electing small business corporation, to reflect the value of services rendered by them to the corporation.

Neither the gift tax nor the estate tax would appear to apply to such informal income-shifting arrangements.[3] The gift tax is imposed on the transfer of property,[4] not services, and the estate tax is similarly based on property owned at death [5] or transferred in specified ways during life.[6]

[2] Loans and Use of Property

LESTER CROWN v. COMMISSIONER

United States Court of Appeals, Seventh Circuit, 1978.
585 F.2d 234, 78-2 USTC ¶ 12,260.

HARLINGTON WOOD, Jr., Circuit Judge.

The primary question presented in this appeal is whether a taxpayer who lends money to his children and other close family members in the form of no-interest loans and open accounts payable on demand must include in the computation of gifts taxable during a particular tax year the value of the interest foregone on the indebtedness outstanding during that year. The tax court ruled in favor of the taxpayer's argument that no taxable gift occurred. We affirm.

As the relevant facts have been set out in the Tax Court's opinion in this case reported at 67 T.C. 1060 (1977), we need only briefly summarize them here. Appellee is an equal partner along with his two brothers in Areljay Company, Not Incorporated ("Areljay"). Prior to and during 1967, Areljay made loans totaling approximately $18 million to a series of 24 trusts that had been established for the benefit of the children and other close relatives of the three brothers. The loans were made to enable the trusts to acquire interests in another investment partnership known as Henry Crown and Company (Not Incorporated) ("HC Not Inc."). Approximately 13% of the trusts' indebtedness to Areljay was represented by notes payable on demand. The remaining 87% consisted of loans on open account. Neither the open accounts nor the demand notes contained any provision for the payment of interest except after demand. Nor was any interest paid on the outstanding balances of the loans during the tax year in question.

In the notice of deficiency sent to the appellee on November 30, 1973, the Commissioner of Internal Revenue determined that the loans to the trusts resulted in gifts from the Areljay partners in 1967 in the amount of $1,086,407.75, one-third of which was allocated to the appellee. In calculating the amount of the gifts the Commissioner applied an interest rate of 6% per annum to the daily balance of the loans outstanding during the year. The Commissioner theorized that the loans involved the transfer of a valuable property right to the trusts equal to the market rate of interest charged on similar loans. After the matter was heard by the Tax Court, a decision

---

3. One court has held that an agreement of a father (F) to manage his brother's investment property without compensation, in exchange for the brother's promise to bequeath one-half of his estate to F's daughter, constituted a taxable gift from F to his daughter. See Ray Dodge v. United States, 443 F.Supp. 535, 78-1 USTC ¶ 13,242 (D.Or.1977).

4. § 2501(a).

5. § 2031(a).

6. See, e.g., § 2036.

was filed on March 31, 1977, holding that the appellee could not be subject to the gift tax on his proportionate share of the partnership's outstanding loans because the making of non-interest-bearing loans under these circumstances is not a taxable event.   There were three dissenters.   *   *   *

The Commissioner begins his argument for finding a gift in these loans with the proposition that the granting of a loan over a period of time at less than the true economic rate of interest bestows an economic benefit on the recipient.   As with any productive asset the ability to employ that asset in productive activity gives rise to "income" in an economic sense.[7]   When money is loaned at zero interest over a period of time the recipient is enriched by the amount of income that the money generates for him.   At the same time, the person who lends the money is poorer by the amount of interest foregone.   His nominal wealth may not decline, but he misses out on a chance to increase his net worth.   This is the "opportunity cost" of his loan. In order for an economic benefit to be transferred to the recipient, it is not necessary that the interest rate be set at zero, but only that the interest rate on the loan be less than the appropriate market rate of interest at the time.

The Commissioner argues that this transfer of economic benefit by means of interest-free loans is inimical to the two major purposes of the gift tax statute—protection of the income tax and the estate tax.[8]   The argument is clearly correct with respect to the income tax, a fact which the Tax Court majority failed to note.   The concern here is that people will use gifts of income producing property to split up an income taxable in a high tax bracket into smaller incomes taxable in lower brackets.   No-interest loans do just that.[9]   Moreover, where the loans are payable on demand, the maker of the loans is able to achieve this result without the inconvenience of losing access to the principal should the need arise.   The situation with regard to the estate tax is more complex.   Because of the time-value of money, when a no-interest loan is made for a definite term, the estate of the person making the loans is reduced in that the economic value of the promise to pay off the loan in the future is less than the value of the money which was loaned out.[10]   The Commissioner suggests that the same thing is true of the loans in the case at bar.   However, as the appellee points out, since the estate could require the loans to be repaid on demand, there

---

7.   Even with consumption rather than production goods, the use thereof gives rise to "income" during the period of use if one employs the economic definition of income as the sum of consumption during the period plus the net change in wealth.

8.   Petitioner argues that protection of the income tax is only a "natural consequence" of the gift tax rather than one of its purposes.   But there is authority to the contrary.   With regard to the 1932 Act, see 65 Cong.Rec. 3120, 8095–96; H.R.Rep.No. 708, 72nd Cong., 1st Sess. (1932); S.Rep.No. 665, 72nd Cong., 1st Sess. 40 (1932).   See generally Lowndes, Kramer & McCord, Federal Estate and Gift Taxes, §§ 22.2 and 26.15 (3d ed. 1974);   Harris, Legislative

History of Federal Gift Taxation, 18 Taxes 531, 533 (1940).

9.   We do not mean to express any view with regard to the Commissioner's contention, not part of this appeal, that the loans in this case gave rise to constructive income to the Areljay partners taxable under the income tax.

10.   As the date of maturity of the loan approaches, the fair market value of the promise to pay increases.   All other things being equal, at the date of maturity the market value and the face value of the note would be equal.

is no reason to expect that the fair value of the promise to repay would be substantially less than the face amount of the loans.[11]   This fact led the Tax Court below and the district court in Johnson v. United States, 254 F.Supp. 73 (N.D.Tex.1966)—the only reported decision on all fours with the case at bar—to conclude that the government's interest in taxing the estate of the lender had not been affected.   But the Commissioner goes on to argue that if the lender had retained the money loaned out and invested it in income-producing assets, his taxable estate would have grown larger by the amount of income earned.   See Note Gift Taxation of Interest-Free Loans, 19 Stan.L.Rev. 870, 874 (1967).   Appellee's counter-argument, which was accepted by the majority in the Tax Court, is that

> our income tax system does not recognize unrealized earnings or accumulations of wealth and no taxpayer is under any obligation to continuously invest his money for a profit.   The opportunity cost of either letting one's money remain idle or suffering a loss from an unwise investment is not taxable merely because a profit *could have been made* from a wise investment.

67 T.C. 1060, 1067 (1977) (emphasis in the original).

It is true that under our system a taxpayer is not under any duty to cultivate the fruits of his capital (or labor) and will not be taxed as if he had when he hasn't.   However, by actively placing others in a position to enjoy the fruits of his capital, the taxpayer in a sense vicariously "realizes" the economic potential thereof.[12]   Permitting others to enjoy the economic benefits of an asset can be seen as one means of exerting control over the asset's economic potential.   This might serve as a theoretical basis for distinguishing gifts such as those involved here from situations where the taxpayer lets his productive properties lie totally fallow.   However, whatever the value of this consideration as a policy factor favoring the gift taxation of loans such as those present in the instant case, the Commissioner has not been able to point to any authority suggesting that the congressional purpose of protecting the estate tax was concerned with the use of gifts to diminish a taxpayer's potential estate as well as his actual one.

The Commissioner also points out that a failure to tax the use of interest-free demand loans would be inconsistent with the tax treatment of other practical alternatives for the transfer of an economic benefit to another. The appellee has conceded that had the interest-free loans been made for

---

11.   There might be some difference because of the lack of credit worthiness of the promisor, or because there is an anticipation of practical delays in procuring payment. There is no evidence of either in this case.

12.   A similar argument might be made with respect to donations of personal services. Yet, the IRS has apparently made an administrative determination that a donor's free offering of his personal services is not subject to the gift tax.   Lowndes, Kramer & McCord, Federal Estate and Gift Taxes, § 26.1 (3d ed. 1974), and what little judicial authority there is on the question is to the same effect, see, e.g., Comm'r of Internal Revenue v. Hogle, 165 F.2d 352 (10th Cir. 1947).   However, although the situation with regard to labor may be analogous in an economic sense, a different set of policy considerations are involved.   It has been suggested that:

> The opportunities for deflection of the relative income tax burdens clearly appear to distinguish interest-free loans from gifts of services and justify the backstop use of the gift tax to minimize the potential loss to the federal fisc.   (Footnotes omitted).

Lowndes, Kramer & McCord, supra § 26.15 at 686.

a definite term, a taxable gift might have occurred.[13]   Similarly, if the taxpayer had contributed the money to a trust made irrevocable for a certain duration, then the present discounted value of the income interest payable to the beneficiaries would have been considered a gift taxable to the taxpayer at the time that the trust was established.   See Treasury Regulations on Gift Tax (1954 Code), § 25.2511–1(e) (26 C.F.R.).   More analogous to the situation of no-interest loans repayable on demand is the establishment of a revocable trust.   There the income payments to the beneficiary are considered gifts from the grantor during the calendar years received.   If the power to revoke terminates, a gift of the corpus is considered to occur.[14] See H.Rep.No. 708, 72d Cong., 1st Sess., 28 (1932); Treasury Regulations on Gift Tax (1954 Code), §§ 25.2511–1(e), 2(f), 25.2512–5(c).

It is not enough for the Commissioner to demonstrate that there are good policy reasons for taxing interest-free demand loans and that to fail to do so will lead to inconsistent tax treatment of transactions constituting practical alternatives.   He must also show that the taxation of such loans is within the contemplation of the gift tax statute.   The Commissioner attempts to carry his burden in this respect by relying on Sections 2501 and 2512(b) of the Code, 26 U.S.C.A. §§ 2501 and 2512(b).   No statutory language or statements in the legislative history have been cited dealing specifically with interest-free loans.[15]   Instead, reliance is placed on the broad general sweep of these statutory sections.   * * *   Congress intended the gift tax statute to "cover and comprehend all transactions   * * * whereby and to the extent   * * *   that property or a property right is donatively passed to or conferred upon another, regardless of the means or device employed in its accomplishment."   H.Rep.No. 708, 72d Cong., 1st Sess. 22 (1932); S.Rep.No. 665, 72d Cong., 1st Sess. 39 (1932); both reprinted in 1939–1 Cum.Bull. (Part 2) 476, 524.   The purpose was to "reach every kind and type of transfer by gift."   Robinette v. Helvering, 318 U.S. 184, 187, 63 S.Ct. 540, 542, 87 L.Ed. 700 (1943).[16]   In enacting the predecessor to Section 2512, Congress dispensed with the common law test of "donative intent" in favor of a "workable external test."   "The language of the gift tax statute, 'property   * * *   real or personal, tangible or intangible,' is broad enough to include property, however conceptual or contingent."   Smith v. Shaughnessy, 318 U.S. 176, 180, 63 S.Ct. 545, 547, 87

13. Although the Commissioner characterized the petitioner's concession at oral argument as being a concession as to taxability, in fact the appellee only conceded that the present discounted value of a no-interest term loan would be less than its face amount.   However, it may be possible to characterize the differential as a gift under Section 2512(b) of the Internal Revenue Code.   See Blackburn v. Comm'r, 20 T.C. 204 (1953); Mason v. United States, 513 F.2d 25 (7th Cir. 1975).   The question has not yet been decided.

14. The important distinction between a revocable trust and an interest-free demand loan is that in the former case, the beneficiary is given the income already produced by the capital, while in the latter the borrower receives only the opportunity to use the capital productively.

15. Although the petitioner attempts to distinguish between the open account loans in the case and those evidenced by demand notes, we find them to be equivalent for present purposes.   Both forms involved loans of money repayable on demand and with no provision for the payment of interest.

16. Justice Frankfurter found that Congress desired "to hit all the protean arrangements which the wit of man can devise that are not business transactions within the meaning of ordinary speech * * * ."   Commissioner v. Wemyss, 324 U.S. 303, 306, 65 S.Ct. 652, 654, 89 L.Ed. 958 (1944).

L.Ed. 690 (1942). The Congressional reports also evidence a broad concept of "property":

> The terms "property," "transfer," "gift," and "indirectly" are used in the broadest and most comprehensive sense; the term "property" reaching every species of right or interest protected by law and having an exchangeable value.

H.Rep.No. 708, supra, at 27–28; S.Rep.No. 665, supra, at 39.

Yet, in spite of the broad sweep of the gift tax statutes the Commissioner's attempt to bring interest-free demand loans within their scope presents a number of difficulties. His argument seems to alternate between at least two analytically distinguishable approaches. He first attempts to characterize the transaction as an "unequal exchange" within Section 2512(b), focusing on the time of the loan. The lender is seen as transferring "property" (money) in exchange for a promise that a like amount of money will be repaid upon demand. This promise is seen as being less in "money's worth" than the money loaned. The Commissioner presents no evidence in support of the latter proposition, but only the argument that the promise is to repay the loan at some indefinite time in the future and that given the time-value of money this must be worth less than its face value. Although this may be true in the abstract in that instantaneous repayment is impossible, from a realistic point of view the value at the time the loan is extended of the right to repayment is both unknown and unknowable. The Commissioner has not produced any evidence showing that demand notes systematically trade at a significant discount from face value in the market place. Nor can a present discounted value formula be successfully applied given the absence of knowledge as to when the loan will be repaid.[17] The most that can be said is that the eventual value of the notes expressed in terms of a present discounted value as of the time of the loan will range somewhere between zero and the face amount of the notes.[18] The reason that the value at the time of the loan cannot be determined with greater certainty is that the transfer of the economic benefit is incomplete at that point, being yet totally dependent on the lender's continuing willingness to refrain from demanding repayment.

The Commissioner's method for determining the timing and amount of the taxable gift generated by interest-free demand loans permits the calculation of a definite value, but is not entirely consistent with the "unequal exchange" theory. The Commissioner would find a gift to have occurred during any quarter in which there were no-interest loans outstanding and would measure the amount of the gift by multiplying the outstanding balances by the market interest rate on similar notes. The imputation of interest in subsequent time periods is not a theoretically accurate measure of the difference in value of the time of the loan between the money loaned and the promise to repay. The "unequal exchange" approach of Section 2512(b) implicitly assumes that the values being compared will be measured

---

17. The Commissioner has not suggested that there was a collateral agreement or plan that would have precluded demanding repayment of the notes over any predetermined period.

18. If payment is demanded immediately after the loan is made, the present value will approximate the face value. If the loan remains perpetually unpaid, the present value approaches zero.

at the same point in time, just as Section 2512(a) requires that an outright gift of property be valued as of the date of the gift. The failure to discount the interest imputed in subsequent periods back to the time of the loan leads to the seeming paradox that if the lender were to permit the interest-free loan to remain outstanding for a sufficiently long period before demanding repayment, he would end up paying more in gift taxes than he would have had he made an outright gift of the loan principal.[19] The other problem is that as a measure of the "unequal exchange" differential, the Commissioner's formula would imply that at the time of the loan it was predetermined that the loan would be outstanding during the period in which interest is sought to be imputed. There is no basis for this assumption.

At other times, instead of characterizing the loans as an "unequal exchange," the Commissioner seems to suggest that there is an outright gift of a "property right"—namely, the right to use the money for an indefinite period. To use a real property analogy, it is as if the lender gives the borrower a "tenancy at will" with respect to a sum of money while retaining the "reversion." See Simes & Smith, The Law of Future Interests § 83 (2d ed. 1966). The question is whether such an "at will" interest can properly be characterized as "property" under the gift tax laws; i.e., whether it is "protected by law" and has an "exchangeable value." H.Rep.No. 708, supra, at 27; S.Rep.No. 665, supra, at 39. Certain "at will" interests have been the subject of legal protection vis-a-vis third parties. A real property tenancy at will clearly gives the tenant a possessory interest against third parties. There is also authority to the effect that an action may be maintained against third parties for interference with a contract right even if the latter was terminable at will. See W. Prosser, Law of Torts § 129 at 932 (4th ed. 1971). However, we have seen no authority suggesting that the recipient of a loan payable on demand has a legally protectible interest vis-a-vis the lender. Moreover, the Commissioner has produced no evidence showing that the borrower's "at will" interest has an exchangeable value.[20] Even if the theoretical existence of the possibility of an exchangeable value were conceded, as discussed above the imputation of interest in subsequent time periods is seriously deficient as a measure of that value as of the time of the loan.[21]

---

19. For example, if a lender makes a $1,000 no-interest loan and the "proper" interest rate is 10%, under the IRS formula he would be treated as having made a gift of $100 in each year the loan remains outstanding for 20 years, he will be treated as having made gifts totaling $2,000, whereas he would only have been taxed on $1,000 if he had made a gift of the principal in the first place. However, the paradox is one of nominal rather than real values. In the case of the outright gift the tax is paid immediately, while under the loan the tax is paid at various points in the future. Because of the time-value of money, the present value of the two alternatives may be about the same.

20. Money itself, of course, has an exchangeable value. However, the interest posited here is not money itself, but the right to use a sum of money until the lender demands repayment. It is also noteworthy that at common law a tenancy at will terminates if transferred, and therefore has no exchangeable value. See Restatement, Second, Landlord and Tenant § 1.6.

21. Appellee cites a number of cases in which courts rejected the IRS's attempt to tax as a gift a series of payments received by virtue of an earlier transferred right, in favor of the taxation of the value of the right itself at the time it was irrevocably transferred. See, e.g., Galt v. Comm'r, of Internal Revenue, 216 F.2d 41 (7th Cir. 1954), cert. denied, 348 U.S. 951, 75 S.Ct. 438, 99 L.Ed. 743 (1955). However, the present case is distinguishable since the right transferred was revocable. See Lowndes, Kramer & McCord, supra, § 26.10.

A third variant of the Commissioner's argument abandons the idea that the gift occurs at the time of the making of the loan in favor of the view that although it begins at that time, it is completed only as, and to the extent that the lender continues to refrain from demanding repayment. This view of the gift as occurring continuously during the period that the loan is outstanding is in harmony with the Commissioner's formula for measuring the amount and timing of the gift. Yet, bringing this version of the Commissioner's argument under the aegis of the gift tax statute involves a certain amount of stretching of the latter. To characterize the mere use of property as a transfer of a property right implies a broader concept of what constitutes a property right under the gift tax laws than has heretofore been recognized.[22] The application of the Commissioner's theory to the case at bar is the equivalent to viewing the appellee as constructively receiving a hypothetical interest payment on the money loaned which he then constructively transfers to the borrower. This raises the problem, discussed previously, of whether a tax is being imposed on what the lender could have done rather than what he did. A finding of a taxable gift is also equivalent to saying that the lender had a right to receive interest from the borrower—which "indebtedness" he then forgave. It is true that a lender has a "right" to charge interest in that he is legally empowered to do so. But absent a contract provision providing otherwise there is no legal obligation for the borrower to pay interest, which might occasion the application of a cancellation of indebtedness approach. See Lowndes, Kramer & McCord, supra, § 26.12.

The Commissioner cites little precedent in support of his interpretation. Blackburn v. Commissioner, 20 T.C. 204 (1953), Mason v. United States, 513 F.2d 25 (7th Cir. 1975), and Commissioner v. Edwards, 135 F.2d 574 (7th Cir. 1943), constitute only indirect support for the subsumption of interest-free term loans within the "unequal exchange" approach of Section 2512(b). The only case directly on point here, Johnson v. United States, 254 F.Supp. 73 (N.D.Tex.1966), is squarely contrary to the Commissioner's position. The Tax Court also noted that the courts have consistently rejected the IRS's attempts to impute taxable income to the recipients of interest-free loans. See J. Simpson Dean, 35 T.C. 1083 (1961); Saunders v. United States, 294 F.Sup. 1276, rev'd on other grounds, 450 F.2d 1047 (9th Cir. 1971); Joseph Lupowitz Sons, Inc. v. Commissioner, 497 F.2d 862 (3d Cir. 1974). In fact, courts have generally been inhospitable to the Commissioner's attempts to make the granting of interest-free or low-interest loans a taxable event, absent an express statute or regulation. The courts refused to give in to the Commissioner's efforts to impute interest on interest-free or low-interest loans between related business entities until the IRS promulgated Regulation 1.482–2 under newly granted authority. Compare Tennessee-Arkansas Gravel Co. v. Commissioner of Internal Revenue, 112 F.2d 508 (6th Cir. 1940), with B. Forman Co. v. Commissioner of Internal Revenue, 453 F.2d 1144 (2d Cir.), cert. denied, 407 U.S. 934,

---

22. It is of interest that the IRS has consistently maintained that a donation of the use of property that is not a "legally enforceable conveyance" does not constitute a gift of "property" within the meaning of the charitable contribution provisions of the Internal Revenue Code. See, I.T. 3918, 1948–2 Cum.Bull. 33; Rev.Rul. 70–477, 1970–2 Cum.Bull. 62.

92 S.Ct. 2458, 32 L.Ed.2d 817 (1972). That regulation embodied the same basic principle that the Commissioner espoused in the courts, but provided for a "safe harbor" with respect to the taxpayer's choice of interest rate. The courts also refused to impute interest income in connection with interest-free installment sales until Congress added Section 483 to the Code. See, e.g., Clay B. Brown, 37 T.C. 461 (1961), aff'd, 325 F.2d 313 (9th Cir. 1963), aff'd, 380 U.S. 563, 85 S.Ct. 1162, 14 L.Ed.2d 75 (1965); Pretzer v. United States, 61–1 USTC ¶ 9477 (Ariz.1961). When Congress dealt with the problem, it also gave recognition to the basic principle espoused by the Commissioner, but limited its applicability by excluding sales of certain types of assets and transactions of less than one year or involving less than $3,000.

Adoption of the Commissioner's position in the present case by judicial construction would involve the courts in the difficult task of determining an appropriate interest rate for imputation. The lack of statutory or regulatory guidelines on this question would also make it difficult for a taxpayer to know in advance whether a particular loan would give rise to a taxable gift, and if so, in what amount. This uncertainty as to valuation would make it difficult to comply with the reporting provisions of Section 6019(a) of the Code. A "safe harbor" in the form of a minimum acceptable interest rate might be desirable, such as that provided in Regulation 1.482–2.

Another problem with adopting the judicial construction urged by the Commissioner is the extremely broad potential reach of the principles that would be at least implicitly recognized. The same reasoning that leads to the finding of a taxable gift when $18 million is loaned by a parent to his children for investment purposes would find a gift where a father lends a thousand dollars to his son graduating from college until he can get established, or even where an office worker lends a fellow employee $10 "until next payday." Similar reasoning might find the presence of a gift when a neighbor borrows your lawnmower and fails to return it immediately, or when out-of-town guests are provided a night's lodging by friends instead of going to a hotel.[23] As in Section 483, it might be desirable to set out a clear set of rules exempting from taxation certain types of property and/or transactions below some threshold duration or dollar value.

Lastly, our hesitancy to adopt the result advocated by the Commissioner by judicial construction is reinforced by equitable considerations. See Central Illinois Public Service Co. v. United States, 435 U.S. 21, 98 S.Ct. 917, 55 L.Ed.2d 82 (1978) (Brennan, J., concurring). Although we recognize that the Commissioner has broad discretion in applying a ruling retroactively, Wisconsin Nipple and Fabricating Corp. v. Commissioner, 581 F.2d 1235 (7th Cir. 1978), as the majority opinion in the Tax Court recognized, the Commissioner has only recently begun to assert that the making of non-interest bearing loans is a taxable event, even though the statutory authorities offered in support of that position have been in existence since the creation of the gift tax laws. When the Commissioner's

---

23. Of course, these kinds of problems would only arise if the taxpayer has already hit the ceiling on gift tax exclusions and deductions because of other transactions. It is also unlikely that the IRS would seek to impose a tax in many of the situations hypothesized. Yet, it may be desirable to rely on something more than the Commissioner's discretion in this area.

position on the same issue involved in the case at bar was squarely rejected by the court in Johnson v. United States, 254 F.Supp. 73 (N.D.Tex.1966), no appeal was taken. Moreover, the Commissioner's non-acquiescence in that decision was not made public until seven years later, six years after the alleged gifts now before us were made. See Rev.Rul. 73–61, 1973–1 Cum.Bull. 408. Until that time there was no administrative or judicial authority suggesting that interest-free demand loans would give rise to a taxable gift.

In conclusion, although we are sympathetic to the Commissioner's desire to fill in what may be a significant loophole in the gift tax laws, a number of theoretical and practical problems make it undesirable to do so by judicial construction. Accord, Note, 9 Rut.-Cam.L.J. 579, 586 (1978). We express no view here as to whether a prospective regulation making such loans taxable would be valid or whether, on the other hand, the problem would best be left to Congress.

The judgment of the Tax Court is

Affirmed.

ROBERT VAN PELT, Senior District Judge, dissenting:

It is with reluctance that I note my dissent. The judges who constitute the majority are men of honor and competence and I respect their judgment. The fact that the Tax Court was divided on this issue, with four judges dissenting, I mention only to show that I am not alone in the views herein expressed.

While the amount involved in the notice of deficiency is only slightly more than a million dollars, the overall interest-free loans, as the majority opinion recognize, totalled approximately $18,000,000. I conclude gifts of such magnitude, and of lesser amounts also, if not de minimis, embody a gift. That a gift is being given seems evident to me when you consider the example used by Judge Simpson who dissented in the Tax Court. He says, if the taxpayer here had

> arranged for the borrowers to obtain the money from financial institutions and agreed to pay the interest thereon, clearly, the payment of such interest would constitute a taxable gift

Crown v. Commissioner of Internal Revenue, 67 T.C. 1060, 1066 (1977). The taxpayer here has in effect paid the interest on these loans when he does not demand payment or interest at the prevailing rate. The majority recognized the recipient has been enriched. Under the majority decision, the disparate treatment of gift-giving taxpayers becomes more obvious when we follow through with what has happened. We have here a lender loaning money to his children and other close family members without interest in an amount which, if placed in U.S. Government Bonds, even by one "not bright" in the handling of money, could hardly help resulting in annual income of a million dollars. All of this is received without any gift tax or other transfer tax being paid, if the Tax Court is affirmed.

On the other hand, a grandparent who, without tax advice of lawyers and accountants, gives a grandchild $10,000 in one year, and has previously used his or her gift tax exclusion, pays tax on what by comparison with eighteen million dollars could be called "the widow's mite." I use the populist expressions and comparisons in this paragraph only to point up more graphically my feelings that the decision of the Tax Court's majority "just ain't right."

This dissent is not based solely on what I think is right or wrong. The moral sense and conscience of the majority of this panel is as trustworthy as mine. I dissent, mainly, because I feel Internal Revenue Code §§ 2501, 2511 and 2512 are broad enough to cover this transaction. Where the Congressional history, as related in the majority opinion, indicates that Congress intended the gift tax statutes to "cover and comprehend all transactions * * * whereby and to the extent * * * that property or a property right is donatively passed to or conferred upon another, regardless of the means or device employed in its accomplishment," there is little need to specifically enumerate interest-free loans as a taxable gift or as included in the term "all transactions." I can only conclude, as the Commissioner of Internal Revenue and four members of the Tax Court have concluded, that the authority for treating this as a taxable event has long been available in the statutes as written.

I would reinstate the decision of the Commissioner of Internal Revenue and reverse the Tax Court.

QUESTIONS

1. In *Crown*, what would be the tax consequences of the running of the statute of limitations on the right of the lender under state law to sue to collect the note? See Estate of Grace E. Lang, 64 T.C. 404 (1975), aff'd 613 F.2d 770, 80-1 USTC ¶ 13,340 (9th Cir. 1980).

2. Will the Commissioner treat interest-free or low-interest loans from a parent to his child as giving rise to taxable income to the parent?

3. What significance might follow from the fact that the loans in *Crown* were to trusts, rather than individuals? See § 676.

––––––––

Arrangements less formal than loans from the client to a beneficiary may enhance the financial position of the latter without subjecting the client to as great a risk that such an enhancement will be taxable income for the client who made it possible. For example, it is common for parents to guarantee repayment of loans made to their children and such guarantees may be essential in order to permit the child to borrow or to obtain a favorable interest rate. Such guarantees have not, as yet, given rise to income to the parent. Many parents undoubtedly allow their children to enjoy the use of property, either rent-free or at below-market rentals, without being required to include the value of such use in the parent's taxable income.

[3] Diversions of Business or Investment Opportunities

A classic illustration of diversion of business opportunities to children is provided by *Robert P. Crowley*.[24] In that case, the taxpayer controlled a savings and loan association, whose business generated fees and commis-

––––––––

24.   34 T.C. 333 (1960), acq. 1961-1 CB 4.

sions for appraisals, insurance, abstracts, and title policies. This work was done by a partnership owned by the taspayer's minor children, and the income it produced was held to be taxable to them, rather than to their father. Here, as elsewhere, existing law has yet to treat parents who use their business relationships to generate income for their children in the same manner as taxpayers who seek, by means of an assignment, to make income taxable to someone else after it has been earned.

¶ 8.02   SALES AND EXCHANGES

Sales and exchanges are often an attractive way to move wealth into the hands of a beneficiary (or into a trust for his or her benefit) without making a gift for purposes of the gift tax or a transfer that will be includible in the transferor's estate when he dies. In order to achieve this tax objective, the consideration received must be "full and adequate" [25] for gift tax purposes. However, the rules that are used in valuing the consideration received, particularly if it takes the form of the transferee's unsecured promise to pay an annuity to the transferor of his life, often produce such an unrealistically high value that the net effect of the transaction is to permit a tax-free movement of wealth.[26]

Although a sale or exchange for a full and adequate consideration is free of gift tax and estate tax consequences, it is subject to income tax if the consideration received exceeds the transferor's basis in the property. However, if such consideration is payable as an annuity or in installments, substantial deferral of tax may be achieved.[27] This deferral of income taxes is the substantial equivalent of obtaining an interest free loan from the Treasury, and may even reduce the total taxes which must be paid if the seller's income tax bracket is lower in years after the transfer has been made.

Sales to individual beneficiaries or trusts may also be used to convert what would otherwise be ordinary income to a client into capital gain for him or his beneficiary.

For example, the client may own a tract suitable for development as a subdivision. He may anticipate that if he undertakes the development himself he will be denied capital gain treatment on profits realized.[28] One

---

25. See Reg. § 25.2511–1(g)(1). If only partial consideration is received, there is a gift to the extent of the difference. If the transfer would (but for such partial consideration) be included in the transferor's estate under §§ 2035–2038, it is included under § 2043, with a reduction for the consideration received.

26. For a discussion of such valuation rules, see ¶ 8.03[3][a] infra.

27. The Installment Sales Revision Act of 1980, Pub.L. 96–471, has substantially reduced the effectiveness of installment sales to achieve deferral if the buyer is a relative or controlled entity, but does not deal "directly" with intra-family sales for an annuity. See H.R.Rep.No. 1042, 96th Cong., 2d sess. 10 n. 12 (1980).

For a discussion of possible effects of the Act on such arrangements, see Ginsburg, 39 N.Y.U.Inst. on Fed. Tax § 43.09 (1981). The author concludes that it would be wise for the Treasury in its regulations to "exclude annuity transactions from installment sale treatment." Id. at § 43.09[4].

28. The common reason for denying such treatment is that the property is held for sale to customers within the meaning of § 1221(1). Although § 1237 sometimes avoids this result, practical problems often make compliance with its requirements difficult, particularly for developers of residential subdivisions.

solution to this problem is to sell the tract to individual beneficiaries (or to set up trusts for their benefit) before development has been started, while the client still is able to treat gain on such a sale as capital gain.[29] If the purchase price is not unrealistically high, it will be the purchaser's basis.[30] He can then proceed with development of the tract. Although the purchaser's gains from such development may be ordinary income, the amounts taxable as such will be reduced as a result of the step-up in basis obtained when the first sale was made by the client. If a similar sale were made to a controlled corporation or a partnership, it would risk recharacterization as a contribution to capital of the corporation or a nonrecognition exchange of property for stock [31] or a partnership interest,[32] with no step-up in basis.

Gifts and sales are not mutually exclusive, as a single transaction may have elements of each if property is transferred for less than its current fair market value. For example, if a client has an asset worth $100,000 with a basis of $20,000, a sale to a non-charitable purchaser [33] for $20,000 has the advantage of avoiding realization of gain and at the same time limiting the amount of the seller's taxable gift [34] to the purchaser to the amount of the appreciation of $80,000.

JOHN M. KING v. UNITED STATES

United States Court of Appeals, Tenth Circuit, 1976.
545 F.2d 700, 76–2 USTC ¶ 13,165.

BARRETT, Circuit Judge.

The respective parties cross-appeal from the district court's findings of fact, conclusions of law and order of January 28, 1975, relating to a determination of the amount and the validity of taxes assessed by the United States through the Internal Revenue Service (IRS) against John McCandish King (King) and the liens filed pursuant to the assessments, in proceedings

29. If depreciable property, such as a building, is sold to the seller's spouse or other "related person" as defined in § 1239(b), § 1239(a) recharacterizes gain realized on the sale as ordinary income. The section has no application to non-depreciable assets, such as land.

30. Of course, a purported sale may be recharacterized for tax purposes as a joint venture (or partnership) between the seller and the purchaser. See, e.g., Raymond Bauschard v. Commissioner, 279 F.2d 115, 60–2 USTC ¶ 9533 (6th Cir. 1960): Horace Fishback Jr. v. United States, 215 F.Supp. 621, 63–2 USTC ¶ 9555 (D.S.D.1963). In this situation, the seller in effect contributes the property to a partnership. Section 723 provides generally that the partnership basis shall be that of the contributing partner.

31. See, e.g., Burr Oaks Corp., 43 T.C. 635 (1965), aff'd 365 F.2d 24, 66–2 USTC ¶ 9506 (7th Cir. 1966), cert. denied 385 U.S. 1007 (1967).

32. See, e.g., Horace E. Oliver, 13 TCM 67 (1954), aff'd per curiam 218 F.2d 352, 55–1 USTC ¶ 9175 (5th Cir. 1955) (1939 Code). See generally, Westfall, "Corporate Analogues in Partnership Taxation," 80 Harv.L.Rev. 765 (1967).

33. For the treatment of bargain sales to charities, see § 1011(b) and Reg. § 1.1011–2. In general the result is to require realization of a portion of gain corresponding to the consideration received. In the example in the text, the client would be treated as (1) selling one-fifth of the asset, with a basis of $4,000, for $20,000, realizing gain of $16,000; and (2) contributing four-fifths of the asset. See §§ 170(e)(2), 1011(b); Reg. §§ 1.170A–4(c)(2), 1011–2(a); Winston F. C. Guest, 77 T.C.No. 2 (1981).

34. If the purchaser is a charity, the gift would appear to qualify for the charitable deduction as an "undivided portion of the donor's entire interest in the property. See Reg. § 25.2522(c)–3(c)(2).

for an arrangement under Chapter XI of the Bankruptcy Act, 11 U.S.C.A. § 701, et seq.

*   *   *

I.

Whether a clause in an agreement for the sale of the debtor's corporate stock to his children's trusts requiring a price adjustment in the event the Internal Revenue Service determined the stock was sold for less than its fair market value may be enforced to defeat a gift tax assessed under § 2512(b) of the Code.

The IRS contends that the amount of the tax is the difference between its then market value and the value of the consideration received.

In 1967, King appointed his attorney, Timothy Lowry, as trustee for separate trusts he then created for each of his four children. These trusts were designated and referred to at trial as Trusts No. 1. They were intended to exist for the full period of time permitted by the rule against perpetuities, for the benefit of King's children, grandchildren and even great grandchildren. Of course, under these circumstances, the trusts provided for distribution restrictions to King's children. A Denver attorney, James Bye, was contacted by King in October of 1969, and was asked to prepare some documents reflecting recent sales King had made of stock he held in The Colorado Corporation to Timothy Lowry, as trustee of Trusts No. 1. Bye obtained confirmation from Mr. Lowry that such a transaction had taken place. Thereafter, Lowry prepared drafts of the documents dated as of January 1, 1969. Four letter agreements were prepared bearing that date and executed by King and Lowry after October of 1969, one for each of King's four children. Each provides that King is to retain title to the stock as security for payment of the purchase price and each contains this language:

> *   *   *   However, if the fair market value of The Colorado Corporation stock as of the date of this letter is ever determined by the Internal Revenue Service to be greater or less than the fair market value determined in the same manner described above, the purchase price shall be adjusted to the fair market value determined by the Internal Revenue Service.

Attached to each of the four letters was a formal "Declaration of Trust" executed by Lowry who acknowledged that he would execute formal trust agreements. This he did, following the October 1969 discussions. The formal trust agreements, prepared by Mr. Bye, were also dated January 1, 1969. The property granted in each trust agreement was the 400 shares of King's stock in The Colorado Corporation.

The valuation formula employed for the shares sold by King to the trusts was identical to the valuation plan used for a qualified stock option plan of The Colorado Corporation. Under that formula, each share was valued at $1250.00. The four trusts executed notes for $2,000,000.00. Later, as a result of a 1000 for 1 stock split, the total shares transferred were 1,600,000 at a value of $1.25 per share.

At a later date, Bye inserted a provision in the trust agreements for a redetermination of the purchase price because of the uncertainty of the value of The Colorado Corporation stock in light of the fact that it was a closely held corporation and few sales of its stock had been made.

The district court found that King created the four Trusts No. 1 on October 20 1969; that the shares of his stock held in The Colorado Corporation were transferred to the trusts in exchange for the promissory notes on that same date; and that there was an intention to cause the trusts to pay full and fair consideration for the stock and to make an actual adjustment of the price paid upon the event of a determination by the IRS.

* * *

The agreed price was later computed at $1.25 per share. The IRS, however, determined the stock had a fair market value of $16.00 per share at the date of transfer and assessed a gift tax against King for the difference. The court, of course, rejected the IRS view, finding that it was intended that the trusts pay the fair market value of the stock and that the price-adjustment clause overcame the difficulty of determining its fair market value. IRS contends that this finding is clearly erroneous, and that the sole issue is whether the price adjustment clause in the sale agreements may be given effect to alter the terms of a completed transfer and thus avoid a gift tax. IRS relies substantially upon Commissioner v. Procter, 142 F.2d 824 (4th cir. 1944), cert. denied 323 U.S. 756, 65 S.Ct. 90, 89 L.Ed. 606 (1944), which held that when the taxpayer there transferred certain property to a trust he had previously established (retaining the income therefrom during his lifetime with the remainder of the trust property to be distributed to his children upon his death) the price adjustment clause contained therein was void as against public policy. The trust agreement provided that if a federal court should ever rule that any portion of the trust res was subject to gift tax, the taxable portion of the transfer would automatically revest in the taxpayer as if the conveyance in trust had not been made. The court held that the transfer was a completed gift of the remainder to the children and that it was contrary to public policy to enforce the "savings clause" to avoid the tax on a completed gift.

The district court distinguished the facts in the case at bar from those in *Procter*, supra, finding that the parties intended that the trusts pay a full and adequate consideration for the stock and that the clause was a proper means of overcoming the uncertainty in ascertaining the fair market value of the stock. The court concluded that there was an intention to cause the trusts to pay full and fair consideration for the stock and to make an actual adjustment of the price paid upon the event of a determination by the IRS. We agree. It is important to observe that the IRS does not dispute the contention that it was difficult, if not impossible, to accurately value the stock at the time of its transfer in 1969 and that the parties inserted the specific valuation paragraph in the agreement because the transaction was intended as a sale and not as a gift. The trial court's determination was one of fact. That finding is not clearly erroneous.

We believe that the IRS reliance on *Procter*, supra, is misplaced. Here, there was at no time or in any way an attempt to alter or negate the plain terms of the valuation clause and no attempt by the trustees was made to reconvey the stock to King or to cancel the notes in anticipation of an unfavorable valuation ruling.

Authorities relied upon by the Government dealing with contingencies which, upon fruition, alter, change or destroy the *nature* of the transaction do not apply here. The proviso for adjustment of the purchase price of the stock to equal its fair market value did not affect the *nature* of the transaction. But, argues the IRS, even though the parties may have intended to pay full consideration for the stock, still this fact is immaterial for gift tax purposes because the test is solely objective, i.e., whether the transfer was made for full and adequate consideration. In a nutshell, IRS contends that if King's intent to make a sale would not be sufficient to prevent the gift tax were the price adjustment clause absent, "that intent obviously cannot be used to legitimate the presence of the clause so as to avoid the tax". [Br. of Appellant, p. 16]. Treasury regulations, references and citations are relied upon. The IRS presents persuasive arguments, based upon its rules that (a) for accounting purposes, absent specific statutory language to the contrary, tax consequences attach at the end of fixed and regular accounting periods, regardless how subsequent events might affect the economic or tax results of the transaction, (b) taxpayers cannot amend a transaction retroactively to avoid the federal tax consequences of prior taxable periods and (c) the difficulty of valuing the property transferred does not make the gift tax inapplicable. IRS further contends that the record does not show an attempt by the parties at the time of suit to make an actual price adjustment and the gift tax would be virtually emasculated if the parties' intention to effect a transfer for a full consideration were enough to satisfy the requirements of 26 U.S.C.A. § 2512(b) of the Internal Revenue Code of 1954.

The trial court's finding that there was no donative intent and that the transaction was made in the ordinary course of business at arms length is not clearly erroneous. Further, it does not work an abuse upon the operative intent of § 2512, supra, i.e., to reach donative transfers and to exclude transfers whose consideration is not reducible to money or money's worth. The transfers involved here can be ultimately reduced to money's worth and are, accordingly, excluded from the gift tax consequences. No diminution of King's estate can result from the trial court's finding.

* * *

The IRS contention that the price adjustment clause violates public policy in that it deters administrative enforcement of the gift tax provisions is valid *only* if the transaction be construed as an inter vivos transfer undertaken to reduce King's estate. The IRS argument would be applicable if we were to hold that the trial court's finding that King intended that the trust pay full and adequate consideration predicated upon the price-adjustment proviso is clearly erroneous. It is not. Under the facts found, King is not subject to the gift tax under Treas.Reg. § 25.2512–8 because the transaction was made in the ordinary course of business at arm's length, free from any donative intent. We hold that the trial court did not err in holding that the aforesaid stock transfers are not subject to a gift tax.

To be sure, it has been held that the absence of a donative intent will not alone prevent a transfer from being subject to gift taxation, but this is not the controlling factor when the transfer has been found to have been made "at arm's length in the ordinary course of business". Commissioner of Internal Revenue v. Wemyss, 324 U.S. 303, 307, 65 S.Ct. 652, 654, 89 L.Ed. 958 (1945). *See also* 156 A.L.R. 1022. Interpretive of the Code requirements of "an adequate and full consideration in money or money's worth" the Supreme Court has held that the return must be an adequate and full equivalent and that the requisite consideration cannot be equated with mutual promises satisfying common law consideration sufficient to support an agreement, Taft v. Commissioner, 304 U.S. 351, 58 S.Ct. 891, 82 L.Ed. 1393 (1938); 116 A.L.R. 346.

Significant, we believe, is the fact that perhaps the main purpose of the gift tax was to prevent or compensate for the avoidance of death taxes by taxing the gifts of property inter vivos which, but for the gifts, would be subject in its original or converted form to the tax laid upon transfers at death. Sanford's Estate v. Commissioner, 308 U.S. 39, 60 S.Ct. 51, 84 L.Ed. 20 (1939). No such risk is involved in the instant case.

We hold that the trial court did not err in finding that the stock sold to Trusts No. 1 under the "price adjustment" proviso is not subject to the gift tax provisions.

* * *

We affirm.

WILLIAM E. DOYLE, Circuit Judge (dissenting).

I respectfully dissent from the decision of the majority of the court that the transaction in question was a sale and not a gift subject to gift tax. The several differences follow.

I.

I disagree with the majority's ruling that intent of Mr. King governed the entire transaction and was a factual matter which had the effect of rendering the finding unimpeachable.

The source of my disagreement on this ground is that intent of the donor is not the determining factor in deciding whether it is a gift or sale. Treas.Reg. Section 25.2511–1(g)(1) (26 C.F.R.) provides as follows:

> Donative intent on the part of the transferor is not an essential element in the application of the gift tax to the transfer. *The application of the tax is based on the objective facts of the transfer and the circumstances under which it is made, rather than on the subjective motives of the donor.* (Emphasis supplied.)

Id.

Also, the Supreme Court said in this regard in Commissioner of Internal Revenue v. Wemyss, 324 U.S. 303, 306, 65 S.Ct. 652, 89 L.Ed. 958 (1945), that: "Congress chose not to require an ascertainment of what too often is an elusive state of mind." See also Commissioner of Internal Revenue v. Berger, 201 F.2d 171 (2d Cir. 1953). Thus, even if the taxpayer expresses an intent to make a sale, which is questionable evidence in most instances, the inquiry does not end there. The court as a matter of law must determine gift tax consequences by looking to the application of the statute and regulations and to the facts and circumstances. The court's view, then, must be objective.

II.

Nor do I agree with the majority's determination that the evidence shows immunity from gift tax because the transfer was in the ordinary course of business within Treas.Reg. Section 25.2512–8 (26 C.F.R.). This latter regulation provides in part:

> * * * a sale, exchange, or other transfer of property made in the ordinary course of business (a transaction which is bona fide, at arm's length, and free from any donative intent), will be considered as made for an adequate and full consideration in money or money's worth.

By its very terms the above regulation excludes transfers from the gift tax where the consideration is less than full and adequate. See Commissioner of Internal Revenue v. Berger, supra, at 173. Under this regulation business transfers for less than full and adequate consideration are excluded from the gift tax regardless of a price adjustment clause. See Commissioner of Internal Revenue v. Berger, supra, at 173. If, then, the transfer were a genuine sale in the ordinary course of business, no gift tax is due. And this is true even though the consideration may be adequate. The regulation itself brings this about and the price adjustment clause would be unnecessary.

III.

Moreover, the determination of the majority that this is in the ordinary course of business cannot be upheld because the regulation requires that a transaction be bona fide, at arm's length, and without donative intent in order to be considered as in the ordinary course of business. The evidence establishes that this transaction rather than being in the ordinary course of business was an intra-family transaction, the main object of which was to transfer some of King's wealth to his children. Such a transfer must be scrutinized with great care. It is presumed to be a gift. Estate of Reynolds v. Commissioner of Internal Revenue, 55 T.C. 172 (1970); Clark v. Commissioner of Internal Revenue, 205 F.2d 353 (2d Cir. 1953), aff'g 18 T.C. 780 (1952). It is difficult to conceive of a transaction being intra-family in character having the purpose of transferring wealth within the family and also having the character of a business transaction. Cf. Robinette v. Helvering, 318 U.S. 184, 63 S.Ct. 540, 87 L.Ed. 700 (1943). This conclusion is supported, to the extent that it is supported, by the fact that the price adjustment clause is included. It would be unnecessary if the transfer were truly one in the ordinary course of business.

It becomes all the more clear, therefore, that the intent was to avoid the gift tax and this court ought not to allow Mr. King to use this clause solely to avoid the tax.

IV.

The clause is not justified by the reason of difficulty of evaluation which is no bar to the imposition of the tax. See Smith v. Shaughnessy, 318 U.S.

176, 63 S.Ct. 545, 87 L.Ed. 690 (1943). And, since the regulations are guides to the valuation of corporate shares, the responsibility for making evaluations for the purpose of determining tax consequences ought not to be shifted to the IRS as the clause apparently seeks to do.

V.

I disagree also with the argument of the majority that giving effect to the price adjustment clause does not conflict with the purposes and the administration of the tax laws. By allowing the taxpayer to make retroactive price adjustment in respect to completed transactions, the court is allowing him to avoid tax consequences and to give effect to this effort would certainly deter the enforcement of the tax. Indeed if it were allowed to stand, and it is doubtful that it will, the effect would be substantial. The majority opinion attempts to distinguish Commissioner of Internal Revenue v. Procter, 142 F.2d 824 (4th Cir.), cert. denied, 323 U.S. 756, 65 S.Ct. 90, 89 L.Ed. 606 (1944), wherein a savings clause which provided that property transferred in trust would revert to the settlor if found subject to gift tax was void as against public policy. The same result was reached in Van Den Wymelenberg v. United States, 397 F.2d 443 (7th Cir.), cert. denied, 393 U.S. 953, 89 S.Ct. 377, 21 L.Ed.2d 364 (1968). The majority opinion says that the cited cases involve changes in the nature of the transaction, whereas the instant clause did not so operate, but the price adjustment clause is intended to work a change in the nature of the transaction in that it attempts to transform what would be a gift into a sale.

It is to be noted that the Supreme Court has held that Internal Revenue provisions are to be interpreted to conform to the basic premise of annual tax accounting. If you give effect to the price adjustment clause you are in effect saying that a private agreement can effect a retroactive change in a completed transaction and its tax consequences. To allow non-business transfers to remain unsettled until the Service makes an adverse determination would render tax liability unsettled at least until the statute of limitations had run. Van Den Wymelenberg v. United States, supra, at 445.

Accordingly, the price adjustment clause is in conflict with the principle that once a transaction and a tax year are completed, the tax consequences attach and retroactive adjustments in the transaction are not allowed to alter these tax consequences.

On its face this transaction is not and cannot be a sale. Surely the law of gift taxation does not call for an entirely different set of definitions and principles. Unless it does, the present holding cannot be sustained.

¶ 8.03 SALES FOR PRIVATE ANNUITY PAYMENTS

If more clients and their advisors fully appreciated the impressive estate-planning potential of sales for private annuity or installment payments, these important tools would be more widely used. For income tax purposes, they sometimes offer the best of two worlds: For the seller, recognition of gain may be largely deferred, but for the buyer, payments to be made in the future are immediately reflected in his basis for determining gain on resale of the property and for depreciation if the property is depreciable. These income tax advantages may be combined with important gift and estate tax savings for the seller if the buyer is a family member or other object of his bounty.

The Installment Sales Revision Act of 1980 [35] substantially restricted the use of intra-family sales to achieve deferral and other advantages under the income tax. The Act does not deal "directly" with sales for private annuities.[36] Nor does it deal with estate and gift tax aspects of either kind of sale.

An "annuity" literally is any series of fixed payments at regular intervals over some period of time.[37] It is used here to describe a series of payments for the life (or lives) of one or more annuitants (to whom the annuity is paid). Payments for a fixed term of years or months, rather than for the life of the seller, are "installment" payments. The tax consequences of sales for each kind of payments will be discussed separately.

[1] Income Tax Consequences for the Seller

Most clients are familiar with commercial annuities paid by insurance companies, in which the company makes monthly, quarterly, or annual payments for the life of the annuitant in exchange for a lump sum paid in advance. In estate planning, however, it is the private rather than the commercial annuity [38] that offers important tax saving potential, because of the way in which the annuity is valued for estate and gift tax purposes and the income tax treatment of the annuitant.

A "private annuity" is one paid by someone not regularly engaged in issuing annuity contracts. Indeed, in order to insure treatment as such, the annuity may have to be essentially a unique venture for the payor.[39] It commonly is paid as a result of a sale by a client to a family member or other object of his bounty in exchange for the buyer's unsecured promise to pay fixed sums to the seller periodically for the rest of his life.

> *Example 8.1.* A father (*F*), aged 73, sells the family farm to his daughter (*D*) in exchange for her unsecured promise to pay *F* $25,000 per year for *F*'s life, beginning one year after the date of the sale. When the farm is sold, its fair market value is $154,000, and *F*'s basis is a total of $50,000 for the farm land and buildings. The present value for gift tax purposes of the payments that *F* will receive, as determined by the Commissioner's actuarial tables, is approximately equal to the

35. Pub.L. 96–471, 96th Cong., 2d sess. (1980).

36. ¶ 8.02 note 27 supra.

37. See Reg. § 1.72–2(b)(2).

38. Annuity contracts issued by a corporation, trust, fund, or foundation (other than a commercial life insurance company) that "from time to time" enters into such contracts are valued on the same basis as those issued by commercial insurance companies. See Rev.Rul. 62–137, 1962–2 CB 28. A

transfer of property in exchange for such a contract, if its value exceeds the basis of the property transferred, results in recognized gain in the year of exchange to the extent of such excess. Rev.Rul. 62–136, 1962–2 CB 12.

39. See Rev.Rul. 62–137, 1962–2 CB 28, supplemented by Rev.Rul. 62–216, 1962–2 CB 30 and Rev.Rul. 67–39, 1967–1 CB 18, which equates annuities from organizations that issue annuities "from time to time" with commercial annuities.

fair market value of the farm.[40]   Because of this equality, no gift tax is due, and the farm is not included in *F's* taxable estate when he dies, even though his death occurs before the expiration of his actuarially determined life expectancy.   In addition, the gain *F* realizes on the transaction is recognized for income tax purposes only as annuity payments are received from *D*.

Under the general rules for income tax treatment of annuities contained in § 72, each payment received by the seller is divided into two parts: One part, deemed to be economically equivalent to interest, is taxed as ordinary income; the other part is deemed to represent recovery by the seller of the cost of the annuity.   The tax treatment of the cost-recovery portion depends upon whether the annuity was acquired for cash or for property.

If the annuity is acquired for cash, the cost-recovery portion of each payment is not included in income, even though the annuitant lives longer than was his actuarial life expectancy when the annuity was acquired and therefore receives tax-free more than he paid for the annuity.   If the annuity is acquired in exchange for property, however, as is usually true in the case of annuities that are important in estate planning, the treatment of the cost-recovery portion of the annuity payments is more complex. Typically, the fair market value of the property transferred exceeds the seller's basis, so that the cost-recovery portion of each annuity payment includes part of the appreciation in value of such property.

In *Example 8.1* above, the Regulations under § 72 give *F* an actuarial life expectancy of ten years at the time the exchange is made.[41]   This means that according to the Commissioner's tables, the amount *F* will receive if he lives his exact life expectancy and no more is $250,000 ($25,000 per year for ten years).   The fair market value of the farm transferred in exchange for the annuity was $154,000, so that it might appear that the portion of each annuity payment to be excluded from income as representing the cost-recovery portion would be 154/250, or 61.6 percent of each payment.   However, under Revenue Ruling 69-74,[42] only the basis of the property transferred, or $50,000 in the example, is permitted to be recovered tax-free, rather than the higher fair market value of $154,000.   The difference of $104,000 ($154,000—50,000) represents gain to the seller [43] and is taxable as annuity payments are received by him.   In this case, each annuity pay-

---

40.   See Reg. § 25.2512–9(f), Table A(1), giving a factor of 6.1752 for a life annuity payable to a 73-year-old male. Applying this factor to an annual payment of $25,000 produces a value of $154,380 for the annuity, assuming the annuity is payable annually at the end of each year.   See Reg. § 25.2512–9(b)(1). If payments were due at more frequent intervals or at the beginning of each period, a higher value would result.   See Reg. § 25.2512–9(b)(2), (3).

41.   This is the life expectancy assumed in Table 1 in Reg. § 1.72–9, with the adjustment called for in § 1.72–5(a)(2).

42.   1969–1 CB 43.   The validity and effect of this Ruling are considered in Note, 23 Vand.L.Rev. 675 (1970); Comment, 47 Tex.L.Rev. 1395 (1969).

43.   Normally gain is measured by the value of what is received, which should equal the value given up in an arm's-length transaction.   With a private annuity, any substantial discrepancy between the value of the transferred property and the actuarial value of the annuity is likely to constitute a gift. See Estate of Lloyd G. Bell, infra; Rev.Rul. 69–74, 1969–1 CB 43.   In *Example 8.1*, the values are roughly equal.

ment consists of three portions, rather than two as in the case of an annuity acquired for cash:

(1) A portion of each payment, equal to the basis of the transferred property divided by the seller's actuarial life expectancy (ten years in *Example 8.1*), is excluded from income. In this example, the portion is one-fifth (50/250), so that for each annual payment of $25,000, $5,000 is excluded. This exclusion ratio continues to apply even if *F* lives longer than his actuarial life expectancy. Even if *F* lives to be age 100 or older, one-fifth of each annual payment will continue to be excluded from his income.

(2) A second portion of each payment, equal to the gain of $104,000 divided by the seller's ten-year life expectancy, or $10,400 of each $25,000 payment in *Example 8.1*, is taxed as gain realized from the sale of the transferred property. Ordinarily, sound planning requires that the property is a capital asset in the hands of the seller and has been held for more than one year, so the gain will be long term capital gain. Taxation of this portion of each payment as such gain continues, however, only until the excess of the value of the property over its basis when the sale was made has been taxed in full. This will occur if and when the seller has lived his actuarial life expectancy, determined as of the date of the transfer. Thereafter, this second portion of each annual payment is taxed as ordinary income.

(3) The balance of each payment, after deducting the portions described at 1 and 2 above, is taxable as ordinary income.

Some support may be found for more favorable tax treatment of private annuity payments.[44] But from a planning standpoint, Revenue Ruling 69–74 appears to represent the current Service position on income tax consequences of sales for unsecured private annuity payments. It is relatively favorable, from the seller's standpoint, in allowing recognition of gain to be spread over the period during which annuity payments are received. In order to obtain such treatment for the seller, the buyer's obligation to pay the annuity must be unsecured. If the obligation is secured, by a lien on the property sold or otherwise, the seller may be required to recognize gain in the year of sale, measured by the excess of present actuarial value of the annuity payments over his basis in the property.[45] In *Example 8.1*, this would mean recognition of gain of $104,000 in the year the sale occurred. For many sellers, such immediate recognition of gain would go far to offset any gift tax or estate tax savings which might be obtained by the sale.

---

44. See Reg. § 1.1011–2(c), *Example (8)*, dealing with a bargain sale to a charitable organization in exchange for an annuity and finding no further tax on the capital gain portion of each payment after the total gain has been reported. The possibility that *Example (8)* constitutes a partial repudiation of Revenue Ruling 69–74 is examined in Stewart, "Private Annuities–Revenue Ruling 69–74 Partially Repudiated, *Sub Silentio*, by Treasury Regulations Section 1.011–2(c), *Example (8)*," 24 Mercer L. Rev. 585 (1973).

45. See Estate of Lloyd G. Bell, infra; 212 Corp., 70 T.C. 788 (1978).

ESTATE OF LLOYD G. BELL

United States Tax Court, 1973
60 T.C. 469.

QUEALY, Judge.

*   *   *

FINDINGS OF FACT

*   *   *

Pursuant to an "Annuity Agreement" dated December 6, 1967, Lloyd and Grace Bell transferred community property consisting of 822½ shares of Bell & Bell, Inc., capital stock and 2,034 shares of Bitterroot, Inc., capital stock to William and Beverly Bell and Calvin A. and Betty Bell Reinertson in exchange for a promise by the transferees to pay them $1,000 per month for so long as either shall live. The stock was placed in escrow as security for the promise of the tranferees. As further security, the agreement provided for a cognovit judgment against the transferees in the event of a default. William Bell and Betty Bell Reinertson are the son and daughter, respectively, of Lloyd and Grace Bell.

Bell & Bell, Inc., and Bitterroot, Inc., are both closely held farming corporations. Neither is traded on a stock exchange. Both corporations were formed in 1965 by Lloyd Bell and his son, William Bell, as successors to an informal partnership carried on between father and son.

Lloyd Bell owned one-third of the stock of Bell & Bell, Inc., and two-thirds of the stock of Bitterroot, Inc. William Bell owned the balance of the stock in these corporations.

At the time of the transfer, Lloyd and Grace Bell's basis in the stock of Bell & Bell, Inc., was $9,559.94, and the basis of their stock in Bitterroot, Inc., was $11,497.63, or a total of $21,057.57. The total fair market value of such stock was $207,600.

Lloyd Bell was 72 years of age and Grace Bell was 68 years of age at the time of transfer. They had a joint life expectancy of 18.7 years. The expected return from the annuity, based upon such life expectancy, was $224,400. The discounted value of the annuity at the time of the transfer was stipulated to be either $142,573 or $126,200.38, depending upon whether the Court finds the correct method of valuation to be the representative cost of a comparable commercial annuity, as petitioners contend, or the tables under section 20.2031–7, Estate Tax Regs., as respondent contends.

Pursuant to the "Annuity Agreement" of December 6, 1967, Lloyd and Grace Bell received payments totaling $13,000 during 1968 and $12,000 during 1969.

OPINION

*   *   *

The rules for the inclusion in income of said payments are prescribed in section 72. Insofar as material herein, that section provides:

SEC. 72. ANNUITIES; CERTAIN PROCEEDS OF ENDOWMENT AND LIFE INSURANCE CONTRACTS.

(a) GENERAL RULES FOR ANNUITIES—Except as otherwise provided in this chapter, gross income includes any amount received as an annuity (whether for a period certain or during one or more lives) under an annuity, endowment, or life insurance contract.

(b) EXCLUSION RATIO—Gross income does not include that part of any amount received as an annuity under an annuity, endowment, or life insurance contract which bears the same ratio to such amount as the investment in the contract (as of the annuity starting date) bears to the expected return under the contract (as of such date).   *   *   *

(c) DEFINITIONS—

(1) INVESTMENT IN THE CONTRACT—For purposes of subsection (b), the investment in the contract as of the annuity starting date is—

(A) the aggregate amount of premiums or other consideration paid for the contract, minus

(B) the aggregate amount received under the contract before such date, to the extent that such amount was excludable from gross income under this subtitle or prior income tax laws.

The respondent argues that petitioners' "investment in the contract," as defined in section 72(c), is petitioners' adjusted basis for the stock transferred in consideration of the transferees' promise of an annuity.   Rev. Rul. 69–74,[46] 1969–1 C.B. 43.   The petitioners argue that their "investment in the contract" is the fair market value of the stock transferred, relying on Rev. Rul. 239, 1953–2 C.B. 53, which applied to a similar computation under section 22(b)(2) of the Revenue Act of 1939.   Petitioners further contend that the fair market value of the stock was not less than $207,600.

In our opinion, we need not pass on the applicability of either Rev. Rul. 239 or Rev. Rul. 69–74, supra, since both involve "unsecured" private annuities.   Here, we are dealing with an annuity which is amply secured, not only by the property transferred, but also by a cognovit judgment that would subject all the property of the transferees to attachment without court proceedings.

Section 72(c)(1) defines "investment in the contract" as "the aggregate amount of premiums or other consideration paid for the contract."   Section 22(b)(2) of the 1934, 1936, and 1939 Revenue Acts, predecessors to section 72, contained similar language.   Under such Acts, this language has uniformly been construed to mean the amount required to purchase the annuity, which in an arm's-length transfer, is the fair market value of the property

---

46. [The *Bell* case and its relationship to Rev. Rul. 69–74 are considered in Croft & Hipple, "Planning Lifetime Property Transfers: Private Annuities, Installment Sales and Gift-Leasebacks," 11 Real Prop., Prob. & Trust J. 253, 255 (1976); Note, 52 Tex. L. Rev. 149 (1973).—ed.]

transferred. F. A. Gillespie, 38 B.T.A. 673 (1938); Hill's Estate v. Maloney, 58 F.Supp. 164 (D.N.J. 1944); Jane J. de Canizares, 32 T.C. 345 (1959). Nothing in the statute, the legislative history, or the regulations interpreting section 72 indicates that "consideration paid" on our facts should have a different meaning than it had under section 22(b)(2) of the prior Acts. Here the consideration paid consisted of stock of two closely held farming corporations having an aggregate fair market value of $207,600.

In determining the "consideration paid," however, the statute presupposes a transaction between unrelated parties dealing at arm's length. The petitioners claim that the consideration paid for the annuity amounted to $207,600, while at the same time petitioners concede that the discounted value or cost of a commercial annuity providing for the same payments was $142,573. We can only account for such excess as being attributed to the family relationship between the annuitants and the transferees. Such excess therefore, whether predicated upon the cost of a commercial annuity, as contended for by the petitioners, or upon the annuity tables under section 20.2031–7(f), Estate Tax Regs., as contended for by the respondent, must be deemed to be a gift. In Commissioner v. Wemyss, 324 U.S. 303, 306 (1945), the Supreme Court makes this clear:

> Congress chose not to require an ascertainment of what too often is an elusive state of mind. For purposes of the gift tax it not only dispensed with the test of "donative intent." It formulated a much more workable external test, that where "property is transferred for less than an adequate and full consideration in money or money's worth," the excess in such money value "shall for the purpose of the tax imposed by this title, be deemed a gift * * *." * * * [Sec. 2512(b).]

[Citations omitted.]

Our determination that the transfer was a partial gift if further buttressed by the fact that the annuitants did not seek to ascertain the price at which they could have purchased a similar annuity from an insurance company. Nor did the transferees investigate whether the obligation, which they were assuming, was more or less than the value of property received. Their concern was merely whether they could pay the required monthly amounts. The consideration paid for the annuity under these circumstances, therefore, is limited to the commuted value of the annuity contract irrespective of the fair market value of the property transferred.

The parties further disagree on the correct method of valuing the annuity. Petitioners have valued it at $142,573, using the representative cost of a comparable commercial annuity. Respondent, on the other hand, has valued it at $126,200.38, using the Table I under section 20.2031–7(f), Estate Tax Regs., as provided by section 1.101–2(e)(1)(iii)(*b*)(*3*), Income Tax Regs.

Respondent's determinations are presumptively correct. To overturn his use of the estate tax tables, petitioners must prove that their use under the circumstances is arbitrary and unreasonable. John C. W. Dix, 46 T.C. 796 (1966), affd. 392 F.2d 313 (C.A.4, 1968).

Petitioners object to the actuarial table used by respondent because it is based on the life expectancies of the general population in 1939–41, which does not reflect the longer longevity of the population in 1967, the year of the transfer.   Nor does it provide separate tables for men and women, experience indicating that the latter live longer.

Petitioners contend that the cost of a comparable commercial annuity would be a more correct indication of the value of the transferees' promise. Respondent, however, has presented an expert witness who testified that the rates charged by commercial life insurance companies are affected by factors not present in private annuity transfers.   For instance, the commercial price contains a "loading factor" for anticipated expenses and expected profits.   Commercial annuitants, as a self-selected class, have a longer life span than the general population.   These factors operate to increase the cost of a commercial annuity.   So does the fact that commercial companies, being regulated by the State, are restricted in their investments and required to maintain sufficient reserves to assure annuity payments can be made.   All these factors have been recognized in prior cases which have rejected using the cost of a commercial annuity to value a private annuity [Citations omitted.]

The petitioners have presented no evidence to show that the longer life expectancy of commercial annuitants should be attributed to the annuitants in this case, Lloyd and Grace Bell.   Indeed, the record indicates that Lloyd Bell died less than 3 years after the transfer.   The fact that the table used by the respondent does not distinguish between males and females is of itself not sufficient to prove the use of such tables was arbitrary and unreasonable.   John C. W. Dix, supra.

On the basis of the evidence presented, the petitioners have failed to show that respondent's use of the table under section 20.2031–7(f), Estate Tax Regs., to value the annuity promise of the transferees was arbitrary and unreasonable.   We therefore adopt the respondent's determination of $126,200.38 as the value of the annuity promise at the time of transfer.

Finally, having determined that the consideration paid by the petitioners for the annuity within the meaning of section 72(c) amounted to $126,200.38, the petitioners must likewise be deemed to have realized a taxable gain on the transfer, measured by the difference between petitioners' adjusted basis in the stock and the fair market value of the annuity.

Petitioners argue that they should be able to use the cost recovery approach of J. Darsie Lloyd, 33 B.T.A. 903 (1936), before having to report any gain since the value of the promise received is too contingent to be valued for purposes of section 1001.   See also Frank C. Deering, 40 B.T.A. 984 (1939);   Hill's Estate v. Maloney, supra;   Commissioner v. Kann's Estate, 174 F.2d 357 (C.A.3, 1949).

We think that petitioners' reliance on *Lloyd* is misplaced.   That case involved the transfer of certain appreciated stock by a father in exchange for his son's unsecured promise to make certain annuity payments to him for life.   In permitting the father to recover his basis first before having to report any capital gain, the Court held that the son's promise was too contingent to value for purposes of section 111(c) (now 1001) due to "the uncertainty as to whether or not the one agreeing to make payments will be able to make them as agreed when the time for payment actually arrives." Cf. Burnet v. Logan, 283 U.S. 404 (1931).

The facts in this case are clearly distinguishable from *Lloyd* and the cases cited by petitioners. Both petitioners and respondent have elected to treat the exchange of stock for an annuity as a viable transaction for income tax purposes. The annuity was amply secured not only by the stock transferred but also by an agreement providing for a cognovit judgment against the transferees in the event of a default. It was agreed that the stock transferred by Lloyd and Grace Bell had a value of $207,600. It was further agreed that the annuity promise received in return had a substantial value, ranging from $126,200.38, as contended by respondent, to $142,573, as contended by petitioners. This Court has sustained the respondent's determination with respect to that value.

We thus have a transfer of stock in exchange for a consideration, subject only to a lien to secure payment thereof. Under the laws of the State of Washington, as well as prevailing tax law, this constituted a completed sale. [Citations omitted.] In fact, except for the uncertainty as to the ultimate amount payable under the contract, it is no different than any other installment sale. The actuarial tables provide a recognized basis for determining the value of the consideration received notwithstanding such uncertainty. John C. W. Dix, supra. Under such circumstances, we find no grounds for the application of the cost recovery rule in Burnet v. Logan, supra.

It would be manifestly inconsistent to find that the annuity contract had a fair market value for purposes of determining a taxpayer's cost or investment in the contract under section 72(c), and yet to hold it had no determinable value for purposes of section 1001.

Since the transfer occurred prior to the taxable years [1968 and 1969— ed.] before the Court, no part of the amounts received are taxable as gain realized during the years before the Court.

Reviewed by the Court.

Decision will be entered under Rule 50.

SIMPSON, J., dissenting:

I must dissent from the majority opinion with respect to its holding that the gain resulting from the exchange of the stock for the private annuity was taxable in the year of the exchange. Such conclusion was not sought by the respondent. Although the majority opinion results in no part of the gain on the exchange being taxable in 1968 and 1969, it may ultimately result in the petitioners having a larger tax burden than that contended for by the respondent. If section 1311, I.R.C. 1954, is applicable, as may be the case, the entire gain of $105,142.81 will be taxable to the petitioners in 1967; whereas, under the respondent's approach, none of the gain would be taxable in that year, but a portion of each annuity payment would be treated as capital gain until the entire gain is reported. See Rev.Rul. 69–74, 1969–1 C.B. 43.

The opinion states in part:

It would be manifestly inconsistent to find that the annuity contract had a fair market value for purposes of determining a taxpayer's cost or investment in the contract under section 72(c), and yet to hold it had no determinable value for purposes of section 1001.

Such statement implies that the actuarial value of an annuity constitutes its fair market value in all cases, whether or not there is security for the performance of the obligation. Such statement ignores the long-established position of this Court. Frank C. Deering, 40 B.T.A. 984 (1939); J. Darsie Lloyd, 33 B.T.A. 903 (1936); see Commissioner v. Kann's Estate, 174 F.2d 357 (C.A.3, 1949), affirming a Memorandum Opinion of this Court; Bella Hommel, 7 T.C. 992 (1946). In J. Darsie Lloyd, 33 B.T.A. at 905, this Court held that the transfer of property to an individual, in consideration for an unsecured promise to pay an annuity, did not require the reporting of gain in the year of the transfer because of "the uncertainty as to whether or not the one agreeing to make payments will be able to make them as agreed when the time for payment actually arrives." The Court found that the annuity had no fair market value even though the application of the tables would have rendered an actuarial value. We have found no cases which deviate from such holding where a private, unsecured annuity was involved.

The security present in this case may provide a basis for distinguishing *Lloyd,* but it should not result in gain being reported on the transfer of the stock for the private annuity. This Court has held many times that a cash method taxpayer does not include in the computation of the "amount realized" under section 1001(b) the right to receive future income unless that right is readily transferable in commerce. [Citations omitted.] * * *

The peculiar characteristics of a private annuity require a finding that the right to receive income during a person's life is not ordinarily a right which is readily transferable in commerce. The span of each person's life is so speculative that it is impossible to determine with any degree of certainty the number of annuity payments that will be made prior to the annuitant's death. Actuarial estimates may be accurate in the macrocosm where the margin of error in forecasting one life will be offset by the margin in forecasting other lives. However, if a taxpayer is considering the purchase of an annuity on another's life, there is no margin of error to offset the extremely speculative nature of the lifespan. See Mancina, "The Private Annuity,'" 43 Taxes 255, 258–259 (1965); Note, "Private Annuities: Revenue Ruling 69–74—Its Significance, Effect, and Validity," 23 Vand.L.Rev. 675, 688 fn. 77 (1970). For example, in this case, although the expected return on the private annuity was $224,400, there was no obligation to pay that amount. In fact, it was almost certain that the annuitants would receive, not that amount, but more or less than that amount. A right as speculative as a life annuity, or, in this case, a joint annuity for two lives, cannot be said to have a readily realizable market value or to be freely and easily negotiable or to be of the type that commonly changes hands in commerce. Indeed, in 1954, Congress rejected a proposal to tax the gain on the exchange of property for a private annuity in the year of the exchange. S.Rept.No. 1622. 83d Cong., 2d Sess., p. 116 (1954).

The question remains of how the gain on the transfer of property for a secured private annuity should be treated within the framework of the present law. Under pre-1954 law, Congress adopted a 3-percent formula in taxing annuities. As explained by the Senate Finance Committee, the rule taxed an annuitant on the annuity payments he received to the extent of 3 percent of the amount paid for the annuity. Any payments he received above this amount were considered to be the return of his capital and were excluded from tax until the total amount excluded equaled the amount he paid for the annuity. Thereafter, the annuity payments were taxable in whole. S.Rept.No. 1622, supra, at p. 11. Section 72 was enacted because the 3-percent rule was erratic. After the annuitant recovered his investment, the rule could lead to a situation in which:

> the annuitant finds that after being retired for a few years and becoming accustomed to living on a certain amount of income after tax, he suddenly has to make a sizable downward adjustment in his living standard because, when his exclusion is used up, the annuity income becomes fully taxable. [S.Rept.No. 1622, supra at p. 11.]

Congress intended to eliminate this difficulty by enacting section 72, under which there is a proration of the cost of the annuity—a portion of each annuity payment is treated as annuity income, and the balance is treated as a return of cost. The treatment of the gain from the transfer of the property for an annuity should, insofar as possible, be in accord with this legislative treatment of annuities.

I agree with the majority that the investment in the contract for the purposes of section 72 is, in this case, equal to the actuarial value of the annuity, and, in this respect, I would reject Rev.Rul. 69–74, 1969–1 C.B. 43. The investment in the contract is the fair market value of the stock exchanged for the annuity, and in view of the family relationship in this case and the fact that a gift was obviously made as to a portion of the stock, it is reasonable to conclude that the amount of stock exchanged for the annuity is equal to the value of the annuity. Thus, stock worth $126,200.38 was paid for the annuity.

Section 72(b) provides that gross income does not include that part of any amount received as an annuity which bears the same ratio to such amounts as the investment in the contract bears to the expected return under the contract. Hence, the exclusion ratio in this case is $126,200/$224,400 or approximately 56 percent. Of each annuity payment of $1,000, approximately $437.62 is includable under section 72 as annuity income, and the remaining $562.38 is not taxable under section 72. However, in this case, a gain of $105,142.81 has been realized on the exchange of the stock for the annuity, and there is no indication that by the enactment of section 72(b), Congress intended for any such gain to be excluded from taxation. Such provision was designed to exempt that portion of the annuity payment from taxation under section 72 which was a return of cost, but since the annuity payments also constitute payment for the stock exchanged for the annuity, a part of each payment must be treated as taxable gain. Cf. Hill's Estate v. Maloney, 58 F.Supp. 164 (D. N.J.1944).

If the rule of Burnet v. Logan, 283 U.S. 404 (1931), were adopted, approximately $562.38 of each annuity payment would be excluded until the recovery of the petitioners' entire basis in the stock of $21,057.57. After the recovery of basis, then such portion would be wholly taxable as capital gain, until the $105,142.81 of gain was all reported. Such an approach is manifestly inconsistent with the objective of section 72; whereas, an approach which prorates the capital gains would be consistent with the approach taken by that section. Under the latter approach, the gain resulting from the exchange of the stock for the annuity would be divided by the life expectancy of the annuitant at the time of the exchange; that is, the gain of $105,142.81 would be divided by Mr. and Mrs. Bell's joint life expectancy of 18.7 years. Each year the portion of the gain allocable to the annuity payments received in that year would be subjected to taxation. If the annuitant lives less than his life expectancy and received less than expected, only a part of the estimated gain would be taxable. When the entire gain is reported, no additional amounts would be taxable as gain. The American Law Institute proposed in 1953 that the portion of each annuity payment allocable to the gain on the exchange should be treated as capital gain, however long the annuitant lived, but that approach would require legislation. See 1 ALI Fed. Income Tax Stat. sec. X126 (Feb. 1954) [Citations omitted].

Under my suggested approach, Mr. and Mrs. Bell would treat each $1,000 monthly payment as follows: Approximately $437.62 as ordinary income, approximately $468.54 as capital gain income, and approximately $93.84 as excludable from income. If Mrs. Bell lives beyond the joint life expectancy of herself and Mr. Bell, the capital gain will not be reportable thereafter, and she can exclude approximately $562.38 of each payment. The $437.62 will continue to be taxable as ordinary income.

The suggested approach does not necessarily require that a similar approach be used in the case of a commercial annuity, where such other factors as cash surrender value and guaranteed benefits might be involved. Moreover, a commercial annuity is usually purchased for cash, and the question of how to tax gain resulting from a transfer of property for a commercial annuity would not arise in such a situation.

DRENNEN, DAWSON, TANNENWALD, HALL, and WILES, JJ., agree with this dissent.

QUESTION

How should the annuity be valued to determine the amount includible in the transferor's estate for estate tax purposes? See Estate of Lloyd G. Bell, 80–2 USTC ¶ 13,356 (E.D.Wash.1980).

[2] Income Tax Consequences for the Purchaser

For the purchaser, the private annuity transaction is treated favorably in that as soon as the transaction occurs, his basis includes the present value of the payments he is obligated to make in the future, if the seller lives his actuarial life expectancy.[47] The primary disadvantage of the transaction from the purchaser's standpoint is that no part of the annuity payments is deductible as interest;[48] each payment is treated entirely as a capital ex-

---

47. See Rev.Rul. 55–119, 1955–1 CB 352, which deals with the computation of basis in various circumstances and for various purposes.

48. See, e.g., John C. W. Dix v. Commissioner, 392 F.2d 313, 68–1 USTC ¶ 9322 (4th Cir. 1968); F. A. Gillespie & Sons Co. v. Commissioner, 154 F.2d 913, 46–1 USTC ¶ 9207 (10th Cir. 1946), cert. denied 329 U.S. 781.

penditure to acquire the property, and accordingly becomes part of the purchaser's basis.

Initially, the purchaser's basis, determined in the manner just described, is used in computing depreciation if the property is depreciable or in determining gain or loss on a resale of the property.[49]   Thus, in *Example 8.1* above, if *D* resells the farm before *F* dies, it is necessary to determine her basis in order to compute her gain or loss on the sale.   For purposes of gain, her basis equals the sum of the payments already made and the actuarial value of the payments to be made over *F*'s remaining life expectancy as of the date of the sale.   For purposes of determining loss, on the other hand, *D*'s basis is limited to payments actually made up to the time when she sells the property.   If the amount for which *D* sells the property falls between the two amounts just described, no gain or loss is recognized.

Thus, if *D* resells the property for $200,000 after paying *F* $75,000, when the present actuarial value of payments required to be made over *F*'s remaining life expectancy is $150,000, no gain or loss is recognized by *D* when the sale is made.   This follows from the fact that her basis for purposes of gain is $225,000 and her basis for purposes of loss is only $75,000.   Subsequent events, however, will affect this computation and will be reflected by *D* as giving rise to either income or a deduction for the year in which they occur.   If *F* lives long enough so that the total amount *D* pays to him exceeds $200,000, *D* has a deductible loss each year in which she pays the annuity to *F*.   And if *F* dies after *D*'s sale and before *D* pays him a total of $200,000, *D* has a gain measured by the difference between that amount and the payments *D* in fact made.

In *Example 8.1*, as the property sold is depreciable, a similar computation of basis is required in order to compute the depreciation deduction of *D*.   For this purpose, the actuarial value of the payments to be made when the annuity commences is allocated between the depreciable and nondepreciable property in proportion to their relative values. [50]   The depreciation is then based on the amount allocated to the depreciable property until the amount actually paid by *D* exceeds the initial actuarial value of such payments.   Thereafter, each payment increases the amount to be allocated until the death of *F* freezes basis by eliminating further payments by *D*.

[3] Gift Tax and Estate Tax Consequences

The most important function of private annuity sales in estate planning is to enable the seller to remove property from his prospective taxable estate without incurring liability for a gift tax.   In order to achieve that goal, the actuarial value of the annuity payments to be made by the purchaser must equal or exceed the fair market value of the property sold.   In theory, such equality should mean that the sale does not reduce the seller's prospective taxable estate;   the property sold is merely replaced by annuity payments which cause the estate to be as large as it would have been if no sale had been made.   In practice, the transfer of property often may reduce the seller's taxable estate.   This is the result of the unrealistic manner in which the annuity is valued in determining its adequacy as consideration for gift

49. See Rev.Rul. 55–119, 1955–1 CB 352.   50. See Rev.Rul. 69–74, 1969–1 CB 43.

tax and estate tax purposes.   In addition, general valuation-reducing techniques may be used to minimize the value for gift tax purposes of the
property transferred.[51]

[a] Valuation of the Annuity

Valuation of the annuity to determine whether it is equal in value to
the property transferred has generally been based on the tables in the gift
tax and estate tax regulations.[52]   These tables often may overvalue the
annuity for two reasons:

(1) They fail to reflect the seller's health; and

(2) They are based on an assumed 6 percent interest rate.[53]

[i] **Relevance of Seller's Health.**   If the seller's health is poor, he is
likely to live a shorter time than that assumed in the relevant actuarial
tables.   Yet, the courts reason, "the United States is in business with
enough different taxpayers so that the law of averages has ample opportunity to work." [54]   An individual taxpayer, on the other hand, may enter
into the transaction because he believes the facts in his case weight the odds
in his favor.

Revenue Ruling 80–80 [55] deals at some length with the circumstances
under which the physical condition of an individual will justify departure
from using the actuarial tables to value property interests for estate and
gift tax purposes.   It concludes that such departure is justified only if the
individual whose life interest is being valued

> * * *   is known to have been afflicted, at the time of the trans-
> fer, with an incurable physical condition that is in such an advanced
> stage that death is clearly imminent.   Death is not clearly immi-
> nent if there is a reasonable possibility of survival for more than
> a very brief period.   For example, death is not clearly imminent
> if the individual may survive for a year or more and if such a
> possibility is not so remote as to be negligible.

The Ruling expressly applies to "every situation that involves valuation
of an interest that is dependent upon the life of one or more individuals for
federal estate or gift tax purposes," including valuation for purposes of the
estate tax or gift tax charitable deduction.   The only exception made is the
valuation of reversionary interests, for purposes of § 2037 or § 2042(2), in
determining whether the value is large enough to require inclusion of interests subject to a requirement of survival of a decedent-transferor in his
gross estate.[56]   For that purpose, the actuarial tables must be applied in
every case.

51. For a discussion, see ¶ 6.03[2] supra.

52. See, e.g., 212 Corp., 70 T.C. 788, 798
(1978); Rev.Rul. 69–74, 1969–1 CB 43.

53. For decedents dying after 1970, the estate tax regulations are Regulations
§ 20.2031–10(f); the gift tax regulations,
which are similar, are Regulations
§ 25.2512–9(f).   The latter admittedly deals
with valuation of annuities transferred,
rather than those received.   Reg.
§ 25.2512–9(a).   It seems unlikely, however, that the Commissioner would use
different rules to value the latter.

54. Rose Gelb v. Commissioner, 298 F.2d
544, 552, 62–1 USTC ¶ 12,060 at 84,523 (2d
Cir. 1962).   See also George G. McMurtry,
203 F.2d 659, 53–1 USTC ¶ 10,895 (1st Cir.
1953).

55. 1980–1 CB 194.

56. ¶ 5.02[4][b][i] note 103 supra.

[ii] **Assumed 6 Percent Interest Rate.** In recent years, a 6 percent interest rate (except for tax-exempt securities) has become another item of nostalgic Americana. It is particularly low for the unsecured promise of an individual, especially if he has no established credit rating and could not obtain a similar loan from an institutional lender. Thus the use of a 6 percent rate in the Commissioner's tables may substantially overvalue the purchaser's promise to pay the annuity. Yet attacks on this assumed rate, whether by taxpayers [57] or by the Commissioner,[58] generally have been unsuccessful, as have sellers' efforts to use the cost of a comparable commercial annuity.[59]

[b] Use of Price Adjustment Provisions

In sales for private annuities, as in other areas of estate planning, clients and their advisors seek to fortify their tax positions by incorporating relevant tax criteria into the governing documents. For any sale to a related purchaser, whether the purchase price is payable as an annuity or otherwise, the seller has reason to be concerned about the adequacy of the selling price. If it is too low, the difference may be a gift for gift tax purposes.[60] If the price is payable as an annuity, the seller may be required to include the property in his taxable estate because of retention of an interest in income.[61]

To guard against such risks, sellers should obtain reliable estimates of the value of the property sold. Even with such estimates, risks remain, as the value of any asset which must be determined by appraisals rather than by market quotations [62] often is a matter of dispute between the taxpayer and the Commissioner. As additional protection, the seller in a private annuity transaction may provide for an increase in the annuity payments if the Commissioner determines that their value is less than that of the property transferred. Such a provision was held to bar assessment of a gift tax in King v. United States.[63] Although the sale in that case was

---

57. See John H. Vernon, 66 T.C. 484 (1976) (value of term of years for gift tax purposes); Merchants Nat'l Bank v. United States, 583 F.2d 19, 78–2 USTC ¶ 13,257 (1st Cir. 1978) (value of charitable remainder).

58. See Leonard Rosen v. Commissioner ¶ 6.03[1][a], supra; B. Calhoun Hipp v. United States, 215 F.Supp. 222, 63–1 USTC ¶ 12,126 (D.S.C.1962).

59. The taxpayer succeeded in attacking the Commissioner's reliance on actuarial tables in valuing a private annuity for gift tax purposes in James B. Dunigan v. United States, 434 F.2d 892, 70–2 USTC ¶ 12,727 (5th Cir. 1970). There, however, the attack was based on evidence that the taxpayer's life expectancy was greater than average and that the tables (which antedate those presently in use) were obsolete. But see Rev.Rul. 80–80, note 55 supra.
For a discussion of the use of actuarial tables for valuation purposes under the fed-

eral transfer taxes, see Comment, 29 U.Chi.L.Rev. 728 (1962); Note, 53 N.C.L.Rev. 161 (1974).

60. See Simon M. Lazarus v. Commissioner, 513 F.2d 824, 75–1 USTC ¶ 9387 (9th Cir. 1975). In that case, an additional factor supporting recharacterization of the "sale" was the fact that the purchasing trust had only nominal assets apart from the property transferred. See also Reg. § 25.2512–8.

61. § 2036(a).

62. The availability of market quotations does not necessarily eliminate disputes. See Reg. § 25.2512–2(e), recognizing that selling prices may not represent the fair market value of securities because of factors such as a thin market or the need to value a large block of stock.

63. ¶ 8.02 supra.

not for private annuity payments, the principle involved in the holding does not appear to be dependent upon the manner in which the price is payable.

¶ 8.04   INTRA-FAMILY INSTALLMENT SALES

A sale to a family member (or family trust) qualifying for installment method reporting of gain under § 453, as amended by the Installment Sales Revision Act of 1980,[64] is similar to a sale for private annuity payments. Both combine deferral of recognition of gain by the seller with immediate acquisition of increased basis by the buyer.   The moment the sale occurs, the installment payments the buyer is obligated to make become part of his basis both for gain on a resale of the property and for depreciation if the property is depreciable.[65]   In one respect, the installment sale is more favorable from the buyer's standpoint than the sale for private annuity payments—his payments of interest on unpaid installments will be deductible, whereas no part of his annuity payments qualify even though economically they too may represent interest.[66]

The use of the intra-family installment sale as an estate-planning tool has been substantially curtailed by the 1980 Act.   Its effects are twofold:

(1) Such sales no longer serve as readily or in as many situations to defer recognition of gain by the seller, if the buyer is a "related person" [67] who resells to a third party for cash or for a price payable in installments at earlier dates than those provided in the prior intra-family sale. [68]

(2) If depreciable property is sold for installment payments to a spouse or "80-percent owned entity" [69] the seller nevertheless must report the entire gain in the year of sale, rather than as payments are received.   Thus, installment sales to such purchasers may not be used to achieve an increased basis for depreciation for the buyer without a corresponding recognition of gain by the seller.

Apart from these new restrictions on its use in estate planning, the intra-family installment sale does not have the same potential for removing property from the seller's estate without a gift or estate tax as in the case of a sale for private annuity payments.   Current market interest rates must

---

64. Pub.L. 471, 96th Cong., 2d Sess. (1980). Section 453(a), as amended by the Act, makes gain from an "installment sale," defined generally in § 453(b)(1) as "a disposition of property where at least 1 payment is to be received after the close of the taxable year in which the disposition occurs," includible in income under the "installment method."   Under it, gain is reported pro rata as payments are received (see § 453(c)) unless the taxpayer elects to have § 453(a) not apply to the disposition. See § 453(d)(1). There no longer is a limit on payments in the year of sale of 30 percent of selling price, as under former § 453(b)(2).

65. Crane v. Commissioner, 331 U.S. 1, 67 S.Ct. 1047, 91 L.Ed. 1301, 47–1 USTC ¶ 9,217 (1947).

66. See ¶ 8.03[2] note 48 supra, and accompanying text.

67. The definition in § 453(f)(1) is generally in terms of the attribution rules of § 318.

68. § 453(e), discussed at ¶ 8.04[1] infra.

69. § 453(g), referring to the definition of "related persons" in § 1239(b).   As amended by the Act, that definition includes, in addition to the taxpayer's spouse, a corporation in which he owns 80 percent of the stock or a partnership in which he owns 80 percent of the capital or profits interest.   See § 1239(b).   In determining ownership, the attribution rules of § 318 generally are applicable.   See § 1239(c).   The provision is inapplicable if tax avoidance was not a principal purpose of the sale.   See § 453(e)(7).

be taken into account in valuing the installment obligation to determining whether it is adequate consideration for the transferred property,[70] and the seller in poor health derives no benefit in an installment sale from an actuarial estimate of his life expectancy.   The installment sale does, however, offer other opportunities to minimize taxes, which may make it an attractive tool for some clients.

Example 8.2.   A father (*F*) sells the family farm to his daughter (*D*) for a total selling price of $150,000, with $15,000 down and $15,000 per year for nine years thereafter, plus interest on the unpaid balance at the current market rate as of the time the sale was made.   If the farm had a basis of $50,000, *F*'s gain of $100,000 will, under § 453, be reportable only as payments are received from *D*.   Each payment of $15,000 will be treated as including $10,000 of gain.

From the standpoint of *D*, her basis for depreciation or for gain or loss on resale of the farm reflects both the installment payments she has already made and those she is obligated to make in the future.   In addition, her interest payments are fully deductible by her (and includible in income by *F*).

[1] Income Tax Consequences for the Seller

For the seller, the installment sale spreads taxable gain over the period during which payments are received.   Unlike the annuity sale, provision for a lien on the property sold or other security may be made without loss of the income tax deferral offered by installment sales.   The intra-family installment sale is attractive as a vehicle for sales to unrelated buyers for cash, if the Installment Sales Revision Act of 1980 does not apply to the purchaser's resale of the property to a third party.   Under § 453(e) as amended by the Act, payments received by the related purchaser on sale of the property to a third party while both the original seller and original purchaser are living [71] generally cause recognition of gain by him unless the purchaser held the property for two years before selling it.   If the property sold was a "marketable security," [72] such recognition of gain occurs on receipt of payments from the third party during the joint lives of the original seller and purchaser, no matter how long the original purchaser held the property.

---

70. If the interest rate is less than the usual rate on such transactions (or if no interest is specified), the difference between the value of the property and the value of the buyer's obligation, discounted at the market rate, constitutes a gift in the year of sale.   See Gertrude H. Blackburn, 20 T.C. 204 (1953).   If the stated rate is less than the test rate under § 483(c)(1)(B), a portion of principal payments will be treated as interest.   See § 483(a).   The current test rate is 9 percent.   See Reg. § 1.483–1(d)(1)(ii)(C).

For any sale or exchange of land by an individual to family members described in § 267(c)(4), the test rate cannot exceed 6%, to the extent the aggregate sales price for sales between the individual and the particular family member does not exceed $500,000 during the calendar year.   See § 483(g), added by § 126(a) of the Economic Recovery Tax Act of 1981, limiting the maximum rate to be used in determining "total unstated interest" under § 483(b). § 483(c)(1) requires that the test rate used to determine whether or not there is "total unstated interest" be not less than one percentage point lower than the rate used to compute the amount of such interest.   Thus if a 6% rate is provided in such a sale, there is no total unstated interest subject to § 483.   If a rate below 6% is provided, unstated interest is computed on the basis of a 7% interest rate.

71. See § 453(e)(6)(C).

72. See § 453(e)(2).   For the definition of "marketable securities," see § 453(f)(2).

In *Example 8.2*, if D sold the farm for $200,000 cash within the two years following her purchase from F, this would require F to report the portion of his gain which he had not reported previously. If he had received $30,000 from D when she made the sale, F would have reported 30/150th of his gain of $100,000, or $20,000, before her sale, and would be required to report the balance of his gain, $80,000, when she received payment from her purchaser. If the property sold was a "marketable security," the same result would follow on a sale while both D and F were living, no matter how long D waited to make her sale. D's basis for computing gain or loss will be $150,000, so her gain is $50,000.

The judicial and administrative limitations which had been imposed on the use of the installment sale technique before the new Act presumably are still applicable. The Act was a response to "unwarranted tax avoidance by allowing the realization of appreciation within a related group without the current payment of income tax." [73] There is no inference from the legislative history that the two year provision eliminates other bases for attributing the resale to the original seller. Thus, if the resale to the third party had already been arranged when F sold the property to D, that sale will be disregarded and F will be treated as having sold directly to the third party.[74] Similarly, the Internal Revenue Service will disregard a sale between husband and wife if it was intended that the purchasing spouse would resell, even though no specific purchaser was contemplated.[75] On the other hand, the Tax Court has declined to attribute to the grantor, a resale of stock by family trusts, where the grantor had sold it to the trusts on the installment basis, even though the resales were contemplated when the first sale was made.[76]

[2] Income Tax Consequences for the Purchaser

From the purchaser's standpoint, the installment sale has the usual tax consequences in terms of basis and interest deductions of any purchase on credit. Payments to be made in the future are included in his basis immediately, both in determining any allowable deduction for depreciation and in computing his gain or loss on a resale of the property.[77]

[3] Gift Tax and Estate Tax Consequences

Intra-family installment sales may minimize gift taxes and estate taxes in two important ways:

(1) By "estate freezing" [78] (diverting future increases in the value of

---

73. See H.Rep.No. 1042, 96th Cong., 2d Sess., 12 (1980).

74. See Arnold Malkan v. Commissioner, 54 T.C. 1305 (1970); Rev.Rul. 73–157, 1973–1 CB 213. The same result was reached where the terms of the installment sale required the purchaser to sell and reinvest the proceeds. See Paul G. Lustgarten v. Commissioner, 639 F.2d 1208, 81–1 USTC ¶ 9273 (5th Cir. 1981).

75. Rev.Rul. 73–536, 1973–2 CB 158. Compare Charles B. Nye v. United States, 407 F.Supp. 1345, 75–1 USTC ¶ 9510 (M.D.N.C.1975), allowing installment reporting of the first sale, with Philip W. Wrenn, 67 T.C. 576 (1976), denying such treatment for lack of a bona fide reason for the installment sale apart from tax avoidance.

76. William D. Pityo, 70 T.C. 225 (1978); Clair E. Roberts v. Commissioner, 643 F.2d 654, 81–1 USTC ¶ 9380 (9th Cir. 1981).

77. See note 65 supra.

78. For a discussion, see ¶ 5.02[1][a] supra.

the property sold to the purchaser—either a family member or family trust); and

(2) By allowing the gift of an asset to be spread over a number of years ("piece-meal giving") to facilitate maximum use of the present interest exclusion and to postpone liability for gift tax.

Any intra-family sale of an appreciating asset may be used as an estate-freezing technique. Whether or not the sale is for installment payments, any increase in the value of the property after the sale is made is removed from the seller's estate and inures instead to the purchaser. The installment sale offers the additional advantages of permitting a family member or family trust to purchase despite the buyer's lack of funds (or credit from unrelated sources).

[a] Piece-Meal Giving

An installment sale may allow a client to make a gift over a period of years. The result may be to reduce or even eliminate any gift tax that would be due if the gift were made immediately. This is accomplished by "piece-meal giving," in which an asset is sold for installment payments and the seller cancels the buyer's obligations to make the payments as they come due.

For example, assume that a father (F) wants to give the family farm to his son (S) without using any portion of his unified credit (or paying any gift tax, if his unified credit has already been exhausted). If the present fair market value of the farm is $200,000, F must arrange to give a portion of the farm worth $10,000 to S each year (or $20,000 if F's wife consents to treat one-half of each gift as having been made by her).[79] Even with her consent, a gift of $200,000 would require 10 years to complete if the value of the farm did not change during that period, which is unlikely. Thus, if F gave S an undivided 1/10 interest in the farm each year, an annual appraisal of the property would be required to establish the value of each year's gift, with the likelihood that in some years such value would exceed the combined $20,000 present interest exclusions of F and his wife. In addition, for the entire period (unless F died before the 10 years elapsed and devised his remaining interest in the farm to S), the property would be owned jointly by F and S, with no one person having sole authority for its management.

An installment sale provides an alternative method of transferring the farm to S that may avoid these complications. If F sells the farm to S for $200,000, payable in installments of $20,000 per year with interest on the unpaid balance at the market rate prevailing when the sale is made,[80] F can make an annual gift to S by forgiving each $20,000 principal payment in the year in which it comes due. Any appreciation in value accrues solely to S and the property need not be reappraised each year to determine the amount of F's gift. Although S must also pay interest on the installment obligation, the property itself may produce enough income to cover the required interest payments. The net effect of the arrangement is to give F some income in the form of diminishing annual interest payments while removing the property from his estate without any gift tax.

---

79. § 2513. For a discussion, see ¶ 6.03[1][b] supra. 80. See note 70 supra.

The Internal Revenue Service generally has been unsuccessful in its attempts to treat such piece-meal gifts as all being made in the year of the sale, even in Estate of J. W. Kelley,[81] where it was intended from the start that the notes given by the buyers would be forgiven as they came due and that the buyers had no resources to pay the notes other than the property sold. However, the Service persists in its view that piece-meal giving arrangements constitute gifts of the full value of the property "sold" in the year in which it is transferred.[82] The resulting planning risk should be borne in mind.

[b] Use of Price Adjustment Provisions

To avoid adverse gift or estate tax consequences if the Commissioner determines that the value of the installment obligation of the buyer is less than the value of the property sold, taxpayers may include in the relevant documents a provision for an increase in the amount payable to make it equal to such value. The function of such price adjustment provisions was discussed in connection with annuity sales.[83] Similar considerations are relevant to the use of such provisions in intra-family installment sales as well.

¶ 8.05 TRANSFERS IN CONNECTION WITH SEPARATION AGREEMENTS OR DIVORCE

Transfers in connection with separation agreements or divorce differ from most other estate-planning tools in that the transferor often is not motivated by a voluntary desire to confer benefits but rather is seeking to discharge a legal obligation and no more. Thus, from the transferor's standpoint, the transfer is for consideration and for income tax purposes it generally is so treated.[84] The result may be that the wife gets the house and the husband has to pay income tax on "gain" he is deemed to have realized when he transferred the house to her. For estate and gift tax purposes, however, such consideration may not be recognized.[85] Thus, it is theoretically possible—although rare in practice—for a transfer of appreciated property by a husband to his former wife (or in trust for her benefit) to be subject to income tax on the appreciation,[86] to gift tax on the

81. 63 T.C. 321 (1974), nonacq. 1977–2 CB 2. See also John R. Hudspeth v. Commissioner, 509 F.2d 1224, 75–1 USTC ¶ 9224, (9th Cir. 1975); Nelson Story III, 38 T.C. 936 (1962). But see Minnie E. Deal, 29 T.C. 730 (1958).

82. Rev.Rul. 77–299, 1977–2 CB 343.

83. See ¶ 8.03[3][b] supra.

84. See United States v. Davis, 370 U.S. 65, 82 S.Ct. 1190, 8 L.Ed.2d 335 62–2 USTC ¶ 9509 (1962), requiring recognition of gain by the transferor of appreciated property, and Worthy W. McKinney, 64 T.C. 263 (1975), allowing recognition of loss by the transferor of property with a basis in excess of its fair market value.

85. See § 2043(b), which provides that a relinquishment of "marital rights in the de-

cedent's property or estate" is not consideration for a transfer of property for purposes of the estate tax. Although there is no similar provision in the gift tax sections, the estate tax rule was read into the gift tax by the Supreme Court in Merrill v. Fahs, 324 U.S. 308, 65 S.Ct. 655, 89 L.Ed. 963, 45–1 USTC ¶ 10,180 (1945) and Commissioner v. Wemyss, 324 U.S. 303, 65 S.Ct. 652, 89 L.Ed. 958, 45–1 USTC ¶ 10,179 (1945).

86. See United States v. Davis, 370 U.S. 65, 82 S.Ct. 1190, 8 L.Ed.2d 335, 62–2 USTC ¶ 9509 (1962) (outright transfer); Estate of H. B. Hundley, 52 T.C. 495 (1969), acq. 1978–1 CB 2, aff'd per curiam 435 F.2d 1311, 71–1 USTC ¶ 12,736 (4th Cir. 1971) (transfer in trust). Some states recognize a kind of joint ownership of property acquired by joint efforts of the spouses during marriage, at least for purposes of its division on divorce, with the result that a trans-

value of the property, and to inclusion of such value in his estate when he dies.[87]

As a practical matter, however, it usually is possible with proper planning to avoid any gift tax in this situation. There may even be an opportunity to use a transfer in connection with divorce to achieve a gift tax saving if the transfer is in part for the support of minor children.[88]

[1] Avoiding Gift Tax

Many divorcing spouses do not remain good friends and, thus, it is surprising to find that transfers between them may be subject to the gift tax. But § 2512(b) defines a gift as any transfer of property not in the ordinary course of business that is "for less than an adequate and full consideration in money or money's worth * * * ," and the Regulations negate any requirement of donative intent.[89] With this mechanical application of the gift tax and decisions that consideration for gift tax purposes does not include a release of marital rights,[90] such as dower or an elective share of the spouse's estate when he dies, transfers in connection with divorce may be completed gifts for gift tax purposes.

If the transfer is made before the divorce, it may qualify for the gift tax marital deduction. If it fails to qualify, gift tax usually may be avoided on one of three grounds:

(1) § 2516 provides an exemption for transfers which satisfy its requirements and offers additional planning possibilities for transfers for the support of minor children;

fer to make such division does not result in gain to the transferor. See Ray C. Imel v. United States, 523 F.2d 853, 75–2 USTC ¶ 9698 (10th Cir. 1975) (Colorado law); George F. Collins, Jr. v. Commissioner, 412 F.2d 211, 69–2 USTC ¶ 9471 (10th Cir. 1969) (Oklahoma law). See also Lillian H. Bosch v. United States, 590 F.2d 165, 167, 79–1 USTC ¶ 9229 at 86,472 (5th Cir. 1979), cert. denied, 444 U.S. 1045 (1980), in which the court stated:

Florida has long recognized a 'special equity' in a wife where she has made identifiable contributions to her husband's property during marriage even though the special equity only comes into actual identifiable form upon the termination of the marriage status.

It held that the existence of such a "special equity" made a decree of a Florida divorce court a division of property interests between the former spouses, rather than a transfer in exchange for a relinquishment of the wife's marital rights. The wife's basis therefore was the cost of the property when purchased, rather than its value at the time of the division. A corollary of this holding is that amounts paid by reason of such "special equity" are not deductible by the payor as alimony. See George W. Mann, 74 T.C. 1249 (1980).

No gain or loss is recognized on an equal division of the value of community property as part of a divorce settlement. See

Rev.Rul. 76–83, 1976–1 CB 213. But if the husband is required to pay cash from his separate property to equalize the division or promises to pay for the property out of his future earnings, there is to that extent a taxable sale on which the wife must recognize gain. Jean C. Carrieres, 64 T.C. 959 (1975), acq. 1976–1 CB 1, aff'd per curiam 552 F.2d 1350, 77–1 USTC ¶ 9425 (9th Cir. 1977).

If a division of community property is unequal, a basis adjustment is required. See Courtney L. Siewert, 72 T.C. 326 (1979), where the Tax Court held that the husband, who had received more than one-half of the community property, had a basis equal to one-half of the community's basis in the assets of which he obtained full ownership, plus consideration given by him to his wife for the settlement.

87. Such inclusioon could be based on any of the grounds specified in §§ 2035–2038.

88. See § 2516.

89. Reg. § 25.2511–1(g)(1). Transfers in the ordinary course of business are treated as being for a full consideration, see Reg. § 25.2512–8, thus freeing bad business bargains from the gift tax.

90. See note 85 supra.

(2) Transfers "founded on" a divorce decree are exempt from gift tax under *Harris v. Commissioner*,[91] which may be important if the transfer fails to satisfy the requirements of § 2516; and

(3) Transfers which discharge the transferor's obligation to support his or her spouse are exempt from the gift tax under Revenue Ruling 68–379.[92]

The requirements of § 2516 for gift tax exemption are relatively easy to satisfy in the case of an outright transfer from one spouse to the other. It is merely necessary that the transfer be:

(a) Pursuant to a written agreement relative to the marital and property rights of the spouses; and

(b) In settlement of the spouses' marital or property rights or to provide a reasonable allowance for the support of issue of the marriage during minority.

In addition, a final decree of divorce must occur within two years of the written agreement. If, however, the transfer is in trust, it becomes necessary to determine separate values for:

(1) The interest of the wife;

(2) The interest provided for support of children during minority; and

(3) Any other interests, such as that given to adult children.

Only (1) and (2) are covered by the exemption unless the husband can prove that his ex wife "purchased" other interests in exchange for a release of her marital or property rights.[93]

Sometimes such agreements are found to have been based upon a relinquishment of support rights by the wife in return for the husband's undertaking to bequeath property to the children, so that the children's bequest has been held deductible as a claim against the husband's estate.[94]   Although the Commissioner treats such a relinquishment as a taxable gift by the wife to the children,[95] it may have the advantage from the husband's standpoint of allowing him to make deductible bequests to his children—bequests he might have wished to make even without regard to any bargaining with his wife.

Transfers that fail to satisfy the requirements of § 2516 may nevertheless be exempt under the decree or support exemptions, but in practice these are less important than transfers under § 2516.

---

91.   340 U.S. 106, 71 S.Ct. 181, 95 L.Ed. 111, 50–2 USTC ¶ 10,786 (1950).   If the divorce court had no power under local law to modify the parties' agreement, the transfer is not "founded" on the court's decree and does not come within the *Harris* exemption. Preston L. Spruance, 60 T.C. 141, 153–154 (1973), aff'd without published opinion 505 F.2d 731 (3d Cir. 1974).   In that situation, additional amounts paid in accordance with a voluntary agreement to modify the original agreement to provide increased payments are gifts.   See Rev.Rul. 79–118, 1979–1 CB 315.

92.   1968–2 CB 414.

93.   See Preston L. Spruance, note 91 supra, 60 T.C. at 151–153; Rev.Rul. 79–363, 79–1 CB 284.

94.   See A. Frederic Leopold v. United States, 510 F.2d 617, 75–1 USTC ¶ 13,053 (9th Cir. 1975).   But see Mary B. Lovering v. United States, 318 F.Supp. 215, 70–2 USTC ¶ 12,704 (S.D.N.Y.1979).

95.   Rev.Rul. 77–314, 1977–2 CB 349.

[2] Minimizing Estate Tax

Transfers made or obligations assumed in connection with separation agreements or divorce may be relevant in determining a client's estate tax in either of two ways:

(1) Such a transfer may or may not be includible in the transferor's estate for any of the reasons specified in §§ 2035–38; and

(2) Payments that the transferor's estate is obligated to make after death may or may not be deductible from the gross estate, under § 2053, in determining the taxable estate.

[a] Inclusion of Transfers in *H*'s Estate

Section 2043(a) requires inclusion of a portion of the value of transfers described in §§ 2035–2038, for which consideration was received but which did not constitute "a bona fide sale for an adequate and full consideration in money or money's worth." Section 2043(b) denies status as such consideration to "a relinquishment * * * of dower or curtesy * * * or of other marital rights in the decedent's property or estate * * *." Superficially, this language would suggest that a transfer in exchange for a release by *W* of her support rights would not be supported by consideration. If the transfer would otherwise be includible in *H*'s estate, such a release would appear to be insufficient to take it out.

However, the Internal Revenue Service has stated here, as in connection with the gift tax,[96] that support rights are not within the scope of "other marital rights" and their release thus may constitute consideration for estate tax purposes.[97]

WILLIAM P. GRAY v. UNITED STATES

United States Court of Appeals, Ninth Circuit, 1976.
541 F.2d 228, 76–2 USTC ¶ 13,153.

McWILLIAMS, Circuit Judge.

The question here to be resolved is whether the trial court erred in holding that the proceeds of a life insurance policy on decedent's life, which were paid to the decedent's former wife in accordance with the terms of a pre-existing property settlement agreement, were deductible from decedent's gross estate under Section 2053(a) of the Internal Revenue Code of 1954, as a claim against the estate. We conclude that the trial court did err, and the matter is remanded for further proceedings.

William Robertson, the decedent, and Jane Robertson, his wife, separated on August 15, 1966, after 22 years of marriage and four children. On August 24, 1966, William and Jane entered into a property settlement agreement which provided in pertinent part as follow:

I

RECITALS

* * *

1.04 The parties desire to make a full and final settlement and adjustment of their rights with reference to each other as to alimony and with

---

96. See Rev.Rul. 68–379, 1968–2 CB 414.   97. Rev.Rul. 71–67, 1971–1 CB 271.

respect to the property of the other, and to liquidate and settle the rights and claims of each in and to their property, whether joint tenancy, community or separate; and, without limiting the particularity of the foregoing, it is the intention of the parties to make this agreement integrated in that there exists reciprocal consideration for the agreements with regard to the division of property under Article IV and the provisions for support of Wife under Article V. *It is the further intent of the parties that this agreement shall not be modifiable other than by an instrument in writing executed by both parties, and that the court having jurisdiction of any divorce action between the parties shall not have the power to modify this agreement* other than as it pertains to the custody and support of the children of this marriage as provided in Article VI.

* * *

IV

DIVISION OF PROPERTY AND DISPOSITION OF DEBTS
* * *

4.03 Husband shall pay Wife the sum of $15,000 within thirty days following the execution of this agreement. Husband shall pay Wife an additional $40,000 on or before June 1, 1968.

* * *

V

SUPPORT OF WIFE

5.01 Husband agrees to pay to Wife for her support and maintenance $600 per month commencing on the first day of the first month following the execution of this agreement and continuing until the death or remarriage of Wife or the death of Husband.

* * *

VIII

GENERAL PROVISIONS
* * *

8.02 Husband agrees that after the date hereof and during Wife's life he shall maintain a life insurance policy or policies in full force and effect insuring his life having an aggregate face value of not less than $50,000 and designating Wife as the beneficiary.

* * *

8.07 *This agreement shall survive its incorporation or merger into, or court approval in, an interlocutory judgment of divorce and is not dependent upon the filing or obtaining of a divorce by either party and shall be in full force and carried out pursuant to its terms whether or not a divorce is filed and/or obtained.* (Emphasis added.)

* * *

Divorce proceedings were subsequently instituted by William in the Superior Court of the State of California for the County of Los Angeles.

An interlocutory decree in divorce was entered on January 31, 1967. The decree itself made no specific reference to William's obligation to maintain an insurance policy on his life, payable on his death to his former wife. However, the decree did contain the following provision:

The Property Settlement Agreement between the parties hereto, dated August 24, 1966, received in evidence herein as plaintiff's exhibit No. 1, is hereby approved, and the parties are ordered to carry out the executory provisions thereof.

A final decree in divorce was entered on November 20, 1967, and on that same date William was killed in an airplane crash. At the date of his death, a life insurance policy providing for payment of $50,000 to Jane upon William's death was in effect. The proceeds of this life insurance policy were paid by the insurance company directly to Jane, and hence the latter never did make any claim against William's estate for this particular amount. Jane did file a claim against William's estate for the $40,000 still owing her under the property settlement.

On the tax return filed by William's estate, Gray, the executor, included the life insurance proceeds ($50,000) as a part of the gross estate but claimed the same amount as a deduction in computing the taxable estate. The Commissioner disallowed the deduction, and the executor paid the resulting deficiency in estate taxes. The estate thereafter filed a claim for refund and, upon disallowance of that claim, instituted the instant suit for refund of federal estate tax erroneously assessed and collected.

* * *

The parties agree that where a court decision underlays and is the basis for a claim against an estate, such obligation is deemed to be founded on other than a promise or obligation, and is deductible under section 2053(a) as a claim against the estate without reference to 2053(c). In other words, section 2053(c), requiring that the claim be bona fide and contracted for an adequate and full consideration, applies only to claims founded on promises or agreements, and has no application with respect to claims which are founded upon court decrees. See Lowndes, Kramer and McCord, Federal Estate and Gift Taxes, § 14.6, p. 360 (3d ed. 1974).

In the instant case, the trial court held, in effect, that on the basis of the stipulated facts, Jane had a claim against the estate for the proceeds of the insurance proceeds ($50,000) which was founded on the divorce decree and that accordingly, such claim was properly deductible from the gross estate. * * *

The Government's position in this court is embodied in Rev. Rul. 60–160, 1960–1 Cum. Bull. 374. That ruling holds where a claim against an estate has its origin in a property settlement agreement which has been approved and adopted in a subsequent divorce decree, the claim can be considered as being founded on the court decree, rather than the prior property agreement, only if the court entering the decree had the power to modify or alter the terms of the agreement. Conversely, then, if the court entering the divorce decree had under local law *no* power to modify the terms of the property agreement, the claim is deemed as being founded on the property agreement, and not the divorce decree. And this is true even though the court entering the divorce decree may have approved and adopted the property agreement and ordered its enforcement.

In the instant case it is agreed that under local California law, the California court entering the divorce decree had no power to modify or alter the terms of the property settlement agreement entered into between William and Jane.   Adams v. Adams, 29 Cal.2d 621, 177 P.2d 265 (1947).   In such circumstances we now hold that the claim of William's former wife against William's estate is not founded on the divorce decree, but is founded on the property agreement between the parties.   [Citations omitted.]

We believe our holding that Jane's claim was founded on the property agreement, and not the divorce decree, is in complete accord with the property agreement itself.   In that agreement appear the following pertinent provisions: (1) the agreement is not modifiable other than by an instrument in writing executed by both parties; (2) a court having jurisdiction to entertain a divorce action between the parties shall *not* have the power to modify the terms of the property agreement, except as to custody and support of minor children;   (3) the agreement survives its incorporation or merger into, or court approval in, an interlocutory decree in divorce;   and (4) the property agreement is not dependent upon the obtaining of a divorce by either party, and is in force and to be carried out pursuant to its several terms whether a divorce is ever obtained.

In view of these several provisions in the property agreement itself, coupled with the additional fact that under California law a California court entering a divorce decree, in the absence of fraud, has no power to modify or alter the property agreement, we are of the firm view that the claim of Jane's against the estate was indeed founded on the property agreement, and not the divorce decree.   The fact that the decree ordered the parties to carry out the terms of the property agreement does not alter the situation.   Such only imposed an additional method for enforcing the terms of the property agreement, and in no wise alters what is to us the inescapable fact that Jane's claim had its origin in, and was in fact founded on, the property agreement between the parties.

The executor relies heavily on the reasoning in Commissioner of Internal Revenue v. Watson's Estate, 216 F.2d 941 (2d Cir. 1954).   We do not regard our holding in the instant case to be at odds with the holding in *Watson*.   In *Watson* the property settlement between the parties was incorporated into a divorce decree in a proceeding in the state courts of Nevada.   In Nevada, however, unlike California, a divorce court has the power to modify and alter the terms of a property settlement presented to it in a divorce proceeding.   It was in this factual setting that the Second Circuit in *Watson* held that the claim was founded on the decree, and not the property settlement, and was accordingly deductible as a claim under § 2053(a).   Similarly, in both Harris v. Commissioner of Internal Revenue, 340 U.S. 106, 71 S.Ct. 181, 95 L.Ed. 111 (1950) and Commissioner of Internal Revenue v. Maresi, 156 F.2d 929 (2d Cir. 1946), the property agreement in question was incorporated into a divorce decree entered in the State of Nevada.   So, in *Watson*, *Harris*, and *Maresi* the property settlement was in each instance incorporated into a Nevada divorce decree where the Nevada court was not obligated to accept the property settlement presented to it. On the contrary, under Nevada law the divorce court had the power to modify or alter the terms of the agreement. Under Rev.Rul. 60–160, 1960–1 Cum.Bull. 374, such a claim is deemed to be founded on the court decree, and not the antecedent property settlement. Such, however, is not the present case.

Having held that Jane's claim against the estate is founded on the property settlement, and not the divorce decree, does not end the matter. The Government concedes that such claim may still be deductible under § 2053(c) if it be founded on a promise or agreement which was contracted bona fide and for an adequate and full consideration in money or money's worth. In this regard, the trial court held that based on the stipulated facts, the claim was founded on a promise and agreement which was contracted bona fide and for adequate and full consideration. The Government contends that there is nothing in the stipulation of facts which would support such a finding. We agree. Mere recitals in the property agreement, such as the reference to "reciprocal consideration" in the present property agreement, are insufficient. There must be further inquiry to ascertain whether Jane's claim was in fact founded on a promise or undertaking which was bona fide and for adequate and full consideration.

In support of the foregoing, see Leopold v. United States, 510 F.2d 617 (9th Cir. 1975), where this Circuit upheld a finding by the trial court that a testamentary gift to decedent's child was contracted bona fide and for an adequate and full consideration. In *Leopold* the trial court held an evidentiary hearing on the question whether the decedent's promise as embodied in the property settlement agreement was bargained for or merely gratuitous. It is of passing interest to note that in *Leopold* there was apparently no contention that the claim was founded on a court decree, even though the property settlement agreement had been approved and incorporated into the California divorce decree.

Judgment reversed and cause remanded for further proceedings.[98]

ESTATE OF HOWARD L. DAVIS v. COMMISSIONER

United States Court of Appeals, Third Circuit, 1971.
440 F.2d 896, 71–1 USTC ¶ 12,767.

HASTIE, Chief Judge.

The matter in dispute on this appeal from a decision of the Tax Court is a determination of an estate tax deficiency that resulted from including in the estate an inter-vivos trust that the decedent had established primarily for the benefit of his estranged wife, who survived him. For the estate, the decedent's executrix, who is also his daughter, concedes that the settlor had retained until the time of his death such shared control over the trust as normally would have caused the trusted property to be taxable as part of his estate, as the gross estate is defined in sections 2036 and 2038 of the Internal Revenue Code. However, she contends that particular provisions

---

98. [On remand, the District Court found that the decedent's promise to maintain the life insurance policy with his former wife as beneficiary was supported by full and adequate consideration. 440 F.Supp. 684, 78–1 CCH USTC ¶ 13,244 (D.C.Cal.1977)—ed.]

of those sections that exclude from the taxable estate property transferred for "adequate and full consideration in money or money's worth" apply here and make the Tax Court's decision erroneous.

The decedent was a graduate engineer who from January 1, 1926 until his retirement at age 61 on December 31, 1938, served as Director of Technical Employment and Training for New York Telephone Co. During that period his annual salary ranged from $9,000 to $11,000. He also received small royalty income from two publications. From his retirement until his death on May 9, 1963, he received a pension that varied slightly between $318 and $314 per month. From 1938 to 1947 he earned income between $5,000 and $6,000 per year as a teacher.

The decedent married his wife Ione in 1902 and they had three daughters. He provided a well appointed home of thirteen rooms and four baths for his family in a good neighborhood and generally provided well for his wife. He employed domestic help and made it possible for his family to enjoy various luxuries.

During the 1930s marital difficulties arose and, in contemplation of divorce, the spouses separated and sold their home. On April 13, 1936, when the decedent was 58 years of age, his wife 54, and all daughters were over 25, the spouses executed two documents, one entitled "Articles of Separation" and the other, "Deed of Trust."

In the separation agreement the husband undertook to pay the wife $170 monthly for her support. In the trust he conveyed securities, valued at $26,307.38 at the date of transfer, to a trustee, directing that the entire net income, as well as so much of the corpus as he might direct or, after his death, the daughters might agree, be paid to the wife for life and thereafter the net income to a daughter Alma, whose health had become impaired, for her life. Power to terminate the trust was reserved to husband and wife jointly so long as both should live.

The trust was to terminate upon the death of the survivor of the spouses. The corpus was then to be paid to any surviving daughter or daughters and the issue of any deceased daughter or daughters, *per stirpes*. And finally, the settlor reserved the right to modify the trust, provided the life interests of his wife and Alma were not altered.

Husband and wife were domiciled in New Jersey when the trust was created, and the instrument provided that it was in all respects to be governed by New Jersey law.

The Tax Court found, and it is not now disputed, that the "separation agreement and trust were integrated parts of a larger agreement between decedent and Ione * * * the purpose and effect of which was to settle out of court * * * the provisions decedent was to make for Ione's support. The trust created for Ione, as well as the $170 monthly payments under the separation agreement, were in consideration of her relinquishing her right of support." 51 T.C. at 274. Therefore, for a determination whether all or any part of the property placed in trust came within the nontaxable category of property transferred "for an adequate and full consideration in money or money's worth," the court found it necessary to value the right of support that Ione surrendered in consideration of benefits under the trust and the separation agreement.

To that end, the Tax Court, sitting in 1968, undertook to assign dollar value to Ione's right of support as it existed in 1936 under New Jersey law. There was some evidence of family discussions before the trust was executed in which Ione's minimum requirements were estimated as at least $300 per month. One daughter testified that "the summation of them [family discussions] was that it [the wife's support] would have to be at least $300 per month." She added: " * * * and we really thought, the three of us, she needed more." A second daughter testified that her mother "couldn't have lived on less than $300 per month." An expert called by the taxpayer testified as to the factors a New Jersey court would have considered in translating the right to support into dollars and concluded that in the light of the husband's income and assets, the family history and station, and all related circumstances, a New Jersey court would have awarded Ione not less than $100 per week. Upon the basis of this evidence, the Tax Court stated in its findings of fact that the "family, including decedent, decided that Ione should have $300 per month for her support." And in its opinion the court characterized this amount as "reasonable" and added that "the agreement reached by the parties * * * more accurately reflects the value of Ione's support rights than * * * the expert testimony offered by petitioner as to what the New Jersey courts would have awarded Ione had she litigated the matter." The court then concluded the $300 per month for the life of the wife represented the dollar value of her legal right to support, of which $130 was the consideration for the establishment of the trust, the difference being supplied by the separation agreement. In addition, it found that in 1936 the commuted value of the wife's right to $130 per month for life was $17,150.35 as contrasted with the $26,307.38 that the husband transferred in trust. A determination of the tax consequences of these disparate values involved troublesome problems of estate taxation to which the Tax Court addressed itself,[99] but which we find it unnecessary to consider.

In our view, the valuation of the right of support as $300 per month is not warranted by the evidence. The testimony of the daughters disclosed no more than a family consensus that the wife could not live on less than $300 per month. There is nothing in the record to show that the decedent had provided merely a minimum subsistence for his wife or that a court would so restrict her right of support. The record shows a family living very well and comfortably. The husband's annual salary was $11,000 and he had significant accumulations, which were used to provide the $26,000 corpus of the trust now in question. These circumstances suggest ability and responsibility to contribute substantially more than $300 monthly for support of the wife in a situation where there were no minor children. The conclusion of the expert witness that a New Jersey court would have awarded the wife at least $100 per week was supported by an elaboration of the expert's reasoning and was not refuted by any other witness. In

---

99. Difficult problems of statutory interpretation, valuation of powers and other interests, and at times harsh results, enter the picture when it is necessary to apply section 2043 of the Internal Revenue Code which controls the taxation of property transferred so that various interests are created for consideration less than full and adequate.

these circumstances, we can find no rational basis for valuing the support right as low as $300 per month.

We recognize, as does the dissenting opinion of Judge Hoyt in the Tax Court, that it is impossible 30 years after the time in question, to make an exact retrospective valuation of the wife's intangible legal right of support as a court would have determined it in 1936. In the nature of the case, the evidence on this issue could not be very satisfactory. However, if the family had agreed that $300 per month would be adequate, that might well have sufficed to support the Tax Court's finding. But the testimony, that the wife could not live on less than $300 and in fact needed more, was at best evidence that the value of the right was something more than $300, particularly when the husband's economic situation and his record as a provider are considered. Moreover, since $300 was only an estimated minimum of subsistence needs, that estimate provides no basis for disparaging the only expert testimony on the issue to the effect that a New Jersey court would have valued the support right at not less than $100 per week. The expert properly considered that the husband's income in 1936 from salary, securities and royalties was more than $12,000. And, although he made passing reference to a judicial "rule of thumb * * * to give the wife at least a third of her husband's income," he emphasized that the courts attempt to reach an equitable result in all of the circumstances of a given case.

Sitting as a trial court we might well have been disposed to accept the expert's minimum estimate as a reasonable figure meriting adoption for present purposes. However, since the Tax Court valued the right to support at only $300 per month our legitimate concern as a reviewing court is to do no more than determine how conservative a valuation the evidence permits. We hold that a sum about midway between the family estimate of minimum subsistence needs and the expert estimate of minimum judicial allowance is as low an estimate of the value of the right of support as can reasonably be made on the present record. Accordingly, we hold that at least $370 per month rather than $300, should be the basis upon which the value of the relinquished right of support is calculated.

Since $170 per month was provided by the separation agreement, the discharge of the husband's obligation to pay the remaining $200 per month (rather than $130 as found by the Tax Court) was the consideration received by him for establishing the trust.

Determined by the Tax Court's method of computation the cost in 1936 of an annuity that would have paid the wife $200 per month for life would have been $26,385.15. This compares with the Tax Court's finding that the value of the property transferred in trust was $26,307.38. Thus, in 1936 the husband transferred property worth about $26,300 in trust in return for the release from an unliquidated obligation of approximately equal value.

We again emphasize that precise valuation of the wife's right to support as it existed in 1936 is impossible. But we think and hold that the present record requires the conclusion that the dollar value in 1936 of the trusted property and of the wife's right of support, which the Tax Court found to have been relinquished in consideration of the creation of the trust, were substantially equal.   Certainly, no such disparity appears between the trusted property and the released unliquidated obligation as would prevent one from being full and adequate consideration for the other.

The decision of the Tax Court will be reversed and the cause remanded for appropriate disposition in recognition of that substantial equivalence.

---

[b] Deduction of Payments by the Transferor's Estate

If a client's obligation to make support payments to a former spouse will continue after the client's death, it is highly desirable that it be deductible either as a claim against the estate, under § 2053(a)(3), or as indebtedness against property included in the estate under § 2053(a)(4).   In order to be so deductible, a claim or indebtedness based on a promise or agreement must, under § 2053(c)(1), be supported by consideration, which has been construed to include discharge of a support obligation.[100]   An alternative ground for deduction is that the payments discharge an obligation which is founded on a divorce decree.[101]   This basis for deduction is not available unless the divorce court had the power to modify the parties' agreement.[102]

---

100. See Estate of Robert F. Iversen v. Commissioner 552 F.2d 977, 77–1 USTC ¶ 13,184 (3d Cir. 1977) (Pennsylvania law); William P. Gray v. United States, supra (California Law); Estate of Robert G. Fenton v. Commissioner, 70 T.C. 263 (1978) (New York law).

101 Commissioner v. Estate of Myles C. Watson, 216 F.2d 941, 54–2 USTC ¶ 10,973 (2d Cir. 1954); Rev.Rul. 60–160, 1960–1 CB 374.

102. See William P. Gray v. United States, supra.

Chapter 9

NON-CHARITABLE TRUSTS

The major varieties of inter vivos trusts were introduced in summary fashion in ¶ 6.05. This chapter examines in greater depth the three kinds of non-charitable trusts which are important in minimizing taxes for the grantor during his life:

(1) Short-Term (Clifford) Trusts;

(2) Long-Term (Non-Reversionary) Trusts;

(3) Minors' Present Interest Trusts (and Trust Substitutes).

Chapter 10 will deal with charitable split-interest trusts.

The focus here is primarily on the tax consequences for the grantor and his estate. Both inter vivos and testamentary trusts have important tax consequences for beneficiaries as well, and will be examined in Part III.

¶ 9.01 SHORT-TERM (CLIFFORD) TRUSTS

The general scheme for taxation of trust income allocates taxability either to a beneficiary who received a distribution deemed to represent income or to the trust itself.[1] But important exceptions exist in which either the grantor or the holder of a power to vest income or principal in himself may be taxed on income, even though such income is distributed to someone else or is accumulated in the trust. These exceptions stem chiefly from the 1940 case of Helvering v. Clifford,[2] in which the Supreme Court held that the grantor of a trust was taxable on the trust income under the predecessor of § 61 because of his "dominion and control" over the trust. Two major factors contributed to this result:

(1) The trust term was five years, with the principal reverting to the grantor at the end of that period; and

(2) The grantor was the trustee with extensive administrative powers, as well as the power to determine the time at which income should be paid to his wife, who was the income beneficiary.[3]

The *Clifford* holding was later codified in §§ 671–677. These sections now provide detailed and specific rules as to when a trust grantor is treated for income tax purposes as owner of all, or a portion, of a trust. In addition to the time when the trust principal will revert to the grantor,[4] the relevant factors are the power of the grantor or someone else to:

(1) control beneficial enjoyment of trust income or principal; [5]

---

1. For a discussion, see ¶ 11.01 infra.

2. 309 U.S. 331, 60 S.Ct. 554, 84 L.Ed. 788, 40–1 USTC ¶ 9265 (1940).

3. The taxable year in the case antedated the income-splitting provisions for spouses. See § 6013.

4. § 673. For a discussion, see ¶ 9.01[3] infra.

5. § 674. For a discussion, see ¶ 9.01[4] infra.

(2) administer the trust without being required to act as a fiduciary, and the borrowing of trust funds by the grantor; [6]

(3) cause the trust to be revoked and the principal returned to the grantor; [7] and

(4) use trust income to discharge the legal obligations of the grantor or his spouse, or to pay premiums on insurance policies on the lives of either of them.[8]

These rules not only provide greater certainty in estate planning but also include features, such as a definition of "portion," [9] that may be highly favorable from the standpoint of a grantor. As a result, taxpayers today may plan with confidence and succeed, where Clifford failed, in shifting the taxability of income by creating short-term trusts. Significant changes from the terms of Clifford's trust are required to achieve recognition of a trust today for federal income tax purposes:

(1) The trust term must be a minimum of ten years before either income or principal can revert to the grantor; [10]

(2) Either the grantor must choose someone else as trustee,[11] or his own powers as trustee must be appropriately limited; [12]

(3) The beneficiary must be someone other than the grantor's spouse.[13]

The rules do not deal with the questions of whether the transaction in which the trust was created will be regarded as having "substance" and "economic reality," so as to be recognized for income tax purposes,[14] or whether the grantor will continue to be taxed under the assignment of income doctrine.[15]

The rules of §§ 671–677 are relevant for long-term trusts as well. Long-term (non-reversionary) trusts are discussed separately, however, because of the additional considerations involved in their creation and use.

The major variations in the different forms of Clifford trusts involve the choice of beneficiaries and the way the beneficiaries' interests are defined. With properly selected trustees, a wide range of alternatives is available. The following examples do not begin to exhaust the possibilities. Each example is designed to fit within a different provision of § 674 in order to avoid taxing the grantor on trust income (other than capital gains added

---

6. § 675. For a discussion, see ¶ 9.01[7] infra.

7. § 676. For a discussion, see ¶ 9.01[8] infra.

8. § 677. For a discussion, see ¶ 9.01[9] infra.

9. See Reg. § 1.671–3(b); ¶ 9.01[1][b][i] infra.

10. § 673(a). The life of the beneficiary also may be used as the trust term. See § 673(c). The Regulations permit use of such life or a ten-year term, whichever ends first. See Reg. § 1.673(a)–1(b).

11. He may choose trustees, one-half of whom are "independent," with broader powers, § 674(c), discussed in ¶ 9.01[5] infra. Or he may choose "related or subordinate" trustees with narrower powers, § 674(d), discussed at ¶ 9.01[6] infra.

12. For example, certain powers may be given to trustees other than the grantor.

13. § 677(a).

14. For a discussion, see ¶ 4.01[2][b] supra.

15. For a discussion of the doctrine, see ¶ 4.01[2][a] supra.

to principal) because of his dominion and control over the trust property.[16] Each provision creates an exception to the general rule of § 674(a) that the grantor is treated as owner of any portion of the trust as to which enjoyment of income or principal is subject to a power of disposition without the approval of an adverse party. At this point, § 674 deserves a careful reading.

Example 9.1, below, illustrates § 674(b), which creates an exception to the general rule for certain powers "regardless of by whom held."

> *Example 9.1.*   G transfers property to himself as trustee with the usual fiduciary powers to control investment of the trust property. Such powers do not include discretion to determine who shall receive income or principal. The income is payable to G's mother M for ten years or until she dies, whichever occurs first,[17] and then the principal is to be returned to G.

Example 9.2, below, illustrates § 674(c), which creates an exception to the general rule for broader powers of trustees than those allowed by § 674(b) if none is the grantor and if "no more than half   *   *   *   are related or subordinate parties who are subservient to the wishes of the grantor   *   *   * ."

> *Example 9.2.*   G transfers property to his wife (W) and his son-in-law (S) as trustees. In their discretion, the trustees may distribute income from time to time to such one or more of the living descendants of G as the trustees determine. Any income not so distributed shall be accumulated for distribution to the descendants of S who are living when the trust terminates, such descendants to take *per stirpes*. The trust shall end after ten years and the principal shall be returned to the grantor.

Example 9.3, below, illustrates § 674(d), which creates an exception to the general rule for powers that are broader than those allowed by § 674(b) but not as broad as those allowed by § 674(c). Section 674(d) applies to certain powers to allocate income held by trustees "none of whom is the grantor or spouse living with the grantor   *   *   * ." It thus includes such powers that do not qualify under § 674(c) because the holders are related or subordinate parties who are subservient to the wishes of the grantor.

> *Example 9.3.*   The terms of the trust are the same as in *Example 9.2* except that:
>
> (1) The trustees are G's son and daughter;
> (2) Their power to distribute income is phrased as follows: The trustees shall distribute to each descendant of G (excluding such trustees) such amounts of income as they determine in their discretion are required for his reasonable support and maintenance,[18] adding any excess income to principal at the end of each year.

---

16. Whether the grantor (or anyone else) will be taxed on income used to discharge the legal obligation of one person to support another is a separate problem. For a discussion, see ¶ 9.01[9] infra (dependents of the grantor or his spouse); ¶ 1.05 supra (dependents of other persons).

17. The use of these as alternatives is permissible. See Reg. § 1.673(a)–(1)(b).

18. Applying such a standard could present difficult problems for the trustees if the amounts required to meet the standard exceed the available trust income.

[1] Income Tax Consequences for Grantor

A gift to a short-term trust may achieve significant income tax savings by shifting the taxability of income produced by the property given from the donor to another individual or to a trust.   The result may be to move income from the top income tax bracket to the bottom bracket, or may even cause such income to be tax-free because of the donee's personal exemption. Although income that is taxable to a trust when received may be subject under the so-called throwback rule [19] to an additional tax when it is distributed, income accumulated for a beneficiary who is unborn or under age 21 often is exempt from any such additional tax.[20]

The major problem in short-term trusts is whether income will be taxed to the grantor under the Clifford sections (§§ 671–677), which define the circumstances under which a grantor is treated as owner for income tax purposes of all, or a portion, of a trust.   In applying those provisions, it is necessary to determine:

(1) Who is the grantor?

(2) What is the effect if he is taxed as owner either of the entire trust or of a portion?

(3) What is the effect of requiring the consent of an adverse party to the exercise of a given power over the trust?

[a] Who Is the Grantor: Reciprocal Trusts

Taxpayers sometimes seek to avoid the Code provisions taxing a grantor as owner of all or a portion of a trust by creating trusts on a reciprocal basis. For example, A may create a trust with B as trustee, giving B uncontrolled discretionary power to distribute or accumulate income and principal among members of a group of beneficiaries which includes B's spouse, and B may in turn create a similar trust with A as trustee, giving A uncontrolled discretionary power over distributions of income and principal for a group of beneficiaries which includes A's spouse.   If either A or B had created a trust with his own spouse as a beneficiary, income which could be paid to the spouse would be taxable to the grantor whether or not it was in fact so paid.[21]   Under the reciprocal trust doctrine, A is treated as grantor of B's trust and B as grantor of A's, to the extent of the value of the smaller trust.[22]

---

19. §§ 665–667.   The throwback rule imposes an additional tax on beneficiaries who receive certain distributions that are deemed to represent accumulated trust income. For a discussion, see ¶ 11.02 infra.

20. See § 665(b).   For a discussion, see ¶ 11.05[2] infra.

21. § 677(a)(1).   See note 22 infra with respect to the effective date of this provision.

22. See Adolph K. Krause, 57 T.C. 890 (1972), aff'd 497 F.2d 1109, 74–1 USTC ¶ 9470 (6th Cir. 1974), cert. denied 419 U.S. 1108 (1975).   In *Krause*, A and B, who were husband and wife, were themselves beneficiaries of each other's trusts but the trusts were created before the amendment of § 677, which, in effect, treats an income interest in a spouse as the equivalent of an income interest in the grantor himself for purposes of applying the grantor trust provisions to tax income to him.   (The amendment is inapplicable to transfers on or before October 9, 1969.)   Thus, the decision does not deal with the effect of creation of reciprocal trusts in which the grantors were not beneficiaries of each other's trusts, but merely had powers to control enjoyment thereof.   However, the reciprocal trust doctrine has been applied for estate tax purposes despite the absence of beneficial interests in the trust grantors.   See Estate of Bruno Bischoff, ¶ 5.03 supra.

Example 9.4. Assume that *A*'s trust is funded with $100,000 and *B*'s trust is funded with $50,000. *A* is treated as grantor of *B*'s trust for income tax purposes, but *B* is treated as grantor of *A*'s trust only to the extent of one-half of its value.

If *B* makes a gift to a trust already created by *A*, *B* is treated as the grantor of an appropriate part of *A*'s trust.[23] And if community property is transferred in trust, each spouse is a grantor and consideration of tax consequences must take this into account.

[b] Effect if Grantor Taxed as Owner of All, or a "Portion," of Trust

A grantor who is taxable on trust income under the Clifford rules is taxed as "owner" of all, or a portion, of the trust,[24] not as a trust beneficiary. Taxation as owner differs in its consequences from taxation as a trust beneficiary under §§ 652 and 662 (for simple and complex trusts respectively). A beneficiary is taxable only on his share of the trust's "distributable net income."[25] If the grantor is taxed as owner of a trust, the trust income is treated as if he had received it directly, the deductions and credits of the trust are also included in computing his taxable income,[26] and the beneficiary is not taxed on amounts he receives. For this purpose, the trust's taxable year[27] and method of accounting[28] are ignored, and those of the grantor are used.

If the grantor is taxed as owner of a portion (or all) of the trust, he is entitled to the deductions relating to such portion even though they exceed the income. If the grantor is not taxed as owner, beneficiaries who are taxable on income of a trust generally may not use any of the trust's deductions except as they may reduce distributable net income. For example, a net loss may not be claimed on a beneficiary's return unless it represents a share of depreciation,[29] depletion[30] or amortization,[31] an unused loss carryover, or an "excess deduction" on termination of the trust.[32]

[i] Meaning of "Portion."

For planning purposes, the most useful aspect of the concept of "portion of a trust," as developed in the Regulations[33] dealing with taxation of the grantor as owner, is the characterization of ordinary income and corpus (principal) as separate portions. This means that the grantor may reserve the right to income without thereby incurring

---

23. See Nicholas A. Stavroudis, 27 T.C. 583 (1956), acq. 1957-1 CB 5.

24. § 671.

25. For a discussion, see ¶ 11.01[2] infra. "Distributable net income," defined in § 643(a), limits the amount deductible by the trust (§ 651) and includible by beneficiaries of a simple trust (§ 652), and limits similar deductions (§ 661) and inclusions (§ 662) by trustees and beneficiaries of a complex trust. No provision is made therein for deduction of losses.

26. See Reg. § 1.671-2(a).

27. See William Scheft, 59 T.C. 428 (1972); Rev.Rul. 57-390, 1957-2 CB 326.

28. Rev.Rul. 57-390, note 27 supra.

29. § 167(h).

30. § 611(b).

31. § 642(f). See Reg. § 1.642(f)-1, requiring apportionment of amortization deductions between the trust and its beneficiaries in the same manner as that provided for depreciation and depletion.

32. § 642(h).

33. See generally Reg. § 1.671-3. For a discussion of different meanings of "portion," see Larry W. Benson, 76 T.C.No. 86 (1981).

tax on capital gains realized by the trust (and without being entitled to deduct capital losses).[34]   Conversely, he may reserve the right to principal on termination of the trust without thereby incurring tax on ordinary income during the trust term.[35]   He will nevertheless be taxed on capital gains of the trust because they are, in effect, accumulated for future distribution to him.[36]

Thus, the "portion" rule is useful from an estate-planning standpoint both in preventing a reversionary interest in principal from causing the grantor to be taxed on ordinary income and in preventing a retained interest in income from causing the grantor to be taxed on capital gains.   The latter, however, is the more striking of the two consequences of the rule.   It is not particularly surprising that a grantor who will receive principal on termination of a trust, assuming such termination cannot occur before the time specified in § 673, is not taxed on ordinary income as a result, because in no meaningful sense does such ordinary income inure directly to the benefit of the grantor.[37]   The result with respect to a retained interest in income is more surprising.

If a 21-year-old female creates a trust of $100,000 under which she retains the right to receive the ordinary income for her life, the Commissioner's tables assign a value of $93,724 to her retained income interest so that the taxable gift to the remainderman is only $6,276.[38]   This result is based on the reasonable assumption that the bulk of the present worth of the trust is represented by the income interest, and hence that capital gains realized by the trust and reinvested will for many years benefit the grantor as income beneficiary.   Yet such gains are taxed to the trust and not to the grantor.[39]   Thus, the "portion" rule permits use of a trust as a vehicle for the realization of capital gains—both long-term and short-term—at a lower effective rate of tax without loss of income from the property sold.[40]

[ii] Possible Advantage in Taxation as Owner: Use to Hold Tax Shelter Properties.

Taxation of the grantor as owner of all, or a portion, of the trust could be advantageous if the trust assets included one or more tax shelter properties.   During the early years, when the shelters were generating losses, a related or subordinate party could be given such powers as trustee as to cause the grantor to be taxable as owner and hence able to

---

34. See Reg. § 1.671–3(b)(1).

35. See Reg. § 1.671–3(b)(2).

36. § 677(a)(2).

37. It may, of course, benefit the grantor indirectly if the income is used by the beneficiary in the same manner that the grantor would have used the income.   See ¶ 9.01[9] infra.

38. See Reg. § 25.2512–9(f), Table A(2).

39. There may be no advantage from having such gains taxed to the trust if the gain is realized from the sale or exchange of property within two years of its transfer in trust.   Such gain, to the extent of unrealized appreciation at the time of the transfer, is subject to the same tax that would have been imposed on the grantor if she had made the sale or exchange herself.   See § 644, discussed at ¶ 9.02[2][a] infra.

40. Revenue Ruling 60–370, 1960–2 CB 203, seeks to avoid this result by taxing the grantor on gains realized where the transfer is made with the understanding, express or implied, that the property will be sold and the proceeds invested in tax-exempt securities.   The reason given is that the transfer, in that situation, is of the proceeds of sale rather than of the securities transferred.   The Ruling deals only with reinvestment in tax-exempt securities.

deduct the losses.　When the shelters ceased to generate losses and began producing taxable income, the related or subordinate trustee could resign so that the powers that caused the grantor to be treated as owner would be held by an "independent" trustee designated as his successor.[41]　This change would shift the taxability of the income to the trust or its beneficiaries, if the grantor retained no reversionary interest in income or principal which would cause him to be taxable under § 677(a)(1)—a consideration which would be likely to require that a long-term, rather than a short-term trust be created for this purpose.

It is not surprising, however, to find this use of the grantor trust provisions resisted by the Commissioner.　He has ruled that, where the grantor's retained powers as trustee made him taxable as owner of a trust holding a partnership interest, a change to an independent trustee constituted a sale of the partnership interest.　The result was a realization of income by the grantor to the extent that the trust's share of partnership liabilities exceeded its basis in the partnership interest.[42]

[c]　Effect of Adverse Party's Required Consent

Powers or interests retained by a grantor that may cause him to be taxed on trust income under §§ 674–677 generally do not have that effect if their exercise or enjoyment requires the approval or consent of an adverse party.[43]　Section 672(a) defines "adverse party" as "any person having a

---

41.　§§ 674(c) and 674(d) delineate the powers that may be held by such trustees, respectively, without causing the grantor to be taxed as owner of the trust.

42.　Rev.Rul. 77–402, 1977–2 CB 222.　See also Reg. § 1.1001–2(c), *Example* (5).　In Glenn E. Edgar, 56 T.C. 717 (1971), the 11th issue was whether the grantor/life beneficiary of certain trusts could deduct the trusts' shares of partnership operating losses. The Tax Court, applying Reg. § 1.671–3(c), denied the deduction on the ground that the losses were attributable to the remainder rather than to the grantor's income interest.　The court did note that the economic effect of the losses did not fall on the current income beneficiary.　"Thus, the tax law accords with the economic realities."　56 T.C. at 762.　An economic reality test would be unfavorable from the standpoint of a grantor who sought to deduct trust losses because of retained powers over enjoyment of the trust, if he retained no interest in corpus.　See ¶ 4.01[2][b] supra. The *Edgar* case is discussed extensively in Schmolka, "Selected Aspects of the Grantor Trust Rules," 9th Inst. on Est. Planning ¶¶ 1400, 1403.2 (1975).

Commentators have expressed various views as to possible tax consequences of a change in the status of the trust where the grantor had been treated as owner for income tax purposes but is no longer so treated.　Compare Kantor, "Real Estate Tax Shelters," 51 Taxes 770 (1973), with Ginsburg, "The

Leaky Tax Shelter," 53 Taxes 719, 723–24 (1975) and Cowan, "Use of Grantor Trusts to Escape a Tax Shelter Without Detrimental Tax Effects," 41 J.Tax. 346 (1974).

The treatment under former § 453(d) (renumbered without change as § 453B(a)) of installment obligations transferred to trusts implies that a taxable transfer would occur on a change in status of the transferee trust. The Commissioner has ruled that a transfer of an installment obligation to a revocable trust is not a "disposition" on which gain must be recognized under former § 453(d). See Rev.Rul. 74–613, 1974–2 CB 153.　The same rule applies to a trust under which the grantor is, because of his retained reversionary interest, treated as owner of the portion consisting of the deferred profit included in the installment obligation.　See Rev.Rul. 67–70, 1967–1 CB 106.　Where the grantor is not so treated, the transfer to the trust is taxable.　See Rev.Rul. 67–167, 1967–1 CB 107; A.W. Legg v. Commissioner, 496 F.2d 1179, 74–1 USTC ¶ 9464 (9th Cir. 1974); Harold W. Smith, 56 T.C. 263 (1971), acq. 1972–1 CB 2.　If the grantor's powers prevent the initial transfer to the trust from being a disposition, failure to treat a change in the status of the trust, so that the grantor no longer is taxed as owner, as being such a disposition would mean that § 453B(a) never would apply to tax to the grantor gain represented by subsequent installment payments.

43.　See, e.g., § 674(a).

substantial beneficial interest in the trust which would be adversely affected by the exercise or nonexercise of the power which he possesses respecting the trust." The Regulations require that the value of the interest not be insignificant "in relation to the total value of the property subject to the power   *   *   *." [44] They further characterize the interest of a remainderman as being "adverse to the exercise of any power over the corpus of a trust   *   *   *," [45] but do not state that such an interest is necessarily "substantial," so as to cause the remainderman to be an adverse party.

Such an assumption was made in Floyd G. Paxton v. Commissioner: [46]

> For a sole remainderman, each dollar of trust corpus revested in the grantor costs a dollar.   His adversity is as strong as the grantor's advantage, so that we may fairly say his decision is beyond the grantor's control   *   *   *.

The Commissioner's tables, however, reflect a more realistic view of the dollar value of a remainder interest, which may be quite low if the life tenant is young.   For example, such tables give a present actuarial value of only 3.83 percent [47] to a remainder following a life estate in a two-year-old male. This is less than the value of the interest in *Paxton*, which was found to be too slight to make the holder an adverse party as to the entire trust, but sufficient to make him adverse as to his share.

If the court's dictum in *Paxton* as to the adversity of a sole remainderman is to be relied on without regard to the actuarial value of his interest, it is possible to construct a hypothetical case in which the adverse party exception could be used to avoid provisions that would otherwise tax the grantor as owner of the trust income.

Of course, the adverse party, by consenting to the exercise of a power which diminishes the value of his interest, makes a taxable gift to the person who benefits as a result. [48]   But the value of the gift may be small in a given case.

Example 9.5.   G establishes a trust with T as trustee to pay income to L for life, remainder to R.   During the life of L, principal may be paid to G with the consent of R.

If R were not an adverse party, his power to distribute principal to the grantor would cause the grantor to be taxed on the trust income under § 676.   If his remainder makes him an adverse party, however, the requirement of his consent keeps the grantor from being taxed on the trust income.   When R gives consent to a distribution of principal, which thereby diminishes the value of his remainder, he makes a taxable gift to G.   But if L is comparatively young when consent is given, the value of the gift will be small.   Under this view, G could receive principal throughout the life of L without being taxed on trust income as a result of the existence of the power.

44.   Reg. § 1.672(a)–1(a).

45.   Reg. § 1.672(a)–1(d).

46.   520 F.2d 923, 927, 75–2 USTC ¶ 9607, at 87,856 (9th Cir. 1975), cert. denied 423 U.S. 1016 (1975).

47.   Reg. § 25.2512–9(f), Table A(1).

48.   See, e.g., Reg. § 25.2514–3(e), *Example* (4).

This result seems unduly favorable to *G*, particularly in view of the fact that "adverse party" is defined in § 672(a) as being "any person," with no exclusion for "related or subordinate" parties as defined in § 672(c). Thus *G*'s wife or parent could be *R* in *Example 9.5* without changing the tax consequences to *G*.

Even if the *Paxton* dictum is not to be relied on, the Regulation's test of substantiality merely requires that the value of the interest not be "insignificant." [49] Thus, it is possible that the "adverse party" exception may be used to avoid some of the bite of §§ 673–677.

[2] Income Tax Consequences for Beneficiaries, Power Holders and Trust

If a trust is effective to shift the taxability of trust income from the grantor, the taxpayer to whom such income is shifted may be:

(1) the holder of a power to vest trust principal or income in himself; [50]

(2) a beneficiary who receives (or is entitled to receive) a distribution [51] or whose legal obligation to support a dependent is discharged by a distribution; [52] or

(3) the trust itself. [53]

Income that is taxed to a power holder is not subject to a second tax when it is distributed to him. [54] However, a power holder continues to be taxable on future trust income, or a portion thereof, if his power to vest income or principal in himself has been partially released and after such release the holder would be taxable as owner of the trust, or a portion thereof, under §§ 671–677, if he were a trust grantor. [55]

If trust income is accumulated, rather than being distributed currently each year, distributions in a later year in excess of the trust's distributable net income for that year may be subject to an additional tax under the throwback rule. [56] In that case, the tax paid by the trust for the year in which the income was earned is only a downpayment on the tax ultimately to be paid by the beneficiary receiving accumulated income.

In some situations, the trust may be regarded as having an identity for tax purposes separate from that of the beneficiaries or the grantor. However, a short-term trust which provides that principal shall be paid to the grantor when the trust terminates is likely to enjoy only limited recognition as a separate entity during the life of the grantor. If the potential advan-

---

49. Reg. § 1.672(a)–1(a). Cf. Prop.Reg. § 26.2613–2(b)(3)(ii) (right to withdraw 5 percent of the value of a trust is "substantial" for generation-skipping transfer tax purposes).

50. § 678.

51. § 652 (simple trusts); § 662 (complex trusts). For a discussion, see ¶ 11.01[2] infra.

52. Reg. § 1.662(a)–4. For a discussion, see ¶ 9.01[9][6] infra.

53. See § 641, discussed at ¶ 11.01[3] infra.

54. See Rev.Rul. 67–241, 1967–2 CB 225.

55. § 678(a)(2). For a discussion, see ¶ 12.01[3][c][ii] infra.

56. §§ 665–667. For a discussion, see ¶ 11.02 infra.

tages of separate status [56a] are important to the client, they are more likely to be secured by creating a non-reversionary trust.

[3] Effect of Retained Reversionary Interest (§ 673)

Section 673 taxes the grantor as "owner of any portion of a trust in which he has a reversionary interest in either the corpus or the income therefrom," if such interest will take effect the earlier of either ten years from the transfer in trust or upon the death of the income beneficiary (or beneficiaries).[56] The section presents little difficulty, from a planning standpoint, with respect to the initial creation of a trust, other than that arising from a time lag between the execution of the instrument and the transfer of property in trust, which starts the period running.

Additions to an existing trust and postponements of the date of reacquisition of the trust assets by the grantor also must satisfy the ten year or life of the beneficiary test. In the case of additions, the section will be applied separately to each transfer of property in trust.[57] Thus, a failure to satisfy the test will produce adverse tax consequences by causing the grantor to be taxed as owner of a portion of the trust representing the added property.[58]

The exception in § 673(c) for a reversionary interest taking effect on the death of "the person or persons to whom the income therefrom is payable" is available even though the life expectancy of the beneficiary is less than ten years.[59] Presumably, the exception requires that all beneficiaries of either current income or income accumulated for future distribution be included in the group whose lives measure the duration of the trust. Otherwise, it would be possible to give a trustee discretion to pay income to *A*, an octogenarian, or to accumulate it for ultimate distribution to *B*, a younger person, and to use *A*'s as the only measuring life for purposes of reversion. Such an interpretation would enhance the prospect of reversion to the grantor before ten years have expired even though the trust income is in fact paid to someone who lives longer than the trust term.

[4] Effect of Power to Control Beneficial Enjoyment (§ 674)

Many taxpayers would gladly transfer property in trust in order to shift the tax on the income produced by the property, if only they could retain the power to decide who should receive income for a given year, whether income should be accumulated, or how principal should be paid out. Indeed, if such a trust were effective for income tax purposes, it would offer the best of two tax worlds. The grantor's retained powers would make the transfer incomplete for gift tax purposes [60] and, thus, would avoid any gift tax until income or principal was in fact distributed.

Section 674, with stated exceptions, purports to block such avoidance

---

56a. See ¶ 9.02[2][b] infra.

56b. See Reg. § 1.673(a)–(1)(b).

57. See Rev.Rul. 58–567, 1958–2 CB 365, modified by Rev.Rul. 73–251, 1973–1 CB 324.

58. A "portion" may be either specific trust property, see Reg. § 1.671–3(a)(2), or an undivided fractional interest in the trust. See Reg. § 1.671–3(a)(3).

59. See Reg. § 1.673(a)–1(b). If the reversionary interest is to take effect on the death of the grantor, with income payable to others until then, the exception is inapplicable. See Rev.Rul. 58–567, note 57 supra.

60. See Reg. § 25.2511–2(c).

of taxes by treating the grantor as owner for income tax purposes if he or any non-adverse party has power to control the beneficial enjoyment of income or principal. As is so often true in tax matters, however, the exceptions are the heart of the rule. They permit numerous arrangements which allow grantors to retain a large measure of control, in one way or another, over the selection of beneficiaries of income and principal from time to time, without causing the grantor to be taxed on trust income.

Congress has provided three sets of powers for taxpayers interested in using trusts in this manner to shift taxable income. The first set may be exercised by the grantor, his spouse, or anyone else, without adverse income tax consequences to the grantor.[61] The second set of powers includes all those in the first set plus others. These additional powers may be exercised by trustees other than the grantor or his spouse (if living with him).[62] Permissible trustees include the grantor's relatives or subordinate employees. A third set of additional powers may be exercised by one or more trustees not including the grantor, if at least one-half of the trustees are not "related or subordinate parties who are subservient to the wishes of the grantor." [63]

The choice among these alternatives in a given case may be essentially between having the trustee preferred by the grantor exercise limited discretionary powers and having a trustee chosen from a restricted list exercise broader powers. Grantors may nevertheless avoid a choice and "have it both ways" if trustees chosen from the restricted list are sufficiently responsive to their wishes. Indeed, the grantor or his spouse may also be a trustee, as long as he or she is excluded by the terms of the instrument from formally participating in the exercise of objectionable powers. In this manner, the grantor may, without adverse income tax consequences, participate as trustee in investment decisions and business activities of the trust. He may also informally influence the exercise by other trustees of their powers to affect beneficial enjoyment, as long as his influence does not constitute the exercise of a power under express provisions of the trust instrument.[64]

Nevertheless, reliance on informal influence over other trustees strikes some clients as a risky proposition. Institutions may last forever but their trust officers do not. Clients may fear that the departure of those they know will mean that their wishes as to trust administration will no longer receive the same respectful attention. Even more marked risks may occur with individual trustees. The devoted son-in-law or daughter-in-law—a natural candidate for the office of independent trustee [65]—may, as a result of all-too-common marital vicissitudes, become an embittered, separated, or divorced spouse.

---

61. § 674(b). See ¶ 9.01[4] infra.

62. § 674(d).

63. § 674(c). "Related or subordinate party" is defined in § 672(c).

64. See Estate of Hilton W. Goodwyn, infra. Before the advent of the Internal Revenue Code of 1954, with its highly detailed and specific provisions delineating the circumstances under which grantors are and are not treated as owners for trust income tax purposes, a court could more readily treat a grantor as owner because of his general control over the trust. See Edward M. Goemans v. Commissioner, 279 F.2d 12, 60–2 USTC ¶ 9495 (7th Cir. 1960) (taxable years 1945–1947).

65. § 672(c) includes no relatives by marriage (except the grantor's spouse) in the definition of "related or subordinate party."

It is possible to guard against these eventualities in a variety of ways. The power to remove one "independent" trustee and substitute another may be reserved by the grantor [66] or given to someone else. The trust instrument may provide for removal of any trustee whose marriage to a beneficiary is terminated by divorce. In the absence of such a provision, arrangements for separation or divorce could include resignation of trusteeships. Finally, the grantor may decide to be trustee himself even though it narrows the permissible discretionary powers over distribution of income and principal that the trustee may hold without adverse income tax consequences for the grantor.

Such permissible powers, even though they are without objection from an income tax standpoint, may cause the trust property to be included in the grantor's estate for estate tax purposes if the trust does not terminate before his death.[67] And a power in the grantor to remove one "independent" trustee and substitute another, even though presently permissible under the Regulations without adverse income tax consequences, may cause inclusion of the trust property in the grantor's estate under Revenue Ruling 79–353.[68] The Ruling treats the decedent as having the powers of the trustee for estate tax purposes if he may remove the trustee at will and appoint another trustee, even if the decedent cannot substitute himself. Although there is some basis in existing decisions to question the validity of the Ruling, it may be sustained in relation to the estate tax and conceivably could lead to a modification of the trust income tax Regulations [69] in this respect as well. Thus, cautious advisors may prefer to give any power to remove a trustee to someone who is neither the grantor nor a beneficiary.

ESTATE OF HILTON W. GOODWYN

Tax Court of the United States, 1976.
35 T.C.M. 1026.

QUEALY, Judge—

FINDINGS OF FACT

*   *   *

From the outset until shortly before his death, the decedent exercised control over the investment and management of the trusts hereinbefore

---

66. See Reg. § 1.674(d)–2(a). For a case reaching a result that is inconsistent with these Regulations, see Warren H. Corning, 24 T.C. 907 (1955), aff'd per curiam 239 F.2d 646 (6th Cir. 1956) (taxable years 1946–1950). There the Tax Court held the grantor taxable on trust income because of an unrestricted power to remove the corporate trustee, reasoning that the "petitioner could substitute an independent corporate trustee after first ascertaining that such trustee would follow his directions. Should this corporate trustee subsequently fail to follow his instructions, petitioner could then replace it with another * * *. We cannot say that a trustee who is subject to removal without cause is to be presumed to be able to resist the grantor's influence in the allocation of in-

come or corpus among members of the grantor's family, for even if the trustee is, the grantor would probably substitute him with a trustee who would accede to the grantor's demands." 24 T.C. at 915.

If the grantor could substitute himself as trustee, the trust would not qualify under either §§ 674(c) or 674(d). See Reg. § 1.674(d)–2(a).

67. §§ 2036(a)(2); 2038. See ¶ 5.02[5] supra.

68. 79–1 CB 265, discussed at ¶ 5.02[5][b] supra.

69. See note 66 supra.

described, making all decisions with respect to sales and purchases of property, including transfers as between the respective trusts and other Goodwyn-related entities, and determining the income, if any, to be distributed to the beneficiaries. The actual functions performed by any of the individual trustees in relation to the attention required of these trusts was minimal.

All of the records of each of the aforementioned trusts were kept in the business office of the decedent and were maintained at his discretion. Separate books of account were not set up for each of the trusts. No individual accounting statements or balance sheets were prepared for any of these trusts. However, the individual transactions for each of the various trusts as well as other entities were recorded on the books of account maintained by the decedent. The income and assets of the trusts could be determined from these records.

A common bank account was maintained in the names of Richards and Russell for all of the trusts for which they were trustees. The records of this account were also maintained at the decedent's office. As the occasion required, decedent had checks drawn on this account in payment of mortgages or other assets acquired for the trusts, to pay the expenses of administering the trust, and for distribution to the beneficiaries. Such checks were thereupon signed by the trustees. At other times, blank checks were signed by the trustees to be used by the decedent for such purposes.

The decedent determined the amount of any distributions to the beneficiaries, and that determination was accepted without question by the trustees. Up until a few years prior to the decedent's death, the beneficiaries were not aware of the existence of the trusts.

In no instance did any of the individual trustees undertake any action independently of the decedent. The decedent determined what assets were to be acquired, the means of financing those acquisitions, from whom they were to be purchased, and in most, if not all, instances, the prices to be paid for them. He performed the same functions with the sale of trust assets. The decedent also controlled the making of loans between one entity and another. Besides the responsibilities he exercised over the trusts he personally created, he also managed other trusts created by his wife through powers of attorney executed to him by the respective trustees.

While there was considerable self-dealing between the decedent and the trusts, there appears no basis for any claim that the decedent profited thereby. In fact, respondent's determination in this case is predicated in part upon the fact that the trusts benefited by reason of the investment of the trusts' funds and management of the trusts' properties by the decedent.

* * *

OPINION

Trusts Created by Hilton W. Goodwyn

* * *

There is no question that Goodwyn created legally valid trusts under state law. The provisions of these trust instruments, including those regarding the rights, duties and obligations of the trustees demonstrate the grantor's intent to relinquish the ownership of the involved assets. Although many of the beneficiaries were unaware of the existence of these trusts, such notice is not a requirement for a valid trust.

Regarding the effect of the Federal income tax laws on these trusts, it is not contended here that the decedent reserved any right or power in any of the trusts whereby the income of these trusts could be attributed to the grantor. Additionally, it is clear that during the years in issue the trustees were not related or subordinate parties within the definition of 672(c) whose discretionary power to distribute or accumulate income to beneficiaries would attribute the income to the grantor. Rather, these trustees were independent trustees within the meaning of section 674(c), who may have such a discretionary power over income.

While the record indicates that the legal formalities have been complied with, it also indicates that the designated "independent" trustees, whether by agreement or otherwise, entrusted the management of the trusts' assets and the distribution of income therefrom to the sole discretion of the decedent. The decedent kept all the records, made all of the investments and decided the amount to be distributed to beneficiaries. The trustees merely acquiesced in these actions.

On the basis of these facts, the judicial decisions following the Supreme Court's decision in Helvering v. Clifford, 309 U.S. 331, 60 S.Ct. 554, 84 L.Ed. 788 (1940), and the later so-called *Clifford* regulations might well warrant the attribution of the income from these trusts to the decedent. However, to the extent these previous principles are not embodied in the present statutory provisions of the Code, they must be considered no longer applicable. Section 671 provides that subpart E represents the sole criterion of dominion and control under section 61 (relating to the definition of gross income) and thereby also under the *Clifford* doctrine.

The Report of the Committee on Ways and Means on the Internal Revenue Code of 1954 explains clearly that this exclusivity was the intent of Congress:

> It is also provided in this section [671] that no items of a trust shall be included in computing the income or credits of the grantor (or another person) solely on the grounds of his dominion and control over the trust under the provisions of section 61 (corresponding to sec. 22(a) of existing law). The effect of this provision is to insure that taxability of *Clifford* type trusts shall be governed solely by this subpart. However, this provision does not affect the principles governing the taxability of income to a grantor or assignor other than by reason of his dominion and control over the trust. Thus, this subpart has no application in situations involving assignments of future income to the assignor, * * * whether or not the assignment is to a trust; nor are the rules as to family partnerships affected by this subpart.[70]

Consequently, in order for a grantor to be held taxable pursuant to subpart E on the income of a trust which he has established, he must have one of the powers or retained interests proscribed by subpart E.

---

70. H.Rept.No. 1337, to accompany H.R. 8300 (Pub.L.No. 591), 83d Cong., 2d Sess. (1954), page a212.

The grantor's power to control beneficial enjoyment of either the principal or the income, within the limits defined in section 674, would result in attribution of the income to the grantor. Section 674 provides as a general rule:

> (a) General Rule.—The grantor shall be treated as the owner of any portion of a trust in respect of which the beneficial enjoyment of the corpus or the income therefrom is subject to a power of disposition, exercisable by the grantor or a nonadverse party, or both, without the approval or consent of any adverse party.

$$* \quad * \quad *$$

Although the trustees here would not be adverse parties, section 674(c) excepts the application of the general rule in certain circumstances which are applicable here.

Respondent would concede that none of the provisions of the trusts in issue would give the decedent the power proscribed by this section. It is respondent's argument, however, that although grantor does not specifically have such a power, his relationship to the trust res through its management and to the administration of these trusts generally is such that he should be deemed to be a trustee, in fact, during his life. Being considered a trustee, the trustee's power under the trust agreement to distribute or accumulate the income from these trusts would then make such income attributable to him under subpart E.

Respondent's contention in this respect is similar to that respondent raised in the Estate of Hilton W. Goodwyn, 32 T.C.Mem. 740 (1973). As relevant here, respondent argued in that case that the decedent should be treated as trustee, in fact, possessing such rights and powers as to cause the inclusion of the assets thereof in his gross estate under section 2036(a)(2). That section requires the inclusion in decedent's gross estate any property for which the decedent has retained the right, either alone or in conjunction with any person, to designate the persons who shall possess or enjoy the property or the income therefrom.

We found in that case there was no basis for such inclusion. The Supreme Court has held in United States v. Byrum, 408 U.S. 125, 136–7, 92 S.Ct. 2382, 2390, 33 L.Ed.2d 283, reh. denied 409 U.S. 898, 93 S.Ct. 94, 34 L.Ed.2d 157 (1972), that the right, upon which the inclusion under section 2036(a)(2) is predicated, is "an ascertainable and legally enforceable power," reserved in the trust instrument or by some other means. See also Estate of Charles Gilman, 65 T.C. 296, 316 (1975), on appeal (2d Cir., February 6, 1976). We found that Goodwyn had not retained such a right in the case of the Richards and Russell Trusts of which he was grantor.

In this case, while a different test is applicable, the tests are similar in character. Where section 2036(a) uses the term "right," section 674 uses the term "power." The House Ways and Means Committee Report, cited supra,[71] in its explanation of this section uses the term power in the legal sense of having an enforceable authority or right to perform some action. The use of this term in this legal sense suggests that the power of a grantor upon which he will be taxed is a power reserved by instrument or contract

---

71. H.Rept.No. 1337, supra, at pages a214–216.

creating an ascertainable and legally enforceable right, not merely the persuasive control which he might exercise over an independent trustee who is receptive to his wishes.   Such interpretation is also, we believe, indicated by the holding in the *Byrum* case.

In this case, the trustees in question accepted the rights, duties and obligations granted them in the trust instruments.   Regardless of the fact they had entrusted to the decedent the complete management and control of these trusts, this informal delegation did not discharge them from the legal responsibility they had as the trustees.   As a matter of law, the trustees were liable and answerable for the decedent's acts on their behalf. See 2 Scott, Trusts 1388, 1391 (3rd ed., 1967); 3 Scott, Trusts 1794 (3rd ed., 1967).

There is nothing in the record to show that the trustees could not have undertaken exclusive control of the trust res if they had elected to do so. Whatever power Goodwyn exercised over the trust assets, administration or distribution, he did so on the trustee's behalf and not in his own right.

Because of Goodwyn's failure to have a legally enforceable right, we have already held, following *Byrum*, that the assets of these trusts were not includable in the decedent's estate under 2036(a)(2).   Since a similar legal right or power is a prerequisite under section 674(a), consistency appears to require the same decision with respect to the applicability of this section.   We see no other possible decision.

Section 671 precludes attributing the income to Goodwyn on any other theory of dominion and control under the definition of gross income, including the *Clifford* doctrine.   We interpret this limitation to mean that if Goodwyn cannot be considered as a trustee, in fact, under the statutory provisions of subpart E, he cannot be considered as such by virtue of the judicial doctrines arising from the *Clifford* case which Congress intended to limit through the enactment of subpart E.   But the protection of section 671, as explained in the House Ways and Means Committee Report, cited supra, does not extend to situations involving the assignments of future income.

As heretofore stated, the respondent concedes that the decedent's stewardship greatly enhanced the value of the trusts.   No claim can be made that the decedent took advantage of his role as manager of the trusts and custodian of the trusts' assets.   In fact, there is no record to show that the decedent ever took any compensation for his efforts.

In recognition of the fact that the trusts realized substantial income as a result of the decedent's management, respondent would attribute such income to the decedent.   Respondent therefore argues that there resulted, through the manipulation of the trusts, an assignment by the decedent of income attributable to his efforts, citing Lucas v. Earl, 281 U.S. 111, 50 S.Ct. 241, 74 L.Ed. 731 (1930); Lyman A. Stanton, 14 T.C. 217 (1950). Respondent contends that decedent enjoyed the income, which was realized as a result of his management, in that the decedent determined to which beneficiaries the income would be distributed, if at all.   Helvering v. Horst, 311 U.S. 112, 61 S.Ct. 144, 85 L.Ed. 75 (1940).

Respondent is not arguing here that any portion of the income from these trusts should be allocated to the decedent as compensation for the services provided. Rather respondent is contending that decedent should be taxed on the total amount of the trust income because his arrangements amount to no more than [an] attempt to assign income produced by his industry, efforts, contacts and reputation through his control of the administration of the trust.

According to the cases relied upon by the respondent, either capital could not have been the primary factor in the production of the trust income, as in the *Stanton* case, or, as in the *Horst* case, Goodwyn must have retained control over the capital merely assigning the income therefrom.

In the *Stanton* case, we found that capital was a relatively unimportant factor in the production of trust income compared with the services provided the trust by the grantor-trustee. In the present case, there is little question that the capital represented by the mortgages and the real property comprising the assets of these trusts was the primary factor in the production of the trust income. Goodwyn merely managed and directed the investment of that capital.

His managerial role was clearly not indispensable to the production of the trust income. Shortly before Goodwyn's death the real estate firm of Bailey & Childress, Inc., took over his management of the assets of these trusts. Bailey & Childress is a firm which specializes in providing the management of mortgages and real property of the kind contained in these trusts.

Respondent would concede that the income earned by these trusts was not taxable to Bailey & Childress. If this firm is willing to provide management of these assets for a reasonable fee, such a management function cannot constitute an assignment of income as alleged by respondent. Consequently, it is clear in this case that capital was the primary factor in the production of the trust income. Where income is derived from capital, tax liability for such income follows ownership. Lyman A. Stanton, supra, at 225.

We have already amply discussed Goodwyn's control of the trust res. As he had relinquished all legal right to the corpus of the trusts, respondent's contentions in this regard cannot be sustained.

* * *

[a] Trustee's Power to Control Investments

An important power to affect enjoyment, as between the income beneficiary and the remainderman, is control over investments. Without committing a breach of trust, it often is possible for a trustee to favor securities providing a high current yield but generally regarded as offering minimal prospects for price appreciation, or securities with little or no current yield but generally believed to have impressive growth prospects. At some point, an overbroad investment power could have adverse gift tax consequences by causing an otherwise allowable present interest exclusion to be denied.[72] But the permissible scope in choice of investments appears to be quite broad and provides, in effect, a large measure of control over enjoyment.

---

72. See ¶ 9.01[10][b][ii] infra.

[b] Powers Over Income

Permissible powers over income generally provide as much latitude as a client is likely to want if the trust is primarily for a single beneficiary. Income may be withheld during the beneficiary's legal disability, or while he is under age 21, and added to corpus even though the corpus may ultimately be distributed to other beneficiaries.[73] Income may also be withheld temporarily if it must ultimately be paid to the beneficiary, his estate, or his appointees [74] or if it is part of irrevocably specified shares of corpus.[75]

If there is more than one beneficiary, it is often difficult to fit the powers the client is likely to want within the narrow confines of § 674(b). In that situation, the client often does not wish to commit himself as to the manner in which income will be allocated among the beneficiaries, but § 674(b) requires that their shares be specified in the trust instrument rather than left to the trustees to determine from time to time. If the trustees are to have such a power, they should be so chosen as to qualify under § 674(c) as "independent" trustees.

Section 674(d), which permits certain related or subordinate trustees who are not "independent" within the meaning of § 674(c) to allocate income if their power is limited by an appropriate standard, is a less attractive alternative. Applying such a standard in allocating income between two or more beneficiaries is complicated.

None of the permissible powers over income under §§ 674(b)(6), 674(b)(7), 674(c), or 674(d) may include the power to add beneficiaries, except to provide for after-born or after-adopted children. If the description of the beneficiaries in the trust instrument if broad enough to include everyone the grantor might wish to receive distributions from the trust, however, there is no need to give the trustee a power to amend the description to add others.

[c] Powers Over Principal

Permissible powers to distribute principal generally provide as much latitude as a client is likely to want if the trust is primarily for a single beneficiary. Section 674(b)(5)(B) permits a power to distribute principal "to or for any current income beneficiary" if the distribution must be charged against the share held for the payment of income to him. If he is the only beneficiary, this standard is easily met and it becomes unnecessary to resort to the alternative in § 674(b)(5)(A), which permits a power to distribute principal if limited by "a reasonably definite standard which is set forth in the trust instrument."

If there is more than one primary beneficiary, the desired powers over principal may not fit comfortably within § 674(b)(5)(B). Charging distributions to different income beneficiaries against the respective shares from which they receive income makes bookkeeping more complicated. If sep-

---

73. § 674(b)(7). Of course if the grantor has a reversionary interest in corpus, he will be taxed under § 677(a)(2), notwithstanding compliance with the requirements of § 674(b). This follows from the fact that income added to principal is accumulated for future distribution to him.

74. See Reg. § 1.674(b)–1(b)(7).

75. § 674(b)(6).

arate shares are to be maintained, it might be preferable to create a separate trust for each income beneficiary. The alternative is a power limited by a standard under § 674(b)(5)(A), and the Regulations contain several illustrations of acceptable standards [76] that give a trustee a large measure of discretion.

None of the permissible powers over principal under §§ 674(b)(5) and 674(c) may include the power to add beneficiaries, except to provide for after-born and after-adopted children.

The tax problem with powers to distribute principal, other than a power exercisable by the donor either alone or in conjunction with someone having no adverse interest, is that such powers may make it impossible to value the donor's retained reversionary interest in the trust. In that case, the gift for purposes of the gift tax will be of the entire value of the property transferred in trust, without any deduction for the value of the interest retained by the grantor. [77]

[d] Power to Allocate Receipts and Disbursements Between Principal and Income

Section 674(b)(8) permits creation of a power to allocate receipts and disbursements between principal and income. It is often useful to avoid recourse to the sometimes uncertain or unsatisfactory rules provided for this purpose by local law.

[e] Powers of Appointment

Any power of appointment by its nature is a power to affect beneficial enjoyment. Its existence, therefore, will cause the grantor to be taxed, under § 674(a), on income of any portion of a trust subject to the power, unless the power fits within one of the exceptions in § 674(b). If the power is held by one or more trustees, an exception in § 674(c) or § 674(d) may apply. The exceptions in § 674(b) which are particularly relevant to powers cover:

(1) Powers exercisable only by will (other than certain powers over income held by the grantor); [78] and

(2) Powers to appoint among charitable beneficiaries. [79]

The list does not include powers to appoint by deed (i.e., during the holder's life) among non-charitable beneficiaries. If a power is created that is not covered by one of the exceptions in § 674, it should be made exercisable only after the death of the grantor, when he no longer may be taxed as owner of trust income. [80]

The exception for powers exercisable by will covers only the existence of the power, not the revisions of the trust terms that may result from its exercise. For example, if G creates a trust over which P is given a testamentary power of appointment, it may be exercised to create another

76. See Reg. § 1.674(b)–1(b)(5)(i).

77. See Reg. § 25.2511–1(e).

78. § 674(b)(3).

79. § 674(b)(4).

80. See D. G. McDonald Trust, 19 T.C 672 (1953), acq. 1953–2 CB 5, aff'd sub nom. Chase Nat'l Bank v. Commissioner, 225 F.2d 621, 55–2 USTC ¶ 9649 (8th Cir. 1955), cert. denied 350 U.S. 965 (1956).

power to control beneficial enjoyment, which power is not covered by any of the exceptions from the general rule of § 674(a).   As a result, the grantor would become taxable as owner of the trust as soon as *P*'s exercise of his power takes effect.

[f] Powers to Apply Income for Support of a Dependent

The practical significance of this exception is unclear because it is difficult to determine, either from the Code or the Regulations, what kind of power it covers.   Section 674(b)(1) refers to "a power described in section 677(b)."   However, § 677(b) deals with the tax consequences of powers which may be exercised to support a dependent of the grantor.   Such consequences do not turn on the disposition which would be made of the income if the power to use it to discharge the grantor's support obligation is not exercised.

Section 674(b), on the other hand, deals with powers which allow choices to be made.   Certain choices, such as distributing or accumulating income for a single primary beneficiary, are permissible, and others, such as allocating income among beneficiaries, may cause the grantor to be taxed as owner of the trust.   Section 674(b)(1) makes permissible a power to make some kind of choice, but the scope of that choice remains unclear.

> *Example 9.6.*   G creates a trust with *W*, his wife, as trustee, to pay income to *C*, *G*'s 10 year old child.   In *W*'s discretion, any income may either be accumulated or may be used for *C*'s support;   accumulated income is to be paid to *C* when the trust terminates and the principal is to be returned to *G*.

It appears that § 674 should cover *Example 9.6*, if it is to have any effect whatsoever, as the power to use income for support in that *Example* does not permit it to be diverted from any other beneficiary.   In *Example 9.7* below, on the other hand, income otherwise payable to one beneficiary may be used to support another beneficiary as a result of the exercise of the trustee's support power.   It is questionable whether the section covers that case.

> *Example 9.7.*   G creates a trust with *W*, his wife, as trustee, to pay income to his mother, *M*, for her life, and on her death to return the principal to *G*.   *W* may in her discretion from time to time use income to support *C*, a minor child of *G*.

[g] Postponed Powers

Section 674(b)(2) exempts a power which is exercisable only to affect enjoyment after expiration of the period specified in § 673.   The grantor may, of course, be unwilling to surrender his control over principal and income for a longer period.   If he wants to have control after ten years, he could provide that the trust terminate at the end of that period and the principal be returned to him.   When that has happened, he can, if he wishes and is still competent, create a new trust.   This course, however, may cause termination commissions to be due the trustee and cannot be followed if the grantor is no longer competent (unless state law permits estate planning transfers to be made on behalf of incompetent individuals).[81]   Providing

---

81.   See, e.g., Mass.Gen. Laws Ann.Ch. 201,
    § 38.   (West Supp.1980).

a longer initial term, coupled with powers (exercisable only after the required minimum period) to revoke the trust or alter its terms, may avoid these problems.

[5] Permissible Powers of "Independent" Trustees

Section 674(c) further broadens the permissible powers over both income and principal which may be exercised by trustees if none is the grantor and if "no more than half   *   *   *   are related or subordinate parties who are subservient to the wishes of the grantor   *   *   * ."   Such trustees may be given unlimited discretion to distribute or accumulate income or to pay out principal, as long as beneficiaries cannot be added (except for after-born or after-adopted children).   The section invites a grantor to use trustees who are formally independent but who are likely to be responsive to his wishes.   In a given case, the candidates may include a lawyer or accountant or a relative not on the forbidden list, such as a niece, a nephew, or an in-law.   And a professional fiduciary is also likely to turn to the grantor, for his special knowledge of the needs and circumstances of the beneficiaries, to guide the exercise of discretionary powers over distributions.

Support for a formalistic interpretation of "independent" is provided by Estate of Goodwyn,[82] in which the court rejected the Commissioner's attempt to treat as the trustee a grantor to whom designated "independent" trustees "entrusted the management of the trusts' assets and the distribution of income therefrom   *   *   * ." [83]

The Regulations even permit a further check on any undue display of independence by a trustee, in the form of a power in the grantor to remove him and substitute another "independent" trustee in his place.[84]   That power may not insure that the named trustee will be responsive to the grantor's wishes, but if he is not, someone else may be substituted who will be.

[6] Planning Aspects of Power to Control Enjoyment

The preceding paragraphs suggest that the choice among practical alternatives under § 674 is between § 674(b), if the grantor wants to be trustee himself or to choose from a list which includes his wife, descendants, siblings, and employees, and § 674(c) if he is willing to forego having a completely free hand in selection of trustees.   Section 674(d) provides a third alternative if he is willing to forego naming himself or his wife but wants the freedom to choose as trustee, persons who are descendants, siblings, or employees.   But the advantages of doing so, rather than using "independent" trustees under § 674(c), are likely to be outweighed by the more limited scope of the discretionary powers which are permissible under § 674(d).

Section 674(b) is useful for trusts with one primary beneficiary, where the convenience and economy of naming the grantor or a close relative as trustee is desired and greater discretionary powers are not necessary. Although the grantor may be trustee of such a trust without adverse income tax consequences, in many instances he should not be trustee if he is seeking

---

82.   ¶ 9.01[4] supra.   84.   See note 66 supra.

83.   35 T.C.M. at 1038.

to remove the trust property from his taxable estate. The discretionary powers over income or principal, which are permissible for the grantor from an income tax standpoint under § 674(b), may nevertheless make the trust property includible in his taxable estate.[85]

Trusts that do not fit within the pattern just described for § 674(b) should be qualified under § 674(c) by naming one-half "independent" trustees. The grantor should not be a trustee, or, if he is, he should be excluded by the terms of the trust from participation in the exercise of any objectionable power.

[7] Effect of Administrative Powers and Loans to the Grantor (§ 675)

Section 675 reflects a recognition that powers of administration may have the substantial effect of permitting a grantor to control the beneficial enjoyment of a trust. Basically, the section provides that if either the grantor or a non-adverse party can dispose of principal or income of a trust without being required to act as a fiduciary, the grantor will be treated as the owner for tax purposes. This section gives this effect to the following powers:

(1) To acquire or deal with trust property or income "for less than an adequate consideration in money or money's worth; "[86]

(2) To borrow trust property or income "without adequate interest or without adequate security" except under a general lending power exercisable by a trustee other than the grantor;[87]

(3) to vote securities, or to control investments, in a non-fiduciary capacity;[88] and

(4) "To reacquire the trust corpus by substituting other property of equivalent value."[89]

Section 675(3) treats the grantor as owner of any portion[90] of a trust if he "has directly or indirectly borrowed the corpus or income and has not completely repaid the loan, including any interest, before the beginning of the taxable year." The section then excepts loans with adequate interest and security that are made by independent trustees.

[8] Effect of Power to Revoke (§ 676)

Section 676 treats the grantor as owner of any trust subject to a power to revest title in him prior to expiration of the period specified in § 673. In most cases, such a power would be covered by § 674, so that it is unnecessary to apply § 676 to tax the grantor. Section 676 does close one loophole: A power in an "independent" trustee to pay principal to the grantor is within the exception in § 674(c)(2), if "beneficiary" includes the grantor himself. Such a power over principal is covered by § 676 and renders the grantor taxable as the owner of any portion of the trust subject to the

---

85. See § 2036(a)(2) and § 2038, discussed at ¶ 5.02[5] supra.

86. § 675(1).

87. § 675(2).

88. § 675(4).

89. Id.

90. For a discussion of the meaning of "portion," see Larry W. Benson, 76 T.C. No. 86 (1981).

power.　Such a power to pay him income (but not principal) is covered by § 677(a)(2).

New York Estates, Powers & Trusts Law 7—1.11(a) provides:

Notwithstanding any contrary provision of law, the trustee of an express trust, unless otherwise provided in the disposing instrument, may, from time to time, pay from principal to the creator of such trust an amount equal to any income taxes on any portion of the principal with which he is charged.

Subsection (b) makes the provision inapplicable to certain trusts with charitable future interests.　The provision would appear to create a power in a trustee which would cause the grantor to be taxable as owner of at least a portion of the trust under § 676 by authorizing principal to be paid to him. The extent of that power would ordinarily depend upon the amount of capital gains realized by the trust (and any other income allocable to principal) taxable to the grantor because of being accumulated for distribution to him when the trust terminates.　In a given case it might be possible to establish that the portion of principal which could be paid to the grantor pursuant to the statutory provision and within the period specified in § 673 is less than the entire trust.　But even if the grantor's liability could be thus limited, the part of prudence is to exclude the application of the statutory provision altogether.

[9] Effect of Possible Use of Income for Benefit of Grantor (or His Spouse) (§ 677)

Section 677 is captioned "Income for Benefit of Grantor," and, if the judicial and administrative construction of the section reflected as broad a view of "benefit" as that commonly taken by grantors themselves, a great deal of estate planning to save income taxes by lifetime transfers in trust would be thwarted.　For example, many parents would agree that the use of trust income to provide for the education of their children in college or in a professional school substantially benefits the parents, even though they may not be obligated to provide such education as a matter of state law. And many grandparents feel that the accumulation of trust income for their grandchildren similarly benefits the grandparents as well by carrying out their desires to transmit wealth to the oncoming generation.　In fact, however, both the language of the section and its construction by courts and administrators embody a far narrower view.　Indeed, the section refers to only three forms of "benefit":

(1) Distribution of income to the grantor or his spouse; [91]　and

(2) Payment of premiums on insurance on the life of either of them;

(3) Discharge of obligations of support.

Discharge of legal obligations is generally treated in the same manner as a distribution; [92] otherwise, it would be possible for the grantor to incur bills which could then be paid out of trust income without causing him to

---

91. Spouses were added here and elsewhere in § 677 by the Tax Reform Act of 1969. The revision is effective only for amounts transferred in trust after October 9, 1969. See Reg. §1.677(a)–1(b)(2).

92. See Reg. § 1.677(a)–1(d).

be taxed on it.   But support obligations are treated differently from all other obligations of the grantor or his spouse.   With respect to support of their dependents, the mere possibility that income may, in a trustee's discretion, be used to discharge the obligation is not enough to make the grantor taxable.[93]   His liability is limited to income which is in fact used for this purpose.   With respect to the possible distribution of income to the grantor or to his spouse, or its use to discharge any of their obligations other than support of dependents, the mere possibility is enough to cause the grantor to be taxed on such income even though none is ever in fact used for that purpose.

Four major problems arise in dealing with the use of trust income for the benefit of the grantor:

(1) What constitutes a "support obligation" for federal income tax purposes;

(2) When has such a support obligation been discharged with trust income;

(3) When is the grantor taxable because the trust income may be used to pay off the grantor's debts and taxes, or the property is subject to liabilities when it is transferred in trust; and

(4) When is the grantor taxable because the trust income may be used to pay off premiums on insurance on his life, or that of his spouse.

[a] What Constitutes a "Support Obligation" for Federal Income Tax Purposes?

This paragraph will focus on the meaning of "support obligation" for trust income tax purposes.   The term may have a different meaning for estate, gift, and generation-skipping transfer tax purposes.[94]

Use of trust income to discharge a support obligation may affect the taxation of trust income in three situations:

(1) A grantor who is legally obligated to provide support for another person may establish a trust naming that person as the beneficiary. When the trust income discharges the grantor's support obligation within the meaning of § 677(a)(2) that income is taxable to the grantor under § 677.   In effect, the trust income is treated as though it had first passed through the hands of the grantor, who then paid it to the beneficiary to meet the support obligation.

(2) A related situation arises when income from a trust established by someone other than the obligor is used for the beneficiary's support (e.g., income a child receives from a trust established by his grandparents).   In this situation also, the trust income may be taxable to the obligor even though he is not the grantor, under Regulations § 1.662(a)(4).

(3) Finally, a trustee may, at his discretion, be authorized to apply trust income to the support of a person that the trustee is legally required to support.   To the extent such income is used for such support, it is taxed to the trustee rather than to the beneficiary.[95]

---

93. § 677(b).   95. § 678(a), as limited by § 678(c).

94. See ¶ 5.02[4][a][i] supra.

Regulations Section 1.662(a)–(4) generally [96] provides that an obligor will be taxed on any trust income used to discharge a legal obligation. It states that·

> The term 'legal obligation' includes a legal obligation to support another person if, and only if, the obligation is not affected by the adequacy of the dependent's own resources. For example, a parent has a 'legal obligation' within the meaning of the preceding sentence to support his minor child if under local law property or income from property owned by the child cannot be used for his support so long as his parent is able to support him   *   *   * .

State law is important here because it determines whether the independent resources of a person entitled to support affect the support obligation within the meaning of this Regulation.[97]

The point that this Regulation makes is best illustrated by way of example: In State *A*, a parent may be required to provide support for a minor child regardless of the magnitude of the child's independent resources—i.e., the child's resources do not affect the extent of the parent's support obligation. In this case, the parent will be taxed on the child's trust income if that income is applied to the child's support.[98] By contrast, in State *B*, the existence and extent of a support obligation may depend on the child's resources. Those resources "affect" the support obligation because, if they are sufficient to support the child, the parent's legal obligation to provide support is reduced or eliminated. Thus in State *B*, even though the trust income is used to discharge the support obligation, the income is not taxable to the parent.

Since all states require that a parent provide some minimal support for his minor child, the most significant obligations in connection with the taxation of trust income are those of parent to child. Support obligations between spouses can be important in determining the tax consequences of transfers in connection with separation or divorce.[99] These obligations usually are not significant in an ongoing marriage, however, because the great majority of spouses file joint returns, and the problem of which spouse the trust income should be taxed to does not arise.

Obligations to parents and other relatives ordinarily are affected by the resources of the person to whom the obligation is owed,[100] and thus are outside the scope of the definition in the Regulations.

---

96. Alimony payments governed by § 71 and alimony trusts governed by § 682 are excluded.

97. This Regulation deals with complex trusts, but is made applicable to simple trusts as well. See Reg. § 1.652(a)–1, last sentence. Regulations Section 1.662(a)–4 deals with taxation of beneficiaries and does not expressly apply to other situations in which trust income may be taxed to a support obligor because of its use to discharge his obligations. However, cross references to it appear in regulations dealing with trust grantors, see Reg. § 1.677(b)–1(b), and nongrantors who hold powers to apply principal or income to the discharge of their support obligations. See Reg. § 1.678(c)–1.

98. Although Reg. § 1.662(a)–4 purports to tax obligors on any trust income which discharges his or her support obligation, there is some case law which implies that income from a trust established by someone other than the obligor will not be taxed to the obligor, even though it is used to provide support for his or her dependent. See William B. J. Tibbitts, 24 TCM 663 (1965); Frank E. Joseph, 5 T.C. 1049 (1945), acq. 1946–1 CB 3; Helen V. Stern v. Commissioner, 137 F.2d 43, 43–2 USTC ¶ 9541 (2d Cir. 1943).

99. For a discussion, see ¶ 8.05 supra.

100. See, e.g., Cal.Civ.Code § 242 (West Supp.1980).

Determining whether a support obligation is affected by a child's resources is by no means easy in light of variations in state law. State law is often fragmentary and incomplete, and little case law has developed since it is still unusual for a child to sue a parent for support.[101] Most litigation arises between divorced or divorcing spouses over who will pay the child's expenses,[102] or occasionally it arises in suits by third parties for "necessaries" furnished to minor children.[103] The only safe generalization is that states lie along a spectrum, beginning with those in which a parent fairly clearly has an obligation to support his child regardless of the child's resources.[104] At the other end of the spectrum are a few states such as Louisiana, where a child's independent resources may eliminate any parental support obligation,[105] and Georgia, where use of trust or estate income that is available for the benefit of a dependent for the dependent's support reduces the obligation to the extent that such income is so used.[106]

In California, for example, there is some basis for contending that a child's independent wealth and income may be considered in fixing the amount of the parental obligation in excess of basic support.[107] And Rhode Island provides:

> To the extent that any such minor child has property or an estate of his or her own, or that there is income or principal of any trust for his or her benefit, which may be used to provide such child with an education in a college, university or private school, such [parents] shall not be obligated either jointly or separately to provide such an education.[108]

A literal reading of Regulations Section 1.662(a)–4 conceivably could free parents in these two states from taxation on most trust income used to support their children, since the child's resources *affect* the parental obligation. Other relevant variations in parental obligations under state law include whether the mother's obligation differs from the father's,[109] and

---

101. But see Armstrong v. Armstrong, 15 Cal.3d 942, 126 Cal.Rptr. 805, 544 P.2d 941 (1976); In re Roe v. Doe, 29 N.Y.2d 188, 324 N.Y.S.2d 71, 272 N.E.2d 567 (1971).

102. See, e.g., Anderson v. Anderson, 437 S.W.2d 704 (Mo.App.1969).

103. See, e.g., Greenspan v. Slate, 12 N.J. 426, 97 A.2d 390 (1953) (payment of medical bills).

104. See, e.g., In re Estate of Weisskopf, 39 Ill.App.2d 380, 188 N.E.2d 726 (1963) (mother with sufficient means required to support children although they had independent resources); In re Guardianship Estates of Kaufman, 429 S.W.2d 612 (Tex.Civ.App.1968) (child's resources may be used for support only if parent is unable to provide support); Slaughter v. Slaughter, 313 S.W.2d 193 (Mo.App.1958) (child's resources cannot be used for support, except income from trust established expressly to provide support).

See generally, Report of Committee on Taxation of Trust Income, "Trust Income Tax-

ation and the Obligation of Support," 1 Real.Prop., Prob. & Tr.J. 327 (1966).

105. See Maggio v. Papa, 206 La. 38, 18 So.2d 645 (1944).

106. See Ga. Code Ann. § 23–2311 (1978), construed in McElrath v. Citizens & Southern Nat'l Bank, 229 Ga. 20, 189 S.E.2d 49 (1972).

107. Armstrong v. Armstrong, 15 Cal.3d 942, 126 Cal.Rptr. 805, 544 P.2d 941 (1976).

108. R.I. Gen. Laws § 33–15–1 (Supp.1980).

109. Compare, e.g., Tex. Fam. Code Ann., tit. 1, § 4.02 (Vernon Supp.1980), and Conway v. Dana, 456 Pa. 536, 318 A.2d 324 (1974) (interpreting Pennsylvania constitution), imposing an equal duty upon each spouse to contribute according to his or her means, with Mo.Ann.Stat. § 452.340(1) (Vernon 1977) and Ohio Rev.Code Ann. § 3103.03 (Page 1980), imposing the primary obligation on the father. Such sex-based distinctions may be constitutionally

whether the obligation terminates when the child reaches age 18 or continues until the child has reached age 21.[110]

Exactly what expenses are deemed to be within the scope of the parental obligation, for purposes of taxing trust income to the obligor, is often unclear. On the one hand, a support obligation may be viewed as a requirement to expend a certain amount each year. Under this unitary view of the obligation, trust income used for any aspect of a child's support in a state like Rhode Island would not be taxable to the parent. On the other hand, the duty to support a child may be viewed as a number of distinct obligations—to provide food, housing, clothing, education, etc. Each obligation could be viewed separately to determine whether it is affected, under state law, by the resources of the child. If, as in Rhode Island, the obligation to provide education is so affected, trust income used to educate a child would not be taxable to the parent, but such income used to feed or clothe the child would be so taxable unless those obligations were also affected by the child's resources.

Generally, the items included within the obligation are determined by the parent's "station in life," [111] and the obligation ordinarily is held to include college expenses during minority,[112] doubtlessly reflecting the predominant economic class of litigants in such cases. In states in which minority ends at age 18, however, there may be no significant parental obligation for such expenses unless the child starts college early.[113]

Whether a private secondary school education will be held to be within the scope of the parental support obligation is more debatable. Two cases have refused to tax parents on amounts expended for tuition at such schools and for fees for various lessons.[114] However, a further hurdle taxpayers

impermissible after Stanton v. Stanton, 421 U.S. 7, 95 S.Ct. 1373, 43 L.Ed.2d 688 (1975), where the Court invalidated a state statute requiring parents to support male children to a greater age than female children. See also Orr v. Orr, 440 U.S. 268, 99 S.Ct. 1102, 59 L.Ed.2d 306 (1979) (Alabama statute requiring only husbands to pay alimony held unconstitutional); Califano v. Goldfarb, 430 U.S. 199, 97 S.Ct. 1021, 51 L.Ed.2d 270 (1977) (sex-based difference in Social Security benefits held unconstitutional).

110. Compare, e.g., N.Y.Dom.Rel.L. §§ 32(2), 32(3), (McKinney 1980) (21 years), with Cal.Civ. Code §§ 25, 241(d), 242 (West Supp.1980) (18 years). The California statute also imposes a parental obligation to support a child "of whatever age who is incapacitated from earning a living and without sufficient means." Id. § 241(d).

111. See, e.g., Buchanan v. Buchanan, 353 Mass. 351, 231 N.E.2d 570 (1967); Cal.Civ.Code § 246(g) (West Supp.1980).

112. See, e.g., Herzmark v. Herzmark, 199 Kan. 48, 427 P.2d 465 (1967).

But see Emrick v. Emrick, 445 Pa. 428, 431, 284 A.2d 682, 683 (1971): "[A] father has no duty to aid in providing a college edu-

cation for his child, no matter how deserving, willing or able a child may be, unless the father has sufficient estate, earning capacity or income to enable him to do so without undue hardship to himself." Such hardship was held to preclude paternal liability for any support for a child attending college in Commissioner ex rel. Hanerkam v. Hanerkam, 221 Pa.Super 182, 289 A.2d 742 (1972).

113. In New York, however, even though minority ends at age 18 (N.Y. EPTL 1-2.9-a) a father is liable for support until the child reaches age 21. See N.Y.Dom. Rel.L. 32(2).

Liability for support after a child reaches majority, including college expenses, may also be imposed by a separation agreement or divorce decree. See, e.g., Bugay v. Bugay, 53 Ohio App.2d 285, 373 N.E.2d 1263 (1977).

114. See C. T. Wyche v. United States, 74-9 SFTR ¶ 7911 (Ct.Cl. Comm'r's Rep. 1974) (South Carolina law); C. P. Brooke v. United States, 300 F.Supp. 465, 69-1 USTC ¶ 9366 (D.Mont.1969), aff'd 468 F.2d 1155, 72-2 USTC ¶ 9594 (9th Cir. 1972) (guardianship which court treated as trust for income tax purposes) (Montana law).

face with educational expenses of younger children is that the parent may have incurred a contractual obligation to the school. In that situation, trust income used to pay tuition is taxable to the parent because it is used to discharge his contractual obligation without regard to the scope of required support under state law.[115]

[b] When Has a Support Obligation Been "Discharged"?

As noted above, the Regulations tax the obligor on trust income used to "discharge" his or her support obligation. When has such a "discharge" occurred?

For example, assume that under state law, *F*, the father, is obligated to pay the expenses of *D*, his minor daughter, at a private school, and *D* has trust income available to her. It is not uncommon for a trustee to be authorized to use trust income for a minor in a variety of ways, including the payment of his or her expenses directly, as well as payment to a guardian, or directly to the minor. How does a trustee's choice among these alternatives affect the taxability of trust income used to pay the school expenses of *D*?

If the trustee uses trust income to pay the school directly,[116] it is difficult to avoid the conclusion that this is a discharge of *F*'s support obligation, which should cause the income to be taxable to *F*. If the trustee pays the minor's guardian and the guardian uses the money to pay the school, it would not be unreasonable to treat the income as having been used, through a conduit, to discharge *F*'s support obligation, with the same tax result. The more difficult case is that in which payment is made to *D*, with no strings attached, and *D* then pays the school. Is this a discharge of *F*'s support obligation? Because parents often exert a large measure of influence over their children's behavior, and may thereby secure substantial compliance with parental wishes as to how trust income will be spent, it would not be difficult for a court to find that *D*'s voluntary payment of her school expenses is, in substance, a discharge of the parent's support obligation, although as yet no case appears to have reached this result.[117]

---

115. See George B. Morrill, Jr. v. United States, 228 F.Supp. 734, 64–1 USTC ¶ 9463 (D.Me.1964).

116. In deciding to make such a payment, the trustee should be satisfied that it is clearly authorized by the terms of the trust agreement. Otherwise, the beneficiary may have a basis for surcharge on the ground, for example, that a provision authorizing payment of expenses for his or her "benefit" does not cover a payment that a parent would otherwise be legally obligated to make.

117. In F. B. Cooper v. United States, 60–2 USTC ¶ 9751 (E.D.Wash.1960), trust distributions to minor children "used by the said children without restrictions" were not taxed to the parents under an earlier version of § 677. The court's findings do not state how such income was used.

Section 677(a) was amended in 1969 to tax the grantor of a trust if income may, without the consent of an adverse party, be distributed to the grantor's spouse. It applies only to property transferred in trust after October 9, 1969. Before this amendment, most cases dealing with voluntary application of distributions by a beneficiary to discharge the grantor's legal obligations dealt with a wife rather than a child, and have refused to tax the grantor. See e.g., Lura H. Morgan, 2 T.C. 510, 515 (1943), acq. 1944–1 CB 20: "[The predecessor to § 677] does not reach income that is payable absolutely to a beneficiary without restriction as to use * * * although the beneficiary may thereafter apply it voluntarily to the benefit of the grantor."

See also John W. Parker v. Commissioner, 166 F.2d 364, 48–1 USTC ¶ 9212 (9th Cir. 1948) (trust income payable to wife for her support); William P. Anderson, 8 T.C. 921 (1947), acq. 1947–2 CB 1; Ralph W. Conant, 7 T.C. 453 (1946), acq. 1946–2 CB 2.

Even if *D*'s voluntary payment of her school expenses from her trust income is not considered a discharge of *F*'s obligation, which will cause the income to be taxed to *F* for income tax purposes, there may nonetheless be gift tax consequences. Such a voluntary assumption by *D* of *F*'s legal obligation may constitute a gift from *D* to *F* for purposes of the gift tax.[118] If such a gift is subject to disaffirmance within a reasonable time after *D* reaches her majority,[119] the gift would be made when the time for such disaffirmance has expired.[120]

[c] Payment of the Grantor's Debts and Taxes and Transfers Subject to Liabilities

A transfer in trust of property subject to a liability, or subject to payment of the transferor's gift tax, may create two possible bases for taxing the transferor. One is that to the extent the liability or debt to be paid by the trust exceeds the transferor's basis, the transferor may be taxable on gain realized by the transfer if his basis is lower than the amount of the liability or debt.[121] The other basis for taxing the grantor is under § 677(a), if trust income may, in the discretion of the trustee, be used to pay a debt for which the transferor is personally liable.[122]

In *Victor W. Krause*,[123] the taxpayer transferred property with a total value of $807,000 to trustees in September, 1963. His basis in the transferred property was $21,000. The trusts required the trustees to pay all federal gift taxes attributable to the transfers, which amounted to approximately $134,500. The following April, the trustees borrowed that amount from a bank and paid the gift tax of the taxpayer and his wife, who had consented to have one-half the gifts treated as being made by her. Between 1964 and 1970, the trusts made periodic payments from dividend income to discharge the bank loan. The Commissioner contended that the provision in the trust instruments for payment of the grantor's gift taxes constituted a reservation of an income interest by him, so that he was taxable on the trust income of $14,000 for 1964 and so that payment by the trust of his gift tax liability constituted a purchase in liquidation of his income interest, resulting in ordinary income of approximately $120,000.

The Tax Court sustained the Commissioner only as to income of the trusts received prior to payment of the taxpayer's gift tax, on the ground that the trustees had discretionary power to use such income to pay the tax but that no trust income received after that date was taxable to him because

A beneficiary's use of trust income to pay premiums on insurance on the grantor's life, on the other hand, is sufficient to make such income taxable to the grantor. See ¶ 9.01[9][d], note 128 infra.

118. Cf., Gloria V. Stokowski v. Pedrick, 52–2 USTC ¶ 10,861 (S.D.N.Y.1952) (guardian's payments for support of ward's mother constitute gifts).

119. See generally H. Clark, Jr., Law of Domestic Relations § 8.2 (1968).

120. See Commissioner v. Dorothy A. D. Allen, 108 F.2d 961, 40–1 USTC ¶ 9133 (3d Cir. 1939), cert. denied 309 U.S. 680 (1940).

121. See Reg. § 1.1001–2. For a discussion see ¶ 6.01[2][c].

122. Rev.Rul. 54–516, 1954–2 CB 54.

123. 56 T.C. 1242 (1971). See also Estate of Annette S. Morgan, 37 T.C. 981 (1962), aff'd mem. 316 F.2d 238, 63–1 USTC ¶ 9401 (6th Cir. 1963), cert. denied 375 U.S. 825 (1963).

"the payment of the gift taxes denuded petitioner of every interest in the trusts * * * ." [124]   The end result was highly favorable from the taxpayer's standpoint.   His gift tax was largely paid with borrowed funds which were, in turn, repaid out of trust income which was not taxed to him.

If such cases could be relied upon, such net gifts would be a highly attractive estate-planning tool which would, in effect, permit a major portion of the gift tax cost of a transfer in trust to be financed out of savings in taxes on the income used by the trust to pay the donor's gift tax.   But the apparent distinction between the case in which the gift tax is paid from proceeds of a loan to the trust, which is then repaid out of trust income, and the case in which the gift tax is paid directly from trust income without any borrowing, does not provide the most convincing basis for reliance in planning. [125]

[d] Payment of Premiums on Insurance on the Life of the Grantor (or His Spouse)

Section 677(a)(3) provides that the grantor is taxable on trust income which may (without the consent of an adverse party) be "applied to the payment of premiums on policies of insurance on the life of the grantor or the grantor's spouse" [126] (with an exception for certain policies irrevocably payable to charity).   A literal reading would indicate that if such policies could be taken out by the trustees or assigned to them and, thereafter, trust income could be used to pay the premiums thereon, such income would be taxable to the grantor even though no such policies were in existence at any time.   However, the courts, with the acquiescence of the Service, have read into predecessor versions of the section an implied limitation restricting its scope to premiums on policies in existence. [127]

The cautious draftsman may want to include an explicit prohibition on the use of trust income to pay premiums on policies of insurance on the life of either the grantor or his spouse, rather than relying on case authority to limit income taxable to the grantor to the amount of premiums on existing policies.

Although voluntary use of trust income to discharge his support obligations has not been held to make the grantor taxable, use of income to pay premiums has. [128]   The difference in result may reflect the fact that use of

---

124.   56 T.C. at 1246.

125.   See Estate of Craig R. Scheaffer, 37 T.C. 99 (1961), aff'd 313 F.2d 738, 63–1 USTC ¶ 9272 (8th Cir. 1963), cert. denied 375 U.S. 818 (1963), in which the grantor was held taxable on trust income used to pay his gift tax on the ground that it had been constructively received by him.

126.   The references to spouses applies only to transfers after October 9, 1969.   See note 91 supra.

127.   See Genevieve F. Moore, 39 B.T.A. 808 (1939), acq. 1939–2 CB 25.   See also Frank C. Rand v. Helvering, 116 F.2d 929, 41–1 USTC ¶ 9192 (8th Cir. 1941), cert. denied 313 U.S. 594 (1941).

128.   See Henry A. B. Dunning, 36 B.T.A. 1222 (1937), nonacq. 1938–1 CB 40, appeal dismissed 97 F.2d 999 (4th Cir. 1938), in which H was taxed on trust income used by W, at his suggestion, to pay premiums on insurance on his life but was not taxed on income used by her for household purposes and children.   Dunning was followed, with respect to payment of insurance premiums, in L. B. Foster, 8 T.C. 197 (1947), acq. 1947–1 CB 2.

In Rev.Rul. 66–313, 1966–2 CB 245, the grantor was held to be taxable on trust income used to pay premiums on insurance on the life of the grantor with the consent of the trust beneficiaries, her children.

income at the grantor's suggestion for such a relatively specific purpose reflects a greater degree of dominion over it than use of income for general household expenses.

[10] Gift Tax and Estate Tax Consequences

Creation of a short-term trust is a completed gift for purposes of the gift tax. Whether or not any tax will be incurred as a result depends upon the availability of any exclusions and deductions as well as the availability of any unused portion of the donor's unified credit. Any gift tax cost must be balanced against anticipated savings in income taxes and estate taxes from the creation of the trust. For most clients, both the gift tax cost and the anticipated savings in estate taxes have been substantially reduced by the Economic Recovery Tax Act of 1981. As a result, income tax savings have become relatively more important.

Since the Tax Reform Act of 1976 generally has required inclusion of post-1976 gifts in excess of the present interest exclusion in determining the grantor's estate tax bracket when he dies,[129] it is sometimes asserted that creation of a short-term trust actually will increase the grantor's combined gift and estate taxes. The basis for this assertion is that the trust may terminate before the grantor dies, so that both the trust principal and the gift when the trust was created will be included in determining his estate tax bracket. Even if the principal has not reverted to the grantor during his life, both the gift and his reversionary interest at the time of his death will be included in determining his estate tax bracket. As a result, it is said that more than 100 percent of the value of the trust property will be subject to transfer tax because of his creation of the short-term trust.

As the following examples illustrate, however, this is an over-simplified view of the estate and gift tax consequences of the creation of a short-term trust.

> *Example 9.8.* Assume that *G* transfers $100,000 to himself as trustee to pay the income to his mother, *M*, for her life, and then to return the principal to *G*. If *M* is 72 years old when the trust is created, the value of the gift of her income interest is $44,088 [130]—approximately the same as the value of a gift of income for a ten-year term.[131]

If *M* dies at age 82 and the principal then reverts to *G*, who dies immediately thereafter, did creation of the trust increase or decrease his combined estate and gift taxes? The answer is by no means clear.

Assuming that there was no change in the value of the trust property, the amount included in computing *G*'s taxable estate [132] will be $100,000 plus

129. § 2001(b), last sentence. For an illustration of the mechanics, see ¶ 6.01 note 8 supra.

130. Reg. § 25.2512–9(f), Table A(2).

131. Id. Table B.

132. If *G* possessed at his death (or retained until within three years of his death) a power described in § 2036(a)(2) or § 2038, the interest he gave to M would be included in his taxable estate. See ¶ 502[3][b][i], 5.02[5]. But such inclusion merely affects the time the gift will be valued in determining its estate tax consequences by causing it to be valued as of the date of death (or alternate valuation date). If it were not so included, it would still be taken into account, at the value when the gift was made, in determining *G*'s estate tax bracket. See § 2001(b), last sentence.

the gift to M at the time the trust was created [133] ($44,088 less a $10,000 present interest exclusion, or $34,088 net), or a total of $134,088.[134]   If no trust had been created, G's taxable estate might have been larger by more than $100,000, for three reasons:

(1) Unless G spent or gave away the net income (after income taxes) from the $100,000, it would augment his taxable estate, just as any other savings do.   And the net income (after income taxes) from the trust property may exceed the 6 percent rate used in valuing a gift of the income interest to M, further increasing G's taxable estate.

(2) If G gave away the income, gifts not covered by the present interest exclusion would be included in determining his estate tax bracket.

(3) Any gift tax paid on the gift to M reduces G's taxable estate, if he lives for more than three years after the gift is made.[134a]

[a] Limiting Gift to Value of Income Interest

Because the short-term trust is not a transfer of the grantor's entire interest in the trust property, it is important to insure that only the income interest will be a completed gift for the purposes of the gift tax.   In other words, a deduction should be allowable for the value of the grantor's reversionary interest, since that interest has not been given away.

If the grantor's retained interest "is not susceptible of measurement on the basis of generally accepted valuation principles, the gift tax is applicable to the entire value of the property   *   *   *." [135]   Thus, it is crucial that the interests of the trust beneficiaries fit within the familiar structure of life estates and terms of years, for which rules of valuation are prescribed.[136]   Here, as elsewhere in estate planning, nonconformity carries its price.

For example, in Revenue Ruling 77–99,[137] a trust provision for payment of capital gains to the income beneficiary was held to make the grantor's retained reversionary interest incapable of valuation, so that the entire amount transferred was taxed as a gift.   The same result was reached in Revenue Ruling 76–275,[138] where a trust provision authorized investment in oil, gas, or mineral royalties and provided that the entire proceeds be treated as income although state law would have allocated 27½ percent to principal.   These rulings make it clear that any significant broadening of the rights of an income beneficiary, unless it is so defined as to be capable of actuarial valuation, is likely to bar any deduction for gift tax purposes for a reversionary interest retained by the grantor.

Grantors may be tempted to rely on a bootstrap clause to avoid loss of the deduction for the value of a retained interest because of trust provisions

---

133.   § 2001(b)(1)(B).

134.   Any tax payable with respect to the gift is deducted in computing G's estate tax. § 2001(b)(2).

134a.   If he dies within the three year period, any gift tax paid by G or his estate is included under § 2035(c).   See ¶ 5.02[3][c].

135.   Reg. § 25.2511–1(e).

136.   Reg. § 25.2512–5.

137.   1977–1 CB 295.

138.   1976–2 CB 299.

which may depart from the state law norms in describing beneficiaries' interests.　A bootstrap clause seeks to limit the operation of trust provisions which might otherwise prevent achievement of a given tax objective.　Such reliance is hazardous in view of Revenue Ruling 65–144,[139] where a similar effort to protect a charitable deduction for income tax purposes was unsuccessful.

[b]　Securing Gift Tax Present Interest Exclusion

The annual limit on the present interest exclusion [140] $10,000 per donee (or $20,000 with gift-splitting with the donor's spouse) [141]—often is less than the value of the gift when the trust is created.　In *Example 9.8*,[142] where the trust principal was $100,000, the value of the income interest given was $44,088.　The exclusion would cover less than one-fourth of the gift; even with gift-splitting, it covers less than half.　For many grantors, marginal gift and estate tax rates are high enough to make the tax on the balance of the gift well worth trying to save.

One way to increase the amount that qualifies for the exclusion is to spread the funding of the trust over several years.　However, if the grantor wants to follow this course, in order to keep him from being taxed on part of the income it will be necessary for the trust term to be either for the life of the income beneficiary or for a period of not less than ten years from the date of the last transfer to be made to the trust.[143]

> *Example 9.9.*　Assume that on January 1, *G* creates a trust to pay the income to his mother (*M*) for twelve years and two days.　At the end of that period, the principal is to revert to *G*.　If *G* transferred, on January 1 of each year, the amounts given below, substantially all of the gifts would qualify for the exclusion if *G*'s wife consented to treat one-half as having been made by her:

Year	Transfers	Value of Term Interest [144]	Amount Qualifying for Exclusion
1	$ 40,000.00	$20,121.00	$20,000.00
2	42,000.00	19,875.00	19,875.00
3	18,000.00	7,949.00	7,949.00
Totals	$100,000.00	$47,945.00	$47,824.00

As the above totals indicate, only $121 would fail to qualify for the exclusion.

The advantage of qualifying the bulk of the gift for the present interest exclusion must be weighed against the tax disadvantage to *G* of continuing to be taxable on the income from part of the property until it is transferred to the trust, as well as the fact that his reversion will not take effect for twelve years and he may want to get his hands on the trust property after only ten years.　In this situation a compromise may best carry out *G*'s

---

139.　1965–1 CB 442.

140.　§ 2503(b).　For a discussion, see ¶ 6.03[1][a] supra.

141.　§ 2513.

142.　See ¶ 9.01[10] supra.

143.　§ 673.

144.　See Reg. § 25.2512–9(f), Table B.

objectives—for example, *G* may fund the trust over two years instead of in a single calendar year—for example, on December 31 of one year and January 1 of the following year.

If the trust term is the life of the income beneficiary, no advance decision is required as to the period over which it will be funded, as the reversion cannot take effect sooner than is permitted by § 673. In that situation, the grantor may make a substantial transfer in the first year knowing that he will be free to make such additions in later years as may be appropriate in the light of his current tax and financial position and such position of the beneficiary.

The gift tax advantage in qualifying for the exclusion must be balanced against the tax [115] and non-tax disadvantages of requiring distributions of income to one or more beneficiaries in specified shares in order to qualify. If the grantor prefers to make such distributions discretionary, either as to the recipient or their timing, he must forego the present interest exclusion to achieve [146] this result unless the trust qualifies under § 2503(c) as a minor's present interest trust, permitting the exercise of discretion as to timing.

If the decision is to qualify for the exclusion, three major pitfalls are:

(1) No postponement of beneficial enjoyment is permitted except in a trust which qualifies under § 2503(c);

(2) The trustee's powers must not make it impossible to value either the entire income interest or the shares of individual beneficiaries; and

(3) The trust property must not be of such a nature as to make valuation of the income interest impossible.

Additional problems are present in gifts to minor beneficiaries because of the legal disabilities and practical handicaps of minority. Such problems are discussed in connection with minors' present interest trusts.[147] But it should be borne in mind that a short-term trust also may be the vehicle for a gift to a minor beneficiary if his interest satisfies the requirements for a "present interest."

[i] **Effect of Postponement of Beneficial Enjoyment.** The Regulations state that the term "future interest" includes interests "limited to commence in use, possession, or enjoyment at some future date or time." [148] Literally, this makes *any* postponement, however brief, fatal to the exclusion. It has been applied with severity to cases in which the right to income commenced after a delay of three months, for example.[149] Where the right commences as soon as the gift is made, a reasonable postponement of the time of payment has been allowed.[150] Here, it seems wiser to make no

---

145. Required distributions of income may create tax problems for the beneficiary by increasing his taxable income and prospective taxable estate. See ¶ 11.04[4] infra.

146. The grantor may prefer to have the trustee's distribution of income take into account the needs of the beneficiaries from year to year and may also wish to influence their behavior by granting or withholding distributions.

147. See ¶ 9.03 infra.

148. Reg. § 25.2503–3(a).

149. See, e.g., Estate of Louise Jardell, 24 T.C. 652 (1955).

150. See, e.g., Helvering v. Blanche S. Rubinstein, 124 F.2d 969, 42–1 USTC ¶ 10,128 (8th Cir. 1942).

explicit provision for postponed payment and to rely, instead, on local law rather than inviting a challenge to the exclusion.

[ii] Effect of Trustee's Powers. Broad administrative powers granted to a trustee do not cause the income interests of beneficiaries to fail to qualify for the exclusion, as long as such powers do not permit the trustee to divert income.[151] But in Wymelenberg v. United States,[152] the trustee was given the power to "sell, exchange or alter the trust assets, the power to allocate receipts to principal or income, and the power to apportion expenditures to principal or income." The gifts of trust income were held to be incapable of valuation because of the extent to which the exercise of such powers could affect the amount of income. The court did not discuss the possibility that state law would restrict the trustee's ability to exercise such powers in this manner, and the holding should not preclude the inclusion of usual fiduciary powers in a short-term trust. However, overly broad powers of trustees may be effectively limited, so as to secure the exclusion, by a savings clause.[153]

Even if the income interest for the trust term could be valued, no present interest exclusion is allowed if the trustee has discretion in determining how income shall be allocated among different beneficiaries.[154] Moreover, if the grantor cannot establish the value of his retained reversionary interest, the entire value of the transferred property will be treated as a completed gift.[155]

[iii] Effect of Nature of Trust Property. Some cases have, not surprisingly, denied a present interest exclusion for gifts of income interests in non-income producing property. Two prime examples are non-dividend paying stock and life insurance policies.

The Commissioner and two Courts of Appeals have denied the exclusion for gifts of income interests in trusts of non-dividend paying stock in closely held corporations.[156] The Fourth Circuit reached a contrary conclusion in Rosen v. Commissioner.[157] Clients who seek the present interest exclusion by this route should (1) authorize the trustee to sell the stock; and (2) be prepared for controversy with the Commissioner.

151. See Cherlyn C. C. Martinez, 67 T.C. 60 (1976), acq. 1977–2 CB 1; Frances C. Brown, 30 T.C. 831 (1958), acq. 1959–1 CB 3.

152. 397 F.2d 443, 446, 68–2 USTC ¶ 12,537 at p. 78,321 (7th Cir. 1968), cert. denied 393 U.S. 953 (1968). See also G. Fischer v. Commissioner 288 F.2d 574, 61–1 USTC ¶ 12,014 (3d Cir. 1961) (income interest incapable of valuation where trust instrument required deduction of mortgage amortization from income).

153. Letter Ruling 7905088, 3 CCH E&GT ¶ 12,264 (Nov. 1, 1978).

154. Reg. § 25.2503–3(c), *Example (3)*.

155. Reg. § 25.2511–1(e). For a discussion, see ¶ 9.01[10][a] supra.

156. In Fred A. Berzon v. Commissioner, 534 F.2d 528 (2d Cir. 1976), the trustees could not sell the stock and reinvest in income producing property because of restrictions on its disposition. No such restrictions are referred to in Lera H. Stark v. United States, 477 U.S. 131, 73–1 USTC ¶ 12,921 (8th Cir. 1973), cert. denied 414 U.S. 975 (1973). See Horvitz, "How the Nature of Trust Property Can Kill the Gift Tax Exclusion," 113 Tr. & Est. 490 (1974). See also Maryland Nat'l Bank v. United States, 609 F.2d 1078, 79–2 USTC ¶ 13,322 (4th Cir. 1979), denying the exclusion for an interest in a non-income producing partnership.

157. ¶ 6.03[1][a] supra. But see Rev.Rul. 69–344, ¶ 6.03[1][a] supra, declining to follow Rosen.

Whether a trust of life insurance policies qualifies depends on its terms. If the beneficiaries can demand the corpus [158] or it vests in them on the death of the insured,[159] the trust may qualify.   In addition, courts have held that trust provisions authorizing the use of trust assets to pay premiums did not bar the exclusion,[160] although such a provision was a ground for its denial in Revenue Ruling 69–344.[161]   But if the beneficiaries only have a right to income after the insured dies, the trust will not qualify.[162]

[c] Gift-Splitting by Married Grantors

Gift-splitting with the grantor's spouse often is desirable to minimize the gift tax on creation of a short-term trust.   Under § 2513, gift-splitting is available with respect to gifts made by husband or wife to third parties. If the spouse is a beneficiary of the short-term trust, gift-splitting will not be available unless her interest is capable of being separately valued from that of other beneficiaries.   The result is that inclusion of the spouse as one of the beneficiaries to whom income may be paid in the trustee's discretion will bar use of gift-splitting because such separate valuation will not be possible.   Moreover, for income tax reasons, such inclusion of the spouse is undesirable in any event, as it will cause the trust income to be taxed to the grantor.[163]

[11] Planning

Two important planning considerations in creating short term trusts are:

(1) Choosing beneficiaries who combine desirable tax and nontax attributes (or delegating the choice to trustees);

(2) Choosing property to be transferred which is appropriate in the light of the grantor's estate planning objectives.

A third objective (recognition of the trust as a taxable entity separate from the grantor and the beneficiaries) may be significant in the creation of a non-reversionary trust,[164] but is unlikely to be as important in a short-term trust.   Such recognition may serve two major purposes:

(1) Qualifying for additional exemptions under dollar-limit Code provisions; [165]

(2) Serving as a party in intra-family sales, exchanges, or leases.

---

158. Harbeck Halsted, 28 T.C. 1069 (1957), acq. 1958–2 CB 5.

159. See Rev.Rul. 76–490, 1976–2 CB 300. But see Commissioner v. Warner, 127 F.2d 913, 42–1 USTC ¶ 10,177 (9th Cir. 1942). If the trust consists substantially of insurance on the life of the donor or his spouse, the Commissioner will not rule on whether it is a present interest.   See Rev.Proc. 81–37, IRB 1981–34, 22, 3 CCH E&GT ¶ 12,444 P.

160. Duncan v. United States, 368 F.2d 98, 66–2 USTC ¶ 12,434 (5th Cir. 1966); James T. Pettus, Jr., 54 T.C. 112 (1970).

161. ¶ 6.03[1][a] supra.

162. See Reg. § 25.2503–3(c), *Example (2)*.

163. § 677(a)(1).

164. For a discussion, see ¶ 9.02[2](b) infra.

165. The most obvious is the deduction for personal exemption in § 642(b).   See note 196 infra.

The first purpose may be achieved by a short-term trust, to the extent that income is accumulated and is not taxable to the grantor. And short-term trusts have been used to achieve the second as well.[166] But if recognition of the trust as a taxable entity separate from the grantor is an important goal, it may be desirable to create a nonreversionary trust for this purpose.

[a] Choosing the Beneficiaries (or Delegating the Choice to Trustees)

As in outright gifts, the prime tax consideration in choosing beneficiaries is the effect on the beneficiary's own tax position. Short-term trusts have a potential advantage over outright gifts because properly selected trustees may be given the power to choose to whom income will be distributed from time to time, rather than being bound by a fixed choice made by the grantor when the trust was created. This degree of flexibility frees the grantor from the need to anticipate in advance what the respective tax positions of the various beneficiaries may be from time to time during the term of the trust.

Even if the trust has only one beneficiary to whom income may be distributed, the ability to determine how much he gets in any given year may be highly useful in minimizing his income taxes. This power may be given to any trustee without adverse income tax consequences for the grantor.[167] If the grantor holds the power himself, however, the income interest will be included in his taxable estate if he dies before the trust terminates.[168]

[b] Choosing the Property to Be Transferred

It is obvious that the assets that maximize income-shifting are those that produce a high current return as a percentage of their fair market value when the trust is created. And it does not require a boundless confidence in the rationality of the investment markets to support the assumption that a high current return tends to accompany either minimal prospects for growth in asset value or a high risk that such value may decline.

Thus, if a high-yield investment is transferred to a short-term trust or purchased by the trustee, the income actually shifted may exceed the 6 percent rate used in valuing the income interest for gift tax purposes.[169] Thus, the creation of the trust may combine income tax savings with savings in gift taxes because of the undervaluation of the income interest.

Differences between basis and fair market value of property transferred to a short-term trust are less significant than in a non-trust gift of property. The grantor's ownership of the reversionary interest ordinarily causes him

---

166. See, e.g., Quinlivan v. Commissioner, 599 F.2d 269, 79–1 USTC ¶ 9396 (8th Cir. 1979), cert. denied 444 U.S. 996 (1979) (gift and leaseback to short-term trust); Hobart A. Lerner, 71 T.C. 290 (1978) (same). But compare C. James Mathews v. Commissioner, 520 F.2d 323, 75–2 USTC ¶ 9734 (5th Cir. 1975), cert. denied 424 U.S. 967 (1976), discussed at ¶ 4.01[2][b] supra. See also ¶ 9.02 note 191 infra.

167. § 674(b)(6).

168. § 2038. For a discussion, see ¶ 5.02[5] supra.

169. See Reg. § 25.2512–9(f), Table B.

to be taxed on capital gains realized by the trust (and he also is entitled to deduct capital losses).[170]   As there has been no gift of trust principal, it would seem logical for basis to be the transferor's cost under § 1015(b), which applies to a transfer in trust other than by gift, bequest, or devise. It is difficult, however, to find explicit support for this conclusion.[171]

A further factor to be taken into account is the prospective new basis, under § 1014, for property included in the grantor's estate when he dies.[172] If the grantor dies before the termination of the trust, what he held on the date of his death, and what was therefore includible in his gross estate, was a reversionary interest in a trust.   In this situation, Revenue Ruling 72–466 [173] held that under the basis rule of § 1014 the basis adjustment was limited to the proportionate part of the value of the trust that was includible in the grantor's gross estate.

Other tax consequences flow from the fact that property is held in a short-term trust when the grantor dies.   For example, property that would be eligible for special use valuation under § 2032A,[174] if included in the grantor's taxable estate, would appear to be disqualified if it is owned by a short-term trust at the time of the grantor's death.

¶ 9.02   LONG-TERM (NON-REVERSIONARY) TRUSTS

A trust in which the grantor retains no reversionary interest need not be of long duration in order to save income and estate taxes.   But aside from present interest trusts for minors, short-term trusts in which the grantor retains no reversionary interest are not widely used in estate planning.   If the grantor is going to incur the trouble and expense required to create a trust, it is more reasonable to provide a term of substantial length, so that the advantages a trust may offer can be enjoyed for some time.

An outright gift also may save income and estate taxes, and is even better suited to shifting taxability of any gains realized from a sale of the transferred property within two years of the gift.[175]   But a long-term trust offers additional non-tax advantages from the grantor's standpoint including:

(1) The ability to give beneficiaries a great variety of interests—present and future, vested and contingent, limited and absolute—without unduly hampering the management of the property given; [176]

(2) The ability to provide management of property for beneficiaries who are incapable of providing effective management themselves;

(3) The ability to leave the size and dimensions of each beneficiary's interest, as well as the determination of who will be included as a beneficiary, for future determination by persons or institutions chosen by the grantor [177] and who may be responsive to the grantor's views while he lives.

---

170. § 677(a).

171. See, however, note 166 supra.

172. For a discussion, see ¶ 4.03 supra.

173. 1972–2 CB 466.

174. For a discussion, see ¶ 16.02 infra.

175. §644. For a discussion, see ¶ 9.02[2][a] infra.

176. For a discussion, see ¶ 6.05 supra.

177. For a discussion, see ¶ 9.01[6] supra.

The last factor is particularly important for many grantors, in that it may allow the tax advantages of an outright gift to be enjoyed without, as a practical matter, surrendering complete control to someone else over the property given.

Although an outright gift and a long-term trust are equally effective ways to get income off the donor's return and property out of his taxable estate, there may be a vast difference in the effect of each on the tax positions of the trust beneficiaries. The donee of an outright gift is immediately placed in a less favorable tax position; the income will be included in his return until he disposes of the property and the property itself will be in his taxable estate if he continues to own it until he dies. If he receives an interest in a trust instead, it may be possible to give him access to the property or the income it produces, whenever it is desirable for him to have it, without his incurring tax liabilities for income or wealth he neither needs nor wants. From this standpoint, a trust offers potential advantages which no outright gift can provide.

At some point, the continuation of a trust may cease to be financially desirable either because the trust has become too small to justify incurring the expense of its administration or because it no longer achieves the anticipated tax savings for beneficiaries. A well-drafted trust instrument anticipates this contingency by providing ways by which a trust may be terminated before the expiration of its stated term.[178]

By definition, a non-reversionary trust satisfies the requirements of § 673 as to the minimum period during which principal may not return to the grantor. If the trust is to shift the taxability of the grantor's income from him to the beneficiaries (or the trust itself), it must comply with the other rules for short-term (Clifford) trusts found in §§ 671–677. But a non-reversionary trust which satisfies these rules offers income tax planning possibilities not present in a short-term trust in which the grantor has a reversionary interest. The possibilities include:

(1) Shifting the taxability of capital gains, as well as ordinary income, from the grantor to the trust or its beneficiaries;

(2) Recharacterizing gains as tax-exempt receipts, through the use of discretionary distributions of appreciated assets; and

(3) Achieving greater recognition of the trust as a taxable entity separate from either the grantor or the beneficiaries.

From the standpoint of the grantor's income taxes, the major variations in the different forms of non-reversionary trusts are the same as those for short-term (Clifford) trusts. Thus, the examples given in that connection are equally appropriate here so long as each is modified to eliminate the reversionary interest in the grantor. The following three examples illustrate trusts whose income will not be taxable to the grantor under § 674 because of a power to control enjoyment:

> *Example 9.10.*[179] G transfers property to himself as trustee to pay the income to his mother (*M*) for her life, remainder to G's de-

---

178. For example, a trustee may be given discretionary power to terminate the trust by distributing any remaining principal. Or the holder of a power of appointment may exercise the power to direct such a distribution.

179. § 674(b).

scendants living on the death of *M*, such descendants to take *per stirpes*, or if no such descendant is then living, to THE CHILDREN'S DE-FENSE FUND, a charitable corporation of the District of Columbia.

Example 9.11.[180] *G* transfers property to his wife (*W*) and to his son-in-law (*S*) as trustees.   In their discretion, the trustees may distribute income and principal from time to time to such one or more of the living descendants of *G* as the trustees determine.   Any income not so distributed shall be accumulated and added to principal.   The trust shall terminate twenty-one (21) years after the death of the survivor of the descendants of *G* who are living when the trust is created. On such termination, any remaining principal and accumulated income shall be distributed to *G*'s descendants then living, such descendants to take *per stirpes*, or if no such descendant is then living, to the CHILDREN'S DEFENSE FUND, a charitable corporation of the District of Columbia.   (Appropriate provisions are included for the appointment of successor trustees if either *W* or *S* ceases to serve, so as to insure that the trustees shall at all times satisfy the requirements of § 674(c).)

Example 9.12.[181]   The terms of the trust are the same as in *Example 9.11* except that:

(1) The trustees are *G*'s son and daughter; and

(2) Their power to distribute income and principal is phrased as follows: "The trustees shall distribute to each descendant of *G* (other than such trustees) such amounts of income and principal as they determine in their discretion are required for his reasonable support and maintenance."

Whether the grantor (or anyone else) will be taxed on income used to discharge the legal obligation of one person to support another is a separate problem.[182]

[1] Income Tax Consequences for Grantor

The previous discussion of this topic in connection with short-term trusts is equally applicable to non-reversionary trusts, with one important qualification.   Ordinarily, a major tax objective of a long-term trust is to shift the taxability of all of the trust income from the grantor to the beneficiaries (or to the trust itself).   Thus, the possibility that the grantor will be taxable as owner of a "portion" of the trust usually is not present in such trusts.

[2] Income Tax Consequences for Beneficiaries, Power Holders, and Trusts

The previous discussion of income tax consequences for beneficiaries and power holders of short-term trusts is applicable to non-reversionary trusts as well.   One important difference between short-term and non-

---

180. § 674(c).

181. § 674(d).

182. See ¶ 9.01[9] infra.

reversionary trusts is that only in the latter is it practical to authorize discretionary distributions of appreciated assets and thus minimize or eliminate any tax on the appreciation.[183]

The tax consequences for the trust itself, however, are often substantially different in a non-reversionary trust. One of the tax objectives of such a trust usually is to shift the taxability of all the income either to the beneficiaries or to the trust. Consequently, in *Example 9.10*, the income payable to *M* will be taxable to her (and deductible by the trust) to the limit of the trust's distributable net income,[184] and income allocated to principal, typically including capital gains, will be taxed to the trust. In *Examples 9.11* and *9.12*, if distributions in a given year are less than the trust's distributable net income (DNI),[185] the excess will be taxable to the trust (reduced by any deductions, such as a net capital loss, not reflected in DNI).

If trust income is accumulated, rather than being distributed currently each year, distributions in a later year in excess of the trust's distributable net income for that year may be subject to an additional tax under the throwback rule.[186] But the exemptions from throwback treatment for accumulations while the recipient was unborn or under age 21 are far more likely to apply because the longer trust term provides additional time for the birth of potential beneficiaries. Thus, the possibility is greatly enhanced in *Examples 9.11* and *9.12* that the tax paid by the trust on all or part of a year's income will be the final income tax liability on such income.

[a] Gains Realized by Trusts

If gains on appreciated assets are realized by a trust in which the grantor has no reversionary interest, usually those gains are taxable to the trust rather than to the beneficiaries. Even though the trustee makes distributions in the year such gains are realized, the gains ordinarily are not includible in "distributable net income" (DNI).[187] Nor will distributions of accumulated income change this result: the throwback rule, which may impose an additional tax on trust beneficiaries as a result of such distributions, does not include in its measure accumulations of capital gains,[188] except in the unusual case in which such gains are included in DNI.

The major obstacle to shifting gain on appreciated assets to a trust or its beneficiaries is § 644, which taxes at the grantor's rates gain recognized by the trust within two years of the transfer, but does so only to the extent of appreciation at the time the transfer in trust was made. Section 644 applies to gain recognized by the trust and not to distributions to beneficiaries that do not satisfy a dollar obligation of the trust. Thus, discretionary distributions of principal to give the beneficiary an increased basis [189] may be made even within the two-year period.

183. For a discussion of this technique, see ¶ 4.07 supra.

184. § 652 (inclusion by beneficiary); § 651 (deduction by trust).

185. § 662 (inclusion by beneficiary); § 661 (deduction by trust).

186. §§ 665–667. For a discussion, see ¶ 11.02 infra.

187. See § 643(a)(3), discussed ¶ 11.01[2] infra.

188. See § 665(a), discussed at ¶ 11.02 infra.

189. See ¶ 4.07 supra.

[b] Use of Trust as Separate Entity for Tax Purposes Other Than Income Shifting

An important factor in achieving income tax savings through the use of trusts is the extent to which a trust will be recognized as a separate entity. Two valuable results (in addition to income shifting) may stem from such recognition:

(1) The trust may qualify for an additional set of exemptions under various dollar limit provisions of the Code; and

(2) It can facilitate intra-family sales and leases to achieve savings.

In these matters, the threshold question is whether the trust will be recognized as a separate taxable entity during the life of the grantor. Revocable trusts are not; [190] for some purposes short-term trusts likewise are denied such recognition if the grantor is taxable as owner of the trust principal, even though he is not taxed as owner of the income interest during the term of the trust.[191] On the other hand, a number of cases have accorded recognition for tax purposes to leases by a grantor to the trust, where he was not treated as owner.[192]

Regardless of whether the trust is recognized as a separate entity, the further question arises as to whether a single trust or two or more separate trusts are more advantageous from the standpoint of the beneficiaries. If it appears to be desirable to achieve recognition for tax purposes of two or more separate trusts,[193] it then becomes necessary to take account of the factors relevant in securing this result.[194]

[i] Additional Exemptions Under Dollar-Limit Provisions. The most obvious example of a dollar-limit exemption provision [195] for which a trust may provide an additional exemption is the deduction for personal exemption of $300 for a trust which "is required to distribute all of its income currently" and $100 for any other trust.[196] For a single trust, this deduction is of minor importance because the tax thereby saved may not even begin to cover the additional cost of preparation of the trust's income tax return by a paid professional. For multiple trusts with identical income and deductions, the saving may become significant if mass production of the tax returns for the trusts reduces accounting expenses and the trusts are treated as separate entities for income tax purposes.[197]

---

190. This conclusion would seem to follow from the fact that the grantor is taxable as owner under § 676. See also Rev.Rul. 74–613, 1974–2 CB 153. In Estate of O'Connor, 69 T.C. 165 (1977), a marital deduction trust over which W held a power to withdraw all of the corpus, which she exercised, was held not to be a recognizable tax entity. The result was to deny the estate a deduction for distributions to the trust, which had been assigned by W to a charity.

191. See Rev.Rul. 67–70, 1967–1 CB 106, holding that a transfer of an installment obligation to a short-term trust is not a "disposition" on which gain must be recognized under former § 453(d) (renumbered without change as § 453B(a)).

192. See note 166 supra.

193. For a discussion, see ¶ 11.07 infra.

194. For a discussion, see ¶ 11.07[1] infra.

195. Unit exemption limits are less common. One is contained in § 1237(b)(1) with respect to the character of gain on the sale of a sixth lot or parcel in the same tract.

196. § 642(b). The $100 maximum exclusion of qualifying dividends provided by § 116, as amended by § 302 of the Economic Recovery Tax Act of 1981, should also be considered.

197. For a discussion of whether or not multiple trusts will be recognized for tax purposes, see ¶ 11.07[1] infra.

Dollar limits with greater significance are the $10,000 exemption for purposes of the minimum tax imposed on "items of tax preference," [198] and the $20,000 exemption for purposes of the alternative minimum tax.[199]   Both are allowed in full for a trust for which no items of tax preference are allocable to beneficiaries.[200]   The $10,000 exemption from disallowance of "investment interest," on the other hand, is expressly denied to a trust by § 163(d)(1).

[ii] **Intra-Family Sales and Leases.**   Trusts are given more favorable treatment as parties to intra-family sales than are other taxable entities in at least two instances:

(1) Section 1239, which recharacterizes gain on certain sales of depreciable property as ordinary income, applies to sales between husband and wife and between other "related persons" (as defined) but does not apply to grantors and trusts or beneficiaries and trusts; and

(2) Section 707(b)(2), which recharacterizes gain on sales or exchanges of property (other than capital assets, as defined in § 1221) as ordinary income, applies to certain sales between a partnership and a partner and between two partnerships but again does not apply to grantors and trusts or beneficiaries and trusts.

Section 267(a), on the other hand, which denies any deduction for losses from sales between certain related taxpayers, covers certain grantor-trust, beneficiary-trust, and trustee-to-trustee transactions.

Family trusts may also facilitate the avoidance of § 1091, which denies a deduction for losses on the sale and purchase within thirty days of substantially identical stock or securities.   If the purchase and sale are made by two different taxpayers, the provision literally is inapplicable.[201]   Here, as elsewhere, however, an "economic reality" test may be invoked by a court in order to deny the claimed loss.[202]

[3] Gift Tax and Estate Tax Consequences

Creation of a non-reversionary trust is, of course, a completed gift for purposes of the gift tax, unless the gift is incomplete because of a power reserved by the grantor.   Whether or not any tax will be incurred as a result depends upon the availability of any exclusions and deductions, as well as any unused portion of the donor's unified credit.   Any gift tax cost must be balanced against anticipated savings in income taxes and estate taxes from the creation of the trust.

For estate tax purposes, the critical question is whether the grantor has retained (or possesses at death) such interests or powers as to require inclusion of all or part of the trust property in his taxable estate.[203]   If he

---

198. § 56(a)(1).

199. § 55(a).

200. § 58(c).

201. But see McWilliams v. Commissioner, 331 U.S. 694, 47-1 USTC ¶ 9289 (1947) (predecessor provision applied to sales by one spouse and purchases by the other).

202. See David M. Fender v. United States, 577 F.2d 934, 78-2 USTC ¶ 9617 (5th Cir. 1978).   The court disallowed a loss on a trust's sale of depreciated bonds to a bank in which the grantor-trustee had a substantial stock interest, followed by repurchase of the bonds 42 days later, finding no bona fide sale.

203. §§ 2036-2038.   For a discussion, see ¶¶ 5.02[4], [5] supra.

does retain any such interest or power and disposes of it within three years of his death, the gift will be included in his taxable estate under § 2035, unless the exemption for gifts within the present interest exclusion applies.[204]

[4] "Net Gifts" and Other Transfers Subject to Liabilities

Reasons for not making gifts of property subject to liabilities in excess of the donor's basis have already been discussed.[205]   The same principles generally apply to gifts in trust.   With regard to non-reversionary trusts, some taxpayers have successfully used the "net gift" technique, whereby transfers are made subject to the transferee's payment of the donor's gift tax.   To the extent that the tax is paid out of principal of the property given, the relevant considerations are basically similar to those discussed in connection with non-trust "net gifts."   Payment of the tax out of income of the transferee trust, however, differs in its possible consequences for the grantor.

Section 677 taxes the grantor if trust income may be used for his benefit and such benefit clearly includes payment of a gift tax for which he is personally liable.   Thus, the grantor is taxable on trust income that may be used for this purpose until the gift tax has been paid.   After payment, however, use of trust income to discharge a loan to the trust used to pay the gift tax has not caused income to be taxed to the grantor.[206]

¶ 9.03   MINORS' PRESENT INTEREST TRUSTS (AND TRUST SUBSTITUTES)

Many clients wish to make gifts to minor beneficiaries that will qualify for the present interest exclusion but are deterred by the legal disabilities or practical handicaps of property ownership by minors.   Such deterrence is unwarranted in view of the range of alternatives available in making such gifts.   The four most important are:

(1) Guardianship or custodianship;

(2) Section 2503(c) trusts;

(3) Section 2503(b) trusts; and

(4) Trusts subject to a *Crummey* power.

A fifth possibility is direct ownership of wealth by the minor, without need for a guardian or custodian.   This may be feasible if the minor can open a savings account or if he is made the owner of an insurance policy.   However, it will be difficult during his minority to change the form in which the investment is held, without appointment of a guardian.   For example, if the insured dies, the insurance company can be expected to insist that the policy proceeds be paid to a guardian, rather than directly to the minor himself.

The four major ways to make such gifts are arranged above in the order of the degree of flexibility they offer the client, beginning with the least flexible and progressing to the most flexible alternative.

---

204. For a discussion of this rule, see ¶ 5.02[3] supra.

205. See ¶ 6.01[2][c] supra.

206. See ¶ 9.01[9] supra.

[1] Guardianship or Custodianship

Clients who wish to make gifts to minor beneficiaries without creating a trust need advice on the relative merits of guardianships and custodianships as vehicles for such gifts.

[a] Guardianship

The time-honored method of making gifts to minors is to make the gift to a guardian.

> *Example 9.13.* *C* transfers property to *G* as guardian for *B*, the beneficiary. Until *B* reaches his majority (usually age 18, depending on state law), *G* will hold and dispose of the property in accordance with state law. When *B* attains his majority, *G* will turn over any property he holds as guardian to *B*.

The conventional wisdom is that guardianship is cumbersome and expensive and that a custodianship or trust is preferable as a more flexible and streamlined medium for gifts to minors. Modern practice and legislative revision have reduced the traditional disadvantages of guardianships, so that in many states accounting formalities are minimized and termination of the guardianship may be handled without court proceedings on the basis of an informal settlement of the guardian's accounts. Where this is true, there may be no major difference in formalities between a guardianship and a custodianship—although the scope of permissible investments may be more restricted for the former by state law. In other states, where important differences persist, the custodianship may be significantly more streamlined.

On the other hand, guardianship is more all-inclusive from the standpoint of what kinds of property may be given. The custodianship statutes often apply only to a gift of "a security, a life insurance policy or annuity contract or money." [207] Thus, if the donor wishes to give a valuable painting, for example, a guardianship is an available medium but a custodianship may not be, depending upon the relevant state statute.

Guardianships and custodianships share one distinctive characteristic: Neither is a trust for most federal income tax purposes.[208] Income received by the guardian or custodian is taxable to the minor individually, which means that his "exemption amount" [209] is deductible, rather than the smaller exemption for a trust.[210] Moreover, the income level for which a return is

---

207. See, e.g., Minn.Stat. § 527.02(1)(1976).

208. Custodianships: Joseph Anastasio, 67 T.C. 814 (1977), aff'd per curiam 78–1 USTC ¶ 9153 (2d Cir. 1977); Rev.Rul. 56–484, 1956–2 CB 23. But income from custodianship property which is used to discharge a support obligation is taxable to the person whose obligation is discharged, whether or not he is the donor. See id.; Rev.Rul. 59–357, 1959–2 CB 212.

Guardianships: Reg. § 1.641(b)–2(b). But see Charles P. Brooke v. United States, 468 F.2d 1155, 72–2 USTC ¶ 9594 (9th Cir. 1972), in which the court stated that under Montana law a guardianship must be considered a trust for purposes of taxation under § 677.

209. § 151(b). See note 211 infra.

210. The deduction for personal exemption is $300 if the trust is required to distribute all of its income currently and $100 of the governing instrument contains no such requirement. See § 642(b).

required is higher for an individual [211] than for a trust.[212]   And if a return is required for the ward, it will be the familiar individual return instead of the more exotic form required for a trust.   A nonprofessional is more likely to be able to handle the former without help and, if professional help is needed, the spread of computerized services for individual returns tends to hold the cost below that of a professionally prepared trust return.

[b] Custodianship

Custodianships are a recently developed substitute for guardianships which may offer important advantages in simplified procedures for the custodian.

> *Example 9.14.*   C transfers property to G "as custodian for B under the State X Uniform Gifts to Minors Act." [213]   G will hold and dispose of the property in the same manner as in *Example 9.13* except that the state laws governing G often provide greater flexibility and impose fewer requirements than in the case of a guardianship.   In some states the custodianship may end at a later age.

Custodianships have both the advantages and the disadvantages of a statutory short-form substitute for a trust.   They are less expensive to create—all that is required is registration in appropriate form of the kind of property specified in the statute.   Typically, it must be "a security, a life insurance policy or annuity contract or money." [214]   The statute becomes, in effect, the governing instrument.   Naturally, it is not tailor-made for the needs of a particular client and his beneficiaries and the statutory provisions may not deal satisfactorily, for example, with the problems created by the custodian's death or incapacity.

A more significant deterrent for many donors is that the property held by either a guardian or a custodian must be turned over to the minor at majority or shortly thereafter, depending on state law.   For many donors, the prospect of turning over any substantial amount of wealth to a college freshman (or school dropout) is uninviting, and leads to a preference for other vehicles.

[2] Section 2503(c) Trust

The § 2503(c) trust qualifies, to the extent of all interests in the property transferred (including the interests of takers in default of appointment by the minor), for the present interest exclusion, up to the limit of $10,000 per donee per year contained in § 2503(b).   To achieve that result, however, the client must be willing to:

---

211.   § 6012(a)(1)(A) requires a return for individuals with gross income of the "exemption amount" (defined in § 151(f) as $1,000, with a cost-of-living adjustment beginning in 1985) or more, with specified exceptions. The exception most often applicable to minors is that which generally frees from filing requirements, unmarried individuals with a gross income of less than the sum of the "exemption amount" and the "zero bracket amount" (defined in § 63(d)).   See § 6012(a)(1)(A)(i).   However, it is inapplicable to an individual with unearned income of the "exemption amount" or more who is described in § 63(e)(1)(D), referring to individuals for whom a dependency exemption is allowable to another taxpayer. See § 6012(a)(1)(C)(iv).

212.   §§ 6012(a)(4) requires a return for a trust having either gross income of $600 or any taxable income.

213.   See, e.g., N.Y. EPTL 7–4.1—7–4.11.

214.   See, e.g., Minn.Stat. § 527.02(1)(1976).

(1) Authorize a trustee to spend the property and the income for the benefit of the minor; [215] and

(2) Give the minor whatever is not spent when he reaches age 21, or if he dies before that date, give it to his estate or as he appoints under a general power of appointment.[216]

Example 9.15. G transfers property to T as trustee, the income or principal or both to be used at T's discretion for the benefit of B, any excess income to be added to principal at the end of each year. When B attains age 21, any remaining income and principal shall be paid over to him. If B dies under age 21, such income and principal shall be paid to B's estate.[217]

The required grant of discretion to the trustee is not a major sticking point because a properly chosen trustee usually may be counted on not to exercise the discretionary power in a manner unacceptable to the donor. The only major problem in this connection is to avoid naming as trustee either the donor or an individual who has a legal obligation to support the minor and whose power might therefore constitute a general power of appointment,[218] with adverse estate tax consequences to the trustee himself. Attempts to avoid this result by limiting the scope of the trustee's discretion risk loss of the exclusion.[219]

Major factors to be taken into account in the use of the § 2503(c) trust include:

(1) The required distribution to the minor at age 21;

(2) The costs of trust administration;

(3) Income tax consequences during the initial trust term;

(4) Estate tax consequences during the initial trust term; and

(5) Income and estate tax consequences of the beneficiary's nonexercise of a power of withdrawal (and resulting extension of trust term).

[a] Required Distribution to Minor at Age 21

The major sticking point for most clients is the requirement that the unexpended principal and income pass to the minor at age 21. Clients tend to relate the age of judgment and maturity in handling wealth to their own age when the gift is made, and that normally is well beyond age 21. The unrest of the late 1960s and the marked desire of many young people to

---

215. § 2503(c)(1).

216. Either a general power of appointment exercisable by the minor by will or such a power exercisable by him during his lifetime is required in order to qualify for the gift tax present interest exclusion. See § 2503(c)(2) and Reg. § 25.2503–4(b). If under local law the minor is under a disability to exercise the power, the exclusion nevertheless is allowed. Id.

217. In lieu of payment to the minor's estate, the trust could give him a general power of appointment, whether or not he has capacity under local law to exercise the power. See note 216 supra.

218. See Reg. § 20.2041–1(c).

219. See Rev.Rul. 69–345, 1969–1 CB 226, finding a substantial restriction where income could be used for the minor beneficiary only if his needs could not be met by his parents or from his own resources. But see, e.g., the following cases in which restrictions contained in the trust instrument were held not to be substantial because they were not in excess of those imposed by state law for guardians: Geraldine F. Williams v. United States, 378 F.2d 693, 67–2 USTC ¶ 12,474 (Ct.Cl.1967); Paul Mueller v. United States, 69–1 USTC ¶ 12,592 (W.D.Mo.1969).

experiment with a variety of life styles did nothing to bolster clients' confidence in the wisdom of the next generation from this standpoint.

Devices are available which may avoid entrusting wealth to a beneficiary of a § 2503(c) trust at age 21. The Internal Revenue Service now permits the trust instrument to authorize the beneficiary to extend its term or to provide that such extension shall be automatic if he fails to request the principal.[220] If such an extension occurs, the tax treatment of the trust will change.[221]

COMMISSIONER v. ARLEAN I. HERR

United States Court of Appeals, Third Circuit, 1962.
303 F.2d 780, 62–2 USTC ¶ 12,079.

GOODRICH, Circuit Judge.

This case involves the question of what is a present interest in a trust for a minor under section 2503(c) of the Internal Revenue Code of 1954, 26 U.S.C.A. § 2503(c). The issue arises in connection with the gift tax return of the settlor of a trust. The settlor in 1954 set up four trusts, all the same except for the identity of the beneficiaries, who were his grandchildren. He made additions to each trust in 1955. As to each of the trusts, the trustee was to pay over the income to the beneficiary until his arrival at age thirty and then to pay over the principal. By Article Third of the trust the trustee was to retain the income payable to any minor, reinvesting it and paying over so much of the income and principal as he deemed necessary for the maintenance and support of the minor. All unexpended sums of accumulated income were to be paid to the minor at his majority.

The Commissioner disallowed the annual exclusions on the gift tax return for 1955 on the ground that the transfers were gifts of future interests. The Tax Court held, in a very able opinion by Judge Raum, that those parts of the gifts which were of income during minority were present interests entitling the taxpayers to the claimed deductions. 35 T.C. 732 (1961).

* * * The question in this case is limited to the tax-free nature of the trust income to the minor during minority. There is no claim that the income following majority up to age thirty and the right to the principal at age thirty are present interests. The Government's argument turns upon the phrase "if the property and the income therefrom." It argues strenuously that "property" is equivalent to "corpus," and therefore both the corpus and the income must meet both statutory conditions in order not to be treated as a future interest.

* * *

To bring out our problem here, let us suppose this case: A settlor creates a trust, the income of which is to go to M, a minor, until M is twenty-one. When M is twenty-one the corpus of the trust is to be given to X. Can there by any doubt that in this case the income of the trust is a "present interest" to M as he receives the payments year after year? If we add an additional provision that the minor is to receive, until he is twenty-one, so much of the income as is necessary for his support and that any undistributed income and interest thereon is to go to him at twenty-one, does he not still have a present interest?

If this is right, does it change the situation, if instead of the corpus going to X when M is twenty-one, it is to go to M when he is thirty? That is this case. We think the Tax Court was right in looking at this problem in the light of division of interest in the thing (corpus) in the way it did. The right to income during minority is a present interest; the right to income and principal after minority are future interests.

* * *

ESTATE OF DAVID H. LEVINE v. COMMISSIONER

United States Court of Appeals, Second Circuit, 1975.
526 F.2d 717, 76–1 USTC ¶ 13,115.

IRVING R. KAUFMAN, Chief Judge:

* * *

I.

The facts in this case have been stipulated. On December 30, 1968 David H. Levine, a Connecticut resident, established identical irrevocable trusts for five grandchildren whose ages then ranged from 2 to 15 years. The corpus of each trust consisted of common stock of New Haven Moving Equipment Corporation. The shares were valued at $3,750. Unless a designated "Independent Trustee" saw fit in his discretion to direct otherwise, the trustees were to retain all income generated until the grandchild-beneficiary reached age 21. At that time, the accumulated income would be distributed *in toto*. Thereafter, the beneficiary would receive payments at least annually of all income earned by the trust. If the grandchild died before his or her twenty-first birthday, all accumulated income would go to the estate of the grandchild.

During the lifetime of the beneficiary, control over the trust corpus was vested exclusively in the "absolute and uncontrolled discretion" of the Independent Trustee. He could permit the principal to stand untouched or he could pay out any portion directly to, or for the benefit of, the beneficiary. In addition, the trustee could terminate the trust at any time by distributing the entire corpus. The trust also provided the beneficiary with a limited power of appointment in the event that any of the principal remained in the trust upon his or her death. The corpus, or any part of it, could be designated to pass to some or all of David H. Levine's lineal descendants. The original beneficiary could not elect to leave corpus to his or her own estate, his or her creditors, or the creditors of the original beneficiary's estate.

* * *

II.

The dispute focuses on the interpretation and interrelation of §§ 2503(b) and (c) of the Internal Revenue Code of 1954. Section 2503(b) permits a donor to escape gift tax on the first $3,000 of gifts to each donee yearly, so long as the gift is *not* "of future interests in property." Although the term "future interests" is nowhere defined in the Code, the Supreme Court has instructed that "the question is * * * when enjoyment [of the property] begins." Fondren v. C. I. R., 324 U.S. 18, 20, 65 S.Ct. 499, 500, 89 L.Ed. 668 (1945). The gift is of a future interest if "limited to commence in use, possession, or enjoyment at some future date or time." Id.; Treas.Reg. § 25.2503–3(a). The gift of a remainder interest in a trust has, thus, been considered a future interest. C. I. R. v. Disston, 325 U.S. 442, 447, 65 S.Ct. 585, 89 L.Ed. 1397 (1945). An income interest for life, however, is a present interest if payments commence immediately. Fondren, supra, 324 U.S. at 21, 65 S.Ct. 499.

Despite the attractions of the § 2503(b) gift tax exclusion, donors hesitate to make outright gifts of principal or income to minors. In response to such understandable concerns, and the existence of many state statutory prohibitions against minors accepting and exercising dominion over property, but see Rev.Rul. 54–400, 1954–2 Cum.Bull. 319, 320, Congress in 1954 added § 2503(c) to the Code. The section provides:

> Transfer for the Benefit of Minor.—No part of a gift to an individual who has not attained the age of 21 years on the date of such transfer shall be considered a gift of a future interest in property for purposes of subsection (b) if the property and the income there from—
>
> (1) may be expended by, or for the benefit of, the donee before his attaining the age of 21 years, and
>
> (2) will to the extent not so expended—
>
>> (A) pass to the donee on his attaining the age of 21 years, and
>>
>> (B) in the event the donee dies before attaining the age of 21 years, be payable to the estate of the donee or as he may appoint under a general power of appointment as defined in section 2514(c).

At first blush, it might seem that the Levine trusts clearly fail to satisfy the requirements of § 2503(c)(2). The "property"—if defined as the corpus—would not pass to the donee when the beneficiary turned 21. Nor would it be payable to the donee's estate if death occurred before the age of 21 years. The power of appointment established by each trust over the corpus also fails the tests set forth in § 2514(c).[222]

The problem, however, is somewhat more complex. The Supreme court in *Disston* and *Fondren*, supra, recognized that a gift may be divided into component parts for tax purposes. One or more of those elements may qualify as present interests even if others do not. The Tax Court applied these principles in a 1961 decision involving a trust similar to Levine's. Herr v. C. I. R., 35 T.C. 732 (1961). Treating the income to be accumulated to age 21 (the "pre-21 income interest") as a separate element of "property ," id. at 737, the Tax Court held that this segment satisfied the requirements of § 2503(c) and the taxpayer could therefore benefit from the

---

222. Section 2514(c) requires, in part, that [T]he term 'general power of appointment' means a power which is exercisable in favor of the individual possessing the power * * * , his estate, his creditors, or the creditors of his estate * * * .

§ 2503(b) exclusion.   The Third Circuit affirmed the Tax Court, 303 F.2d 780 (3d Cir. 1962).   The Commissioner has acquiesced in the *Herr* decision, 1968–2 Cum.Bull. 2, and accordingly concedes in the present case that the pre-21 income interest is eligible for the gift tax exclusion.

The pre-21 income interests in the Levine trusts do not, however, exhaust the $3,000 per donee annual exclusion.[223]   Knowing that the remainder interests cannot qualify as present interests under either § 2503(b) or § 2503(c), the Levines have concentrated their attention on the post-21 income interests.   Although the taxpayer in *Herr* did not suggest that the post-21 segment could properly be considered a present interest, the Tax Court explicitly spoke to the issue:

> [I]ncome [after] 21   *   *   *   [is a] future interest.

35 T.C. at 736.   And the Court of Appeals commented similarly:

> [T]he right[s] to income and principal after minority are future interests.

303 F.2d at 782.   The taxpayers ask us to disregard these views and to extend the holding of *Herr* so that the post-21 income interests will be treated as present interests.   We decline to do so.

III.

If the post-21 income interests are looked upon as separate gifts, they cannot be considered present interests under § 2503(b).   As in the case of the remainder interests, initial enjoyment is delayed until a time in the future.   Moreover, the requirements of § 2503(c)(2) are not satisfied.

The taxpayers urge that we are required to treat the post-21 income interests as one with the pre-21 income interests, but that the remainder interests should be considered a separate gift.   The taxpayers recognize that the combined pre- and post-21 income interests do not qualify as a present interest when viewed solely in the light of § 2503(b).   This is so because the accumulation of income before age 21 works as a postponement of immediate enjoyment.   In addition, the combined income interests fail to meet the criteria of § 2503(c)(2).

The Levines seek to overcome these obstacles by means of an ingenious argument.   The combination of pre-21 and post-21 income interests resembles a unitary life estate, they argue.   The only reason it cannot qualify as a § 2503(b) present interest, they urge, is the accumulation provision that permits enjoyment to be delayed until age 21.   But, they say, § 2503(c) as interpreted by *Herr* permits the future interest characteristic of the pre-21 income interests to be disregarded for the purpose of receiving the § 2503(b) exclusion.   In other words, they assert that *Herr* and § 2503(c) in effect transform the pre-21 income interests into present interests.   Then, by a giant leap, the taxpayers conclude that a single, lifetime present interest is produced by linking the pre-21 *constructive* present interests with the post-21 income interests.

Accordingly, we reverse the decision of the Tax Court and remand.

---

223.   Using actuarial tables, the value of each gift is allocated between the present values of the pre-21 income interest, post-21 income interest, and remainder interest.   See Treas.Reg. § 25.2512–5.

In the case of very young children, particularly if the transferred property consists of low-yield, high-growth assets which are unlikely to generate much income before the child reaches age 21, the *Herr* approach may be satisfactory. For a one-year-old child, the right to income until age 21 represents approximately ⅔ of the value of the transferred property.[224] For teenage children, the portion of the gift that qualifies under § 2503(c) is likely to be relatively small if the *Herr* approach is used. Therefore, for such beneficiaries the §2503(b) trust may be preferable, even though only the income interest qualifies for the exclusion.

[b] Costs of Trust Administration

From the standpoint of costs of administration, § 2503(c) trusts are often expensive—in time if not in money—for the amount involved. At least initially, the cost of a professional trustee or custodian is likely to be prohibitive because of the small size of the trust. A family member is likely to serve as trustee and do his own custodial work in keeping track of the trust property. If the trust property consists of a limited number of securities or of shares in a single mutual fund, the trustee's work may not be unduly time consuming until it becomes necessary to prepare income tax returns. At that point he either must cope with the trust form himself or subject the trust to the cost of a professionally prepared return.

If the trust grows—from additions, appreciation of the trust assets, and accumulation of income—custodial and accounting costs may cease to be a major proportion of the trust income. Indeed, the trust property may accumulate more quickly than the donor has anticipated. In that situation, it is useful to be able to make distributions to a custodian for the minor beneficiary if such a course is authorized by state law. This will mean that only part of the income will be taxed to the trust and that the balance will be taxed to the beneficiary individually.

If the trust fails to grow to the extent anticipated by the donor, either as a result of unfavorable investment results or as a result of the donor's inability or unwillingness to make anticipated additions to the trust, the result may be a small trust for which custodial and accounting costs are uneconomically large. This possibility should be pointed out to the client when the trust is being created.

[c] Income Tax Consequences During Initial Trust Term

Income of a § 2503(c) trust during its initial term is taxable to the trust unless it is distributed. This is true even if the donor is the trustee [225] (although it is undesirable for him to be the trustee, from the standpoint of estate taxes, unless he is willing to assume he will survive the termination of the trust). A distribution will cause income to be taxed to the beneficiary, to the extent of the trust's distributable net income,[226] unless the distribution

---

224. The value for gift tax purposes of a twenty-year term interest is 68.8195 percent of the whole. See Reg. §25.2512–9(f), Table B. Presumably, the reduction for the chance that the child would die under age 21 would be relatively small.

225. The required powers over income and principal fit readily within the exceptions provided in §§ 674(b)(5)(B) and 674(b)(7) from the general rule of § 674(a) taxing the grantor because of a power to control beneficial enjoyment of the trust. See ¶ 9.01[4][b], [c] supra.

226. See § 643(a), discussed at ¶ 11.01[2] infra.

discharges a parent's support obligation.   In the latter situation, the parent is taxed on such income.[227]

Income accumulated in prior years is not subject to throwback treatment [228] unless the distributee receives distributions from more than two trusts which are thrown back to the same year and those distributions cause the multiple-trust rule of § 667(c) to apply.   This freedom from throwback treatment enhances the attractiveness of § 2503(c) trusts.

[d] Estate Tax Consequences During Initial Trust Term

From an estate tax standpoint, the donor of a § 2503(c) trust should not be the trustee and should be co-trustee only if powers which are objectionable from an estate tax standpoint are made exercisable solely by one or more other co-trustees.   The required power of the trustee to distribute principal would cause the property to be included in the donor's estate if he held the power.[229]   Some donors prefer to assume the risk that they will not survive the termination of the trust and choose to act as trustee themselves.   Ordinarily, it should be possible to find someone else as trustee who will be responsive to the donor's views and at the same time will avoid having the property includible in the donor's estate.

[e] Income and Estate Tax Consequences of the Beneficiary's Nonexercise of a Power of Withdrawal (and Resulting Extension of Trust Term)

If the beneficiary does not automatically receive the principal at age 21 but instead merely has a power to withdraw it, what are the consequences of his failure to exercise such power of withdrawal?   The power of withdrawal is a general power of appointment for estate and gift tax purposes and is a grantor power for income tax purposes under § 678(a)(2).   Often, the terms of the trust during the extended term are likely to give the beneficiary enough power so that he does not make a gift by failing to exercise his power of withdrawal.   If that is true, the power that prevents gift tax consequences will cause the property to be included in the beneficiary's estate under § 2041, if he dies during the extended term of the trust.

It is impossible to generalize in similar fashion as to the income tax consequences of the beneficiary's nonexercise of the power of withdrawal.   Under § 678(a)(2), his position is that of a trust grantor and usually the provisions of the trust during the extended term will be such as to cause him to be treated as owner of the trust for income tax purposes.

[3] Section 2503(b) Trust

For older minors, the § 2503(b) trust offers an attractive alternative to § 2503(c).

> *Example 9.16.*   G transfers property to T as trustee to pay the income to B for his life, and on B's death, to pay the principal to B's descendants then living, *per stirpes*, or if none are then living, to THE

---

227. See Reg. § 1.662(a)–4, discussed at ¶ 9.01[9][a], [b] supra.

228. See § 665(b), discussed at ¶ 11.02[2] infra.

229. See § 2038(a)(1), discussed at ¶ 5.02[5] supra.

PRESIDENT AND FELLOWS OF HARVARD COLLEGE, a Massachusetts charitable corporation.

If the trust requires that income be paid to the beneficiary for his life, the income interest—which is never less than 91 percent of the value of the property [230]—will qualify for the exclusion. The remainder following his life estate will be a future interest but its value will be small in relation to the amount transferred. And the property will not be subject to estate tax when he dies unless he is given a general power of appointment over it—although it may be subject to the generation-skipping transfer tax if it passes to a younger generation beneficiary who is not a grandchild of the donor.

[4] **Trust With "Crummey" Power**

D. CLIFFORD CRUMMEY v. COMMISSIONER

United States Court of Appeals, Ninth Circuit, 1968.
397 F.2d 82, 68–2 USTC ¶ 12,541.

BYRNE, District Judge:

*   *   *

On February 12, 1962, the petitioners executed, as grantors; an irrevocable living trust for the benefit of their four children. The beneficiaries and their ages at relevant times are as follows:

	Age	12/31/62	12/31/63
John Knowles Crummey		22	23
Janet Sheldon Crummey		20	21
David Clarke Crummey		15	16
Mark Clifford Crummey		11	12

Originally the sum of $50 was contributed to the trust. Thereafter, additional contributions were made by each of the petitioners in the following amounts and on the following dates:

$ 4,267.77	6/20/62
49,550.00	12/15/62
12,797.81	12/19/63

The dispute revolves around the tax years of 1962 and 1963. Each of the petitioners filed a gift tax return for each year. Each petitioner claimed a $3,000 per beneficiary tax exclusion under the provisions of 26 U.S.C.A. § 2503(b). *   *   *

The Commissioner of Internal Revenue determined that each of the petitioners was entitled to only one $3,000 exclusion for each year. This determination was based upon the Commissioner's belief that the portion of the gifts in trust for the children under the age of 21 were "future interests" which are disallowed under § 2503(b). The taxpayers contested the determination of a deficiency in the Tax Court. The Commissioner conceded by stipulation in that proceeding that each petitioner was entitled

---

230. See Reg. § 25.2512–9(f), table A (1), giving a range of values for life estates in   males aged 20–21 of over 91 percent of the whole.

to an additional $3,000 exclusion for the year 1963 by reason of Janet Crummey having reached the age of 21.

The Tax Court followed the Commissioner's interpretation as to gifts in trust to David and Mark, but determined that the 1962 gift in trust to Janet qualified as a gift of a present interest because of certain additional rights accorded to persons 18 and over by California law. Thus, the Tax Court held that each petitioner was entitled to an additional $3,000 exclusion for the year 1962.

The key provision of the trust agreement is the "demand" provision which states:

> "THREE. *Additions.* The Trustee may receive any other real or personal property from the Trustors (or either of them) or from any other person or persons, by lifetime gift, under a Will or Trust or from any other source. Such property will be held by the Trustee subject to the terms of this Agreement. A donor may designate or allocate all of his gift to one or more Trusts, or in stated amounts to different Trusts. If the donor does not specifically designate what amount of his gift is to augment each Trust, the Trustee shall divide such gift equally between the Trusts then existing, established by this Agreement. The Trustee agrees, if he accepts such additions, to hold and manage such additions in trust for the uses and in the manner set forth herein. *With respect to such additions, each child of the Trustors may demand at any time (up to and including December 31 of the year in which a transfer to his or her Trust has been made) the sum of Four Thousand Dollars ($4,000.00) or the amount of the transfer from each donor, whichever is less, payable in cash immediately upon receipt by the Trustee of the demand in writing and in any event, not later than December 31 in the year in which such transfer was made. Such payment shall be made from the gift of that donor for that year. If a child is a minor at the time of such gift of that donor for that year, or fails in legal capacity for any reason, the child's guardian may make such demand on behalf of the child. The property received pursuant to the demand shall be held by the guardian for the benefit and use of the child."* (Emphasis supplied.)

The whole question on this appeal is whether or not a present interest was given by the petitioners to their minor children so as to qualify as an exclusion under § 2503(b). The petitioners on appeal contend that each minor beneficiary has the right under California law to demand partial distribution from the Trustee. In the alternative they urge that a parent as natural guardian of the person of his minor children could make such a demand. As a third alternative, they assert that under California law a minor over the age of 14 had the right to have a legal guardian appointed who can make the necessary demand. The Commissioner, as cross petitioner, alleges as error the Tax Court's ruling that the 1962 gifts in trust to Janet (then age 20) were present interests.

It was stipulated before the Tax Court in regard to the trust and the parties thereto that at all times relevant all the minor children lived with the petitioners and no legal guardian had been appointed for them. In addition, it was agreed that all the *children* were supported by petitioners and none of them had made a demand against the trust funds or received any distribution from them.

* * *

The Commissioner and the Tax Court both placed primary reliance on the case of Stifel v. commissioner of Internal Revenue, 197 F.2d 107 (2d Cir. 1952). In that case an irrevocable trust was involved which provided that the beneficiary, a minor, could demand any part of the funds not expended by the Trustee and, subject to such demand, the Trustee was to accumulate. The trust also provided that it could be terminated by the beneficiary or by her guardian during minority. The court held that gifts to this trust were gifts of "future interests". * * *

* * *

Under the provisions of this trust the income is to be accumulated and added to the corpus until each minor reaches the age of 21, unless the trustee feels in his discretion that distributions should be made to a needy beneficiary. From 21 to 35 all income is distributed to the beneficiary. After 35 the trustee again has discretion as to both income and corpus, and may distribute whatever is necessary up to the whole thereof. Aside from the actions of the trustee, the only way any beneficiary may get at the property is through the "demand" provision, quoted above.

One question raised in these proceedings is whether or not the trust prohibits a minor child from making a demand on the yearly additions to the trust. The key language from paragraph three is as follows:

"If a child is a minor at the time of such gift of that donor for that year, or fails in legal capacity for any reason, the child's guardian may make such demand on behalf of the child."

The Tax Court interpreted this provision in favor of the taxpayers by saying that "may" is permissive and thus that the minor child can make the demand if allowed by law, or, if not permitted by law, the guardian may do it. Although, as the Commissioner suggests, this strains the language somewhat, it does seem consistent with the obvious intent in drafting this provision. Surely, this provision was intended to give the minor beneficiary the broadest demand power available so that the gift tax exclusion would be applicable.

There is very little dispute between the parties as to the rights and disabilities of a minor accorded by the California statutes and cases. The problem comes in attempting to ascertain from these rights and disabilities the answer to the question of whether a minor may make a demand upon the trustee for a portion of the trust as provided in the trust instrument.

It is agreed that a minor in California may own property. Estate of Yano, 188 Cal. 645, 206 P. 995 (1922). He may receive a gift. DeLevillain v. Evans, 39 Cal. 120. A minor may demand his own funds from a bank (Cal.Fin.Code, §§ 850 & 853), a savings institution (Cal.Fin.Code, §§ 7600 & 7606), or a corporation (Cal.Corp.Code, §§ 2221 & 2413). A minor of the age of 14 or over has the right to secure the appointment of a guardian and one will be appointed if the court finds it "necessary or convenient".

Cal.Prob.Code, § 1406; Guardianship of Kentera, 41 Cal.2d 639, 262 P.2d 317 (1953).

It is further agreed that a minor cannot sue in his own name (Cal.Civ.Code, § 42) and cannot appoint an agent.   (Cal.Civ.Code, § 33). With certain exceptions a minor can disaffirm contracts made by him during his minority.   Cal.Civ.Code, § 35.   A minor under the age of 18 cannot make contracts relating to real property or personal property not in his possession or control.   Cal.Civ.Code, § 33.

The parent of a child may be its natural guardian, but such a guardianship is of the person of the child and not of his estate.   Kendall v. Miller, 9 Cal. 591; Cal.Civ.Code, § 202.

After examining the same rights and disabilities, the petitioners, the commissioner, and the Tax Court each arrived at a different solution to our problem.   The Tax Court concentrated on the disabilities and concluded that David and Mark could not make an effective demand because they could not sue in their own name, nor appoint an agent and could disaffirm contracts.   The court, however, concluded that Janet could make an effective demand because Cal.Civ.Code, § 33 indirectly states that she could make contracts with regard to real and personal property.

The Commissioner concentrated on the inability to sue or appoint an agent and concluded that none of the minors had anything more than paper rights because he or she lacked the capacity to enforce the demand.

The petitioners urge that the right to acquire and hold property is the key.   In the alternative they argue that the parent as a natural guardian could make the demand although it would be necessary to appoint a legal guardian to receive the property.   Finally, they urge that all the minors over 14 could make a demand since they could request the appointment of a legal guardian.

The position taken by the Tax Court seems clearly untenable.   The distinction drawn between David and Mark on the one hand, and Janet on the other, makes no sense.   The mere fact that Janet can make certain additional contracts does not have any relevance to the question of whether she is capable of making an effective demand upon the trustee.   We cannot agree with the position of the Commissioner because we do not feel that a lawsuit or the appointment of an agent is a necessary prelude to the making of a demand upon the trustee.   As we visualize the hypothetical situation, the child would inform the trustee that he demanded his share of the additions up to $4,000.   The trustee would petition the court for the appointment of a legal guardian and then turn the funds over to the guardian.   It would also seem possible for the parent to make the demand as natural guardian.   This would involve the acquisition of property for the child rather than the management of the property.   It would then be necessary for a legal guardian to be appointed to take charge of the funds.   The only time when the disability to sue would come into play, would be if the trustee disregarded the demand and committed a breach of trust.   That would not, however, vitiate the demand.

All this is admittedly speculative since it is highly unlikely that a demand will ever be made or that if one is made, it would be made in this fashion.

However, as a technical matter, we think a minor could make the demand.

Given the trust, the California law, and the circumstances in our case, it can be seen that very different results may well be achieved, depending upon the test used. Under a strict interpretation of the *Stifel* test of examining everything and determining whether there is any likelihood of present enjoyment, the gifts to minors in our case would seem to be "future interests." Although under our interpretation neither the trust nor the law technically forbid a demand by the minor, the practical difficulties of a child going through the procedures seem substantial. In addition, the surrounding facts indicate the children were well cared for and the obvious intention of the trustors was to create a long term trust. No guardian had been appointed and, except for the tax difficulties, probably never would be appointed. As a practical matter, it is likely that some, if not all, of the beneficiaries did not even know that they had any right to demand funds from the trust. They probably did not know when contributions were made to the trust or in what amounts. Even had they known, the substantial contributions were made toward the end of the year so that the time to make a demand was severely limited. Nobody had made a demand under the provision, and no distributions had been made. We think it unlikely that any demand ever would have been made.

*   *   *

We decline to follow a strict reading of the *Stifel* case in our situation because we feel that the solution suggested by that case is inconsistent and unfair. It becomes arbitrary for the I.R.S. to step in and decide who is likely to make an effective demand. Under the circumstances suggested in our case, it is doubtful that any demands will be made against the trust— yet the Commissioner always allowed the exclusion as to adult beneficiaries. There is nothing to indicate that it is any more likely that John will demand funds than that any other beneficiary will do so. The only distinction is that it might be easier for him to make such a demand. Since we conclude that the demand can be made by the others, it follows that the exclusion should also apply to them. *   *   *

*   *   *

———

Although neither the *Crummey* case nor Rev.Rul. 73–405, [231] which accepts the result reached, required that the beneficiary be aware of his power to withdraw amounts added to the trust, a subsequent Ruling [232] based denial of the deduction in part on the donor's failure to inform the donee of his demand right. Thus, it is advisable to require that the trustee

231. 1973–2 CB 321.

232. In Rev.Rul. 81–7, 1981–1 IRB 27, 3 CCH E&GT ¶ 12,440U, the present interest exclusion was denied because the donor's conduct was held to make the demand right illusory and to effectively deprive the donee of the power. The trust was created December 29 and the demand right lapsed by its terms on December 31, neither the grantor nor the trustee having informed the beneficiary of the demand right. The Ruling notes that the beneficiary was a legally competent adult, thus leaving open the possibility that an even more rigorous standard could be applied in the case of a minor or incompetent adult beneficiary.

give the beneficiary written notice of additions to the trust and a reasonable period within which to exercise his right to demand such additions. [233]

Even with such notice, many young beneficiaries will be in no position to make a free and informed choice with respect to exercising the demand right or allowing it to lapse. They may be insufficiently mature to be aware that failure to exercise the right will put the trust property beyond their reach or they may be unwilling to risk incurring the disapproval of a donor or parent. Clients may be understandably uncomfortable in facing the prospect that beneficiaries ultimately will learn of the significance of the lapsed demand right and will know then that they never had an opportunity to make a free, timely, and informed choice in the matter.

Clients who are considering use of *Crummey* powers should be advised of this problem and, also, of the income tax consequences to the power holder. Although the lapse of a power to withdraw the greater of $5,000 or 5 percent of the property subject to the power is not a taxable transfer for estate [234] or gift tax [235] purposes, it does cause the power holder in future years to be treated for trust income tax purposes as the grantor of the portion that could have been withdrawn. [236]

---

233. See Letter Rul. 8004172, 3 CCH E&GT ¶ 12,377, Nov. 5, 1979 (exclusion allowed where beneficiaries given 30 days in which to make demand).

234. § 2041(b)(2). For a discussion of the tax consequences of such a lapse, see ¶ 12.03[1][a] infra.

235. § 2514(e).

236. § 678(a)(2). For a discussion, see ¶ 12.01[3][c][ii] infra.

Chapter 10

CHARITABLE SPLIT-INTEREST TRUSTS

¶ 10.01 TYPES OF CHARITABLE SPLIT-INTEREST TRUSTS

Charitable split-interest trusts are trusts in which both charitable and non-charitable beneficiaries have interests. Such trusts are of three basic types:

(1) The charitable remainder trust, in which non-charitable beneficiaries receive periodic payments until the trust terminates, at which time any undistributed principal and income is paid to one or more charities;

(2) The charitable lead trust, in which the charitable beneficiary receives periodic payments for a limited time. When the interest of the charity has terminated, any undistributed principal and income is either paid to one or more non-charitable beneficiaries or continues to be held in trust for their benefit;

(3) The pooled income fund, which is basically a charitable remainder trust to which more than one donor may make contributions and which qualifies under the definition in § 642(c)(5).

Despite their denomination as "charitable," these trusts are primarily important in estate planning to save income, estate and gift taxes on wealth passing to non-charitable beneficiaries. All three kinds may be established either during the grantor's life (inter vivos) or by will (testamentary). Charitable remainder trusts (and pooled income funds) are used primarily to save income taxes, while charitable lead trusts are used primarily to save estate and gift taxes on wealth that ultimately passes to non-charitable beneficiaries.

This chapter deals with charitable split-interest trusts that become irrevocable during the life of the grantor, and Chapter 19 discusses such trusts that become irrevocable on the death of the grantor or are created by his will. Pooled income funds will not be discussed further, as they generally allow gifts of two or more grantors to serve purposes comparable to those served by individually created charitable remainder trusts.

¶ 10.02 CHARITABLE REMAINDER TRUSTS

Charitable remainder trusts offer such impressive income tax savings that they deserve much wider use than they now enjoy. They combine an opportunity for tax-free accumulation of income by the trust [1] with an income tax deduction for the value of the remainder interest if the grantor creates the trust during his life.[2]

---

1. See § 664(c), discussed at ¶ 10.02[2] infra.

2. Section 170 provides generally for a deduction for charitable contributions. However, no deduction is allowed for remainder interests in trust other than those described in § 664 and pooled income funds described in § 642(c)(5). See § 170(f)(2)(A). An otherwise allowable deduction is subject to the various percentile and other limitations contained in § 170, including that provided in § 170(e)(1)(A), with respect to property which would not be long-term capital gain property if sold by the taxpayer.

A charitable remainder trust may be either an annuity trust or a unitrust. An annuity trust requires annual payments of a fixed dollar amount or percentage of the initial value of the trust principal, either for the lives of one or more persons or for a period of years, not exceeding twenty, with the remainder (including any undistributed income) payable to one or more charities.[3] The annual payments must not be less than 5 percent of the initial value of the trust principal. The unitrust differs in that the required annual payments are a specified percentage (not less than 5 percent) of the value of the principal as determined each year [4] rather than a percentage of its initial principal value.

The creation of the trust is a taxable transfer for gift or estate tax purposes to the extent of the interests of the non-charitable beneficiaries. But if the trust is created during the grantor's life, his income tax deduction for the value of the charitable remainder interest [5] may reduce his income taxes enough to wholly or partially offset any gift tax incurred.

It is unclear what minimum value the charitable remainder interest must have in order for the trust to qualify as a charitable remainder trust for income tax purposes under § 664,[6] which also controls qualification for gift tax purposes under § 2522(c)(2)(A).

[1] Income Tax Consequences for Grantor

The income tax consequences for the grantor of either type of inter vivos charitable remainder trust are quite favorable. When the trust is created, the grantor is entitled to an income tax charitable deduction for the present actuarial value of the remainder interest,[7] even though the charity will not be entitled to possession of any of the trust property until the non-charitable interests have terminated.

As soon as the trust is created, the grantor ceases to be taxable on the income from the trust property as long as the trust satisfies the Clifford sections, under which trust income sometimes is taxable to the grantor as owner.[8] Such income-shifting would also be achieved if the grantor created a trust with no charitable remainder. But for such non-charitable trusts,

3. § 664(d)(1)(A).

4. § 664(d)(2)(A).

5. See note 2 supra.

6. Regulations Section 1.664–1(a)(1)(ii) defines "charitable remainder trust," inter alia, as "a trust with respect to which a deduction is allowable under section 170, 2055, 2106, or 2522 * * * ." This suggests that the remainder must have some minimum actuarial value, although one commentator has suggested otherwise. See Covey, "Estate, Gift and Income Taxation—1974 Developments," 9 Univ.Miami Inst. on Est.Planning, ¶¶ 100, 112.15 (1975).

Revenue Ruling 77–374, 1977–2 CB 329, disallowed an estate tax charitable deduction for the value of a charitable remainder on the ground that there was more than a 5 percent possibility the charity's remainder interest would be defeated because the non-charitable beneficiary might live long enough to exhaust the trust assets. See also Rev.Rul. 70–452, 1970–2 CB 199, disallowing a gift tax deduction under prior law for the same reason. However, the tables in the Income Tax Regulations that show the present worth of a remainder interest in a charitable remainder unitrust give values below 1 percent for a remainder following an annual payment to a young female at an adjusted pay-out rate in excess of 8 percent. See Reg. § 1.664–4(b)(4), Table E(2). If the implication is correct that this small a charitable interest is sufficient, the cost of qualifying under § 664 may be modest indeed.

7. See note 2 supra.

8. §§ 671–677. For a discussion, see ¶ 9.01 supra.

income that is not distributed and taxed to the beneficiaries is taxable to the trust itself.[9]   In addition, gain recognized by the trust from a sale or exchange of property within two years of its transfer to the trust is, to the extent of appreciation at the time of such transfer, taxed to the trust at the grantor's rates.[10]   Other income attributed to a non-charitable trust for income tax purposes is taxed at the trust's rates.

Charitable remainder trusts, on the other hand, are generally exempt from income taxes and thus are free from both the two-year rule [11] and the income taxes applicable to the income of non-charitable trusts.   As a result, such trusts are an ideal vehicle for disposing of appreciated property.

[2] Income Tax Consequences for Trust and Beneficiaries

Charitable remainder trusts are taxed under § 664(c), which provides that the trust is exempt from income taxes unless it has unrelated business taxable income.[12]   This makes such trusts ideal for the tax-free realization of gains without diverting from non-charitable beneficiaries the enjoyment of the portion of trust principal that such gains represent.

Investment advisors differ as to the extent to which an investment policy of realizing gains by selling appreciated securities is likely, over the long run, to improve investment results.   Advisors generally are likely to favor such realization if sales of such securities are required to permit the trust investments to be diversified, as in the case of a trust initially funded largely with a single security.   To whatever extent the trustee wishes to follow a policy of realizing gains, either for diversification or in an effort to improve investment performance, use of a charitable remainder trust frees such realization from tax as long as the ordinary trust income is sufficient to cover required payments to non-charitable beneficiaries.

If the practice of realizing gains in fact increases the value of the principal of the trust, the increase may benefit the non-charitable beneficiary even though any remaining principal and accumulated income will be payable to a charity when the trust terminates.   In a unitrust, increases in the value of principal directly affect the amount payable to the non-charitable beneficiary because that amount is based on the value of the principal, determined annually.   In an annuity trust, gains have no such direct effect on the amount payable but provide greater security that funds will be available to make the fixed annual payment.

Taxation of trust beneficiaries is governed by § 664(b).   Distributions are treated as consisting of the following items, in the order listed:

(1) Ordinary income;

(2) Capital gains;

(3) Tax-exempt income;

(4) Corpus.

---

9. For a discussion, see ¶ 9.02[2] supra.

10. See § 644.   For a discussion, see ¶ 9.02[2][a] supra.

11. See § 644(e)(3).

12. Unrelated business taxable income is defined in § 512.

If such distributions exceed the ordinary income of the trust, beneficiaries may be taxed on trust capital gains.[13]   In this respect, beneficiaries are treated less favorably than are beneficiaries of a non-charitable trust, whose taxable income from trust distributions is limited by the trust's distributable net income [14] and, thus, does not ordinarily include capital gains except those for the year in which the trust terminates.[15]

If the trust pays the annuity or unitrust amount in property, it is treated as realizing the value of the property and the beneficiary takes such value as his basis.[16]   As the distribution is required, rather than being discretionary, it does not result in a step-up of basis without realization of gain by the trust, unlike certain discretionary distributions of appreciated property by non-charitable trusts.[17]   However, the realized gain is tax exempt, like other income of a charitable remainder trust, and is never taxable to the non-charitable beneficiary unless distributions on a cumulative basis exceed the ordinary income of the trust.

[3] Gift Tax and Estate Tax Consequences

The creation of a charitable remainder trust during the grantor's life is a completed gift for gift tax purposes at the time when the trust becomes irrevocable, if interests are created in non-charitable beneficiaries other than the grantor himself.   The grantor is entitled to a gift tax charitable deduction for the value of the charitable remainder interest.[18]

The actuarial tables used in computing the deduction are based on an assumed 6 percent interest rate.[19]   At a time when the prevailing return on a variety of investment vehicles is substantially in excess of 6 percent, the tables may provide a distorted estimate of the value of the charitable remainder interest.   Such distortion could result both from unrealistic assumptions with respect to the accumulation of income (or invasion of principal) during the trust term and from failure to discount the assumed value of the charitable remainder sufficiently to reflect the postponement of its receipt by the charity.

For example, if the non-charitable annuity or unitrust payments are at a rate of 6 percent, the tables assume that there will be no increase in the charitable remainder from the accumulation of income.   If such payments are at a rate in excess of 6 percent, the tables assume that the remainder will be reduced by invasion of principal for the benefit of the non-charitable beneficiaries.   In each case, the assumption may be incorrect if the trust in fact yields income at a rate in excess of 6 percent.

On the other hand, when the prevailing interest rate exceeds 6 percent, the tables overstate the present value of a charitable remainder interest

---

13. See Reg. § 1.664–1(d)(1).   Thus, a capital gain realized by the trust is never taxed if distributions, on a cumulative basis, never exceed ordinary income.

14. See §§ 652, 662.   Distributable net income is defined in § 643(a).   For a discussion, see ¶ 11.01[2] infra.

15. § 643(a)(3).

16. See Reg. § 1.664–1(d)(5).

17. Reg. § 1.661(a)–2(f)(3).   For a discussion, see ¶ 4.07 supra.

18. § 2522(c)(2)(A).

19. See Reg. § 25.2522(c)–3(c)(2)(iv), referring to Reg. §§ 1.664–2(c), 1.664–4.

because a realistic discount for the delay in payment would exceed 6 percent. Thus the distorting effects of an interest rate below the rates which prevail in the investment markets tend to offset each other.

The gift of the non-charitable interests will either reduce the grantor's unified credit [20] or, to the extent it exceeds the unused portion of his credit, will constitute a taxable gift.   However, any gift tax due may be offset in whole or in part by the reduction in the grantor's income tax because of the charitable deduction when the gift is made.[21]   If he dies within three years of the transfer, any gift tax paid by him or by his estate is included in his taxable estate.[22]

The charitable remainder trust is included in the grantor's taxable estate if he retains an annuity or unitrust interest.[23]   If the trust is so included, an estate tax charitable deduction is allowed for the value of the charity's remainder interest [24] as of the grantor's death.

[4] Planning

Because inter vivos charitable remainder trusts offer such unusually favorable income tax advantages, the Commissioner insists upon meticulous compliance with statutory and administrative requirements for qualification.[25]   Revenue Ruling 72-395 [26] sets forth both mandatory and optional provisions for creating charitable remainder trusts.   Any deviation from the prescribed pattern risks disqualification unless it is specifically covered in advance by a private ruling.

Some of the major considerations encompassed by Revenue Ruling 72-395 are:

(1) Choosing between an annuity trust and a unitrust;

(2) Selecting the trustee;

(3) Determining the pay-out rate and the duration of the trust;

(4) Selecting the beneficiary; and

(5) Choosing assets to fund the trust.

[a] Choosing Between an Annuity Trust and a Unitrust

For an individual client, the optimum choice between an annuity trust and a unitrust would require an ability to anticipate the future to an extent not given to mortal beings.   The most that an advisor can hope to do is to identify the considerations which point in favor of one alternative or the other.   The major differences are:

(1) The effect of fluctuations in the value of trust assets.   If the client is primarily concerned with maximizing the amounts payable to the non-charitable beneficiaries over the term of the trust, the unitrust

---

20.   § 2505.

21.   § 170(f)(2)(A).

22.   § 2035(c).

23.   § 2036. If the retained interest is equal to less than the right to all the income from the transferred property, only a portion of the value of the property is includible.   See Rev. Rul. 76-273, 1976-2 CB 268.

24.   § 2055(e)(2)(A).

25.   See, e.g., Rev. Rul. 74-19, 1974-1 CB 155 (provision for charging portion of trustee's fee against unitrust amount disqualifies trust because of failure to meet "fixed percentage" requirement).

26.   1972-2 CB 340, as modified by Rev. Rul. 80-123, 1980-1 CB 205.

is better suited to this objective if the trust assets in fact appreciate in value.   Conversely, if the value of trust assets declines, an annuity trust will produce a larger return for non-charitable beneficiaries, as they are guaranteed a fixed annual sum regardless of that value.

(2) The effect of difficulties inherent in an annual valuation of trust assets.   Where determination of the value of trust assets is likely to be a problem (e.g., where the assets have no readily ascertainable market value and their value must be established by appraisal),[27] the annuity trust has the advantage of requiring only one such determination, at the time when the trust is created.   A unitrust, on the other hand, requires the determination to be made annually, which may entail significant expense and uncertainty.

(3) Whether the client may wish to spread the funding of the trust over two or more years.   The annuity trust must by its terms prohibit any additions,[28] but the unitrust may permit additions if appropriate provisions for adjusting the pay-out amount are included.[29]   Thus, if a client may wish to spread the funding of the trust over two or more years, the unitrust is the only vehicle which permits this.

[b] Selecting the Trustee

Selection of the trustee is governed by the same considerations that are relevant in non-charitable trusts.   The charitable remainder trust will be disqualified if anyone holds a spray power (to allocate income or principal) that would cause the grantor or anyone else to be taxable as owner if the rules contained in §§ 671–678 applied to the trust.[30]   Some commentators have expressed concern that selection of the grantor as trustee would cause disqualification of the trust.   Such concerns appear to be unfounded in view of the express recognition in Revenue Ruling 77–285 [31] that a right to remove

---

27.   For the valuation required by § 664(d)(2)(A), the legislative history includes the following:

"It is contemplated that a charitable contribution deduction would be denied where assets which do not have an objective, ascertainable market value, such as real estate or stock in a closely held corporation are transferred in trust, unless an independent trustee is the sole party responsible for making the annual determination of value."

See H.R.Rep.No. 413, 91st Cong., 1st Sess., 60 (1969).

The view of the Ways & Means Committee just quoted does not appear in § 664 or in the Regulations.

Revenue Ruling 80–83, 1980–1 CB 210, deals with the situation in which stock in a publicly held corporation was donated to a charitable remainder unitrust.   The board of directors of the corporation periodically established a price at which it would buy a limited number of its shares.   Although the donor was both a director and one of two

trustees of the unitrust, his power to determine the value of the shares, hence the value of the charitable interest, was held not to make such value unascertainable. The reason given is that "the donor is bound by a fiduciary duty in each capacity to exercise independent judgment   *   *   *   ." Accordingly, a gift tax charitable deduction was allowed for the remainder interest.

28.   Reg. § 1.664–2(b).

29.   Reg. § 1.664–3(b);   Rev.Rul. 72–395, § 6.06, 1972–2 CB 340, 348.

30.   Reg. § 1.664–2(a)(3)(ii) (annuity trust); Reg. § 1.664–3(a)(3)(iii) (unitrust).

31.   1977–2 CB 213.   See also Rev.Rul. 77–73, 1977–1 CB 175, holding that an independent trustee may be given power to allocate income among beneficiaries without causing disqualification as long as the power would not cause anyone to be taxed as owner of the trust if §§ 671–678 were applicable.

the trustee for any reason and substitute any other person, including the grantor, does not disqualify a trust in which distributions are to be made to the grantor for life. The Ruling gives no indication that the result would be different if the beneficiary were someone other than the grantor, as long as the powers of the trustee would not cause the grantor or anyone else to be taxable if §§ 671–678 applied to the trust.

[c] Determining the Pay-Out Rate and Term of the Trust

The minimum pay-out rate for an annuity trust is 5 percent of the initial net fair market value of the property placed in trust "as finally determined for Federal tax purposes." [32]   For the unitrust, the minimum is 5 percent of the net fair market value of the trust assets, determined annually.[33] Setting the rate requires balancing the client's desire to use a low rate in order to maximize the income and gift tax charitable deductions against a desire to use a high rate in order to maximize the amount payable to the non-charitable beneficiaries.

As the tables that determine the amount of such deductions are based on an assumed 6 percent return, a rate below 6 percent produces a larger deduction for income tax and gift tax purposes if an annuity trust rather than a unitrust is used.   In this situation, the assumed additions to principal of income in excess of the annual payment increase the amount of unitrust payments in future years, while annuity payments would remain fixed.   If the rate is above 6 percent, the deduction is larger with a unitrust because of the opposite assumption that the unitrust payments will decline as principal is depleted by payments in excess of each year's income.[31]   Of course, neither assumption takes into account the fact that the actual investment experience of the trust is unlikely to be exactly equal to the assumed 6 percent return reflected in the actuarial tables.

The term may be either a fixed period of time of twenty years or less or it may be measured by the lives of the income beneficiaries.[35]   With either a fixed term of years or a term measured by lives of the beneficiaries, the trustee may be given discretion to allocate the amounts payable to each beneficiary as long as the required total payment must be made each year and such discretion fits within the provisions of § 674, so that the grantor would not be taxable as owner if that section applied to the trust.[36]   However, if lives of the income beneficiaries are used to measure the term of the trust, the beneficiaries must be living and ascertained when the trust is created.[37]   No such requirement applies to a trust measured by a term of years; its beneficiaries may include unborn and unascertained persons,[38] such as grandchildren born after the trust is created.

In setting the pay-out and term, it should be borne in mind that the actuarial value of the charity's interest may have to be at least some min-

---

32. Reg. § 1.664–2(a)(1)(iii).

33. § 664(d)(2)(A); Reg. § 1.664–3(a)(1).

34. See Polasky, "The Numbers Game—Using the Actuarial Tables in Estate Planning," 5 Univ.Miami Inst. on Est.Plan. ¶¶ 71,800, 71.814.3, 71.814.4.   (1971).

35. §§ 664(d)(1)(A), 664(D)(2)(A).

36. Reg. §§ 1.664–2(a)(3)(ii), 1.664–3(a)(3)(ii).

37. Reg. §§ 1.664–2(a)(3)(i), 1.664–3(a)(3)(i).

38. Rev.Rul. 72–395, § 5.03(1), 1972–2 CB 340, 345 (annuity trust); id. § 7.03(1), 1972–2 CB at 350 (unitrust).

imum percentage of the value of the trust property at the time of its creation in order for the trust to qualify as a charitable remainder trust.[39]

[d] Selecting the Beneficiaries

The only explicit requirement as to income beneficiaries is that at least one must not be a charity.[40]   The grantor may be a beneficiary and the references to "persons" in §§ 664(d)(1)(A) and 664(d)(2)(A) appear to include trusts, estates and partnerships or corporations, as well as individuals.[41] The only other requirement with respect to beneficiaries is that, in order to avoid disqualification of the trust, the manner in which they are selected— either under the terms of the trust or in the discretion of the trustee—must not be such as to cause the grantor or anyone else to be taxable as owner if §§ 671–678 were applicable to the trust.[42]

[e] Choosing Assets to Fund the Trust

In order to maximize the income taxes saved by shifting income to a charitable remainder trust and its non-charitable beneficiaries, the trust should be funded with assets that either produce a high current return in relation to their fair market value or have a substantial amount of unrealized appreciation or both.   Some caveats to be borne in mind in choosing assets are:

(1) If appreciated property is used that would not qualify for long term capital gains treatment if sold, the grantor's income tax deduction will be reduced under the provision disallowing part of the value of such property for purposes of the deduction.[43]

(2) If an asset that is subject to a liability in excess of its basis is used, income will be realized by the grantor as a result of the transfer.[44]

(3) If a unitrust is used, ease of valuation of transferred assets is a particularly important factor because of the need for annual valuation to determine the unitrust amount.

¶ 10.03 CHARITABLE LEAD (INCOME) TRUSTS

Charitable lead trusts are primarily useful to save estate and gift taxes on assets that will ultimately pass to non-charitable beneficiaries.   Like a charitable remainder trust, the charitable lead trust may either provide for payment of a guaranteed annuity or it may provide for payment of a percentage of the fair market value of the trust property, determined annually. Unlike the charitable remainder trust, the payee of the annuity or percentage of principal is a charity and there is no requirement that the payout rate be a minimum of 5 percent.   Here again, the actuarial tables used to compute the charitable deduction use an assumed 6 percent interest rate.[45] At a time when the prevailing return on a variety of investment vehicles is substantially in excess of 6 percent, the tables may provide a distorted estimate of the relative values of the charitable and non-charitable interests

39. See note 6 supra.

40. §§ 664(d)(1)(A), 664(d)(2)(A).

41. § 7701(a)(1).

42. See note 30 supra.

43. § 170(e)(1)(A).

44. See ¶ 6.01[2][c] supra.

45. See Reg. § 25.2522(c)–3(d)(3), referring to Reg. § 25.2512–9.

in the trust. Such distortion could result from unrealistic assumptions with respect to the accumulation of income (or invasion of principal) during the charitable term and from failure to discount the assumed value of the non-charitable remainder sufficiently to reflect the postponement of its receipt by the beneficiaries.

For example, if the charitable annuity or unitrust payments are at a rate of 6 percent, the tables assume that there will be no increase in the non-charitable remainder from the accumulation of income.   If such payments are at a rate in excess of 6 percent, the tables assume that the remainder will be reduced by invasion of principal for the benefit of the charity.   In each case, the assumption may be incorrect if the trust in fact yields income at a rate in excess of 6 percent.   Such errors may be greater in an annuity trust than in a unitrust.   In the latter, any build-up (or failure to deplete) principal inures in part to the charity because the amount payable is recomputed annually.

On the other hand, when the prevailing interest rate exceeds 6 percent, the tables overstate the present value of a non-charitable remainder interest because a realistic discount for delay in payment would exceed 6 percent. Thus the distorting effects of an interest rate below the rates which prevail in the investment markets tend to offset each other.   But in an annuity trust, the offsetting effect is not as great, as any build-up of principal inures wholly to the benefit of the remainder interest.

For most clients, the estate and gift tax advantages of charitable lead trusts are not a sufficient reason to make their use appropriate.   Usually, the client's wealth does not allow provisions for his family to be postponed, even as to a portion of that wealth, until after a charitable lead interest of sufficient length to produce significant estate or gift tax savings.   Therefore, the following discussion of lead trusts will merely highlight the major tax consequences of their use.

[1] Income Tax Consequences for Grantor

In order for the grantor to be entitled to an income tax deduction when a lead trust is created, its terms must be such as to cause him to be taxed on the trust income.[46]   In that situation, he is entitled to a current deduction for the present value of the charitable income interest but is taxed on the trust income each year of its term.   Thus, the lead trust which creates an income tax deduction for the grantor does not remove trust income from his tax return but instead allows him to take a current deduction for the present value of the charity's income interest.   The effect is to allow the grantor to anticipate the charitable deduction for amounts to be paid to charity in future years.[47]   Only the taxpayer with an unusual bulge in income for a given year benefits sufficiently from this arrangement to warrant creation of a charitable lead trust to save income taxes.

Thus, the grantor usually is not entitled to an income tax deduction for the charitable contribution he makes when he creates a charitable lead trust.

---

46.   § 170(f)(2)(B).

47.   If the grantor ceases to be taxable on the trust income under § 671, there is a recap-

ture of a portion of the charitable deduction he received when the trust was created. Id.

However, the creation of the trust does have the effect of shifting the taxability of the income from the trust property from the grantor to the beneficiaries if it complies with the Clifford rules.[48]

[2] Income Tax Consequences for Trust and Beneficiaries

Taxation of the lead trust and its beneficiaries is not controlled by a special provision, as in the case of the charitable remainder trust,[49] but rather by the general rules governing complex trusts.[50]   Thus, the trust is entitled to a charitable deduction for amounts paid for charitable purposes from gross income.[51]   The trust instrument should specify the order in which trust income is to be used to make up charitable payments.[52]

The trust's net income, after deductions, is taxable in the same manner as for trusts with no charitable interests.   Gains on sales of assets within two years of their transfer to the trust may be taxable at the grantor's rates under § 644.[53]   Any accumulated income that is ultimately distributed to non-charitable beneficiaries may be subject to an additional tax in the hands of the distributee under the throwback rule, unless an exemption from throwback treatment is available.[54]

[3] Gift Tax and Estate Tax Consequences

The creation of a charitable lead trust during the grantor's life is a completed gift for gift tax purposes, at the time when the trust becomes irrevocable, to the extent that interests are created in non-charitable beneficiaries other than the grantor himself.   The grantor is entitled to a gift tax charitable deduction for the value of the charitable lead interest.[55]   The actuarial tables used in computing the deduction are based on an assumed 6 percent interest rate [56] and may provide a distorted estimate of the value of the portion of the trust property which passes to non-charitable beneficiaries if the income actually realized by the trust differs from 6 percent.

The gift of the non-charitable interests will either reduce the grantor's unified credit [57] or, to the extent it exceeds the unused portion of his credit, will constitute a taxable gift.

48. §§ 671–677. For a discussion of these rules, see ¶ 9.01 supra.

49. § 664. For a discussion, see ¶ 10.02[2] supra.

50. For a discussion of these rules, see ¶¶ 11.01, 11.02 infra.

51. § 642(c).

52. The object in specifying such order is, of course, to cause items with the least desirable tax characteristics, such as ordinary income, to be carried out to the charity first. See Muchin, Lubelcheck & Gras, "Charitable Lead Trusts Can Provide Substantial Estate Planning Benefits," 49 J.Tax 2, 3 (1978). Compare § 664(b)(1), providing that in a charitable remainder trust, such items are carried out to the non-charitable beneficiary first. See note 13 supra.

53. For a discussion, see ¶ 9.02[2][a] supra.

54. §§ 665–667. For a discussion of the rule, see ¶ 11.02 infra.

55. 2522(c)(2)(B).

56. Reg. § 25.2512–9(f).

57. § 2505.

Part III

ARRANGEMENTS FOR BENEFICIARIES AND POWER HOLDERS

Many estate plans, particularly those for smaller estates, dispose of all of the owner's wealth outright, so that each beneficiary receives full ownership of his share.   But other plans often include the creation of limited interests in property, either outright or in trust, and powers to control its disposition.   Beneficiaries who receive less than full ownership of property and the holders of such powers may be affected by all four of the federal taxes important in estate planning: income, estate, gift, and generation-skipping (GST).   This Part deals with ways to minimize the impact of each of these taxes on beneficiaries and power holders.   Trust and will provisions for this purpose often include the creation of powers of appointment, powers of withdrawal, and discretionary powers of fiduciaries.

Most of the material in this Part deals with trusts, because of their widespread use in contemporary estate plans.   However, many of the same problems and possibilities may arise in connection with legal present and future interests and powers over property which is not in trust.

Chapter 11

INCOME TAX ASPECTS

¶ 11.01   TAXATION OF CURRENT TRUST INCOME

"Income" has different meanings for federal income tax purposes and for state-law trust accounting purposes in determining the relative rights of income beneficiaries and remaindermen.   Capital gains are included in the tax definition of income but generally are not included in the trust accounting definition.   State income taxes on such gains, as well as other expenditures chargeable to principal as a matter to trust law, such as local taxes on unproductive property, are deducted in computing income for tax purposes but not in the trustee's income account.

Section 643(b) recognizes this dichotomy of meaning by providing generally that for purposes of Subparts A–D, which include §§ 641–669, income, if not preceded by "taxable," "distributable net," "undistributed net," or "gross," means fiduciary accounting income.   This definition is inapplicable to Subpart E, which includes the sections dealing with taxation of trust grantors and power holders.   Subpart E contains no explicit definition; it appears to refer to income in the usual sense in which the term is used elsewhere in the Code.

It is in this latter sense that the term is used in this chapter, except where the context indicates otherwise.

Trust income may be taxed to a trust grantor during his life under the Clifford sections (§§ 671–677).[1]   Any income not taxed to the grantor while

---

1. For a discussion, see ¶ 9.01 supra.

he lives, as well as all income received after his death,[2] is allocated for tax purposes, in the following order of priority, to:

(1) the holder of a power exercisable solely by himself to vest such income (or trust principal) in himself; [3]

(2) a beneficiary who receives a distribution deemed to constitute such income or to whom a distribution is required to be made,[4] either directly or through discharge of his legal obligations; [5] and

(3) the trust itself.[6]

Income that is initially accumulated and taxed to the trust may be subject to an additional tax under the throwback rule [7] when it is distributed to a beneficiary, unless an exemption from the rule applies.

[1] Income Taxable to Power Holders

If someone has the power at any time during the taxable year to vest trust income or principal in himself, under § 678(a)(1) he is taxed in accordance with § 671 as "owner" of the portion that he may vest in himself. Similarly, if he had such a power described in § 678 and partially released it, he may continue to be taxed as owner under the Clifford sections (§§ 671–677).[8] For example, if after the partial release he has a § 674(a) power to affect beneficial enjoyment that is not covered by one of the exceptions in § 674(b), he will be taxed as if he were a grantor who had retained such a power.[9]

Being taxed as "owner" is quite different from being taxed as "beneficiary." The measuring rod of "distributable net income" (DNI), as defined in § 643(a), limits the amount taxable to beneficiaries [10] but has no application to taxation as "owner." Conversely, if the trust generates losses or deductions in excess of its income, someone who is taxable as "owner" is entitled to the benefit of such deductions. A trust beneficiary, on the other hand, generally cannot deduct net losses of the trust.[11]

---

2. See ¶ 15.01 infra.

3. § 678. Section 671 states that taxation as owner has priority over taxation under subparts A through D, which deal with taxation of trusts and beneficiaries.

4. See § 652, requiring inclusion of such income by the beneficiary of a simple trust, and § 662, requiring such inclusion by the beneficiary of a complex trust, and the corresponding provisions for a deduction by the trust in §§ 651 and 661. The terms "simple" and "complex" are found in the Regulations, rather than in the Code itself. See Reg. §§ 1.651(a)–1, 1.661(a)–1. The statutory definition of trusts governed by § 652 ("simple" trusts) specifies that all current income is required to be distributed, no distributions are made from principal, and there are no charitable beneficiaries. See § 651(a). Trusts that in a given year fail to satisfy this test fall under the complex trust rules.

5. See Reg. § 1.662(a)–4. For a discussion of the income tax consequences of the existence and discharge of support obligations, see ¶ 9.01[9][a], [b] supra.

6. § 641.

7. §§ 665–667, discussed at ¶ 11.02 infra.

8. § 678(a)(2), discussed at ¶ 12.01[3][c] infra. The Clifford sections are discussed in ¶ 9.01 supra.

9. For a discussion of powers to affect enjoyment, see ¶ 9.01[4] supra.

10. See §§ 652(a) (simple trusts), 662(a) (complex trusts).

11. There are exceptions. See §§ 167(h) (depreciation); 611(b)(3) (depletion); 642(h) (unused loss carryover and excess deductions on termination of trust).

[2] Income Taxable to Beneficiaries: The Distributable Net Income (DNI) Measuring Rod

Sections 652 and 662 provide generally that a beneficiary who receives (or is entitled to receive) a distribution, either directly or through discharge of his legal obligations, is taxed on his share of the distributable net income (DNI) of the trust for the year in which the distribution is made (or required to be made). However, § 663(a) creates an exception to the general rule by exempting from such treatment a gift of a specific sum or specific property that is not payable solely from income and is paid in no more than three installments. Thus, the recipient of such a gift is not taxed on his share of DNI.

DNI, as defined in § 643(a),[12] constitutes a ceiling on the total required to be included in income by beneficiaries because of trust distributions in a given year, aside from distributions deemed to represent accumulated income, which are taxable under the throwback rule.[13] The starting point in computing DNI is "taxable income" but it normally does not include capital gains (and is not reduced by capital losses)[14] except for the year in which the trust terminates.[15] Allocation of DNI among the beneficiaries is governed by §§ 652 and 662 for "simple" and "complex" trusts respectively.[16]

[3] Income Taxable to the Trust

Income that is not taxed to a power holder or to a beneficiary is taxed to the trust itself. Section 641(b) provides that the taxable income of a trust "shall be computed in the same manner as in the case of an individual, except as otherwise provided in this part." The most important difference is the deduction for distributions[17] which, in effect, allocates taxable income between the trust and the beneficiaries so that income which is distributed currently is taxed only once.

Although the rate schedule for trusts is the highest applicable to individuals (that for married persons filing separate returns),[18] income that is taxed to a trust may be subject to a lower effective tax rate than if it were distributed currently to the beneficiaries, who in most cases have other taxable income. Income that is initially accumulated and taxed to the trust may be subject to an additional tax under §§ 665–667, dealing with the throwback rule, when such income is distributed to a beneficiary.

---

12. For a discussion, see ¶ 15.05 infra.

13. §§ 665–667. See ¶ 11.02 infra.

14. Reg. §§ 1.643(a)–3(a), 1.643(a)–3(b). Any state income tax paid on such gains by the trust, however, ordinarily reduces DNI even though it is paid from principal. See Rev.Rul. 74–257, 1974–1 CB 153.

15. Gains and losses for that year are necessarily reflected in the final distribution of principal. See Reg. § 1.643(a)–3(d), *Example (4)*.

16. See note 4 supra.

17. See §§ 651 (simple trusts), 661 (complex trusts).

18. The rates for married individuals filing separate returns provided by § 1(d) differ from the rates for trusts in § 1(e) only in that the former schedule has an initial tax-free bracket of $1,700. However, the deduction for the "exemption amount" for an individual is $1,000, with a cost-of-living adjustment beginning in 1985. See §§ 151(a), 151(f). For a trust "which is required to distribute all of its income currently," the deduction is $300; for any other trust, it is $100. See § 642(b).

¶ 11.02   TAXATION OF ACCUMULATED TRUST INCOME: THE THROWBACK RULE FOR DOMESTIC[19] TRUSTS

The throwback rule is intended to limit the potential tax advantage of accumulating income in a trust, having such income taxed at the trust's rates, and later distributing the accumulation to a beneficiary in a higher marginal tax bracket than that of the trust. Until the throwback rule was introduced with the enactment of the Internal Revenue Code of 1954, the procedure just described could produce significant savings because no additional tax was incurred by the beneficiary who received a distribution representing accumulated trust income. The effect of the rule is to impose an additional tax in some instances on a beneficiary who receives such a distribution. To simplify computation, the amount of the additional tax is based on the average amount accumulated by the trust each year and the average increase in the beneficiary's taxable income that would have occurred if the accumulated income had been taxable to him in prior years rather than the exact increase in tax he would have paid each year.

Thus, the throwback rule may impose an additional tax on a beneficiary who receives an "accumulation distribution" [20] (AD) from a trust which has "undistributed net income" [21] (UNI) from a "preceding taxable year" [22] (PTY). The amount, if any, of such additional tax is determined by comparing the average increase in tax that the beneficiary would have paid if the amount of the AD had been added to his taxable income for three of the five years preceding the distribution, with the actual tax that the trust paid on the amount of the AD when the income was accumulated.[23] For this purpose, the AD is allocated ("thrown back") to the first PTY in which the trust had UNI.[24] If the AD exceeds UNI for that year, a further allocation is made to the next PTY in which the trust had UNI, until either the entire AD has been allocated or there is no more UNI for any PTY of the trust.

The beneficiary includes in income for the year of distribution the AD. Except in the case of multiple trusts,[25] he then adds the tax paid on the AD by the trust, and receives credit for the amount of such tax.[26] An averaging provision applies in computing the beneficiary's tax, using his tax bracket for three of the five taxable years preceding the distribution. The year in which his taxable income was highest and that in which it was lowest are excluded from the computation.[27] If the AD is allocated to two or more

19. Different rules apply to foreign trusts as defined in § 7701(a)(31). For a discussion, see Peschel & Spurgeon, Federal Taxation of Trusts, Grantors and Beneficiaries, Ch. 15 (1978).

20. § 665(b).

21. § 665(a).

22. § 665(e).

23. § 667. For an illustration of the mechanics of the computation, see Reg. § 1.666(c)–2A, which, however, does not reflect the adjustment for estate taxes and generation-skipping transfer taxes provided by § 667(b)(6). See note 29 infra.

24. § 666(a). Taxable years beginning before 1969 are not PTYs for the purpose of determining the tax consequences of ADs by domestic trusts made in taxable years beginning after 1973. See § 665(e)(1)(B). Certain taxable years of simple trusts are excluded by the Regulations. See note 35 infra.

25. § 667(c)(1), dealing with multiple trusts, is discussed at ¶ 11.02[3] infra.

26. §§ 666(b), 666(c) (taxes deemed distributed); § 667(b)(1) (credit for taxes paid by trust).

27. § 667(b)(1).

PTYs of the distributing trust, the beneficiary's tax computation is based on an average of the amounts allocated to each PTY, disregarding certain low-allocation years.[28]　If the tax thus computed for the beneficiary is higher than his share of the tax previously paid by the trust, he owes the amount of such excess;[29] if the tax paid by the trust is higher, the beneficiary receives no refund or credit.[30]

The throwback rule thus operates as an averaging provision for recipients of accumulated trust income that may provide substantially different treatment than that which would otherwise apply under the general averaging provisions of §§ 1301–1305, which are inapplicable to ADs.[31]　If instead ADs were fully includible in the recipient's income (together with trust taxes paid thereon), with relief available only through general averaging, the consequence for many recipients of ADs would be unfavorable. If a taxpayer elects [32] general averaging, his tax on averageable income is computed by adding one-fifth thereof to 120 percent of his average base period income and multiplying the resulting increase in tax by 5.[33]　For example, if averageable income for a given year is $60,000 and average base period income is $20,000, a taxpayer who elects averaging would use the brackets applicable to his income between $24,000 (120 percent of his base period income) and $36,000.

If instead the item had been an AD (and trust taxes attributable thereto), averaging for throwback purposes would not be elective.　If the base period income for such purposes was again $20,000 (the average of the five years preceding the distribution, excluding therefrom the highest and lowest years), any additional tax on the AD would be determined by adding to $20,000 the average allocation to each PTY.　Thus the bracket of the AD recipient is not increased 20%, as in general averaging.

The practical impact of the throwback rule in a given case is greatly affected by two factors:

(1) The number of PTYs to which the AD is allocated.　The possibilities range from one year to the number of PTYs of the trust commencing after 1968; [34]

(2) The extent to which the trustee can and does choose the year in which trust distributions are made in such fashion as to minimize taxes for the recipient.

The throwback rule generally is inapplicable to:

(1) simple trusts, except for the year in which the trust terminates; [35] and

---

28. Years in which the allocation is less than 25 percent of the average for the years involved are disregarded.　See § 667(b)(3).

29. § 667(b).　Under § 667(b)(6), the tax on an AD is reduced by any generation-skipping transfer taxes attributable to the AD and by any estate taxes of decedents dying after 1979 attributable thereto.

30. § 666(e).

31. § 1302(a)(2)(B).

32. § 1304(a).

33. § 1301.

34. § 665(e)(1)(B).

35. As to years prior to that in which the trust terminates, this conclusion rests on § 665(b): "If the amounts properly paid, credited, or required to be distributed by the trust for the taxable year do not exceed the income of the trust for such year, there shall be no accumulation distribution for

(2) capital gains, which ordinarily are excluded from distributable net income (DNI) [36] and hence from UNI. [37]

In view of the lower maximum effective tax rate resulting from the partial exclusion of long-term capital gains from income, the exemption of capital gains from throwback treatment has a much greater effect on short-term gains. Such gains are fully taxable, with the top rate the same as for other income.

[1] Undistributed Net Income (UNI) and Preceding Taxable Year (PTY)

The definitions of "undistributed net income" (UNI) [38] and "preceding taxable year" (PTY) [39] are closely related in that together they determine whether or not an accumulation distribution (AD) [40] may have tax consequences for the recipient. Only if the trust has UNI for a PTY is it possible for an AD to have such consequences. [41]

Taxable years beginning before 1969 are not PTYs for the purpose of determining the tax consequences of ADs by domestic trusts made in taxable years beginning after 1973. [42] Thus, for a calendar year trust, only amounts of UNI accumulated in taxable years beginning after 1968 will be relevant in determining the throwback consequences of ADs made from now on.

UNI is defined as the amount by which distributable net income (DNI) exceeds deductible distributions and taxes imposed on the trust. [43] For example, if a trust had DNI of $25,000 for a given year and made distributions to beneficiaries which were deductible under § 661 in the amount of $15,000 and paid a tax of $2,000 on the remaining $10,000 of income, its UNI for that year would be $8,000.

[2] Accumulation Distribution (AD)

An "accumulation distribution" (AD) is the excess of distributions as defined in § 661(a)(2) over DNI, reduced (but not below zero) by required distributions as defined in § 661(a)(1). [44] However, in any year in which distributions do not exceed trust income, there is no AD. [45] And distributions to a beneficiary of income accumulated before he was born or while he was under age 21, although not excluded from the definition, are ignored in allocating AD to prior years, except in the case of multiple trusts. [46] In

such year." This covers any trust which is within the statutory definition of "simple trust" for a given year. See note 4 supra. In addition, § 665(b) covers other trusts as well which fail to satisfy that definition either because income is not required to be distributed or because there are charitable beneficiaries.

In the year of termination § 665(b) does not bar an AD by a simple trust. However, even though there is an AD that year, there may be no UNI because of Reg. § 1.665 (e)–1A(b). These Regulations exclude from "preceding taxable year" (PTY) any year in which a trust was a simple trust and received no "outside income," such as income in respect of a decedent (§ 691) or certain distributions from another trust.

36. § 643(a)(3).

37. § 665(a).

38. Id.

39. § 665(e).

40. § 665(b).

41. § 666(a).

42. § 665(e)(1)(B).

43. § 665(a). As used in § 665(a)(2), "taxes imposed on the trust" means those taxes allocable to undistributed DNI.

44. § 665(b).

45. Id.

46. Id.; § 667(c).

effect, a beneficiary is free from throwback treatment with respect to distributions from two trusts of income accumulated while he was unborn or under age 21. If distributions of such income are made to him from a third trust, the exemption for accumulations while he was unborn or under 21 disappears for such trust (but not for the first two trusts) for any prior taxable year if the amount deemed distributed to him from each trust for such year is $1,000 or more. In addition, as in other such distributions from a third trust, the beneficiary is denied credit for taxes paid by the trust (and is not required to include such taxes in income).

[3] Treatment of Multiple Trusts for Throwback Purposes

If a beneficiary receives cumulatively, from each of three or more trusts, amounts deemed distributed in a given year (i.e., "thrown back" to that year) of $1,000 or more, he is denied credit for taxes paid by all but two of such trusts (and is not required to include such taxes in income).[47] In addition, the under-21 or unborn exclusion from throwback allocations [48] is inapplicable to all but two of such trusts.[49] The multiple trust rule is applied on a cumulative basis to distributions in two or more years that are thrown back to a given PTY. The ADs need not be made by all three trusts in the same year, nor must the $1,000 threshold be reached in a single year, in order for the rule to apply.

Since the marginal tax rate for a trust with taxable income of $10,000 is less than 30 percent, two such trusts may provide a substantial tax shelter for a beneficiary who is in a higher marginal bracket than 30 percent while he is under age 21. Of course, the marginal tax bracket for many beneficiaries under that age is below 30 percent. In that situation, the lowest tax may be achieved by causing all or part of the trust income to be taxed currently to the beneficiary, either by distributing it to him (or to his guardian or some other authorized person) or by giving him the power to demand distributions.[50] The optimum allocation of income for tax purposes between the beneficiary and any trusts which are accumulating income for him depends on the amount involved in the particular case. The addition of trusts as separate taxable entities permits the total to be divided between a larger number of income tax rate schedules.

¶ 11.03   AVOIDING TAXATION AS POWER HOLDER

In order to keep a trust beneficiary from being taxed on trust income under § 678, any power over the trust must be given to someone other than the beneficiary in whose favor it can be exercised. For example, a power to distribute income or principal to A may be given to A's sibling, parent, or spouse [51] without adverse income tax consequences either to A or to the power holder, as long as the power may not be exercised in favor of the holder.

---

47. § 667(c)(1). Distributions from more than 1 trust in the same taxable year of a beneficiary are deemed to be made in such order as he shall determine. See § 667(b)(5).

48. § 665(b).

49. Id.; § 667(c)(1).

50. § 678.

51. See Rev. Rul. 67–268, 1967–2 CB 226.

A would also not be taxable on trust income because of his possession of a power to pay income or principal to himself, if the power could be exercised only with the consent of someone else.   For example, *A* and *B* may have the power to pay income or principal to *A*.   Alternatively, *A* and *B* may have the power to make such payments to either *A* or *B*.   Literally, neither power is exercisable "solely" by a power holder in his own favor as required by § 678 and thus does not provide a basis for taxing trust income to either *A* or *B*.   In the first case, this clearly is the result.

In the second case, where the power may be exercised in favor of either *A* or *B*, it would be possible for a court to conclude that the likelihood of mutual back-scratching is great enough to justify treating each of them as having a § 678(a) power over one-half of the trust property.[52]   To do so, however, requires reading "solely" out of the section.   However, for estate and gift tax purposes, unless *B* either was the creator of the power or had a substantial interest which was adverse to his exercise of the power in favor of *A*, *A* would be taxable as holder of a general power of appointment.[53]   Thus, the creation of such a joint power is inadvisable from a tax standpoint unless *A* also is to be given a general testamentary power over the property, which will subject him to gift or estate taxes in any event.[54]   A similar analysis applies to *B*'s power.

This paragraph has dealt only with avoiding income taxation because of a power presently exercisable in favor of the holder, not with the tax consequences of a power formerly held, which has been released or allowed to lapse.[55]   It has not dealt with a power to invade income or principal for the support of the holder, which should have no income tax consequences in years in which the absence of a need for support precludes exercise of the power.[56]   It also has not explored the income tax consequences of possession and exercise of a limited power of withdrawal, permitting the holder to vest only a portion of trust income or principal in himself.[57]

¶ 11.04 MINIMIZING TAXATION AS BENEFICIARY OF CURRENT TRUST INCOME

A beneficiary avoids taxation on current trust income when no distribution is made to him or is required to be made by the terms of the instrument, or when items he received are not taxable for one of four reasons:

(1) under the "character" rules [58] the distribution represented tax-exempt income of the trust;

---

52. Section 678(a)(1) appears to supersede the holding in Anna Spies v. United States, 180 F.2d 336, 50–1 USTC ¶ 9202 (8th Cir. 1950).   In that case, beneficiaries who held a joint power to vest income in themselves were taxed on such income under the Internal Revenue Code of 1939.

53. See §§ 2041(b)(1)(C) (estate tax), 2514(c)(3) (gift tax).   See ¶ 12.02[3] infra.

54. The common situation in which *A* would be given such a general testamentary power is in order to qualify for the marital deduc-

tion.   See § 2056(b)(5).   In that situation, the client may wish to give *A* an additional power exercisable during *A*'s life.

55. See § 678(a)(2).   For a discussion, see ¶ 12.01[3][c][ii] infra.

56. For a discussion of support powers, see ¶ 12.01[3][a] infra.

57. For a discussion, see ¶ 12.01[3][c] infra.

58. See §§ 652(b) (simple trusts), 662(b) (complex trusts).

(2) under § 663 the distribution did not carry out trust distributable net income (DNI) to the recipient;

(3) under the tier system,[59] any trust DNI was carried out by distributions to other beneficiaries; and

(4) what the beneficiary received was a loan, rather than a distribution.[60]

[1] Allocating Tax-Exempt Income to High-Bracket Beneficiaries

If a trust has, for example, tax-exempt interest income, each beneficiary who receives a distribution of trust distributable net income (DNI) generally is regarded as receiving a proportionate share of such tax-exempt income.[61] A specific allocation required by the terms of the instrument or by local law will be recognized only if it "has an economic effect independent of the income tax consequences of the allocation." [62] Thus, it is possible to direct that any such tax exempt income received by the trust shall be paid entirely to a high bracket beneficiary. Such a rigid provision, however, may be undesirable for other non-tax reasons, as it causes the allocation of income among beneficiaries to be determined without regard to their respective needs.

[2] Using the Exceptions in § 663 to Avoid the General Rule that Distributions Carry Out Trust Distributable Net Income (DNI)

Section 663 creates exceptions to the general rule of §§ 661 and 662 that distributions carry out DNI of a complex trust for tax purposes.[63] Section 663 provides that the general rule is inapplicable to a gift of specific property or a specific sum, which is not payable solely from income and is paid in not more than three installments. Such gifts are relatively more important for beneficiaries of an estate [64] than for beneficiaries of a long-term trust because the three-installment limit does not permit distributions to be spaced at frequent intervals over the life of a trust of even moderate duration. It is not uncommon for a funded revocable trust to provide cash bequests to be paid after the death of the grantor; here the § 663 exemption may be very helpful.

[3] Distributing Income to Low-Bracket Beneficiaries and Principal to Others

In order to permit the use of trust distributions to allocate income to low-bracket taxpayers, two kinds of trust provisions may be useful:

(1) empowering the trustee (or someone else) to determine from year to year which members of a described group shall receive any distributions; and

(2) confining high-bracket beneficiaries to distributions of principal.

59. Under § 662(a)(1), required distributions out of income (or out of income or principal, to the extent income is sufficient to cover the required distribution) are in the first "tier" and carry out trust DNI before any DNI is carried out by other distributions.

60. See ¶ 11.04[5] infra.

61. See Reg. §§ 1.652(b)–2(a) (simple trusts); 1.662(b)–1 (complex trusts).

62. See § 1.652(b)–2(b).

63. See ¶ 11.01[2] infra.

64. See ¶ 17.01[2] infra.

Creating the kind of "spray" power described at (1) enables the power holder to take account of beneficiaries' tax positions, and other relevant factors as they may change from year to year, in determining who shall receive distributions.   Such powers are a major tool of estate planning.[65]

In order to confine high-bracket beneficiaries to distributions of principal, the client's will or trust instrument may make use of the rules contained in §§ 661 and 662.   The general rule of these sections treats trust distributions as being deductible by the trust and includible by the beneficiary to the extent of the trust's "distributable net income" (DNI) for the year in which the distribution is made.   However, beneficiaries to whom distributions are required to be made out of income, or out of either income or principal (to the extent income is sufficient to cover the required distribution), are placed in the first "tier" of distributees.[66]   First tier distributees are taxed on their respective shares of DNI up to the amounts they receive. The second "tier" consists of the remaining beneficiaries—those to whom distributions may be made only from principal, or from income or principal to the extent income is insufficient to cover such distributions after deducting distributions required to be made out of income alone.[67]   Second tier distributees are taxed only on their respective shares of so much of DNI as is not taxable to the first tier.   Thus, the will or trust instrument may control who is taxable on trust income by confining some beneficiaries to principal distributions, thereby placing them in the second tier, and requiring that all income be distributed to others, so that none will be taxable to the second tier beneficiaries.

Problems may arise in using this technique, however, if the trust is a generation-skipping trust as defined in § 2611(b), as is likely to be true of most long-term trusts and many short-term trusts as well.   The generation-skipping transfer tax (GST) applies to a distribution that is not out of trust income (as defined in § 643(b)) to a younger generation beneficiary if there is another younger generation beneficiary in a generation above that of the distributee.[68]   In that situation, confining a younger generation beneficiary in a high income tax bracket to distributions of principal (and requiring that all income be distributed to others) may have the effect of making distributions to that beneficiary subject to GST.

[4] Limiting a Beneficiary's Interest so That He Is Entitled to No More Income and Principal Than He Will Consume

If a trust beneficiary is given an unqualified right to income or principal, he may be taxed on more income than he will consume.   To avoid this result, it is possible to limit or qualify his interest in various ways in order to protect his tax position.   For example, the right to income or principal may be postponed so that it will commence only when the need arises as indicated by the occurrence of a particular event or contingency.   In the case of a married beneficiary who is expected to be supported by his or her

---

65. See ¶ 12.01[2] infra.

66. Reg. § 1.662(a)–2.

67. Reg. § 1.662(a)–3(c).

68. For a discussion, see ¶ 14.05[2][a] infra.

spouse, such rights might be postponed to commence only on the death, divorce,[69] or total disability of the spouse.

If a beneficiary's needs are expected to diminish over the years, his rights may be limited, so that they either will terminate at the end of a specific period of time or will be reduced on a sliding scale basis. For example, a young professional person's income may be expected to rise substantially over his working life, so that trust income currently needed to maintain his standard of living may in later years become more of an embarrassment from a tax standpoint. His right as income beneficiary may be limited so that it will terminate at the end of ten years, for example, or so that it will diminish by one-tenth each year, unless he shall become totally disabled in the meantime.

More complicated definitions of a beneficiary's interest in income can be devised with a view to making income available when he needs it without subjecting him to tax on income that he would not choose to spend. But no amount of ingenuity in anticipating such needs and defining them in advance is likely to operate as satisfactorily as the informed judgment of a trustee or power holder, exercised from year to year in the light of the relative needs of all present and future beneficiaries, as well as changes in the tax laws. Thus, a non-general power of appointment in someone who may be expected to be responsive to the beneficiary's needs, or a trustee's discretionary power to distribute income, is likely to be a preferable method of tailoring a beneficiary's rights to his needs and those of other beneficiaries as well.

There is some risk, of course, depending upon the personalities involved, that the trustee may find himself in a difficult position in making determinations of relative needs of different beneficiaries. Those who feel slighted—and need is, after all, likely to be viewed subjectively by the person most directly affected—may become sufficiently disgruntled to petition a court having jurisdiction over the trust to remove a "hostile" trustee.

For these or other reasons, there may be situations in which it is not feasible to rely upon the exercise of either variety of power. For example, all of the potential trustees may be interested parties and the grantor may prefer not to include any non-family trustee. In that situation, a fixed definition of the rights of beneficiaries may be desirable, rather than reliance upon the exercise of discretionary powers, both from the standpoint of protecting the trustee's tax position and of avoiding intra-family conflict and controversy.

[5] Using Loans to Beneficiaries as a Substitute for Distributions

A beneficiary who receives a distribution may be subject to tax on all or part of the current income of the trust and may incur an additional tax if the distribution represents accumulated income subject to throwback treatment. Borrowers, on the other hand, generally incur no income tax because the proceeds of a loan do not constitute taxable income.[70]

---

69. In some circumstances, such a provision may be invalidated on public policy grounds as tending to promote divorce. See, e.g., In re Estate of Gerbing, 61 Ill.2d 503, 337 N.E.2d 29 (1975).

70. See, e.g., Rev.Rul. 72-2, 1972–1 CB 19 (Answer to Question 1).

The Commissioner has had a large measure of success in treating some loans by corporations, for example, as informal dividends.[71]   To date, he has not generally applied this approach to loans by trustees to trust beneficiaries.[72]   The House Ways and Means Committee has directed the Commissioner to scrutinize loans to determine whether they are in fact disguised distributions, stating: "A loan, particularly if it is unsecured and bears no interest (or only nominal interest), may be substantially equivalent to a distribution." [73]   Whether this directive will curtail the use of loans as an alternative method of making trust resources available to beneficiaries remains to be seen.   If not, such loans are a useful technique to save taxes for beneficiaries.   If the technique is to be available, express provision for it should be included in the trust instrument.

¶ 11.05   MINIMIZING TAXATION UNDER THE THROWBACK RULE

Taxation under the throwback rule may be minimized in four major ways:

(1) avoiding a build-up of undistributed net income (UNI) in the trust;

(2) using the exemptions that are allowed in applying the rule;

(3) qualifying for the credit for taxes paid by the trust; and

(4) using the tax computation rules.

In view of the frequent changes in the throwback rule since it was first introduced by the Internal Revenue Code of 1954, there is a substantial risk that trust provisions keyed to the current statutory framework may become unsuitable as a result of Code amendments.   A sounder basis for throwback savings may be provided by giving the trustee discretionary powers that can be exercised in the light of changes in the operation of the rule over the years.

A further caveat is that the pursuit of throwback savings may interfere with minimizing generation-skipping transfer taxes (GST).   Only by taking account of all relevant federal and state taxes, including estate and gift taxes, can the optimum program to minimize their total impact be developed.

[1] Avoiding a Build-Up of Undistributed Net Income (UNI)

Presence of undistributed net income (UNI) [74] in a trust is a prerequisite for application of throwback treatment to an accumulation distribution (AD).[75]   A build-up of UNI may be avoided by limiting the distributable net income (DNI) of the trust or by draining off the DNI by means of distributions.   Limiting trust DNI may be achieved by investment policies

---

71. See, e.g., Joseph Binenstock's Trust v. Commissioner, 321 F.2d 598, 63–2 USTC ¶ 9585 (3d Cir. 1963).

72. In Frederick M. Tobin Trust, 10 TCM 1251 (1951), a beneficiary who received trust distributions loaned equivalent amounts to the trust.   Nevertheless, the result was held to be a deductible distribution by the trust, taxable to the beneficiary, where the loans were not prearranged.

73. H.R.Rep.No. 1380, 94th Cong., 2d Sess. 1, 52, reprinted in [1976] U.S. Code Cong. & Ad. News 3356, 3406.

74. UNI is defined in § 665(a) as the excess of DNI for the taxable year over the sum of distributions and the trust's tax attributable to such DNI.

75. See § 666(a).

that, pursuant to authority conferred by the trust instrument, emphasize capital gains, realized or unrealized, rather than income items which are included in DNI.[76]   Draining off trust DNI may take the form of distributions either to individual beneficiaries or to other trusts.   Either form of distribution may leave the distributing trust untainted by UNI and, thus, in a position to make distributions in the future that will not be subject to throwback treatment.[77]   Although trusts that receive such distributions will be tainted, it may be feasible to postpone making distributions from them until distributees are available who were unborn or under age 21 when the income was accumulated.

Sometimes it is not feasible to determine the exact amount of DNI in time to distribute it before the end of the grace period in § 663(b) for distributions made within 65 days of the close of the trust's taxable year.   In that situation, an overdistribution of income, subject to refund of the excess when the amount of DNI has been determined, may be a practical solution in avoiding a build-up of UNI.

[2] Using Exemptions

Exemptions from throwback treatment are provided for:

(1) distributions of income accumulated while the distributee was under age 21 or unborn; [78]

(2) distributions that do not exceed trust income.[79]

In addition, a year in which the distributing trust was a simple trust and had no "outside income" is not a "preceding taxable year" (PTY).[80] "Outside income" is defined as amounts included in trust DNI which are not trust accounting income,[81] such as items of income in respect of a decedent within the meaning of § 691.[82]   As distributions cannot be thrown back to a year that is not a PTY,[83] UNI accumulated in such a year is, in effect, ignored for throwback purposes.

Distributions of income accumulated while the beneficiary was under age 21 or unborn are not excluded from the definition of "accumulation distribution" (AD).   Instead, if the multiple trust provision [84] is inapplicable, such distributions are not taken into account in computing any additional tax imposed on the distributee by § 667.[85]   This would appear to leave § 666 applicable to such distributions.   Under § 666(a) the amount thereof would be deemed distributed in preceding taxable years, thereby

---

76.   Capital gains ordinarily are not included in DNI except for the year in which the trust terminates.   See § 643(a)(3).   For a discussion, see ¶ 15.05 infra.

77.   If the distributing and distributee trusts were treated as a single trust for tax purposes, this goal would not be achieved.   See Reg. § 1.641(a)–0(c), quoted at ¶ 11.07[1] infra, providing for such treatment.   In many instances, the two trusts will not be within the scope of these regulations.   And judicial recognition has been accorded to multiple trusts, even though created for tax avoidance purposes.   See ¶ 11.07[1] infra.

78.   § 665(b).

79.   Id.

80.   Reg. § 1.665(e)–1A(b).

81.   Id.

82.   For a discussion of § 691, see ¶ 15.02 infra.

83.   Reg. § 1.665(e)–1A(a)(1)(i).

84.   § 667(c).

85.   § 665(b).

reducing trust UNI and the extent to which future distributions would be subject to throwback treatment.

[3] Qualifying for the Credit for Taxes Paid by the Trust

If a beneficiary receives, cumulatively, from each of three or more trusts, amounts deemed distributed in a given year of $1,000 or more, he is denied credit for taxes paid by all but two of such trusts (and is not required to include such taxes in income).[86]   Loss of such credit results in taxation of trust income both to the trust and to the beneficiary, to the extent of the excess over the trust's tax on such income.   Such double taxation may amount to a substantial penalty on the use of more than two trusts to accumulate income for a given beneficiary.   Whether or not the penalty may be avoided if one or two trusts receive distributions from other trusts and in turn make all trust distributions to the beneficiary is unclear. The Commissioner may be expected to resist any such attempt to use trust-to-trust distributions to "launder" income accumulated by multiple trusts and thereby avoid the multiple trust rule.[87]

[4] Using the Tax Computation Rules

The additional tax imposed under the throwback rule is based on the taxable income of the recipient for three of the five years preceding the distribution, disregarding the highest and lowest of such five years.[88] Trustees who make discretionary distributions may take the beneficiary's tax position into account and time the distribution in light of the throwback tax computation.   The beneficiary also may be given advance notice that a distribution may be made.   This may allow him to arrange his other affairs in anticipation of receiving a distribution.   For example, he may seek to defer income from other sources until the year of distribution.   If the distributee was not in existence during the five-year period, a tax rate applicable to the recipient for throwback purposes often will not exceed the tax paid by the distributing trust.[89]   Thus a newly created trust may be an ideal distributee from a tax standpoint.

¶ 11.06 SECURING INCOME TAX ADVANTAGES FROM TAXATION AS POWER HOLDER OR BENEFICIARY

The previous discussion has assumed that freedom from taxation as power holder or beneficiary would produce optimum income tax results. This is not necessarily the case in at least two situations:

---

86. By determining the order in which distributions in a given taxable year are deemed to have been made to him, see § 667(b)(5), the beneficiary can select the two trusts whose distributions will not be subject to multiple trust treatment.

87. Cf. Reg. § 1.665(b)–1A(b)(1): "A distribution from one trust to another trust is generally an accumulation distribution." The distribution will be deemed to have been made to the ultimate beneficiary if the primary purpose is to avoid the former capital gain distribution provisions (former

§ 669).   Id.   A similar exception could be applied to a trust-to-trust distribution made for the purpose of avoiding the multiple trust rule.

88.   § 667(b)(1).

89. A tax at the distributee's rate for throwback purposes could exceed the tax paid by the distributing trust if rates had increased since the years the income was accumulated or if the distributee received ADs from more than one trust.   See note 108 infra.

(1) If a trust is generating net losses because of ownership of tax shelters or for other reasons, taxation as owner because of possession of a power to vest income or principal in the holder may enable the holder to deduct such losses from his other income; or

(2) If a trust makes a discretionary distribution of appreciated property that is included in income by the distributee, the result may be a tax-free step-up of basis.

[1] Deduction of Trust Losses by Power Holder

Section 678(a)(1) provides that the holder of a power to vest a portion of trust income or principal in himself shall be treated as owner of such portion. Taxation as owner could be advantageous to the power holder if the trust assets included one or more tax shelter properties, just as in the case of a trust grantor taxed as owner. In the latter case, the Commissioner has ruled that when the grantor ceases to be so taxable, on a change to an independent trustee, the grantor realizes income to the extent that the trust's share of liabilities of a tax shelter partnership exceeded the trust's basis in its partnership interest.[90]

The ruling just referred to did not deal with taxation of a non-grantor as owner nor with tax shelters held by a trust other than in the form of an interest in a partnership.

[2] Increase of Basis From Discretionary Distributions of Appreciated Property

Discretionary distributions of appreciated property produce a tax-free step-up of basis in the hands of the distributee only to the extent that the distribution is includible by him in income.[91] In that situation, a tax benefit results from such inclusion that may reduce the combined taxes of the trust and the beneficiary, although, from the standpoint of the beneficiary's individual tax position, the step-up of basis often will not fully offset the tax he incurs on the distribution.[92]

¶ 11.07 DIVIDING A SINGLE FUND INTO TWO OR MORE SEPARATE TRUSTS

If having income from property taxed to one trust, rather than to a beneficiary, may reduce the effective tax rate on such income, does it follow that dividing such property between two or more trusts may produce additional savings? Such a division may occur in any one of at least six ways:

(1) The grantor may make an initial division of property and create two or more trusts at the same time;

(2) The grantor may create two or more trusts at different times during his life;

(3) The grantor may create one or more trusts during his life and one or more additional trusts by his will;

---

90. Rev.Rul. 77–402, 1977–2 CB 222.

91. Reg. § 1.661(a)–2(f)(3); Rev.Rul. 64–314, 1964–2 CB 167. For a discussion, see ¶ 4.07 supra.

92. For a discussion, see ¶ 11.01[2] supra.

(4) The terms of a trust may require that the property be divided into two or more trusts on the occurrence of a stated event—the death of a beneficiary or his attainment of a designated age;

(5) The holder of a power of appointment may exercise his power by directing the trustee to hold a portion of the trust property as a separate trust or to transfer such portion to another trustee for that purpose; or

(6) The trustee may exercise a discretionary power to make distributions in trust for a beneficiary in such fashion as to create a separate trust.

The manner in which such division occurs may affect whether or not each trust is recognized as a separate entity for tax purposes.

Whether or not such a division of property between two or more trusts will, on balance, be in the best interest of the beneficiaries depends on a number of factors, including the answers to the following questions:

(1) Will the trusts be treated as separate entities for income tax purposes or will they be consolidated and treated as a single trust?

(2) Assuming that the trusts are treated as separate entities for income tax purposes, how does such treatment affect the beneficiaries' taxes on amounts distributed currently?

(3) Assuming that the trusts are treated as separate entities for income tax purposes, how does such treatment affect the application of the throwback rule to accumulation distributions?

(4) Do additional expenses incurred for record keeping, accounting, and preparation of income tax returns for separate trusts offset any resulting tax saving?

(5) Will the creation of two or more trusts affect the generation-skipping transfer tax?

[1] Recognition as Separate Taxable Entities

The Regulations provide:

Multiple trusts that have—

(1) No substantially independent purposes (such as independent dispositive purposes),

(2) The same grantor and substantially the same beneficiary, and

(3) The avoidance or mitigation of (a) the progressive rates of tax (including mitigation as a result of deferral of tax) * * * as their principal purpose, shall be consolidated and treated as one trust for the purposes of subchapter J.[93]

Before these Regulations were promulgated, the Commissioner had occasionally succeeded in persuading a court to consolidate multiple trusts for tax purposes, but generally only in extreme cases. For example, in Boyce v. United States,[94] the grantor created ninety trusts with his son as

---

93. Reg. § 1.641(a)–0(c).

94. 190 F.Supp. 950, 61–1 USTC ¶ 9257 (W.D.La.1961), aff'd per curiam 296 F.2d

731, 62–1 USTC ¶ 9150 (5th Cir. 1962). See also Ray R. Sence v. United States, 394 F.2d 842, 68–1 USTC ¶ 9368 (Ct.Cl.1968).

sole beneficiary and the trustee failed to establish that he had treated the trusts as separate entities.   But in Estelle Morris Trusts,[95] twenty trusts created by the same grantors for the same beneficiaries were not consolidated, even though the Tax Court found that twenty trusts, rather than two, were "created principally for tax-avoidance reasons." [96]   In that case, the trustee did maintain separate records and bank accounts for each trust. The Tax Court based its holding in part on the fact that "Congress has taken no action to restrict the use of multiple trusts," [97] even though it "was fully aware of the tax-avoidance possibilities afforded by [their] use * * * ." [98]

Whether the Commissioner will enjoy any greater success in attacking multiple trusts in the future than he has in the past remains to be seen. His successes to date have been in cases in which the grantor made an initial division of property, rather than those in which two or more trusts came into being in any of the other five ways described above.   No case involved the consolidation of trusts for different beneficiaries.

In practice, the most important check on the creation of multiple trusts for a single beneficiary is likely to be the tax consequences for the beneficiary under the throwback rule and the additional expenses likely to be incurred in administering each added trust.   In addition, creation of multiple trusts for two or more beneficiaries in the same generation may affect the application of the generation-skipping transfer tax.[99]

[2] Effect on Beneficiaries' Taxes on Current Distributions

If two or more trusts for the same beneficiary are treated as separate entities for income tax purposes, such treatment may reduce a beneficiary's tax on amounts distributed currently by causing a portion of such distributions to be treated as principal.   This results from the fact that distributable net income [100] (DNI) of one trust does not affect the character of distributions made by another, as long as the two trusts are treated as separate taxable entities.

> *Example 11.1.*   Assume that *H* in his will creates *Trust A* for his wife *W* to qualify for the marital deduction [101] and *Trust B*, also for the benefit of *W*.   The trustee is required to distribute the income of *Trust A* to *W* and, in addition, has discretion to distribute principal to her. The trustee also has discretion to either distribute income and principal of *Trust B* to *W* or to accumulate the income and add it to principal. On the death of *W*, she has a general power to appoint the principal of *Trust A* by her will.   To whatever extent she does not effectively exercise that power, the principal of *Trust A* goes to *H*'s descendants then living, *per stirpes*.   The principal of *Trust B* also goes to such

---

95.   51 T.C. 20 (1968), aff'd per curiam 427 F.2d 1361, 70–2 USTC ¶ 9490 (9th Cir. 1970).

96.   Id. at 34.

97.   Id. at 42.

98.   Id.

99.   For a discussion, see ¶ 14.05[4][c][i].

100.   § 643(a).

101.   § 2056.   For a discussion of power of appointment marital deduction trusts, see ¶ 18.04[2] infra.

descendants on the death of *W* in default of appointment, but she has only a limited power of appointment over that trust.

If the trustee distributes to *W* the income of *Trust A* and *Trust B*, she will be taxable on whatever she receives, up to the limit of the distributable net income (DNI) of both trusts. If instead the trustee distributes to *W* only the income of *Trust A*, as required by the terms of the trust, and an amount of principal of *Trust A* equal to the income of *Trust B*, as long as the two trusts are treated as separate entities for income tax purposes, *W* will be taxed only on the DNI of *Trust A*. The income of *Trust B* will be accumulated and taxed to the trust.

If *Trust A* eventually is exhausted as a result of distributions of principal to *W*, the trustee may then make distributions to her from *Trust B* that are in excess of DNI of that trust. Such distributions will constitute accumulation distributions for purposes of the throwback rule [102] and may subject *W* to an additional tax.[103] But, in the meantime, there will have been deferral of tax, without interest, to the extent *W* was in a higher tax bracket than that of the trust when it was accumulating income.

Exhausting *Trust A* also has an estate tax advantage, in that whatever remained at the death of *W* would have been includible in her gross estate because of her possession of a general power of appointment over the trust property.[104] *Trust B* is not so includible. Thus, the exhaustion of *Trust A* and off-setting build-up of *Trust B* may result in a reduction in *W*'s estate tax.

[3] Effect on the Application of the Throwback Rule

If two trusts for the same beneficiary are treated as separate entities for income tax purposes, such treatment may reduce the beneficiary's tax on distributions of accumulated income by causing a portion of such distributions to be treated as principal. This results from the fact that undistributed net income (UNI) of one trust does not affect the character of distributions made by another trust, as long as the two trusts are treated as separate taxable entities. But if income is accumulated for a beneficiary in three or more trusts, treatment of such trusts as separate entities for income tax purposes may increase the beneficiary's tax on distributions of accumulated income. This results from application of the multiple trust provision of the throwback rule.[105]

A further possible consequence of a recognition of two or more trusts for the same beneficiary (or for different beneficiaries) as separate entities for income tax purposes is to permit trust-to-trust accumulation distributions of appreciated property to be made in order to secure a step-up of basis. This technique is recognized for current distributions to beneficiaries.[106] Its application to a distribution by one trust to another trust is based upon the explicit position taken in the Regulations that ordinarily such distributions of accumulated income do constitute throwback distri-

102.   § 665(b).

103.   § 667(b).

104.   § 2041(a)(2).

105.   § 667(c). For a discussion, see ¶ 11.02[3] supra.

106.   See note 91 supra.

butions.[107] Thus, such distributions are included in income by the distributee and appear to satisfy the requirements in the Regulations for an increased basis.

If this route is effective to achieve an increased basis for the property distributed, it often may have the advantage of doing so without causing additional tax to be incurred under the throwback rule. If, for example, the distributee trust is newly created, often no such additional tax will be due as a result of the accumulation distribution, as the relevant brackets of the distributee may be no higher than the brackets of the distributing trust for the years in which such income was accumulated.[108]

[4] Effect of Additional Expenses for Separate Trusts

Creating two or more trusts is likely to cause additional expenses for accounting and legal fees, record-keeping, and preparation of tax returns. Although such expenses are deductible in computing the distributable net income (DNI) [109] as well as any taxable income [110] of the trust, they may nevertheless significantly reduce the net economic advantage from the existence of the trusts as separate taxable entities. For this reason, it is desirable to include a provision for the termination of trusts that have become uneconomic or whose continued existence is undesirable for any reason.

Such a provision may be directed specifically to the factors just referred to or it may be in a more general form. For example, the trustee may have a discretionary power to distribute all or any portion of the trust principal, or someone other than the trustee may have a power of appointment. Either power may be exercised to terminate the trust by causing the trust property to be distributed directly to the beneficiary. Or the power may be exercised, if its terms so permit, by causing such property to be distributed to another trust.

[5] Effect of Separate Trusts on Generation-Skipping Transfer Tax (GST)

Creation of separate trusts for each of two or more beneficiaries in the same generation may have adverse consequences from the standpoint of the generation-skipping transfer tax (GST). If a single trust is created, payment of the tax may be deferred until the termination of the interests of all beneficiaries assigned to the same generation.[111] If separate trusts are created for each member, there will be no such deferral of GST.

107. See Reg. § 1.665(b)–1A(b)(1). For a discussion, see Dasburg & Eittreim, "How to Cut Taxes by Using the Throwback Rules With In-Kind Distributions," 44 J.Tax. 284 (May 1976).

108. Under § 667(b), such tax is determined by adding the distribution to the other income of the beneficiary in three of the five taxable years preceding the distribution. See § 667(b)(1). If the distributee trust was not in existence during such preceding years, it would have had no such other income, unless it had previously received an accumulation distribution from another trust that was thrown back to one or more of such

years. Cf. Reg. § 1.668(b)–2A, dealing with provisions of § 668 prior to amendment. However, a change in rates might cause its top rate to be higher than that paid by the accumulating trust.

109. See § 643(a), defining DNI by reference to taxable income.

110. Reg. § 1.212–(1)(i). Expenses allocable to production of tax-exempt income are, of course, nondeductible. Id.

111. For a discussion, see ¶ 14.05[4][c][i] infra.

Chapter 12

ESTATE, GIFT, AND INCOME TAX ASPECTS OF POWERS

Estate and gift tax aspects of arrangements for beneficiaries and power holders turn largely on the treatment of powers of appointment under § 2041 and § 2514. As a general rule, a beneficiary or power holder who is not taxable under either of those sections avoids estate and gifts taxes altogether unless he owns the property or it is insurance on his life.

A third exception has been created by the Economic Recovery Tax Act of 1981. Sections 2056(b)(7) and § 2533(f) now provide for the use of "qualified terminable interests" as marital deduction gifts, and sections 2044 and 2519 provide that termination or transfer of such interests is a taxable transfer for estate and gift tax purposes.

Income tax aspects of powers are governed by § 678, discussed in ¶ 12.01[3][c].

¶ 12.01   USE OF POWERS IN ESTATE PLANNING

Arrangements that give someone the power to determine who shall enjoy a client's wealth, at what time, and in what manner, are among the most important tools of estate planning. Either during the client's life or after his death, such arrangements may enable one or more individuals, or a corporation, or a combination of both, to exercise the same judgment in disposing of wealth that the client himself could have exercised if he were living and still owned it. A client may undertake to determine in advance exactly who will enjoy his wealth, as well as when and how. Some clients insist on doing so in meticulous detail. But in an estate plan that may be operating over a span of 80 to 100 years, the foresight of a genius may be unable to anticipate the most desirable disposition under the broad range of unforeseen circumstances that may arise. By comparison, the judgment of an average individual based on events as they unfold may be far superior. Arrangements to delegate the power to dispose of wealth and, thus, to permit future developments to be taken into account in shaping its disposition include powers of appointment and discretionary powers of fiduciaries.

A power of appointment, "the most efficient dispositive device that the ingenuity of Anglo-American lawyers has ever worked out," [1] is defined in the Restatement of Property as: "[A] power created or reserved by a person (the donor) having property subject to his disposition enabling the donee of the power to designate, within such limits as the donor may prescribe, the transferees of the property or the shares in which it shall be received." [2] The Restatement definition, however, does not reflect the use of powers in tax-oriented estate planning. It includes powers reserved by the donor, although such powers are of limited use in such planning because of their

---

1. Leach, "Powers of Appointment," 24 A.B.A.J. 807 (1938).   2. Restatement of Property § 318(1) (1940).

generally adverse consequences.[3]   The Restatement excludes discretionary trusts, as well as powers to cause a gift of income to be augmented out of principal.[4]   Discretionary powers of fiduciaries—both executors and trustees—are of great importance in tax-oriented estate planning, as are powers of withdrawal that enable the holder to require distribution to him of portions of trust principal.   It is unfortunate that lawyers and other professionals involved in estate planning are often not fully aware of the potential uses of powers and that as a result those uses remain "sadly neglected."[5]

Estate planning advisors are concerned both with handling powers held by clients under existing estate plans and with the creation of new powers as part of a client's own plan.

The major tax consequences of the possession or exercise of powers held by someone other than the donor generally are as follows:

(1) For trust income tax purposes, the holder of a power presently exercisable solely by him that enables him to vest trust income or principal in himself is taxable as owner of such income or principal.[6]

(2) For both gift and estate tax purposes, the possession, exercise, or release of a general power of appointment created after October 21, 1942—one exercisable in favor of the holder, his estate, or the creditors of either—ordinarily is treated in the same manner as if the holder had owned the property subject to the power and had transferred such property.[7]

(3) For purposes of the generation-skipping transfer tax, the termination of any presently exercisable power of appointment may result in a "taxable distribution"[8] or "taxable termination"[9] unless the power is a general power and hence subject to estate tax or gift tax, or the power fits within an exemption provided by § 2613(e), or it is within the "grandfather" protection accorded pre-existing instruments.[10]

(4) Except for purposes of the generation-skipping transfer tax, a non-general power (one not exercisable in favor of the holder, his estate,

---

3. Powers are commonly reserved by the grantor of a revocable trust but such trusts ordinarily are not created in order to save taxes.   See ¶ 6.05[1] supra.   Some powers may be reserved by the grantor of a trust created to save taxes without interfering with achievement of that objective.   See ¶¶ 5.02[5][a] (estate taxes) 9.01[4] (income taxes) supra.

4. Restatement of Property, supra note 2, at § 318(2).

5. Report of Subcommittee of the Committee on Estate and Tax Planning, "Use and Drafting of Powers of Appointment," 1 Real Prop., Prob. & Tr.J. 307 (1966).

6. § 678(a)(1).

7. §§ 2514(b), 2041(a)(2).   In the case of a general power created on or before October 21, 1942, only the exercise is taxable.   See

§§ 2514(a) and 2041(a)(1), which also exempt the exercise of such a power if it was partially released before November 1, 1951, or within six months of the termination of the legal disability of the donee of a power who was under such disability on October 21, 1942, whichever is later.

If a testator created a power in a will executed on or before October 21, 1942, and died before July 1, 1949, "without having republished such will, by codicil or otherwise, after October 21, 1942," the power is deemed to have been created on or before that date.   See § 2041(b)(3); § 2514(f).

8. § 2613(a)(1).   For a discussion, see ¶ 13.11 infra.

9. § 2613(b)(1).   For a discussion, see ¶ 13.10 infra.

10. See ¶ 13.15 infra.

or the creditors of either) does not subject the holder to any adverse tax consequence [11] (whether exercised or not) unless he previously held (and partially released) a general power.[12]

(5) Although a lapse of a general power ordinarily is treated as a release,[13] there is a limited exemption for purposes of estate and gift [14] taxes (but not for trust income tax) [15] for lapses of powers of withdrawal during the life of the holder.

(6) Joint powers exercisable in favor of one or more of the power holders may be general powers for estate and gift tax [16] purposes but are not so treated for trust income tax [17] purposes.

[1] General Powers of Appointment

Ever since the introduction of the marital deduction by the Revenue Act of 1948, the most important function of general powers of appointment in estate plans has been to qualify otherwise non-qualifying terminable interests for the marital deduction.[18]   The Economic Recovery Tax Act of 1981 has made it unnecessary to give the spouse such a power in order to qualify for the marital deduction under federal tax law.[18a]   Under state law, however it may still be necessary to give the spouse either ownership of property or a general power of appointment over it in order to secure a state estate tax marital deduction.[19]   Thus general powers may continue to be used in estate planning for the same reasons that lead to their use before the 1981 Act changed the federal marital deduction requirements.

Some transferors may prefer to qualify for the deduction for state estate tax purposes by giving the surviving spouse a general power of appointment exercisable during her life, rather than giving her ownership of property. This is because the transferor is willing to have his surviving spouse exercise full control over the trust property but prefers to require that she act affirmatively to do so, by requesting a withdrawal.   Accordingly, he may give her a power exercisable during her lifetime (by deed).   The need for making such a request may cause her to allow property to stay in the trust and be managed by the trustee rather than undertaking to manage it herself.

11. There is an esoteric exception for powers that are exercised to create new powers exercisable without regard to the date of creation of the first power.   See § 2041(a)(3), discussed at ¶ 12.03[2] infra.

12. See § 678(a)(2), discussed at ¶ 12.01 [3][c][ii] infra, under which the power holder may continue to be taxed on trust income despite the partial release.   See also § 2041(a)(2); Reg. § 25.2514–3(c).

13. See, e.g., § 2041(b)(2).

14. Id.; § 2514(e).

15. § 678(a)(2), discussed at ¶ 12.01[3][c][ii] infra.

16. See §§ 2041(b)(1)(C) and 2514(c)(3), both of which except joint powers exercisable only in conjunction with the creator or with the holder of a substantial adverse interest.

17. See § 678(a)(1), which appears to supersede the holding in Anna Spies v. United States, 180 F.2d 336, 50–1 USTC ¶ 9202 (8th Cir. 1950).   In that case, beneficiaries who held a joint power to vest income in themselves were taxed on such income under the Internal Revenue Code of 1939.

18. See §§ 2056(b)(5), 2056(b)(6).   For a discussion of such use, see ¶ 18.04[2] infra.

18a. See ¶ 18.04[4] infra.

19. See, e.g., Mass.Gen.Laws Ann. ch. 65C, § 3(b) (West Supp.1981), referring to deductions allowable in determining the federal taxable estate, with exceptions.   Under § 1(a), references to the Internal Revenue Code are as it was in effect January 1, 1975.

If the transferor does not want his surviving spouse to have this degree of control over the trust property throughout her life, he may still qualify the transfer for the marital deduction by giving her a general power exercisable only by will.[20]   It is commonly believed that such a power will be exercised in the light of a more mature judgment, as the holder's will necessarily constitutes the final formal expression of her dispositive wishes and is free from the competing claims for gratification of her own desires while she lives.   Such a general power by will is treated as the equivalent of ownership for federal estate and gift tax purposes but not for federal income tax purposes.   The result is that the holder will be taxable as beneficiary on the trust's accounting income [21] but not on income allocable to principal such as capital gains, because her general power is not presently exercisable.

General powers are also used in connection with present interest gifts to minor under § 2503(c), which requires either that the minor have such a power if he dies under age 21 or that the property be paid to his estate on such death.[22]   And a general power likewise may be used in connection with the generation-skipping transfer tax to qualify property for the grandchild's exclusion if it is retained in trust instead of being distributed to the grandchild.[23]

The creation of a postponed general power may be appropriate for non-tax reasons as well.   For example, the transferor may be willing to allow the beneficiary to control all or a portion of the property after he attains a designated age, but may again prefer that the property not be distributed to the beneficiary unless he affirmatively acts to exercise the power.   In effect, creating a power rather than directing that distribution be made results in an informal presumption in favor of continued retention of the property by the trustee.   In a given case, however, the beneficiary may be well advised to exercise his power of withdrawal in order to act as his own investment manager (or to employ a non-fiduciary manager to act for him), rather than to continue paying trustee's fees on the trust portfolio.

HORACE S. MILLER v. UNITED STATES

United States Court of Appeals, Third Circuit, 1968.
387 F.2d 866, 68–1 USTC ¶ 12,504.

FREEDMAN, Circuit Judge:

This case presents the recurring problem of the taxability as part of a decedent's estate of a power of appointment over trust corpus which the decedent possessed but did not exercise.   Here, as in other such cases, the legal question is mixed with the apparent injustice of the imposition of an estate tax on a power which was never exercised and which would clearly

---

20. Such a power may, if the transferor wishes, be supplemented by a power exercisable during her life after she attains a specified age.

21. § 2056(b)(5) requires that the wife be given the trust income for her life in order to qualify for the marital deduction under the power of appointment exception to the terminable interest rule.   See ¶ 18.04[2] infra.

The amount taxable to the beneficiary is limited by the distributable net income (DNI) of the trust.   See § 643(a), discussed at ¶ 11.02[2] supra.

22. For a discussion, see ¶ 9.03[2] supra.

23. For a discussion, see ¶ 13.12 infra.

have been exempt from tax as a limited power had the words of grant been more narrowly chosen.

Decedent's husband created by his will a residuary trust whose net income was to be paid to decedent for life with remainder on her death to their children. The testamentary trust contained a provision authorizing the trustees, who were the decedent and a trust company to make disbursements out of the principal of the trust to decedent "at such times and in such amounts as my said Trustees, in their discretion, shall deem necessary or expedient for her proper maintenance, support, medical care, hospitalization, or other expenses incidental to her comfort and well-being."

Decedent died three years after her husband's death. She had lived modestly, had substantial assets of her own and in the period following her husband's death she had not received nor had she requested any payment from the corpus of the trust. Her executors did not include the value of the trust in her gross estate for federal estate tax purposes. The Commissioner of Internal Revenue, however, assessed a deficiency on the ground that the trust was property over which the decedent had held a general power of appointment at the time of her death and that it therefore was includable in her gross estate under § 2041 of the Internal Revenue Code of 1954. The executors paid the assessment and brought his suit for refund in the district court. On cross-motions for summary judgment and a stipulation of facts the district court entered judgment for the executors. 267 F.Supp. 182 (W.D.Pa.1967). The United States has appealed.

The standard of taxability of a general power of appointment, which includes a power to consume, and the extent of the exceptions thereto are explicitly laid down in § 2041 of the Code. Section 2041(a)(2) provides that the value of the gross estate of the decedent shall include the value of property with respect to which the decedent at the time of his death possesses a general power of appointment created after October 21, 1942. A general power of appointment is defined in subsection (b)(1) as "a power which is exercisable in favor of the decedent, his estate, his creditors, or the creditors of his estate," but an exception is made by subsection (b)(1)(A) that a "power to consume, invade, or appropriate property for the benefit of the decedent which is limited by an ascertainable standard relating to the health, education, support, or maintenance of the decedent shall not be deemed a general power of appointment."

The Regulations provide that a power is limited by an ascertainable standard "if the extent of the holder's duty to exercise and not to exercise the power is reasonably measurable in terms of his needs for health, education, or support (or any combination of them)," deeming maintenance to be synonymous with support.

It is by this measuring rod that we must judge whether the trust provision here falls within the exception or outside it. It is clear, and indeed it is conceded by the government, that the power to consume for decedent's "proper maintenance, support, medical care, hospitalization," as the trust provides, if there were nothing more, would bring the case clearly within the exception from taxability. The dispute, therefore, revolves around the remaining phrase, "or other expenses incidental to her comfort and well-being."

We had occasion not long ago in Strite v. McGinnes, 330 F.2d 234 (3 Cir. 1964), affirming 215 F.Supp. 513 (E.D.Pa.1963), cert. denied, 379 U.S. 836, 85 S.Ct. 69, 13 L.Ed.2d 43, rehearing denied 379 U.S. 910, 85 S.Ct. 185, 13 L.Ed.2d 182 (1964), to consider a problem quite similar, although not precisely identical.   There the power to consume was exercisable "at any time necessary or advisable in order to provide for the reasonable needs and proper expenses or the benefit or comfort" of decedent, and there were indicia in the will itself that the decedent had been the main object of the testatrix's bounty and that the power to invade principal should therefore be given its broadest meaning.[24]   We held that the power to consume when necessary or advisable for the decedent's "benefit" fell outside the exception and we therefore found it unnecessary to decide the effect of the word "comfort," which the district court had held was also beyond the exception.

The extent of the decedent's interest in the testator's estate under the power to consume must be determined by Pennsylvania law, although the taxability of the interest will be determined by federal law.   In ascertaining the extent of decedent's property interest under Pennsylvania law we recognize its guiding principles that each will is unique and that the intention of the testator must be found within the four corners of the instrument. We must determine this meaning uninfluenced by our present knowledge that decedent died without ever having sought to invade the principal of the trust and we must view the trust in the same way that a Pennsylvania court would have done in considering an application by the decedent for the consumption of principal in her lifetime.   Of course, we may not disregard the plain meaning of words used in a testamentary trust on any representation or plea that they may have been selected without a discriminating understanding of their meaning.   In Strite v. McGinnes the district court said: "In ascertaining the meaning of [the language of the power to consume] * * * we may not dismiss the language used as 'boiler plate,' although it is so characterized by plaintiff's counsel, perhaps with some justice. Boiler plate it may be, in the sense that the words may have been chosen indiscriminately by the scrivener without the imaginative understanding which is the hallmark of the skillful draftsman.   Executors confronted with substantial tax liability because of the carefree use of words in a will, especially words which never were put to use, must view a scrutiny of their meaning as an academic intrusion into the world of reality.   But we deal here with the *power* to consume property, regardless whether the power was exercised or lay dormant.   The grant of power in the will is the test of taxability, and the reality which governs is the language of the grant rather than the extent of its exercise."   215 F.Supp. at 515–516.

The district court, applying the rule of *ejusdem generis*, considered "incidental" as the significant word, so that the phrase "or other expenses *incidental* to her comfort and well-being" should be made to read as if it had provided for expenses incidental to her maintenance, support, medical care or hospitalization, and thus "comfort or well-being" was to be limited to such items.

---

24.   330 F.2d at 239, quoting 215 F.Supp. at 517.

This construction is erroneous. The word "incidental" relates to the decedent's "comfort and well-being," and not to her maintenance, support, medical care or hospitalization. To read the phrase "or other expenses incidental to her comfort and well-being" as limited by what has gone before would cut down to meaninglessness the words "comfort and well-being." It is impossible to adopt such a meaning in reading the language, as we must, as a Pennsylvania court would have done if decedent in her lifetime had sought to exercise the power to consume granted by her husband, rather than with the eyes of a reversioner's lawyer poring over the language of a condition subsequent. An artificial rule of construction such as the doctrine of *ejusdem generis* has very limited application and is to be exercised with caution, and in any event is applicable to a will only where the intention of the testator is ambiguous. The words "comfort and well-being" must be given their ordinary meaning and as such go far beyond support and medical and hospital care. * * * Here "comfort" is joined with "well-being" and without referring to dictionary definitions or authorities which have considered one or the other of the words, it is clear that much like the words "benefit or comfort" in the *Strite* case, they conferred a power to consume which extended beyond the statutory exception of an ascertainable power for health, education and support. Indeed, the Regulations make this plain beyond doubt. They provide: "A power to use property for the comfort, welfare, or happiness of the holder of the power is not limited by the requisite standard." [25]

The power to consume in the present case therefore exceeds the limit fixed for exception from a general power of appointment which is taxable to the estate of the holder of the power.

Appellant argues that in any event the power is not taxable to the decedent's estate because it falls within the exception of § 2041(b)(1)(C)(ii) as a power not exercisable by the decedent except in conjunction with a person "having a substantial interest in the property, subject to the power, which is adverse to the exercise of the power in favor of the decedent." Here a trust company was cotrustee with decedent. The power to invade principal was granted to the trustees jointly and not to the decedent alone, and it was exercisable "at such times and in such amounts as my said Trustees, in their discretion, shall deem necessary or expedient. * * * "

The corporate trustee had no substantial interest in the property of the trust adverse to the decedent's exercise of the power. Its only interest was in the administration of the trust as trustee; it was not a beneficiary of the trust and would have lost no right to obtain any property that might have been turned over to the decedent on the exercise of the power. The trust company's right to compensation for serving as a trustee, even though dependent to some extent on the amount of the corpus of the trust, is not a substantial adverse interest within the meaning of the statute. The substantial adverse interest must be one, as the statute declares, "in the property itself" and not an interest in continuing in the office of trustee. * * *

---

25. 26 C.F.R. § 20.2041–1(c)(2).

[2] Non-General or Limited Powers

The Regulations define a non-general power as a power that is not exercisable in favor of the holder, his estate, or the creditors of either.[26] This allows the power holder to be given the ability to roam the world over to choose his appointees, without being treated as owner of the property for federal income, estate, or gift tax purposes.   The exercise or termination of any power, however, may be a "deemed transfer" by the power holder for purposes of the generation-skipping transfer tax.[27]   This result may be avoided if the exercise or termination of the power causes property to vest in one or more grandchildren of the grantor and is within the cumulative exclusion of $250,000 allowed for transfers to all grandchildren who are the offspring of the same child of the grantor.[28]   Alternatively, the power may come within one of the exemptions for certain powers of independent trustees and certain powers to appoint among lineal descendants of the grantor.[29]

If the transferor does not wish to give the power holder a completely unrestricted freedom of choice of appointees, a power to appoint among members of a more limited group may be a highly desirable feature of an estate plan.   For example, giving the spouse the power to appoint among the issue of the settlor may serve several important purposes.   Revisions of the transferor's plan for such issue may become desirable as a result of changes in their individual circumstances or in the tax laws.   And it does not require an overly cynical view of human nature to suggest that the spouse's possession of a power to affect the distribution of wealth among her descendents may cause them to be more attentive and respectful, particularly if she can only exercise the power by her will.

[3] Powers of Withdrawal

No saving in income, estate, and gift taxes results for an individual who is given an unlimited power of withdrawal (or its equivalent for tax purposes, a general power of appointment exercisable during the holder's life, i.e., by deed).   Possession of such a power over a trust causes the trust income to be taxed as if the power holder were the owner of the trust.[30]   If the holder either exercises the power during his life in favor of someone else or releases it, he makes a taxable gift.[31]   A release requires affirmative action of the power holder to surrender his right to exercise the power.

A lapse, on the other hand, occurs whenever the holder fails to exercise the power during the period in which such exercise is authorized by the terms of the instrument creating the power.   A lapse is treated for gift tax purposes as a release, subject to a limited exemption described below.[32]

---

26. See Reg. §§ 20.2041–1(c)(1), 25.2514–1 (c)(1).   If a power to appoint to the children of the power holder may be exercised to satisfy his obligation to support them, the Commissioner will treat the power as a general power.   See Rev.Rul. 79–154, 79–1 CB 301.

27. § 2613(a)(1), § 2613(b)(1).

28. See §§ 2613(a)(4), 2613(b)(5), 2613(b)(6). For a discussion, see ¶ 13.12 infra.

29. See § 2613(e).   This provision merely exempts the power and does not exempt the passage of property which occurs pursuant to the exercise of the power or which may occur at the time of its termination.   For a discussion, see ¶ 13.13 infra.

30. § 678(a)(1).

31. § 2514(b).

32. § 2514(e).   For a discussion, see ¶ 12.01[3][b] infra.

Whether or not such exercise or release causes the property subject to the power to be included in the holder's gross estate is determined in accordance with the rules applied to transfers of owned assets.[33]   Again, a lapse is treated as a release, with the same exemption as that provided for gift tax purposes.[34]   And if the holder still has the power when he dies, the appointive property is likewise includible in his gross estate.[35]   Thus, an unlimited power of withdrawal should not be created unless it is required in order to qualify for a particular tax deduction or unless the client believes that the non-tax advantages of the power for the holder outweigh any adverse tax consequences from it.

Ordinarily, however, such non-tax advantages can be largely achieved by giving the beneficiary a package of powers and interests that does not include an unlimited power of withdrawal but that does afford him as much power over the property as the client wants him to have.   Important elements in that package can be the following two forms of limited powers of withdrawal:

> (1) a support power, enabling the holder to withdraw each year such amounts as are required for his support in accordance with a standard specified in the trust instrument; [36]

> (2) a "5 or 5" power, enabling the holder to withdraw each year the greater of $5,000 or 5 percent of the value of the trust principal at the end of the year.[37]

It is possible to give the same individual both kinds of powers over a single trust, and to provide as well that additional amounts may be distributed to him in the discretion of the trustee or through the exercise of a power of appointment held by someone else.

[a] Support Powers

A power to invade either income or principal or both for the "health, education, support, or maintenance" of the holder, in accordance with a standard that meets the tests specified in the Regulations,[38] has no federal estate or gift tax consequences because it is excluded from the definition of

33. § 2041(a)(2).

34. § 2041(b)(2).

35. § 2041(a)(2).

36. See §§ 2041(b)(1)(A), 2514(c)(1).

37. §§ 2041(b)(2), 2514(e).

38. See Reg. §§ 20.2041–1(c)(2), 25.2514–1 (c)(2).   The Commissioner's application of the statutory standard has been quite strict in some respects.   In Rev.Rul. 77–60, 1977–1 CB 282, a power to invade corpus "to continue the donee's accustomed standard of living" was a general power of appointment because (1) it was not limited to one or more of the four statutory objectives and (2) under applicable state law it did not impose an objective limitation on exercise of the power.   In Letter Rul. 7914036, 3

CCH E&GT ¶ 12,266 Jan. 3, 1979 on the other hand, a power to "maintain the standard of living to which [the donee] was accustomed" was held not to be a general power because of the restriction to "maintenance," one of the statutory objectives.

Judicial application of the statutory standard has sometimes been more liberal.   In John C. Brantingham v. United States, 631 F.2d 542, 80–2 USTC ¶ 13,373 (7th Cir. 1980), the power was limited to withdrawal of amounts needed for the holder's "maintenance, comfort and happiness," but the inclusion of "happiness" did not make the power a general power even though it is not one of the statutory objectives.   The court reasoned that under applicable state law the power would be limited by " an ascertainable standard."

general power of appointment.[39]   However, whether the power relates to income or principal or both, it may have income tax consequences under § 678.[40]

It is not easy to reconcile the exemption of support powers with the statement in the Regulations that a power to discharge a legal obligation of the holder is a general power of appointment.[41]   As a matter of state property law, it is reasonable to assume that a power to invade principal for the support and maintenance of a married man would be construed to include support and maintenance of his wife and minor children.[42]   Otherwise, the power holder may theoretically be placed in a dilemma: Either he eats while his wife and children starve or he feeds them with his support money while he starves.[43]

A power to invade principal or income for the support of dependents could be considered a non-general power of appointment if such use is merely an aspect of supporting the power holder himself.   Otherwise, it may be viewed as a general power of appointment.   But it is difficult to find persuasive justification for such a distinction.[44]

In practice, however, the Commissioner does not appear to treat support powers as general powers of appointment because support of dependents is included in support of the power holder as a matter of state law. Whether or not a support power is within the statutory exemption is generally viewed as turning on whether the language creating the power tracks that in the Regulations.

For purposes of the generation-skipping transfer tax (GST), the holder of a support power is a beneficiary and the termination of his power may be subject to the tax.[45]   However, the power holder usually is also given an interest in income whose termination may be taxable [46] even if he had

---

39. § 2041(b)(1)(A); § 2514(c)(1).

40. See ¶ 11.01[1]. At least one case dealing with taxable years prior to the enactment of § 678 as part of the Internal Revenue Code of 1954 declined to tax the holder of an unexercised support power. See Mary A. Smither v. United States, 108 F.Supp. 772, 52–2 USTC ¶ 9455 (S.D.Tex.1952), aff'd 205 F.2d 518, 53–2 USTC ¶ 9482 (5th Cir. 1953). See also Eleanor M. Funk v. Commissioner, 185 F.2d 127, 50–2 USTC ¶ 9507 (3d Cir. 1950), reaching a similar result where the power referred merely to "needs."

41. See Reg. §§ 20.2041–1(c)(1), 25.2514–1 (c)(1). It may be significant that these regulations do not include the following statement in Reg. § 20.2036–1(b)(2), dealing with transfers with retained life estate: "The term 'legal obligation' includes a legal obligation to support a dependent during the decedent's lifetime."

42. "Where a trust is created for the support of a beneficiary, and the beneficiary is a married man, the inference is that he is en-titled to receive enough to support his wife and minor children also." 2 Scott, Trusts § 128.4 (3d ed. 1967). In In re Estate of Rockwell, 26 Misc.2d 709, 205 N.Y.S.2d 928 (Surr.Ct.1960), this rule was applied to a provision for invasion of trust principal. Contrary views are found in Old Colony Trust Co. v. Rodd, 356 Mass. 584, 254 N.E.2d 886 (1970), and Cavett v. Buck, 397 P.2d 901 (Okl.1964).

43. The dilemma may be avoided if the beneficiary has other resources which he is not required to exhaust before resorting to the trust. See Reg. §§ 20.2041–1(c)(2), 25.2514–1(c)(2).

44. A possible basis is the omission in the power of appointment regulations of the reference to obligations to support dependents included in connection with retained life estates. See note 41 supra.

45. See § 2613(b)(1). For a discussion, see ¶ 13.10 infra.

46. See ¶ 13.07 infra.

no other interest in or power over the property.   In this situation, the addition of the support power or limited power of withdrawal does nothing to make the generation-skipping transfer tax picture less favorable than it otherwise would have been.

[b] Estate and Gift Tax Consequences of "5 or 5" Powers

The Code creates an exemption for gift and estate tax purposes for lapses of powers that do not exceed $5,000 or "5 percent of the aggregate value, at the time of such lapse, of the assets out of which, or the proceeds of which, the exercise of the lapsed powers could have been satisfied." [47] The exemption also applies to the lapse of a power to withdraw more than $5,000 or 5 percent of the trust property.   But in that situation, the excess over the exempt amount may be a taxable transfer for gift tax [48] and estate tax [49] purposes.

A power to withdraw each year the greater of $5,000 or 5 percent of the property subject to the power enjoys very favorable estate and gift tax treatment.   Such a power is not excluded from the definition of "general power of appointment." [50]   Thus, any property that the holder could withdraw from the trust at the time of his death will be included in his gross estate.   But the lapse of such a power during the holder's life is not treated, as are lapses of general powers, as a release for either gift tax or estate tax purposes.[51]   The favorable treatment of such powers is with respect to lapses during the life of the holder, and is an exception to the general rule that a lapse of a general power is treated for gift and estate tax purposes as a release.[52]   Under the general rule, the holder of a power that lapses during his life is regarded as having made a transfer to whoever takes as a result of the lapse.   The amount of any gift for gift tax purposes, and whether any portion of the property is includible in the power holder's gross estate, depends upon whether he retained other interests, or powers over the property, after the lapse.[53]

In order to fit wholly within the exemption, the power must be non-cumulative, or "use it or lose it," with respect to the holder's rights for any

47. §§ 2041(b)(2), 2514(e).

48. The starting point in determining the amount of the transfer for gift tax purposes is the amount which could have been withdrawn in excess of the exemption.   See Reg. § 25.2514–3(c)(4).   Whether or not the power holder would be regarded as having made a gift of that amount would also depend upon whether he retained other interests in or powers over the trust after the lapse which would reduce the amount given or make the gift incomplete.   See ¶ 12.03[1][a] infra.

49. Whether or not the lapse requires inclusion of any of the property subject to the power in the holder's gross estate is determined by the same tests that are applied for transfers of owned assets.   See § 2041(a)(2).   If any of the property is includible because of the lapse, the starting point in determining the amount of the

transfer for estate tax purposes is the amount which could have been withdrawn in excess of the exemption.   See Reg. § 20.2041–3(d)(4).   The result is that a fraction of the trust will be included for each year in which such a lapse occurs.   The Regulations magnanimously limit the total amount required to be included to 100 percent of the value of the trust property when the holder dies.   See Reg. § 20.2041–3(d)(5).

50. §§ 2041(b)(1), 2514(c).

51. §§ 2514(e), 2041(b)(2).

52. Id.

53. See notes 48 and 49 supra.   Whether or not the lapse occurred within three years of the power holder's death also is relevant in determining whether the property is includible in his gross estate.   See § 2035 (d)(1), discussed at ¶ 5.02[3][b][i].

given year.   If 5 percent not withdrawn in *Year 1* can be withdrawn in *Year 2*, in addition to another 5 percent for that year, there is no lapse at the end of *Year 1* to which the exemption can apply.   The result is that the holder has not made a taxable gift by failing to exercise his power in any given year, because the amount subject to withdrawal that year may be withdrawn in a later year.   When he dies, however, there may be an accumulation of unexercised powers for many years that will require inclusion of a substantial part of the trust property in his gross estate because such part is subject to a power exercisable at the time of his death.[54]

For purposes of the generation-skipping transfer tax (GST), the holder of a "5 or 5" power is a beneficiary and the termination of his power may be subject to the tax.[55]   However, the power holder usually is also given an interest in income whose termination would be taxable [56] even if he had no other interest in or power over the property.   In this situation, the addition of the support power or limited power of withdrawal does nothing to make the GST picture less favorable than it otherwise would have been.

In drafting a "5 or 5" power, problems may arise with respect to:

(1) the time when the power may be exercised; and

(2) the effect of other powers of the holder.

Thus, the language should make clear in any case that the power is exercisable over principal, rather than income, as the 5 percent exemption is computed on the value of the fund out of which the exercise of the power may be satisfied.[57]   In addition, the income tax treatment of a power over principal often is far more favorable than that of a similar power over income.

CLARENCE B. FISH v. UNITED STATES

United States Court of Appeals, Ninth Circuit, 1970.
432 F.2d 1278, 70–2 USTC ¶ 12,718.

TAYLOR, District Judge.

Clarence Blagen Fish (taxpayer), as administrator of the estate of Minnie C. Blagen, has appealed from an adverse judgment of the District Court on his suit for refund of federal estate taxes   *   *   *

The stipulated facts reveal that Clarence G. Blagen, the husband of Minnie C. Blagen, died on May 28, 1951.   The residuary clause of his will established a trust, the terms of which provided that Minnie C. Blagen should have, during her lifetime, the right in any calendar year to demand payment to her of all or part of the net income of the trust for that year, but that any income not so claimed by her would be added to the corpus of the trust.   Upon the death of Minnie C. Blagen, the trust corpus, including such accumulated income added to the corpus, was to be distributed to the grandchildren of Clarence G. Blagen.

Minnie C. Blagen (decedent) never exercised or released her power over the income of the trust in any year from the inception of the trust until

---

54. See note 49 supra.

55. See § 2613(b)(1).   For a discussion, see ¶ 13.08 infra.

56. See § 2613(b)(1).   For a discussion, see ¶ 13.07 infra.

57. §§ 2041(b)(2)(B); 2514(e)(2).   See Clarence B. Fish v. United States, infra.

her death on July 13, 1960, except insofar as the annual lapse of the power, if any such lapse occurred, constituted a release of the power as a matter of law under Section 2041(b)(2) of the Internal Revenue Code. The Commissioner, in assessing the tax deficiency, included in the decedent's gross estate the net income of the trust, less allowable exemptions, for the years 1955, 1956, 1957, 1958 and 1959. The inclusion of accumulated income which had been added to the trust in those years resulted in an increase in the decedent's gross estate of $116,045.36. The taxpayer had not included this amount in the estate tax return which he had filed for the estate.

The Commissioner determined that the decedent possessed a general power of appointment over the trust income and that the failure of the decedent to exercise this power constituted a lapse of the power in each year in which it was not exercised. The Commissioner contends that the lapse constitutes a release of the power under Section 2041(b)(2) in such a way that, if it were a transfer of property owned by the decedent, the property would have been includible in the decedent's gross estate as a transfer with a retained life estate under Section 2036(a)(1).[58]

The taxpayer agrees that the decedent possessed a general power of appointment, and that the "transfer" each year, had the property been owned by the decedent, would be a transfer with a retained life estate. The taxpayer contends, however, that the decedent was incompetent for some seven years prior to her death and her general power of appointment could not have been lawfully exercised or released by her or by anyone acting in her behalf and that therefore the annual expiration of her power over the trust income was not a "lapse" and thus not a release of the power within the meaning of Section 2041(b)(2). Alternatively, the taxpayer contends that if the incompetency of the decedent is immaterial and a lapse of the power occurred in each year, the Commissioner and the District Court erred in computing the allowable exemption under Section 2041(b)(2) on the basis of five per cent of the net income of the trust instead of, as taxpayer contends, five per cent of the total trust assets.

We agree with the District Court that the competency of the decedent is immaterial in determining whether a lapse or release of the power occurred. The statute provides, without equivocation, that a lapse of the power shall be considered a release, and does not purport to qualify the manner in which the lapse occurs. While no case has been discovered which is precisely on all fours with the facts in the instant case, it nevertheless appears from closely analogous cases that taxability and the inclusion of the assets in a decedent's gross estate are determined by the existence of the power and by circumstances which bring its release or exercise within the ambit of Sections 2041(a)(2) or 2041(b)(2). The precise manner of exercising or releasing the power is immaterial for purposes of determining taxability. Thus it is sufficient here that the power was released by its annual expiration

---

58. As income was added to the trust each year as a result of the decedent's inaction; that income generated additional income in following years which was subject to the decedent's lifetime power of appointment; and thus the "transfer" each year by the decedent was one which left her with a life-time interest in the property. Such a transfer, resulting from the exercise or release of a power of appointment, becomes includible in the gross estate of the decedent under the provisions of Section 2041(a)(2) of the Internal Revenue Code.

or lapse, and it is immaterial whether the lapse occurred through a designed failure to exercise the power or through the indifference or incompetency of the decedent.   Round v. Commissioner, 332 F.2d 590 (1st Cir. 1964); Townsend v. United States, 232 F.Supp. 219 (E.D.Tex.1964).[59]   Since we hold the matter of the decedent's competency to be immaterial, we need not decide whether the decedent was in fact incompetent or whether the power could have been exercised by a guardian acting in her behalf.

The taxpayer next contends that the District Court erred in computing the exemption allowed under Section 2041(b)(2).   That section allows as an exemption to the amount includible in the taxable estate an amount equal to five per cent of "the aggregate value of the assets out of which, or the proceeds of which, the exercise of the lapsed powers could have been satisfied," or the sum of $5,000, whichever is the greater.   The District Court, in determining the amount of the exemption, computed the exemption on the basis of five per cent of the trust income.   Since for each year in question, the sum of $5,000 was greater than five per cent of the trust income, the District Court allowed an exemption of $5,000 for each year, as the Commissioner had done.   The taxpayer argues that the exemption should be $5,000 or five per cent of the total trust assets, and since five per cent of the total assets would exceed the net income for three of the five years in question and would nearly equal net income in the other two years, the end result should be that the amount includible in the decedent's estate should be reduced to $15,858.47.   The taxpayer argues that since the income payable to the decedent, had she demanded it, would have been payable either from corpus or income, the entire trust represents "assets out of which, or the proceeds out of which, the exercise of lapsed powers could be satisfied," and thus the entire trust assets should serve as the basis for the five per cent computation.   We do not agree.   Even if the trustee could have satisfied a demand for income out of either corpus assets or income funds, a point which we do not here decide, the distribution would necessarily have been a distribution of income as a matter of federal tax law or as a matter of trust accounting, since the decedent had no power whatever to invade the corpus of the trust.

While the language of Section 2041(b)(2)(B), like much of the statutory tax law, is hardly a model of precision and clarity on the point, we are satisfied from a reading of the statute together with its legislative history that the applicable basis for computation of the allowable exemption is the trust or fund in which the lapsed power existed.   The District Court correctly determined that the power of appointment in the instant case existed only with respect to the trust income, and properly allowed an exemption of $5,000 for each year in question.

The District Court correctly resolved the material issues in the case, and its judgment is accordingly affirmed.

---

59. We note parenthetically that if the position contended for by the taxpayer were adopted, the result would be an open invitation to contest the competency of the decedent in every similar case, since the competency of any decedent who held a similar power of appointment, and many of whom suffer mental debilitation to some degree prior to death, would be subject to the same posthumous inquiry which the taxpayer seeks here.   It should be noted that the decedent was never adjudicated an incompetent prior to her death.

[i] When the Power May Be Exercised. In order to be wholly within the statutory exemption for lapses, a 5 percent power must be based on the value of the trust assets "at the time of such lapse." [60] Thus, if the power is exercisable throughout the year this means the value of the assets at the end of the year. However, there is an estate tax disadvantage in making the power exercisable over such an extended period: It will result in inclusion in the holder's estate of 5 percent of the trust property, less whatever he had withdrawn in the year of his death. [61]

Such inclusion may be avoided by making exercise of the power in any year effective only if the power holder is living on a given date and requiring the assets to be valued for this purpose as of that date. For example, the power could be made exercisable if the holder gave appropriate notice during the calendar year and was living on December 31st, with assets to be valued on that date to determine the amount that can be withdrawn. Such a provision should mean that if the power holder died before that date, no inclusion of property in the holder's gross estate would be required because of his possession of the power when he died. It also has the advantage of keeping the trustee from being required to forecast what the value of the principal will be on the last day on which the power may be exercised, [62] if the power holder may request a distribution earlier in the year.

[ii] Multiple "5 or 5" Powers. The Code does not indicate clearly the manner in which the exemption is to be applied if the power holder has two or more "5 or 5" powers. For example, the power holder may have the power to withdraw the greater of $5,000 or 5 percent from principal of *Trust A*, worth $100,000, and also have an identical power to withdraw principal from *Trust B*, worth $60,000. In this situation, if the exemption is applied on a per-trust basis, there will be no taxable lapse from the holder's failure to exercise his powers. But if the holder is limited to a single exemption, there may be such a taxable lapse. He has the power to withdraw a total of $10,000, which is greater than either $5,000 or 5 percent of the combined value of the two trusts, $160,000. The result is an exempt lapse of $5,000 with respect to *Trust A* and a non-exempt lapse with respect to $2,000 in *Trust B*, the excess of $5,000 over 5 percent of the value of the trust.

Logically, the exemption should be applied on a "one per holder" rather than "one per trust" basis. Otherwise, it would theoretically be possible to create 100 trusts of $5,000 each for a beneficiary, giving him a "5 or 5" power over each trust. He would thus have complete control over the trust property without its being includible in his gross estate. The problem just described would not arise if both powers were merely powers to withdraw 5 percent of the trust principal, without the alternative of $5,000. Of

---

60. § 2041(b)(2)(B). Although § 2514(e)(2) does not include the quoted language, the general rule of § 2512(a) that gifts are valued as of the date of the gift would apply.

61. § 2041(a)(2).

62. No such forecast is required if the power is $5,000 or 5 percent and the requested withdrawals earlier in the year do not aggregate more than $5,000. Another alternative is to limit withdrawals to 5 percent of the value of the trust when the request is made, with the amount which may be withdrawn to be reduced by previous withdrawals during the year. Under this formula, the amount which may be withdrawn at any given time never exceeds the exemption, and no forecast of year-end value need be made by the trustee.

course, a beneficiary who has the power to withdraw 5 percent from one trust and the power to withdraw $5,000 from a second trust of less than $100,000, so that the lapse of his powers is not entirely within the exemption, may act to avoid a taxable lapse. He need merely exercise the power to the extent that $5,000 exceeds 5 percent of the property in the second trust, in order to bring the lapse within the scope of the 5 percent exemption. But situations may arise in which it is impractical or undesirable for a beneficiary to exercise such a power. For example, he may be incapacitated or incompetent.

[c] Income Tax Consequences

[i] Possession and Exercise of Power. The income tax consequences of the possession and exercise of a power of withdrawal turn on whether it is expressed as a power to withdraw income or principal.[63] The following examples illustrate the difference between the two varieties:

> *Example 12.1.* Assume that a trust created for the benefit of *P* provides that income shall be accumulated and added to principal, but that *P* may withdraw in any year out of income the greater of $5,000 or 5 percent of the value of the trust principal at the end of the year. Assume further that the trust principal remains constant at $300,000 and the trust has distributable net income [64] of $20,000 per year (and no other income).

> *Example 12.2.* Assume that *P*'s power in *Example 12.1* is to withdraw out of principal the greater of $5,000 or 5 percent of the value of the trust principal at the end of the year.

In *Example 12.1*, *P* has a § 678(a)(1) power to vest $15,000 of income in himself and is taxable in *Year 1* on that amount of trust income whether or not he exercises the power of withdrawal. The tax consequences are the same in *Year 2* if *P* exercises the power of withdrawal in *Year 1*. If he allows the power to lapse in *Year 1*, in whole or in part, a different set of tax consequences apply.[65]

In *Example 12.2*, *P* also has a § 678(a)(1) power, but it relates to principal, rather than income. As a result, *P* is taxable under that section as owner of 5 percent of the principal,[66] rather than as owner of $15,000 of income, as in *Example 12.1*. Thus, he is taxable under § 678(a)(1) on $1,000 of trust income (the portion attributable to 5 percent of the principal) whether or not he exercises the power of withdrawal. If he does exercise that power in *Year 1*, he nevertheless is taxable on only $1,000 of trust income because §§ 661(a)(2) and 662(a)(2) are inapplicable to the portion of trust principal considered owned by him when it is distributed to him.[67]

---

63. This follows from the treatment of income and principal (or corpus, in the Code's latinate terminology) as separate portions in taxing a grantor or non-grantor as the owner thereof. See Reg. § 1.671–3(b). For a discussion of similar principles applied in taxing trust grantors, see ¶ 9.01[1][b] supra.

64. See § 643(a), discussed at ¶ 11.01[2] supra.

65. See ¶ 12.01[3][c][ii] infra.

66. See Rev. Rul. 67–241, 1967–2 CB 225.

67. Id. The ruling deals with a trust in which income was payable to other beneficiaries, rather than being required to be accumulated. However, the conclusion as to the tax treatment of the power holder does not appear to be dependent upon that factor.

The trust would be taxable on its remaining income of $19,000, with a tax of roughly $5,000 at current rates.

The income tax consequences of the exercise of a limited power to withdraw principal thus are initially much more favorable than such consequences with respect to a power over income. If the power holder exercises such a power in *Year 1* to withdraw 5 percent of the trust principal, or $15,000 in the above example, he nevertheless is taxable on only 5 percent of the trust income, or $1,000 in the above example. Thus, he is enabled to receive $14,000 from the trust without being required to include that amount in income, even though the trust had DNI in excess of $15,000 in *Year 1*. However, the corollary of this treatment of the exercise of the power in *Year 1*—that receipt of the amount paid pursuant to such exercise does not cause DNI to be taxable to the power holder—is that there is a build-up of undistributed net income (UNI) in the trust.

Such a build-up of UNI is relevant if the power of withdrawal is exercised in a second year, as the Regulations treat amounts paid pursuant to the exercise of a power of withdrawal as constituting an accumulation distribution [68] for the purposes of the throwback rule.[69] Thus, *P* may be subject to an additional tax on the withdrawal in such second year.

Thus, in *Year 2*, if *P* again exercised his power and withdrew $15,000, he would be taxed as owner on $1,000, as in *Year 1*. The distribution would also be an accumulation distribution of $15,000 [70] and would be subject to throwback treatment to the extent of the trust's undistributed net income (UNI), $14,000 (income accumulated in *Year 1* of $19,000 [71] less $5,000 tax paid by the trust). Accordingly, *P* would include in income in the manner prescribed for throwback distributions both the UNI of $14,000 and the tax

---

68. § 665(b). See ¶ 11.02[2] supra. Amounts which could have been withdrawn pursuant to an unexercised power of withdrawal are not treated as a throwback distribution. See note 77 infra.

69. See Reg. § 1.665(b)–1A(a)(2). It has been suggested that these Regulations are inconsistent with § 665(b), which defines accumulation distributions with reference to amounts specified in § 661(a)(2), and hence are invalid. See Warren, "Estate Trust Provides Income Splitting Possibilities as Well as a Marital Deduction," 6 Est.Plan. 224, 226–227 (1979).

70. Note that the amount paid pursuant to *P*'s exercise of his power over principal carries out UNI accumulated in a prior year for purposes of the throwback rule even though such amount does not carry out DNI for the year in which the payment is made. See notes 66, 69 supra.

The accumulation distribution here is $15,000 rather than $14,000 because the Regulations treat amounts taxable to either a grantor or non-grantor as owner—here $1,000—as not reducing the amount of an accumulation distribution. See Reg. § 1.665(b)–1A(d), *Example (4)*. The defi-

nition in § 665(b) does not limit the amount of the accumulation distribution to the trust's UNI. But to the extent it exceeds such UNI, it has no tax consequences for the distributee. Thus, the fact that the amounts taxable to *P* in *Year 1* and *Year 2* do not reduce the accumulation distribution of $15,000 in *Year 2* has no practical significance here because a distribution of $14,000 would equal the UNI of the trust. If there were additional UNI from earlier years, the treatment of the entire $15,000 as a throwback distribution would be significant because such additional UNI from years preceding *Year 1* would also become taxable up to the excess of $1,000 over the UNI from *Year 1*. See Peschel & Spurgeon, Federal Taxation of Trusts, Grantors and Beneficiaries ¶ 3.04[C][7] (1978).

71. UNI is $19,000 less tax rather than $20,000 less tax because § 671 excludes from the application of the throwback rule of §§ 665–667, amounts taxable to a power holder under § 678.

thereon paid by the trust, or $5,000,[72] or a total of $19,000,[73] and would receive credit for the trust's tax.

It therefore appears that for income tax purposes, the difference between a limited power of withdrawal over income and such a power over principal is relatively unimportant if the power is exercised each year. The net result, if the power is over principal rather than income, is deferral for one year of the difference between the tax on such income at the trust's rates and the beneficiary's tax under the throwback rule. Although such deferral may continue throughout the term of the trust, the cost of achieving it is an annual throwback computation that may result in increased accounting costs for the power holder. If the trust initially adopts a fiscal year ending January 31 and the beneficiary is on a calendar year basis, the resulting deferral is almost as great,[74] without comparable accounting complexities.

The income tax treatment of an unexercised power to withdraw principal, on the other hand, is significantly more favorable than that of an unexercised power to withdraw income. Even more striking differences exist in estate and gift tax consequences for such unexercised powers. Accordingly, a power of withdrawal should ordinarily be expressed as a power over principal, rather than income, if it is anticipated that the power is not likely to be exercised every year and the trust income is expected to be accumulated.

[ii] Failure to Exercise Power. The income tax consequences of a failure to exercise a power of withdrawal depend primarily on whether it is expressed as a power to withdraw income or principal. The latter receives a more favorable tax treatment. In *Example 12.1*, if *P* fails to withdraw the $15,000 in *Year 1*, he is taxable in *Year 2* under § 678(a)(2) because of his partial release of the power of withdrawal in *Year 1*. When *P* failed to exercise his right to withdraw the $15,000, he is treated under that section as having become for income tax purposes the grantor of a trust. A grantor who retains the power to withdraw income from a portion of a trust is taxed as owner of such portion under § 677.

Arguably, that portion is not the full amount added to principal in *Year 1* because *P*'s right of withdrawal may not cover the entire trust income in future years. But it will in any year in which the trust earns 5 percent or less. Section 677 taxes as owner a trust grantor who may have trust income distributed to him before the end of the period specified in § 673 (10 years or the life of the beneficiary). *P* cannot prove that he may not receive all of the income at some time within that period. Thus, he is taxable in *Year 2* as owner of the portion of the trust he could have withdrawn in *Year 1*, if he had exercised his power. He could have withdrawn $15,000 from a trust of $300,000. Accordingly, ignoring changes in value of the trust principal due to adding accumulated income to principal or to market fluctuations, that portion is 5 percent.

---

72. § 666(b).

73. For an illustration of the mechanics of the throwback rule, see Peschel & Spurgeon, supra note 70, at ¶ 3.04[B].

74. Under § 662(c), the beneficiary would include in his taxable income for *Year 2* his share of the trust's DNI for its fiscal year ending January 31 of *Year 2*. Eleven months of the period covered by such year would be in the beneficiary's *Year 1*.

In *Year 2*, whether or not he exercised the power of withdrawal, he would be taxed as owner of $15,000 of trust income under § 678(a)(1) and on an additional $1,000 of trust income under § 678(a)(2), representing the 5 percent of the trust of which he is treated as having become the grantor. The reason that the result is not affected in any given year by whether or not *P* exercises his power of withdrawal for that year is that his tax under § 678 is based on current possession, or past partial release, of a power, rather than on receipt of a trust distribution. Thus, whether or not he exercises his power in *Year 2* does not affect his tax for for that year, but does affect his tax for *Year 3*.

In *Year 3*, P would again be taxed as owner of $15,000 of trust income under § 678(a)(1) because of his current power to withdraw that amount. If he had allowed his power to lapse in both *Year 1* and *Year 2*, he would be taxable on an additional $2,000 of trust income under § 678(a)(2), representing the two 5 percent portions of the trust of which he is treated as having become the grantor. This build-up of P's tax liability under § 678(a)(2) would continue until he was treated as owner of 100% of the trust (95% under § 678(a)(2) and 5% under § 678(a)(1)). At that point he would be taxable on the entire trust income.

In *Example 12.2*, on the other hand, *P*'s unexercised power over principal makes him taxable as owner of only 5 percent of the trust.[75] In *Year 1* he would be taxed as owner of 5 percent, or on $1,000 of trust income. If he did not exercise his power of withdrawal in *Year 1*, in *Year 2* he would be again taxed as owner of 5 percent under § 678(a)(1) because of his power to withdraw 5 percent currently in *Year 2*. He would also be taxed as owner of an additional portion of the trust under § 678(a)(2) because of his failure to withdraw 5 percent in *Year 1*. Such failure appears to be a partial release of his power of withdrawal for *Year 1*. The partial release left *P* with a power of revocation over part of the trust because of his ability to withdraw 5 percent each year thereafter. Possession of such a power causes a trust grantor to be taxed as owner under § 676. Under § 676(b), however, he is thus taxable only to the extent the power can be exercised within the period specified in § 673 (ten years or the life of the beneficiary, whichever is shorter). Ignoring for the moment the alternative of the life of the beneficiary, the question is what portion of the trust is regarded as revocable by a grantor within ten years, if he has a non-cumulative power to withdraw 5 percent of the trust principal each year?

The Regulations provide no precise guidance but the portion is susceptible of actuarial determination. It would, of course, be less than 50 percent because each exercise of the power reduces the amount that may be withdrawn in a later year.

Thus in *Year 2*, if P did not exercise his power of withdrawal in Year 1, he would be taxed as owner of 5% under § 678(a)(1) and as owner of an additional percentage under § 678(a)(2). Such percentage would be 5% multiplied by the portion of principal which could be withdrawn by exercising a 5% power annually for ten years. If he likewise did not exercise his power in *Year 2*, in *Year 3* he would be taxed as owner on the same portion

---

75. See note 67 supra.

of principal as in *Year 2*, increased by the same portion as the increase in Year 2 over Year 1.   This build-up of P's tax liability under § 678(a)(2) would continue until he was treated as owner of 100% of the trust (95% under § 678(a)(2) and 5% under § 678(a)(1)).   At that point he would be taxable on the entire trust income.

This relatively favorable treatment of an unexercised power to withdraw principal rests on the Regulations, which contain a favorable definition of "portion" for trust income tax purposes [76] and provide that an unexercised power does not constitute a throwback distribution.[77]   The estate and gift tax treatment of limited unexercised powers over principal is even more favorable[78] and is sufficient reason for choosing such a power in preference to a power over income.

¶ 12.02   HANDLING A CLIENT'S GENERAL POWERS OF APPOINTMENT

Many clients hold general powers of appointment under existing estate plans of others.   An important responsibility of their advisors is to determine how such powers should be handled in the light of all of the relevant tax and non-tax factors, the client's desires, and the circumstances of the beneficiaries.   In some cases, the conclusion may be that the power should not be exercised.   In that event, it may be advisable for the client either to make a disclaimer or a release of the power or merely to make explicit in his will his intent not to exercise the power.

In addition to the possible tax consequences, the decision as to how to deal with an existing power should take into account the manner in which the property will be disposed of in default of exercise of the power.   Are the takers in default the persons whom the holder would most like to benefit? Are the terms of the gift in default sufficiently ambiguous that an exercise of the power would be desirable to avoid uncertainty and possible litigation?

A variety of tax considerations may be involved in the exercise of a general power, including those relating to the tax consequences to the power holder as well as the effect on the tax positions both of the takers in default of exercise of the power and of the persons in whose favor the power is to be exercised.   For example, assume that W has a general power to appoint the assets of a marital deduction trust by her will, and in default the trust property will pass to her children.   If a child has ample resources apart from the trust property, it may be in his best interest for W to exercise her power in such manner as to keep the trust property from increasing his taxable income or prospective taxable estate.   Thus, W might bypass the child in favor of his descendants, or she might limit the child's rights so that the trust property will only be distributed to him if he has need for it.   Such arrangements, of course, should take into account the generation-skipping transfer tax as well as the estate and gift taxes, as the former is more comprehensive in its sweep than are either of the latter.

---

76. See Reg. § 1.671–3(b), discussed at ¶ 9.01[1][b] supra.

77. Reg. § 1.665(b)–1A(a)(2).   This is not consistent with the usual treatment of

amounts "constructively received" by a taxpayer.   See Reg. § 1.451–2.

78. See ¶ 12.01[3][b] supra.

If the power is exercised, the exercise must comply with the terms provided by the creator of the power. In addition to making specific reference to the power, which is desirable for clarity whether or not expressly required by its creator, the exercise must comply with any limits imposed either by the creator or by local law in the absence of an express provision to the contrary. Such limits most often relate to non-general powers and may preclude their exercise to create limited interests instead of appointing outright, to create new powers of appointment, or to appoint in trust.

If the holder decides to refrain from exercising the power or to make such exercise contingent on the occurrence or non-occurrence of one or more events, his will should expressly state that he does not intend to exercise any powers except as specifically provided therein. This is to avoid the view in some states that a general residuary clause is presumed to exercise any general powers held by the testator.[79] Although some commentators favor the blind exercise of powers, the results may be undesirable from various standpoints. For example, a disposition which is valid for the power holder's owned assets, under the local version of the Rule Against Perpetuities, may be invalid for property over which he has only a testamentary power of appointment.[80]

[1] Powers of Appointment Created on or Before October 21, 1942

Possession of a general power of appointment created on or before October 21, 1942, has no adverse estate tax consequences for the holder of the power.[81] Release of such a power is similarly tax-free.[82] Exercise of such a power, however, is treated in the same manner for estate and gift tax purposes as is exercise of a post-1942 general power, unless the power was partially released so as to be converted into a limited power before November 1, 1951.[83] If such a release was made, a subsequent exercise of the power will be treated as the exercise of a limited power.[84]

A joint power created on or before October 21, 1942, is not a general power.[85] However, the exercise of the power may cause a transfer of an interest of one of the joint holders in the property subject to the power. Presumably in that case there would be a completed gift by such joint holder.[86]

[2] Powers of Appointment Created After October 21, 1942

No saving in estate and gift taxes results for an individual who is given a general power of appointment after October 21, 1942, whether it is exercisable by deed (i.e., during life) or only by will. If the holder either exercises or releases a general power during his life in favor of someone

79. See, e.g., N.Y. EPTL 10–6–1(a)(4). Powers exercisable only by deed may be included too, as a will can also be used to exercise such powers unless expressly prohibited by the instrument creating the power. Restatement of Property § 347, Comment b (1940); Cal.Civ.Code § 1385.1 (West Supp.1980); N.Y. EPTL 10–6.2.

80. See, e.g., N.Y. EPTL 10–8.1(a)(2).

81. § 2041(a)(1).

82. See Reg. § 20.2041–2(d).

83. See §§ 2041(a)(1); 2514(a). Both also provide a further extension for persons under legal disability on October 21, 1942.

84. Id.

85. §§ 2041(b)(1)(B), 2514(c)(2).

86. Cf.Reg. § 25.2514–3(e), *Example (4)*. See also ¶ 12.03[1] infra.

else, he makes a transfer of property for gift tax purposes.[87]   Whether or not such exercise or release causes the property subject to the power to be included in the holder's gross estate is determined in accordance with the rules applied to transfers of owned assets.[88]   And if the holder still has either a general power by deed or by will when he dies, the appointive property is likewise includible in his gross estate,[89] even if he is not legally competent to exercise the power immediately before his death.[90]

[3] Powers Created After October 21, 1942 Which are Exercisable Jointly by the Beneficiary and Another

Example 12.3.   Assume that *C* creates a trust with *T* as trustee under which income is payable to *B* for life, remainder to *R*.   *B* and *X*, acting jointly, have the power to direct *T* in writing to pay principal to *B* or to any descendant of *B* (excluding *X* himself).   The power possessed by *X* is attributed to *B* for estate and gift tax purposes, even though *X* may be *B*'s hostile former spouse.   Thus, if *B* and *X* direct that principal be paid to *G*, *B*'s grandson, such payment constitutes a gift by *B*.   And the trust property will be included in *B*'s gross estate because of the joint power he possesses with *X*.[91]

The unstated premise of the provisions governing joint powers is that unless *X* has a substantial interest adverse to the exercise of the power in favor of *B*, he will willingly go along with any request by *B* for a distribution of property to *B* himself or to whomever else *B* may choose.

In *Example 12.3*, the result is that if both *B* and *X* must sign the letter directing *T* to pay principal to a descendant of *B*'s, such payment is a completed gift by *B*.[92]   But if *X*'s signature alone is sufficient, there is no such gift by *B*.   In this respect, the Code provision is clear, but difficult to rationalize.

The provision governing joint powers exercisable in favor of two or more power holders is equally clear, and less difficult to justify, as the following example illustrates:

Example 12.4.   Assume that *C* creates a trust with *T* as trustee. *B* and *X* have a joint power as long as both of them are living to pay principal and income to a group consisting of *B*, *X*, and the descendants

---

87. § 2514(b).   The transfer may not be a completed gift if the transferor retains another power over the property.   See ¶ 6.03[3] supra.

88. § 2041(a)(2).

89. Id.

90. See, Pennsylvania Bank & Trust Co. v. United States, 597 F.2d 382, 79–1 USTC ¶ 13,299 (3d Cir. 1979), cert. denied 444 U.S. 980 (1979);   Estate of Fannie Alperstein v. Commissioner, 613 F.2d 1213, 80–1 USTC ¶ 13,326 (2d Cir. 1979), cert. denied sub nom. Greenberg v. Commissioner 446 U.S. 918 (1980);   Estate of Anna L. Gil-

christ, v. Commissioner, 630 F.2d 340, 80–2 USTC ¶ 13,378 (5th Cir. 1980).

91. § 2041(b)(1)(C).   In Henry Garfield v. United States, 80–2 USTC ¶ 13,381 (D. Mass. 1980), the decedent was held to be barred from participating, as trustee, in the exercise of a power vested in the trustees to pay income or principal to the decedent. The holding was based on the general rule that a trustee-beneficiary may not participate in decisions to distribute principal to himself, unless a contrary intent is expressed in the instrument.

92. § 2514(c)(3).

of either.   The power may not be exercised after the death of either of them.   If B and X direct payment of $10,000 to B, such payment is a completed gift by X of $5,000.   If B and X direct payment of $10,000 to G, a descendant of B's, such payment is a completed gift of $5,000 by each of them.[93]

The unstated premise here is that B and X will agree to scratch each other's backs, if neither of them has a substantial interest which is adverse to the exercise of the power.   In this situation, each has an economic incentive to cooperate with the other joint power holder because each may thereby receive a distribution himself.   Therefore, each is treated as owner of one-half of the trust property for gift and estate tax purposes.

In *Example 12.3*, on the other hand, X cannot receive a distribution himself, no matter how complete his cooperation with B.   If X dislikes B (or prefers R to B), X has a reason not to cooperate with B and may act accordingly.   Yet B nevertheless is treated for estate and gift tax purposes as if he held the power alone.

[4] Disclaimers

Some powers may be effectively disclaimed for one or more federal tax purposes.   Disclaimers are discussed separately because of their importance as a tool of estate planning.[94]   The advantage of disclaiming a power, if the disclaimer is recognized as such for purposes of a given federal tax, rather than releasing it (or merely failing to exercise it), is that such a disclaimer causes the tax in question to be applied as if the power had never been given to the client.   Thus, the result may be that no transfer tax is payable as a result of the disclaimer, whereas the existence of a general power created after October 21, 1942, may cause the holder to be subject to gift tax or estate tax whether or not he exercises the power,[95] and a termination of a non-general power may be subject to the generation-skipping transfer tax.[96]   Of course, if the power was created to satisfy the requirements of a particular Code provision, such as the estate tax marital deduction,[97] a disclaimer will frustrate the creator's objective.   But in a given case, the tax advantage to the disclaimant may more than offset the tax cost of failing to achieve the creator's objective.

[5] Releases

If the time within which a qualified disclaimer may be made has passed, it may still be desirable for the power holder to release the power in whole or in part, so that his ability to exercise the power will either cease altogether or be curtailed.

---

93.   § 2514(c)(3)(C).   If B and X could each exercise the power after the death of the other, the interest of each would be adverse to the exercise of the power in favor of the other and neither would have a general power as long as both were living.   See Reg. § 25.2514–3(b)(2).   The survivor would have such a power, however.

94.   See ¶ 17.02 infra.

95.   §§ 2041(a)(2), 2514(b).

96.   § 2613(b)(1).

97.   §§ 2056(b)(5), 2056(b)(6).   § 2056(b)(7), added by § 403(d)(1) of the Economic Recovery Tax Act of 1981, allows a marital deduction for "qualified terminable interests," even though the spouse has no power of appointment over the property.

For estate and gift tax purposes, a release of a general power created after October 21, 1942,[98] is treated as if the power holder had owned the property subject to the power.[99] Thus, the release may constitute either a gift for purposes of the gift tax or a transfer that will cause the property to be includible in the transferor's estate, or both. For example, if *W* has a life estate in a trust created by her husband (*H*) and a post-1942 general power to appoint the remainder by her will, a release of her power will be treated as a gift of the remainder interest for purposes of the gift tax [100] and a transfer retaining a life estate requiring inclusion of the property under § 2036 for purposes of *W*'s estate tax.[101]

A release of a non-general power of appointment does not constitute a transfer by the holder for gift tax or estate tax purposes, but may constitute a taxable termination of a power for purposes of the generation-skipping transfer tax.[102]

If a release is only partial, the usual result is that there are no immediate tax consequences for the power holder. The fact that he has retained some portion of his power makes any transfer incomplete at the time the partial release becomes effective.[103]

From a tax standpoint, deciding to make a complete release of a general power of appointment created after October 21, 1942,[104] turns on the same factors that are involved in deciding to make a gift of owned assets. On the other hand, the decision to make a partial release of a general power normally does not turn on tax factors, as there are no immediate tax consequences as long as the partial release leaves the power holder with some degree of control over the choice of recipients of the appointive property so that there is no completed gift to any of them. If the power, after having been thus partially released, is thereafter exercised or released completely, the exercise or release will have the same gift and estate tax consequences as if the partial release had not been made.[105]

There may be valid non-tax reasons, however, for making a partial release of a general (or non-general) power. For example, in connection with separation or divorce, *W* may seek assurance that *H* will not exercise a non-general power in favor of his children of a later marriage to the exclusion of his children by *W*. If *H* partially releases his power so that it may only be exercised in favor of his children by *W*, he will still have the ability to take their individual needs and circumstances into account, but cannot divert the appointive property to children of another marriage.

---

98. In the case of a general power created on or before October 21, 1942, a release, whether partial or complete, is not treated as a transfer for gift or estate tax purposes. See §§ 2514(a), 2041(a)(1).

99. Reg. §§ 20.2041–3(d)(1), 25.2514–3(c)(1).

100. Reg. § 25.2514–3(a).

101. Reg. § 20.2041–3(d)(1).

102. § 2613(b)(1).

103. Reg. § 25.2514–3(c)(1).

104. See note 98 supra for the different treatment of complete or partial releases of powers created on or before October 21, 1942.

105. There is an exception for any power created after October 21, 1942, which was partially released before June 1, 1951, so that it no longer constitutes a general power. Such a power may thereafter be exercised without the gift tax consequences that normally attach to the exercise of a general power. See Reg. § 25.2514–3(c)(2).

The effectiveness of a partial or complete release of a power depends on governing state law. State statutes typically authorize either kind of release.[106]

¶ 12.03 HANDLING A CLIENT'S NON-GENERAL OR LIMITED POWERS AND POWERS OF WITHDRAWAL

The Regulations provide that a power of appointment is not a general power if it is either:

(1) exercisable only in favor of one or more designated persons or classes other than the holder, his estate, or the creditors of either; or

(2) expressly not exercisable in favor of the holder, his estate or the creditors of either.[107]

Thus, the holder's estate and gift tax position may be protected by the required express exclusions, leaving him free to choose from all the rest of humanity in exercising his power. For reasons other than estate and gift taxes, limited powers are usually less broad than this, confining the holder to his lineal descendants, or some similarly restricted group. Such restrictions also may be important in qualifying under the provisions of the generation-skipping transfer tax for exempt powers of appointment,[108] which are far narrower than their estate and gift tax counterparts.

A client who exercises a limited power of appointment may incur adverse gift or estate tax consequences in two situations:

(1) Where the exercise of the power has the incidental effect of transferring another interest of the holder; and

(2) Where the power is exercised to create a new power of appointment that may be exercised without regard to the date of creation of the first power, under applicable local law relating to perpetuities or suspension of the absolute power of alienation.

Both are consequences of the exercise of a limited power, rather than of the mere possession of such a power. Neither, therefore, is a reason to avoid creating such a power.

[1] Exercise, Release, or Lapse of Power Causes Transfer of Another Interest of Power Holder

The exercise, release, or lapse of a limited power may have gift tax consequences for the holder where the result is to cause a transfer of another interest of the holder, as illustrated in the following example:

Example 12.5. Assume that *C* creates a trust under which income is payable to *B* for life and *B* has the power to appoint principal, either during his life or by his will, to one or more of *B*'s descendants. If *B* exercises his power by directing the trustee to pay $10,000 from principal to his grandson (*G*), *B*'s exercise of the power is not taxable as such. But payment of principal to *G* has the effect of terminating *B*'s

---

106. See, e.g., N.Y. 10–9.2 EPTL.

107. See Reg. §§ 20.2041–1(c)(1), 25.2514–1 (c)(1).

108. See § 2613(e). For a discussion, see ¶ 14.05[2][c] infra.

right to income for his life from the principal thus paid. The Regulations accordingly treat B as having made a completed gift of an interest in income on $10,000 for his life.[109] Although there is case authority to the contrary,[110] for planning purposes the position taken in the Regulations should be regarded as controlling.

In *Example 12.5*, it would be possible to give B control over the disposition of principal without subjecting him to adverse gift tax consequences on an exercise of his power. This result could be achieved by giving B only a limited power to appoint principal by his will, rather than during his life. However, there is no persuasive tax reason to restrict B to appointment by will. Although exercise of the power during his life will constitute a completed gift, the mere possibility of doing so will not itself have any gift tax consequences. Giving B the power to appoint principal during his life thus gives him an option which he need not exercise unless he chooses to incur whatever gift tax may result.

The value of the interest transferred by B in *Example 12.5*, as a result of his exercise of a power during life to direct payment of principal to someone else, can readily be determined from actuarial tables. More complex questions may arise if the interest transferred by B includes a release of:

(1) a "5 or 5" power to withdraw principal;

(2) a support power to invade principal; or

(3) the possibility of receiving principal or income in the discretion of someone else.

[a] Release or Lapse of "5 or 5" Power to Withdraw Principal

What is the effect, if, in *Example 12.5*, B had in addition to income for life, the noncumulative right to withdraw the greater of $5,000 or 5 percent of the value of the principal at the end of each year? The Code provides an exemption, for estate and gift tax purposes, for lapse of such a "5 or 5" power during life.[111] But that exemption is from the general rule that a lapse of a power exercisable in favor of the holder is a release, and a release is a transfer of property for gift and estate tax purposes.[112] Thus, it appears that B's exercise of a limited power to appoint principal, where he was entitled to income and also had the right to withdraw $5,000 or 5 percent of the value of the principal at the end of each year, conceivably could be treated for gift tax purposes as a gift of the combined value of the rights given up.[113] An argument for such treatment is that B's exercise of his limited power effects a release of both his income interest and his power to withdraw principal, and that the statutory exemption is for the lapse of such a power, rather than its release. A contrary argument for limiting B's gift

---

109. Reg. § 25.2514–1(b)(2); Rev.Rul. 79–327, 1979–2 CB 342. Ordinarily, the gift will qualify for the present interest exclusion.

110. See James C. Self, Jr. v. United States, 142 F.Supp. 939, 56–2 USTC ¶ 11,613 (Ct.Cl.1956). The Service declines to follow the Self case. See Rev.Rul. 79–327, supra note 109.

111. §§ 2041(b)(2), 2514(e).

112. §§ 2041(a)(2), 2514(b). See notes 48 and 49 supra.

113. Cf. Lockard v. Commissioner, ¶ 6.03[3] supra.

to the transfer of his income interest is that there is no substantial difference between a lapse and a release of a power, as § 2514(e) recognizes to be the general rule.

[b] Release or Lapse of Power to Invade for the Support of the Holder

What is the effect, if, in *Example 12.5*, B had in addition to income for life, the right to withdraw principal for his support in accordance with an appropriate standard set forth in the trust instrument? The Code expressly excludes such a support power from the definition of a general power of appointment for estate and gift tax purposes.[114] Unlike the "5 or 5" power, the holder's possession of a support power at his death does not require inclusion of any of the property subject to the power in his gross estate. Its release during his life should also be free from estate or gift tax consequences.

[c] Release of Possibility of Receiving Principal or Income in the Discretion of Someone Else

What is the effect, if, in *Example 12.5*, B had in addition to income for life, the right to receive principal in the discretion of X, as well as the right to direct X to distribute principal to persons other than B? If B gives such a direction to X, he thereby reduces both his right to income and the amount of principal that X could distribute to him. Is such reduction to be considered in determining the amount of B's gift? It is difficult to find an explicit answer. But for planning purposes, the safe assumption is that B's gift may be of the full amount paid in accordance with his direction to X, unless B is merely one of a number of objects of X's power.[115]

[2] Exercise of Power Creates New Power That May Be Exercised Without Regard to the Date of Creation of the First Power

The prevailing view as a matter of state property law is that for purposes of determining the validity of appointed interests under the Rule Against Perpetuities, the period starts to run from the creation of the power, rather than its exercise, except in the case of a general power to appoint by deed.[116] Thus, in *Example 12.5*, if B exercises [117] his power to appoint principal in trust, the interests B creates must be certain to vest, if at all, no later than 21 years after the death of one or more persons [118] who were living when C created the trust. Similarly, if B exercises his power to create a new limited power (or general power to appoint by will only) in his grandson G, G may validly exercise his power only to create interests which also are certain to vest, if at all, no later than 21 years after the death of one or more persons who were living when C created the trust.

---

114. §§ 2041(b)(1)(A), 2514(c)(1).

115. Cf. Reg. § 25.2511–1(e).

116. See ¶ 3.03 at pp. 91–92 supra.

117. Whether a power may be exercised by appointing in trust, by creating limited interests instead of appointing outright, or by creating new powers of appointment depends on local law. See generally, Report of Subcommittee of the Committee on Estate and Tax Planning, "Use and Drafting of Powers of Appointment," 1 Real Prop., Prob. & Tr.J. 307 (1966).

118. According to Restatement of Property § 374 (1944), the lives selected must not be "so numerous nor so situated that evidence of their death is likely to be unreasonably difficult to obtain."

The effect of this prevailing characteristic of local law is to require that property transferred in trust vest, and thus be potentially subject to a gift tax or estate tax, at the expiration of the period of the Rule Against Perpetuities.   Where, as in Delaware,[119] the holder of a limited power of appointment gets a new start for perpetuities purposes, there is no such requirement of vesting under local law.   In Delaware, it is possible for *B* to exercise his power (if he has appropriate authorization) to create successive life interests in his son and grandson, with a limited power in the latter, which may in turn be exercised to create further life interests.   The property need never, as a matter of state law, vest outright.   Thus, but for § 2041(a)(3), the trust property theoretically could remain free from estate and gift taxes for centuries.

Section 2041(a)(3) seeks to limit such avoidance of taxes [120] by removing the exemption from *B*'s power if it is exercised to create a new power which does get a new starting date for perpetuities purposes as a matter of local law.   The significance of this provision, however, is not confined to Delaware.   It is the prevailing rule that the holder of a general power of appointment by deed gets such a new start because he has the same degree of control over the appointive property that he would over wealth owned outright.[121]   Thus, in *Example 12.5*, if *B* exercises his limited power to appoint by will to create in an appointee, a general power to appoint by deed, the result will be that such exercise causes the appointive property to be included in *B*'s gross estate.   Unless this result is desired, *B* [122] should not exercise his power in this fashion.   What is the result if the limited power is exercised to create another limited power which does not get a new start under the applicable local law, but the perpetuities period nevertheless does not run under such law as long as the trustee has the power to sell the trust property?   Even though the power of sale keeps the perpetuities period from running, § 2041(a)(3) does not apply, and the limited power remains tax exempt.[123]

---

119.   Del. Code Ann., tit. 25, § 501 (1975).

120.   The generation-skipping transfer tax also limits such avoidance possibilities.   See Chapter 13.

121.   See ¶ 3.03 at pp. 91–92 supra.

122.   In some situations, such inclusion of the appointive property might be desirable in order to secure a new basis under § 1014.

123.   See Estate of Mary M. Murphy, 71 T.C. 671 (1979), acq. 1979–1 CB 1 (Wisconsin law).

Chapter 13

GENERATION-SKIPPING TRANSFER TAX (GST) ASPECTS

A tax on generation-skipping transfers was first imposed by the Tax Reform Act of 1976, which added Chapter 13 to the Internal Revenue Code. The new tax substantially restricts the effectiveness of some major tax-saving tools. But it stops far short of eliminating the potential tax advantages of various forms of generation-skipping.

The Code provisions leave many uncertainties, and the Final Regulations promulgated to date deal merely with the extent to which the tax applies to interests created or instruments executed before its enactment.[1] Regulations have been proposed which deal with other aspects of the new tax.[2] Although the Final Regulations may be substantially different, the proposed regulations highlight major problems and provide a useful framework for discussion.

¶ 13.01 VARIETIES OF GENERATION-SKIPPING

A great many estate plans involve some kind of generation-skipping. In non-technical terms, it may take either of two forms, as follows:

> *Example 13.1.* A client (*C*) has a son (*S*) and a grandchild (*G*), the child of *S*. *C* makes a gift to *G*, skipping *S*'s generation. This form of generation-skipping, in which no member of the skipped generation receives any interest in the property or any power over its disposition, is *not* subject to GST.

> *Example 13.2.* Assume that in *Example 13.1*, *C* made a gift in trust to pay the income to *S* for life, and on the death of *S*, to pay the principal to *G*. Here *S*'s generation is not completely skipped, as *S* receives an interest in trust income for his life, although that interest will not cause the trust property to be included in *S*'s gross estate when he dies. This form of generation-skipping, in which there is "a splitting of the benefits between two or more generations which are younger than the generation of the grantor of the trust,"[3] is subject to GST.[4]

Before the advent of the GST, both forms of generation-skipping were widely used. The disposition in *Example 13.1* achieved estate and gift tax savings for members of the skipped generation by avoiding giving them ownership of wealth or any power over its disposition. This movement of wealth to members of one or more younger generations often carried out

---

1. Reg. § 26.1601, discussed at ¶ 13.15 infra. Temp.Reg. § 26a.2621–1 deals with tax returns.

2. See 46 Fed.Reg. 120 (Jan. 20, 1981); 3 CCH E&GT ¶ 11.923.

3. See H.R.Rep.No. 1380, 94th Cong., 2d Sess. 1, 47, reprinted in [1976] U.S. Code Cong. & Ad.News 3356, 3401.

4. A limited exclusion is allowed for generation-skipping transfers which cause property to vest in a grandchild of the grantor. See §§ 2613(a)(4)(A), 2613(b)(5)(A). For a discussion, see ¶ 13.12 infra.

the basic estate planning objectives of members of the skipped generation: to add to the incomes and wealth of their children and grandchildren.

The disposition in *Example 13.2*, on the other hand, permitted estate and gift tax savings to be achieved even though various interests and powers were given to members of the skipped generation. Thus, in *Example 13.2*, *S* might be given, in addition to the trust income, one or more of the following interests or powers:

(1) The power to invade principal for his own benefit if the power is limited by an appropriate standard; [5]

(2) The power to give principal to anyone except himself, his estate, or the creditors of either; [6]

(3) The power to withdraw an amount of principal not exceeding in any calendar year the greater of $5,000 or 5 percent of the value of the trust property. [7]

None of such interests would cause the trust property to be included in the gross estate of *S*, except for the last-mentioned power, and then only such amounts as he could have withdrawn at the time of his death. [8] Nor would there be adverse gift tax consequences from *S*'s possession of such powers, although the exercise of (2) during his life would constitute a gift of interests given up by *S* as a result of such exercise. [9]

The GST was enacted to restrict what were perceived to be opportunities to avoid estate and gift taxes through the use of generation-skipping as illustrated in *Example 13.2* and the variations just described. The result is to make the use of certain limited interests and powers potentially very expensive for beneficiaries. In *Example 13.2*, GST would apply on the death of *S* if he lived for as little as one day after the trust was created and thus had no opportunity to enjoy the income. [10] Consequently, the tax may be astronomical in relation to the total economic benefit derived by the holder of the terminated interest that triggered GST. If *C*'s transfer was subject to estate tax, the GST due on the death of *S* would be offset, in whole or in part, by a credit for an appropriate part of *C*'s estate tax. [11] But the credit might be far less than the GST if the tax bracket applicable to death-time transfers by *S* was substantially higher than the average estate tax rate for *C*'s estate. And if *C*'s transfer was subject to gift tax

5. §§ 2041(b)(1)(A), 2514(c)(1). For a discussion, see ¶ 12.01[3][a] supra.

6. See Reg. §§ 20.2041–1(c)(1), 25.2514–1 (c)(1). For a discussion, see ¶ 12.01[2] supra.

7. §§ 2041(b)(2), 2514(e). For a discussion, see ¶ 12.01[3][b] supra.

8. The lapse of the power during life is free from estate and gift tax consequences (see §§ 2041(b)(2), 2514(e)), but not its possession at death.

9. See Reg. § 25.2514–3(e), *Example* (1). But see James C. Self v. United States, 142 F.Supp. 939, 56–2 USTC ¶ 11,613 (Ct.Cl.1956). The Service declines to follow the Self case. See Rev.Rul. 79–327, 1979–2 CB 342.

10. Indeed, there is no indication that *S* must survive any minimum period in order for GST to apply. If he was alive when the trust was created, he acquired an interest within the meaning of § 2613(d)(1). Unless it constitutes a future interest, there is no basis for avoiding the conclusion that its termination is taxable under § 2613(b)(1), subject to the limited exclusion for transfers to grandchildren. See note 4 supra.

11. See § 2602(c)(4). Complex issues are raised by the credit provision. For a discussion, see Covey, Generation-Skipping Transfers in Trust 193–205 (3d ed. 1978 and Supp. 1980).

rather than estate tax or if no estate tax was due because of the unified credit, no credit would be available against the GST due on the death of *S*. Therefore, clients should be warned of the potential tax cost of creating such interests or powers.

¶ 13.02 TRANSFERS SUBJECT TO GST

Section 2611(a) defines "generation-skipping transfer" as "any taxable distribution or taxable termination with respect to a generation-skipping trust or trust equivalent." "Generation-skipping trust," in turn, is defined as a trust having beneficiaries assigned to two or more generations that are younger than the generation of the grantor.[12] A "beneficiary" is "any person who has a present or future interest or power in the trust," [13] and "interest" [14] and "power" [15] are likewise broadly defined. Elaborate rules are provided for the assignment of beneficiaries to generations.[16]

The tax applies to a taxable distribution [17] and to a taxable termination [18] of an interest or power. Either event is treated as a transfer by the "deemed transferor," [19] as defined. The termination of an interest or power of a person who never had anything other than a future interest or future power is not taxable.[20] Thus the definitions of "present interest" [21] and "present power" [22] are crucial. The relationship between the interests of different beneficiaries is determined in the light of a "separate share rule." [23] An exclusion is provided for certain transfers to grandchildren of the transferor,[24] as well as exemptions for certain powers [25] and for transfers subject to estate tax or gift tax.[26]

Provisions for computation [27] and payment of GST,[28] as well as the possibilities for deferring payment,[29] are major subjects in themselves. A "grandfather clause" [30] and transition rule [31] limit the extent to which GST applies to pre-existing instruments and transfers.

[1] Generation-Skipping Trust

The classic illustration of a generation-skipping trust is *Example 13.2*.[32] The essential feature is the splitting of benefits between members of two or more generations younger than that of the grantor.

12. § 2611(b).

13. § 2613(c)(3).

14. § 2613(d)(1).

15. § 2613(d)(2).

16. § 2611(c). See ¶ 13.05 infra.

17. § 2613(b)(1). See ¶ 13.11 infra.

18. § 2613(a)(1). See ¶ 13.10 infra.

19. § 2612. See ¶ 13.06 infra.

20. § 2613(b)(1).

21. See Prop.Reg. § 26.2613–4(d); ¶ 13.07 infra.

22. See Prop.Reg. § 26.2613–4; ¶ 13.08 infra.

23. See Prop.Reg. § 26.2613–5; ¶ 13.09 infra.

24. §§ 2613(a)(4)(A), 2613(b)(5)(A). See ¶ 13.12 infra.

25. § 2613(c). See ¶ 13.13 infra.

26. §§ 2613(a)(4)(B), 2613(b)(5)(B).

27. § 2602. See ¶ 13.14 infra

28. § 2603. See ¶ 13.14 infra.

29. See ¶ 14.05[4] infra.

30. See ¶ 13.15[1] infra.

31. See ¶ 13.15[2] infra.

32. See ¶ 13.01 supra.

[2] Generation-Skipping Trust Equivalent

The Code and Proposed Regulations reflect a recognition that generation-skipping may take place without the use of a trust and provide a broad definition of generation-skipping trust equivalent. It includes:

> any legally enforceable arrangement whether effectuated by contract, deed, will, agreement, understanding, plan or by any other means (including any combination of the preceding at the same or different times) which splits the beneficial enjoyment of assets among two or more younger generation beneficiaries who are assigned to more than one generation.[33]

For this purpose, the effect of the arrangement, and not the grantor's motives, is controlling.

Of the seven examples given in the Proposed Regulations,[34] two particularly merit consideration here: estates and custodianships.

[a] Estates

Example (5) would generally treat as a generation-skipping trust equivalent, any non-residuary bequest of money or property to a younger generation beneficiary if the residue were bequeathed to another beneficiary in a generation older than that of the first legatee but younger than that of the testator.   For example, a legacy of $100,000 to a great-grandson and a residuary bequest to a child or grandchild would together constitute a generation-skipping trust equivalent, with payment of the legacy a taxable termination of an interest of the child or grandchild.   This follows from the fact that a pecuniary legacy not in trust generally does not carry with it any right to a share of estate income during administration.[35]   Income from property used to pay the legacy usually augments the residue and thus benefits the residuary legatees.   That income interest necessarily ends when the legacy is paid.   If the Final Regulations incorporate this treatment of non-residuary legacies, it may be anticipated that fractional shares of residue will increasingly be substituted for ordinary cash legacies in wills. Alternatively, a cash legacy may be accompanied by gifts of income during administration so as to constitute a separate share.[36]

[b] Custodianships

Example (7) treats as a generation-skipping trust equivalent, a custodianship under the Uniform Gift to Minors Act for the benefit of the transferor's grandchild.   This conclusion is based not upon the power of the custodian to make distributions to or for the minor, but rather on the possibility that such distributions will discharge his parent's obligation to support him, thus causing the parent to be treated as a beneficiary as well. However, if no money is ever spent to discharge that obligation, the parent never had anything other than a future interest in the generation-skipping trust equivalent.[37]   Accordingly, there is no taxable termination in this

33. See Prop.Reg. § 26.2611–4(a).

34. See Prop.Reg. § 26.2611–4(b).

35. See, e.g., N.Y. EPTL 11–2.1(d)(2). State law may provide for the addition of interest if payment of a legacy is unduly delayed.

36. See Prop.Reg. § 26.2613–5, discussed at ¶ 13.09 infra.

37. Prop.Reg. § 26.2613–4(e), Example (3).

situation when a distribution is made to the minor.[38]   If the Final Regulations retain this characterization of custodianships without providing similar treatment for alternative vehicles for gifts to minor beneficiaries, such as a guardianship, the present popularity of custodianships is likely to be significantly curtailed.

[3] Exception for Transfers Subject to Estate Tax or Gift Tax

As the purpose of GST is to restrict the use of generation-skipping to avoid estate and gift taxes, it is logical that a termination or distribution is exempt from GST to the extent that it is a transfer subject to either of such taxes.[39]

> *Example 13.3.*   In *Example 13.2*, if S had a general power to appoint the trust property by will, the trust property would be includible in his gross estate.[40]   There would therefore be no taxable termination on the death of S.

¶ 13.03   WHO IS THE "GRANTOR" [41]

Determining who is the "grantor" of a trust or trust equivalent is a first step in assigning beneficiaries to generations in order to determine whether there is generation-skipping.[42]   Generally one becomes a grantor by making a contribution to a trust which is included in the contributor's gross estate or is subject to a gift tax without regard to the present interest exclusion allowed by § 2503(b).[43]   Thus the holder of a general power of appointment becomes a grantor if he allows the power to lapse, but only to the extent that the property subject to the power exceeds the $5,000 or 5% estate tax and gift tax exemptions for such lapses.[44]

Problems arise in situations in which more than one grantor is involved, depending upon whether there are:

(1) Two or more contributors to one trust; or

(2) Two or more contributors to separate trusts or trust equivalents.

[1] Two or More Contributors to One Trust

The Proposed Regulations treat contributions by two or more contributors to a single trust as causing each contributor to be treated as grantor

---

38. Id.   Example (3) deals with the possibility of a taxable termination when the beneficiary reaches the legal age of majority. Presumably, however, such a termination could occur if custodianship income or principal is used to discharge a parental support obligation and subsequently a distribution which does not discharge that obligation is made to the minor, whether or not the minor has reached majority when the distribution is made to him.

39. §§ 2613(a)(4)(B), 2613(b)(5)(A).

40. § 2041(a)(2).

41. See Prop.Reg. § 26.2611–2.

42. See § 2611(c).

43. See Prop.Reg. § 26.2611–2(a).

44. Id.   The exemptions are provided in §§ 2041(b)(2), 2514(e).   The termination of the nontaxable power is a taxable termination, however, for GST purposes.   For this purpose, the value of the entire property subject to the power, valued as of the date of its termination, is taken into account.   See Prop.Reg. § 26.2613–3(b).   It should be noted that this treatment of nontaxable powers does not take account of the fact that the estate tax exemption in § 2041(b)(2) is only for lapse of the power during life and not for its possession at death.   To the extent the property subject to the power is includible in the holder's estate under § 2041(a)(2), the termination of the power would appear to be exempt for GST purposes under § 2613(b)(5)(B).

in proportion to his contribution.[45]   The principle of proportionality is readily applied to simultaneous contributions.[46]   If contributions are made at different times, the proportion attributable to a grantor "must be redetermined based upon the latest contribution to the trust." [47]   In each case, determinations of relative values are required, creating problems inherent in the elusive concept of "fair market value" as applied to given kinds of assets.   But the proportionality principle itself should present no serious difficulty.

[2] Two or More Contributors to Separate Trusts or Trust Equivalents

The Proposed Regulations do not address the problem of reciprocal trusts and transfers which may arise when there are two or more contributors to related trusts or trust equivalents.

> *Example 13.4.*   A husband (H) transfers property into Trust #1, providing for the payment of income and principal in the discretion of an independent trustee to his son (S) for life, remainder to the issue of S who survive him.   At the same time, H's wife (W) transfers property into Trust #2, providing for the accumulation of income for the life of S, with the principal and accumulated income payable on the death of S to the issue who survive him.

If either H or W had created a single trust for S for life with remainder to the issue of S, there would be a taxable termination on the death of S with respect to the then value of the trust [48] (reduced by any previously unused grandchild's exclusion,[49] to the extent that the transferees were children of S (rather than more remote issue).   If the separate trusts created by H and W are treated as such for GST purposes, only the amount remaining in H's trust (#1) will be taxable when S dies, and that amount will have been diminished by any distributions of principal to S.   At the same time, the amount passing to the issue of S would be augmented by income accumulated in W's trust (#2).

Instead of creating trusts for the benefit of a child and his issue, respectively, H and W might have created trusts for each other.   In this situation, under the "reciprocal trust doctrine" each spouse may be treated as the grantor of the other spouse's trust (to the extent of the value of the smaller trust), for estate tax [50] and for trust income tax purposes.[51]   Whether the doctrine will be similarly invoked for GST purposes remains to be seen.

¶ 13.04   WHO IS A "BENEFICIARY"[52]

In view of the definition of "generation-skipping trust" as a trust having "younger generation beneficiaries" assigned to more than one generation,[53]

---

45.   See Prop.Reg. § 26.2611–2(b)(1).

46.   See Prop.Reg. § 26.2611–2(b)(3), Example (1).

47.   See Pro.Reg. § 26.2611–2(b)(2).

48.   § 2613(b)(1).

49.   § 2613(b)(5)(A).

50.   See ¶ 5.03 supra.

51.   See ¶ 9.01[1][a] supra.

52.   § 2613(c)(3).

53.   § 2611(b).

the meaning of the term is crucial in applying the tax.   It is initially defined as "any person who has a present or future interest or power in the trust." [54] "Interest" [55] and "power" [56] are likewise broadly defined.   Any permissible object of a presently exercisable power of appointment has an interest. And § 2613(d)(2) provides:

> The term "power" means any power to establish or alter beneficial enjoyment of the corpus or income of the trust. [57]

Finally, the terms include indirect interests and powers of legatees, heirs, trust beneficiaries, partners, and shareholders. [58]

¶ 13.05   GENERATION ASSIGNMENTS

Elaborate rules are provided for the assignment of beneficiaries to generations. [59]   Such assignment is made along conventional family lines for beneficiaries who are descendants of a grandparent of the grantor. [60]   This class, including as it does the grantor's own lineal descendants as well as those of his brothers and sisters, doubtless encompasses the great bulk of trust beneficiaries.   The generation assignment thus determined also applies to anyone who was at any time married to the grantor or any such descendant. [61]   Other beneficiaries are assigned to generations on the basis of the number of years between their birth dates and that of the grantor. [62]

¶ 13.06   TRANSFEREES AND DEEMED TRANSFERORS

The "deemed transferor," whose tax brackets are used in computing GST on a taxable transfer or distribution, generally is the "parent of the transferee   *   *   *   who is more closely related to the grantor of the trust than the other parent of such transferee." [63]

> *Example 13.5.*   Assume that *C* made a gift in trust for his daughter-in-law (*D*) for life, then for the children of his son (*S*) who survive *D*.   The deemed transferor is *S*, even though he is not a trust beneficiary and may have died long before the trust was set up, because he is more closely related to *C* than *D* is.

If, as in *Example 13.5*, the parent more closely related to the grantor is not a younger-generation beneficiary, but an ancestor of the transferee related to the grantor is such a beneficiary, the youngest of such ancestors is the deemed transferor. [64]

> *Example 13.6.*   Assume that *C* made a gift in trust for his son (*S*) for life, remainder to the great-grandchildren of *C*.   On the death of *S*, the deemed transferor is not a parent of the great-grandchildren

---

54. § 2613(c)(3).

55. § 2613(d)(1).

56. § 2613(d)(2).

57. See Prop.Reg. § 26.2613–4(c)(3).

58. See Prop.Reg. § 26.2611–3(e).

59. § 2611(c).   See Prop.Reg. § 26.2611–3.

60. § 2611(c)(1).   See Prop.Reg. § 26.2611–3(a).

61. § 2611(c)(2).

62. § 2611(c)(5).   See Prop.Reg. § 26.2611–3(b).

63. § 2612(a)(1).

64. § 2612(a)(2).

but instead it is S himself.   However, if S were not a beneficiary, the parent of the great-grandchildren would be the deemed transferor.

If neither parent of a transferee is related to the grantor, under the Proposed Regulations the choice of which parent is the "deemed transferor" is based on which has a "closer affinity" [65] to the grantor, based on specified factors.[66]

The transferee in a taxable termination under § 2613(b) that results in a distribution of the trust property, or a taxable distribution under § 2613(a), usually is clear, unless the transferee's identity is affected by a support obligation.   For example, a distribution purportedly for the "benefit" of A, a beneficiary, which has the effect of discharging a legal obligation of X to support A, may cause X, rather than A, to be treated as the transferee.[67]

If a taxable termination occurs without actual distribution of trust assets, the Proposed Regulations contain rules for the determination of the "deemed transferees." [68]

¶ 13.07   INTERESTS: PRESENT, FUTURE, AND NOMINAL

"Interest" is broadly defined for GST purposes.   A person has an interest if he either has a right to receive income or principal or is a "permissible" recipient thereof [69]—i.e., someone in whose favor a power of appointment could be exercised.   If the person has an interest, the next analytical step is to determine whether it is present or future.   If it is a present interest, it also needs to be classified as either substantial or nominal.   Termination of the interest of someone who never had anything other than a future interest [70] or a present interest that is classified as nominal is not a taxable termination.[71]

This paragraph will deal with the interests which arise from the existence of powers in two situations:

(1) Powers exercisable in favor of persons other than the power holder himself.   For example, P has a discretionary power to distribute trust income or principal to beneficiaries B–1 and B–2.

(2) Powers exercisable in favor of the holder.   For example, P can withdraw either a stated amount of income or principal from a trust, or an amount determined by reference to a standard, such as the amount needed for his reasonable support and maintenance.

The focus here, however, will be on the person, whether or not he is also the power holder, in whose favor the power may be exercised.   The tax treatment of powers exercisable in favor of persons other than the power holder is discussed in ¶ 13.08 infra.

65. § 2612(a)(1).

66. § Prop.Reg. § 26.2612–1(a).

67. See Prop.Reg. § 26.2613–4(c)(3), defining "beneficiary" to include "any person who is or may be relieved of a legal obligation." But see ¶ 13.07[1][a] infra.

68. See Prop.Reg. § 26.2613–3(a).

69. § 2613(d)(1).

70. § 2613(b)(1).

71. Prop.Reg. § 26.2613–2(b)(3).

[1] Present and Future Interests

The definition of "present interest or power" [72] in the Proposed Regulations leaves many questions unresolved.   The first two sentences are relatively non-controversial:

A beneficiary's interest or power is a present interest or power if the beneficiary has an unrestricted right to receive income or corpus from a trust.   A right is restricted if it is contingent upon the happening of an event which is wholly outside the beneficiary's control. [73]

However, the reassuring words of the second sentence are contradicted by the treatment of discretionary powers exercisable in favor of persons other than the power holder himself.

[a] Interests of Objects of Discretionary Powers

The Proposed Regulations generally treat every object of a discretionary power as having a present interest:

If a beneficiary may currently receive income or corpus upon the exercise of a trustee's or other person's discretion, the interest is a present interest although it may be a nominal interest under § 26.2613–2(b)(3). [74]

This appears to be inconsistent with the preceding statement that a right is restricted if it is contingent upon the happening of an event which is wholly outside the beneficiary's control—here the exercise of a discretionary power by someone else.

The breadth of the definition of "present interest" as applied to objects of discretionary powers is limited by the concept of nominal interests, [75] which, however, only applies to certain persons who are not descendants of the grantor's grandparent. [76]   If the beneficiary in whose favor the power may be exercised is such a descendant, he has a substantial interest without regard to whether or not he ever receives anything as a result of the exercise of the power. [77]   If he is not such a descendant, he has a substantial interest "if at least 5 percent of the value of the trust (valued on the first day of the tax year of the trust) is distributed to the nonlineal descendant (or descendants) annually." [78]   Even though less than 5 percent is distributed, the Proposed Regulations recognize that "unusual facts and circumstances" [79] may indicate that it is substantial.

On the other hand, with respect to a power to discharge an individual's legal obligation, the Proposed Regulations take the position that the individual's interest "becomes" a present interest upon the exercise of the power by the trustee or custodian. [80]   Until the power is exercised to discharge

72. Prop.Reg. § 26.2613–4(d).

73. Id.

74. Prop.Reg. § 26.2613–4(d).

75. Prop.Reg. § 26.2613–2(b)(3).

76. Prop.Reg. § 26.2613–2(b)(3)(iii).

77. Id.

78. Id.

79. Id.

80. Prop.Reg. § 26.2613–4(d), fourth sentence.

a legal obligation of the individual, such as his obligation to support his child, the individual has only a future interest.[81]

Thus it appears that if T as trustee has a discretionary power to use trust income and principal for the support of B (a descendant of the grantor's grandparent), B has a present interest even though T never exercises the power in B's favor.   But if T has instead a discretionary power to use trust income and principal for the support of B's legal dependants, B has only a future interest until T exercises his power.   It is not easy to find support in the legislative history for this distinction between a power to support a beneficiary and a power to support his dependents.

[b] Interests of Holders of Powers Exercisable in Favor of the Power Holder.

The Proposed Regulations treat powers exercisable in the holder's favor which are limited by an ascertainable standard within the meaning of section 2041(b)(1)(A) as substantial if "the beneficiary's need for the income or corpus is not so remote as to be negligible." [82]   If the power is expressed as a right to withdraw income or corpus (or both), the test of substantiality turns on whether, at the time the power terminates, the present value of that which the beneficiary could withdraw is at least 5 percent of the value of the trust.[83]

[2] Substantial and Nominal Interests

Classification of an interest or power as "nominal" may have two important consequences:

(1) termination of a nominal interest or power is not a taxable event; [84] and

(2) a taxable termination will not be postponed because of the interest of a remaining beneficiary, if that interest is nominal.[85]

For example, G may create a trust under which the trustee has discretion to pay income to any of his children or grandchildren or to N, an unrelated individual who is 25 years younger than G.[86]

Under the general rule, the taxable termination on the death of the first child of G to die would be postponed until the death of other beneficiaries in the child's generation.[87]   If N's interest were not classified as nominal, N would be counted as a beneficiary in the generation of G's children, so that when the children had all died, there would be no taxable termination until N also had died.[88]   Meanwhile the trustee could continue to make distributions to G's grandchildren without depletion of the trust to pay GST on the death of the children.

---

81. Prop.Reg. § 26.2613–4(3), example (3).

82. Prop.Reg. § 26.2613–2(b)(3)(ii).

83. Id.

84. Prop.Reg. § 26.2613–2(b)(3)(i).

85. Id.

86. Because of his age, N will be assigned to the first generation younger than the grantor.   See § 2611(c)(5)(B).

87. See § 2613(b)(2)(A);   Prop.Reg. § 26.2613–2(b)(1).

88. Id.

The treatment of nominal interests, however, keeps the creation of such interests in unrelated beneficiaries from causing postponement of liability for GST.[89]   Here, N's interest is nominal unless (and only so long as) he receives annually 5 percent of the value of the trust.[90]

¶ 13.08   POWERS: PRESENT, FUTURE AND NOMINAL

"Power" is defined as "any power to establish or alter beneficial enjoyment of the corpus or income of the trust."[91]   The Proposed Regulations give the definition a broad construction:

> A power is a present power if the property subject to the power would have been included in the estate of the power holder under section 2036 or 2038 had the power holder been the settlor of the trust.[92]

Thus the definition includes non-general powers that do not subject their holders to gift tax or estate tax,[93] no matter how restricted the permissible scope of exercise, unless the power fits within either of two rather narrow statutory exemptions.[94]   As might be expected, the distinction between present and future powers turns on whether or not the power is "currently exercisable"[95] and presents problems similar to those discussed with respect to present and future interests.   Termination of a power held by someone who never had anything other than a future power is not a taxable termination.[96]

A power exercisable by the holder in his own favor may or may not be classified as "substantial."[97]   If the power is nominal, rather than substantial, its continued existence does not cause postponement of liability for GST otherwise due,[98] and its termination is not taxable.[99]

¶ 13.09   SEPARATE SHARE RULE

A broadened version of the separate share rule for trust income tax purposes[100] applies for GST purposes.   The rule requires interests of beneficiaries having "substantially separate and independent shares" in a single trust to be treated as "separate trusts."[101]   Such treatment may affect the time of termination of an interest or power, under the rules for postponing such termination for GST purposes.[102]

---

89.   Prop.Reg. § 26.2613–2(b)(3)(i).

90.   Prop.Reg. § 26.2613–2(b)(3)(i), (iii).

91.   § 2613(d)(2).

92.   Prop.Reg. § 26.2613–4(d).

93.   For a discussion, see 12.01[2] supra.

94.   § 2613(e).   For a discussion, see ¶ 13.13 infra.

95.   See Staff of Joint Comm. on Taxation, General Explanation of the Tax Reform Act of 1976, 94th Cong., 2d Sess., 567 (Comm. Print 1976).

96.   § 2613(b)(1).

97.   See Prop.Reg. § 26.2613–2(b)(3)(ii); ¶ 13.07[1][b] supra.

98.   See Prop.Reg. § 26.2613–2(b)(3)(i).

99.   Id.

100.   See § 663(c), discussed at ¶ 15.06 infra.

101.   See Prop.Reg. § 26.2613–5.

102.   See Prop.Reg. § 26.2613–2(b)(1).

¶ 13.10 TAXABLE TERMINATION

The general definition of "taxable termination" is quite broad: "[T]he termination (by death, lapse of time, exercise or nonexercise or otherwise) of the interest or power * * * of any younger generation beneficiary who is assigned to any generation older than the generation assignment of any other * * * younger generation beneficiary * * * ." [103]

> *Example 13.7.* Assume that C made a gift in trust for his wife (W) for life, then for his son S for life, then for his grandson G for life. On the death of G, the trust will terminate and the principal will be distributed to the then living issue of C, such issue to take *per stirpes*. If the order of deaths is W, S, and G, and on the death of G, the property is distributed to a great-grandchild, GG, the tax consequences would be as follows:
>
> (1) There would be no taxable termination on the death of W because she is not a younger generation beneficiary; [104]
>
> (2) There would be taxable terminations for GST purposes on the deaths of S and G.

There are three major exceptions or exclusions from the definition of "taxable termination" set forth above:

(1) any transfer to the extent it is subject to estate or gift taxes;[105]

(2) any transfer to the extent it is within the grandchild's exclusion; [106] and

(3) a termination of a future interest or power of someone who never had any other interests or powers.[107]

There are additional provisions that may cause postponement of the time when a taxable termination is deemed to occur, if:

(1) There are two or more younger generation beneficiaries assigned to the same generation; [108]

(2) The same beneficiary has more than one interest or power; [109] or

(3) The order of termination is unusual.[110]

¶ 13.11 TAXABLE DISTRIBUTION

Section 2613(a) defines "taxable distribution" as a distribution that is not out of trust income (as defined in § 643(b)) to a younger generation beneficiary if there is another younger generation beneficiary in a generation above that of the distributee.

> *Example 13.8.* In *Example 13.7*, if the trustee had discretion to distribute principal to G during the life of S, such a distribution would

---

103. § 2613(b)(1).

104. § 2611(c)(2).

105. § 2613(b)(5)(B).

106. § 2613(b)(5)(A).

107. § 2613(b)(1).

108. § 2613(b)(2)(A).

109. § 2613(b)(2)(B).

110. § 2613(b)(2)(C).

be within the definition, although it might be exempt from GST because of the grandchild's exclusion.[111]

The exclusion of distributions out of income is an important avenue of relief from GST.

Other exclusions from the definition of "taxable distribution" include:

(1) any transfer to the extent that it is subject to estate or gift taxes; [112] and

(2) any transfer to the extent that it is within the $250,000 grandchild's exclusion, which is applied cumulatively to terminations and distributions.[113]

If the same occurrence is a taxable termination and also requires a distribution which is within the above definition, only a taxable termination is deemed to have occurred with respect to the portion subject to such required distribution.[114]

The Proposed Regulations treat payment of the tax out of trust income or corpus which was not subject to the tax as another GST transfer.[115] They do not indicate whether the process of treating payment of the tax as a transfer is repeated if the tax on the tax is paid in this manner, etc.

Loans to beneficiaries also may constitute a GST transfer if not bona-fide.[116]

¶ 13.12   GRANDCHILD'S EXCLUSION

A transfer that causes property to vest in a grandchild of the grantor,[117] up to a cumulative total of $250,000 for each child of the grantor,[118] is excluded from the definitions of "taxable termination" and "taxable distribution." [119]

> *Example 13.9.*   Assume that C made a gift in trust for his son (S) for life, then for the children of S who survive him.   On the death of S, the trust property, valued at $300,000, is divided among the children of S.   If no part of the grandchild's exclusion has been exhausted by previous transfers to such children for which S was the deemed transferor, only $50,000 is subject to GST on the death of S.

The grandchild's exclusion is applied on a "deemed transferor" basis. If C had four children and each had children of his own, a total of $1 million could pass to C's grandchildren free of GST.   For transfers of which a given child is deemed transferor, however, only a maximum of $250,000 is excluded.[120]   If the exclusion is likely to be exhausted by transfers made by one parent (either during his life or by his will), the other parent should be

---

111. § 2613(a)(4)(A).

112. § 2613(a)(4)(B).

113. § 2613(a)(4)(A).

114. 2613(b)(7).

115. See Prop.Reg. § 26.2613–1(e).

116. See Prop.Reg. § 26.2613–1(f)(1).

117. § 2613(b)(6).

118. § 2613(b)(5)(A).

119. § 2613(a)(4)(A).

120. See Prop.Reg. § 26.2613–4(a)(1).

warned that no further exclusion is likely to be available for subsequent transfers by her.

The Proposed Regulations provide:

> This exclusion is available only if the property would be includable in all events in the grandchild's federal gross estate if the grandchild died at any time after the generation-skipping transfer.[121]

Accordingly, a grandchild may be given a general power of appointment [122] over property instead of an outright interest, in order to qualify for the deduction, as long as no interest is given to someone other than a grandchild.

¶ 13.13 EXEMPT POWERS

The definition of "power" for GST purposes exempts:

(1) a power to allocate income or corpus among lineal descendants of the grantor who are in one or more generations younger than that of the power holder,[123] and

(2) a power held by an "independent trustee," as defined,[124] to allocate income or corpus among a designated class of beneficiaries.

Thus, the choice of exempt powers is between the limited power described at (1), which may be given to anyone who is in an older generation than that of the beneficiaries, and the broader power described at (2), which may only be given to an "independent trustee."

"Independent trustee" is defined in § 2613(e)(2) as an individual "who has no interest in the trust (other than as a potential appointee under a power of appointment held by another)" and is not "related or subordinate." [125] An independent trustee may be given a power (if he has no other present or future power in the trust) "to dispose of the corpus * * * or the income therefrom to a beneficiary or a class of beneficiaries designated in the trust instrument." [126]

The power described at (1) is useful to allow a child of the grantor to allocate income or corpus among grandchildren or great-grandchildren of the grantor, if separate trusts are being created for each generation of beneficiaries. However, if a single trust is created with the expectation that distributions may be made to both grandchildren and great-grandchildren, the exemption of the power to make distributions may not provide complete protection from GST. Distributions to great-grandchildren will be taxable unless covered by the income exemption.[127] There will be a taxable termination when the interests of the grandchildren have ended.[128]

---

121. Id.

122. See § 2041(b).

123. § 2613(e)(1).

124. § 2613(e)(2).

125. § 2613(e)(2)(B). The definition of "related or subordinate" for this purpose is far more sweeping than the similar definition

for trust income tax purposes in § 672(c). It includes, inter alia, spouses and employees of beneficiaries, as well as many other individuals who would not be thus classified under § 672(c).

126. § 2613(e)(2).

127. § 2613(a)(1).

128. § 2613(b)(1).

The power described at (2) is useful if it is desired to authorize discretionary distributions to persons other than lineal descendants of the grantor, such as spouses of beneficiaries or charities.   Like the power described at (1), however, the exemption is merely for the power itself and not for distributions made as a result of its exercise, or for terminations of the interests of objects in whose favor it could be exercised.

¶ 13.14   COMPUTATION AND PAYMENT OF GST

The stated objective of GST is to impose a tax that is "substantially equivalent to the estate tax which would have been imposed if the property had been actually transferred outright to each successive generation." [129] The Code provisions seek to carry out this goal for transfers that occur at or after the death of the deemed transferor as follows:

(1) GST is computed under the unified rate schedule by adding the deemed transfer to the sum of:

    (a) prior GST transfers of the deemed transferor;

    (b) adjusted taxable gifts of the deemed transferor; and

    (c) the taxable estate of the deemed transferor, if he dies the same time as the transfer, before the transfer, or within three years thereafter.[130]   (For GST purposes, the treatment of transfers during the three year period preceding the death of the transferor was not changed by the Economic Recovery Tax Act of 1981, although the Act extensively revised the treatment of such transfers for estate tax purposes.) [131]

A tentative tax is computed thereon.   The tax on the total of (a), (b), and (c) is then subtracted, and the difference is the GST payable.[132]

(2) GST provisions are generally similar to estate tax provisions for:

    (a) alternate valuation; [133]

    (b) the charitable [134] deduction; and

    (c) various credits against the tax.[135]

No marital deduction is allowed for GST purposes, but this difference is unimportant, as transfers to spouses are not subject to GST.   The overall result falls short of complete conformity with the estate tax in other respects as well,[136] but often these other differences are unimportant in planning a client's estate.

For transfers that occur during the life of the deemed transferor (and more than three years before his death),[137] different rules apply.   Just as lifetime transfers of owned assets may be less expensive than transfers at

---

129. H.R.Rep.No. 1380, 94th Cong., 2d Sess. 1, 47, reprinted in [1976] U.S. Code Cong. & Ad. News 3356, 3401.

130. See § 2602(e).

131. See ¶ 5.02[3] supra.

132. § 2602(a).

133. § 2602(d).

134. § 2602(c)(2).

135. §§ 2602(c)(3), 2602(c)(4), 2602(c)(5)(B).

136. See Covey, note 11 supra, at 211–214.

137. See § 2602(e).

the owner's death,[138] these rules often will produce a lower tax than those for transfers at or after the death of the deemed transferor. This saving follows from the fact that, in this situation, GST is calculated under the unified rate schedule by adding the deemed transfer to the sum of:

(1) prior GST transfers of the deemed transferor; and

(2) "adjusted taxable gifts" of the deemed transferor.

A tentative tax is computed thereon. Tax on the total of (1) and (2) is then subtracted; the difference is the GST payable.[139]

The result of this computation of GST on transfers deemed to occur during the life of the deemed transferor is to produce a tax that may be equivalent to the gift tax (before deduction of any unused portion of the donor's unified credit) that would have been incurred on a gift of the amount subject to GST.[140] But unlike gifts,[141] transfers subject to GST are not taken into account in computing the deemed transferor's gift tax on subsequent gifts or his estate tax when he dies.

Disparities between computation of GST and gift tax may arise from the treatment of a trust's payment of GST as itself constituting a transfer subject to the tax.[142]

> *Example 13.10.* Assume the C made a gift in trust for his descendants. The terms of the trust authorize the trustee, in his discretion, to pay income and principal to C's descendants from time to time living. At a time when such descendants include a son (S), a grandchild (G), and a great-grandchild (GG), the trustee distributes $10,000 from principal[143] to G. Assume that prior transfers have exhausted the grandchild's exclusion.[144] This distribution constitutes a taxable distribution with S the deemed transferor. If, pursuant to the terms of the trust, GST of $3,000 is paid by the trust, this payment of GST constitutes a further transfer also subject to GST.[145]

Such treatment may make GST on a distribution greater than the tax on a gift of the same amount. In the case of a gift, the donor's payment of the gift tax would not be an additional taxable gift.[146]

---

138. For a discussion, see ¶ 6.01[1][a] supra.

139. § 2602(a)(1).

140. The gift tax may be higher if the donor had made taxable gifts before 1977, which are taken into account in determining his gift tax bracket under § 2504(a), but are not included in "adjusted taxable gifts" as defined in § 2001(b). It is only the latter which are taken into account in computing GST. See § 2602(a)(1)(C).

Major difference also may result from the general denial of deductions and exclusions for GST purposes under § 2602(c)(1). The only exception to the general rule that appears to be applicable to transfers subject to GST during the life of the deemed transferor is the charitable deduction. See § 2602(c)(2). Thus, no present interest exclusion is available. The gift tax marital deduction would not be relevant in any case,

as spouses (and former spouses) are in the same generation. § 2611(c)(2).

141. For an illustration of the mechanics of the computation of estate tax for a decedent who made taxable lifetime gifts, see ¶ 6.01 note 8 supra.

142. § 2613(a)(3); Prob.Reg. § 26.2613–1(e).

143. If the distribution were from income, it would not be taxable. See § 2613(a)(1).

144. § 2613(a)(4)(A).

145. See note 142 supra. Whether payment of GST by the trust on the $3,000 tax payment will in turn be subject to GST remains to be determined. See Covey, note 11 supra, at 83.

146. See ¶ 6.03[1][f] supra.

¶ 13.15 APPLICATION OF GST TO PRE-EXISTING INSTRUMENTS AND TRANSFERS

An effective dates provision limits the application of GST to trusts and instruments that were in existence on June 11, 1976, in two ways:

(1) A grandfather clause makes GST inapplicable to any generation-skipping transfer under a trust which was irrevocable on that date, "but only to the extent that the transfer is not made out of corpus added to the trust after June 11, 1976 * * * ";[147] and

(2) A transition rule makes GST inapplicable to any generation-skipping transfer pursuant to a will or revocable trust of a decedent dying before 1983 if the instrument was in existence on June 11, 1976, and was not thereafter amended to create or increase the amount of a generation-skipping transfer.[148] An extension is provided for certain decedents who were under a mental disability on that date so that they could not change the disposition.[149]

[1] Trusts Irrevocable on June 11, 1976—Grandfather Clause

Interpretation of the grandfather clause, which applies to trusts that were irrevocable on June 11, 1976, except to the extent a generation-skipping transfer is made out of corpus added to the trust after that date, raises two major questions:

(1) Under what circumstances is a trust "irrevocable" for this purpose?

(2) What constitutes an addition of corpus to such an irrevocable trust?

[a] **When Trust Irrevocable.** Under the Regulations, the test generally is whether a trust in existence on June 11, 1976, would have been included in a decedent's gross estate under § 2038 if he had died on that date (without regard to powers relinquished within the prior three-year period).[150] Thus, the existence of a power of appointment or a power to withdraw trust principal that is exercisable by someone other than the grantor does not keep a trust from being regarded as irrevocable.[151] Neither such power causes a trust to be includible in a decedent's estate under § 2038,[152] which applies to powers held by a transferor, although the trust may be includible under § 2041 in the gross estate of a power holder who is not the transferor.

[b] **Additions to Corpus.** An addition after June 11, 1976, to the corpus of a trust that was irrevocable on that date, generally will cause Chapter 13 (the GST provisions of the Code) to apply to a proportionate part of the generation-skipping transfers from the trust.[153] Thus, the addition of $100,000 on June 12, 1976, to an irrevocable trust worth $900,000 on that date prior to the addition, will cause one-tenth of subsequent gen-

---

147. See Tax Reform Act of 1976, Pub.L.No. 94–455, § 2006(c)(2)(A), 90 Stat. 1889, as amended by Revenue Act of 1978, Pub.L.No. 95–600, § 702(a)(1), 92 Stat. 2935.

148. See Tax Reform Act of 1976, Publ.L.No. 94–455, § 2006(c)(2)(B), 90 Stat. 1890, as amended by Revenue Act of 1978, Pub.L.No. 95–600, § 702(n)(1), 92 Stat. 2935, and § 428 of the Economic Recovery Tax Act of 1981.

149. Id.

150. See Reg. § 26.2601–1(c)(1).

151. See Reg. § 26.2601–1(c)(2), *Example* (2).

152. But see ¶ 5.02[5][b] supra.

153. See Reg. § 26.2601–1(e)(1).

eration-skipping transfers from the trust to be subject to GST.[154]   The fraction will be applied to the trust as augmented by subsequent appreciation in the value of the corpus and additions of accumulated income.   Except to the extent of such fractional parts of appreciation and income accumulated after an addition to corpus has been made, neither constitutes an addition to corpus for the purpose of applying GST.[155]

The Regulations also recognize a category of "constructive" additions to corpus.   A "constructive" addition occurs if property remains in a trust after the post-June 11, 1976 exercise, release, or lapse of a power of appointment in a transaction treated to any extent as a taxable transfer for either gift or estate tax purposes.[156]   For example, the death after that date of the holder of a general testamentary power of appointment over a trust would, if the power were created after October 21, 1942, cause the trust property to be included in the holder's taxable estate under § 2041(a)(2) and, thus, would constitute a "constructive addition" of such property to the corpus of the trust.

The Regulations provide: "Any addition to a trust made pursuant to a trust meeting the requirements of the effective date rule [i.e., an irrevocable trust qualifying under the grandfather clause] * * * will not be treated as an addition to corpus for purposes of this section." [157]   Presumably, this covers both required and discretionary distributions from a grandfathered trust to another grandfathered trust.   For example, if the terms of an irrevocable trust in existence on June 11, 1976, as to which there have been no subsequent additions (including constructive additions) to corpus, authorize or direct the trustees to distribute all or part of the trust property to a second trust which was also irrevocable on such date, the distribution should not constitute an "addition" to the second trust for GST purposes.

[2] Revocable Trusts and Wills in Existence on June 11, 1976; Transition Rules

The statutory transition rule makes GST inapplicable to any generation-skipping transfer pursuant to a will or revocable trust of a decedent dying before 1983 if the instrument was in existence on June 11, 1976, and was not thereafter amended to create or increase the amount of a generation-skipping transfer.[158]   For decedents who were under a mental disability on that date so that they could not change the disposition, the transition rule applies if they die within two years of the termination of such disability without having thus amended the instrument.[159]

Revocation of an outright bequest of $10,000 makes the transition rule inapplicable to a will creating a generation-skipping residuary trust, which

---

154. See Reg. § 26.2601–1(e)(7), *Example* (1).

155. See Reg. § 26.2601–1(e)(5).

156. See Reg. § 26.2601–1(e)(3). The Regulations also cover the more esoteric case of a power "exercised in a manner that may postpone or suspend the vesting, absolute ownership or power of alienation of an interest in property for a period, measured from the date of creation of the trust, ex-

tending beyond any life in being at the date of creation of the trust plus a period of 21 years." For a discussion of state law permitting such an exercise of a power, see ¶ 12.03[2] supra.

157. See Reg. § 26.2601–1(e)(4).

158. See note 148 supra.

159. See note 148 supra.

is thereby augmented by $10,000,[160] and the same result presumably would follow if the revoked bequest were as little as one cent, as no de minimis provision is included.　The regulations exempt any amendment that is "basically administrative or clarifying in nature and only incidentally increases the amount transferred," [161] or that is "designed to insure that an existing bequest or transfer qualifies for the applicable marital, charitable, or minor child (orphan's) deduction　*　*　*." [162]

The Regulations provide that additions to a revocable trust or will covered by the transition rule after June 11, 1976, but before the death of the settlor generally will cause Chapter 13 (the GST provisions of the Code) to apply to *all* subsequent generation-skipping transfers involving the trust, "unless the corpus of the trust as it existed on June 11, 1976, is severed from the additions thereto." [163]　However, if the decedent dies before January 1, 1982, inter-vivos transfers will not be treated as additions "if the same property or money would have been added to the trust pursuant to a will or trust described in the transition rule, or passed in the same way, but for the inter-vivos transfer." [164]　The governing date for the transition rule was changed from January 1, 1982, to January 1, 1983 by Section 428 of the Economic Recovery Tax Act of 1981.　Presumably this change will be applied to the earlier date in these Regulations.

160.　See Reg. § 26.2601–1(d)(3), *Example* (4).

161.　See Reg. § 26.2601(d)(1)(i).

162.　See Reg. § 26.2601(d)(1)(ii).　The orphan's deduction formerly allowed by § 2057 was repealed by § 427 of the Economic Recovery Tax Act of 1981.

163.　See Reg. § 26.2601–1(e)(2).

164.　See Reg. § 26.2601–1(e)(4).

Chapter 14

SAVING ESTATE, GIFT, AND GENERATION-SKIPPING
TRANSFER TAXES

All too often, clients fail to realize that they may help a child or a spouse more by giving him less. Arrangements that limit his exposure to estate and gift taxes may permit more wealth to pass to his children or grand-children instead. And a well-considered plan may at the same time allow the child or the spouse to have as much for his own use as he would wish to spend if he received his full share of the client's wealth.

Any such use of techniques to save estate and gift taxes for a beneficiary should also take account of the new tax on generation-skipping transfers (herein GST) which was introduced by the Tax Reform Act of 1976. Arrangements that minimize estate taxes for a beneficiary may leave the client's wealth exposed to tax upon a generation-skipping transfer of such wealth, either during the life of the beneficiary or upon his death. In that situation, planning to minimize only his estate tax is grossly inadequate.

Nevertheless, it is appropriate to analyze techniques that save estate and gift taxes for beneficiaries separately from those that save GST, for two reasons:

(1) Different techniques are effective in minimizing estate and gift taxes, on the one hand, and GST, on the other, requiring separate analysis for each before they can be integrated effectively into a client's plan; and

(2) GST is inapplicable to many trusts and wills that were in existence on June 11, 1976, including revocable trusts and wills of grantors and testators who were living on that date.[1]

Of course it is desirable, in planning to minimize estate and gift taxes, to bear in mind ways to minimize GST as well.

¶ 14.01 ARRANGEMENTS TO SAVE ESTATE AND GIFT TAXES

A beneficiary may incur estate or gift taxes because he owns property when he dies [2] or makes a transfer of property during his life,[3] including transfers implicit in certain dispositions of employee benefits.[4] Property that he never owns will cause him to incur such taxes only if he had a general power of appointment over it,[5] or, with respect to insurance on his life, if it is payable to his estate or if he had incidents of ownership.[6] Techniques

---

1. See Tax Reform Act of 1976, Pub.L.No. 94–455, § 2006(c), 90 Stat. 1889, as amended by Revenue Act of 1978, Pub.L.No. 95–600, § 702(n)(1), 92 Stat. 2935, and § 428 of the Economic Recovery Tax Act of 1981. For a discussion, see ¶ 13.15 supra.

2. See §§ 2033 (property owned at death), 2040 (joint interests).

3. See §§ 2035–2038.

4. See § 2039.

5. See § 2041. For an esoteric exception with respect to the exercise of a special power to create another power, see § 2041(a)(3), discussed at ¶ 12.03[2] supra.

6. See § 2042.

that minimize his exposure to estate and gift taxes may be grouped under three headings:

(1) Avoiding giving the beneficiary ownership of more wealth than he will consume;

(2) Avoiding giving the beneficiary a general power of appointment; and

(3) Avoiding giving the beneficiary incidents of ownership with respect to insurance policies on his life, or making such policies payable to his executor.

Often, the use of these techniques may be inconsistent with another tax objective of the client.   For example, arrangements which include giving a spouse a general power of appointment are a popular method of qualifying for the estate tax marital deduction.[7]   The result, however, is to expose the spouse to estate tax because of her possession of the general power. Similarly, giving a beneficiary ownership of wealth is a common way to qualify for the gift tax present interest exclusion [8] but, again, it may expose him to gift taxes if he disposes of such wealth and to estate taxes if he retains it until he dies.   In these situations, the client must determine whether his tax objective should be given priority even if it results in tax exposure for the beneficiary or whether it can be achieved without causing such exposure.

¶ 14.02   AVOIDING GIVING A BENEFICIARY OWNERSHIP OF WEALTH HE WILL NOT CONSUME OR ENJOY

As the beneficiary's taxable estate generally will include anything he owns when he dies, as well as certain transfers he makes during his life,[9] an obvious way to limit his exposure to estate tax is to give him only that which he will consume or enjoy while he lives.   Before the Tax Reform Act of 1976 introduced the tax on generation-skipping transfers, the classic way to limit a beneficiary to that which he might consume was to give him only a life estate in property or in a trust, rather than outright ownership of it. For example, a father might create a trust to pay income to his daughter for her life, remainder on her death to her children, instead of giving her outright ownership of the trust property.

The life estate clearly is a valuable interest in property but because it terminates on the daughter's death, nothing is includible in her estate except such income as she received and saved during her life (and any income due her when she dies).   If the trust income proved to be more than she spent, there would be a build-up of her estate.   But it would not be as great as the build-up which would have resulted from giving her the principal transferred in trust.   A further refinement to avoid swelling the daughter's taxable estate with accumulated income, as well as to avoid making income taxable to her that she would not in fact spend, is to give her no absolute right to income.   Instead, a trustee other than the daughter may be given

---

7. § 2056(b)(5).   For a discussion, see ¶ 18.04[2] infra.

8. § 2503.   For a discussion, see ¶ 6.03[1][a] supra.

9. §§ 2035–2038.   Certain employee death benefits and individual retirement benefits are barred from inclusion under any Code section.   See §§ 2039(c), 2039(d), 2039(e). For a discussion, see Ch. 21.

a discretionary power to distribute income or principal (or both) to a group consisting of the daughter and her descendants. In this situation, the daughter has only the possibility of receiving a distribution in the discretion of the trustee. Nothing is includible in her estate when she dies except such distributions as she may have received during her life and saved until her death.

If a discretionary power is created in order to keep her from having a general power of appointment,[10] the daughter must not be given the power (as trustee or otherwise) to make distributions to herself, unless her power is a properly limited power to use income or principal (or both) for her own support, or to withdraw specified amounts.[11] But an unlimited power to pay income or principal (or both) to the daughter can be given instead to someone else who can be expected to act with the daughter's interest in mind.

The alternatives just described continue to be effective in saving estate tax for the daughter but may be subject to the new tax on generation-skipping transfers. However, with appropriate modifications, it may be possible to minimize the impact of that tax as well.[12]

Provisions to facilitate a "qualified disclaimer"[13] by a beneficiary also may permit him to reduce or eliminate the amount he receives from the client's estate without thereby making a taxable transfer for gift or estate tax purposes. Such a reduction or elimination may appear to be desirable in the light of the situation existing after the client's death. Inclusion of provisions dealing with the effect of a disclaimer, as well as the procedure to be followed in disclaiming, also serve as a useful reminder that the tool is available.

¶ 14.03 AVOIDING GIVING A BENEFICIARY A GENERAL POWER OF APPOINTMENT

The permissible scope of a non-general power of appointment is extremely broad. A beneficiary may be given a variety of interests in wealth without having a general power of appointment for estate tax purposes. Such interests may include:

(1) Income for his life;[14]

(2) The power to invade principal for his own benefit if the power is limited by an appropriate standard;[15]

(3) The power to give principal to anyone he chooses except himself, his estate, and the creditors of either;[16]

10. § 2041.

11. For a discussion of such powers which may be created without significant adverse estate and gift tax consequences, see ¶ 12.01[3] supra.

12. For a discussion, see ¶ 14.05 infra.

13. See § 2518. For a discussion, see ¶ 17.02 infra.

14. Section 2036, requiring inclusion of transfers with retained life estate, does not apply to life estates received by the decedent from someone else.

15. § 2041(b)(1)(A). For a discussion, see ¶ 12.01[3][a] supra.

16. See Reg. § 20.2041–1(c)(1). For a discussion, see ¶ 12.01[2] supra.

(4) The power as trustee to manage the trust property and to control the manner in which it is invested; [17] and

(5) The possibility of having principal paid to him in the discretion of someone else.

In addition to these five kinds of interests, which do not constitute a general power of appointment, there is a limited exemption, for estate and gift tax purposes, for the lapse of a power of withdrawal during the holder's life. The exemption frees the possession of the power from adverse gift tax or estate tax consequences during the holder's life, to the extent that the value of the property that may be appointed does not exceed the greater of $5,000 or 5 percent of the aggregate value of the property subject to the power.[18] Only in the year of his death will there be possible adverse estate tax consequences from his possession of the power and then only to the extent of the amount that could have been withdrawn at the time he died.

¶ 14.04 AVOIDING ESTATE TAXATION OF INSURANCE ON THE LIFE OF A BENEFICIARY

The concept of "incidents of ownership" under § 2042 is so broad that what would be a non-taxable, non-general power of appointment with respect to other property may cause insurance on the life of the holder to be includible in his taxable estate. The definition includes the power, as trustee or otherwise, alone or with others, "to change the beneficial ownership in the policy, or its proceeds, or the time or manner of enjoyment thereof * * *." [19] Accordingly, it is desirable to avoid giving an insured either powers as trustee or an explicit power of appointment with respect to policies of insurance on his own life, as well as not making policies payable to his estate.

¶ 14.05 ARRANGEMENTS TO SAVE GENERATION-SKIPPING TRANSFER TAXES (GST)

Some of the major ways to minimize the impact of GST upon new trusts not protected by the effective dates provision [20] include:

(1) using separate gifts or trusts for each generation (layering);

(2) using statutory exclusions and exemptions such as:

[a] the income exclusion;

[b] the grandchild's exclusion;

---

17. See Reg. § 20.2041–1(b)(1), next to last sentence.

18. §§ 2041(b)(2) (estate tax), 2514(e) (gift tax).

19. See Reg. § 20.2042–1(c)(4). In Estate of Hector R. Skifter, 468 F.2d 699, 72–2 USTC ¶ 12.893 (2d Cir. 1972), the Court of Appeals declined to apply these Regulations to require inclusion of policies in the insured's estate. He had previously transferred the policies to his wife, who predeceased him and bequeathed such pol-

icies to a trust of which he was trustee. Although the Commissioner refuses to follow the cases, see Rev. Rul. 76–261, 1976–2 CB 276, there continue to be decisions favoring taxpayers in comparable situations. See, e.g., Sue Ann Hunter v. United States, 80–2 USTC ¶ 13.362 (8th Cir. 1980).

20. Tax Reform Act of 1976, Pub. L. No. 94–455, § 2006(c), 90 Stat. 1889, as amended by Revenue Act of 1978, Pub. L. No. 95–600, § 702(n)(1), 92 Stat. 2935, and § 428 of the Economic Recovery Tax Act of 1981, discussed at ¶ 13.15 supra.

[c] the exemptions for future interests and powers, and for certain limited powers;

(3) changing the deemed transferor; and

(4) postponing payment of GST.

[1] Using Separate Gifts or Trusts for Each Younger Generation (Layering)

As GST applies to trusts with interests in members of two or more younger generations, an obvious way to avoid the tax is to make separate provisions for each generation. For example, if the client would otherwise leave $1 million in trust for his son (S) for life, then to his grandson (G) for life, then to his great-grandchildren, the fund may be divided into three separate trusts, for S, for G, and for the great-grandchildren. To whatever extent the trust for S is not exhausted during his lifetime, it will be subject to GST when he dies and the trust passes to G or to the great-grandchildren (unless it passes to G in such form as to qualify for the grandchild's exclusion); [21] and G's trust would likewise be subject to GST to whatever extent it was not exhausted during his life and passed to the great-grandchildren when G died. But this division—popularly referred to as "layering"—could substantially reduce GST as long as the three trusts were regarded as separate and not as interests in a single trust. [22]

Similar results could be produced by making an outright gift to S instead of a gift in trust. In that case, to whatever extent S did not spend or give away what he received during his lifetime, the gift would be included in his taxable estate when he died.

The problem in using a separate gift for S, either outright or in trust, is one of allocation between generations. Ideally, S should receive, outright or in trust, an amount that, with the use of both income and principal, will suffice for his lifetime but leave little or nothing to be subjected to estate tax or GST when he dies and the residue passes to a younger generation. If S has no other resources, the client may be fearful that the income from a trust for S funded with, say, $400,000, may be insufficient for his needs and that the principal may be exhausted if he spends part each year and lives longer than anticipated. Thus, this approach is more feasible if the client's wealth is sufficiently substantial to allow him to make generous provision for S, or if S has enough resources of his own to make him independent. In the latter case, the client may wish to bypass S altogether.

If a gift is made to S, he may prefer to receive a sum of money outright, rather than in trust, in order to buy an annuity. If he is able to acquire a commercial annuity on attractive terms, it could last as long as he lives and thus avoid the inevitable risk of dissipation that arises if he spends portions of the principal of a trust. However, the terms on which commercial annuities are offered are often relatively unattractive and frequently make no provision for inflation.

---

21. See ¶ 13.12 supra. If G received only an income interest, the exclusion would not be allowed, as the principal would not "vest" in G.

22. See Prop.Reg. § 26.2611–4(a), defining "generation-skipping trust equivalent" broadly. For a discussion, see ¶ 13.02[2] supra.

If, instead of a sum of money, *S* received a major income-producing asset such as the family farm or an interest in the family business, he might at some time sell the asset to his child or grandchildren in return for private annuity payments.[23]　If there were a prior understanding between the client and his beneficiaries that such a sale would be made,[24] *S* might be regarded as having received a life interest in the farm or business, the termination of which would be a transfer for GST purposes.　But if the later annuity transaction were not combined with the client's dispositions for such purposes, this series of events might provide an assured income for *S* for his life and freedom from GST when he dies.

[2] Using Statutory Exclusions and Exemptions

The major statutory exclusions and exemptions from GST include:

(1) the income exclusion;

(2) the grandchild's exclusion;

(3) the exemption of future interests and powers; and

(4) the exemption for certain limited powers.

[a] The Income Exclusion

If family resources do not permit creation of a separate trust for each generation, an obvious alternative is to use a single trust in conjunction with the exemption for distributions out of income.[25]　For example, the trustee may be given discretion to pay income or principal to the client's descendants from time to time living.　A distribution of current income [26] to a grandchild is not a "deemed transfer" by a child and thus is not subject to GST and does not exhaust any available grandchild's exclusion.　Such distributions also reduce the amount which would be subject to GST on the death of a child if income were accumulated.　But at the same time, the principal (and the income it produces in the future) remains available for the child's use if it is needed in a later year.

Such a trust should avoid making distributions in excess of current income to beneficiaries in two different generations in the same year, because for GST purposes the distribution to the older generation comes out of income first and to that extent makes the exclusion unavailable for distributions to the younger generation.[27]　Thus, such trusts have sometimes been referred to as "AC-DC" trusts, to reflect the alternation between distributions to children and grandchildren in different years.　If the trustee periodically distributes to children an amount of principal equal to several years' income, this scheme of distribution may allow them to enjoy the trust while they live.　At the same time, it allows significant amounts to pass to the grandchildren free of GST in the form of income distributions in years when nothing is distributed to the children.

23.　For a discussion of such sales, see ¶ 8.03.

24.　See note 22 supra.

25.　§ 2613(a)(1).

26.　The Proposed Regulations treat distributions made within the first 65 days of the following taxable year as having been made in the preceding taxable year to the extent provided in § 663(b), if the trustee makes the required election thereunder.　See Prop. Reg. § 26.2613–1(a)(2).

27.　§ 2613(a)(2).

[b] The Grandchild's Exclusion

The exclusion for transfers to the grandchildren of the transferor [28] is available for interests that "vest" in a grandchild, defined as "property interests [that] will be taxable in the grandchild's estate." [29] This vesting requirement permits continuation in trust of the grandchild's interest after his death, if he has a general power to appoint the property by will or if the trust property is distributable to his estate on his death.[30]

[c] The Exemption of Future Interests and Powers

The exemption for future interests and powers [31] allows provision to be made for contingencies that may arise but does not cause GST to be imposed if they do not. For example, the client's son (S) may be given a lump sum or separate trust under the layering approach [32] with the expectation that it will be sufficient to meet his needs unless he lives beyond a specified age or is totally disabled. Another trust for the children of S could provide for distributions to S, either as a matter of right or in the discretion of the trustee, from and after the date upon which S either attained age 70 or had been totally disabled for twelve consecutive months. If S died before age 70 without having become disabled, his interest in the second trust would have always been a future interest, and its termination would not be subject to GST, as long as the two trusts were not combined for GST purposes.[33]

A further refinement would authorize the trustee to postpone the date on which distributions to S were to commence, for example, by changing the age to 75 or by requiring total disability for a five-year period. This provision would allow the trustee to revise the terms of the trust if it became apparent that the needs of S would not be sufficiently pressing at 70 to justify giving him an interest, the termination of which would be subject to GST. The anticipated saving would not be achieved, however, if the trustee's power were not itself exempt under § 2613(e)(1) or § 2613(e)(2) and a taxable termination of the power occurred during the life of S.[34]

[3] Changing the Deemed Transferor

As GST is computed with reference to other transfers of a "deemed transferor," [35] savings may be achieved by causing a different individual to be so identified. For example, GST rates may be high if a client's child is the deemed transferor because of the size of the child's lifetime gifts, other deemed transfers for GST purposes, or because of the size of his prospective taxable estate.[36] GST rates may be lower if some other individual, such as a relative by marriage, is caused to be treated as the deemed transferor

---

28. §§ 2613(a)(4)(A), 2613(b)(5)(A).

29. H.R.Rep. 94–1515, 94th Cong. 2d Sess. 1, 618, reprinted in [1976] U.S. Code Cong. & Ad.News 4118, 4256.

30. See Prop.Reg. § 36.2613–4(a)(1), discussed at ¶ 13.12 supra.

31. § 2613(b)(1). For a discussion, see ¶¶ 13.07[1], 1308 supra.

32. See ¶ 14.05[1] supra.

33. See note 22 supra.

34. For a discussion of the exemptions for certain limited powers under these sections, see ¶ 13.13 supra.

35. § 2612(a)(1), discussed at ¶ 13.06 supra.

36. For a discussion of computation of GST, see ¶ 13.14 supra.

instead of the client's child if such relative has made smaller transfers for gift tax and GST purposes or can be expected to have a smaller taxable estate.

> *Example 14.1.*   Assume that C made a gift in trust for his son (S) for life, then for D (the wife of G, the son of S) for her life or until her marriage to G is terminated by divorce, then to the children of G and D.   On the death of S, the deemed transferee would appear to be D, so that the "deemed transferor" would be the parent of D having "closer affinity" [37] to C.

Of course, this arrangement may be inappropriate in a particular family situation for non-tax reasons.   Here, as elsewhere, tax considerations should not be allowed to interfere with arrangements that will carry out the basic dispositive preferences of the client.

[4] Deferring Payment of Generation-Skipping Transfer Taxes (GST)

Techniques to defer payment of GST may be an important adjunct to techniques to minimize or avoid liability for the tax.   As in deferral of income taxes, the result of successful use of the technique to postpone payment of GST is to obtain an interest-free loan from the Treasury.   It does not follow, however, that maximum deferral of GST will, in the long run, reduce the burden of the tax for a client's beneficiaries.

[a] Reasons Not to Defer Payment

(1) GST is computed on the basis of the value of the property when the taxable distribution or termination occurs.[38]   If payment of GST is deferred, the value of the property may go up and thus increase the amount subject to GST.   If the increase in value is large enough, it may more than offset the advantage of an interest-free loan of the amount of tax that would have been due earlier in the absence of deferral.   This is even more true if the increase in the amount subject to GST is due to accumulation of income, which could have been distributed free of GST under the income exemption.[39]

(2) The manner in which GST is calculated may cause substantial increases in the tax rate for transfers during the course of a deemed transferor's life and a further substantial increase for taxable terminations or distributions occurring at or after his death.   Such increases result from the fact that GST is calculated under the unified rate schedule by adding the deemed transfer to the sum of:

  (a) prior GST transfers of the deemed transferor;

  (b) prior adjusted taxable gifts of the deemed transferor; and

  (c) the taxable estate of the deemed transferor, *if* he died at the same time as the transfer, before the transfer, or within three years thereafter.[40]

---

37. § 2612(a)(1).

38. § 2602(a)(1)(A).   In the case of certain taxable terminations, § 2602(d) allows use of the alternate valuation provided in § 2032 for estate tax purposes.

39. See § 2613(a)(1), discussed at ¶ 14.05[2][a] supra.

40. §§ 2602(a), 2602(e).

The result is that every time a deemed transferor makes a taxable gift or a GST transfer, the marginal tax rate for his subsequent lifetime GST transfers may [41] go up.   The rate never goes down (assuming no change in the rate schedule itself) during his life. When he dies, the rate may go up again if he leaves a taxable estate. If his taxable estate is not large enough to exhaust his unified credit, the rate of GST may be lower for transfers at or after his death than it was during his life.[42]

(3) Until the estate tax provisions of the Economic Recovery Tax Act of 1981 were enacted, the long range trend of estate tax rates had been upward, particularly if account is taken of the effect of inflation on asset values.   Since GST rates are linked to the estate tax,[43] a GST at today's rates may prove, with the omniscience of hindsight, to have been a bargain, even if the deemed transferor makes no subsequent taxable gifts or transfers subject to GST and leaves no taxable estate.

Even if techniques for deferral of GST do, in fact, reduce the economic burden of the tax for the client's beneficiaries, the arrangements which are made to employ such techniques may have adverse income, estate, or gift tax consequences for the beneficiaries.   It is not uncommon to find that the use of a given estate planning tool to minimize one federal tax has the opposite effect on liability for another.

Finally, tax-deferral arrangements may be unsatisfactory for non-tax reasons.   For example, substituting a single trust for separate trusts for different branches of a family may lead to resentments over what may appear to be a trustee's discriminatory treatment of beneficiaries in different branches of the family.   The resulting ill will may more than offset the economic advantage achieved by deferral of GST.   Thus, in most family situations it is desirable to provide for division into separate trusts for each child and his family by the time all the children have completed their education.

[b] Reasons to Defer Payment

Deferring payment of GST may achieve tax savings in addition to providing an interest-free loan of the amount of tax deferred.   If the taxable termination occurs at or after the death of the deemed transferor, the computation of GST is more favorable in at least three [44] respects:

(1) The deemed transferor's unused unified credit, to the extent it exceeds his estate tax and prior GST taxes, is applied against the GST; [45]

41.   The relatively wide brackets of the estate tax rate schedule, which is used for GST purposes, see § 2602(a)(1), may mean that a substantial taxable gift or GST transfer has no effect on the deemed transferor's marginal tax rate for GST purposes.   For example, between $250,000 and $1,500,000 the brackets increase in increments of $250,000.   See § 2001(c).

42.   Section 2602(c)(3) allows a credit for so much of the deemed transferor's unified credit as exceeds his "tentative tax" under § 2001 and prior GST taxes if a transfer subject to GST occurs at or after his death.

43.   § 2602(a)(1).

44.   A credit also may be available for state death taxes paid on the transfer subject to GST.   See § 2602(c)(5)(B).

45.   § 2602(c)(3).

(2) A deduction may be allowed for certain expenses described in §§ 2053 and 2054,[46] and certain expenses relating to the tax on a taxable distribution; [47] and

(3) The alternate valuation under § 2032 may be elected if the deemed transfer occurs on the death of the deemed transferor and in certain other cases as well.[48.]

The practical importance of these potential tax advantages for purposes of GST necessarily depends upon the particular fact situation. Only the first is likely to be a significant factor in the decision to arrange to defer GST, and then only for deemed transferors whose taxable gifts, taxable estates, and prior transfers subject to GST are expected to be well below the amount covered by the unified credit.

[c] Deferral Techniques

If the potential advantages of deferral make it a worthwhile goal to pursue in a given case, the following techniques merit consideration. Reliance on any of them, however, must necessarily be somewhat tentative. The proposed regulations interpreting the statutory deferral provisions provide that if the rules described at (1) and (2) below are used primarily for postponement of the taxable termination, it will be deemed to occur in accordance with the general rule without regard to these exceptions.[49] Similarly, if a beneficiary's remaining interest is classified as nominal, it will not cause postponement under the rules described below.[50]

Major deferral techniques are based on § 2613, which, in simplified form, provides for deferral in three situations:

(1) Where there are two or more beneficiaries in the same generation. If there are two or more younger generation beneficiaries assigned to the same generation, there is no taxable termination for any beneficiary in that generation until the interests of all such beneficiaries have terminated.[51]

(2) Where a beneficiary has two or more present interests or powers. If a younger generation beneficiary has both a present interest and a present power, or more than one of either, there is no taxable termination until all such interests and powers have terminated.[52]

(3) Where there is an unusual order of termination. Where the interest or power of a younger generation beneficiary terminates when an older generation beneficiary still has a present interest or power, there is no taxable termination until all of the older generation beneficiary's present interests and powers have terminated.[53]

---

46. § 2602(c)(5)(A)(i).

47. § 2602(c)(5)(A)(ii).

48. § 2602(d).

49. See Prop. Reg. § 26.2613–2(b)(3).

50. Id.; Prop. Reg. § 26.2613–2(d).

51. § 2613(b)(2)(A); Prop. Reg. § 26.2613–2(b)(1).

52. § 2613(b)(2)(B); Prop. Reg. § 26.2613–2(b)(1).

53. § 2613(b)(2)(C); Prop. Reg. § 26.2613–2(d).

Techniques which may be used in an effort to achieve deferral include:

(1) Using a single trust for several children instead of separate trusts for each child and his family; and

(2) Including additional beneficiaries who are in the generation of the grantor or in an older generation.

[i] Using a Single Trust for Several Children Instead of Separate Trusts for Each Child and His Family.   This technique may be illustrated by the following example:

> *Example 14.2.*   Assume that *C* made a gift in trust under which the trustee was authorized, in his discretion, to make distributions of income and principal to *C*'s descendants from time to time living.   The trust is to terminate 21 years after the death of the survivor of such descendants who were living when the trust was created.   All of *C*'s living descendants have present interests but there will be no taxable termination of any of their interests until all of *C*'s children have died.[54] If a separate trust had been created for each child and his descendants, a taxable termination would have occurred each time a child died (unless the grandchild's exclusion applied).[55]

Use of the technique is subject to "separate share" rules prescribed in the regulations, under which interests of beneficiaries having "substantially separate and independent shares" are "treated as separate trusts." [56]   However, a relevant example of the "separate share" rule in the Proposed Regulations is a trust with specified percentile allocations of income and principal to each child and his descendants.[57]   It should be rather easy to avoid any such rule, as long as each child is given a significant but indivisible interest in the trust.

Other factors weigh against creation of a single trust despite any advantage resulting from deferral of GST.   To whatever extent income is accumulated and taxed to the trust, the income tax may be higher if the accumulations are taxable to one entity instead of several.   And other advantages from the use of separate trusts may also be lost.[58]

[ii] Including Beneficiaries Who Are in the Grantor's (or an Older) Generation.   This technique is based on the Code provision dealing with an unusual order of termination.[59]   Where the interest or power of a younger-generation beneficiary terminates while an older-generation beneficiary still has a present interest or power, there is no taxable termination until all of the older-generation beneficiary's present interests and powers have terminated.

The problem in using this technique is that if the interest or power of the older-generation beneficiary is substantial, rather than merely nominal, the client has significantly altered his dispositive plan to achieve deferral

---

54. §§ 2613(b)(2)(A), 2613(b)(2)(C).

55. § 2613(b)(6).

56. See Prop.Reg. § 26.2613–5(a).

57. See Prop.Reg. § 26.2613–5(c), Example (1).

58. For a discussion, of both advantages and disadvantages, see ¶ 11.07 supra.

59. § 2613(b)(2)(C); Prop.Reg. § 26.2613–2 (d)(1).

of GST when such deferral may not ultimately prove to have been advantageous.   On the other hand, if such interest or power is merely nominal, the technique will fail to achieve deferral.[60]

60. Id.   For a discussion of nominal interests, see ¶ 13.07[2] supra.

Part IV

ARRANGEMENTS EFFECTIVE UPON DEATH

A variety of arrangements for the disposition of a client's wealth may become effective upon his death. Some may be used to dispose of the bulk of his estate: wills; revocable (living) trusts; and state intestacy statutes. Other arrangements, which are more specialized and deal with only a particular asset, include joint ownership with a right of survivorship; [1] beneficiary designations for proceeds of insurance on the life of the decedent; [2] and beneficiary designations for employee death benefits, individual retirement arrangements (IRAs), and deferred compensation arrangements. [3]

Wills and revocable trusts usually are the primary tools for the disposition of a client's wealth. Reliance on state intestacy statutes to provide a major part of a client's estate plan may be necessary if he lacks legal capacity to adopt a plan of his own [4] or if his wealth is too small to justify the expense of a professionally prepared plan. In other cases, such reliance usually reflects a decedent's failure either to obtain or to act upon sound estate planning advice.

Even if the intestacy statute specifies the exact disposition that the client wants as to beneficiaries and their respective shares, his advisor usually can make significant improvements in the arrangements for administration of his estate over those provided if the client dies intestate. One or more executors may be named to carry out the process instead of allowing the choice to be controlled by the statutory list of persons entitled to priority in applying for appointment as administrator. [5] And the will usually may waive bond for the executor if bond would otherwise be required, [6] thus saving the estate the substantial expenses of premiums on a surety bond for an administrator. [7] Shares of minor or incompetent adult beneficiaries may be bequeathed in trust in order to avoid the expense and inconvenience of administration of property by a guardian or conservator. Therefore, few clients with significant assets are well-advised to rely upon the intestacy statute if they have the legal capacity to make a will or create a revocable trust instead.

1. For a discussion, see ¶ 7.01.

2. For a discussion, see ¶ 20.02.

3. For a discussion, see ¶ 21.01.

4. In some states, by statute or court decision it is possible to obtain judicial approval of lifetime transfers on behalf of an incompetent individual based on tax and other estate-planning considerations. See Mass.Gen.Laws Ann., Ch. 201, § 38 (West Supp.1980); In re Irénée duPont, 41 Del.Ch. 300, 194 A.2d 309 (1963).

5. See, e.g., N.Y.Surr.Ct.Proc.Act 1002(1).

6. Id. at § 806.

7. Id. at § 801.

Of the four federal taxes important in estate planning, only the income tax and the estate tax will be discussed in this chapter.   The gift tax applies only to transfers completed during a client's life,[8] and the generation-skipping transfer tax (GST) is discussed in connection with arrangements for beneficiaries.[9]

---

8. 2501(a)(1).

9. See Chapter 13.

Chapter 15

INCOME TAX ASPECTS

A basic decision to be made in planning a client's estate is whether, and to what extent, a revocable trust should be used as the vehicle to control the disposition of his wealth. Either a revocable trust or a will is usually chosen for the disposition of a major portion of such wealth, although other arrangements may control substantial amounts. In order to make the choice intelligently, it is necessary to compare the rules governing taxation of income received by probate estates with such rules for income received by revocable trusts after the death of the grantor. Often this comparison is favorable to the probate estate, and hence to the will, as a vehicle to control the disposition of wealth. Revocable trusts, on the other hand, may offer advantages that have nothing to do with taxes [10] but are sufficiently important for a given client to overcome any income tax disadvantages.

An appropriate starting point in comparing the income tax treatment of estates and revocable trusts after the death of a client is to consider the treatment of the decedent's final taxable year.

¶ 15.01   THE DECEDENT'S FINAL TAXABLE YEAR

For income tax purposes, a decedent's final taxable year ends the day he dies [11] and his executor or the administrator of his estate is responsible for filing the decedent's final return.[12] Unless he happens to die at midnight on December 31 (or on the final day of his fiscal year, if he is a fiscal year taxpayer), his dying cuts short a taxable year that would otherwise have included twelve full months. Apart from usually covering a shorter period, the final return is generally similar to returns for the previous years of the taxpayer's life. Full personal exemptions are allowed without reduction for the short period,[13] and the Regulations provide: "In computing taxable income for such year, there shall be included only amounts properly includible under the method of accounting used by the taxpayer." [14] Thus, whichever method, cash or accrual, the taxpayer was using before he died is used for the year of his death.

Applying this rule creates problems when the taxpayer's death comes, as it often does, while he is engaged in income-producing activities or owns income-producing property. For example, he may have rendered services for which he is yet to be paid when he dies. Or he may have sold property

---

10. For a discussion, see ¶ 6.05[1] supra.

11. Reg. § 1.443–1(a)(2). If a joint return is filed by the surviving spouse and the personal representative of the decedent's estate, the decedent's taxable year ends on the same date as that of the surviving spouse. § 6013(c). As a result, unless she also dies before the end of her taxable year, the joint return will include her income for a full year and that of the decedent for the period prior to his death.

12. § 6012(b)(1).

13. Reg. § 1.443–1(a)(2), fourth sentence.

14. Reg. § 1.451–1(b). Items accrued solely by reason of the decedent's death are not includible in his final return.

424

without having received payment of the full selling price in such form that it will be reflected in income tax returns during his lifetime (including his final return).[15]   Given the policy decision not to require that such items be accrued because of his death and, thus, included in his final return, the obvious way to tax them is to require the taxpayer who receives them as a result of the decedent's death to include them in his tax return.   This requirement is applied to a statutory category of items called "Income in Respect of a Decedent" (IRD), which receive special treatment under § 691.

¶ 15.02   INCOME (AND DEDUCTIONS) IN RESPECT OF A DECEDENT (IRD)

[1] Effect of § 691

Section 691 requires the person who receives an item of "Income in Respect of a Decedent" (IRD) as a result of a decedent's death to include it in his own income "for the taxable year when received * * * ."   The section also allows a deduction for the increase in the federal estate tax attributable to the inclusion of the item in the decedent's estate.[16]   In view of the Pickwickian meanings sometimes given to "received," it is appropriate to point out that for most purposes in this context it means "collected." [17] Thus, an estate beneficiary to whom the right to receive an IRD item is distributed by the executor does not "receive" it when the right is distributed, but rather when he collects cash on account of the IRD item.

> *Example 15.1.*   A decedent, *D*, is entitled to $5,000 in salary at the time of his death and his executor distributes the right to receive that amount to the sole beneficiary, *B*.   *B* includes the $5,000 in income in the year he collects it and deducts the federal estate tax attributable to inclusion of the right to the unpaid salary in *D*'s estate.   If payment of the $5,000 could be expected shortly after *D*'s death, the claim would be valued for estate tax purposes at its face amount without any discount and the gross estate would be increased by $5,000, assuming none of the deductions specified in § 691(c)(2)(B) were applicable to the unpaid salary.   If this causes the estate tax to be $2,000 more than it would otherwise have been, *B* would include $5,000 in income and be entitled to a § 691(c) deduction of $2,000.

The estate tax attributable to the IRD item, which may be deducted in computing the taxable income of the recipient, is computed at the estate's marginal rate (or rates, if the aggregate amount of IRD items is large enough that more than one estate tax bracket is involved in the computation).   Thus, it is first necessary to determine what the estate tax would have been if the estate had not included the IRD item.   It is also necessary to recompute all deductions as if the IRD item did not exist.[18]

The character of an IRD item for tax purposes is that which it would have had for the decedent.[19]   However, if the item is long-term capital gain,

---

15. The time for reporting gain on a sale may be affected by the taxpayer's election to forego use of the installment method under § 453.   See § 453(d)(1).

16. § 691(c).

17. See, e.g., Reg. § 1.691(a)–2(b), *Example (1)*.

18. Reg. § 1.691(c)–1(a)(2).

19. Reg. § 1.691(a)–3(a).

the amount treated as such is reduced by the deduction under § 691(c)(1).[20] Thus, if the $5,000 item referred to above were long-term capital gain, the amount subject to the tax on such gains would be $2,000 ($5,000 minus $3,000), and the long-term capital gains deduction would be computed as a percentage of $2,000, not $5,000.

[2] Items Within the Scope of § 691

Far more confusing than the rules for treating IRD items is the question of whether something is an IRD item. The Code provides no definition of "income in respect of a decedent." The Regulations under § 691 are somewhat more helpful:

> In general, the term "income in respect of a decedent" refers to those amounts to which a decedent was entitled as gross income but which were not properly includible in computing his taxable income for the taxable year ending with the date of his death or for a previous taxable year under the method of accounting employed by the decedent * * *. Thus, the term includes:
>
> (1) All accrued income of a decedent who reported his income by use of the cash receipts and disbursements method:
>
> (2) Income accrued solely by reason of the decedent's death in case of a decedent who reports his income by use of an accrual method of accounting; and
>
> (3) Income to which the decedent had a contingent claim at the time of his death.[21]

The most common example of an IRD item is unpaid salary. Other examples noted in the Regulations include an insurance agent's renewal commissions on insurance sold by him during his life and the proceeds of sales completed by the decedent during his life.[22]

[a] **Reasons for Provision.** The history leading to the enactment of § 691 is helpful in understanding the problem of defining IRD items.[23] Prior to 1934, items of income that had accrued, but had not yet been received by a cash basis taxpayer, were not includible in his final return. Because these items were viewed as entering the estate as corpus, and not as income, they were not taxable to the estate. As a result, they escaped the income tax altogether. In 1934, Congress, in an attempt to close this gap, required that all income items not previously taxed to the decedent be included in his final return. This rule, however, created what many considered to be a serious bunching problem; not only was a tax levied on money not yet

---

20. The reduction of long-term capital gains by the amount of the § 691(c)(1) deduction is required by § 691(c)(4), added by the Tax Reform Act of 1978 and applicable to decedents dying after November 6, 1978. Under prior law, no such reduction was required. See Eleanor Quick v. United States, 503 F.2d 100, 74–2 USTC ¶ 9700 (10th Cir. 1974); Robert F. Goodwin v. United States, 458 F.2d 108, 72–1 USTC ¶ 9355 (Ct.Cl.1972); Edna R. Meissner v. United States, 364 F.2d 409, 66–2 USTC

¶ 9547 (Ct.Cl.1966); J. T. Bridges, Jr., 64 T.C. 968 (1975), acq. 1976–2 CB 1.

21. Reg. § 1.691(a)–1(b).

22. Reg. § 1.691(a)–2(b).

23. The legislative history of the provision is recounted in Ard E. Richardson, Jr. v. United States, 294 F.2d 593, 61–2 USTC ¶ 9660 (6th Cir. 1961), cert. denied 369 U.S. 802.

received, but the tax was also at a relatively high rate due to the inclusion of all such income items in one year.

Although some sort of averaging provision might have solved this problem, Congress instead chose to enact the predecessor of § 691, which by taxing these items to the recipient—be it the estate, a trust, or some other beneficiary—assured that the character of these items as income would not be lost.   Thus, the provision is best understood as a compromise between two goals: to preserve the income character for tax purposes of items that would have been income to the decedent, had he lived, and to relieve the burden that would occur if they were taxed before they were actually received.

[b] **Examples of IRD Items.**   Identifying an item as IRD is relatively easy where it is clear that a right to it accrued during the decedent's lifetime. Far more difficult is the situation where the decedent's right to the item is less well-defined.   For example, a common problem involves payments made to a decedent's spouse that do not reflect explicit contractual obligations of the employer.   In Estate of Edgar V. O'Daniel v. Commissioner,[24] the Second Circuit decided that a discretionary year-end bonus, although its amount was not determined until after the employee's death, was nevertheless an IRD item.   The court found it unimportant that the decedent had no enforceable right to the payment, so long as it was clear that the payment was compensation for the decedent's economic activities.   In Trust Co. of Georgia v. Ross [25] and in George W. Keck v. Commissioner,[26] on the other hand, the Fifth and Sixth Circuits held that the existence of such a right is crucial to the determination that an item constituted IRD, and that in the absence of the right, the extent of the decedent's economic activity in relation to the item is irrelevant.

Another area of controversy concerns a decedent's executory sale contracts.   Section 1014 generally provides a new basis for property included in a decedent's estate,[27] but with an exception in § 1014(c) for IRD items. If the sale is made before the decedent's death, and either the executor or the beneficiary receives the proceeds of the sale, there obviously is a tax liability for any gain not fully accounted for in the decedent's final return. Such gain therefore is taxable to the recipients as an IRD item.[28]   If, on the other hand, the sale is not completed before the decedent's death, and either the executor or the beneficiary completes the sale, there is a stepped-up basis for the property sold, with any taxable gain limited to appreciation after the decedent's death (or alternate valuation date, if applicable).

¶ 15.03   TAXATION OF THE ESTATE

The executor or administrator is responsible for filing the estate's income tax returns.   Section 641(b) provides that the taxable income of an

---

24.   173 F.2d 966, 49–1 USTC ¶ 9235 (2d Cir. 1949).

25.   392 F.2d 694, 68–1 USTC ¶ 9133 (5th Cir. 1967), cert. denied 393 U.S. 830 (1968).

26.   415 F.2d 531, 69–2 USTC ¶ 9626 (6th Cir. 1969).

27.   For a discussion, see ¶ 4.03 supra.

28.   See Reg. § 1.691(a)–2(b), *Examples (4)*, *(5)*.

estate "shall be computed in the same manner as in the case of an individual, except as otherwise provided in this part." The Code does not undertake to determine how long an estate is recognized as a taxable entity. The Regulations state that "[t]he income of an estate $*$ $*$ $*$ is that which is received by the estate during the period of administration or settlement," defined in terms of the period "actually required $*$ $*$ $*$ to perform the ordinary duties of administration $*$ $*$ $*$." [29] Although the rate schedule for estates is the highest applicable to individuals (those for married persons filing separate returns), and the personal exemption is only $600,[30] income that is attributed to an estate for tax purposes may be subject to a lower effective tax rate than if it were distributed currently to the ultimate recipients of estate assets, who in most cases have other taxable income.

As the estate is regarded as a new taxpayer, rather than a continuation of the decedent, the executor may elect a different method of accounting and a different taxable year from that of the decedent. For example, if D dies September 1, D's executor may elect a fiscal year ending on the last day of any month other than December or he may use the calendar year.[31] The result of his election may be a very short initial taxable year; he may, for example, choose September 30 as the closing date for the estate's fiscal year. The estate's income tax for that initial year will nevertheless be computed as if its income had been received over a full twelve-month period.

The tax may be paid by an estate in four equal installments.[32] For a calendar year estate, only 25 percent of the tax for 1980 is due April 15, 1981; the balance is payable, without interest, three, six, and nine months thereafter.[33] This privilege of deferred payment is given to neither individuals nor trusts.

[1] Gross Income

Gross income of an estate encompasses the usual range of items that would have been gross income to the decedent had he lived longer. It includes income from his personal property, which the executor or administrator controls after his appointment and which does not become the property of the legatees until he has distributed it. Real property, on the other hand, is often treated differently because under state law it may vest immediately in the devisees under the will. If it does, the devisees are taxed on the rental income and are entitled to the benefit of deductions for expenses.[34] If, however, the real property and the income it produces remain subject to administration and to assessment for the decedent's debts, such income received by the estate remains taxable to it.[35]

---

29. Reg. § 1.641(b)–3(a).

30. § 642(b). The rates for married individuals filing separate returns contained in § 1(d) differ from the rates for trusts and estates in § 1(e) only in that the former schedule has an initial tax-free bracket of $1700. However, the deduction for the "exemption amount" for an individual is $1,000, with a cost-of-living adjustment beginning in 1985. See §§ 151(a), 151(f).

31. Reg. § 1.441–1(b)(3).

32. § 6152(a)(2).

33. § 6152(b)(1).

34. See, e.g., Guaranty Trust Co., 30 B.T.A. 314 (1934) (New York law).

35. Estate of B. Brasley Cohen, 8 T.C. 784 (1947) (California law).

[2] Deductions

In keeping with the manner in which its gross income is calculated, an estate generally is entitled to the same deductions as an individual. The major departure from this principle relates to distributions made to beneficiaries. Because the goal of the income tax provisions in this area is to insure that the income earned during the administration of the estate is taxed either to the estate or to a beneficiary, the estate is allowed a deduction for those distributions taxed as income to the recipient. Whether a distribution causes all or part of the estate's income to be taxable to the beneficiary is determined by the rules contained in §§ 661–663. The general rule is that distributions do cause income, for the year in which the distribution is made, to be taxable to the recipient and deductible by the estate up to the limit of the "distributable net income" (DNI) of the estate for that year. However, the general rule is subject to major exceptions contained in § 663, which may permit substantial distributions of specific assets or sums of money to be made without causing estate income to be taxable to the recipient.

Another important income tax deduction for estates is for certain expenses of administration, if the right to a deduction for such items under § 2053 for estate tax purposes is waived.[36] Such deductions may be split in any manner desired between the income and estate tax returns,[37] so that careful planning is required to maximize their tax effect.

In at least one instance, a payment by the estate may give rise to a deduction on the decedent's return, rather than on that for the estate. Under § 213(d), medical expenses paid out of the decedent's estate during the year following his death may be deducted as if he had paid them when they were incurred, but only if the right to deduct the item for estate tax purposes as a claim under § 2053 is waived. On the other hand, if the expense is actually paid by the decedent before he dies, that amount may be deducted (to the extent authorized by § 213) for income tax purposes in the year in which it is paid and at the same time is removed from his taxable estate. Thus, the last act of a tax-conscious invalid might well be to pay his attending physician for services to date. If a client's estate plan includes the creation of a funded revocable trust, a more realistic alternative to payment of medical expenses by the client himself on his death bed may be to authorize the trustee to make such payment on his behalf.

¶ 15.04 TAXATION OF A REVOCABLE TRUST

A trust that is revocable by the grantor, acting alone, does not achieve any federal income tax advantage for him during his life because the income is taxable to him under § 676. Such a trust is the only kind discussed here, as it is the only kind that serves a purpose similar to that served by a will. It allows the client to control the devolution of his wealth when he dies without surrendering his control while he lives.

Once the grantor has died, the income tax situation changes because trust income no longer can be attributed to him.[38] The trust then becomes

---

36. See § 642(g); Reg. § 1.212–1(i).   37. See Reg. § 1.642(g)–2.

a separate taxable entity and the trustee may elect to use either the calendar year or a fiscal year for income tax purposes.[39]   Taxation of the trust and its beneficiaries is then governed by the same rules as those that apply to other trusts after the death of the grantor or testator.[40]   Such rules differ in important respects from the rules that apply to estates and estate beneficiaries.[41]

¶ 15.05   TAXATION OF TRUST AND ESTATE BENEFICIARIES— THE DISTRIBUTABLE NET INCOME (DNI) MEASURING ROD

Distributable Net Income (DNI) [42] is a statutory measuring rod that limits both the amount deductible by the estate, under § 661, for distributions made to beneficiaries and the amount includible by them as their shares of the income of an estate (or trust) for the year in which the distribution is made.   Estate DNI is defined as the taxable income of the estate, with specified modifications and before any deduction has been taken for distributions.[43]   The most important difference between DNI and taxable income is that capital gains and losses ordinarily are not taken into account in computing DNI,[44] except for the year in which administration of the estate ends.[45]

The general rule that distributions cause income for the year in which the distribution is made to be taxable to the recipient and deductible by the estate, up to the limit of estate DNI for that year, is subject to exceptions contained in § 663.   The most important is § 663(a)(1), which excludes "a gift or bequest of a specific sum of money or of specific property * * * paid or credited all at once or in not more than [three] installments."   Thus, a will or trust may provide for substantial cash legacies or gifts that can be distributed without thereby causing estate or trust income to be taxed to the recipient.

For example, a cash bequest to a beneficiary may provide funds for her support during the period of estate administration without causing her to be taxed on any estate income.   If she is the surviving spouse, the bequest may also qualify for the marital deduction.

The following *Example* illustrates the operation of the rules governing taxation of estates and estate beneficiaries.

   Example 15.2.   Assume that in 1982, the Estate of *D* has the following receipts and payments:

Received interest and dividends	$25,000
Realized capital gains	10,000

---

38.   See D. G. McDonald Trust, 19 T.C. 672 (1953), acq. 1953–2 CB 5, aff'd sub nom. Chase Nat'l Bank v. Commissioner, 225 F.2d 621, 55–2 USTC ¶ 9649 (8th Cir. 1955), cert. denied 350 U.S. 965 (1956).

39.   See Rev. Rul. 57–51, 1957–1 CB 171.

40.   For a discussion, see ¶ 11.01 supra.

41.   See ¶ 15.06 infra.

42.   The definition is in § 643(a).

43.   § 643(a).

44.   § 643(a)(3).

45.   Gains and losses for that year are necessarily reflected in the final distribution of principal.   See Reg. § 1.643(a)–3(d), *Example (4)*.

Paid state income tax on capital gains	1,000
Paid L $5,000 in cash in satisfaction of legacy of that amount	5,000
Paid R, the residuary legatee, $30,000 in cash as a partial distribution	30,000

Assume further that no other distributions were made in 1982 and that all taxpayers are on the calendar year basis. The estate's DNI is $24,000 (interest and dividends less state income tax). R includes that amount in income and the estate has a corresponding distributions deduction of $24,000. Nothing is included or deducted because of the payment to L, as his legacy is within the exception provided by § 663(a)(1). The capital gains remain taxable to the estate.

HARKNESS v. UNITED STATES

United States Court of Claims, 1972.
469 F.2d 310, 199 Ct.Cl. 721, 72–2 USTC ¶ 9740, cert. denied 414 U.S. 820.

PER CURIAM:

In her 1955 federal income tax return, plaintiff included in her gross income $413,379.04 as income received during that year from her husband's estate. In 1961, the District Director of Internal Revenue for the Manhattan District, New York, took the position that, instead of such sum, plaintiff should have included the amount of $630,740.04, i.e., an additional $217,361. The inclusion of such larger amount in plaintiff's gross income resulted (after the making of various adjustments) in plaintiff's allegedly owing an additional $188,153.35 in income tax for such year, and the Director at that time assessed plaintiff in such amount, plus interest thereon in the amount of $60,103.40, or a total of $248,256.75. Plaintiff paid the additional tax and interest so assessed, and then filed a timely claim for refund therefor. Having received neither a notice of disallowance nor any refund, plaintiff instituted the instant suit to recover such assessed amount, plus interest.

Plaintiff's husband died on August 12, 1954. But his will, he gave plaintiff one-half of his residuary estate. The remaining half was, after the deduction therefrom of any "legacy, succession, transfer, estate or inheritance taxes payable by [the] estate with respect to any property disposed of by [the] Will or payable by any recipient of any such property," given, in equal shares, to the trustees of four testamentary trusts for the children of plaintiff and the decedent (i.e., the issue of their or prior marriages). The will provided that such taxes "shall be paid by [the] Executors out of [the] estate as part of the expenses of administration thereof," with the proviso that "no part of such taxes shall be deducted from or payable out of the one-half (½) of [the] residuary estate" which the decedent bequeathed to plaintiff.

During 1955, and prior to the ultimate distribution of the residuary estate, the executors made distributions to the five beneficiaries thereof in the total sum of $36,004,082.23. Of this amount plaintiff, by eleven payments, received $27,467,768.51. The four trusts, by ten payments to each, received the balance of $8,436,295.75 (in equal shares of approximately $2,134,000). All the distributions were in the form of cash, stocks and bonds. None of the distributions were required by the will to be made prior to the ultimate distribution of the residuary estate.

The federal fiduciary income tax return filed by the executors on behalf of the estate showed distributable net income for 1955 in the amount of $1,005,682.94. A deduction of $826,758.68 was shown on the return for distributions of such income to the five residuary estate beneficiaries, the difference of $178,924.26 between such two figures consisting of tax-exempt income (and expenses allocable thereto).

Section 662(a)(2)(B) of the Internal Revenue Code of 1954 (26 U.S.C.A. § 662(a)(2)(B) (1958)) provides that, where the amounts distributed to all beneficiaries of an estate accumulating income or distributing corpus exceed the distributable net income of the estate, each beneficiary shall include in his gross income an amount which bears the same ratio to distributable net income as the total amount distributed to him bears to the total of the amounts distributed to all the beneficiaries.

The amount of $27,467,768.51 which plaintiff received in 1955 from the residuary estate equaled 76.2907 percent of the total amount of $36,004,082.23 distributed to all beneficiaries during such taxable year. Since such total amount distributed exceeded the distributable net income, the District Director concluded that the provisions of Section 662(a)(2)(B) were applicable and accordingly applied the same percentage to the taxable distributable net income of the estate, the resulting figure being regarded as the amount which plaintiff should have included in her gross income. Application of such 76.2907 percent to the taxable distributable net income figure of $826,758.68 produces the aforementioned figure of $630,740.04 as the amount the District Director concluded plaintiff was required by the statute to have included in her gross income. The inclusion of such amount in plaintiff's gross income produced the additional income tax which is the subject of this suit.

Plaintiff contends that, pursuant to accurate accounting by the executors in calculating the amount of the estate corpus and income which they distributed to the five beneficiaries in 1955, she in fact actually received during the year only the taxable amount of $413,379.34, which amount was but one-half of the taxable distributable net income, and not 76.2907 percent thereof, the figure that the statutory formula produces. Such accounting in the administration of the estate was, plaintiff says, in no way tax motivated, but was in accordance with common practices followed at that time by executors in New York in the administration of estates, and was permitted by the terms of the will and applicable local law. Furthermore, she points out, the accounts of the executors for the year 1955, which set forth the income distributions to plaintiff and the four trusts on a basis of one-half to plaintiff and the other half to the trusts, were judicially settled and allowed by the Surrogate Court of New York County, New York.

Although the approximately $27,500,000 paid to plaintiff during the year greatly exceeded the aggregate amount of approximately $8,500,000 paid to the four trusts, each of such total payments concededly consisting of both corpus and income, plaintiff says that such unequal amounts nevertheless included the equal amounts of $413,379.34 of taxable net income. For this result, plaintiff relies upon the manner in which the executors made their distributions of what they designated as "corpus." The executors, in accordance with a common New York practice, made simultaneous distributions of "principal" and "income" among all the residuary legatees on a basis proportionate to their respective interests in the residuary estate. Further, since here the will directed that all legacy, succession, transfer, estate, or inheritance taxes (sometimes collectively referred to as "death taxes") were to be paid as administration expenses of the estate, but with plaintiff's share of the residuary estate to be undiminished thereby, whenever the executors made any such tax payments (which were, according to their accounting, entirely out of corpus), they also made, again following a common New York practice where wills provided for payment of death taxes out of one or more shares of the residue but not out of one or more other shares, "corpus" distributions to the plaintiff simultaneously with and in the same amounts as such tax payments. Thus, these simultaneous distributions to plaintiff always served, says plaintiff, to keep the remaining corpus interests of the plaintiff and the four trusts in the residuary estate in equal balance, with such equal corpus shares therefore always generating equal amounts to income. The result of adopting these simultaneous distribution practices was the avoidance of complicated calculations of shares of income earned, over varying periods of time, by unequal shares of principal (or by undistributed income). (In this case the decedent's will specifically provided that the income should be distributed proportionately to the residuary legatees, and that if distribution of the residuary estate was not made simultaneously, "an adjustment of the income shall be made by my Executors.") To illustrate, when, on January 1, 1955, the executors distributed $1,125,000 to each of the trusts—amounts which the executors designated as coming entirely from corpus—they simultaneously paid plaintiff $4,500,000, also designated as a corpus distribution. And when, on February 8, 1955, they paid $4,310,000 on account of the New York estate tax, they distributed the identical amount (again designated as principal on their accounts) to plaintiff. Similarly, when on November 14, 1955, they paid $14,621,454.81 on account of the federal estate tax, plus an amount aggregating $3,524,558.49 to the four trusts, such sums totaling $18,146.013.29, they distributed the identical total sum to plaintiff (all amounts again being designated as coming entirely out of principal). In accordance with the will, the New York and federal estate tax payments were deducted from the trusts' aggregate one-half interest in the residuary estate. The several 1955 distributions to plaintiff and the four trusts which the executors designated as distributions of estate income were so calculated by the executors that the amount of such income distributed to plaintiff on any date equaled the aggregate amount distributed to the trusts on the same date.

It is on the above basis that plaintiff argues she actually received only one-half of the distributable net income of the estate in 1955, and not 76 percent.

In a situation such as the instant one, plaintiff contends, Section 662(a)(2)(B) was not intended to be applicable for the formula there prescribed would attribute to plaintiff income which she in fact did not receive. She should not, she argues, have attributed to her more than her actual share of estate income simply because the executors, in their authorized discretion, made principal distributions to her in order to balance the death tax payments and other principal distributions to the trusts. The purpose of the statutory provision here involved was, she contends, to prevent fiduciaries, where the estate had principal, current income, and accumulated income, from controlling tax consequences by manipulating distributions, as, for instance, making distributions designated as coming from "income" to beneficiaries in low income tax brackets, while distributions designated as coming from "principal" are made to beneficiaries in high brackets, and therefore not taxable at all. There was no intent here on the part of the executors, she argues, to gain any kind of income tax advantage for plaintiff.

These contentions cannot be accepted as justifying recovery. There can be no doubt but that plaintiff's situation falls squarely within the literal provisions of Section 662(a)(2)(B), and plaintiff is not understood to contend otherwise. The nub of her contention is that the payments here involved should not be treated as being covered by the statute because the executors' actions were not tax motivated. Even so, the section applies. Clear statutory coverage of this kind, based upon a presumption that any distribution is deemed to be a distribution of the estate's income to the extent of its income for the year, does not and cannot be made to depend on such intangible factors as the subjective intent of executors.

Section 662(a)(2)(B) was specifically intended, for the purposes of that section, "to avoid the necessity for tracing of income." [46] Such tracing was required by the 1939 Code, which provided that distributions by an estate or trust to its beneficiaries were taxed to the beneficiaries for the taxable year in which they received the distributions only if the distributions were made from the current income of the estate or trust. As shown, this lent itself to various kinds of manipulations by executors in the labeling of estate moneys as "income" or "principal." To eliminate such manipulations and tax consequences based upon such estate tax accounting designations of what was "principal" and "income" and from which source a distribution has been made, the "tracing" requirement was, for such distribution purposes, eliminated. Instead, "[t]he beneficiary's proportionate share of the distributable net income   *   *   *   is determined by taking the same fractional part of [the] distributable net income   *   *   *   as the   *   *   *   amounts   *   *   *   distributed to him   *   *   *   bear to the total of [the] amounts   *   *   *   distributed to all beneficiaries." [47] In short, Congress wished to establish an easily useable formula, and to avoid both the necessity of "tracing" and an inquiry into the subjective intention of executors or trustees.
*   *   *

*   *   *   Around this concept of "distributable net income" the Code builds its provisions for (a) the deduction allowed the trust for its current distributions to the beneficiaries, and (b) the distributions which the beneficiaries must include in their own gross incomes. "Thus, distributable net income has been termed the

46. H.R.Rep.No.1337, 83d Cong., 2d Sess. A199, 3 U.S.C.Cong. & Adm.News, pp. 4017, 4339 (1954); S.Rep.No.1662, 83d Cong., 2d Sess. 349, 3 U.S.C.Cong. & Adm.News, pp. 4621, 4990 (1954).

47. 3 U.S.C.Cong. & Adm.News, supra n. 6, at pp. 4340, 4990. The portions of the House and Senate Reports here involved are identical. Id., at pp. 4339–40, 4989–90.

measuring rod or yardstick to be employed in determining, on the one hand, the maximum deduction for distributions which may be allowed to the estate or trust and for gauging, on the other hand, the extent to which beneficiaries may be taxable on the distributions." 6 Mertens "Law or Federal Income Taxation" § 36.04.

We accept plaintiff's contention that there were no tax motivations on the part of the executors in making the distributions at the times and in the amounts they did, and that they made the "balancing" corpus distributions to plaintiff only to avoid complicated calculations of estate income due to the beneficiaries which would result from their having disproportionate interests in the residuary estate.[48] The fact nevertheless remains that, by making the discretionary "balancing" distributions as they did—required neither by the will nor state law—plaintiff received, under their estate accounting, less of the distributable net income than she probably otherwise would have. There is no showing that—either by not making distributions until the estate was wound up finally, or otherwise—the residuary estate could not have been so managed as to produce the same result as the statutory formula. Thus, in that sense (and not in the sense of tax avoidance), the distributions were "manipulated" so that plaintiff, who received over 75 percent of the 1955 payments, is nevertheless said to have received in that year only 50 percent of the taxable distributable net income. On its face and as its purpose is shown by its development and legislative history, the statute was designed to prevent such a result for tax purposes. Indeed, the statutory formula could be considered as providing the more natural and logical result—income earned during the administration of the residuary estate is allocated to the beneficiaries in the same ratio as their interest in the corpus of such estate. Generally, of course, various percentages of corpus will produce like percentages of income. It is thus plain that plaintiff's situation is, by the unambiguous provisions thereof, covered by the statute and although recognizing, of course, the difficulties involved in envisaging every specific situation that could arise under general statutory language, it would nevertheless appear to constitute the type of situation that Congress intended should be covered.

Plaintiff further contends that, even if Section 662(a) is applicable, its formula was erroneously applied because the death taxes should be included in the "amounts properly paid, credited, or required to be distributed to * * * beneficiaries." Crediting the trusts with such taxes as if they constituted distributions to the trusts would result in plaintiff and the trusts receiving equal total amounts. Accordingly, they would, under the statutory formula, be considered as having received equal amounts of the taxable distributable net income.

Plaintiff's basis for treating the payment of the death taxes as distributions to the trusts is based upon the provisions of Regulations § 1.662(a)–4 (26 C.F.R.) that "[a]ny amount which, pursuant to the terms of a will * * * is used in full or partial discharge or satisfaction of a legal obli-

---

48. Such as would occur after the death taxes were paid and deducted from the shares of the trusts, thereby diminishing the interests of the trusts in the residuary estate from the dates of such payments, with proportionate diminutions in the income which would be produced after such dates from such diminished shares.

gation of any person is included in the gross income of such person under section 662(a) * * * (2) * * * as though directly distributed to him as a beneficiary, * * * ." Since the taxes were not deductible from or payable out of plaintiff's one-half of the residuary estate, they therefore were, argues plaintiff, a charge upon, or obligation of, the remaining one-half passing to the trusts. As such an obligation, they should, plaintiff says, be considered, under the Regulations, as expenditures made on behalf of the trusts.

This contention too cannot be sustained. The death tax moneys never constituted a part of, nor were they ever incorporated in, the trusts. The will bequeathed one-half of the residuary estate to the trusts "*after* the deduction therefrom of all of the [death] taxes * * * ." (Emphasis supplied.) There is, therefore, no warrant for adding to the amounts paid to the trusts the amount of the death taxes, an amount which was never paid or payable to the trusts and which the trusts were, under the will, never to receive. Furthermore, these taxes were the legal obligations of the estate, and not of the trusts, the will specifically so recognizing and providing that such taxes, "payable by my estate * * * shall be paid * * * out of my estate as part of the expenses of administration thereof * * * ." The taxes were a "charge" upon, or an "obligation" of, the trusts only in the loose sense that, in calculating the net amount of the residuary estate which the trusts were to receive, the amount of the taxes was to be deducted from the share left to the trusts. They were not a "legal obligation" of the trusts in the sense used by the regulation upon which plaintiff relies.

The trusts received $8,536,313.72 from the estate in 1955. It is such amount that is properly to be considered as the amount "properly paid, credited, or required to be distributed to" them under the statute. The $18,931,454.81 in death taxes paid during the year by the executors, described by the will as part of the administration expenses of the estate, were not "amounts properly paid, credited, or required to be distributed to * * * beneficiaries" within the meaning of the statute or the regulation.

Finally, plaintiff contends that if Section 662(a), properly construed, does cover the instant situation, it is unconstitutional as applied to her because it would impose an unapportioned direct tax on principal or capital in violation of Article I of the Constitution. * * *

* * *

In upholding constitutionality, defendant urges the broad proposition that, even though the disputed amount ($217,361) which taxpayer received in 1955 may have constituted corpus, still the challenged sections (as applied here) are valid on two alternative grounds, first, that the receipt of a bequest, devise or inheritance (whether or not it be from corpus) properly falls within the Sixteenth Amendment as "income" to the recipient, and, second, that in any event the sections impose an indirect tax upon the receipt of property which under the Constitution need not be apportioned. On either of these views, plaintiff's invocation of the Fifth Amendment would also fail because the taxpayer would clearly not be taxed on the income or property of others.

We do not have to delve into the difficult issues of large scope which the Government presents because, as we see it, there is a much narrower ground upon which to sustain the statute as applied to plaintiff's case. That more limited approach stresses the factor (which plaintiff underplays) that the executors did have a choice in 1955 whether to make the distributions in the form they did or, instead, so to manage distributions, to the extent governed by Section 662(a), that the several beneficiaries would not be taxable under Section 662(a) on more than their share of the estate's income. Plaintiff has failed to show that this could not be done. There was no legal compulsion, in the will or in New York law, to make the "balancing" distributions of corpus and income which were made. That course was selected because the other would have been much more burdensome, requiring over the years complicated calculations of shares of income, earned either by principal or by undistributed income, which were due to the various residuary legatees. But the choice was not a forced one, and the other route could have been picked (though at the cost of more work and trouble). If the application of Section 662(a)(2)(B) was deemed unfair to plaintiff taxwise, when such "balancing" distributions were made, the presumed inequity could be avoided by not making "balancing" distributions but employing the other methods of distribution which were available.

That these other methods would have occasioned more trouble (and possibly some more expense) does not invalidate the statutory formula. As we have already indicated, Congress could properly assume, as it did, that in the generality of instances the formula would correspond to reality and not be unfair to any beneficiary. At least where an option is open to avoid an unfair and unrealistic result, use of the formula is not prohibited in the minority of instances in which it may be thought harsh or inequitable.

* * *

* * *

It may be said that Mrs. Harkness, the taxpayer, did not have or make the choice here—the executors did. Technically that is the situation, but there is no hint that plaintiff objected in any way to the estate's course of action, or suggested the other course, or was compelled to accept the large distributions of principal in 1955. It is unrealistic to suppose that, if she had objected on the ground that the estate's mode of distribution increased her own taxes, the executors would nevertheless have forced her to accept those large payments. Indeed, there is no reason to believe that under the will the executors could lawfully compel her to accept the large corpus distributions in 1955, if she was unwilling to do so because of the tax consequences to her. Plaintiff's reply brief to the court makes it clear that plaintiff was not so compelled, and suggests that a deliberate chance was taken as to how the law would be applied. The brief indicates that the executors (and probably plaintiff's own counsel) believed that § 662(a)(2)(B) should not be interpreted (in this type of case) as the Internal Revenue Service and we have construed it—and they acted accordingly.

Without intimating in any way that the statute would be invalid if applied where there was no such option as in this case, we hold that the existence of the choice removes whatever defect there might otherwise be. At least where the option is present, Congress can reasonably and validly forbid "tracing" and presume that its formula in § 662(a)(2)(B) gives an accurate reflection of the division of the estate's "distributable net income" among the beneficiaries.   Cf. Smith v. Westover, 191 F.2d 1003 (9th Cir. 1951), aff'g 89 F.Supp. 432 (S.D.Cal.1950).   Normally, use of the formula would be fair and accurate enough.   If discretionary "balancing" payments which include large amounts of corpus are made and accepted, as here, the necessary consequence is to invoke the formula nonetheless, and the taxpayer will not be allowed to "trace" in order to show that the source of part of his receipts was in fact not "distributable net income" but corpus.   If the tax consequences of this approach are deemed sufficiently undesirable, there is the other route which can and should be taken.   In these circumstances, there is no compulsion to accept an unfair or unrealistic division of "distributable net income."

For these reasons, we hold that the tax was lawfully imposed and that plaintiff is not entitled to recover.

SKELTON, Judge (dissenting):

I respectfully dissent.   In my opinion, the majority opinion by failing to hold that Section 662(a)(2)(B) of the Internal Revenue Code of 1954 (26 U.S.C.A § 662(a)(2)(B) (1958)) and the related Treasury Regulations 1.662(a)–3 are unconstitutional and invalid, has placed a stamp of approval upon the acts of the Internal Revenue Service in collecting income taxes from the plaintiff that she did not owe and in exempting the trusts from income taxes that they owned.   This has caused an unconscionable result to be reached in this case.

* * *

¶ 15.06   DIFFERENCES IN INCOME TAXATION OF TRUSTS AND ESTATES (AND THEIR BENEFICIARIES)

Estates are free from three rules applicable to trusts that might otherwise interfere with optimum use of estates as vehicles for minimizing income taxes:

(1) The throwback rule, which may impose an additional tax on trust beneficiaries who receive distributions deemed to represent accumulated trust income; [49]

(2) The substantial ownership rule embodied in § 678, which causes a power holder to be taxed as owner of trust income or principal which he had the power to vest in himself, even if he does not choose to exercise the power; [50]   and

---

49.   §§ 665–667. For a discussion, see ¶ 11.02 supra.

50.   In Trevanion M. F. McCauley v. United States, 193 F.Supp. 938, 61–2 USTC ¶ 9620 (E.D.Ark.1961), the Commissioner contended that the taxpayer, who was executrix and sole beneficiary of her husband's estate, constructively received certain income of the estate in her individual capacity because of her control over estate assets.

The court decided in favor of the taxpayer on the basis of a jury finding that administration of the estate was not "unduly prolonged."   It reasoned: "[T]o the extent that the doctrine of constructive receipt has play in connection with the taxation of the income of decedents' estates, it is encompassed in the concept of an administration being 'unduly prolonged' * * * ."   193 F.Supp. at 945, 61–2 USTC at 81,543.

(3) The separate share rule embodied in § 663(c), which causes substantially separate and independent shares of different beneficiaries of a single trust to be treated as separate trusts, so that distributions to one such beneficiary do not carry out DNI of another beneficiary's share.　Depending on the relative tax brackets of different beneficiaries, however, the separate share rule may in fact reduce total tax burdens, so that the inapplicability of the rule to estates is not necessarily an advantage in all cases.

Since an estate is not subject to these rules, it is unfortunate that a client's estate cannot continue indefinitely to be treated as a separate tax entity.　Such treatment might insulate even a sole beneficiary who is also the executrix from tax on income of the estate.　However, the Regulations limit the period of such recognition to that actually required to complete administration [51]—which in one case was held to be as long as eleven years.[52]

¶ 15.07　ACCUMULATION OF INCOME IN AN ESTATE OR TRUST

Estates are particularly useful estate-planning tools because estate distributions are not subject to the throwback rule.　If a trust accumulates income, the rule may impose a tax on beneficiaries who later receive distributions deemed to represent such accumulated income,[53] in addition to the tax paid by the trust in the year of its accumulation.　Because income of an estate is not subject to throwback treatment, the tax paid by the estate is the only income tax imposed on its accumulated income.　There is no additional tax when it is distributed to a beneficiary in a later year.

Accumulating the optimum amount of income to minimize taxes is made easier by an advantage that estates share with trusts: the fiduciary's option to elect a fiscal year.[54]　The following *Example* illustrates the use of this option to minimize taxes.

Example 15.3.　*D* dies January 1 and income is received by *E*, his executor, at the rate of $5,000 per month during the first year of estate administration.　If *E* uses the calendar year for income tax purposes and makes no distributions that carry out estate income for income tax purposes to the beneficiaries, the estate will be subject to tax on income of $60,000.　If the executor elects a fiscal year ending June 30, the estate's income for its first fiscal year will be only $30,000.　Distributions may be made after June 30 if it is desirable to reduce the estate's income for its second fiscal year and to thereby keep it out of tax brackets in excess of $30,000.　If the distributees are on the calendar year basis, such distributions will not be includible in income until the following calendar year, in accordance with § 662(c).

Causing income to be taxed to an estate or trust is also made easier by the fact that capital gains realized in a given year by the estate or trust

---

51. Reg. § 1.641(b)–3(a).

52. See A. T. Miller v. Commissioner, 333 F.2d 400, 64–2 USTC ¶ 9579 (8th Cir. 1964).

53. See § 667(a).　For a discussion of the rule, see ¶ 11.02 supra.

54. See Reg. § 1.441–1(b)(3).

ordinarily are not included in DNI [55] except for the year in which administration of the estate ends.[56]   Thus, gains realized in a year before administration ends are taxable to the estate even though distributions to beneficiaries are made in the same year.   However, since an estate's holding period for assets received from the decedent is deemed to be long-term [57] and only 40% of long-term gains is taxable,[58] causing such gains to be taxed to an estate has only a limited importance in minimizing income taxes.

If an estate's income or gains are so large in a given year as to push the estate into a comparatively high income tax bracket, so that accumulating all of such income in the estate becomes expensive from a tax standpoint, several options may be open:

(1) The executor may elect to pay certain administration expenses in that year and deduct them for income tax purposes,[59] rather than on the estate tax return;

(2) Distributions may be made that will carry out estate income for tax purposes, so as to equalize the tax brackets of the estate and its beneficiaries; and

(3) Appreciated property may be distributed to the residuary legatees prior to its sale, so that the sale is made, and gain realized, by them rather than by the estate.[60]

¶ 15.08   DIRECTING THAT INCOME BE DISTRIBUTED TO LOW-BRACKET TAXPAYERS AND PRINCIPAL TO OTHERS

In order to allocate the estate's taxable income to low-bracket distributees and tax-free distributions of principal to others, the client may make use in his will or trust agreement of the rules contained in §§ 662 and 663. The general rule of these sections treats trust and estate distributions as being deductible by the trust or estate and includible by the beneficiary to the extent of the "distributable net income" (DNI) [61] for the year in which the distribution is made.   However, beneficiaries to whom distributions are required to be made out of income, or out of either income or principal (to the extent income is sufficient to cover the required distribution), are placed in the first "tier" of distributees.[62]   First-tier distributees are taxed on their respective shares of DNI up to the amounts they receive.   The second "tier" consists of the remaining beneficiaries—those to whom distributions may be made only from principal or from income or principal to the extent income is insufficient to cover such distributions after deducting distribu-

---

55. § 643(a)(3).   For a discussion of the meaning of "distributable net income" (DNI), see ¶ 15.05 supra.

56. See ¶ 15.05, note 45 supra.

57. § 1223(11)(A).

58. See § 1202(a).

59. See Reg. § 1.642(g)–2.

60. The basis of the residuary legatees may be higher than the estate's.   See Reg.

§ 1.661(a)–2(f)(3), discussed at ¶ 4.07 supra.   If the distribution were in satisfaction of a cash legacy, the estate would realize gain.   See ¶ 4.03[1] supra.   It realizes no gain on a distribution to a residuary legatee. See ¶ 17.01[3] infra.

61. For a discussion of DNI, see ¶ 15.05 supra.

62. See § 662(a)(1), last sentence;   Reg. § 1.662(a)–2(b).

tions required to be made out of income alone.[63]   Second-tier distributees are taxed only on their respective shares of so much of DNI as is not taxed to the first tier.   Thus, the will may control who is taxable on estate income by confining some beneficiaries to principal distributions, thereby placing them in the second tier.

Section 663 creates an exception to the general rule that distributions carry out estate income for tax purposes.   It makes the rule inapplicable to a gift or bequest of specific property or a specific sum, payable in not more than three installments.   Such a bequest facilitates accumulating income in the estate or trust for tax purposes while, at the same time, payment of the bequest allows the executor or trustee to make resources available to the beneficiary who receives it.

---

63.   Reg. § 1.662(a)–3(c).

Chapter 16

ESTATE TAX ASPECTS

Arrangements that become effective upon the client's death may minimize estate taxes in four major ways:

(1) Using statutory deductions and exclusions;

(2) Using discounts to reduce asset values;

(3) Paying the tax with bonds bought at a discount; and

(4) Postponing payment of the tax with low interest.

For optimum results, action in addition to inclusion of appropriate provisions in his will or revocable trust is often required during the client's life. For example, the estate tax can be paid by redemption of United States Treasury bonds purchased at a discount only if the bonds were brought before the client died.

¶ 16.01 USING STATUTORY DEDUCTIONS AND EXCLUSIONS

Estate planning to reduce estate taxes is, to a far greater extent than similar planning to save income taxes, based upon use of specific statutory exclusions and deductions rather than any general "common law" tax principles. For purposes of discussion, the major possibilities for such use may be grouped under four headings:

(1) the estate tax marital deduction;

(2) the estate tax charitable deduction;

(3) the exclusion for certain employee death benefits and individual retirement arrangements; and

(4) deductions for debts, claims, and administration expenses.

An orphans' deduction was provided by § 2057, added by the Tax Reform Act of 1976. The provision was repealed by § 427 of the Economic Recovery Tax Act of 1981, effective for estates of decedents dying after 1981.

[1] The Estate Tax Marital Deduction

In common-law states, the biggest single step most married clients can take to reduce estate taxes at their death is to qualify for the estate tax marital deduction. For decedents dying after 1981, there is no limit on the amount of the deduction under § 2056(a). The great majority of clients need not pay any federal estate tax if they are survived by a spouse [1] and make qualifying gifts to her in sufficient amount.

---

1. For this purpose, "if the order of deaths of the decedent and his spouse cannot be established by proof, a presumption (whether supplied by local law, the decedent's will, or otherwise) that the decedent was survived by his spouse" is sufficient under Regulations Section 20.2056(e)–2(e) to the extent that it gives her an interest in property includible in her estate.

For cases dealing with the effect of state law in determining who is the decedent's "surviving spouse" after a divorce, see ¶ 1.03, note 5 supra.

The relatively rare exception occurs when death taxes exceed the amount covered by the client's unified credit. In this case, even though the entire estate is bequeathed to the surviving spouse, the portion required to pay death taxes diminishes the net value of her gift and hence the amount allowable as a marital deduction.[2]

For example, assume that a decedent dies in 1982, bequeathing his entire estate to his surviving spouse. The gross estate, after deductions allowable under §§ 2053 and 2054, is $4 million. The state of the decedent's domicil does not have an unlimited marital deduction, and state death taxes of $250,000 are payable. As a result, the federal estate tax marital deduction cannot exceed $3,750,000, because the net value of the gift to the spouse will be reduced by the state death taxes. In fact, the allowable marital deduction will be further reduced because a federal estate tax will also be payable, likewise diminishing the net value of the gift to the spouse.

Chapter 18 deals at length with how to qualify for the deduction. This paragraph is concerned only with the extent to which it is desirable for a client to do so.

If the client's estate will not be subject to estate tax in any case because of the unified credit, there is no need to qualify any part of it for the marital deduction. Indeed, it is affirmatively undesirable, from a tax standpoint, to do so. That which qualifies must be in a form that will be includible in the estate of the surviving spouse when she dies, unless it is spent or given away during her life. If the client's estate will be subject to some estate tax despite the unified credit, but a marital deduction of less than the maximum allowable amount will be sufficient in combination with the unified credit to eliminate any estate tax, it is likewise desirable from an estate tax standpoint to qualify for the deduction only to the extent necessary to eliminate any tax.

Before the previous limits on the amount of the marital deduction were repealed by Section 403 of the Economic Recovery Tax Act of 1981, some clients chose to further restrict the amount of their marital deduction gifts, even though the result was to incur more estate tax than would have been due if the maximum allowable deduction had been secured. In addition to the variety of non-tax reasons which may lead clients to avoid making qualifying gifts to a spouse, there was sometimes a desire to equalize the taxable estates of husband and wife with a view to minimizing total estate taxes.

A theoretical basis for seeking to cause one-half of the combined wealth of a married couple to be taxed when the first spouse dies and the balance on the death of the survivor is provided by the progressive rate structure of the estate tax. The total tax on two estates of $1 million each is $691,600 before credits; the tax on a single estate of $2 million is $780,800, or $89,200 more. Thus a husband (H) with a taxable estate of $1.5 million may, if his wife (W) already has $500,000 of her own, seek to equalize the two taxable estates by limiting his marital deduction gift to $500,000, even though it leaves his estate subject to an estate tax of $345,800 (before credits).

As a practical matter, for a given client it may be more advantageous than these figures would suggest to qualify for the deduction to the full

2. See ¶ 18.07 infra.

extent necessary to eliminate (or minimize) any estate tax. The apparent saving of $89,200 in estate taxes from the equalization just described may be illusory, for the following reasons:

(1) If H dies first, the use of the money paid in estate tax on his death is lost for whatever period W survives him. According to the Treasury's figures, over one-half of spouses survive ten years or more.[3] If the marital deduction is used to postpone estate tax until W dies, the result is an interest-free loan from the Treasury for as long as she survives H, providing funds which may be invested to produced additional income for W;

(2) If H dies before 1987, when the unified credit will reach its presently scheduled maximum of $192,800, the tax payable on his death (before any credit for state death taxes)[4] on any given amount of wealth will be more than the tax on the same amount when W dies, if she lives until 1987;

(3) W may act during her life to reduce her taxable estate, so that all or part of her marital deduction gift may not be taxable when she dies.

On the other hand, the final results of qualifying for the deduction in *H*'s estate to the full extent necessary to eliminate (or minimize) any estate tax may be less favorable than the foregoing discussion would suggest, because:

(1) W may already own, or subsequently may acquire, other assets that will be included in her taxable estate when she dies, so that her effective estate tax rate will be higher than if she had only the marital deduction gift.

(2) The values of many assets have tended to increase, over time, as a result of inflation and other factors, which may cause the same aggregation of assets to be taxed in a higher estate tax bracket.

(3) Estate tax rates have fluctuated both up and down over the years. A tax at the rates prevailing when *H* dies may prove to be a bargain in comparison to a tax at the rates in force when *W* dies years later.

(4) For state death tax purposes, the marital deduction may be less liberal than that allowed by federal law. Qualifying for the maximum under federal law may mean overfunding for state death tax purposes. The resulting build-up in the amount subject to a state death tax when the wife dies, without an offsetting benefit when *H* dies, is objectionable from a tax standpoint.

Two other factors not involving a comparison of total estate taxes should also be considered:

(1) In order to qualify for the marital deduction, it is necessary either to give W control over the disposition of the gift, or to give her the income from the property for her life.[5] This may cause *H*'s property, or the income it produces, to be enjoyed by *W*'s second husband or relatives, rather than beneficiaries whom *H* might have preferred.

3. See U.S. Treas. Dep't, 91st Cong., 1st Sess., Tax Reform Studies and Proposals, Pt. 3, at 360 (Comm.Print 1969).

4. See §2011.

5. See § 2056(b).

(2) Most forms of gifts that qualify for the deduction cause W to be taxable on the income from the marital deduction gift.[6] If she is in a high income tax bracket, this may be relatively more expensive [7] than a nonqualifying gift that allows income to be accumulated in trust or distributed to other beneficiaries. Although the estate trust is occasionally used to permit income of a marital deduction trust to be accumulated.[8] the consequences of creation of such a trust may, as a matter of state law, be unclear or unsatisfactory, or both.[9]

On balance, for most clients the arguments in favor of using the marital deduction to the extent necessary to eliminate (or minimize) estate tax when the first spouse dies should be given substantial weight, unless the surviving spouse has a relatively short life expectancy or the client's major concern is with limiting her control or enjoyment of his wealth. The estate tax cost of any potential deduction foregone is high. The marginal estate tax rate is currently 32% for amounts not sheltered from tax by the unified credit,[10] and is scheduled to rise to 37% as the increases in the credit are phased in until it reaches $192,800 in 1987.[11] The present top marginal bracket of 65% for taxable estates in excess of $4 million [12] is scheduled to decline to 50% for decedents dying after 1985.[13] Thus the potential tax saving from equalizing the taxable estates of spouses is limited, and the equalization mechanism may carry additional administrative costs.

[2] The Estate Tax Charitable Deduction

Transfers solely for charity are a way to save estate taxes by qualifying for the estate tax charitable deduction.[14] But for the average client, who usually wishes to make the bulk of his wealth available for non-charitable beneficiaries, transfers which are not solely for charity are likely to be far more useful. In order for such transfers to qualify for the estate tax charitable deduction, the charitable interest must be in one of three forms: [15]

(1) A remainder interest in a charitable remainder unitrust, annuity trust, or pooled income fund;

(2) A lead interest in the form of a guaranteed annuity or fixed percentage to be "distributed yearly of the fair market value of the trust property (to be determined yearly)"; [16] or

(3) An interest described in § 170(f)(3)(B), which allows "a remainder interest in a personal residence or farm," as well as other less common varieties of partial interests in property, to qualify for an income tax charitable deduction.

6. Id. For a discussion, see ¶ 18.04 infra.

7. This objection can be overcome by investment in tax-exempt bonds but by hindsight such bonds have often been unattractive investments.

8. See Reg. § 20.2056(e)–(2)(b)(1)(iii).

9. Estate trusts are discussed at ¶ 18.04[3] infra.

10. See §§ 2001(c).

11. See § 2010(b).

12. See § 2001(c)(2)(B).

13. See § 2001(c)(1), (2). The rate will apply to estates over $2.5 million.

14. § 2055.

15. § 2055(e)(2).

16. § 2055(e)(2)(B).

Gifts of remainder interests in personal residences or farms allow the benefit of an estate tax deduction to be combined with present enjoyment of the property by a family member or other beneficiary.

Charitable split-interest trusts, in which either a remainder interest or an income (or lead) interest is given to charity, are discussed in Chapter 19.

[3] The Exclusions for Employee Death Benefits and Individual Retirement Arrangements

Two forms of wealth that are exempt from the estate tax by express Code provision are certain employee death benefits under qualified plans described in § 2039(c), and individual retirement accounts, annuities, and bonds described in § 2039(e).   These two forms provide as nearly an ideal shelter from income and estate taxes as the Code offers because the transfer tax exemption is combined with income shifting and deferral as well.[17]

The estate tax exemption is denied if the employee benefit or individual retirement account, annuity, or bond is payable to the employee's executor [18] or is deemed to be so payable.[19]   Although such items may be made payable to the surviving spouse, it is preferable to use other assets, if they are available, to meet her needs.   Items already exempt under § 2039 do not qualify for the marital deduction because they are not includible in the employee's gross estate.[20]   Ordinarily, it is undesirable to give the spouse amounts in excess of her needs for current consumption that do not qualify for the marital deduction if other items that would qualify for the deduction could be given to her instead.

[4] Deductions for Debts, Claims, and Expenses of Administration

The planning possibilities for deductions allowed for debts, claims, and expenses of administration are limited but are by no means nonexistent. If the deductible item is founded upon a promise or agreement, an explicit requirement is imposed that it have been contracted "bona fide and for an adequate and full consideration in money or money's worth." [21]   This has been held not to allow a deduction for a claim against the estate that arose from a release of marital rights (other than support rights).[22]   Thus, the requirement may be significant in the negotiation of separation agreements in order to insure the deductibility of amounts payable to the former wife after her husband's death.

The Regulations allow a deduction for the "full unpaid amount" of mortgages upon property in the gross estate [23] and do not indicate that the deduction is reduced because the interest rate may be below the currently prevailing market rate.   However, Letter Ruling 8118009 [24] requires such

---

17. For a discussion, see ¶ 21.02[2].

18. §§ 2039(c), 2039(e).

19. See Reg. § 20.2039–2(b)(4), referring to Reg. § 20.2042–1(b).

20. § 2056(a).

21. § 2053(c)(1)(A).

22. See ¶ 8.05[2].

23. See Reg. § 20.2053–7.   But compare Reg. § 20.2031–4 (note may be includible in gross estate at less than amount of unpaid principal, because of the interest rate): Estate of Meyer B. Berkman, 38 TCM 183 (1979) (notes bearing 6 percent interest when prime rate 9.75 percent valued at less than 50 percent of unpaid principal amount).

24. 3 CCH E&GT ¶ 12,443A (Jan. 23, 1981).

a reduction. If the Ruling had not discouraged reliance on the literal language of the Regulations, clients acquiring assets on credit extended by the seller and secured by a mortgage or other lien on the property, might be encouraged to offer to pay a higher principal sum in return for a lower interest rate.[25] The value of the asset will be determined by appraisal, and is not wholly controlled by the price paid to acquire it; the principal balance of the mortgage might be deductible in full without regard to the interest rate.

The Regulations allow a deduction for expenses of sale of assets "if the sale is necessary in order to pay the decedent's debts, expenses of administration, or taxes, to preserve the estate, or to effect distribution." [26] If assets are sold for the benefit of a legatee, no estate tax deduction is allowed; [27] but if the sale is required to be made by the executor, the selling expenses become deductible.[28] Thus, if the client wishes to have an asset sold, it may be more advantageous to direct the executor to make the sale and distribute the proceeds instead of distributing the asset itself. Of course, the different income tax positions of the estate and its beneficiaries should also be taken into account in making this choice.

The executor should bear in mind that, under § 642(g), a deduction under § 2053 precludes a deduction for estate income tax purposes (or treatment for such purposes as an offset against sales price in determining gain or loss). If the income tax deduction or offset is preferred, the estate tax deduction must be waived.

¶ 16.02   USING DISCOUNTS TO REDUCE ASSET VALUES

Discounting the value of assets to be transferred at death may be accomplished either through use of general techniques to minimize asset values [29] or through qualifying under the special use valuation provision of § 2032A, which creates an exception to the general rule.

25. From the standpoint of the seller, a higher purchase price and lower interest rate may be attractive in causing a larger portion of amounts received to be treated as proceeds of sale of a capital asset, thereby qualifying for long-term capital gain treatment. To achieve this result, the stated interest rate must be no lower than the test rate for unstated interest. See § 483(a), discussed at ¶ 8.04 note 70 supra.

26. See Reg. § 20.2053–3(d)(2).

27. See Estate of Thomas W. Streeter v. Commissioner, 491 F.2d 375, 74–1 USTC ¶ 12,970 (3d Cir. 1974). But see Estate of Mary F. C. Park v. Commissioner, 475 F.2d 673, 73–1 USTC ¶ 12,913 (6th Cir. 1973) (expenses deductible to the extent "allowable" under state law, without regard to whether necessary for estate administration). The Internal Revenue Service will not follow the *Park* case in disposing of cases outside of the Sixth Circuit. Letter Rul. 7802006, 3 CCH E&GT ¶ 12,100 (Sept. 30, 1977).

28. In Estate of David Smith v. Commissioner, 510 F.2d 479, 75–1 USTC ¶ 13,046, (2d Cir. 1975), cert. denied 423 U.S. 827 (1975), mere authorization for sales by the executors of the decedent's sculpture was not enough to support a full deduction for sales commissions under § 2053(a), even though the full amount had been allowed as administration expenses by a New York Surrogate in uncontested proceedings. The Second Circuit limited the deduction to commissions on sales required to pay debts, expenses of administration, and taxes. Under this view, a direction that the sculpture be sold and the proceeds remaining after payment of such items be distributed to legatees might have changed the result and caused the deduction to be allowed in full.

29. Such techniques usually involve some form of lifetime arrangement. For a discussion, see ¶ 5.02[1][c] supra.

The general rule is that the value of property for estate tax purposes is the price at which it would pass from a willing seller to a willing buyer,[30] based on the most profitable use of the property. This follows from the fact that a buyer wishing to make such use of it will be willing to pay more than other potential buyers who wish to use it for less profitable purposes. Such a rule of valuation causes estate taxes to be higher than if the property had been valued on the basis of its actual use. This increases the likelihood that property which is not in its most profitable use, will be sold either by the owner during his life, in anticipation of the estate tax when he dies, or by the executor to provide for its payment after the owner's death.

A common example of such sales is the case of a family farm located near an expanding city. Despite the fact that the heirs or devisees may wish to continue to farm the land, under the general valuation rule estate taxes would be based on the value of the land to a developer. The resulting tax burden might force the sale of the farm in order to pay the tax where other assets are insufficient to meet it, as the farm income may not be great enough even to cover the repayment of a loan to pay the taxes or to pay the taxes in installments if that option is available.[31]

Congress felt that it was desirable to "encourage the continued use of property for farming and other small business purposes," [32] and therefore provided, as part of the Tax Reform Act of 1976, for an election by the executor to have "qualified real property," as defined in § 2032A(b), valued in its current use.[33] The resulting reduction in value may not exceed $700,000, for decedents dying in 1982 and $750,000 for decedents dying thereafter.[34] If the property is disposed of or ceases to be used for its qualified purpose within ten years of the decedent's death, part or all of the reduction in estate tax produced by the lower valuation may be recaptured.[35]

"Qualified real property" is defined in § 2032A(b). From a planning standpoint, one significant consequence of § 2032A is its impact on transfers which remove property from a client's gross estate. As there is no counterpart provision for gift tax purposes, a lifetime transfer of property that might qualify under the section if it were owned at death may be subject to a substantially higher tax than would have been incurred if the property had been retained. On the other hand, a lifetime transfer of other property may make it possible for the estate to qualify under § 2032A by reducing the size of the denominator of the fraction applicable to the test for qualification under § 2032A(b)(1), if the executor finds this to be in the best interests of the beneficiaries.

QUESTIONS

If property is designated as "homestead" under state law, does such designation reduce its value for federal estate tax purposes? See Estate of Helen M. Johnson, 77 T.C.No. 10 (1981).

---

30. See Reg. § 20.2031–1(b).

31. H.R.Rep.No. 94–1380, 94th Cong., 2d Sess. 1, 22, reprinted in [1976] U.S.Code Cong. & Ad.News, 3356, 3376.

32. Id. at 22.

33. Formulae are included for determining such value. See §§ 2032A(e)(7), 2032A (e)(8).

34. § 2032A(a)(2).

35. See § 2032A(c).

¶ 16.03   PAYING THE ESTATE TAX WITH BONDS BOUGHT AT A DISCOUNT ("FLOWER BONDS")

Present law offers a discount in estate tax for purchasers of United States Treasury bonds ("flower bonds") eligible for redemption at par to pay the tax.[36] Such bonds in recent years have often sold at a substantial discount from par value, as interest rates have moved above those that prevailed when the eligible bond issues were offered by the Treasury. For example, the 3 percent bonds due in 1995 have sold for as little as 70 percent of par value. No more bonds eligible for redemption for this purpose may be issued [37] but as of mid-1981, nine eligible issues were outstanding.[38]

Such bonds are valued at par for estate tax purposes to the extent of the amount eligible for redemption to pay estate taxes,[39] which is limited to the amount of the decedent's estate tax. Thus, the purchase of bonds, to the extent of the amount eligible for redemption, has the effect of increasing the taxable estate—and hence the estate tax—by the difference between the purchase price and the par value of the bonds. But the total effect of the purchase may be a substantial saving in estate taxes, as illustrated by *Example 16.1.*

> *Example 16.1.*   Assume that a client has made no post-1976 taxable gifts and has a prospective taxable estate of $1 million. He or she faces a prospective estate tax of $249,800 after a unified credit of $62,800 if he dies in 1982,[40] and a maximum credit of $33,200 for state death taxes.[41] To anticipate this obligation, he could buy, for example, $268,000 par value of the 3 percent bonds due in 1995 at a price of about 80 in mid-1981.[42] Any bonds eligible for redemption at par would be valued at 100 for estate tax purposes, rather than at 80, because they would be worth 100 to the estate as a means of paying its tax obligations. On the basis of the values given, all of the bonds purchased would be eligible. The higher value for the bonds would increase the taxable estate by $53,600, the amount by which their value for estate tax purposes ($268,000) exceeded their cost ($214,400). Hence, the estate tax (after reduction for a larger state death tax credit) would go up to $268,774. But only $774 would be paid in cash; the balance would be satisfied with bonds which cost only $214,400. The result is a saving of $34,626 in federal estate tax compared to the $249,800 which would otherwise be paid in cash.

The redemption of the bonds must be taken into account in determining the estate's capital gains for income tax purposes. But the new basis under

---

36. Eligible issue are listed at 2 CCH E&GT ¶ 9764.45.

37. See 31 U.S.C.A. § 757c–4 (1976).

38. See note 36 supra.

39. See Bankers Trust Co. v. United States, 284 F.2d 537, 61–1 USTC ¶ 11,985 (2d Cir. 1960), cert. denied 336 U.S. 903.

40. See § 2010(b).

41. See § 2011(b).

42. This issue combines the lowest coupon of any bonds eligible for redemption to pay estate taxes with a relatively long maturity (the longest is 1998, but for an issue paying 3½ percent). A combination of low coupon and long maturity tends to maximize the discount at which an issue sells. In comparing the relative attractiveness of different issues, however, a higher coupon may mean more income during the period the bond is held. For this purpose, the relevant comparison is current yield, rather than yield to maturity, and the relevant time span is the estimated remaining life expectancy of

§ 1014 for assets included in the gross estate [43] eliminates any gain on redemption of the bonds.

The savings would be reduced by increased state death taxes if the bonds were valued at 100 for such purposes and the result was to increase such taxes so that they exceed the maximum federal credit.[44]

In view of the difficulty in predicting the estate tax that will ultimately be paid, one may be tempted to advise clients to err on the side of liberality in buying flower bonds, in order to be sure to have enough.   There are hazards in this approach, however.   If, in *Example 16.1*, the decedent had purchased $350,000 par value of bonds, his or her executor is placed in a difficult position.   On the basis of the figures given, not all of the bonds would be eligible for redemption at par and the executor might be tempted to sell the excess, either to meet cash needs of the estate or to secure a better yield from another investment.   If he or she does so, however, and the Commissioner determines a deficiency in estate tax that brings the total up to $350,000, all of the bonds owned at the decedent's death are valued at par for estate tax purposes, even though part has already been sold and, thus, is no longer available for redemption at par at the time the deficiency is determined.[45]   Thus, it is prudent to underestimate, rather than to overestimate, the estate tax in determining how many flower bonds to buy unless the executor is prepared to hold all of them until the time for determination of any estate tax deficiency has expired.

In order to be eligible for redemption to pay estate taxes, the bonds must be owned by the decedent (or a trust or individual legally liable for the tax) at the time of his death.   This may present problems if the decedent ceases to be legally competent prior to his death and the purchase is made on his behalf by the holder of a power of attorney.   The common-law rule is that such a power is revoked automatically by the incompetence of the principal.[46]   But the courts have held the result to be merely that the purchase is voidable, with the executor's ratification sufficient to make the decedent the owner at the time of his death.[47]

Clients in community-property states face an additional problem in using flower bonds.   If the bonds constitute community property, only the decedent's one-half interest in the bonds will be eligible for redemption to pay the decedent's estate tax.[48]   If bonds are acquired with community funds or on credit for which community assets are liable for payment, the

the client plus the nine months following his death before the estate tax is due.

43.   For a discussion of § 1014, see ¶ 4.03 supra.

44.   See In re Estate of Behm, 19 A.D.2d 234, 241 N.Y.S.2d 264 (1963), aff'd without opinion 14 N.Y.2d 826, 251 N.Y.S.2d 475, 200 N.E.2d 457 (1964).   But see Estate of Power, 156 Mont. 100, 476 P.2d 506 (1970), in which valuation at market was held to be mandated by statute.

45.   Estate of Elfrida G. Simmie, 69 T.C. 890 (1978), aff'd per curiam 632 F.2d 93, 80–2

USTC ¶ 13,377 (9th Cir. 1980); contra, Colorado Nat'l Bank v. United States, 71–1 USTC ¶ 12,781 (D.Colo.1971).

46.   See, e.g., Foster v. Reiss, 18 N.J. 41, 112 A.2d 553 (1955).   By statute, a number of states authorize a "durable" power of attorney to provide that it will survive the incompetency of the principal.   See, e.g., N.Y.Gen.Oblig.Law 5–1601.

47.   See, e.g., United States v. James C. Manny, 645 F.2d 163, 81–1 USTC ¶ 13,400 (2d Cir. 1981); Estate of Pauline M. Pfohl v. Commissioner, 70 T.C. 630 (1978).

48.   See Rev.Rul. 76–68, 1976–1 CB 216.

bonds will constitute community property as a matter of state law.[49]   However, the Fifth Circuit has held that under Texas law this result can be avoided by an agreement between the purchasing spouse and the creditor that the latter will look only to the purchaser's separate property for payment of the loan.[50]

¶ 16.04   POSTPONING PAYMENT OF THE ESTATE TAX WITH RE-DUCED INTEREST

The estate tax is due nine months after the date of death,[51] but three Code sections authorize extensions of the time for payment for all or a portion of the tax.[52]   The extension provisions are valuable from the estate's standpoint not merely in permitting a more leisurely liquidation of estate assets to discharge the tax liability but also in reducing the real economic burden of the tax.   This results from the manner in which interest is computed for the period during which payment is deferred, for two reasons:

(1) The nominal interest rate sometimes is lower than that which would be charged the estate by a non-governmental lender and may be lower than the estate itself earns on short-term investments; and

(2) Under § 6601(e), interest is not compounded, another departure from the practice of non-govermental lenders.

Under § 6621, the nominal interest rate, which generally applies to deferred payments, is set by reference to the "adjusted prime rate charged by banks," defined in § 6621(c) as "the average predominant prime rate quoted by commercial banks to large businesses   *   *   *."

In the real world of business, the nominal prime rate understates the true cost of borrowing because the lending bank may require the borrower to maintain a "compensating" balance equal to a part of the amount of the loan.   The result may be that such cost of borrowing from a bank, even for large businesses, is 110 percent or 120 percent of the so-called "prime rate" referred to in § 6621(c).   Thus, when interest rates are rising, borrowing from the Treasury may be less costly than borrowing from a bank.[53]

Section 6166 mandates a further departure from business reality if 35 percent of the adjusted gross estate consists of closely held businesses as therein defined.   If that test is satisfied, the applicable interest rate is only 4 percent on a maximum of $345,800,[54] the amount of tax on the first $1 million of the taxable estate that is attributable to the value of the business. On the balance of the tax the interest rate is determined under § 6621.

---

49. For a discussion of what constitutes community property see ¶ 1.08[1] supra.

50. Colletta L. Ray v. United States, 538 F.2d 1228, 76–2 USTC ¶ 13,154 (5th Cir. 1976).

51. §§ 6075(a) (due date for return), 6151 (tax due when return is filed).

52. See the following sections, which provide for extensions either at the election of the executor or in the discretion of the Secretary.   See §§ 6161, 6163, 6166.

53. Under § 6621(b), provision is made for rounding the rate to the nearest full percent, and for adjustment of the rate not oftener than annually.

54. § 6601(j)(2).

The advantages of these low nominal rates are heightened by the free-dom from compound interest provided by § 6601(e). Thus, the elective extensions under §§ 6166 with respect to estate tax attributable to a closely held business may significantly ease the burden and should be kept in mind in planning for clients whose estates may be expected to satisfy the tests contained in those sections. In addition, interest incurred by the estate on the unpaid balance of federal estate taxes may be deductible for estate tax purposes as an administration expense.[55] For some estates, such a deduction may be more valuable than deducting such interest for income tax purposes.

55. If the executor elects to defer payment of the estate tax, only interest actually accrued (and not estimated interest to be incurred over the period of deferral) is deductible under § 2053. See Rev.Rul. 80–250, 1980–2 CB 278. If payment of estate tax in installments is elected in accordance with § 6166, additional accrued interest is deductible under § 2053(a)(2) when each annual installment payment is made, requiring recomputation of the tax. Id. See Estate of Charles A. Bahr, 68 T.C. 74 (1977), acq. 1978–1 CB 1. See Rev.Rul. 79–252, 1979–2 CB 333, noting that interest on income tax and gift tax deficiencies is likewise deductible.

Chapter 17

WILLS AND PROBATE ESTATES

Despite the widespread use of revocable trusts [1] and joint ownership with a right of survivorship [2] as will substitutes, wills remain the most important estate-planning tool.   Although a revocable trust may serve many of the purposes which might otherwise be served by a will, it rarely eliminates the need for a will altogether.   Few clients wish to transfer title to all of their assets to the trustee of a revocable trust and, even if they did, subsequent acquisitions would not become part of the trust unless further transfers are made whenever assets are acquired.   Joint ownership with survivorship is an even less comprehensive alternative to a will, as it does not provide for the possibility that the other joint owner may not be the survivor.

Aside from controlling the disposition of at least the residual assets of a client which are not part of a revocable trust when he or she dies, wills serve other purposes which revocable trusts cannot perform:

(1) To exercise any powers of appointment that the client holds and wishes to exercise [3] and that are exercisable only by will.

(2) To appoint an executor.   Even if all of a client's assets have been transferred to a revocable trust, an executor will be needed to perform various functions after the client's death, such as filing tax returns.

(3) To appoint a guardian [4] of the person or of the estate or both for any minor children of the client.

From the standpoint of saving taxes, the following will provisions are important:

(1) bequests and devises;

(2) elections or disclaimers by beneficiaries; and

(3) payment of taxes.

¶ 17.01 BEQUESTS AND DEVISES

The choice among kinds of bequests and devises is important in determining the tax consequences for both the estate and the legatee, depending on whether he receives his gift in the form of money or property.   In addition, such form is an important factor in qualifying for estate tax deductions for marital and charitable gifts.   The three forms which are significant from an income tax standpoint are bequests of:

(1) specific property;

---

1. See ¶ 6.05[1] supra.

2. See ¶ 7.01 supra.

3. The handling of clients' powers of appointment is discussed in ¶ 12.02 (general powers) and ¶ 12.03 (limited powers) supra.

4. Guardianship is discussed in ¶ 9.03[1] supra.

(2) sums of money; and

(3) shares of residue.

Bequests and devises may be either outright or in trust. Trusts under wills (as well as bequests to trusts created during the client's life) are important tools in saving taxes when the client dies. Such trusts may qualify for the estate tax deductions for marital and charitable gifts. They also may be used to achieve income tax savings as vehicles for distributions of appreciated assets to accomplish a step-up of basis [5] and for the allocation of income to low-bracket individual beneficiaries.[6] In addition, the trust itself may be used to hold accumulated income, either so that the tax paid by the trust is the total tax on such income or so that an additional tax is payable, under the throwback rule, by the beneficiary to whom such income is distributed, with interest-free deferral in the meantime.[7]

[1] Specific Property

A bequest or devise of specific property [8] that is satisfied by delivery thereof to the legatee has the advantage of simplicity.[9] No gain or loss is realized by the estate upon delivery of the property to the legatee; no income of the estate is taxed to the legatee because of its receipt; and the executor's basis for the asset becomes its basis in the hands of the recipient.[10]

Thus, a bequest or devise is a useful means of moving wealth into the hands of a legatee without adverse tax consequences to him or to the estate. In practice, however, such gifts usually are not the vehicle for disposition of the bulk of a client's wealth, except in some instances of gifts of interests in family businesses or family farms. Ordinarily, the form in which the bulk of a client's wealth is held makes substantial bequests and devises in kind not feasible for two reasons:

(1) Clients are more likely to want to give shares of the total value of their wealth to particular beneficiaries, rather than a lengthy list of specific assets of fluctuating value; and

(2) The form in which wealth is held changes from time to time as assets are acquired and disposed of during the client's life, leaving specific bequests and devises vulnerable to disposition of the subject matter.

Therefore specific bequests are most common in disposing of jewelry and other valuable tangibles, such as works of art, antiques, automobiles, and yachts. Specific bequests of shares of cooperative housing corporations and devises of residential real property are also quite common.

---

5. For a discussion of this technique, see ¶ 4.07 supra.

6. For a discussion of this technique, see ¶ 4.01[1][a] supra.

7. For a discussion of this technique, see ¶ 4.01[1][b] supra.

8. "Specific property" is defined in Reg. § 1.663(a)–1(b) supra.

9. Such a bequest may be more complicated than it appears if the item bequeathed is community property, as the survivor has a vested one-half interest in it. This may unintentionally create a "widow's election" will. See ¶ 18.03[3] infra.

10. See Reg. § 1.1014–4(a).

[2] Sums of Money

Although often handled routinely and simply with cash on hand in the estate, a bequest of a sum of money may produce more complex results from an income tax standpoint than a bequest of specific property. Either by agreement with the legatee or pursuant to authority conferred by the will or by local law, such legacies are often satisfied by delivering property to the legatee instead of paying him cash. The satisfaction of a pecuniary legacy with property results in recognition of gain or loss to the estate.[11] Since the estate generally has a new basis in the decedent's property under § 1014,[12] only the post-death appreciation or depreciation is recognized.

Unless the gift is of a "specific sum" within the meaning of § 663(a)(1), the distribution of money or property in satisfaction of it may cause estate income to be taxed to the distributee under § 662.

[3] Shares of Residue

Still a different set of income tax rules governs bequests of shares of residue. An authorized distribution in kind to residuary legatees does not cause gain or loss to be realized by the estate, as no dollar obligation of the estate is being satisfied.[13] But a non-pro rata distribution not authorized by the will or local law but, rather, by agreement between the executor and the beneficiaries is treated as a pro rata distribution followed by a taxable exchange between them.[14]

In addition, a distribution of residue will cause the legatee to be taxed on a share of estate distributable net income (DNI) for the year in which the distribution is made.[15] Thus, if the client wants the executor to be in a position to make distributions that will not carry out estate income, the residuary legatees should also be given specific property or a specific sum of money within the meaning of § 663(a)(1). If, in a given taxable year of the estate, the executor distributes to a legatee only such specific property or specific sum, the distribution will not carry out estate income for the year to him.

A distribution of property as part of a residuary bequest that causes the legatee to be taxed on a share of estate DNI may cause the property to have a different basis in the legatee's hands from that which it had in the hands of the executor.[16] In an appropriate case, the result may be to minimize capital gains from appreciated property that is distributed to legatees, similar to such use of distributions to trust beneficiaries.[17] Such use of bequests is limited, however, by the relatively short period of adminis-

---

11. See William R. Kenan, Jr. v. Commissioner, 114 F.2d 217, 40–2 USTC ¶ 9635 (2nd Cir. 1940); Reg. § 1.1014–4(a)(3).

12. For a discussion of assets denied a new basis under § 1014, see ¶ 4.03[1] supra.

13. Reg. § 1.1014–4(a)(3).

14. The conclusion rests on Rev. Rul. 69–486, 1969–2 CB 159, dealing with a distribution

to trust beneficiaries, but presumably it applies to legatees as well.

15. See § 662(a)(2) and Reg. §§ 1.662(a)–2, 1.662(a)–3 for the manner in which such shares are determined.

16. See ¶ 4.07 supra.

17. Id.

tration of estates,[18] as compared to trusts, and by the fact that legatees may be receiving distributions of property with a fair market value substantially higher than the estate's distributable net income for the year in which the distribution is made.[19]

¶ 17.02   DISCLAIMERS AND ELECTIONS BY BENEFICIARIES

A disclaimer is the refusal by a beneficiary to accept an interest in property.   Ideally, clients should keep their wills current, with frequent revisions to reflect changes in their assets and in the needs and tax positions of their beneficiaries.   If a client (and his advisor) are conscientious in this respect, there is less need for a disclaimer by a beneficiary to be made for the purpose of improving the client's estate plan after he has died.

In practice, plans often are not revised as frequently as they should be to take account of such changes.   And the reason is not necessarily the tendency of clients and their advisors to procrastinate.   A client may become incompetent, and thus lose the ability to make a legally effective change in his estate plan, unless state law authorizes his guardian to make estate-planning transfers on his behalf.[20]   Even if he remains competent and has his plan reviewed and revised as needed, the most omniscient revision may be capable of improvement in the situation that actually develops after his death.

Wills often require a beneficiary to elect between gifts contained in the will and other rights the beneficiary has.   The use of the so-called community property widow's election requires a surviving spouse to acquiesce in the decedent's disposition of her interest in community property in order to receive benefits under his will.[21]   Spouses in non-community-property states also may be required to elect between benefits given to them by a decedent's will and their rights to a forced share of his estate under state law.[22]   In either situation, the spouse gives up one set of rights in order to be entitled to others.

In addition to such required elections between alternative rights, it often is possible under state law for a legatee to disclaim or renounce interests in a decedent's estate even though he receives no other interest as a result, and many states by statute have extended the same privilege to takers of intestate shares as well.[23]   Elections and disclaimers by beneficiaries are important tools of estate planning whose use can often be greatly facilitated by provisions of a client's will or trust agreement.

By means of a disclaimer, a beneficiary may be able to engage in postmortem estate planning to rearrange interests in the client's estate to better

---

18.   See Reg. § 1.641(b)–3(a), limiting recognition of an estate for tax purposes to the time required for its administration.

19.   See ¶ 4.07 supra.

20.   Some state statutes authorize the conservator or guardian to establish, with court approval, an estate plan for his ward. See, e.g., Mass.Gen.Laws Ann., Ch. 201, § 38 (West Supp.1980).

21.   See ¶ 18.03[3] infra.

22.   See, e.g., N.Y. EPTL 5–1.1

23.   See, e.g., N.Y. EPTL 2–1.11.   The prevailing view, in the absence of statute, is that bequests may be disclaimed but intestate shares may not.   See Newman & Kalter, Postmortem Estate Planning 30 (1976).

advantage. Similarly, the client himself may improve his own tax position while he lives by means of disclaimers of interests under the estate plans of others. In either case, instead of receiving an interest and then transferring it, the disclaimant seeks to divert the interest before it reaches him. If the disclaimer is fully recognized as such for federal tax purposes, the resulting shift in property interests does not constitute a transfer for gift, estate or generation-skipping transfer tax purposes. The disclaimant in that situation is regarded as never having had the interest he disclaimed.

In analyzing the use of disclaimers as an estate-planning tool, it is appropriate first to deal with the requirements for their recognition for tax purposes, then with their use by clients with respect to other estates, and finally with provisions to facilitate their use by the client's own beneficiaries.

[1] Recognition of Disclaimers for Federal Tax Purposes

Recognition of disclaimers for federal tax purposes turns on the date of the transfer which created the disclaimed interest, as well as the effectiveness of the disclaimer as a matter of state law. In order to be entitled to such recognition, the disclaimer of an interest created by a transfer made after 1976 must constitute a "qualified disclaimer" under the standards specified in § 2518. If those standards are met, the disclaimer causes Subtitle B of the Code, which includes the estate tax, gift tax, and generation-skipping transfer tax, to be applied as if the interest had never been transferred to the disclaimant.[24] If the interest was created by a transfer made before 1977, whether the disclaimer is entitled to recognition for federal tax purposes is again a question of federal law but is decided without the guidance provided in § 2518 as to what constitutes a "qualified disclaimer."[25] A disclaimer may be recognized for federal tax purposes even though it is not effective as such as a matter of state law. For example, that law may provide a shorter period in which a disclaimer may be made than the period specified in § 2518(b)(2). In that situation, § 2518(c)(3) provides that "a written transfer of the transferor's entire interest in the property" which satisfies § 2518(b)(2) and (3) will be treated as a qualified disclaimer if the transferees would have received the property if a qualified disclaimer had been made.

The holder of a power to vest any portion of trust income or principal in himself generally is treated for income tax purposes as the owner of such portion under § 678(a). Section 678(d), however, makes the rule inapplicable to a power "which has been renounced or disclaimed within a reasonable time after the holder of the power first became aware of its existence." Thus, it is possible that a disclaimer may be timely and effective for federal income tax purposes without being effective for the estate tax, gift tax, and generation-skipping transfer tax.

[a] "Qualified Disclaimers" of Interests Created by Post-1976 Transfers. Section 2518(b) defines a "qualified disclaimer" as an "irrevocable and unqualified refusal" to accept an interest in property (defined in § 2518(c)(2) to include powers) and requires that it be in a writing received by designated persons no later than nine months after (a) the date of the transfer creating

---

24. § 2518(a).

25. H.R.Rep.No. 1380, 94th Cong., 2d Sess. 67–68 (1976).

the interest or (b) the disclaimant's 21st birthday, whichever is later.[26] Such person must not have "accepted the interest or any of its benefits," [27] and the result of the disclaimer must be to cause the interest to pass either to the spouse of the decedent or to someone other than the person making the disclaimer, without any direction on the part of such person.[28]

The provision permitting the disclaimer to cause an interest to pass to the spouse of the decedent was added by § 702(m) of the Revenue Act of 1978.[29] It may be useful in allowing the spouse to disclaim all or part of a marital deduction trust where the effect is to cause the disclaimed portion to pass to a non-marital trust in which she has an income interest. However, in Proposed Regulations, the Commissioner has taken the position that "[i]f the surviving spouse * * * retains the right to direct the beneficial enjoyment of the disclaimed property in a transfer that is not subject to Federal estate and gift tax, such spouse will be treated as directing the beneficial enjoyment of the disclaimed property." [30] Under this view, the spouse's disclaimer would not qualify, if she had a non-general power of appointment over the non-marital trust, unless she also disclaimed the power.[31]

If a disclaimer meets these requirements and, thus, is entitled to recognition as such for purposes of the three federal wealth transfer taxes, it should also be recognized for trust income tax purposes under § 678(d). The converse does not necessarily follow, however. The "reasonable time" specified in § 678(d) does not commence until the holder of the power first becomes aware of its existence; in § 2518, the time clock starts ticking when the transfer that creates the disclaimed interest is made.

Section 2518(c)(1) provides for qualified disclaimers of "an undivided portion of an interest" but does not indicate whether this includes a dollar amount or whether a disclaimant who is not the spouse of the decedent may retain a life estate or other limited interest in the disclaimed property. The Commissioner has taken the position, in Proposed Regulations, that a disclaimant may make a qualifying disclaimer of an income interest while retaining a remainder interest, or vice versa.[32] However, all income interests beneficially owned by one person are to be considered a single interest and all remainder interests shall be similarly viewed.[33]

The Proposed Regulations also recognize a concept of "severable property," which permits a disclaimant to make a qualified disclaimer with respect to a specific item "which can be separated from other property to which it is joined and which, after severance, maintains a complete and independent existence." [34] Thus, some shares of stock may be accepted by a legatee who makes a qualified disclaimer of the remaining shares.[35]

26. See generally Prop.Reg. §§ 25.2518–1 through 25.2518–4, 3 CCH E&GT ¶ 11,920.

27. § 2518(b)(3).

28. § 2518(b)(4).

29. Pub.L.No. 95–600, 92 Stat. 2935.

30. Prop.Reg. § 25.2518–2(e)(2).

31. Prop.Reg. § 25.2518–2(e)(5), *Example* (5).

32. Prop.Reg. § 25.2518–3(a)(i).

33. Id.

34. Prop.Reg. § 25.2518–3(a)(ii).

35. Id.

[b] Disclaimers of Interests Created by Pre-1977 Transfers. In addition to satisfying the varying requirements of applicable state law, the refusal to accept an interest created by a transfer made before 1977 must, in order to be recognized as a disclaimer for gift tax purposes, be "made within a reasonable time after knowledge of the existence of the transfer * * * [and be] unequivocable [sic] and effective under local law." [36] What period of time is "reasonable" is not always clear. In Pauline Keinath v. Commissioner,[37] on the death of a decedent in 1944, a trust had been created to pay income to his widow for life. On her death, the principal was to be divided between the testator's sons. If either son had predeceased the widow, his share was to go to his children. Two months after the widow died, in 1963, one of the sons filed a disclaimer of his interest that the state court held to be effective to cause the remainder interest to pass to the grandchildren. The Commissioner's contention that the disclaimer was not timely and hence was taxable as a gift was rejected. The court stated that an unequivocal disclaimer made by a remainderman within six months of the death of the life beneficiary is made within a reasonable time. On the other hand, in Kathryn S. Fuller,[38] a widow who renounced a three-eighths interest in a testamentary trust 25 years after her husband's death was held to have made a taxable gift. And a legatee who proceeded to exercise a special power of appointment over a renounced interest, as provided in the instrument that created it, likewise made a taxable gift to the appointees.[39]

[2] Disclaimers by a Client of Powers and Interests in Other Estates

Some clients receive powers and interests in other estates that they would be well advised to disclaim, if a disclaimer would be recognized for federal tax purposes under the tests described above. Two of the major uses of disclaimers to save taxes are:

(1) To eliminate an interest which would otherwise keep a gift from qualifying for the marital deduction or charitable deduction; and

(2) To allow property to pass to one or more individuals who will take as a result of the disclaimer, thus permitting the client to make a tax-free gift or an assignment of an income interest which will be effective to shift the taxability of such income.

In the case of a disclaimer of an interest created by a transfer made before 1977, if it is unclear whether the disclaimer will be recognized as such for purposes of the relevant tax, the client may still wish to have the property pass to the individuals who will take as a result of the disclaimer. If so, the disclaimer at least has a chance of avoiding a gift tax which would otherwise apply if the client received the property and then transferred it.

[3] Provisions for Disclaimers in Client's Will or Trust Instrument

The major advantages of an express provision in a will or trust instrument dealing with the consequences of a beneficiary's disclaimer or election are:

---

36. Reg. § 25.2511–1(c).

37. 480 F.2d 57, 73–1 USTC ¶ 12,928 (8th Cir. 1973).

38. 37 T.C. 147 (1961).

39. Rev.Rul. 76–156, 1976–1 CB 292.

(1) To avoid state law consequences that may be inconsistent with the requirements for recognition of the disclaimer as such for federal tax purposes; and

(2) To resolve unsettled questions under state law as to such consequences.

For example, if *F* in his will gives his son (*S*) a general legacy of $100,000 outright and provides a residuary trust under which *S* receives all of the income or may receive income in the discretion of the trustee, a disclaimer of the legacy by *S* may, under state law, cause it to fall into the residue. As *S* is entitled to all (or may receive a portion) of the income from the residuary trust, the disclaimer may not satisfy the requirement of § 2518 that it cause the property to pass to someone other than the disclaimant, *S*. *F*'s will could avoid this result by providing that if *S* disclaimed his legacy, it would pass to his children or to a trust for their exclusive benefit.

In other situations, state law may provide no clear answer as to whether *S* may share in the disclaimed interest. In that case, express provisions in the will may dispell uncertainty and thus (1) make it more likely that *S* will make a disclaimer if it appears advisable for him to do so; and (2) reduce the risk that his doing so will lead to litigation about the effect of the disclaimer.

¶ 17.03 PROVISIONS FOR PAYMENT OF TAXES

The tax clause in a will is important in specifying where the tax burden will ultimately fall or in leaving it to be allocated in accordance with applicable state law. Earlier decisions treated the tax as an expense of administration, payable from the residue.[40] But an increasing number of states, by statute [41] or decision,[42] require the tax to be shared pro rata by persons interested in the taxable estate, except to the extent the decedent otherwise directs in his will. In addition, federal legislation requires such sharing by recipients of insurance [43] and property over which the decedent had a power of appointment requiring its inclusion under § 2041,[44] in the absence of such a contrary direction.

A different rule applies to "qualified terminable interest property" for which a marital deduction was allowed under § 2056(b)(7). Such property is includible in the estate of the recipient spouse under § 2044 even though she had no right to appoint the property or to direct that it be used to pay her estate tax. Section 2207A provides that in the absence of a contrary direction in her will, her estate may recover from the person receiving such property, the amount of the increase in the spouse's estate tax as a result of its inclusion in her taxable estate.

It is quite common to include a tax clause which purports to negate any statutory or judicially required sharing of the federal estate tax burden.

40. See, e.g., YMCA v. Davis, 264 U.S. 47, 44 S.Ct. 291, 68 L.Ed. 558, 1 USTC ¶ 89 (1924); Harrison v. Northern Trust Co., 317 U.S. 476, 63 S.Ct. 361, 87 L.Ed. 407, 43–1 USTC ¶ 10,004 (1943).

41. See, e.g., N.Y. EPTL 2–1.8.

42. See, e.g., Roe v. Estate of Farrell, 69 Ill.2d 525, 14 Ill.Dec. 466, 372 N.E.2d 662 (1978).

43. § 2206.

44. § 2207.

In some instances, this is inappropriate.   If the client has made lifetime transfers that might be includible in his taxable estate,[45] it may be desirable, if the transfers are in fact included, that the transferees bear their respective shares of the federal tax.   Otherwise, the residuary estate may be depleted to pay the tax with respect to lifetime transfers of assets that may have greatly appreciated in value.   Of course, this provision is unnecessary if the residuary legatees are also the recipients of the lifetime transfers, but sometimes the transferees and residuary legatees are different people, particularly if the client has been divorced.

If the client wishes to protect the residuary legatees from possible burdens for taxes attributable to lifetime transfers, the statutes and decisions requiring apportionment of the tax give him a measure of control over the situation.   The tax clause in his will can be limited to taxes imposed on property passing thereunder, leaving the apportionment statute (or decision) effective to throw part of the tax on recipients of any lifetime transfers that may be includible in the taxable estate, if the executor is able to enforce that liability.

---

45.   For example, transfer may be includible under § 2036 or § 2038 because of an interest or power retained or possessed at his death, and there remain uncertainties in applying those sections.   See ¶¶ 5.02[4], [5] supra.

Chapter 18

THE MARITAL DEDUCTION AND COMMUNITY PROPERTY

Before the present provisions for joint income tax returns were introduced by the Revenue Act of 1948, spouses in community-property states often had a substantial federal tax advantage. Because income that constitutes community property generally is automatically divided between the spouses, regardless of which spouse earned it,[1] a spouse's income in a community-property state was often taxed at lower rates than an identical amount of income of a spouse in a common-law state. The 1948 Act largely eliminated this difference by taxing the income of spouses who elect to file joint returns as if it were equally divided between them.[2]

The 1948 Act also recognized the automatic estate-splitting that results under state law from acquisition of community property[3] and it sought to extend similar benefits to spouses in common-law states. The Act introduced a marital deduction for both estate tax[4] and gift tax[5] purposes and also introduced elective gift-splitting for married persons.[6] But, on balance, these provisions often fell short, leaving spouses in community-property states in a more favorable estate and gift tax position than their counterparts in common-law states. This discrimination was largely cured by § 403 of the Economic Recovery Tax Act of 1981, which removed the limits on the amounts allowable as a marital deduction for purposes of both taxes.

Before dealing with estate and gift tax aspects of community and separate property, it should be noted that references to spouses in community-property and common-law *states* may be misleading without further explanation. The character of property is controlled by the law of the state in which the spouses reside when the property is acquired.[7] Unless that

---

1. Poe v. Seaborn, 282 U.S. 101, 51 S.Ct. 58, 75 L.Ed. 239, 2 USTC ¶ 611 (1930). But see § 66, discussed in note 2 infra.

2. The automatic income-splitting under community property laws has been held to cause a spouse to be taxable on income earned by her husband while she was living separate and apart from him and had no control over his income. See Aimee D. Bagur v. Commissioner, 603 F.2d 491, 79-2 USTC ¶ 9607 (5th Cir. 1979). Spouses in common-law states do not incur such liabilities if they do not sign joint returns.

Section 66 has reversed the result in the Bagur case, for spouses who satisfy the section's requirements. It applies to calendar years beginning after 1980.

3. Section 351(a) of the 1948 Act repealed § 811(e)(2) of the Internal Revenue Code of 1939, under which the full value of community property, rather than merely a one-

half interest, was sometimes includible in a decedent's estate.

4. § 2056. For a discussion, see ¶ 16.01[1].

5. § 2523. For a discussion, see ¶ 6.03[1][c].

6. § 2513. For a discussion, see ¶ 6.03[1][b].

7. See Rau v. Rau, 6 Ariz.App. 362, 432 P.2d 910 (1967); Rozan v. Rozan, 49 Cal.2d 322, 317 P.2d 11 (1957). The result of the rule is that if a married person buys land in Washington with funds derived from his earnings while domiciled in New York, the land is separate property although it would have been community property if he had bought the land with money earned while domiciled in Washington. Brookman v. Durkee, 46 Wash. 578, 90 P. 914 (1907). If a Washington spouse buys land in a common law state with earnings from temporary work there, the property is community

462

character is changed by the spouses, it remains though they move to another state and take such property with them.[8]   Thus, the relevant distinction is between kinds of property, rather than between states of residence.   The separate property of spouses in community-property states generally is treated in the same manner for federal tax purposes as is separate property of spouses in a common-law jurisdiction, unless it is derived from a conversion of what was formerly community property.

¶ 18.01   PROPERTY INTERESTS THAT QUALIFY

In order to qualify for the marital deduction, an interest in property must be one that

(1) "passes or has passed from the decedent to his surviving spouse," [9]

(2) "is included in determining the value of the gross estate," [10] and

(3) is not disqualified as a "terminable interest." [11]

Because of the importance and complexity of the terminable interest rule, it will be considered separately.

Passing is defined broadly to include almost every way a surviving spouse may receive assets of a decedent as a result of his own action or as a result of the spouse's exercise of rights under local law, such as dower, curtesy, or inheritance.[12]   It even includes property received by the spouse as a result of a "qualified disclaimer" by another beneficiary.[13]

The requirement that property qualifying for the deduction be included in determining the value of the decedent's gross estate rules out certain employee death benefits,[14] individual retirement accounts, retirement annuities, and retirement bonds.[15]   Of course, there is no reason to seek a deduction for items already excluded from the gross estate.   But if the executor has discretion to fund an otherwise qualifying gift to the spouse with assets that do not qualify, the deduction is reduced by the amount of such assets even though the executor does not choose to include any of them

property.   Snyder v. Stringer, 116 Wash. 131, 198 P. 733 (1921).

8.   See Rau v. Rau, note 7 supra;   In re Thornton's Estate, 1 Cal.2d 1, 33 P.2d 1 (1934), holding unconstitutional a former California statute that purported to change into community property certain separate property of spouses moving to California.   However, a later statute, under which certain separate property is treated as quasi-community property for purposes of distribution in a divorce action, was held constitutional in Addison v. Addison, 62 Cal.2d 558, 43 Cal.Rptr. 97, 399 P.2d 897 (1965).   But see the following cases in which courts in common-law states refused to recognize the community-property interest of the surviving spouse in determining the amount subject to state death taxes on the death of a spouse: In re Hunter's Estate, 125 Mont. 315, 236 P.2d 94 (1951); In re Kessler's Estate, 177 Ohio St. 136, 203 N.E.2d 221 (1964); Commonwealth v. Terjen, 197 Va. 596, 90 S.E.2d 801 (1956).

Some common-law states have undertaken to deal with problems arising from changes of residence of spouses between community-property and common-law states by enacting the Uniform Disposition of Community Property Rights at Death Act.   See, e.g., N.Y. EPTL 6–6.1 et seq.

9.   § 2056(a).

10.   Id.

11.   § 2056(b), discussed at ¶ 18.02 infra.

12.   § 2056(c).

13.   See § 2518, discussed at ¶ 17.02 supra.

14.   § 2039(c).   For a discussion of the circumstances under which the exclusion is applicable, see ¶ 21.02[2] infra.

15.   § 2039(e).

in the spouse's gift.[16]　This reduction applies if either disqualified terminable interests may be used or assets that are not included in the gross estate may be used to fund the gift.[17]　To prevent such a potential loss of the deduction, it is common practice to prohibit funding a marital deduction gift with any nonqualifying property.

¶ 18.02 TERMINABLE INTERESTS

Section 2056(b) includes a general disqualification of life estates or other terminable interests.　It applies to any interest passing to the surviving spouse which will terminate or fail "on the lapse of time, on the occurrence of an event or contingency, or on the failure of an event or contingency to occur," if the result is to allow someone else who did not give full consideration for his interest to possess or enjoy any part of the property.　The classic illustration of a disqualified interest is a life estate given to the wife, followed by a remainder given to the children.　But the rule applies to less common estate planning arrangements as well.[18]

As in the other areas of estate planning, the exceptions, discussed at ¶ 18.04 infra, are the most important aspects of the terminable interest rule. The rule is applied strictly and it is crucial for arrangments intended to qualify under an exception to satisfy all applicable requirements.　Otherwise, any possibility, as of the time of the decedent's death, that an interest may pass to someone other than the spouse results in its disqualification for the deduction.[19]　As a result, it is common practice to include provisions which seek to minimize the risk of disqualification as a result of an unintended violation of the rule.

[1] Reason for Disqualification

The reason for disqualification of terminable interests when the marital deduction was introduced by the Revenue Act of 1948 was Congressional concern that the tax lost because of the marital deduction when the first spouse died might not be collected on the death of the surviving spouse. Prior to the 1948 Act, the prevailing pattern of wills often included a life estate to the wife or during widowhood if the client did not wish to continue to provide income after W's remarriage, with remainder to the children. The husband's entire estate was taxed on his death but if the wife survived him, her interest terminated with her death so that the estate could then pass to the children free of any second tax.　Without sacrificing that tax objective, the husband could, if he wished, give the wife a measure of control

---

16. § 2056(b)(2).

17. The Code provision applies only to assets included in the gross estate.　Id.　The Regulations apply the principle to other assets as well.　See Reg. § 20.2056(b)–2(d), *Example*, last sentence.

18. § 2056(b)(1)(C) disallows the deduction for a terminable interest which "is to be acquired for the surviving spouse, pursuant to directions of the decedent," even though no interest in the property subject to the terminable interest passes to anyone other than the spouse.　See Reg. § 20.2056

(b)–1(f).　The classic example is a direction to the executor to purchase an annuity for the wife.　The amount bequeathed to carry out this direction is nondeductible.　See Reg. § 20.2056(b)–1(g), *Example (7)*.　The rule is puzzling, as an annuity contract purchased by H during his lifetime may qualify if no amount is payable to anyone other than W after her death.　Id. *Example (3)*. And, if W uses a qualifying bequest to purchase an annuity, the bequest is not thereby made nondeductible.

19. See § 2056(c), last sentence.

over principal as well as income, as long as such control did not constitute a general power of appointment within the meaning of the predecessors to § 2041 for purposes of the estate tax and § 2514 for purposes of the gift tax.

For example, assume *H*'s estate was $500,000, and his will followed the common pattern. The entire $500,000 would be subject to an estate tax when *H* died but when *W* died, there would be nothing from *H*'s estate to tax if she had spent or given away all of the trust income during her life. The children would receive the trust principal (which might be either more or less than $500,000, reduced by the estate tax paid when *H* died) free of any second estate tax.

[2] Ways to Avoid Disqualification

When the 1948 Act introduced the marital deduction, limited to one-half of the adjusted gross estate, it made possible the tax-free transfer of half the estate when the first spouse died, or $250,000 in the previous example. But that saving normally carries its price. Because of the terminable interest rule, the $250,000 not taxed on *H*'s death will be taxed when *W* dies unless she spends it or gives it away during her lifetime. Thus, the tax-free transfer of the entire estate on the death of the survivor, which was the prevailing pattern before the 1948 Act, normally cannot be achieved without loss of the marital deduction in the estate of the first spouse to die.

H could seek to minimize taxes on W's death despite the terminable interest rule by giving *W* $250,000 outright and the children $250,000. *W* could use her legacy to buy an annuity to pay her a life income. If the annuity had no refund feature, there would be nothing to tax on her death. Or, alternatively, *W* could spend the $250,000 during her life, again leaving nothing taxable in her estate.

Annuities admittedly are, in theory, an attractive way to insure that one does not outlive one's capital. But most commercial annuities are offered on relatively unfavorable terms. Actuarial experience indicates that annuitants live longer than the general population, either because they have one more thing to live for or because the self-selection process keeps many short-lived individuals from applying. This experience is reflected, of course, in premiums charged. And until variable annuities become more generally available, most annuities will be payable in "frozen dollars," which do not change to reflect increases in the cost of living or in security prices. On the other hand, for wives who shun annuities in favor of seeking to spend their principal gradually over the course of their lives, there is always the risk that they may live longer than they anticipate or that the expenses of illness may exceed their expectations.

A life income interest in a trust, on the other hand, offers advantages that are not available if *W* receives, instead, an outright gift of the actuarial value of that interest. Often, she will feel more secure if she has the income from $500,000 instead of $250,000 outright because she knows that the income will last as long as she needs it. Moreover, she may be given limited powers to invade principal as well without permitting her to dissipate the entire trust at an early date. Thus, relatively few wives who receive outright marital deduction gifts use the money to buy an annuity.

Accordingly, a common pattern in estate planning for married clients has continued to include, as a marital deduction gift, a life income interest in trust for the spouse, with a general power of appointment by will, and a gift in default of appointment to the children, rather than outright gifts to the spouse and children of the actuarial value of a life income and remainder interest, respectively. This means, of course, that the part of the estate of the first spouse to die which qualifies for the marital deduction will be taxed on the death of the survivor, unless it is spent or given away during her life.

Many clients continue to dispose of the non-marital portion of their estates in the classic pre-1948 pattern: in trust for W for life (or, alternatively, during her widowhood), with remainder to the children. Although this avoids a second tax on W's death on the non-marital portion, whatever remains in the marital trust will be taxed when she dies. From a tax standpoint, therefore, a more favorable result could be achieved by using up the principal of the marital trust for W's support during her lifetime, instead of requiring that the income of the non-marital trust be paid to her for this purpose. Accordingly, one popular pattern is to authorize such use of the marital trust principal, by giving either W or a disinterested trustee the power to invade principal for her benefit, and to make distributions of both income and principal from the non-marital trust wholly discretionary with the trustee. Under this approach, if the income of the non-marital trust is accumulated and added to principal, it remains available for W's support after the marital trust is exhausted. If the non-marital trust is not needed for this purpose during her lifetime, it will pass on her death to the children tax-free,[20] augmented by whatever income has been accumulated while W lived. A disinterested trustee may even be authorized to make distributions to the children while W is living if the testator does not wish to keep available for W all of the income and principal of the non-marital trust.

The Treasury's concern about loss of revenue if terminable interests qualified for the marital deduction and the common practice of giving wives income interests in trusts could have been accommodated in a number of ways. For example, the marital deduction in the husband's estate could have been treated as a tax-postponement provision, with the balance due when W died without regard to the size of her estate. Or the disqualification of terminable interests could have been correlated with § 2041, dealing with powers of appointment, so that no interest would fail to qualify if W received the kind of power which would cause the property subject to the power to be includible in her estate when she died if she had not disposed of it in her lifetime. However, neither of these approaches was taken in the 1948 Act. Instead, terminable interests were disqualified unless W received (1) income for life; and (2) a general power of appointment which met specified standards.

When the previous limits on the amount deductible were removed by § 403 of the Economic Recovery Tax Act of 1981, repealing § 2056(b) of the Code, provision was made for "qualified terminable interests" under which

---

20. The accumulated income may, however, be subject to an additional tax under the throwback rule. §§ 665–667. For a discussion, see ¶ 11.02 supra.

W would receive income for life but need not be given any power to dispose of the property.[21] The explanation in the House Ways and Means Committee Report was in part as follows:

> " * * * unless certain interests which do not grant the spouse total control are eligible for the unlimited marital deduction, a decedent would be forced to choose between surrendering control of the entire estate to avoid imposition of estate tax at his death or reducing his tax benefits at his death to insure inheritance by the children.[22]

Such interests are deductible at the election of the decedent's executor.[23] If such an election is made, the deduction is allowed for the entire value of the property in which the interest exists, not merely that which passes to the wife.[24] The corollary of an election to have a terminable interest qualify for the marital deduction is that the wife's disposition of her interest during her life is treated as a transfer of such property by her for gift tax purposes.[25] If she retains the interest until her death, the property in which her interest existed is included in her gross estate,[26] with a right to recover from the recipients of such property the increase in her estate tax which such inclusion causes.[27]

¶ 18.03 RELATIVE TAX BURDENS UNDER MARITAL DEDUCTION AND COMMUNITY PROPERTY

Until the limitations on the amount allowable as a marital deduction for gift and estate tax purposes were removed by § 403 of the Economic Recovery Tax Act of 1981, residents of community property states enjoyed a significant advantage. Income constituting community property is automatically split between the spouses without constituting a gift for gift tax purposes. In order to achieve an equivalent splitting of income which is not community property, the spouse who is entitled to the income must make a transfer to the other spouse. That transfer, unless it merely discharges a legal obligation of the transferor, is a gift for gift tax purposes. As long as there were limitations on the amount allowable as a gift tax marital deduction, the interspousal transfer could reduce the transferor's unified credit for gift and estate tax purposes and might even incur a gift tax.

Removal of the previous limitations on the gift tax marital deduction eliminates the legal discrimination just referred to, as spouses now are free to transfer property back and forth without federal gift tax consequences, without regard to whether the transferred property is community or separate. Whether, as a practical matter, the end result will be lower transfer tax burdens for residents of community property or common law states

21. § 2056(b)(7).

22. H.R.Rep. 97–201, 97th Cong. 1st Sess. 1, 160 (1981).

23. § 2056(b)(7)(B)(v).

24. § 2056(b)(7)(A).

25. § 2519.

26. § 2044.

27. § 2207A, discussed at ¶ 17.03 supra.

depends on the extent to which the freedom to make interspousal transfers is used effectively to minimize total transfer tax burdens.

If equalizing the taxable estates of husband and wife in fact reduces the combined transfer taxes on the two estates, a community property regime would be more likely to achieve such reduction than the common law system of separate ownership of property by married persons. The automatic estate-splitting under community property tends to limit the difference in the size of the spouses' estates without requiring any action by them. Although spouses in common law states could act to achieve such estate-splitting, experience indicates that many couples will not, but instead will let the law take its course. Moreover, even though there is an unlimited marital deduction for federal gift tax purposes, there may be no similar freedom from state gift taxes on transfers between spouses. However, the previous discussion illustrated why equalization of estates through the use of marital deduction gifts does not necessarily reduce the total transfer tax burden.[27a]

Thus, whether the automatic estate-splitting of community property is more advantageous from a tax standpoint than the controlled estate-splitting possible through transfers which qualify for the gift tax or estate tax marital deduction, depends upon the individual client's tax position and estate-planning objectives. These objectives are more likely to be served by such automatic estate-splitting if the spouse who benefits does not already have (and may not be expected to acquire from other sources) substantial assets or income of her own. The most important aspect of this comparison is that clients procrastinate in acting to take advantage of the gift tax and estate tax marital deduction; there is no similar delay in the estate-splitting provided by law under a community property regime.

Three areas in which discrimination between residents of community property and common law states persists are:

(1) The basis adjustment for the survivor's interest in community property;

(2) The methods sometimes used in valuing undivided interests in community property; and

(3) The tax treatment of the community property "widow's election."

The first two areas of difference in the tax treatment of the two kinds of marital property ownership clearly favor residents of community property states. The tax treatment of the widow's election is a more complex affair. It may offer important tax savings for the widow, but it exposes the other party to the transaction to potential adverse income tax consequences.

[1] The Basis Adjustment for the Survivor's Interest in Community Property

The basis adjustment for the survivor's interest in community property is a unique advantage that has no counterpart in common-law states. Under § 1014, the basis of property included in a decedent's estate generally is adjusted to its fair market value as of the date of his death (or alternate

---

27a. See ¶ 16.01[1] supra.

valuation date, if elected for estate tax purposes).[28]　This may result in either a basis "step-up" or "step-down," depending upon whether the value of a particular asset was more or less than its basis before the decedent died.　Over the years, however, as asset values have been pushed up by inflation and other causes, the tendency has been for the adjustment to result in a step-up rather than a step-down.　The result of the adjustment is to exempt from income tax any appreciation that occurs between the acquisition of property by a decedent and the date of his death, as well as to provide an increased basis for depreciation if the property is depreciable.

The basis adjustment applies generally to all property included in a decedent's estate, both community and separate, except for appreciated property transferred to a decedent within one year of his death.　If such property (or the proceeds of its sale) passes from the decedent to the transferor (or his spouse), he will have only his original basis, rather than the value on the decedent's death.[29]　The advantage for spouses in community-property states arises from the fact that the basis of all of the community property is adjusted when the first spouse dies,[30] although only the decedent's one-half interest is included in his gross estate.　Spouses in common law states can obtain a comparable basis adjustment only if the property in question is owned by the first spouse to die.　If they are able to forsee which spouse will die first, the other spouse may transfer all of her appreciated assets to the prospective decedent in anticipation of obtaining a basis adjustment on his death.　But even if the spouses' forecast of their relative mortality is correct, transfers within one year of the death of the first to die will not achieve the desired basis adjustment.[31]　Thus in order to obtain equivalent income tax advantages, spouses in a common law state not only must make transfers of assets on the basis of an accurate forecast as to who will die first, but must do so at least a year before that death occurs.　Again, a state gift tax may be an impediment.　The automatic basis adjustment for the survivor's interest in community property eliminates any need to engage in this guessing game.

[2] Valuation of Undivided Interests in Community Property

Valuation of undivided interests in community property is another area in which the tax laws favor spouses in community property states.　If a decedent and his spouse owned stock or other assets as community property, it is necessary to determine whether the asset should be valued as one-half of a combined block or as a separate one-half interest.　For example, if H and W own 55 percent of the voting stock of a close corporation, on the death of H, should his interest be valued as if it were a minority interest of 27½ percent, or as one-half of a controlling majority interest of 55 percent? Treatment as a minority interest may result in a discount, while treatment as part of a majority interest may result in the value being increased by a control premium.[32]

28.　See ¶ 4.03 supra.

29.　§ 1014(e), discussed at ¶ 4.03[1] supra.

30.　§ 1014(b)(6). For an argument that the community property basis adjustment under § 1014(b)(6) does not offer any unjus-

tified advantage, see Martin, "Community Property and Basis—The Equalization Is Not Complete," 1 Comm.Prop.J. 18 (1974).

31.　See note 29 supra.

32.　For a discussion, see ¶ 5.02[1][c] supra.

In Estate of Mary F. S. Bright v. United States,[33] the Fifth Circuit, over six dissents, refused to include any control premium in valuing such a one-half interest in a 55 percent block of corporate stock. The court declined to apply a doctrine of family attribution for this purpose on the ground that the doctrine is "logically inconsistent with the willing buyer-seller rule set out in the regulations." [34] But the Commissioner nonacquiesced in a similar Tax Court holding.[35]

Spouses in common law states who seek a similar minority discount may be able to achieve comparable results for estate tax purposes by transferring a one-half interest so that only a minority interest remains to be valued in the transferor's estate. But the price for making such a transfer is loss of the basis adjustment for the transferred interest on the transferor's death. If the subject matter were community property, the basis of the interests of both the decedent and the survivor would be adjusted, without requiring that any lifetime transfer be made.[36]

[3] The Community Property "Widow's Election"

The term "widow's election" is commonly used to refer to the situation in which one spouse (assumed here to be the husband (H)) provides in his will for two alternative dispositions of his share of the community property. A typical provision is a bequest of his share of the community property in trust, with directions to the trustee to pay his wife (W) the trust income for her life if she agrees to transfer her share of the community property to the same trust. Upon W's death, the trust principal goes to the children of H and W or continues to be held in trust for their benefit. H's will provides further that if W does not agree to transfer her share to the trust, she will not be a beneficiary of the trust and will receive no interest in H's share. Many variations on this basic pattern are possible, but it illustrates the tax consequences of the election provision.

Of course, H's will cannot deprive W of her share of the community property without her consent. But she may be compelled to choose between transferring her share to the trust and receiving all of the trust income for her life, or keeping her share and receiving no part of H's share or the income it produces.[37]

Some commentators have viewed the tax consequences of the election as being highly favorable to W in some circumstances. The result may be to allow her share of the community property to pass on her death to her children free, in whole or in part, from both gift tax and estate tax. Despite

---

33. 81–2 USTC ¶ 13,436 (5th Cir. 1981). For a discussion of the problem, see Featherson, Parsons & Vaughan, "Estate Tax Valuation of a Community Property Interest in Corporate Stock: The Controversy Continues," 7 Comm.Prop.J. 181 (1980).

34. 81–2 USTC at 18,991.

35. Estate of Elizabeth M. Lee, 69 T.C. 860 (1978), nonacq. 1980-1 CB 2. See also

Ralph Sundquist v. United States, 74–2 USTC ¶ 13,035 (E.D.Wash.1974).

36. See ¶ 18.03[1] infra.

37. See, e.g., Estate of Resler, 43 Cal.2d 726, 278 P.2d 1 (1954); Dakan v. Dakan, 125 Tex. 305, 83 S.W.2d 620 (1935); Andrews v. Kelleher, 124 Wash. 517, 214 P. 1056 (1923).

these savings for *W*, the potential income tax consequences for the other party to the transaction (whether that party is viewed as being *H*'s estate or a trust under *H*'s will) make the widow's election a hazardous estate-planning tool.[38]

[a] Gift Tax Consequences

For gift tax purposes, *W*'s election to transfer her share of the community property to the trust is a gift of the remainder interest in her share to the children, who will receive the trust property on her death. However, in determining the amount of the gift, *W* is permitted to offset the value of what she has received—a life interest in *H*'s share—against the value of what she transferred to the children.[39] Whether or not the value of what she transfers is greater than that of what she gives depends upon her age when *H* dies.

> *Example 18.1.* Assume that *W* is 68 years old when *H* dies and that the value of the community property at that time is $1 million. The Commissioner's tables, based on actuarial calculations, give a present value to that which *W* has transferred—a remainder to the children to take effect on her death—of approximately 49 percent of her $500,000 share of the community property, or $245,000. The same tables give a value for that which *W* has received from *H*'s estate—a life interest in H's share of the community property—of approximately 51 percent of his $500,000 share, or $255,000. When these two amounts are offset, the net result is that *W* has received property worth more than that which she transferred, and that therefore she has made no taxable gift. Her transfer to the children was for "adequate and full consideration."[40]

The result would be quite different if *W* were age 72 when *H* died. In that situation, the Commissioner's tables value the interest she has transferred at $280,000 and that which she has received at only $220,000. The difference of $60,000 is a gift for purposes of the gift tax.

Some commentators have suggested that *W* may avoid liability for gift tax if *H*'s will gives her enough control over the trust to make the transfer of her interest in the community property incomplete for gift tax purposes. Such control may take the form of a limited power of appointment, for example. However, the result may be merely to postpone liability for gift tax. A subsequent release of the power will be a completed gift, with no reduction for the value of the consideration received by *W* when she elected to accept the provisions of *H*'s will.[41]

---

38. See ¶ 18.03[3][c] infra.

39. See § 2512(b); Commissioner v. Mildred I. Siegel, 250 F.2d 339, 57–2 USTC ¶ 11,731 (9th Cir. 1957); Zillah Mae Turman, 35 T.C. 1123 (1961), acq. 1964–2 CB 7; Estate of Isabelle M. Sparling, 60 T.C. 330 (1973), acq. and non-acq. 1978–1 CB 2, 1978–1 CB 3, rev'd on other grounds 552 F.2d 1340, 77–1 USTC ¶ 13,194 (9th Cir. 1977). It should be borne in mind that if any item, such as the federal estate tax, is payable out of the decedent's share of the community property, it will affect the computation of the relative values of the life estate and remainder interests.

40. See § 2512(b).

41. Myra B. Robinson, 75 T.C. No. 29 (1980). See also Estate of Bluma Steinman, 69 T.C. 804 (1978), in which *W* received a general testamentary power of appointment over a trust as a result of her election to take under *H*'s will. Property subject to the power was held to be includible in her taxable estate, with no reduction for consideration received by her.

[b] Estate Tax Consequences

The estate tax consequences of the widow's election are less clear because of differing interpretations by the courts of the relevant estate tax provision, § 2043. This section deals with transfers otherwise includible in the gross estate under §§ 2035–2038 or under § 2041, for which insufficient consideration was received by the transferor to come within the exception in each of those sections for certain transfers for "full consideration." Section 2043 requires inclusion of the property transferred, reduced by the value of the consideration received.

In interpreting "full consideration," some cases use the same test that is applied for gift tax purposes.[42] If the value of what W transferred—the remainder interest in her share of the community property—is no more than the value of her life interest in H's share, then the transfer was for "adequate and full consideration" and no part of W's share of the community property is included in her estate when she dies. This would be the result if, in *Example 18.1*, W was 68 years old when H died.

Under this view, if the comparison of values shows that W received less than what she transferred, then her transfer was for less than "full consideration" and is governed by § 2043. Section 2043 requires inclusion of the value of the transfer as of the date of the transferor's death, reduced by the value of that which was received. For example, if, in *Example 18.1*, W was age 72 when H died, the remainder interest her children received was worth $60,000 more than W's life interest in H's share of the community property. Therefore, her estate would include the full value of her share less the value of the life interest in H's share that she received. Assuming that the value of the trust assets did not change between H's death and W's death, the result is that $500,000 is included in W's estate, reduced by the value of her life interest in H's share of the community property.

Other cases use a different "adequacy of consideration" test for estate tax purposes from that described above for the gift tax. These cases compare the *full* value of what W transferred in trust (not merely the actuarial value of the children's remainder following her retained life estate) with the actuarial value of the life interest she received in H's share.[43] This comparison inevitably leads to the conclusion that the transfer was not for "adequate and full consideration" because the full value of W's share is always greater than the life interest W receives in H's share. Under this view, W's estate always includes the value of her share of the community property at the time of her death as a transfer for insufficient consideration within the meaning of § 2043, with a deduction for the value of the interest in H's share that she received.

Under either view of the "adequacy of consideration" test for estate tax purposes, all or part of W's share of the community property passes to the children without being subjected to gift tax or estate tax.[44]

42. See, e.g., Estate of Lela B. Vardell v. Commissioner, 307 F.2d 688, 62–2 USTC ¶ 12,089 (5th Cir. 1962); Estate of Daisy F. Christ, 54 T.C. 493 (1970), aff'd with respect to certain income tax aspects 480 F.2d 171, 73–1 USTC ¶ 9,454, 12,930 (9th Cir. 1973).

43. See, e.g., United States v. Howard Past, 347 F.2d 7, 65–1 USTC ¶ 12,317 (9th Cir. 1965); Estate of Lillian B. Gregory, 39 T.C. 1012 (1963). For a criticism of the Past case, see Stephens, Maxfield & Lind, Federal Estate & Gift Taxation ¶ 4.15[2][b] (1978).

[c] Income Tax Consequences

The income tax consequences for *W* if she makes the election are relatively favorable.   The basis adjustment for her interest in community property provided by § 1014(b)(6) eliminates any gain, at least if the exchange is deemed to take place as of *H*'s death (or within the six months following his death, if the alternate valuation date is elected for estate tax purposes).[45]   In addition, *W*'s income tax on the income she received from *H*'s share is reduced because she is allowed an amortization deduction from income to permit her to recover, over her estimated life expectancy, her cost of acquisition of the income interest.   Such cost is the remainder in her share, which she was required to transfer to the children.[46]

Serious unresolved questions as to the income tax consequences for *H*'s estate or a trust under *H*'s will, whichever entity is seen as the transferor of the life interest in *H*'s one-half of the community property, make the widow's election a hazardous estate-planning tool.[47]   It has been suggested that such consequences for the other party to the transaction may be either of the following:

(1) The transfer of the life interest in *H*'s share of the community property may trigger the immediate recognition of income by *H*'s estate or the trust under his will, with the amount received (the remainder interest in *W*'s one-half) taxable as ordinary income in the year of the transaction; [48] or

(2) The transfer may be a capital transaction, but with the transferred life interest having a basis of zero, so that the amount received (the remainder interest in *W*'s one-half) is taxable as capital gain, with no basis deduction.[49]

---

44. There is some support for valuation methods other than those noted in the text above.   In cases where standard actuarial calculations that determine values as of the date of the transfer are not feasible, courts have used a "hindsight" approach to determine the value of *W*'s life interest in *H*'s share of community property.   See, e.g., Estate of Lela B. Vardell v. Commissioner, 307 F.2d 688, 62–2 USTC ¶ 12,089 (5th Cir. 1962), where the court held that the lesser of the actuarial value of the life estate *W* received or of the actual dollar amounts she received would be used, because *W*'s "life" interest was to terminate on her remarriage.   See also Paul Nourse v. Riddell, 143 F.Supp. 759, 56–2 USTC ¶ 11,637 (S.D.Cal.1956), in which the court used the actual value of the amounts that a widow received because the applicable actuarial information was extremely outdated.

45. See ¶ 18.03[1] supra.

46. See Estate of Daisy F. Christ, 54 T.C. 493 (1970), aff'd with respect to the valuation of the interest the widow received, 480 F.2d 171, 73–1 USTC ¶¶ 9,454, 12,930 (9th

Cir. 1973); Alice B. Gist v. United States, 423 F.2d 1118, 70–1 USTC ¶ 9,309 (9th Cir. 1970); Bedie L. Kuhn v. United States, 392 F.Supp. 1229, 75–1 USTC ¶ 9,454 (S.D. Tex.1975).

47. For a more detailed discussion of these potential tax consequences, see Wilson, "The Widow's Election Viewed in the Light of the Federal Tax Reform Act of 1976 and the California Probate Code Revision of 1975," 28 Hastings L.J. 1435, 1441 (1977), reprinted in 5 Comm.Prop.J. 60, 63 (1978); Browerman, "Disposition of Community Property: Should One Spouse Receive a Life Estate in Other's Half?," 40 J.Tax 116 (1974).   The latter commentator suggests an alternative plan designed to avoid the problems described in the text.

48. See Commissioner v. P. G. Lake, Inc., 356 U.S. 260, 78 S.Ct. 691, 2 L.Ed.2d 743, 58–1 USTC ¶ 9428 (1958), indicating that a transfer of a term interest may require the immediate recognition of the amount received in exchange as ordinary income.

49. See § 1001(e).

Until the income tax treatment of the transaction has been resolved, there is a substantial risk of adverse tax consequences in using the widow's election.

[d] Use of Election in Common-Law States

Use of a similar election arrangement in common-law states has been suggested.[50]   However, in that context, the election mechanism raises the tax problems described above and others as well.   For income tax purposes, W's separate property is not given the basis adjustment provided by § 1014(b)(6) for the survivor's interest in community property, so that W may realize gain when she exchanges a remainder in her separate property for a life estate in H's.   And for estate tax purposes, transfers by H which give W only a life interest, do not qualify for the estate tax marital deduction unless H's executor elects to treat the life estate as a "qualified terminable interest." [51]   If he makes that election, the property qualifies for the marital deduction but is included in W's estate when she dies.[52]   There is no similar problem in the community property situation because the survivor's half-interest is excluded from the decedent's estate without regard to any marital deduction requirements.[53]

¶ 18.04 EXCEPTIONS TO DISQUALIFICATION OF TERMINABLE INTERESTS

The terminable interest rule is subject to five exceptions:

(1) The spouse may be required to survive for a limited period.[54]

(2) The spouse may be given a life estate in and a general power of appointment over property.[55]

(3) A trust exclusively for the spouse and her estate may be created.[56]

(4) A "qualified terminable interest" may be created.[57]

(5) A "qualified charitable remainder trust" may be created.[57a]

Literally, (3) is not an exception.   Rather, the so-called "estate trust" is outside the definition of a terminable interest.   This follows from the requirement for disallowance, that an interest pass to someone other than the spouse or her estate.[58]   It is discussed here because it may be used as an alternative to the power of appointment trust referred to at (2).

---

50. See Miller & Martin, "Voluntary Widow's Election: Nation-Wide Planning for the Million Dollar Estate," 1 Cal.W.L.Rev. 63 (1965).

51. § 2056(b)(7).

52. See § 2044.

53. If H does seek to qualify for the deduction, the amount allowable is reduced by any interest W is required to surrender in order to receive the marital deduction gift. See United States v. Stapf, ¶ 18.07 infra; Reg. § 22.2056(b)–4(b).   For a discussion, see ¶ 18.07 infra.

54. § 2056(b)(3).

55. § 2056(b)(5).   A similar arrangement for a life insurance, endowment, or annuity contract qualifies.   See § 2056(b)(6).

56. See Reg. §§ 20.2056(c)–2(b)(1)(i), 20.2056(e)–2(b)(1)(ii), 20.2056(c)–2(b)(1)(iii).

57. § 2056(b)(7).

57a. § 2056(b)(8).

58. § 2056(b)–(1)(A).

58. For a discussion, see ¶ 18.04[3] infra.

[1] Spouse Required to Survive for Limited Period

Section 2056(b)(3) allows a qualifying interest to be made terminable on the death of the surviving spouse if she dies within "a period not exceeding [six] months after the decedent's death, or * * * as a result of a common disaster resulting in the death of the decedent and the surviving spouse, or * * * in the case of either such event * * * ." If the interest does in fact terminate as a result of the death of the spouse, no deduction is allowable. But if she survives, the possibility that the interest might have terminated does not result in disqualification.

The provision is useful in permitting reduction or elimination of a qualifying gift to the spouse if she survives the decedent for a relatively short period. In that situation, the marital deduction will not have achieved any major deferral of estate tax and the spouse will have had only a brief opportunity to reduce her taxable estate by lifetime gifts. However, if the taxable estate of the surviving spouse would otherwise be substantially smaller than that of the decedent, it may be desirable to provide a marital gift to her even though she does not survive for more than six months. Such a gift, by reducing the disparity between the two taxable estates which would otherwise exist, may achieve a reduction in total estate taxes. A so-called "equalization clause" may be used to limit the amount of the marital gift to that which is required to equalize the size of the two taxable estates.[58]

[2] Spouse Given Life Estate and General Power of Appointment

The most common way to qualify a gift in trust for the marital deduction is to give the spouse a life estate and a general power to appoint the property by her will. This statutory exception to the terminable interest rule [59] requires that she be given income for life from the entire interest, or a specific portion thereof, and a power to appoint the entire interest, or such specific portion, exercisable in favor of the spouse or her estate. The power of appointment must be exercisable by her "alone and in all events." [60] However, it may be either a power to appoint by will or during life; she need not have both.[61]

Most clients who satisfy the statutory requirement in this way give the spouse a general power to appoint by will and not by deed. This power may be supplemented by a non-general power to appoint during her life, to withdraw limited amounts of principal, or both.[62] Such restrictions on the spouse's powers during her life may produce income tax savings by keeping her from being taxable on all or part of any capital gains realized by the trust.[63] It also reduces the risk that the power may be exercised by the spouse irrevocably without a full and mature consideration of all relevant factors.

The required right to income is satisfied if the trust gives the spouse "substantially that degree of beneficial enjoyment of the trust property

58. See ¶ 18.05[4] infra.

59. § 2056(b)(5).

60. Id., last sentence.

61. See Reg. § 20.2056(b)–5(g)(1).

62. For a discussion, see ¶¶ 12.01[2], 12.01[3] supra.

63. This would follow if she does not have a power to vest income or principal in herself within the meaning of § 678. For a discussion, see ¶ 11.03 supra.

during her life which the principles of the law of trusts accord to a * * * life beneficiary * * * ." [64] A major problem has been the treatment of unproductive property. The Regulations provide:

> * * * a power to retain trust assets which consist substantially of unproductive property will not disqualify the interest if the applicable rules for the administration of the trust require, or permit the spouse to require, that the trustee either make the property productive or convert it within a reasonable time * * * .[65]

Often it may be undesirable to compel the trustee to convert unproductive property if the spouse is willing to have it retained in the trust, even though such retention reduces her income. Indeed, such retention may save income taxes, if the property may be expected to appreciate and the appreciation will ultimately be realized for tax purposes by someone in a lower income tax bracket than the spouse.[66] Thus, it may be preferable to authorize the trustee to retain unproductive property but to provide that it shall not be retained for more than a reasonable period without the consent of the spouse.

There should be no serious problem in creating the required power of appointment in favor of the spouse. A large number of cases deal with the question of whether or not such a power has been given where what the spouse received was a power to invade or consume trust principal.[67] In many instances, the statutory requirement was not satisfied and the deduction disallowed.[68] Such failures, however, should not arise if a general power of appointment is created in express terms.[69]

Similarly, the income requirement can be satisfied by naming the spouse as income beneficiary if other provisions do not unduly restrict her rights as such.[70] But minor departures from the norm under local law may result in loss of the deduction.[71]

To guard against all such risks, it is common practice to include provisions which seek to avoid an unintended failure to satisfy both the income and power of appointment requirements.[72]

---

64. See Reg. § 20.2056(b)–5(f)(1).

65. See Reg. § 20.2056(b)–5(f)(4).

66. A subsequent sale of such property by the trustee may cause such appreciation to be taxable to the trust, rather than to the spouse, if she has no power to vest principal in herself. See § 678(a)(1). Alternatively, the property may not be sold until the trust terminates and distribution is made to other beneficiaries after the death of the wife, when there will be a new basis under § 1014.

67. See, e.g., Jane G. Piatt v. Gray, 321 F.2d 79, 63–2 USTC ¶ 12,160 (6th Cir. 1963).

68. See, e.g., Estate of Ralph G. May v. Commissioner, 283 F.2d 853, 60–2 USTC

¶ 11,976 (2d Cir. 1960), cert. denied 366 U.S. 903 (1961); Reg. § 20.2056(b)–5(g)(3).

69. But see Rev. Rul. 76–502, 1976–2 CB 273 (power to appoint by will does not, under Maryland law, include power to appoint to holder's estate and hence does not qualify for the marital deduction).

70. See Reg. § 20.2056(b)–5(f)(1).

71. See e.g., Rev. Rul. 72–283, 1972–1 CB 311 (deduction disallowed where income earned in preceding year payable quarterly in the following year).

72. For a discussion, see ¶ 18.06 infra.

COMMISSIONER v. ESTATE OF BOSCH

Supreme Court of the United States, 1967.
387 U.S. 456, 87 S.Ct. 1776, 18 L.Ed.2d 886, 67–2 USTC ¶ 12,472.

Mr. Justice CLARK delivered the opinion of the Court.

These two federal estate tax cases present a common issue for our determination: Whether a federal court or agency in a federal estate tax controversy is conclusively bound by a state trial court adjudication of property rights or characterization of property interests when the United States is not made a party to such proceeding.

* * * We hold that where the federal estate tax liability turns upon the character of a property interest held and transferred by the decedent under state law, federal authorities are not bound by the determination made of such property interest by a state trial court.

I.

(a) No. 673, Commissioner v. Estate of Bosch.

In 1930, decedent, a resident of New York, created a revocable trust which, as amended in 1931, provided that the income from the corpus was to be paid to his wife during her lifetime. The instrument also gave her a general power of appointment, in default of which it provided that half of the corpus was to go to his heirs and the remaining half was to go to those of his wife. In 1951 the wife executed an instrument purporting to release the general power of appointment and convert it into a special power. Upon decedent's death in 1957, respondent, in paying federal estate taxes, claimed a marital deduction for the value of the widow's trust. The Commissioner determined, however, that the trust corpus did not qualify for the deduction under § 2056(b)(5) of the 1954 Internal Revenue Code and levied a deficiency. Respondent then filed a petition for redetermination in the Tax Court. The ultimate outcome of the controversy hinged on whether the release executed by Mrs. Bosch in 1951 was invalid—as she claimed it to be—in which case she would have enjoyed a general power of appointment at her husband's death and the trust would therefore qualify for the marital deduction. While the Tax Court proceeding was pending, the respondent filed a petition in the Supreme Court of New York for settlement of the trustee's account; it also sought a determination as to the validity of the release under state law. The Tax Court, with the Commissioner's consent, abstained from making its decision pending the outcome of the state court action. The state court found the release to be a nullity; the Tax Court then accepted the state court judgment as being an "authoritative exposition of New York law and adjudication of the property rights involved," 43 T.C. 120, 124, and permitted the deduction. On appeal, a divided Court of Appeals affirmed. It held that "[t]he issue is * * * not whether the federal court is 'bound by' the decision of the state tribunal, but whether or not a state tribunal has authoritatively determined the rights under state law of a party to the federal action." 363 F.2d, at 1013. The court concluded that the "New York judgment, rendered by a court which had jurisdiction over parties and subject matter, authoritatively settled the rights of the parties, not only for New York, but also for purposes of the application to those rights of the relevant provisions of federal tax law." Id., at 1014. It declared that since the state court had held the wife to have a general power of appointment under its law, the corpus of the trust qualified for the marital deduction. We do not agree and reverse.

(b) No. 240, Second National Bank of New Haven, Executor v. United States.

Petitioner in this case is the executor of the will of one Brewster, a resident of Connecticut who died in September of 1958. The decedent's will, together with a codicil thereto, was admitted to probate by the Probate Court for the District of Hamden, Connecticut. The will was executed in 1958 and directed the payment "out of my estate my just debts and funeral expenses and any death taxes which may be legally assessed * * * ." If further directed that the "provisions of any statute requiring the apportionment or proration of such taxes among the beneficiaries of this will or the transferees of such property, or the ultimate payment of such taxes by them, shall be without effect in the settlement of my estate." The will also provided for certain bequests and left the residue in trust; one-third of the income from such trust was to be given to decedent's wife for life, and the other two-thirds for the benefit of his grandchildren that were living at the time of his death. In July of 1958, the decedent executed a codicil to his will, the pertinent part of which gave his wife a general testamentary power of appointment over the corpus of the trust provided for her. This qualified it for the marital deduction as provided by the Internal Revenue Code of 1954, § 2056(b)(5). In the federal estate tax return filed in 1959, the widow's trust was claimed as part of the marital deduction and that was computed as one-third of the residue of the estate before the payment of federal estate taxes. It was then deducted, along with other deductions not involved here, from the total value of the estate and the estate tax was then computed on the basis of the balance. The Commissioner disallowed the claimed deduction and levied a deficiency which was based on the denial of the widow's allowance as part of the marital deduction and the reduction of the marital deduction for the widow's trust, by requiring that the estate tax be charged to the full estate prior to the deduction of the widow's trust. After receipt of the deficiency notice, the petitioner filed an application in the state probate court to determine, under state law, the proration of the federal estate taxes paid. Notice of such proceeding was given all interested parties and the District Director of Internal Revenue. The guardian *ad litem* for the minor grandchildren filed a verified report stating that there was no legal objection to the proration of the federal estate tax as set out in the application of the executor. Neither the adult grandchildren nor the District Director of Internal Revenue filed or appeared in the Probate Court. The court then approved the application, found that the decedent's will did not negate the application of the state proration statute and ordered that the entire federal tax be prorated and charged against the grandchildren's trusts. This interpretation allowed the widow a marital deduction of some $3,600,000 clear of all federal estate tax. The Commissioner, however, subsequently concluded that the ruling of the Probate Court was erroneous and not binding on him, and he assessed a deficiency. After payment of the deficiency, petitioner brought this suit in the United States District

Court for a refund. On petitioner's motion for summary judgment, the Government claimed that there was a genuine issue of material fact, i.e., whether the probate proceedings had been adversary in nature. The District Court held that the "decrees of the Connecticut Probate Court * * * under no circumstances can be construed as binding and conclusive upon a federal court in construing and applying the federal revenue laws." 222 F.Supp. 446, 457. The court went on to hold that under the standard applied by the state courts, there was no "clear and unambiguous direction against proration," and that therefore the state proration statute applied. Id., at 454. The Court of Appeals reversed, holding that the decedent's will "would seem to be clear and unambiguous to the effect that taxes were to come out of his residual estate and that despite any contrary statute the testator specifically wished to avoid any proration." 351 F.2d, at 491. It agreed with the District Court that, in any event, the judgment of the State Probate Court was not binding in the federal court.

* * *

III.

The problem of what effect must be given a state trial court decree where the matter decided there is determinative of federal estate tax consequences has long burdened the Bar and the courts. This Court has not addressed itself to the problem for nearly a third of a century. In Freuler v. Helvering, 291 U.S. 35, 54 S.Ct. 308, 78 L.Ed. 634 (1934), this Court, declining to find collusion between the parties on the record as presented there, held that a prior *in personam* judgment in the state court to which the United States was not made a party, "[o]bviously * * * had not the effect of *res judicata*, and could not furnish the basis for invocation of the full faith and credit clause * * *." At 43, 54 S.Ct. at 311. In *Freuler's* wake, at least three positions have emerged among the circuits. The first of these holds that

> " * * * if the question at issue is fairly presented to the state court for its independent decision and is so decided by the court the resulting judgment if binding upon the parties under the state law is conclusive as to their property rights in the federal tax case * * *." Gallagher v. Smith, 223 F.2d 218, at 225.

The opposite view is expressed in Faulkerson's Estate v. United States, 301 F.2d 231. This view seems to approach that of Erie R. Co. v. Tompkins, 304 U.S. 64, 58 S.Ct. 817, 82 L.Ed. 1188 (1938), in that the federal court will consider itself bound by the state court decree only after independent examination of the state law as determined by the highest court of the State. The Government urges that an intermediate position be adopted; it suggests that a state trial court adjudication is binding in such cases only when the judgment is the result of an adversary proceeding in the state court. * * *

We look at the problem differently. First, the Commissioner was not made a party to either of the state proceedings here and neither had the effect of *res judicata*, Freuler v. Helvering, supra; nor did the principle of collateral estoppel apply. It can hardly be denied that both state proceedings were brought for the purpose of directly affecting federal estate tax liability. Next, it must be remembered that it was a federal taxing statute that the Congress enacted and upon which we are here passing. Therefore, in construing it, we must look to the legislative history surrounding it. We find that the report of the Senate Finance Committee recommending enactment of the marital deduction used very guarded language in referring to the very question involved here. It said that "proper regard," not finality, "should be given to interpretations of the will" by state courts and then only when entered by a court "in a bona fide adversary proceeding." S.Rep.No. 1013, Pt. 2, 80th Cong., 2d Sess., 4. We cannot say that the authors of this directive intended that the decrees of state trial courts were to be conclusive and binding on the computation of the federal estate tax as levied by the Congress. If the Congress had intended state trial court determinations to have that effect on the federal actions, it certainly would have said so—which it did not do. On the contrary, we believe it intended the marital deduction to be strictly construed and applied. Not only did it indicate that only "proper regard" was to be accorded state decrees but it placed specific limitations on the allowance of the deduction as set out in § 2056(b), (c), and (d). These restrictive limitations clearly indicate the great care that Congress exercised in the drawing of the Act and indicate also a definite concern with the elimination of loopholes and escape hatches that might jeopardize the federal revenue. This also is in keeping with the long-established policy of the Congress, as expressed in the Rules of Decision Act, 28 U.S.C.A. § 1652. There it is provided that in the absence of federal requirements such as the Constitution or Acts of Congress, the "laws of the several states * * * shall be regarded as rules of decision in civil actions in the courts of the United States, in cases where they apply." This court has held that judicial decisions are "laws of the * * * state" within the section. Erie R. Co. v. Tompkins, supra; Cohen v. Beneficial Loan Corp., 337 U.S. 541, 59 S.Ct. 1221, 93 L.Ed. 1528 (1949); King v. Order of United Commercial Travelers, 333 U.S. 153, 68 S.Ct. 488, 92 L.Ed. 608 (1948). Moreover, even in diversity cases this Court has further held that while the decrees of "lower state courts" should be "attributed some weight * * * the decision [is] not controlling * * *" where the highest court of the State has not spoken on the point. King v. Order of United Commercial Travelers, supra, at 160–161, 68 S.Ct. at 492. And in West v. American Tel. & Tel. Co., 311 U.S. 223, 61 S.Ct. 179, 85 L.Ed 139 (1940), this Court further held that "an intermediate appellate state court * * * is a datum for ascertaining state law which is not to be disregarded by a federal court *unless it is convinced by other persuasive data that the highest court of the state would decide otherwise.*" At 237, 61 S.Ct. at 183 (Emphasis supplied.) Thus, under some conditions, federal authority may not be bound even by an intermediate state appellate court ruling. It follows here then, that when the application of a federal statute is involved, the decision of a state trial court as to an underlying issue of state law should *a fortiori* not be controlling. This is but an application of the rule of Erie R. Co. v. Tompkins, supra, where state law as announced by the highest court of the State is to be followed. This is not a diversity case but the same principle may be applied for the same reasons, viz., the underlying substantive rule involved is based on state law and the State's highest court is the best authority on its own law. If there be no decision by that court then federal authorities must apply what they find to be the state law after giving "proper regard" to relevant rulings of other courts of the State. In this respect, it may be said to be, in effect, sitting as a state court. Bernhardt v. Polygraphic Co., 350 U.S. 198, 76 S.Ct. 273, 100 L.Ed. 199 (1956).

We believe that this would avoid much of the uncertainty that would result from the "non-adversary" approach and at the same time would be fair to the taxpayer and protect the federal revenue as well.

The judgment in No. 240 is therefore affirmed while that in No. 673 is reversed and remanded for further proceedings not inconsistent with this opinion. It is so ordered.

*   *   *

[Dissenting opinions of Justices HARLAN, DOUGLAS and FORTAS omitted.]

ESTATE OF FRANCIS S. TILYOU v. COMMISSIONER

United States Court of Appeals, Second Circuit, 1972.
470 F.2d 693, 73–1 USTC ¶ 12,900.

MOORE, Circuit Judge:

*   *   * The Commissioner disallowed a marital deduction for the personalty which passed under the residuary clause of the will of Francis S. Tilyou because he found that the will created a terminable interest in the residuary estate.[73] This created a tax deficiency in the amount of $112,600.21. The Tax Court upheld the Commissioner's decision. We reverse.

I.

Francis S. Tilyou left his entire estate to his wife. His will also provides:

> In the event, however, of the death of my wife herein named before me, or *before she shall have become entitled to any part or share of my residuary estate*, then my said residuary estate shall be paid to my children. *   *   * (emphasis added)

The Commissioner here argues that this "entitled to" clause meant that if Mrs. Francis S. Tilyou had died before distribution, the residuary estate would have passed to the children of Francis S. Tilyou. He, therefore, decided that her interest in the estate was a terminable one under section 2056(b) and disallowed a marital deduction as to the personalty included in the residuary estate.

*   *   *

---

73. All of Francis S. Tilyou's property passed under the residuary clause except that required to pay his "just debts, funeral and testamentary expenses." The Commissioner allowed the marital deduction as to the real property included in the residuary estate since, under the law of the appropriate state, New York, title to real property passes at the instant of death. [Citations omitted.]

II.

We must now consider whether the "entitled to" clause in the will of Francis S. Tilyou created a terminable interest within the meaning of 2056(b), so that the marital deduction for the personalty which passed in the residuary estate of this will should be disallowed.

New York law, in theory, controls the determination of this question, Commissioner v. Bosch, 387 U.S. 456, 87 S.Ct. 1776, 18 L.Ed.2d 886 (1967); *see* Estate of Horton v. Commissioner, 388 F.2d 51 (2d Cir. 1967), but from the briefs of the parties and our own research we are satisfied that there are no New York cases which have construed a similar clause.   *   *   *

By long settled law in New York a legatee takes only an equitable title to personalty passing under the residuary clause of a will; it is the executor who takes legal title.   In re Starbuck, 251 N.Y. 439, 443, 167 N.E. 580 (1929).   The legatee does not gain full legal title to this property until all estate creditors have been satisfied.   Blood v. Kane, 130 N.Y. 514, 517, 29 N.E. 994 (1892).   This is true even where, as here, there is a sole legatee who is also the sole executor.   Id.

Where a New York will contains either an "entitled to possession" or an "entitled to distribution" clause, that will creates a terminable interest which falls squarely within section 2056(b).   Personal property passing under such a clause is, therefore, not to be considered when computing the marital deduction available to the estate created by such a will.

By applying the rule applicable to "entitled to possession" and "entitled to distribution" clauses to the "entitled to" clause in the Francis S. Tilyou will, the Commissioner determined that this clause created a terminable interest in the residuary estate and therefore disallowed the deduction.

While there are no New York cases interpreting a simple "entitled to" clause, the estate has cited Brewster v. Gage, 280 U.S. 327, 50 S.Ct. 115, 74 L.Ed. 457 (1930) to support its argument that this clause means only "entitled as of right" to the property included in the residuary estate.

> Upon the death of the owner, title to his real estate passes to his heirs or devisees.   A different rule applies to personal property. Title to it does not vest at once in heirs or legatees.   [citation omitted]   But *immediately upon the death of the owner there vests in each of them the right to his distributive share* of so much as shall remain after proper administration and the right to have it delivered upon entry of the decree of distribution.   *   *   *   *The decree of distribution confers no new right;* it merely identifies the property remaining, evidences right of possession in the heirs or legatees and requires the administrators or executors to deliver it to them.   The legal title so given relates back to the date of death.   [Citations omitted.]   Petitioner's right later to have his share of the residue vested immediately upon testator's death. 280 U.S. at 334, 50 S.Ct. at 116.   (emphasis added)

The opinion of this Circuit in *Brewster*, which the Supreme Court affirmed, includes even more direct language in support of the estate's argument. After noting that legal title to personalty vests in the personal representative of the deceased as of the date of his death, the opinion continued:

But a legatee under a will * * * acquires that *to which he is entitled* at the instant of the testator's death. Brewster v. Gage, 30 F.2d 604, 605 (1929). (emphasis added)

These Brewster opinions can be read to support the estate's argument here, although the legal question actually involved in *Brewster* was the federal income tax law question of when stock received under a will is "acquired" for the purpose of computing gain or loss on the disposition of that stock. While this case did not determine whether an "entitled to" clause creates a "terminable interest" in a New York will, it is indicative that equitable title, at least, vested as of the date of death. * * *

* * * Since New York law does not tell us whether an "entitled to" clause creates a terminable interest, we believe it appropriate to consider the circumstances which were known to Francis S. Tilyou when he made his will so that we may determine exactly what he did intend by including this clause.

* * *

[Discussion of evidence of the testator's intentions omitted.]

As already established there are no cases interpreting the effect of an "entitled to" clause in a New York will. Given the uncertain impact of this phrase in New York law, the receptiveness of New York courts to extrinsic evidence to determine the circumstances known to the testator when he drew his will, and the substantially uncontroverted explanation of the reasons for including this clause in the will (which explanation clearly established that Francis S. Tilyou did not *intend* to create a terminable interest in his widow), we believe that the clause should not be read to create a terminable interest in this will.

* * *

Since the law of New York is not clear as to the meaning of the questioned clause, since the origin of that clause had nothing to do with creating a terminable interest, and since the Commissioner, in effect, concedes that this is so, we conclude that petitioner is entitled to a marital deduction as to the personalty under the residuary clause of the will of Francis S. Tilyou.

NORTHEASTERN NAT'L BANK v. UNITED STATES

Supreme Court of the United States, 1967.
387 U.S. 213, 87 S.Ct. 1573, 18 L.Ed.2d 726, 67–1 USTC ¶ 12,470.

Mr. Justice FORTAS delivered the opinion of the Court.

The issue in this case is whether a bequest in trust providing for the monthly payment to decedent's widow of a fixed amount can qualify for the estate tax marital deduction under § 2056(b)(5) of the Internal Revenue Code of 1954, 26 U.S.C.A. § 2056(b)(5). That section allows a marital deduction from a decedent's adjusted gross estate of up to one-half the value of the estate in respect to specified interests which pass to the surviving spouse. Among the interests which qualify is one in which the surviving spouse "is entitled for life to * * * all the income from a specific portion [of the trust property], payable annually or at more frequent intervals, with

power in the surviving spouse to appoint   * * *   such specific portion
* * * ."

* * *

At the date of decedent's death, the value of the trust corpus created by his will was $69,246.   The will provided that his widow should receive $300 per month until decedent's youngest child reached 18, and $350 per month thereafter.   If the trust income were insufficient, corpus could be invaded to make the specified payments; if income exceeded the monthly amount, it was to be accumulated.   The widow was given power to appoint the entire corpus by will.

On decedent's estate tax return, his executor reported an adjusted gross estate of $199,750.   The executor claimed the maximum marital deduction of one-half the gross estate, $99,875, on the ground that qualified interests passing to the wife exceeded that amount.   The value of the property which passed to the widow outright was $41,751.   To this the executor added the full value of the trust, $69,246.   The Commissioner, however, determined that the trust did not qualify for the marital deduction because the widow's right to the income of the trust was not expressed as a "fractional or percentile share" of the total trust income, as the Treasury Regulation, § 20.2056(b)–5(c), requires.   Accordingly, the Commissioner reduced the amount of the allowable deduction to $41,751.   The resulting deficiency in estate tax was paid, a claim for refund was disallowed, the executor sued in District Court for refund, and the District Judge gave summary judgment for the executor.   On appeal, the Court of Appeals for the Third Circuit, sitting *en banc*, reversed, with three judges dissenting. * * *   We reverse.

The basis for the Commissioner's disallowance lay in Treasury Regulation § 20.2056(b)–5(c).   This interpretative Regulation purports to define "specific portion" as it is used in § 2056(b)(5) of the Code: "A partial interest in property is not treated as a specific portion of the entire interest unless the rights of the surviving spouse in income   * * *   constitute a fractional or percentile share of a property interest   * * * ."   The Regulation specifically provides that "if the annual income of the spouse is limited to a specific sum   * * *   the interest is not a deductible interest."   If this Regulation properly implements the Code, the trust in this case plainly fails to qualify for the marital deduction.   We hold, however, that in the context of this case the Regulation improperly restricts the scope of the congressionally granted deduction.

In the District Court, the executor initially claimed that the entire trust qualified for the marital deduction simply because, at the time of trial, the corpus had not yet produced an income in excess of $300 per month, and that the widow was therefore entitled "to all the income from the entire interest."   The District Court rejected this contention, observing that the income from the corpus *could* exceed $300 per month, and in that event the excess would have to be accumulated.   The executor's alternative claim, which the District Court accepted, was that the "specific portion" of the trust corpus whose income would amount to $300 per month could be computed, and a deduction allowed for that amount.

Resolution of the question in this case, whether a qualifying "specific portion" can be computed from the monthly stipend specified in a decedent's will, is essentially a matter of discovering the intent of Congress. The general history of the marital deduction is well known. See United States v. Stapf, 375 U.S. 118, 128, 84 S.Ct. 248, 255, 11 L.Ed.2d 195 (1963). The deduction was enacted in 1948, and the underlying purpose was to equalize the incidence of the estate tax in community property and common-law jurisdictions. Under a community property system a surviving spouse takes outright ownership of half of the community property, which therefore is not included in the deceased spouse's estate. The marital deduction allows transfer of up to one-half of noncommunity property to the surviving spouse free of the estate tax. Congress, however, allowed the deduction even when the interest transferred is less than the outright ownership which community property affords. In "recognition of one of the customary modes of transfer of property in common-law States," the 1948 statute provided that a bequest in trust, with the surviving spouse "entitled for life to all the income from the corpus of the trust, payable annually or at more frequent intervals, with power * * * to appoint the entire corpus" would qualify for the deduction.

The 1948 legislation required that the bequest in trust entitle the surviving spouse to "all the income" from the trust corpus, and grant a power to appoint the "entire corpus." These requirements were held by several lower courts to disqualify for the deduction a single trust in which the surviving spouse was granted a right to receive half (for example) of the income and to appoint half of the corpus. Since there was no good reason to require a testator to create two separate trusts—one for his wife, the other for his children, for example—Congress in 1954 revised the marital deduction provision of the statute to allow the deduction where a decedent gives his surviving spouse "all the income from the entire interest, or all the income from a specific portion thereof" and a power to "appoint the entire interest, or such specific portion." The House Report on this change states that "The bill makes it clear that * * * a right to income plus a general power of appointment over only an undivided part of the property will qualify that part of the property for the marital deduction." The Senate Report contains identical language. There is no indication in the legislative history of the change from which one could conclude that Congress—in using the words "all the income from a specific portion" in the statute, or the equivalent words "a right to income * * * over * * * an undivided part" in the committee reports—intended that the deduction afforded would be defeated merely because the "specific portion" or the "undivided part" was not expressed by the testator in terms of a "fractional or percentile share" of the whole corpus.

Congress' intent to afford a liberal "estate-splitting" possibility to married couples, where the deductible half of the decedent's estate would ultimately—if not consumed—be taxable in the estate of the survivor, is unmistakable. Indeed, in § 93 of the Technical Amendments Act of 1958, 72 Stat. 1668, Congress made "The more realistic rules of the 1954 Code" apply retroactively to the original enactment of the marital deduction in 1948, and opened the statute of limitations to allow refunds or credits for overpayments. Plainly such a provision should not be construed so as to impose unwarranted restrictions upon the availability of the deduction. Yet the Government insists that even where there are well-established principles for computing the principal required to produce the monthly stipend provided for in a trust, a "specific portion" cannot be determined in that way. The "specific portion" must, the Government urges, be expressed in the trust as a fractional or percentile share of the total corpus. The spouse of a testator whose will provides for a specific monthly stipend is deprived of any benefit from the marital deduction, according to the Government's view. But we can find no warrant for that narrow view, in common sense or in the statute and its history.

The Government puts most of its reliance upon a phrase which occurred once in the legislative history of the 1948 enactment. The Senate Report stated that the marital deduction would be available "where the surviving spouse, by reason of her [*sic*] right to the income and a power of appointment, is the virtual owner of the property." The Government's argument is that the deduction was intended only in cases where the equivalent of the outright ownership of a community property State was granted, and that this is what the Senate Report meant by the words "virtual owner." Actually, however, the words were not used in that context at all. The section of the Report from which those words derive deals with the rule that, with minor exceptions, the marital deduction does not apply where any person other than the surviving spouse has any power over the income or corpus of the trust. It is in this sense that the Report described the surviving spouse as a "virtual owner." Hence, the Government's argument that only a grant of the income from a fractional or percentile share subjects the surviving spouse to the vagaries and fluctuations of the economic performance of the corpus in the way an outright owner would be, is simply irrelevant. There is no indication whatsoever that Congress intended the deduction to be available only in such a situation, nor is there any apparent connection between the purposes of the deduction and such a limitation on its availability. Compare Gelb v. Commissioner, 298 F.2d 544, 550–551 (C.A.2d Cir. 1962). Obviously Congress did not intend the deduction to be available only with respect to interests equivalent to outright ownership, or trusts would not have been permitted to qualify at all.

The Court of Appeals advanced a somewhat different argument in support of the Government's conclusion. Without relying upon the validity of the Regulation, the Court of Appeals maintained that a "specific portion" can be found only where there is an acceptable method of computing it, and that no such method is available in a case of the present sort. The Court of Appeals noted that the computation must produce the "ratio between the maximum monthly income [producible by the whole corpus] and the monthly stipend [provided for in the trust]." 363 F.2d 476, 484. The following example was given:

> "If the investment factors involved were constant and it could be determined that the *maximum* income that could be produced from the corpus in a month was, for example, $500 then the relationship between the $300 monthly stipend and the $500 maximum income would define 'specific portion' for marital deduction purposes. i.e.:

"$300 being ⅗ of $500 then ⅗ of $69,245.85 would be the 'specific portion' of the trust corpus from which the surviving spouse would be entitled to the entire income of $300 monthly *under maximum production circumstances.*

"Though in reality it might take the entire corpus to produce the monthly stipend, or even the necessity to invade corpus might be present, nevertheless * * * it could be said, after computing the theoretical maximum income, that the surviving spouse's income interest of $300 monthly represented the investment of ⅗ of the corpus. 'Specific portion' would then be accurately defined for marital deduction purposes." (Italics in original.) 363 F.2d, at 484, n. 17.

The Court of Appeals concluded, however, that the computation could not be made because "[t]he market conditions for purposes of investment are unknown" and, therefore, there are no constant investment factors to use in computing the maximum possible monthly income of the whole corpus. 363 F.2d, at 484.

It is with this latter conclusion that we disagree. To be sure, perfect prediction of realistic future rates of return [74] is not possible. However, the use of projected rates of return in the administration of the federal tax laws is hardly an innovation. Cf. Gelb v. Commissioner, 298 F.2d 544, 551, n. 7 (C.A.2d Cir. 1962). It should not be a difficult matter to settle on a rate of return available to a trustee under reasonable investment conditions, which could be used to compute the "specific portion" of the corpus whose income is equal to the monthly stipend provided for in the trust. As the Court of Appeals for the Second Circuit observed in *Gelb*, supra, "the use of actuarial tables for dealing with estate tax problems has been so widespread and of such long standing that we cannot assume Congress would have balked at it here; the United States is in business with enough different taxpayers so that the law of averages has ample opportunity to work." 298 F.2d, at 551–552.

The Government concedes, as it must, that application of a projected rate of return to determine the "specific portion" of the trust corpus whose income is equal to the monthly stipend allotted will not result in any of the combined marital estate escaping ultimate taxation in either the decedent's or the surviving spouse's estate. The Government argues, however, that if analogous actuarial methods were used to compute as a fixed dollar amount the "specific portion" as to which a qualifying power of appointment is given, where the power in fact granted extends to the whole corpus but the corpus is subject to measurable invasions for the benefit, for example, of a child, the result, in some cases, would be to enable substantial avoidance of estate tax. Whether, properly viewed, the Government's claim holds true, and, if so, what effect that should have upon the qualification of such a trust, is a difficult matter. Needless to say, nothing we hold in this opinion has

---

74. An estimated realistic rate of return which a trustee could be expected to obtain under reasonable investment conditions must be used—absent specific restrictions upon the trustee's investment powers—in order to isolate that "part of the corpus which in [all] * * * reasonable event[s]" will produce no more than the monthly stipend, to paraphrase the court below. 363 F.2d, at 483.

reference to that quite different problem, which is not before us. Cf. Gelb v. Commissioner, supra.

The District Court used an annuity-valuation approach to compute the "specific portion." This was incorrect. The question, as the Court of Appeals recognized, is to determine the amount of the corpus required to produce the fixed monthly stipend, not to compute the present value of the right to monthly payments over an actuarially computed life expectancy. Accordingly, we reverse and remand for further proceedings in conformity with this opinion.

Reversed and remanded.

Mr. Justice STEWART, whom Mr. Justice BLACK and Mr. Justice HARLAN join, dissenting.

*   *   *

The Court holds that the widow in this case had an interest in "all the income from a specific portion" of the trust because the stream of payments to her could be capitalized by the use of assumed interest rates. This capitalized sum is then said to constitute the "specific portion" which qualifies for the marital deduction. A corollary of the Court's theory is that a trust which gave the widow the right to the income from a fixed amount (in dollars) of corpus and the right to appoint the entire corpus would support a marital deduction. But if such a bequest qualifies, then one which limits her power of appointment to only that amount of corpus with respect to which she has income rights will also qualify for the marital deduction. For under the statute, the survivor must have only the right to "all the income from a specific portion   *   *   *   with power in the surviving spouse to appoint   *   *   *   *such* specific portion." (Emphasis added.) The way in which such an estate allows a tax avoidance scheme not available to a community-property couple can be easily illustrated.

Assume a trust estate of $200,000, with the widow receiving the right to the income from $100,000 of its corpus and a power of appointment over that $100,000, and the children of the testator receiving income from the balance of the corpus during the widow's life, their remainders to vest when she dies. Now suppose that when the widow dies the trust corpus has doubled in value to $400,000. The wife's power of appointment over $100,000 applies only to make $100,000 taxable to her estate. The remaining $300,000 passes tax free to the children. Contrast the situation in a community property State. The wife's 50% interest in the community property places $200,000 of the expanded assets in her estate and taxable as such; only $200,000, therefore, passes directly to the children. Thus, the Court's interpretation of "specific portion" affords common-law estates a significant tax advantage that community property dispositions cannot obtain.

By changing "specific portion" from the fractional share, which is both described in the Treasury Regulation and used as the basis for community property ownership, into a lump sum bearing no constant relation to the corpus, the Court allows capital appreciation to be transferred from the wife's to the children's interest in the estate without any tax consequence.

Thus, today's decision is directly opposed to what we have previously recognized as the purpose of the marital deduction:

> "The purpose * * * is only to permit a married couple's property to be taxed in two stages and not to allow a tax-exempt transfer of wealth into succeeding generations. Thus the marital deduction is generally restricted to the transfer of property interests that will be includible in the surviving spouse's gross estate." United States v. Stapf, 375 U.S. 118, 128, 84 S.Ct. 248, 255, 11 L.Ed.2d 195.
>
> * * *

In ruling as it does today the Court not only frustrates the basic purposes of the marital deduction, it also ignores or brushes aside guideposts for deciding tax cases that have been carefully established in prior decisions of this Court. Thus, a 10-year-old interpretation of the statute contained in the Treasury Regulations is held invalid, although we have consistently given great weight to those regulations in the interpretation of tax statutes. See, e.g., United States v. Stapf, 375 U.S. 118, 127, n. 11, 84 S.Ct. 248, 255.

Of even greater importance is the sharp change of attitude toward the marital deduction, which today's decision heralds. The Treasury's interpretation of "specific portion" is held invalid because "Congress' intent [was] to afford a liberal 'estate-splitting' possibility." This finding of "liberalism" in the marital deduction leads the Court to reason that "[p]lainly such a provision should not be construed so as to impose unwarranted restrictions upon the availability of the deduction." * * * But we have previously construed the marital deduction to mean what it says and have not discerned a liberal intent that allows us to write new words into the statute, as the Court does here in changing "specific portion" to "ascertainable amount." For example, in Jackson v. United States, 376 U.S. 503, 510, 84 S.Ct. 869, 873, 11 L.Ed.2d 871, eight members of the Court, speaking through Mr. Justice White, declared that "the marital deduction * * * was knowingly hedged with limitations" by Congress, and "[t]o the extent it was thought desirable to modify the rigors of [such limitations], exceptions * * * were written into the Code." * * *

With this change in approach, uncertainty is now introduced into one of the areas of the law where long-range reliance upon the meaning of a statute is essential. Estate planners and tax lawyers are technicians schooled to view the marital deduction as a tightly drawn, precise provision. They are now shown a totally new statute that is to be construed in the manner of a workman's compensation act. * * *

[3] Trust Exclusively for the Spouse and Her Estate

A surprising result of the 1948 Act was that a trust exclusively for the spouse and her estate is not a terminable interest and therefore need not satisfy the requirements of the life estate and power of appointment exception. This follows from the requirement, for disallowance as a terminable interest, that an interest pass to someone other than the spouse or her estate.[75] Thus, a trust to accumulate income for *W*'s life, with principal

---

75. § 2056(b)(1)(A).

and accumulated income payable on her death to *W*'s estate, qualifies for the deduction even though *W* is not given any kind of power of appointment as such (although the necessary effect of a disposition in favor of her estate is to allow her to dispose of the property by her will).[76] Such so-called estate trusts have been little used, however, partly because of uncertainty as to whether a remainder to the estate of a living individual can be effectively created in some states.[77] Where such uncertainties do not exist, the estate trust may be a useful technique to qualify for the marital deduction if the client does not wish to give *W* an absolute right to trust income, either to protect her income tax position or for non-tax reasons.

Clients who choose the estate trust should not undertake to combine some of its features with those of a power of appointment trust. A trust that provides for accumulation of income for *W*'s life, with a general power to appoint the principal and accumulated income by her will and, to whatever extent not so appointed, to pay such principal and income to her estate, does not qualify under either exception.[78] The accumulation provision is incompatible with the power of appointment trust provision and the power prevents qualification as an estate trust.

[4] "Qualified Terminable Interests"

"Qualified terminable interests" were introduced by § 403 of the Economic Recovery Tax Act of 1981, adding § 2056(b)(7) to the Code. The rationale for providing this alternative method to qualify for the marital deduction has already been described, as well as the mechanisms involved in its use.[79] The following discussion will focus on the requirements which must be satisfied to create the interest.

The basic characteristics of a qualified terminable interest are the same as for a power of appointment marital deduction trust or gift except that the spouse need not be given any power of appointment. All that is required is that she be given the income for her life, as in a power of appointment trust or gift, and that no one have a power to appoint the property to anyone else during her life.[80] Upon election by the decedent's executor,[81] the property in which the qualified terminable interest exists qualifies for the marital deduction to the extent of its full value,[82] not merely the value of the spouse's life estate, with concomitant inclusion of the property in the spouse's estate on her death.[83]

[5] "Qualified Charitable Remainder Trusts"

If the trust is a qualified charitable remainder trust and the only non-charitable beneficiary is the spouse, the terminable interest rule is inappli-

---

76. See Reg. § 20.2056(e)–2(b)(1)(iii).

77. See Fox, "Estate: A Word to be Used Cautiously, if at All," 81 Harv.L.Rev. 992 (1968); Huston, "Transfers to the 'Estate of a Named Person,'" 15 Syracuse L.Rev. 463 (1964). Other reasons include the fact that property bequeathed to *W*'s estate is subject to the claims of her creditors and may be included in computing the commissions of her executor.

78. See Rev.Rul. 75–128, 1975–1 CB 308.

79. See ¶ 18.02[2] supra.

80. See § 2056(b)(7)(B)(ii).

81. See § 2056(b)(7)(B)(v).

82. See § 2056(b)(7)(A).

83. See § 2044.

cable.[84]   A marital deduction is allowed for the annuity or unitrust interest, and a charitable deduction is allowed for the remainder.[85]

¶ 18.05   FORMS OF QUALIFYING GIFTS

In order to qualify for the marital deduction, each form of gift listed below may either be made directly to the spouse or to a trust for her benefit, if the trust satisfies the terminable interest rule (or creates a "qualified terminable interest") or if it is an estate trust:

(1) *A specific bequest or devise*: Grasslands (or all of my Xerox stock) to my wife absolutely.

(2) *A general legacy of a specified amount*: $100,000 to my wife.

(3) *A non-formula fractional share*: One-half of my residuary estate (or of my gross estate) to my wife.

(4) *A formula general legacy*: An amount equal to the smallest amount that, if allowed as a deduction in computing the federal estate tax liability of my estate, would reduce such liability (after taking into account all credits allowed against such tax) to zero,[86] diminished by the value for such purposes of all other items in said gross estate that qualify for said deduction and that pass or have passed to my wife under other provisions of this will or otherwise, all such values to be as finally determined for federal estate tax purposes.

(5) *A formula fractional share of residue*: That fraction of my residuary estate of which the numerator is the smallest amount that, if allowed as a deduction in computing the federal estate tax liability of my estate, would reduce such liability (after taking into account all credits allowed against such tax) to zero,[86a] diminished by the value for such purposes of all other items in said gross estate that qualify for said deduction and that pass or have passed to my wife under other provisions of this will or otherwise, and of which the denominator is the value of my residuary estate, all such values to be as finally determined for federal estate tax purposes.

The first three alternatives listed above are not different from standard testamentary dispositions and present no particular problems when used for a marital deduction gift.   However, since a primary purpose of the marital deduction gift is often to transfer the minimum amount of property to the surviving spouse required to eliminate (or minimize) estate taxes in the decedent's estate, it often is desirable to utilize a formula provision, such as (4) or (5).   Formula provisions were common in estate planning before the limitations on the marital deduction were removed.

---

84. See § 2056(b)(8).

85. H.R.Rep. 97–201, 97th Cong. 1st Sess. 1, 162 (1981).

86. In the relatively rare instances in which death taxes may exceed the amount covered by the client's unified credit, appropriate modifications are necessary if this type of formula is to be applied.   See ¶ 16.01[1] supra.

86a. See note 86 supra.

[1] Reasons for Using Formula Gifts

The reasons for the widespread use of formula gifts before the limitations on the marital deduction were removed are not hard to find. Many clients wanted to qualify for the maximum allowable marital deduction in order to achieve the greatest possible saving in estate taxes. But, at the same time, they did not wish to give the surviving spouse, in a form which qualifies for the deduction, any more than the maximum allowable amount. Such excess, unless spent or given away by the surviving spouse during her lifetime, will be taxed when she dies. Use of a formula also avoided the need to revise the will whenever there was a change in the value of the client's property.

Similar considerations continue to apply despite the removal of limitations on the amount of the deduction. The important difference is that the emphasis today is on limiting the marital gift to the amount required to avoid (or minimize) estate tax for the decedent, or, in some instances, to the amount required to equalize the two estates. If the spouse is independently wealthy and dies shortly after the client, such equalization may minimize total estate taxes because of the progressive rate schedule. But the progression is leisurely, with steps of $250,000 each between $250,000 and $1.5 million, and of $500,000 thereafter to $2.5 million, so that precise equalization of the two estates is not required to minimize total estate taxes. Furthermore, use of such equalization provisions requires appraisal of the survivor's assets, resulting in additional expenses that would not otherwise be incurred until the survivor's death.

If the spouse survives for a longer period, it may be more important to minimize estate taxes when the client dies than to minimize the combined taxes on the two estates that would be paid if the spouse survived only for a short time. Use of the maximum allowable deduction will, in effect, postpone payment of estate taxes until the death of the survivor and amounts to an interest-free loan from the Treasury. And she may be able to minimize estate taxes actually to be paid on her death by means of gifts within the annual exclusion. In addition, the impact of a state death tax, particularly if it is an inheritance tax, may affect what might be an ideal arrangement from the standpoint of federal taxes alone.

Of much greater importance than equalizing estates is the relationship between the marital deduction and the portion of the estate that is free from estate tax because of the unified credit. For a decedent who made no taxable gifts after 1976, that portion is equivalent to an exemption of $225,000 if he dies in 1982. If he survives longer, the portion increases annually until 1987, when it is scheduled to reach $600,000. It may be desirable to bequeath the portion of the estate that is free from estate tax because of the unified credit in a form that will keep it from being taxed on the death of the surviving spouse. For example, the spouse could be given the income from a bequest in trust of this amount, with the principal passing to the children on her death. Or the bequest could be made to the children (or in trust for their benefit), by-passing the wife altogether.

It is not necessary to revise the client's will or trust each year to reflect increases in the portion covered by the unified credit. The marital deduction gift can be defined as the smallest amount required to avoid (or minimize) any estate tax, so that it will automatically be decreased whenever the portion covered by the unified credit increases.

Existing wills and trust agreements which include formula provisions should be reviewed in the light of the removal of the limit on the amount of the marital deduction.   If the will was executed, or the trust created, before September 12, 1981, and expressly provides a maximum allowable marital deduction formula gift, the removal of the limitation on the deduction is inapplicable to the decedent's estate unless:

(1) the formula is amended after September 12 (and before the death of the decedent) to refer specifically to an unlimited deduction; or

(2) a state statute is enacted which construes the formula as referring to an unlimited deduction.[87]

If a will or revocable trust was in existence on June 11, 1976, however, the effect of the transition rule for generation-skipping transfer tax purposes [87a] should be considered before any change is made.

[2] Comparison of Formula Legacies and Formula Fractional Share Gifts

The two basic types of formula provisions are the formula legacy and the formula fractional share.   The formula legacy, like any non-formula bequest of a sum of money, does not change in amount with fluctuations in values of estate assets after the date of death (or alternate valuation date). Some advisors formerly sought to further simplify its operation, and to obtain other advantages as well, by authorizing the legacy to be satisfied with assets at their estate tax values, but this practice has been curtailed.[88] On the other hand, the value of what the legatee receives under a formula fractional share gift will change with every change in the value of estate assets after the relevant date, up to the time the share is delivered to the legatee.   If the residuary estate goes up in value after the date of death (or alternate valuation date), the value of a fractional share of the estate will go up also, and the converse is true on a decline in value.

At first glance, the formula legacy might appear to be the preferable device because its use eliminates any need to account for changes in the values of the assets in the residuary estate in order to determine the effect of such changes on the marital deduction gift.   However, these accounting problems may be minimized if the executor has and exercises the power to make a non-pro rata distribution of assets to different residuary legatees. A non-pro rata distribution not authorized by the will or local law, but rather by agreement between the executor and the beneficiaries, is treated as a pro rata distribution followed by a taxable exchange between them.[89]

An executor using appreciated property to satisfy a pecuniary bequest recognizes gain accruing subsequent to the death of the decedent (or alter-

---

87.   § 403(e)(3), Economic Recovery Tax Act of 1981.

87a.   See ¶ 13.15[2] supra.

88.   ¶ See Rev.Proc. 64–19, 1964–1 CB 682. For a discussion, see ¶ 18.05[3] infra.

89.   The conclusion rests on Rev.Rul. 69–486, 1969–2 CB 159, dealing with a distribution to trust beneficiaries, but presumably it applies to legatees as well.

nate valuation date if elected).[90]　　Thus if the executor delivers such property as part of a formula legacy, the estate will realize income as a result, whereas a similar delivery of appreciated property as part of a formula fractional share gift would not give rise to estate income.[91]　　Of course, the formula legatee acquires a new cost basis for the distributed property equal to the fair market value of the property on the date of the transfer.[92]　　But the new basis is of no importance until the property is sold (unless it is depreciable).

On the other hand, if the residuary assets have appreciated, a formula fractional share gift will be worth more when it is delivered than would a formula legacy.　　As noted above, the marital deduction gift will be taxed again when the surviving spouse dies, unless the property is spent or given away during her lifetime.　　Thus, the survivor's estate taxes may be higher as a result of having received a formula fractional share gift instead of a formula legacy.

It is impossible to generalize as to how these conflicting considerations should be resolved in any given case.　　Informal surveys suggest that the majority of advisors prefer to use the formula pecuniary legacy rather than the formula fractional share gift.

[3] Use of Estate Tax Values for Assets

For a time, some advisors sought the best of both tax worlds by using formula legacy provisions in conjunction with an authorization to the executor to satisfy the legacy by distributing assets valued at their values for estate tax purposes.　　If this were permissible, realization of gain by the estate would be avoided without the accounting complications that may accompany fractional share gifts.　　However, such a provision, if construed literally, would allow the formula legacy to be satisfied with assets having little or no value on the date of distribution, as long as their total value for estate tax purposes equalled the amount of the legacy.

Whether or not such a literal reading of an authorization to distribute assets in satisfaction of a legacy at estate tax values is correct as a matter of state law, the tax avoidance possibilities that the technique might open were unacceptable to the Commissioner.　　If the executor could pick the depreciated assets for delivery to the surviving spouse, leaving the appreciated assets for the non-marital shares in the estate, there would be that much less to be subject to estate tax at the death of the surviving spouse.

Accordingly, Revenue Procedure 64–19 [93] was promulgated to deal with the effect on the marital deduction of provisions authorizing pecuniary bequests to be satisfied in kind with assets at their value as finally determined for federal estate tax purposes.　　It requires, for allowance of the deduction, that the fiduciary must be required "by applicable state law or by the express or implied provisions of the instrument" to distribute assets, including cash, which meet one of the following standards:

90.　The estate generally has a new basis in the decedent's property under § 1014, thus eliminating gain from any per-death appreciation.　For a discussion, see ¶ 4.03 supra. Instances in which the new basis is inapplicable are discussed at ¶ 4.03[1] supra.

91.　Reg. § 1.1014–4(a)(3).

92.　Id.

93.　1964–1 CB 682.

    (1) Such assets have "an aggregate fair market value at the date, or dates, of distribution amounting to no less than the amount of the pecuniary bequest or transfer, as finally determined for Federal estate tax purposes * * * ," or

    (2) Such assets are "fairly representative of appreciation or depreciation in the value of all property thus available for distribution in satisfaction of such pecuniary bequest or transfer * * * ."

In view of this Revenue Procedure, it is highly desirable to provide for valuation of assets distributed in satisfaction of a qualifying pecuniary bequest on the date of distribution.

[4] Use of Equalization Clauses

Occasionally, if the spouse has substantial assets of her own, it may be undesirable to make a qualifying gift large enough to eliminate any estate tax in the husband's estate, as the resulting increase in her taxable estate may more than offset the advantage of reducing that of the decedent. To avoid this result, a so-called "equalization clause" is sometimes used to reduce the marital gift by one-half of the assets of the surviving spouse in order to make the two taxable estates more nearly equal in size. The Commissioner's contention that such a clause makes the marital gift a nonqualifying terminable interest has been rejected.[94]

Whether or not such equalization is in fact desirable depends on many factors, including the length of time the spouse survives the decedent.[95]

ESTATE OF CHARLES W. SMITH v. COMMISSIONER

United States Court of Appeals, Seventh Circuit, 1977.
565 F.2d 455, 77–2 USTC ¶ 13,215.

PER CURIAM.

The Commissioner of Internal Revenue has appealed from an adverse decision of the Tax Court. The Commissioner determined a deficiency in the estate tax of Charles W. Smith's estate in the amount of $646,700.50. The deficiency resulted from a disallowance of $1,330,101.62 of a claimed marital deduction of $1,521,245.86. After contesting the assessed amount, Smith's estate sued for a refund on the ground that the marital deduction should have been allowed.

Decedent's 1967 *inter vivos* trust contained an "equalization clause" under which his surviving spouse would take nothing if the values of assets owned by her at his death were subsequently determined, by calculations that could not be made until one year later, to be in excess of certain amounts. The Commissioner insisted that because the amount passing under this provision might be decreased as a result of valuation changes in the alternate valuation period, the wife's interest was contingent and therefore constituted a "terminable interest" under Section 2056(b)(1) which would fail to qualify for the marital deduction for federal estate tax purposes.

     * * *

94. See Estate of Charles W. Smith v Commissioner, infra; Estate of Vilda S. Laurin v. Commissioner, 645 F.2d 8, 81–1 USTC ¶ 13,398 (6th Cir. 1981).

95. For a discussion see ¶ 16.01[1] supra.

The stipulated facts may be summarized as follows: Charles W. Smith (decedent), a Michigan resident, died in 1970. In 1967, he had established a revocable *inter vivos* trust with the Northern Trust Company of Chicago as Trustee. His federal estate tax return reported a gross estate of about $3,500,000. The assets of the trust amounted to approximately $3,300,000.

On decedent's death, Article IV of the trust divided the trust assets into a "Marital Portion" and a "Residual Portion." The Marital Portion was to be held as a Marital Trust designed to qualify for the marital deduction under the federal estate tax laws pursuant to Section 2056 of the Internal Revenue Code. Under the terms of the Marital Trust, decedent's surviving spouse was to receive all the net income for her lifetime, with a special power of appointment over corpus exercisable by deed and a general power of appointment exercisable by will. Decedent's wife, Alice M. Smith, died shortly more than one year after her husband. The critical provision of Article IV of the trust is the "equalization clause." Its purpose was to equalize the size of the estates of Mr. and Mrs. Smith in order to minimize the total combined federal estate taxes on both estates.

Article IV of the trust, dealing with distribution upon decedent's death, provided for allocating to the Residual Portion any assets with respect to which the marital deduction would not be allowed if allocated to the Marital Portion. Article IV then provided:

"(b) There shall then [after allocation of the Residual Portion] be allocated to the Marital Portion that percentage interest in the balance of the assets constituting the trust estate which shall when taken together with all other interests and property that qualify for the marital deduction and that pass or shall have passed to Settlor's said wife under other provisions of this trust or otherwise, obtain for Settlor's estate a marital deduction which would result in the lowest Federal estate taxes in Settlor's estate and Settlor's wife's estate, *on the assumption Settlor's wife died after him, but on the date of his death and that her estate were valued as of the date on (and in the manner in) which Settlor's estate is valued for Federal estate tax purposes*; Settlor's purpose is to equalize, insofar as possible, his estate and her estate for Federal estate tax purposes, based upon said assumptions." (Emphasis added.)

The equalization clause contained in Article IV(b) is the only one at issue.

Decedent's estate tax return claimed a marital deduction of $1,521,245.86, representing the value of the Marital Trust as determined by the estate, plus the value of certain other property interests passing to Mrs. Smith outside of the trust. The estate determined that had Mrs. Smith died after decedent, but on the same day, her individual gross estate, including all assets received from decedent outside the trust, would have had a value of $667,331.47 on the date of decedent's death. Under this assumed fact situation, the value of Mrs. Smith's gross estate would have been $813,630.17 one year from the date of her husband's death, the alternate valuation date. * * * On that date, the values of both decedent's estate and the assumed estate of his wife were higher than the date-of-death values. Consequently, in accordance with the terms of the trust, the estate utilized date-of-death values for federal estate tax purposes and for computing the value of the assets in the marital trust.

The Commissioner took the position that the property interest passing from decedent to his wife under the trust was a terminable interest under Section 2056(b)(1)　*　*　*　and therefore determined an estate tax deficiency in the amount of $646,700.50.　Of the entire Tax Court, only Judge Irwin agreed that Mrs. Smith's interest was a nondeductible terminable interest, and he "reached this conclusion reluctantly" (66 T.C. at 436) in this case of first impression.

First of all, the Commissioner admits that the equalization clause is not a tax avoidance measure, for estate taxes will still be collected from the estate of each spouse and none of the funds will escape taxation.　The clause does have the effect of minimizing the total combined federal estate taxes on both estates by treating the assets of each spouse as if it were pure community property.　Such a clause is frequently used in estate planning. See 1 Casner, Estate Planning 785 and Supplement (3d ed. 1961).　Government counsel candidly admitted at the oral argument that there are no policy grounds for vitiating such a clause.　This litigation was brought ostensibly because supposedly required by the literal language of Section 2056(b).

As taxpayer has put it (Br. 4–5), if decedent's estate had a value of $2,000,000 on the selected valuation date and Mrs. Smith's "estate" then had a value of $400,000, the amount passing to her under the equalization clause would be $800,000.[96]　The agreed reason for using such a clause is that

> "under the graduated estate tax rate structure, a smaller aggregate estate tax in the estates of husband and wife will be due [the total will be due after the second death] if both estates are in the same estate tax rate bracket than if the estates are in disparate brackets as a result of the deferral of the maximum estate tax from the death of the first spouse, through use of the maximum marital deduction, to the death of the surviving spouse" (Taxpayer's Br. 5).

Since Mrs. Smith had an independent estate in Michigan, a non-community property state, this equalization clause was to achieve a "pure" community property result.　This accorded with the purpose of the marital deduction, which was to put residents of non-community and community property states on an equal footing for estate tax purposes.　See Northeastern Pennsylvania Bank & Trust Co. v. United States, 387 U.S. 213, 219, 87 S.Ct. 1573, 18 L.Ed.2d 726.　This equalization clause would determine the amount of property to be received by Mrs. Smith under the trust.　That amount was meant by decedent to qualify for the marital deduction in his estate and to be taxed in full in his spouse's estate.

The Commissioner contends that because of the remote possibility that Mrs. Smith would receive nothing from the equalization clause bequest, the terminable interest rule of Section 2056(b)(1) applies　*　*　*　At the same time, he admits that a formula fractional share bequest [97] "does qualify for

---

96.　$800,000 is one half the amount by which the value of the decedent's estate exceeds the value of Mrs. Smith's "estate." This would be in lieu of the maximum marital deduction of $1,000,000.

97.　Under such a clause, the numerator of the fraction is the maximum allowable marital deduction and the denominator is the value of the residual estate.　See 66 T.C. at 434 n. 3; 1 Casner, supra, at 795.

the marital deduction" (Br. 15) even though the precise fraction and the value of the fractional share cannot be known until the estate makes its choice of valuation dates and the wife there too can theoretically take nothing. To distinguish the formula fractional marital bequest from Mrs. Smith's interest, the Commissioner asserts that there is an additional factor outside decedent's estate that his trustee had to consider, namely, the valuation of Mrs. Smith's "estate" at the alternate valuation date. But, as Judge Drennen responded, "The only possible effect on the spouse's [Mrs. Smith's] interest from [that] 'additional factor' * * * relates to the *value* of that interest. And even that effect is limited solely to the amount of market fluctuation in the value of the assets in the spouses' 'estate'." (66 T.C. at 431; footnote omitted.) Therefore, the Tax Court rightly concluded that both a formula fractional share bequest and an equalization clause bequest should qualify for the marital deduction.

* * *

As the Tax Court explained, the purpose of the terminable interest rule in Section 2056(b)(1) forbidding a marital deduction is "to limit the marital deduction to the value of interests in property passing from the decedent to his surviving spouse which were interests of such a character that, unless consumed or disposed of prior to the surviving spouse's death, would be taxable in the surviving spouse's estate at her death" (66 T.C. at 423). That purpose is fully satisfied because Mrs. Smith's equalization clause share was taxable in her estate when she died in 1971.

* * *

Judgment affirmed.

¶ 18.06 PROVISIONS TO MINIMIZE THE RISK OF DISQUALIFICATION

An advisor who fails to qualify a gift for the marital deduction may substantially increase his client's estate tax. In a field where the rules are often extremely technical and the stakes may be high, it is not surprising that advisors seek to minimize the risks of disqualification. Provisions designed for this purpose commonly take two major forms:

(1) A direction to the executor to use only assets which qualify for the marital deduction in funding the marital deduction gift;

(2) A general limitation on the powers of fiduciaries, making any power which would preclude the allowance of the marital deduction inapplicable to the gift or trust which is intended to qualify.

Provisions of this general type have been accepted for some purposes by the Commissioner [98] and the courts [99] as a basis for removing doubts that might otherwise exist as to whether a bequest qualifies for the marital

---

[98]. See Rev.Rul. 75–440, 1975–2 CB 372, giving effect to the clause to resolve ambiguity as to whether the decedent intended certain powers to apply to the marital trust, as well as to the non-marital trust.

[99]. See, e.g., Estate of James S. Todd, Jr. v. Commissioner, 57 T.C. 288 (1971), acq. 1973–2 CB 4. See also Estate of Jerome

Mittleman v. Commissioner, 522 F.2d 132, 75–2 USTC ¶ 13,108 (D.C. Cir. 1975): "In light of the all-pervasive influence of the tax laws on estate planning, it seems entirely reasonable for courts to presume, absent contrary language, that testamentary provisions in favor of spouses are designed to qualify for the marital deduction."

deduction. However, neither is a substitute for precision in drafting. For example, broad language giving trustees "all powers that I might exercise as owner of the trust property except to whatever extent such powers must be limited to qualify for the marital deduction" is so vague and indefinite as to invite disallowance of the deduction.[100]

¶ 18.07   VALUATION OF QUALIFYING GIFTS

The amount allowable as a marital deduction is the net value of the gift to the spouse after deducting the amount of any mortgage on the property or any obligation imposed on the spouse in connection with the passing of an interest to her.[101] If, for example, a bequest to the spouse is subject to payment by her of any federal or state death taxes, the amount thereof is deducted in arriving at the net value of the marital deduction gift.[102]

ESTATE OF MILTON S. WYCOFF v. COMMISSIONER

United States Court of Appeals, Tenth Circuit, 1974.   506 F.2d 1144, 74–2 USTC ¶ 13,037,
cert. denied 421 U.S. 1000, 95 S.Ct. 2398, 44 L.Ed.2d 667 (1975).

WILLIAM E. DOYLE, Circuit Judge.

This is a federal estate tax case, and the issue is whether the United States Tax Court ruled correctly in determining that the value of the marital deduction available to the estate must be reduced to the extent of inheritance, estate and transfer taxes that the executor was authorized by the will to pay out of the marital trust even though he was not required in the will to pay it from the marital share.

The will of decedent, Milton S. Wycoff, created two trusts. One was in favor of his wife amounting to 50% of his adjusted gross estate; the other trust dealt with the residue of the estate for the benefit of his son. While he directed that inheritance, estate and transfer taxes were to be paid out of the portion of his estate which was not in the marital trust, he, at the same time, granted the executor a discretion to pay these taxes out of this trust estate if the executor considered it prudent from a business standpoint to do so. Based on this authorization, both the Commissioner and the Tax Court ruled that the amount of the marital deduction had to be reduced by the amount of the death taxes. The executor now seeks reversal of the Tax Court ruling.

Decedent died on March 3, 1966 and his will was admitted to probate on March 30, 1966, Zions First National Bank of Salt Lake City being named as the executor. A large part of the estate was composed of shares in the family corporations. The trust in favor of the wife gave her income for life and the power to appoint the corpus together with accrued and undistributed income. The language of the will was such as to seek to maximize the

---

100. See Letter Rul. 7905088, 3 CCH E&GT ¶ 12,264 (Nov. 1, 1978), refusing to give effect to a savings clause purporting to limit the power of a trustee to whatever extent necessary to prevent loss of the gift tax present interest exclusion.

101. See § 2056(b)(4)(B); Reg. § 20.2056 (b)–4(b).

102. See § 2056(b)(4)(A); Reg. § 20.2056 (b)–4(c). For illustrations of the complex mathematical computation required, see Internal Revenue Service Publication 904, Computing the Interrelated Charitable, Marital, and Orphans' Deductions and Net Gifts.

estate tax deduction available under § 2056 of the Internal Revenue Code. A further provision in the will directed that the liquid assets were so far as possible to be given to the wife's trust; this was so as to avoid her having to participate in the family businesses. The residuary trust in favor of the son was created in ARTICLE VII of the will.

* * *

Though he was given discretion to pay the death taxes out of the wife's trust, the executor has not elected to do so. The Probate Court decreed the distribution of the corpus of the estate to the Zions First National Bank as trustee of the two trusts on December 31, 1968.

Some time later, May 25, 1970, the District Director of Internal Revenue gave the bank notice that there was a deficiency in the amount of $57,458.30. Shortly thereafter, the appellant sought a redetermination of the deficiency by the Tax Court. However, that tribunal ruled that in computing the marital deduction, the value of the interest of the surviving spouse had to be reduced by the amount of the death taxes which could have been paid from the widow's share. The deficiency was ruled to be in the amount of $54,888.31.

* * *

Section 2056(b) provides in part:

(4) *Valuation of interest passing to surviving spouse.*—In determining for purposes of subsection (a) the value of any interest in property passing to the surviving spouse for which a deduction is allowed by this section—

> (A) there shall be taken into account the effect which the tax imposed by section 2001, or any estate, succession, legacy, or inheritance tax, has on the net value to the surviving spouse of such interest;

We are required to determine the value of the deductible non-terminable interest in the property which passed to the surviving spouse. In turn, we must decide whether the executor's *authority* to use marital trust assets for the payment of the state and federal death taxes served to reduce the marital deduction in this amount. The bank contends that § 2056(b)(4) is subject to the interpretation that the marital deduction is to be reduced only to the extent that the federal estate or state inheritance tax was actually paid from or charged to the marital share. Its further claim is that the language of § 2056(b)(4) supports this.

It is pointed out that the provision is entitled "valuation of interest passing to surviving spouse." It refers to the "effect" of death taxes upon the "net value to the surviving spouse." It is argued that the purpose was to restrict the effect on the surviving spouse's marital deduction to the amount of taxes actually paid. The only relevant consideration in applying § 2056(b)(4), so it is argued, is whether the property interest passed to the surviving spouse was in fact utilized to pay the taxes.

The regulations relied on by the bank and quoted below are not germane because the thrust of them is to explain the computation of the marital deduction rather than the effect of the taxes payable out of it.

* * *

The value of the marital deduction and the effect of death taxes upon the extent of the marital deduction are to be determined as a matter of federal law. Thus, the orders of state probate courts are not applicable. In this instance the Utah Probate Court ordered the executor to distribute to the widow's trust 50% of the adjusted gross estate unreduced by any federal estate or Utah inheritance taxes. The court also decreed that such taxes were to be charged to the property not included in the marital trust.[103]

* * * since the will speaks as of the date of death, and since it does authorize the payment of taxes from the marital trust within the executor's discretion, it serves the interest of precision and definiteness as well as avoidance of uncertainty to rule that the authorization to pay death taxes from the marital share by its very existence reduces the marital share.
* * *

* * *

The directive in the will at bar authorizing payment of death taxes dispels the executor's claim that decedent failed to vest authority in the executor to apply marital trust assets to the payments of death taxes. The existence of the authority is out of harmony with the notion that the decedent firmly directed the executor to pay taxes out of funds other than marital ones so as in all circumstances to secure the greatest possible marital deduction. Cf. Bauknect v. Kellogg-Citizens National Bank, 49 Wis.2d 392, 182 N.W.2d 238 (1971).

Although ARTICLE XII of the will expresses a preference for payment of the taxes from that part of the estate not included in the marital trust, this is much less than a positive direction that death taxes be paid from that part of the estate not included in the marital share, and as we view it such an express provision would be necessary to justify a ruling for the executor.
* * *

Since we do not have a positive expression in the will we must rule that § 2056(b)(4) renders the marital share available to the surviving spouse subject to the payment of death taxes. As a result of this, the value of the marital deduction is reduced by the amount of these death taxes.
* * *

[Dissenting opinion of MOORE, J., omitted.]

In Putnam v. Putnam,[104] the court construed the will as placing on the non-marital trust the burden of all inheritance taxes imposed with respect to future interests in the marital trust. This construction was sought by the trustees in response to the contention of the Internal Revenue Service that the burden of state inheritance taxes on such interests would fall on the marital trust, and that the marital deduction should therefore be reduced by the maximum amount of such taxes that would be payable if the surviving

103. Although federal law governs payability of estate tax, the impact of the federal tax is governed by state law. Riggs v. Del Drago, 317 U.S. 95, 63 S.Ct. 109, 87 L.Ed. 106 (1942); Thompson v. Wiseman, 233 F.2d 734 (10th Cir. 1956). Thus, the apportionment of payment of death taxes is governed by state law.

104. 366 Mass. 261, 316 N.E.2d 729 (1974).

spouse appointed the principal to a single individual not closely related to the decedent. However, the court expressed no opinion as to the propriety of the Service's interpretation of the federal tax consequences of its construction of the will in this respect.

UNITED STATES v. STAPF

Supreme Court of the United States, 1963.
375 U.S. 118, 84 S.Ct. 248, 11 L.Ed.2d 195, 63–2 USTC ¶ 12,192.

Mr. Justice GOLDBERG delivered the opinion of the Court.

* * *

Lowell H. Stapf died testate on July 29, 1953, a resident and domiciliary of Texas, a community property jurisdiction. At the time of his death he owned, in addition to his separate estate, a substantial amount of property in community with his wife. His will required that his widow elect either to retain her one-half interest in the community or to take under the will and allow its terms to govern the disposition of her community interest. If Mrs. Stapf were to elect to take under the will, she would be given, after specific bequests to others, one-third of the community property and one-third of her husband's separate estate. By accepting this bequest she would allow her one-half interest in the community to pass in accordance with the will, into a trust for the benefit of the children. It was further provided that if she chose to take under the will the executors were to pay "all and not merely one-half" of the community debts and administration expenses.

The relevant facts and computations are not in dispute. The decedent's separate property was valued at $65,100 and the community property at $258,105. The only debts were community debts totalling $32,368. The administration expenses, including attorneys' fees, were $4,073. If Mrs. Stapf had not elected to take under the will, she would have retained her fully vested one-half interest in the community property ($129,052) which would have been charged with one-half of the community debts ($16,184) and 35% of the administration expenses ($1,426). Thus, as the parties agree, she would have received a net of $111,443.

In fact Mrs. Stapf elected to take under the will. She received, after specific bequests to others, one-third of the combined separate and community property, a devise valued at $106,268, which was $5,175 less than she would have received had she retained her community property and refused to take under the will.

In computing the net taxable estate, the executors claimed a marital deduction under [§ 2056] for the full value of the one-third of decedent's separate estate ($22,367) which passed to his wife under the will. The executors also claimed a deduction for the entire $32,368 of community debts as "claims against the estate" under [§ 2053(a)(3)] and for the entire $4,073 of expenses as "administration expenses" under [§ 2053(a)(2)]. The Commissioner of Internal Revenue disallowed the marital deduction and the deductions for claims and administration expenses insofar as these represented debts (50%) and expenses (35%) chargeable to the wife's one-half of the community. * * * For reasons stated below, we hold that the

Commissioner was correct and that none of the disputed deductions is allowable.

I. THE MARITAL DEDUCTION.

By electing to take under the will, Mrs. Stapf, in effect, agreed to accept the property devised to her and, in turn, to surrender property of greater value to the trust for the benefit of the children. This raises the question of whether a decedent's estate is allowed a marital deduction under [§ 2056(b)(4)(B)] where the bequest to the surviving spouse is on the condition that she convey property of equivalent or greater value to her children. The Government contends that, for purposes of a marital deduction, "the value of the interest passing to the wife is the value of the property given her less the value of the property she is required to give another as a condition to receiving it." On this view, since the widow had no net benefit from the exercise of her election, the estate would be entitled to no marital deduction. Respondents reject this net benefit approach and argue that the plain meaning of the statute makes detriment to the surviving spouse immaterial.

Section [2056(a)] provides that "in general" the marital deduction is for "the value of any interest in property which passes　*　*　*　from the decedent to his surviving spouse." [§ 2056(b)(4)] then deals specifically with the question of valuation:

"(4) Valuation Of Interest Passing To Surviving Spouse.—In determining for the purposes of [§ 2056(a)] the value of any interest in property passing to the surviving spouse for which a deduction is allowed by this section—

*　*　*

"(B) where such interest or property is incumbered in any manner, or where the surviving spouse incurs any obligation imposed by the decedent with respect to the passing of such interest, such incumbrance or obligation shall be taken into account in the same manner as if the amount of a gift to such spouse of such interest were being determined."

The disputed deduction turns upon the interpretation of (1) the introductory phrase "any obligation imposed by the decedent with respect to the passing of such interest," and (2) the concluding provision that "such　*　*　* obligation shall be taken into account in the same manner as if the amount of a gift to such spouse of such interest were being determined."

The Court of Appeals, in allowing the claimed marital deduction, reasoned that since the valuation is to be "as if" a gift were being taxed, the legal analysis should be the same as if a husband had made an *inter vivos* gift to his wife on the condition that she give something to the children. In such a case, it was stated, the husband is taxable in the full amount for his gift. The detriment incurred by the wife would not ordinarily reduce the amount of the gift taxable to the husband, the original donor. The court concluded:

"Within gift tax confines the community property of the widow passing under the will of the husband to others may not be 'netted' against the devise to the widow, and thus testator, were the transfer inter vivos, would be liable for gift taxes on the full value of the devise." 309 F.2d 592, 598.

This conclusion, based on the alleged plain meaning of the final gift-amount clause of [§ 2056(b)(4)(B)], is not supported by a reading of the entire statutory provision. First, [§ 2056(a)] allows marital deduction only for the decedent's gifts or bequests which pass "to his surviving spouse." In the present case the effect of the devise was not to distribute wealth to the surviving spouse, but instead to transmit, through the widow, a gift to the couple's children. The gift-to-the-surviving-spouse terminology reflects concern with the status of the actual recipient or donee of the gift. What the statute provides is a "marital deduction"—a deduction for gifts *to the surviving spouse*—not a deduction for gifts to the children or a deduction for gifts to privately selected beneficiaries. The appropriate reference, therefore, is not to the value of the gift moving from the deceased spouse but to the net value of the gift received by the surviving spouse.

Second, the introductory phrases of [§ 2056(b)(4)(B)] provide that the gift-amount determination is to be made "where such interest or property is incumbered in any manner, or where the surviving spouse incurs any obligation imposed by the decedent with respect to the passing of such interest. * * * " The Government drawing upon the broad import of this language, argues: "An undertaking by the wife to convey property to a third person, upon which her receipt of property under the decedent's will is conditioned, is plainly an 'obligation imposed by the decedent with respect to the passing of such interest.' " Respondents contend that "incumbrance or obligation" refers only to "a payment to be made *out of* property passing to the surviving spouse." Respondents' narrow construction certainly is not compelled by a literal interpretation of the statutory language. Their construction would embrace only, for example, an obligation *on* the property passing whereas the statute speaks of an obligation "*with respect* to the passing" gift. Finally, to arrive at the real value of the gift "such * * * obligation shall be taken into account * * * " In context we think this relates the gift-amount determination to the net economic interest received by the surviving spouse.

This interpretation is supported by authoritative declarations of congressional intent. The Senate Committee on Finance, in explaining the operation of the marital deduction, stated its understanding as follows:

> "If the decedent bequeaths certain property to his surviving spouse *subject*, however, *to her agreement*, or a charge on the property, for payment of $1,000 to X, the value of the bequest (and, accordingly, the value of the interest passing to the surviving spouse) is the value, reduced by $1,000, of such property." S.Rep.No.1030, 80th Cong., 2d Sess., Pt. 2, p. 6. (Emphasis added.)

The relevant Treasury Regulation is directly based upon, if not literally taken from, such expressions of legislative intent. Treas.Reg. [§ 20.2056 (b)–4(b)]. The Regulation specifically includes an example of the kind of testamentary disposition involved in this case:

> "A decedent bequeathed certain securities to his wife in lieu of her interest in property held by them as community property

under the law of the State of their residence.   The wife elected
to relinquish her community property interest and to take the
bequest.   For the purpose of the marital deduction, the value of
the bequest is to be reduced by the value of the community property
interest relinquished by the wife."

We conclude, therefore, that the governing principle, approved by Congress
and embodied in the Treasury Regulation, must be that a marital deduction
is allowable only to the extent that the property bequeathed to the surviving
spouse exceeds in value the property such spouse is required to relinquish.

Our conclusion concerning the congressionally intended result under
[§ 2056] accords with the general purpose of Congress in creating the marital
deduction.   The 1948 tax amendments were intended to equalize the effect
of the estate taxes in community property and common-law jurisdictions.
Under a community property system, such as that in Texas, the spouse
receives outright ownership of one-half of the community property and only
the other one-half is included in the decedent's estate.   To equalize the
incidence of progressively scaled estate taxes and to adhere to the patterns
of state law, the marital deduction permits a deceased spouse, subject to
certain requirements, to transfer free of taxes one-half of the non-community
property to the surviving spouse.[105]   Although applicable to separately held
property in a community property state, the primary thrust of this is to
extend to taxpayers in common-law States the advantages of "estate splitting" otherwise available only in community property States.   The purpose,
however, is only to permit a married couple's property to be taxed in two
stages and not to allow a tax-exempt transfer of wealth into succeeding
generations.   Thus the marital deduction is generally restricted to the
transfer of property interests that will be includible in the surviving spouse's
gross estate.   Respondents' construction of [§ 2056] would, nevertheless,
permit one-half of a spouse's wealth to pass from one generation to another
without being subject either to gift or estate taxes.   We do not believe that
this result, squarely contrary to the concept of the marital deduction, can
be justified by the language of [§ 2056].   Furthermore, since in a community
property jurisdiction one-half of the community normally vests in the wife,
approval of the claimed deduction would create an opportunity for tax reduction that, as a practical matter, would be more readily available to couples
in community property jurisdictions than to couples in common-law jurisdictions.   Such a result, again, would be unnecessarily inconsistent with
a basic purpose of the statute.

Since in our opinion the plain meaning of [§ 2056] does not require the
interpretation advanced by respondents, the statute must be construed to
accord with the clearly expressed congressional purposes and the relevant
Treasury Regulation.   We conclude that, for estate tax purposes, the value
of a conditional bequest to a widow should be the value of the property
given to her less the value of the property she is required to give to another.
In this case the value of the property transferred to Mrs. Stapf ($106,208)
must be reduced by the value of the community property she was required

105.   [Section 403 of the Economic Recovery   amount allowable as a marital deduction.—
Tax Act of 1981 removed the limits on the   ed.]

Westfall Estate Planning 2d Ed. UCB—19

to relinquish ($111,443). Since she received no net benefit, the estate is entitled to no marital deduction.

II.   CLAIMS AGAINST THE ESTATE AND ADMINISTRATION EXPENSES

A.   *Claims Against the Estate*

Section [§ 2053(a)(3)] provides for the deduction from the gross estate of "Such amounts * * * for claims against the estate * * * as are [allowable] by the laws of the jurisdiction * * * under which the estate is being administered * * *." The community debts in this case total $32,368, consisting largely of taxes due for past income. The decedent's will directed that his executors pay "all and not merely one-half" of the community debts. Under Texas law, absent this provision, only one-half of the community debts would be charged to the decedent's half of the community. The issue presented is whether, as a result of the testamentary direction, a deduction may be taken for the entire amount of the community debts as "claims against the estate * * * allowed by" state law.

The first question to consider is whether the claim is of the type intended to be deductible. It cannot be denied that where the executors are directed to pay the debts of another party the substance of the direction is to confer a beneficial gift on that party. Respondents' contentions in effect require that [§ 2053]—designed to allow deductions for "expenses, losses, indebtedness, and taxes"—be construed to authorize tax-free gifts despite the general policy that wealth not be transmitted tax free at death. The provisions of [§ 2053] demonstrate that it was not intended to allow deductions for voluntary transfers that deplete the estate merely because the testator described the transfers or payments as the settlement of "claims" or "debts." This intent is evidenced by the treatment of claims or debts founded upon promises or agreements. The section carefully restricts the deductible amount "in the case of claims against the estate * * * or any indebtedness * * *, when founded upon a promise or agreement, * * * to the extent that they were contracted bona fide and for an adequate and full consideration in money or money's worth. * * *" Absent such an offset or augmentation of the estate, a testator could disguise transfers as payments in settlement of debts and claims and thus obtain deductions for transmitting gifts. As this requirement suggests, a deduction under [§ 2053] should not be predicated solely on the finding that a promise or claim is legally enforceable under the state laws governing the validity of contracts and wills. The claims referred to by the statute are those "claims against" the property of the deceased which are allowed by and enforceable under the laws of the administering State and not those claims created by the deceased's gratuitous assumption of debts attaching to the property of another.

The pertinent Treasury Regulation states that the deductible claims are "such only as represent personal obligations of the decedent * * *" [106] We cannot agree with respondents' contention that the debts chargeable to the wife's community property are "personal obligations" of

---

106. Treas.Reg. 105, § 81.36 (1942), now
Treas.Reg. § 20.2053–4 (1958) * * *

the decedent within the meaning of the Regulation. It is true, as the Court of Appeals stated, that under Texas law the husband, as manager of the community property, was personally liable for the full amount of community debts. 309 F.2d 592, 596. His liability for the portion of debts chargeable to his wife's community property was, however, accompanied by a right over against her half of the community. Ibid. The basic rule of Texas law is that the community is liable for its debts, and accordingly, half the debts attach to the wife's community property. Since the will of the decedent cannot be allowed to define what is an "obligation" or a "claim," where, as in this case, the community is solvent, the debts chargeable to the wife's property cannot realistically be deemed "personal obligations" of the decedent or "claims against" his estate.

The provisions of [§ 2053], like those of [§ 2056] allowing marital deductions, must be analyzed in light of the congressional purpose of equalizing the incidence of taxation upon couples in common-law and community property jurisdictions. If the deductible "claims" were to include all community debts that might be, in a literal sense, "personal obligations" of the husband as surety, then a married couple in a community property State might readily increase their tax-free estate transfers. For example, by borrowing against the value of the community property and then requiring that his executors pay all community debts, the husband could obtain a tax deduction for what would in effect be a testamentary gift to his wife.[107] That gift might or might not qualify for treatment as a marital deduction, but it certainly was not intended to be made deductible by [§ 2053]. A contrary interpretation of [§ 2053(a)(3)] would, in our opinion, generally tend to create unwarranted tax advantages for couples in community property States.

B.　*Administration Expenses.*

The testator's will provided that administration expenses, as well as community debts, should be paid entirely out of his half of the community property. The administration expenses totalled $4,073. Under Texas law an allocable share of these costs was chargeable to the surviving spouse's community property. That allocable share was determined to be 35% or $1,426. The issue is whether the executors' payment of the costs attributable to the wife's property are deductible "administration expenses * * * [allowable] by" the law of the State under [§ 2053(a)(2)].

The interpretation of "administration expenses" under [§ 2053(a)(2)] involves substantially the same considerations that determine the interpretation of "claims against the estate" under [§ 2053(a)(3)]. In both instances, the testator, by directing that payment be made of debts chargeable

---

107. 309 F.2d 592, 604 (Wisdom, J., dissenting): "For example, in the twilight of their years, a couple with community property worth $1,000,000 could borrow an additional $1,000,000 and invest it in securities, using the $2,000,000 as collateral. As a result, the community property would be increased from one million to two million dollars, and would have debts against it of one million dollars. If the husband provided by will that all community debts be paid out of his share of the community property, upon his death his share of the community property would be worth $1,000,000. All of this, however, would be matched by deductible community debts. Thus, under the Court's holding, the entire 'net' estate of $1,000,000 would pass, untaxed, to the wife."

to another or to non-estate property, reduces his net estate and in effect confers a gift or bequest upon another.   We believe that the provisions of [§ 2053], like those of [§ 2056] providing the marital deduction, must be read in light of the general policies of taxing the transmission of wealth at death and of equalizing the tax treatment of couples in common-law and in community property jurisdictions.   We hold, therefore, that a deduction may not be allowed for administration costs chargeable to the surviving spouse's community property.

C.   *The Payment of Debts and Expenses as a Marital Gift.*

In our view the payments made as a result of the testator's assumption of responsibility both for his wife's share of the community debts and for her share of the administration expenses are more properly characterized as marital gifts rather than as "claims" or "expenses."   Since these gifts were to the surviving spouse, respondents contend that a marital deduction should be allowed.   Our interpretation of [§ 2053] disposes of this argument, for under any view of the facts, even if these items are deemed to be gifts to the wife, the will required her to surrender property more valuable than the bequests she received.[108]   In the absence of a net benefit passing to the surviving spouse, no marital deduction is allowable.

The judgment of the Court of Appeals for the Fifth Circuit is reversed and the case remanded for proceedings in accordance with this opinion.

It is so ordered.

---

108. Respondents concede that "even with the benefit of the bequest of ⅓ of the separate property to her and the benefit of the debt and expense assumption provisions, Mrs. Stapf ended up with less than she would have owned had she elected to take against the will."   *   *   *

Chapter 19

CHARITABLE DEDUCTION GIFTS

¶ 19.01 QUALIFYING TRANSFERS

Any bequest to a qualifying charity [1] will generate an estate tax charitable deduction. Whether, or to what extent, a client should seek to qualify for the deduction depends on matters of personal preference often having little to do with taxes. It is the responsibility of the client's advisor to help him decide whether to make charitable transfers in light of their net cost, after taking into account any tax savings that they produce, and how to make such transfers in a manner that best achieves his tax and non-tax objectives.

Clients should be reminded that a lifetime charitable gift may produce income tax savings not available from a transfer at death. If the transfer does not occur until his death, either because it is made by his will or is an interest in a trust of which he retained the power to revoke as long as he lived, he is not entitled to any charitable deduction for income tax purposes during his life. [2] His estate (or revocable trust) is entitled to such a deduction only if the amount transferred to charity is payable out of gross income. [3] A lifetime gift, on the other hand, may give rise to an income tax deduction even though it takes the form of a remainder interest in trust principal [4] or in a personal residence or farm, following a life estate or term of years either retained by the client or given to a noncharitable beneficiary. [5]

This advantage for lifetime gifts is available up to the moment of the client's death. If the gift is included in his gross estate because he retained an interest or power when he made the transfer, it is deductible for estate tax purposes. [6] Thus, the net effect of making the gift before he dies, rather than upon his death, may be to secure an income tax deduction not otherwise allowed. It may also avoid state-law limitations on transfers to charity occurring at or shortly before the transferor's death. [7]

---

1. Qualifying charities are described in § 2055(a).

2. The grantor is entitled to a deduction for charitable contributions "made within the taxable year." See § 170(a)(1). His taxable year ends on the date of his death, see Reg. § 1.443–1(a)(2), prior to the transfer to the trust.

3. Section 642(c) allows an income tax deduction for estates and trusts for certain amounts "paid" for a charitable purpose but the Regulations limit the deduction to payments out of gross income. See Reg. § 1.642(c)–(a)(1); Estate of A. Lindsay O'Connor, 69 T.C. 165 (1977).

4. § 170(f)(2)(A).

5. § 170(f)(3)(B)(i).

6. § 2055.

7. See ¶ 1.07[3], note 52 supra.

FRANK E. MOTT v. UNITED STATES

United States Court of Claims, 1972.
462 F.2d 512, 72–2 USTC ¶ 9557
cert denied 409 U.S. 1108, 93 S.Ct. 902, 34 L.Ed.2d 688 (1973).

COWEN, Chief Judge.

This tax case, apparently one of first impression, comes before the court on the parties' cross-motions for summary judgment.   The issue is whether an estate is entitled to a deduction from its gross income, pursuant to Section 661(a)(2) of the Internal Revenue Code of 1954, when it makes a distribution of corpus of an estate to a qualified charitable beneficiary pursuant to a general pecuniary bequest.   We have concluded that the claimed deduction is not available.

The pertinent facts, which have been stipulated, are as follows: Walter C. Teagle died on January 9, 1962, leaving a gross estate in excess of $36,000,000.   Under the terms of his will, two-thirds of the estate, after payment of debts, expenses, and specific bequests, was left to the Teagle Foundation, a tax-exempt charitable corporation.   The residue of the estate, including all income earned during its administration, was left in trust for the benefit of Jane W. Teagle, an alternate life beneficiary, with specified remainders over.

The years involved in this suit are the estate's taxable years ending July 31, 1963, 1964, and 1965.   During this period, the executors of the estate made the following payments out of the corpus of the estate in partial satisfaction of the bequest to the Teagle Foundation:

1963	$13,165,575.75
1964	405,379.02
1965	375,000.00

The executors also made several distributions of income to Jane during the administration period before the trust came into operation, including during the years involved here, a $100,000 payment in 1963.

In computing Mr. Teagle's taxable estate, the executors were allowed an estate tax deduction of $14,107,420.90 for the charitable bequest to the Teagle Foundation.   They now assert that they are also entitled to a deduction, in computing the estate's taxable income for the years involved here, for the payments described above which they made in satisfaction of the charitable bequest.   Briefly stated, they contend that such a deduction is permitted by the plain terms of Section 661(a)(2), which provides in pertinent part that:

> In any taxable year there shall be allowed as a deduction in computing the taxable income of an estate * * * any * * * amounts properly paid * * * for such taxable year * * *.

The Government, while conceding that a literal reading of Section 661(a)(2) would permit plaintiffs to prevail, maintains that that section cannot properly be interpreted without reference to its purpose, and that when the provision is read in the context of the entire statutory scheme of Subchapter J of Chapter 1 of the Code, it is clear that the distribution to the charitable organization in this case cannot qualify for the deduction permitted by Section 661(a)(2).

* * *

* * * Both parties agree that the amount of the payments, although made to a charitable organization, are not deductible under Section 642(c) in computing the estate's taxable income. Mr. Teagle's will did not provide, as Section 642(c) requires, that the payments be made out of the estate's gross income. In fact, the payments here were made out of the corpus of the estate.

In addition, the parties seem to agree that none of the provisions of Section 663(a) expressly excludes the payments here from the operation of Section 661. The exception of Section 663(a)(1), for gifts or bequests of a specific sum or of specific property which is paid or credited all at once or in not more than three installments, is not applicable here because the bequest has not been satisfied in three installments or less. Moreover, it is not a bequest of a specific sum of money since its amount, expressed as a percentage of the estate after payment of administrative expenses and other charges, was not ascertainable at the time of Mr. Teagle's death. See Treas.Reg. § 1.663(a)–1(b)(1) (1956). Section 663(a)(2), which provides that an estate may not deduct under Section 661 any amount paid, permanently set aside, or otherwise qualifying for the charitable deduction permitted by Section 642(c), would also seem to be inapplicable because the amounts here, as noted above, do not qualify under Section 642(c) for the charitable deduction.

Plaintiffs contend that since none of the express exceptions to Section 661 applies here, the amounts paid to the Teagle Foundation are properly deductible under that section because they constitute "amounts properly paid * * * for such taxable year * * * ." The Government contends that "amounts" cannot be read literally and that Section 661(a)(2) does not apply to these charitable distributions. It relies principally on Section 1.663(a)–2 of the Regulations which provides in pertinent part:

> Any amount paid, permanently set aside, or to be used for the charitable, etc., purposes specified in section 642(c) and which is allowable as a deduction under that section is not allowed as a deduction to an estate or trust under section 661 or treated as an amount distributed for purposes of determining the amounts includible in gross income of beneficiaries under section 662. *Amounts paid, permanently set aside, or to be used for charitable, etc., purposes are deductible by estates or trusts only as provided in section 642(c).*

* * *

From our reading of this regulation, two things seem clear. First, the italicized language is dispositive of the issue in this case, since it prevents an estate from claiming as a deduction under Section 661(a)(2) any amounts distributed to a charitable beneficiary except as permitted by Section 642(c). Second, however, there is nothing in Section 663(a)(2), the statutory provision under which this regulation was promulgated, which expressly supports the rule announced in the regulation. Section 663(a)(2) provides only that an estate or trust may not deduct under Section 661 any amounts which are also deductible under Section 642(c); it does not specifically cover situations like the one here, where amounts paid to a charitable organization do not qualify for the charitable deduction.

The validity of this regulation must be sustained unless it is "unreasonable and plainly inconsistent with the revenue statutes   *   *   *." Commissioner of Internal Revenue v. South Texas Lumber Co., 333 U.S. 496, 501, 68 S.Ct. 695, 698, 92 L.Ed. 831 (1948).   See also, e.g., Estate of Bahen v. United States, 305 F.2d 827, 829, 158 Ct.Cl. 141, 145 (1962), and cases cited therein.   After carefully considering the parties' contentions in this case, as well as the entire distribution scheme of Subchapter J, we think that the regulation is valid and also that any other rule would be an unreasonable interpretation of the statute.

We do not adopt plaintiff's argument that Section 661(a)(2) must be read according to its literal terms.   If an estate were entitled to a distribution deduction for "*any* other amounts properly paid," as that section provides, then all payments made by an estate, whether or not to a beneficiary, would be deductible.   For example, contrary to Thomas Lonergan Trust, 6 T.C. 715 (1946), an estate would be allowed a distribution deduction when it makes payments to a creditor in satisfaction of a judgment against the estate.   Moreover, under a literal interpretation of Section 661(a)(2), in many instances an estate would be entitled to a double deduction.   Thus, expenses which are deductible under Section 212 would be deductible again under Section 661.

Obviously, the phrase "any other amounts paid" should not be read as broadly as its literal terms suggest.   It must be interpreted in its own particular context, with reference to its relationship with the other provisions of Subchapter J, and in accordance with the consequences which Congress sought to achieve when it enacted Section 661 in 1954.

The most logical reference point in attempting to delineate the scope of Section 661 is the corollary provision of Section 662.   That the two sections should be read together is not only implicit from the fact that they are similarly structured and in some instances identically worded, but also explicit from Section 662's express reference to Section 661.   Thus, Section 662(a), in imposing its tax on distributees, states that "there shall be included in the gross income of a beneiﬁciary to whom an amount specified in section 661(a) is paid, credited, or required to be distributed   *   *   *   the sum of the following amounts   *   *   *."   By this reference, we think it is proper to confine Section 661 to distributions to *beneficiaries* of the estate, even though Section 661(a) does not specifically so provide.   Such a construction, implied in Section 662(a), prevents the absurd results mentioned above which would occur if the phrase "any other amounts properly paid" in Section 661(a)(2) were applied literally.

Of course, an interpretation which limits Section 661 to distributions to beneficiaries does not put an end to the matter here, since the Teagle Foundation is a beneficiary of the estate.   Therefore, the Government also asks us to interpret Section 661(a) as permitting a deduction only for distributions to *taxable* beneficiaries, based upon its argument that Section 661 must be read as interdependent with Section 662.   That is, as we understand the Government's argument, the incidence of the tax on the income of an estate must be allocated between estate and beneficiary; and to the extent that the beneficiary is exempt from the tax imposed by Section 662, any distributions to that beneficiary would not be deductible by the estate under Section 661.

The Government's position seems to be correct in the context of this case, but we do not hold that it is a general rule which may be applied in every conceivable situation that may arise under the provisions of the Code here considered.   We think it is sufficient to say that, under the facts of this case, the Government's position accords with the general intent of Congress in enacting the distribution rules and, as we discuss below, is in accord with what we believe to be an implied Congressional intent to prevent all charitable distributions, whether or not deductible under Section 642(c), from entering into the operation of the distribution rules.

As we noted above, when Congress enacted the present distribution rules its primary purpose was to eliminate the necessity for tracing the source of distributions.   Under prior law, in general, beneficiaries were taxed only on amounts of current income distributed by an estate or trust. Such a simple rule led to manipulation, and in 1942 Congress attempted to tighten up the statute by enacting the 65-day rules of Section 162(d) of the 1939 Code.   The end result was that the distribution rules became so difficult to apply, and so entrenched in the tracing requirements, that Congress abandoned the old system in favor of the present scheme.   Tracing was eliminated by providing in Section 662 that all amounts distributed to beneficiaries would be considered to be distributions of income, subject to the modifications of Section 663 and the quantitative limitation of D. N. I. Consistent with the conduit principle, an estate or trust making such distributions would be entitled to a deduction under Section 661.

As we read Sections 661(a) and 662(a), Congress intended to do nothing more than combine the conduit principle with a conclusive presumption that distributions subject to the operation of those sections are distributions of income.   Such a presumption is, we think, inapplicable to charitable distributions.   As Section 642(c) provides, a charitable deduction is available only if the source of the distribution is gross income.   Tracing of charitable distributions is still required under Section 642(c), and to the extent that a charitable distribution is not paid out of gross income in accordance with the requirements of Section 642(c), then we think that Congress intended that no deduction is allowable.

Without the distinction between charitable and noncharitable distributions, Congress' general intent in enacting the present provisions—to prevent manipulative distributions—would be seriously thwarted.   The facts of this case are a good illustration.   Both the Teagle Foundation and Jane, the sole income distributee, would be second-tier beneficiaries.   If the estate could deduct under Section 661(a)(2) the payments made out of the corpus of the estate in satisfaction of the charitable bequest, then the following will result: the estate will pay no tax on the income which it accumulates, because that income will be offset by deductions for its distributions of corpus to the Teagle Foundation.   Later on, the estate can distribute the accumulated income to Jane tax-free.   With regard to current payments to Jane, concededly out of estate income, her tax would be greatly reduced.   Thus, in 1963, she received $100,000 while the Teagle Foundation received approximately $13,200,000.   If both amounts were considered distributions to beneficiaries within the meaning of Section 662, then Jane would be taxable on only $\frac{1}{133}$ of the estate's D. N. I. for 1963, up to the amount of her distribution.

Based upon our reading of the distribution sections of Subchapter J and their legislative history, we conclude that Section 1.663(a)–2 of the Regulations, which provides that amounts distributed by an estate or trust to a charitable organization are deductible only under Section 642(c), is consistent with the statutory scheme and a reasonable interpretation thereof. It necessarily follows that plaintiffs are not entitled to a deduction pursuant to Section 661(a)(2) for the amounts of corpus distributed in satisfaction of the charitable bequest.   Accordingly, defendant's motion for summary judgment is granted, plaintiff's motion for summary judgment is denied, and the petition is dismissed.

*   *   *

[1] Major Forms

Qualifying transfers to charity may take five major forms:

(1) a specific bequest or devise of particular property, such as shares of stock, an art collection, or real estate; [8]

(2) a general legacy of a specified dollar amount; [9]

(3) a residuary bequest,[10] under which the charity is entitled to all or part of so much of the estate as remains after debts, taxes, and administration expenses have been paid and specific bequests and general legacies have been satisfied;

(4) a remainder interest in a personal residence or farm;

(5) either a remainder or an income interest in a charitable split-interest trust.

The first three of the alternatives listed above are not different from standard testamentary dispositions to non-charitable beneficiaries.   They present no special problem when used for a charitable gift, unless the bequest is conditional.

For the average client, who usually wishes to make the bulk of his wealth available for his noncharitable beneficiaries, the transfers described at (4) and (5), which combine interests of charitable and non-charitable beneficiaries, are likely to be more useful than the first three alternatives listed above.

[2] Conditional Bequests

The Regulations provide:

> If, as of the date of a decedent's death, a transfer for charitable purposes is dependent upon the performance of some act or the happening of a precedent event in order that it might become

---

8. For a discussion, see ¶ 17.01[1] supra.   10. For a discussion, see ¶ 17.01[3] supra.

9. For a discussion, see ¶ 17.01[2] supra.

effective, no deduction is allowable unless the possibility that the charitable transfer will not become effective is so remote as to be negligible.[11]

There are two exceptions to the general principle, reflected here and elsewhere in the Regulations, that the possibility that the charity will not take must be viewed as of the decedent's death.

First, a qualified disclaimer [12] by a non-charitable beneficiary may increase the amount passing to charity and deductible as a charitable transfer. For example, if a decedent has made specific bequests to his children and a residuary bequest to a charity, a qualified disclaimer by a child that increases the size of the residue will increase the allowable deduction.   In effect, this allows the children to determine after the decedent dies whether they want to receive their bequests or prefer that they pass to charity, without adverse tax consequences from the availability of these options.

Second, the complete termination, before the estate tax return is due and before the power has been exercised, of a power to invade property for the benefit of an individual may eliminate the possibility of diversion of such property from the charity and, thus, may cause a deduction to be allowed for its value.[13]

¶ 19.02   REMAINDER INTERESTS IN A PERSONAL RESIDENCE OR FARM

Under § 2055(e)(2), an estate tax charitable deduction is allowed for the transfer of a remainder interest in a personal residence or farm, as well as for less common varieties of partial interests in property such as certain easements for conservation purposes.[14]   Such transfers generally provide a life estate in the property for a family member or other noncharitable beneficiary, with the charity entitled to the property on the death of the life tenant.   The transfer of the remainder interest allows the transferor's estate the benefit of an estate tax charitable deduction to be combined with immediate enjoyment of the property by a noncharitable beneficiary.

The deduction is based on the actuarial value of the remainder interest, using a 6 percent interest rate.[15]

If the client is willing to transfer the remainder interest during his life, rather than upon his death, he can also enjoy an income tax deduction for the value of the charitable remainder interest.[16]   If the client retains a life interest in the property himself, his gross estate will include the value of all interests following his life estate [17] but an estate tax charitable deduction will be allowable for the value of the charity's remainder.[18]   Such a lifetime

11. Reg. § 20.2055–2(b)(1).

12. Reg. 20.2055–2(c)(1). "Qualified disclaimers" are discussed at ¶ 17.02 [1][a] supra.

13. Reg § 20.2055–2(c)(2).

14. See § 170(f)(3)(B). For a discussion of the use of conservation easements in estate planning, see ¶ 6.03[2][b][ii] supra.

15. See Reg. § 1.170A–12.

16. See § 170(f)(3)(B).

17. See § 2036.

18. See § 2055(e)(2).

transfer allows the client to combine a right to enjoyment of the property for himself while he lives with both income and estate tax advantages from a charitable deduction.

¶ 19.03 CHARITABLE SPLIT-INTEREST TRUSTS

Charitable split-interest trusts are trusts in which both charitable and non-charitable beneficiaries have interests.   Such trusts are of three basic types:

(1) The charitable remainder trust, in which non-charitable beneficiaries receive periodic payments until the trust terminates, when any undistributed principal and income is paid to one or more charities;

(2) The charitable lead trust, in which the charitable beneficiary receives periodic payments for a limited time.   When the interest of the charity has terminated, any undistributed principal and income is either paid to one or more non-charitable beneficiaries or continues to be held in trust for their benefit; and

(3) The pooled income fund,[19] which is basically a charitable remainder trust to which more than one donor may make contributions.

Despite their denomination as "charitable," these trusts are primarily important in estate planning to save income, estate, and gift taxes on wealth passing to non-charitable beneficiaries.   All three kinds may be established either during the grantor's life or upon his death.   Charitable remainder trusts and pooled income funds are used primarily to save income taxes, while charitable lead trusts are used primarily to save estate and gift taxes on wealth that ultimately passes to non-charitable beneficiaries.

This chapter deals with charitable split-interest trusts that are created, or become irrevocable, upon the death of the testator or grantor; Chapter 10 deals with such trusts that are irrevocable during his life.   Pooled income funds will not be discussed further, as they generally allow gifts of two or more grantors to serve purposes comparable to those served by individually created charitable remainder trusts.

¶ 19.04 CHARITABLE REMAINDER TRUSTS

Charitable remainder trusts offer such impressive income tax savings that they deserve much wider use than they now enjoy.   Such a trust may be either an annuity trust or a unitrust.   The former requires annual payments of a fixed dollar amount or percentage of the initial value of the trust principal, either for the lives of one or more persons or for a period of years, not exceeding twenty, with the remainder (including any undistributed income) payable to one or more charities.[20]   The annual payments must not be less than 5 percent of the initial value of the trust principal.   The unitrust differs in that the required annual payments are a specified percentage (not less than 5 percent) of the value of the principal as determined each year,[21] rather than a percentage of the initial principal value.

---

19.   See § 642(c)(5) for the definition.

20.   § 664(d)(1)(A).

21.   § 664(d)(2)(A).

It is unclear what minimum value the charitable remainder interest must have in order for the trust to qualify as a charitable remainder trust for income tax purposes under § 664,[22] which also controls qualification for estate tax purposes under § 2055(e)(2)(A).

[1] Income Tax Consequences for Trust and Beneficiaries

The income tax consequences for the trust and its beneficiaries are not affected by whether it is created during the transferor's life or upon his death.   Reference should be made to the discussion of such consequences in ¶ 10.02[2] supra.

[2] Estate Tax Consequences

An estate tax charitable deduction is allowed for the actuarial value of the remainder interest.   The actuarial tables used in computing the deduction are based on an assumed 6 percent interest rate.[23]   For the reasons discussed at ¶ 10.02[3] supra, at a time when the prevailing return on a variety of investment vehicles differs from 6 percent, the tables may provide a distorted estimate of the value of the charitable remainder interest.

¶ 19.05   CHARITABLE LEAD (INCOME) TRUSTS

Charitable lead trusts are primarily useful to save estate taxes on assets that will ultimately pass to non-charitable beneficiaries.   Like a charitable remainder trust, the charitable lead trust may either provide for payment of a guaranteed annuity or a percentage of the fair market value of the trust property, determined annually.   Here, however, the payee of the annuity or percentage of principal is a charity and there is no requirement that the pay-out rate be a minimum of 5 percent, as in the case of a charitable remainder trust.

As in the charitable remainder trust, the actuarial tables used to compute the estate tax charitable deduction use an assumed 6 percent interest rate.[24]   For the reasons discussed at ¶ 10.03 supra, at a time when the prevailing return on a variety of investment vehicles differs from 6 percent, the tables may provide a distorted estimate of the value of the charitable lead interest.

[1] Income Tax Consequences for Trust and Beneficiaries

Taxation of the lead trust and its beneficiaries is not controlled by a special provision, as in the case of the charitable remainder trust,[25] but rather by the general rules governing complex trusts.[26]   Thus, the trust is entitled to a charitable deduction for amounts paid for charitable purposes from gross income.[27]   The trust instrument should specify the order in which trust income is to be used to make up charitable payments.[28]

---

22.   See ¶ 10.02, note 6 supra.

23.   See Reg. § 20.2055–2(f)(2), referring to Reg. § 1.664–2(c) for annuity payments and Reg. § 1.664–4 for unitrust payments. Reg. § 1.664–2(c) refers, in turn, to Reg. § 20.2031–10.

24.   Id.

25.   § 664.   For a discussion, see ¶ 10.02[2] supra.

26.   For a discussion of these rules, see chapter 11.

27.   § 642(c).   See note 23 supra.

28.   See ¶ 10.03[2], note 52 supra.

The trust's net income, after deductions, is taxable in the same manner as for trusts with no charitable interests. Any accumulated income that is ultimately distributed to non-charitable beneficiaries may be subject to an additional tax in the hands of the distributee under the throwback rule, unless an exemption from throwback treatment is available.[29]

[2] Estate Tax Consequences

The creation of a charitable lead trust upon the client's death gives rise to an estate tax charitable deduction for the value of the charitable lead interest.[30] The actuarial tables used in computing the deduction are based on an assumed 6 percent interest rate [31] and may give a substantially distorted valuation for the portion of the trust property which passes to non-charitable beneficiaries if prevailing interest rates differ from 6 percent.

¶ 19.06 MINIMIZING RISK OF DISQUALIFICATION

An advisor who fails to qualify a transfer at death for the charitable deduction when qualification is consistent with the client's objectives may substantially increase his estate tax. While outright bequests to qualified charities rarely pose problems unless the bequest is conditional,[32] charitable split-interest trusts are subject to extremely technical rules that are strictly applied. In a field where the stakes may be high, advisors understandably seek to minimize the risk of disqualification, and so-called boot-strap provisions cannot be relied on here. Thus, in Revenue Ruling 65-144,[33] a provision that, if broad powers of the trustee made a charitable remainder nondeductible, such powers should be inapplicable to the remainder interest, was held to be ineffective to secure the deduction.

The best protection against disallowance of a charitable deduction is meticulous compliance with the Regulations.[34] Revenue Ruling 72–395,[35] with elaborately articulated mandatory and optional provisions for charitable remainder trusts, is also a major source of guidance. If a client's circumstances make it sufficiently important to include a provision as to which there is any significant doubt, a private letter ruling should be obtained. In order to secure such a ruling it may be necessary to plan to create the trust in question during the client's life rather than upon his death. The National Office of the Internal Revenue Service will not rule on matters "relating to the application of the estate tax to property or the estate of a living person." [36]

¶ 19.07 VALUATION OF QUALIFYING TRANSFERS THAT ARE SUBJECT TO PAYMENT OF DEATH TAXES

If federal or state death taxes are payable out of an otherwise qualifying charitable transfer, the amount of the estate tax charitable deduction will be reduced by the amount of such taxes.[37]

---

29. §§ 665–667. For a discussion of the rule, see ¶ 11.02 supra.

30. § 2055(e)(2)(B).

31. See note 23 supra.

32. See ¶ 19.01[2] infra.

33. 1965–1 CB 442.

34. See generally Reg. § 20.2055–(e)(2).

35. 1972–2 CB 340, as modified by Rev. Rul. 80–123, 1980–1 CB 205.

36. See Reg. § 601.201(b)(2).

The Regulations point out that if the Federal estate tax is payable out of a charitable transfer, thereby reducing the amount otherwise passing to charity, the allowable deduction will also be reduced, increasing the tax.[38] It is difficult to take issue with the further statement: "If, in addition, interdependent State and Federal taxes are involved, the computation becomes highly complicated." [39]

---

37. § 2055(c).

38. Reg. § 20.2055–3(b).

39. Id.

PART V

SPECIALLY TREATED PROPERTY

CHAPTER 20

LIFE INSURANCE

¶ 20.01 USE OF LIFE INSURANCE IN ESTATE PLANNING

Life insurance is a major tool of estate planning that offers important tax and non-tax advantages as:

(1) An asset that is sheltered from income taxes both during the client's life and after his death;

[2] A source of liquid funds to meet death taxes and expenses of the estate and its beneficiaries;

[3] An asset that may often be removed from the client's gross estate at little or no gift tax cost; and

[4] As asset that may often be acquired by a client's beneficiaries, and thus kept out of his gross estate, at relatively little cost to them.

In a given case, it frequently is necessary to forego one advantage in order to achieve another. For example, if insurance proceeds are to be available as a source of liquid funds to meet death taxes, it may not be possible to keep them out of the client's gross estate at the same time. But the range of available alternatives in handling insurance often is impressive.

The two major forms of life insurance are term and whole life. Term provides coverage for a fixed period only, with whatever rights of renewal or conversion the policy contains. Whole life builds a cash value, in addition to providing insurance. Thus, it is a form of investment and may be kept in force by the timely payment of premiums as long as the insured lives. It may be either ordinary life, requiring payment of premiums throughout the life of the insured, or limited-payment life, under which the periodic premium is higher but after a specified period the policy remains in force without further premium payments. The controversy over the relative attractiveness of term and whole life insurance has raged for years and no attempt will be made to resolve it here.

Clients need advice in determining whether to retain ownership of existing policies or to transfer them to their beneficiaries (or trusts). That choice necessarily depends on the role that the policy is destined to play in the client's estate plan, as well as upon gift tax and estate tax considerations. Clients also need advice in the choice of beneficiary designations and settlement options for policies that they own or acquire. Both ownership of policies and designation of beneficiaries are affected by community property laws in the eight states in which they are in force.

[1] As a Shelter From Income Taxes

During the client's life, insurance may serve as a tax shelter in building his estate,[1] but the focus here is on the shelter it offers beneficiaries when he dies. Proceeds payable by reason of the death of the insured are excluded from taxable income.[2]

The exclusion is limited by the "transferee for value" rule. If the proceeds are received by someone who bought the policy from a prior owner, only the price he paid (and subsequent payments of premiums or other amounts by him) is excluded from income.[3] The rule does not apply, however, if the transferee's basis is "determined in whole or in part by reference to" the basis of the transferor, or to a transfer to the insured, his partner or partnership, or to a corporation in which he is a shareholder or officer.[4] The transferee for value rule is likely to come into play in relation to transfers of policies in connection with a divorce settlement, where a surrender of rights by the divorced spouse is consideration for the transfer of the policy.[5]

The exclusion applies only to the amount payable by reason of the death of the insured. If the insurance company holds the proceeds after the death of the insured, any interest paid to the beneficiary is fully taxable,[6] as is the interest element in installment payments,[7] subject to a limited exemption for a surviving spouse. For example, if the face amount of the policy is $120,000 but the installment option is elected and the company will pay the proceeds in installments of $1,250 per month for ten years, the total of the installment payments will be $150,000. Accordingly, the $30,000 excess over the face amount of the policy is the economic equivalent of interest and is taxed as such unless the installments are payable to a surviving spouse of the insured, for whom $1,000 of interest element per year is exempt.[8]

The excludible interest element does provide an opportunity for a surviving spouse to receive tax exempt interest income, if the policy includes an option for payment of the proceeds in installments. However, in a period of rising interest rates there often are other opportunities to receive tax exempt interest on municipal bonds at a higher rate than that used by insurance companies for purposes of the installment option.

[2] As a Source of Liquid Funds

Life insurance is an important source of liquid funds to meet death taxes and expenses of the estate and its beneficiaries. Often, the process of developing an estate plan for a client reveals a need for additional life insurance, either to provide for such expenses or to meet anticipated needs

---

1. Interest on funds borrowed to pay premiums is deductible, subject to the limitations contained in § 264, thus generating a current deduction. But the increase in the policy reserve, which represents income earned by the company's investment of the premiums generally, is not includible in income either by the insured or by the beneficiary who receives the policy proceeds.

2. § 101(a).

3. § 101(a)(2).

4. §§ 101(a)(2)(A), 101(a)(2)(B). The exception for cases in which the transferee's basis is determined by reference to that of the transferor covers gifts of policies. See § 1015(a), discussed at ¶ 4.04 supra.

5. See Sander & Gutman, "Divorce and Separation," 95 T.M. 3d., A–49 (1975).

6. § 101(c).

7. § 101(d).

8. § 101(d)(1)(B).

of beneficiaries.　From this standpoint, insurance is unique in offering a client with insufficient assets the means to create an "instant estate."

If policy proceeds are payable to the insured's estate or to a beneficiary who is legally obligated to use them to discharge estate obligations, the proceeds are includible in the insured's gross estate.[9]　But policy proceeds can aid in meeting the liquidity problems of the estate without thereby becoming subject to estate tax.　If an individual or trust receives the proceeds and thereafter buys illiquid assets from the estate or lends sums to the executor, the immediate cash needs of the estate may be met.　This may permit a more advantageous liquidation of estate assets than would be possible if the executor were under pressure to raise cash.　And if the lender is under no legal obligation to make the funds available to the executor and there is no advance understanding that he will do so, it is difficult to find a basis for treating the insurance proceeds as being payable to the executor so as to require their inclusion in the insured's gross estate.

[3] As a Shelter from Estate and Gift Taxes

Life insurance that a client owns often may be removed from his estate at little or no gift tax cost because of the favorable valuation rules for gifts of insurance.　Valuation for gift tax purposes of ordinary life policies that have been in force for some time generally is based not on the cash surrender value, but, instead, on the higher "interpolated terminal reserve at the date of the gift."[10]　For this purpose, such reserve is increased by a portion of the gross premium last paid covering the period that extends beyond the date of the gift.　If the client's health is such that he is no longer insurable, this method may produce an unrealistically low figure.[11]　And even if he could obtain other insurance, the value for gift tax purposes often is relatively small in relation to the proceeds payable on his death.

Gifts of life insurance policies remain vulnerable to inclusion in the insured's estate, under § 2035, if he dies within three years of the transfer.[12] This is true even if the value of all gifts to the donee for the year did not exceed $10,000 and, thus, were not required to be reported in a gift tax return.[13]　But if the insured survives the three-year period, no part of the policy proceeds is includible under § 2035 even though he continued to pay premiums after the transfer was made.[14]

9.　See Reg. § 20.2042–1(b)(1).

10.　See Reg. § 25.2512–6(a).　*Example (4)* illustrates the computation.

11.　Regulations Section 25.2512–6(a) states that the method described in the text may not be used "if because of the unusual nature of the contract such approximation is not reasonably close to full value * * * ."　However, it is difficult to contend that the client's health or uninsurability makes the nature of the contract unusual.

12.　See § 2035, discussed at ¶ 5.02[3][e] supra.

13.　See § 6019(a)(1).

14.　See Rev. Rul. 71–497, infra.　If the insured dies within the three-year period but one or more premiums were paid by the donee, the amount includible in the insured's estate remains unclear.　In Estate of Morris R. Silverman, 61 T.C. 338 (1973), acq. 1978–1 CB 2, decided under the pre-1976 version of § 2035, the Tax Court required inclusion of a portion of the proceeds corresponding to the portion of total premiums that had been paid by the insured. In affirming, the Court of Appeals noted that the Commissioner merely sought affirmance and did not renew his contention in the Tax Court that the entire proceeds were includible.　Estate of Morris R. Silverman v. Commissioner, 521 F.2d 574, 75–2 USTC ¶ 13,084 (2d Cir. 1975).

[4] As an Estate-Building Asset for Beneficiaries

A client may assist a beneficiary in various ways so that the beneficiary will be in a position to acquire insurance on the client's life, rather than receiving the policy as a gift. Such assistance may take the form of gifts, loans, or any of the various methods by which a client may improve the financial position of a beneficiary.[15] Of course, the three-year rule of § 2035 applies. So, direct payment of premiums by the client on a policy taken out by a beneficiary within three years of the client's death will cause the policy proceeds to be included in the client's estate,[16] as with a policy transferred by the client within that period.[17] Similarly, if the client gives the beneficiary the money and urges him to use it for payment of premiums, such use may be attributed to the client for estate tax purposes.[18] But in the absence of some such direct connection between the client's financial assistance to the beneficiary and the use of the money to pay premiums, it is difficult to find a basis for including the policy in the insured's estate under § 2035. Ordinarily, what is includible under that section is what was transferred, rather than other property into which it may have been converted by the donee.[19]

The same estate-building possibilities for beneficiaries may be present in assets other than insurance that clients assist beneficiaries to acquire, such as real estate or securities with favorable prospects for appreciation in value. What makes insurance unique is the extent of the appreciation that may occur as a result of the client's death. This potential gain is particularly impressive in term insurance acquired by a beneficiary on the life of a client who is relatively young, so that the premiums are low. At the same time, the chance that such gain will be realized in the near future is small unless the client's health deteriorates or his life style is an unusually hazardous one.

Such insurance may be acquired by a trust, rather than by the beneficiary himself. Again, however, it is important that the trustee be under no obligation to use trust assets for this purpose.[20] And to whatever extent trust income may be used to pay premiums on insurance on the life of the grantor or his spouse, such income will be taxable to the grantor.[21] Ownership of insurance on the client's life by a trust, rather than by an individual beneficiary, has the advantage of making it possible to keep the policy from

---

If the present interest exclusion does not cover premiums paid by the insured within three years of his death, such payments will be includible in his gross estate under § 2035. For a discussion of the exclusion in relation to that section, see ¶ 5.02[3][e] supra.

15. See ¶ 8.01 supra for a discussion of the use of informal arrangements for this purpose. Use of trust income to pay premiums on insurance on the life of the grantor or his spouse will cause such income to be taxed to the grantor. See § 677(a)(3), discussed at ¶ 9.01[9][d] supra.

16. See, e.g., Daisy M. B. Bel v. United States, infra; First Nat'l Bank of Oregon v. United States, 488 F.2d 575, 74–1 USTC ¶ 12,966 (9th Cir. 1973).

17. See Revenue Ruling 71–497, infra.

18. See First Nat'l Bank of Oregon v. United States, note 16 supra.

19. See ¶ 5.02[3][d] supra.

20. See Detroit Bank & Trust Co. v. United States, 467 F.2d 964, 72–2 USTC ¶ 12,883 (6th Cir. 1972), cert. denied 410 U.S. 929 (1973).

21. See § 677(a)(3); ¶ 9.01[9][d] supra.

being included in the beneficiary's gross estate.   If it is so included and the beneficiary dies before the death of the client, the policy will be valued in the manner previously described for gifts of policies: not on the basis of the cash surrender value, but, rather, on the basis of the higher "interpolated terminal reserve at the date of the decedent's death." [22]   Such reserve is increased by a portion of the gross premium last paid covering the period that extends beyond the date of death.

Of course, if the beneficiary survives the client, the beneficiary's wealth will be augmented by the policy proceeds.   To whatever extent they have not been spent or given away before he dies, his gross estate will have been increased.

COMMISSIONER v. ESTATE OF NOEL

Supreme Court of the United States, 1965.
380 U.S. 678, 85 S.Ct. 1238, 14 L.Ed.2d 159,
65–1 USTC ¶ 12,311.

Mr. Justice BLACK delivered the opinion of the Court.

This is a federal estate tax case, raising questions under § 2042(2) of the Internal Revenue Code of 1954, 26 U.S.C.A. § 2042(2) (1958 ed.), which requires inclusion in the gross estate of a decedent of amounts received by beneficiaries other than the executor from "insurance under policies on the life of the decedent" if the decedent "possessed at his death any of the incidents of ownership, exercisable either alone or in conjunction with any other person.   *   *   *" The questions presented in this case are whether certain flight insurance policies payable upon the accidental death of the insured were policies "on the life of the decedent" and whether at his death he had reserved any of the "incidents of ownership" in the policies.

These issues emerge from the following facts.   Respondent Ruth M. Noel drove her husband from their home to New York International Airport where he was to take an airplane to Venezuela.   Just before taking off, Mr. Noel signed applications for two round-trip flight insurance policies, aggregating $125,000 and naming his wife as beneficiary.   Mrs. Noel testified that she paid the premiums of $2.50 each on the policies and that her husband then instructed the sales clerk to "give them to my wife.   They are hers now, I no longer have anything to do with them." The clerk gave her the policies, which she kept.   Less than three hours later Mr. Noel's plane crashed into the Atlantic Ocean and he and all others aboard were killed.   Thereafter the companies paid Mrs. Noel the $125,000 face value of the policies, which was not included in the estate tax return filed by his executors.   The Commissioner of Internal Revenue determined that the proceeds of the policies should have been included and the Tax Court sustained that determination, holding that the flight accident policies were insurance "on the life of the decedent"; that Mr. Noel had possessed exercisable "incidents of ownership" in the policies at his death; and that the $125,000 paid to Mrs. Noel as beneficiary was therefore includable in the gross estate.   39 T.C. 466.   Although agreeing that decedent's reserved

---

22. See Reg. § 20.2031–8(a)(2). The computation is illustrated in Reg. § 20.-2031–8(a)(3), Example (4).

right to assign the policies and to change the beneficiary amounted to "exercisable incidents of ownership within the meaning of the statute," the Court of Appeals nevertheless reversed, holding that given "its ordinary, plain and generally accepted meaning," the statutory phrase "policies on the life of the decedent" does not apply to insurance paid on account of accidental death under policies like those here. 332 F.2d 950. The court's reason for drawing the distinction was that under a life insurance contract an insurer "agrees to pay a specified sum upon the occurrence of an *inevitable* event," whereas accident insurance covers a risk "which is *evitable* and not likely to occur." (Emphasis supplied.) 332 F.2d, at 952. Because of the importance of an authoritative answer to these questions in the administration of the estate tax laws, we granted certiorari to decide them. 379 U.S. 927, 85 S.Ct. 330, 13 L.Ed.2d 340.

I.

In 1929, 36 years ago, the Board of Tax Appeals, predecessor to the Tax Court, held in Ackerman v. Commissioner, 15 B.T.A. 635, that "amounts received as accident insurance" because of the death of the insured were includable in the estate of the deceased. The Board of Tax Appeals recognized that "there is a distinction between life insurance and accident insurance, the former insuring against death in any event and the latter * * * against death under certain contingencies * * * ." The court of Appeals in the case now before us considered this distinction between an "inevitable" and an "evitable" event to be of crucial significance under the statute. The Board of Tax Appeals in *Ackerman* did not, stating "we fail to see why one is not taken out upon the life of the policy-holder as much as the other. In each case the risk assumed by the insurer is the loss of the insured's life, and the payment of the insurance money is contingent upon the loss of life." This view of the Board of Tax Appeals is wholly consistent with the language of the statute itself which makes no distinction between "policies on the life of the decedent" which are payable in all events and those payable only if death comes in a certain way or within a certain time. Even were the statutory language less clear, since the Board of Tax Appeals' *Ackerman* case it has been the settled and consistent administrative practice to include insurance proceeds for accidental death under policies like these in the estates of decedents. The Treasury Regulations remain unchanged from the time of the *Ackerman* decision and from that day to this Congress has never attempted to limit the scope of that decision or the established administrative construction of § 2042(2), although it has re-enacted that section and amended it in other respects a number of times. We have held in many cases that such a long-standing administrative interpretation, applying to a substantially reenacted statute, is deemed to have received congressional approval and has the effect of law. See, e.g., National Lead Co. v. United States, 252 U.S. 140, 146, 40 S.Ct. 237, 64 L.Ed. 496; United States v. Dakota-Montana Oil Co., 288 U.S. 459, 466, 53 S.Ct. 435, 77 L.Ed. 893. We hold here that these insurance policies, whether called "flight accident insurance" or "life insurance," were in effect insurance taken out on the "life of the decedent" within the meaning of § 2042(2).

II.

The executors' second contention is that even if these were policies "on the life of the decedent," Mrs. Noel owned them completely, and the decedent therefore possessed no exercisable incident of ownership in them at the time of his death so as to make the proceeds includable in his estate. While not clearly spelled out, the contention that the decedent reserved no incident of ownership in the policies rests on three alternative claims: (a) that Mrs. Noel purchased the policies and therefore owned them; (b) that even if her husband owned the policies, he gave them to her, thereby depriving himself of power to assign the policies or to change the beneficiary; and (c) even assuming he had contractual power to assign the policies or make a beneficiary change, this power was illusory as he could not possibly have exercised it in the interval between take-off and the fatal crash in the Atlantic.

(a) The contention that Mrs. Noel bought the policies and therefore owned them rests solely on her testimony that she furnished the money for their purchase, intending thereby to preserve her right to continue as beneficiary. Accepting her claim that she supplied the money to buy the policies for her own benefit (which the Tax Court did not decide), what she bought nonetheless were policy contracts containing agreements between her husband and the companies. The contracts themselves granted to Mr. Noel the right either to assign the policies or to change the beneficiary without her consent. Therefore the contracts she bought by their very terms rebut her claim that she became the complete, unconditional owner of the policies with an irrevocable right to remain the beneficiary.

(b) The contention that Mr. Noel gave or assigned the policies to her and therefore was without power thereafter to assign them or to change the beneficiary stands no better under these facts. The contract terms provided that these policies could not be assigned nor could the beneficiary be changed without a written endorsement on the policies. No such assignment or change of beneficiary was endorsed on these policies, and consequently the power to assign the policies or change the beneficiary remained in the decedent at the time of his death.

(c) Obviously, there was no practical opportunity for the decedent to assign the policies or change the beneficiary between the time he boarded the plane and the time he died. That time was too short and his wife had the policies in her possession at home. These circumstances disabled him for the moment from exercising those "incidents of ownership" over the policies which were undoubtedly his. Death intervened before this temporary disability was removed. But the same could be said about a man owning an ordinary life insurance policy who boarded the plane at the same time or for that matter about any man's exercise of ownership over his property while aboard an airplane in the three hours before a fatal crash. It would stretch the imagination to think that Congress intended to measure estate tax liability by an individual's fluctuating, day-by-day, hour-by-hour capacity to dispose of property which he owns. We hold that estate tax liability for policies "with respect to which the decedent possessed at his death any of the incidents of ownership" depends on a general, legal power to exercise ownership, without regard to the owner's ability to exercise it at a particular moment. Nothing we have said is to be taken as meaning that a policyholder is without power to divest himself of all incidents of ownership over his insurance policies by a proper gift or assignment, so as to bar its inclusion in his gross estate under § 2042(2). What we do hold is that no such transfer was made of the policies here involved. The judgment of the Court of Appeals is reversed and the judgment of the Tax Court is affirmed.

It is so ordered.

Mr. Justice DOUGLAS dissents.

NOTE

The following case and Revenue Ruling deal with the pre-1977 version of § 2035, under which gifts made by a decedent within three years of his death were included in his gross estate if the gifts were made in contemplation of death.

DAISY M. B. BEL v. UNITED STATES

United States Court of Appeals, Fifth Circuit, 1971.
452 F.2d 683, 72–1 USTC ¶ 12,818
cert. denied 406 U.S. 919, 92 S.Ct. 1770, 32 L.Ed.2d 118 (1972).

GOLDBERG, Circuit Judge:

* * *

Commencing in October of 1957, the decedent, John Albert Bel, purchased annually an accidental death policy on his own life in the principal amount of $250,000. Each policy covered a term of one year, and the last such policy was acquired in October of 1960, less than one year prior to the decedent's death. While the decedent himself executed the original insurance application and paid, with community funds, all of the premiums, the policies from their inception were owned solely by the decedent's three children. The October 1960 policy matured as a result of the decedent's accidental death, and his three children, as beneficiaries under the policy, received the $250,000 proceeds. Plaintiffs Mrs. Daisy Miller Boyd Bel and Richard E. Gerard, as executors of the decedent's estate, duly filed an estate tax return, in which they omitted from the decedent's gross estate an amount equal to John Bel's community share of the policy proceeds. The Commissioner of Internal Revenue thereafter assessed a deficiency, which resulted in part from a determination that the accidental death policy had been transferred by the decedent to his children in contemplation of death. The plaintiffs paid the deficiency, filed a claim for refund, and then instituted this suit.

With respect to the accidental death policy, the district court held (1) that the taxpayers failed to discharge their statutory burden of proving that the decedent's purchase of the policy was not a transfer in contemplation of death within the meaning of 26 U.S.C.A. § 2035, and (2) that the amount includable in the decedent's gross estate as a result of this transfer in contemplation of death was the purchase price of the policy (premiums paid), rather than its matured value at the time of decedent's death (insurance proceeds). 310 F.Supp. 1189. On appeal, the taxpayers assert that the former holding of the district court is erroneous, while the government contends that it is the latter ruling that is incorrect as a matter of law. We affirm the district court's conclusion that the decedent's purchase of the accidental death policy was a transfer in contemplation of death, but we reverse its holding that only the policy premiums are includable in the decedent's gross estate.

* * *

In determining *what* the decedent had transferred to his children as a result of his purchase of the accidental death policy, the district court concluded that only the dollar amount of the policy premiums was includable in the decedent's gross estate. In disposing of this issue the district court relied entirely upon the Tax Court case of Estate of Coleman v. Commissioner, 1969, 52 T.C. 921. In *Coleman* the decedent's children purchased, more than four years prior to the decedent's death, a life insurance policy on her life. The children were the record owners and beneficiaries of the policy, but the decedent paid all of the premiums. While the taxpayers and the Commissioner agreed that approximately one-third of the policy premiums had been paid in contemplation of death, the government, on the basis of Revenue Ruling 67–163, 1967, 2 Cum.Bull. 327, contended that the amounts to be included in the decedent's gross estate was a pro rata portion of the policy proceeds based on the amount of premiums that the decedent had transferred in contemplation of death. The Tax Court rejected this argument. The Court noted that prior to a 1954 amendment, the Internal Revenue Code provided that proceeds of an insurance policy on the life of a decedent which were receivable by beneficiaries other than the decedent's executor were includable in the decedent's gross estate in the proportion that the amount of premiums or other consideration paid directly or indirectly by the decedent bore to the total amount of the premiums paid for the insurance. In 1951 Congress altered the taxability of life insurance by providing in 26 U.S.C.A. § 2042 that includability of the proceeds of life insurance in a decedent's gross estate depends solely upon the decedent's retention of incidents of ownership in the policy. The congressional rejection of the premium-payment test persuaded a majority of the Tax Court in Estate of Coleman to conclude that a mere payment of premiums by a decedent could not operate as a transfer of an interest in the proceeds of insurance. In addition, the Tax Court stated:

> "The purpose of section 2035 is to prevent the avoidance of estate tax through the use of gifts as a substitute for testamentary disposition of what would otherwise be included in the gross estate. Milliken v. United States, 283 U.S. 15, 51 S.Ct. 324, 75 L.Ed. 809 (1931); see Liebman v. Hassett, 148 F.2d at 251. The focus, therefore, must be on what the decedent parted with as a result of her payment of the premiums in contemplation of death. Decedent held no interest whatsoever in the policy or its proceeds. Her children were the sole owners of the policy and only they could deal with rights and benefits flowing therefrom. To be sure, these payments kept the economic substance of that ownership alive.

But the decisive point is that what these payments created or maintained was theirs and not hers. In these circumstances, we can see no basis for concluding that there was a constructive transfer of an interest in the policy. The only thing diverted from her estate was the actual money paid."

52 T.C. at 923.

* * *

In arguing that this court should affirm the lower court's ruling that no part of the insurance proceeds is includable in decedent's gross estate, the taxpayers would have us apply a section of the Code dealing with lemons (section 2042), to one pertaining to oranges (section 2035). Section 2042, which deals strictly with life insurance, provides, *inter alia*, that a decedent's gross estate shall include the value of the proceeds of life insurance policies on which the decedent possessed at his death any of the incidents of ownership. However, section 2035 provides that *all property* which is transferred in contemplation of death is includable in a decedent's gross estate. We do not think that these two code provisions were designed or conceived to be read in *pari materia*. They came into being at different times, their respective targets were diverse, and we perceive no philosophic confluence to twin them. Therefore, we conclude that congressional rejection of the premium-payment test for purposes of section 2042 is foreign to the proper application of section 2035 to the instant case.

More importantly, however, we think that the district court erred in failing to recognize the fundamental factual differences between the case *sub judice* and Estate of Coleman v. Commissioner, *supra*. In *Coleman* the premium payments were made on a policy that was brought into existence more than three years prior to the decedent's death. Thus, the original contractual rights and ownership of the policy in *Coleman* were created outside the presumptive period, and, as the Tax Court noted, those premiums paid in contemplation of death served only to keep "the economic substance of that ownership alive." In the instant case, however, the premium paid by the decedent less than one year prior to his death engendered the entire right, title, and interest which the decedent's children had in the accidental death policy. Essentially, every stick in the bundle of rights constituting the policy and its proceeds had its genesis within three years of the decedent's death. Therefore, we conclude that the Tax Court's rejection of the premium-payment test as the measurement of what the decedent transferred in contemplation of death is inapplicable to the factual situation in the instant case.[23]

Finally, we, unlike the district court, are not convinced that judicial inquiry should focus on what the decedent "parted with" as a result of his purchase of the accidental death policy in contemplation of death. As noted above, the Tax Court in *Coleman* reasoned that only the value of the premiums should be included in the donor's estate because "[t]he only thing

23. Similarly, we conclude that First National Bank of Midland v. United States, 5 Cir. 1970, 423 F.2d 1286, wherein this court rejected Revenue Ruling 67–163 in a factual context essentially identical to the situation in *Coleman*, is inapposite because of factual differences with our case. There, as in the *Coleman* case, the insurance policy had been procured more than three years prior to the decedent's death.

diverted from [the] estate was the actual money paid." The district court adopted this "diversion" principle, since it concluded that the decedent's estate was reduced only by the dollar amount of the policy premiums. However, we decline to follow the *Coleman* standard in this case.

In Chase National Bank v. United States, 1929, 278 U.S. 327, 49 S.Ct. 126, 73 L.Ed. 405, the Supreme Court upheld the constitutionality of the estate tax imposed by §§ 401 and 402(f) of the Revenue Act of 1921, ch. 136, §§ 401, 402(f), 42 Stat. 277, 278. The Court concluded that the Act imposed a tax on a decedent's privilege of transferring property at his death and thus was not invalid because not apportioned as required by art. 1, §§ 2, 9, of the United States Constitution. The plaintiffs in *Chase*, however, asserted that the tax imposed on life insurance proceeds must be deemed to be a direct tax on property because there was nothing to which a transfer or privilege tax could apply, since the beneficiaries' interests in the policies were not transferred to them from the decedent, but rather from the insurer. In answering this contention, the Supreme Court stated:

> "Obviously, the word 'transfer' in the statute, or the privilege which may constitutionally be taxed, cannot be taken in such a restricted sense as to refer only to the passing of particular items of property directly from the decedent to the transferee. It must, we think, at least include the transfer of property procured through expenditures by the decedent with the purpose, effected at his death, of having it pass to another. Sec. 402(c) taxes transfers made in contemplation of death. It would not, we assume, be seriously argued that its provisions could be evaded by the purchase by a decedent from a third person of property, a savings bank book for example, and its delivery by the seller directly to the intended beneficiary on the purchaser's death, or that the measure of the tax would be the cost and not the value or proceeds at the time of death."

278 U.S. at 337, 49 S.Ct. at 128.

* * *

In our opinion the broad legal principle enunciated by the Supreme Court in *Chase* is that the word "transfer" is not limited to the passing of property directly from the donor to the transferee, but encompasses a donation "procured through expenditures by the decedent with the purpose, effected at his death, of having it pass to another." Like the Supreme Court, we perceive little seriousness in the argument that a decedent should be permitted to evade the provisions of section 2035 by funneling property to various beneficiaries through a third-party conduit. Judicial sanctioning of such evasion, we think, would so frustrate the attempted taxation of testamentary substitutes that section 2035 would stand emaciated and skeletonized beyond congressional recognition. We recognize, of course, that John Bel never formally possessed any of the incidents of ownership in the accidental death policy. As noted above, however, we conclude that section 2042 and the incidents-of-ownership test are totally irrelevant to a proper application of section 2035. We think our focus should be on the control beam of the word "transfer." The decedent, and the decedent alone, beamed the accidental death policy at his children, for by paying the premium he designated ownership of the policy and created in his children all of the contractual rights to the insurance benefits. These were acts of transfer. The policy was not procured and ownership designated and designed by some goblin or hovering spirit. Without John Bel's conception, guidance, and payment, the proceeds of the policy in the context of this case would not have been the children's. His actions were not ethereally, spiritually, or occultly actuated. Rather, they constituted worldly acts which by any other name come out as a "transfer." Had the decedent, within three years of his death, procured the policy in his own name and immediately thereafter assigned all ownership rights to his children, there is no question but that the policy proceeds would have been included in his estate. In our opinion the decedent's mode of execution is functionally indistinguishable. Therefore, we hold that the action of the decedent constituted a "transfer" of the accidental death policy within the meaning of section 2035, and that the district court erred in failing to include John Bel's community share of the proceed value of the policy in his gross estate.

* * *

REVENUE RULING 71–497.
1971–2 CB 329

The Internal Revenue Service has given further consideration to the position set forth in Revenue Ruling 67–463, C.B. 1967–2, 327, relating to the amount includible in a decedent's gross estate by reason of the payment by him, in contemplation of death, of premiums on an insurance policy on his life owned by another. Consideration has also been given to the question whether the proceeds of insurance on the life of the decedent in each of the situations described below are includible in his gross estate.

Situation 1. Four years prior to his death a decedent purchased and transferred to his wife all incidents of ownership in a whole life insurance policy and a five-year term policy on his life. However, he continued to pay the premiums on the policies until the time of his death.

Situation 2. Nine months before he died by accidental means, the decedent purchased an accidental death insurance policy on his life for a one-year term, designating his children as owners and beneficiaries. He paid the full premium from his individual funds.

It was determined that all of the actions taken by the decedent with respect to the policies were in contemplation of death.

Section 2035(a) of the Internal Revenue Code of 1954 provides that the value of the gross estate shall include the value of all property to the extent of any interest therein of which the decedent has at any time made a transfer (except in case of a bona fide sale for an adequate and full consideration in money or money's worth) in contemplation of his death.

Section 2035(b) of the Code provides that if the decedent within a period of three years ending with the date of his death (except in case of a bona fide sale for an adequate and full consideration in money or money's worth) transferred an interest in property, such transfer shall, unless shown to the contrary, be deemed to have been made in contemplation of death; but no such transfer made before such three-year period shall be treated as having been made in contemplation of death.

The value of an interest in property includible in a decedent's gross estate under section 2035 of the Code as a transaction in contemplation of death is the value of the interest as of the applicable valuation date (in this case, the date of death since the value of a matured policy would not change if the alternate valuation date were elected).   See section 20.2035–1(e) of the Estate Tax Regulations.

Revenue Ruling 67–463 holds that each premium payment made by a decedent on an insurance policy on his life owned by another was a transfer for an interest in the policy measured by the proportion the premium so paid bears to the total premiums paid.   Accordingly, the value of the proportionate part of the insurance proceeds that is attributable to those premiums paid within three years of death is includible in decedent's gross estate under section 2035 of the Code.   However, in First National Bank of Midland, Texas v. United States, 423 F.2d 1286 (1970), the United States Court of Appeals for the Fifth Circuit rejected the rationale of the Revenue Ruling in a substantially identical factual situation and held that no part of the proceeds of the policies was includible under section 2035.

The Service will follow the decision in *Midland*, insofar as that decision holds that payment, by a decedent, of premiums on a whole life insurance policy on his life that had been owned by another for more than three years prior to his death is not a transfer of an interest in the policy.

Accordingly, it is held with respect to *Situation 1* that no part of the proceeds of the whole life policy on the life of the decedent is includible in his gross estate.   The same conclusion is equally applicable to the five-year term policy that the decedent had transferred more than three years before his death.   However, with respect to both policies the value of any premiums paid by the decedent in contemplation of death within three years of his death is includible in his gross estate under section 2035 of the Code. Kathleen M. Gorman v. United States, 288 F.Supp. 222 (1968); Estate of Inez G. Coleman v. Commissioner, T.C. 921 (1969).

In *Situation 2*, on the other hand, the purchase by the decedent of a one-year term policy on his life, designating his children as beneficiaries and owners, constituted a transfer of the policy to his children just as the purchase of any other asset in their names would have effected a transfer. In Chase National Bank v. United States, 278 U.S. 327, 49 S.Ct. 126, 73 L.Ed. 405 (1929), Ct.D. 40, C.B. VIII–1, 308 (1929), the Supreme Court of the United States upheld the constitutionality of section 402(f) of the Revenue Act of 1921 (section 2042 of the 1954 Code) as applied to tax the proceeds of a life insurance policy taken out by decedent on his own life, as a tax on the indirect transfer of the proceeds from decedent to the beneficiaries   *   *   *.

The Supreme Court's analysis of the "transfer" of life insurance proceeds for estate tax purposes indicates that the estate tax provisions extend to the proceeds of a life insurance policy that are transferred only indirectly by the decedent to the beneficiaries, that the real subject of the estate tax is the shifting of the economic benefits of property at death, and that the gift in contemplation of death provisions cannot be evaded by decedent's purchase of property from a third person and the delivery of the property by the seller directly to the intended beneficiary.

Thus, in *Situation 2*, the economic benefit that the decedent did in substance transfer to his children by the purchase of the insurance policy was not the use of the cash amount of the premium payment, but the right to the insurance coverage for the one-year period of the contract. This coverage matured into the proceeds of the policy at his death. Accordingly, it is held that the value of the insurance in this situation is includible in his gross estate under section 2035 of the Code. See section 2042–1(a)(2) of the regulations.

Revenue Ruling 67–463 is hereby revoked.

¶ 20.02   BENEFICIARY DESIGNATIONS

Insurance proceeds may be made payable to one or more individuals in their own right, to trustees of an existing trust, or to a trust created to hold the policies or to receive the proceeds. If the company will accept the designation, proceeds may be made payable to trustees under the insured's will or to the executors and administrators of his estate. The last designation should be avoided because it subjects the proceeds to the expenses of probate and makes certain that they will be included in the insured's taxable estate under § 2042(1).

Making proceeds payable to a trustee, rather than to a named individual in his own right, allows more flexible arrangements to be made for the enjoyment of the proceeds by the trust beneficiaries. As in other situations where trusts are used to hold assets, beneficiaries may be given limited interests and the trustee may be given discretion in determining the amount to be paid to each of them.

If an individual is named as primary beneficiary, provision may be made for contingent beneficiaries if the primary beneficiary fails to survive the insured or fails to survive for some specified period of time. A requirement of survival for at least thirty days is desirable, if the primary beneficiary is entitled to the full policy proceeds, to provide for the possibility that both will be fatally injured in a common accident. Otherwise, if proceeds are payable to a beneficiary who survives the insured for only a relatively short time, additional taxes [24] and probate expenses may be incurred when the beneficiary dies. If he was entitled to the proceeds when he died, they will be included in his taxable estate even though payment is not made by the insurance company until after his death.

---

24. Section 2013, providing a credit for all or part of the federal estate tax paid with respect to a transfer of property to the decedent if the transferor died not more than ten years before or two years after the death of the decedent, mitigates the effect of successive deaths from the standpoint of federal taxes. But state death taxes may contain no comparable crediting provision.

REVENUE RULING 76–261.
1976–2 CB 276

Advice has been requested whether, under the circumstances described below, the insured-decedent possessed sufficient incidents of ownership in an insurance policy held in a fiduciary capacity to require inclusion of the policy proceeds in the gross estate under section 2042 of the Internal Revenue Code of 1954.

In 1957 the decedent, H, purchased an insurance policy on decedent's life. Decedent's spouse, W, was named beneficiary. In 1962 H transferred complete ownership of the policy to W and added the names of their children as beneficiaries. In 1971 W died. In W's will, H was named executor of W's estate and trustee of a residuary trust established for the benefit of their children. The insurance policy on H's life was included in W's residuary estate.

H, as trustee, was granted absolute and unfettered discretion to distribute the current income from the trust to the beneficiaries or accumulate the income and add it to corpus. In addition, H, as trustee, was empowered in the management and investment of the trust property to do any and all things that a natural person, free from disability of every kind, might legally do with or in respect of such person's own property. Under the terms of the policy, the owner could elect to have the proceeds made payable according to various plans, use the loan value to pay the premiums, borrow on the policy, assign or pledge the policy, and elect to receive the annual dividends.

In 1974, H died and a successor trustee was named.

* * *

In enacting section 811(g) of the Internal Revenue Code of 1939 (the predecessor of section 2042(2) of the 1954 Code), Congress introduced, but failed to define, the term "incidents of ownership." However, the Senate Finance Committee listed in its report the types of powers and interests that Congress meant to be included within the scope of the term. S.Rep.No.1631, 77th Cong., 2d Sess. 235 (1942), 1942–2 C.B. 677. The powers and interests there listed are virtually the same as those now included in section 20.2042–1(c)(2) of the regulations.

At the time of the enactment of section 2042 of the Code, the Senate Finance Committee strongly inferred that Congress intended section 2042 to parallel the statutory scheme governing the interests and powers that will cause other types of property to be included in a decedent's estate under other Code sections, particularly sections 2036 and 2038. S.Rep.No.1622, 83rd Cong., 2d Sess. 124 (1954). Under these sections, it is the decedent's power at the time of death to affect the beneficial interest or enjoyment of the property, or the income therefrom, that requires inclusion, even though the decedent had no right to receive any of the economic benefits.

That Congress had such an intent was recognized by the courts in Skifter v. Commissioner, 468 F.2d 699 (2d Cir. 1972), a case involving an insured decedent's possession of certain incidents of ownership in a fiduciary capacity, and in Lumpkin v. Commissisoner, 474 F.2d 1092 (5th Cir. 1973), a case involving a decedent's incidents of ownership not held in a fiduciary capacity.

The court stated in *Lumpkin* that "by using the 'incidents of ownership' term Congress was attempting to tax the value of life insurance proceeds over which the insured at death still possessed a substantial degree of control." Then, drawing upon cases decided under the predecessors of sections 2036 and 2038 of the Code, the court concluded that the decedent possessed "substantial control" over the time and manner of enjoyment of the proceeds because of the right conferred upon him to elect optional modes of settlement (his only right) under a group term life insurance policy. The court held this right to be an incident of ownership within the meaning of section 2042(2) despite the fact that the decedent could not benefit himself or his estate. See Rose v. United States, 511 F.2d 259 (5th Cir. 1975); United States v. Rhode Island Hospital Trust Company, 355 F.2d 7 (1st Cir. 1966).

Further, the fact that a decedent's control over the insurance is subject to fiduciary restraints over its exercise does not automatically deprive it of the substantiality required for inclusion of the value of the proceeds in the gross estate. Section 20.2042–1(c)(4) of the regulations specifically provides that a decedent is considered to have an "incident of ownership" in a policy held in trust if the decedent has the power (as trustee or otherwise) to change the time or manner of enjoyment, even though the decedent has no beneficial interest in the trust.

In *Skifter*, the Court of Appeals for the Second Circuit concluded that section 20.2042–1(c)(4) of the regulations must be read to apply only to reservations of powers by the transferor as trustee. The Service will not follow this holding nor the dictum to the same effect in Fruehauf v. Commissioner, 427 F.2d 80 (6th Cir. 1970). However, in *Lumpkin*, the Court of Appeals for the Fifth Circuit, in holding that the value of insurance proceeds was includible in the gross estate, stated that "it is enough if at death the decedent merely *possessed* an incident of ownership, the means by which he came into possessing being irrelevant." The principle of *Lumpkin* was again applied in *Rose*, another case involving incidents of ownership held in a fiduciary capacity, where the court pointed out:

* * * Under section 2036 Congress specifically levied the estate tax upon interests *retained* by a decedent in connection with an incomplete transfer; and section 2038 is similar in effect. Under section 2042, however, Congress applied the tax to insurance over which a decedent *possessed* any incidents of ownership. The difference in statutory language is significant. * * * We agree with the Second Circuit that section 2042 "roughly parallels" its cousin sections of the Estate Tax Code in regard to the substantiality of the decedent's control which is prerequisite to includibility in decedent's gross estate. But we cannot ignore Congress' conspicuous variety in statutory idiom, so as to make the tax treatment of insurance identical with the taxation of other interests: section 2042 was not drawn in terms to catch only *retained* incidents of ownership, and we find no basis to infer such a design. * * *

Similarly, the court in Terriberry v. United States, 517 F.2d 286 (5th Cir. 1975), cert. denied 44 U.S.L.W. 3530 (Mar. 22, 1976), held that the insurance proceeds on the decedent's life were includible in the decedent's gross estate under section 2042 of the Code where the decedent's wife transferred the policies to a revocable trust of which the decedent was a co-trustee.

In the instant case, the decedent, as trustee, through the right to elect optional modes of settlement, borrow on the policy, and withdraw dividends pursuant to the terms of the trust and the insurance policy, had a substantial degree of control over the time and enjoyment of the policy proceeds. Such control was an incident of ownership within the meaning of section 2042(2) of the Code.

Accordingly, since the insured-decedent possessed an incident of ownership in the insurance policy at the time of death, the proceeds of such insurance are includible in decedent's gross estate, even though held only in a fiduciary capacity.

¶ 20.03   SETTLEMENT OPTIONS

Policy proceeds normally are payable in a lump sum unless a settlement option is elected by the insured or by the beneficiary. The major types of settlement options are:

(1) Interest or income only payable to the beneficiary, with the principal sum held by the company for distribution at a later date;

(2) Installments payable over a fixed period of years; and

(3) An annuity payable for the life of one or more beneficiaries.

Payments of interest under the first option are fully taxable as income to the beneficiary. In a period of rising interest rates, the rate used to compute the payments is likely to be unattractively low.

The installment option includes an interest element, as each installment payment combines principal and interest. The portion representing interest is fully taxable as income to the recipient unless she is the surviving spouse of the insured.[25] Up to $1,000 per year of interest free of income tax may be received by a surviving spouse, with respect to policies on the life of each deceased former spouse.[26] Estate planners may be intrigued by the image of a thrice-widowed recipient of $1,000 per year of excludible interest with respect to insurance on the lives of each of three former husbands. But other sources of tax-exempt income are available and an investment in tax-exempt bonds may offer a better yield than the income earned by leaving proceeds with the company.

The annuity option is a series of periodic, level payments that combine principal and interest, as in the installment option, but which are contingent, as to some or all of the payments, on the survival of the payee. The $1,000 exclusion for spouses, described above with respect to the installment option, is similarly available under the annuity option.[27]

One disadvantage of settlement options is that they provide only limited flexibility in the payment of policy proceeds. Although some special provisions may be worked out for relating the amount payable to a beneficiary to attainment of a designated age or some other event, insurance companies

---

25. § 101(d)(1).   27. Reg. § 1.101–4(g), *Example (3)*.

26. § 101(d)(1)(B).

are not equipped to administer provisions that require any extended inquiry into a beneficiary's situation or a discretionary judgment as to the amount needed at a particular time. If such an inquiry or judgment is to be made, it is necessary that the proceeds be payable to a trustee to whom discretionary powers are given.

¶ 20.04 USE OF LIFE INSURANCE IN COMMUNITY PROPERTY STATES

The use of life insurance in estate planning is greatly affected by community property laws in the eight states in which they are in force. Such laws affect:

(1) ownership of policy rights during the life of the insured;

(2) beneficiary designations and transfer of policy rights; and

(3) rights to proceeds of the policy on the death of the insured.

In order to determine federal tax consequences of ownership and transfer of policy rights, as well as entitlement to policy proceeds, it is necessary to analyze the effect of state community-property laws.

[1] Rights Under Insurance Policies During the Life of the Insured

Two different rules have been applied in determining ownership of rights under a life insurance policy during the life of the insured, where the premiums were paid, in whole or in part, with community funds:

(1) the proportional payment rule; and

(2) the inception-of-title rule.

It should be kept in mind that if the result of applying the particular rule is that all or part of such rights are held as community property, one spouse may be entitled to exercise such rights as manager for the community but does not become sole owner as a result.[28]

There has been some support by commentators for a third rule (the "risk payment" rule) for term insurance; their support is based on the theory that proceeds of such insurance are directly attributable to the final premium payment made during the life of the insured.[29] The source of that payment determines whether (and to what extent) the proceeds are community property or the separate property of either or both spouses.

[a] Proportional Payment Rule

Under the proportional payment rule (also referred to as apportionment or tracing), ownership of policy rights is determined by the proportion of total premiums paid from the community estate and the respective separate

---

28. Reg. § 20.2042–1(c)(5); Rev.Rul. 48, 1953–1 CB 392; Rev.Rul. 232, 1953–2 CB 268; Commissioner v. Chase Manhattan Bank, 259 F.2d 231, 58–2 USTC ¶ 11,818 (5th Cir. 1958), cert. denied 359 U.S. 913 (1959).

29. See J. Higbee. "Applying the Risk Payment Doctrine to Community and Separate Property Interests in Life Insurance Proceeds: Its Federal Estate Tax Consequences." 4 Comm.Prop.J 87 (Spring 1977);

Comment, "Community and Separate Property Interests in Life Insurance Proceeds: A Fresh Look," 51 Wash.L.R. 351 (1976). Results consistent with this approach, although without explicit reference to "risk payment," were reached in Lock v. Lock, 8 Ariz.App. 138, 444 P.2d 163 (1968); Travelers Ins. Co. v. Johnson, 97 Idaho 336, 544 P.2d 294 (1975). See also, Guy v. Guy, 98 Idaho 205, 560 P.2d 876 (1977) (group term disability insurance).

estates of the spouses.[30]   For example, if total premium payments on a policy on the husband's life were $20,000, of which $10,000 came from community funds, $5,000 from the separate property of the husband, and $5,000 from the separate property of the wife, the policy rights would be owned one-half by the community and one-quarter each by the husband and wife respectively.   This division of ownership would govern federal tax consequences of a gift of the policy during the husband's life,[31] as well as its inclusion in the wife's gross estate if she predeceases him.[32]

Of course, each premium payment may change the proportion of total premiums paid from each source, so that a periodic updating is required to determine the tax characteristics of the policy for estate-planning purposes. And, as with other questions of characterization of property as community or separate, various presumptions are controlling in the absence of evidence to rebut them.[33]

[b] Inception-of-Title Rule

Under the inception-of-title rule, the character of a policy is determined when it is first purchased and is not affected by subsequent premium payments.[34]   Thus, if the first premium is paid with separate funds of the husband, the policy is part of the husband's separate estate.   If the couple's community property is used to pay subsequent primiums, the character of the policy as a separate asset is not changed.   Instead, the premium payments give rise to a claim to reimbursement from the separate estate of the husband in favor of the community.[35]   Again, the characterization of the policy would govern federal tax consequences of a gift of the policy during the life of the insured,[36] as well as whether or not it is includible in the gross estate of the non-insured spouse if she predeceases the insured.[37]

[2] Beneficiary Designations and Transfer of Policy Rights

During the life of the insured, there may be a transfer of policy rights or a designation of beneficiary with or without the consent of both spouses. A designation of beneficiary is necessarily inconclusive except in the rare cases in which it is irrevocable.   Thus, the consequences of such designations, both for purposes of state law and federal taxes, must await the death

---

30.   Polk v. Polk, 228 Cal.App.2d 763, 781, 39 Cal.Rptr. 824, 835 (1964);   McBride v. McBride, 11 Cal.App.2d 521, 54 P.2d 480 (1936);   Modern Woodmen of America v. Gray, 113 Cal.App. 729, 299 P. 754 (1931).

31.   This is an application of the general rule of Reg. § 25.2511-1(h)(8).

32.   Reg. § 20.2042-1(c)(5).   For valuation, see Reg. § 20.2031-3(a)(2); Rev.Rul. 75-100, 1975-1 CB 303.

33.   See ¶ 1.08 [1], note 65 supra.

34.   Beatrice S. Parson v. United States, 460 F.2d 228, 233, 72-1 USTC ¶ 12,847 (5th Cir. 1972) (Texas);   McCurdy v. McCurdy, 372 S.W.2d 381 (Tex.Civ.App.1963), writ ref'd: Connell v. Connell, 331 So.2d 4 (La.1976).

35.   Rev.Rul. 232, 1953-2 CB 268;   Rev.Rul. 54-272, 1954-2 CB 298;   Estate of Bryan Wildenthal, 29 TCM 519 (1970).

36.   Rev.Rul. 48, 1953-1 CB 392;   Rev.Rul. 232, 1953-2 CB 268;   Commissioner v. Chase Manhattan Bank, 259 F.2d 231, 246-7, 58-2 USTC ¶ 11,818 (5th Cir. 1958).

37.   Reg. § 20.2042-1(c)(5);   Rev.Rul. 75-100, 1975-1 CB 303.   If the insured dies first, the insurance proceeds are subject to a claim in favor of the community estate for reimbursement for premiums paid from community funds.   The amount of that claim is deductible in determining how much is includible as insurance in the estate of the insured, but one-half of the claim is includible therein as property owned at death.   See Rev.Rul. 80-242, 1980-2 CB 276.

of the insured and the determination of rights to the proceeds. A transfer of policy rights is another matter and, to whatever extent it is effective under state law, is a completed gift for federal gift tax purposes.[38]

If the non-insured spouse consents to such a transfer of policy rights to a third party, federal gift tax consequences turn on the ownership of such rights as a matter of state law. If such a transfer of a community-property interest in a policy is made by the insured without the consent of the non-insured spouse, whether or not there is a completed gift depends upon whether state law recognizes his authority to make the transfer. States vary as to the extent to which the husband may make gifts of community property that is under his managerial control.[39] If the transfer is within the scope of his authority, it is a gift by the wife of her community-property interest in the policy.[40] If the transfer exceeds the scope of such authority, it is voidable by the wife.[41] There is no gift for federal tax purposes unless and until her right to treat the transfer as voidable has expired.

[3] Proceeds and Related Rights

If the insured spouse dies first, only one-half of the community interest in the proceeds is includible in his estate even if such proceeds are payable to his executor.[42] If the insured held incidents of ownership, he is deemed to have held such incidents with respect to the community interest in the policy as agent of the community rather than as an individual.[43] Again, only one-half of the community interest is includible in his estate.

The surviving (non-insured) spouse is held to have made a gift of her share of the community interest if the proceeds are payable to anyone other than her [44] or the insured's estate,[45] with one important exception. If she has and exercises a legal right to assert an interest in such proceeds by challenging the beneficiary designation, there is no gift of her share. A widow's ability to do so is similar to her ability to challenge other gifts of community property.[46]

---

38. Reg. § 25.2511–1(h)(8).

39. Now that many community property states have equal or joint management, see, e.g., Idaho Code § 32–912 (Supp.1980), the ability to make or challenge gifts may belong to both spouses.

40. See, e.g., Commissioner v. Chase Manhattan Bank, note 36 supra.

41. See note 46 infra.

42. Reg. § 20.2042–1(b)(2); Rev.Rul. 232, 1953–2 CB 268, Example A.

43. Reg. § 20.2042–1(c)(5); Rev.Rul. 48, 1953–1 CB 392.

44. Reg. §§ 20.2042–1(c)(5), 25.2511–1(h)(9); Rev.Rul. 48, 1953–1 CB 392; Rev.Rul. 232, 1953–2 CB 268, Example A(1); Commissioner v. Chase Manhattan Bank, note 36 supra.

45. Generally, community policy proceeds payable to the insured's estate retain their community character when the insured H predeceases W. See, for example, Rev.Rul. 232, 1953–2 CB 268, Example A(3); Berry v. Franklin State Bank & Trust Co., 186 La. 623, 173 So. 126 (1937); In re White's Estate, 41 N.M. 631, 73 P.2d 316 (1937); In re Brown's Estate, 124 Wash. 273, 214 P. 10 (1923). Texas also allows W to recover one-half of the proceeds from a community policy payable to predeceasing H's estate. Blackmon v. Hansen, 140 Tex. 536, 169 S.W.2d 962, 965 (1943) (dictum); Martin v. Moran, 11 Tex.Civ.App. 509, 32 S.W. 904 (1895).

46. See, e.g., Polk v. Polk, 228 Cal.App.2d 763, at 782, 39 Cal.Rptr. 824, at 835 (1964); Francis v. Francis, 89 Wash.2d 511, 573 P.2d 369 (1978).

If the insured is the surviving spouse,[47] the law of some states may lead to inclusion of the entire amount of the proceeds in his estate because he will be awarded ownership when the estate of the non-insured spouse is settled.[48]   In other states, one-half of the community interest therein may be excluded because of the right of the predeceasing (non-insured) spouse to dispose of her share by will.[49]   Regardless of which spouse dies first, the executor in some inception-of-title states may claim reimbursement for separate funds used as premiums on community property policies.[50]   Also, the community estate may claim reimbursement for community property expended on the separate property policies of the deceased.[51]

---

47. For the amount includible in the non-insured's estate due to her community property interest in a policy, see notes 32 and 37 supra.

48. The estate of the noninsured spouse is allocated one-half of the cash surrender value of the policy while the insured receives the other one-half of the cash surrender value plus ownership of the policy. Thompson v. Calvert, 301 S.W.2d 496 (Tex.Civ.App.1957).

49. See Donald Scott v. Commissioner, 374 F.2d 154, 67–1 USTC ¶ 12,460 (9th Cir. 1967) (California law) (sons allowed to take one-half of the value of the community proceeds as *W*'s residuary legatees).

50. See, for example.   Rev.Rul. 232, note 42 supra, *Example D;* Berry v. Franklin State Bank & Trust Co., note 45 supra, 186 La. at 639, 173 So. at 132 (*H* dies first); Succession of Le Blanc, 142 La. 27, 76 So. 223 (1917) (*W* dies first).

51. See note 35 supra.

Chapter 21

EMPLOYEE BENEFITS AND INDIVIDUAL RETIREMENT ARRANGEMENTS (IRAs)

¶ 21.01 USE OF EMPLOYEE BENEFITS AND INDIVIDUAL RETIREMENT ARRANGEMENTS (IRAs) IN ESTATE PLANNING

"Quintessential tax shelter" has been used to describe qualified pension and profit-sharing plans for employees.[1] No other estate-building device offers comparable opportunities to defer or minimize income taxes and to avoid estate and gift taxes.

The major varieties of qualified plans for employees that are important in estate planning include:

(1) Pension, profit-sharing, incentive stock option, and stock bonus plans; and

(2) HR 10 (Keogh) plans, which may include self-employed individuals.

Nonqualified deferred compensation and survivorship plans do not provide comparable tax advantages. A transfer of the employee's interest during his life may be taxable as a gift, and any interest not disposed of during his life may be included in his estate when he dies. No special favorable tax formulas are provided for benefits under such plans paid to employees or their beneficiaries. However, such plans are important in many estates and may be arranged on a case-by-case basis as part of individual negotiations with respect to compensation. Thus, the advisor often may need to review the possibility of negotiating such an arrangement as part of the client's compensation package.

Incentive stock option plans are authorized by § 422A, added by § 251 of the Economic Recovery Tax Act of 1981. The estate planning implications of such plans are outside the scope of this book.

Individual Retirement Arrangements (IRAs) have many of the distinctive tax advantages of benefits under the varieties of qualified plans noted above but are dealt with separately here because (1) an eligible client may set up an IRA for himself; and (2) the low dollar limits on contributions (other than rollovers) make such arrangements of greatest importance as vehicles to receive rollover distributions from qualified plans, as such distributions may be transferred ("rolled over") to IRAs in order to defer tax.

It is not surprising that benefits under plans for employees often form a major part of the estates of executives and highly paid employees. The rules governing the tax treatment of such benefits have become as complex and technical as any in the Code, with severe penalties for even minor deviations from their requirements. Thus, this is an area in which clients are in acute need of sound advice in deciding whether to set up a plan, what

---

1. Hickman, "Pension and Profit Sharing Plans: The Quintessential Tax Shelter," 25th Nat'l Conf. of the Tax Foundation 22 (1974).

kind of plan to establish, and how to exercise any available options under plans for their benefit.

The first two problems, whether to set up a qualified plan and what kind to establish, are outside the scope of this book.[2]   If the client is sufficiently in control of the situation to influence these decisions, the available alternatives should be explored in depth because large sums may turn on the choices made.   Stockholder-employees of a close corporation are often in this position, as are partners, sole proprietors, or self-employed individuals who may qualify for HR 10 (Keogh) plans.   Individuals who receive earned income (as defined in § 401(c)(2)) have the option of setting up an individual retirement arrangement (IRA).

The third problem is to choose among available options under an existing plan.   Before undertaking to do so, the advisor should obtain a description of the plan, the client's current beneficiary designation, and a statement of the value of the employee's account or of the benefits to which he or his beneficiaries will be entitled (if the plan defines such benefits).   With this information, the available alternatives can be analyzed in light of the client's other income and assets.

All forms of employee benefits and individual retirement arrangements are affected by community property laws in the eight states in which they are in force.

¶ 21.02   QUALIFIED PENSION, PROFIT-SHARING, AND STOCK BONUS PLANS

The great attraction of qualified pension, profit-sharing, and stock bonus plans for employees is that within the specified limits the employer may deduct his contributions when they are made [3] but nothing is includible in income by the employee or his beneficiaries at that time.[4]   Employer contributions may be paid through a trust or may be used to purchase annuities, face-amount certificates issued by mutual funds, or retirement bonds issued by the Treasury.   Income of the trust is generally tax exempt.[5]   This advantage of income tax deferral for the employee and his beneficiaries applies not only to the employer's contributions but also to amounts earned thereon (and amounts earned on contributions by the employee as well) until distributions are made.

Somewhat less favorable treatment is provided in the case of annuities purchased by tax exempt organizations or schools.[6]

---

2.   For a discussion, see Bergman & Reynolds, "Plan Selection—Pension, Profit-sharing Plans and ESOPs," 314 T.M.

3.   § 404(a) (pension, profit-sharing, or annuity plan); § 405(c) (bond purchase plan).

4.   § 402(a)(1) (pension, profit-sharing, and stock bonus trusts); § 403(a)(1) (annuity plans); § 405(a) (bond purchase plans).

5.   § 501(a), referring to § 401(a).   The trust is subject to tax on any unrelated business net income.   See §§ 501(b), 511.

6.   Under § 403(b), amounts contributed by the employer above an "exclusion allowance" are included in the employee's gross income for the taxable year in which the contribution is made.   The exclusion allowance is determined through a two-step calculation.   First, 20 percent of the compensation received from the employer for the most recent period is multiplied by the employee's number of years of service.   The excess of this figure over the aggregate of the amounts contributed by the employer for annuity contracts and excludible from the gross income of the employee for any

[1] Options as to Distribution of Benefits

Plans typically give employees and their beneficiaries a variety of options with respect to the method of distribution, which may be in a lump sum, in installments, or as an annuity. "Lump sum distribution" is a statutory term of art, on which important federal tax consequences turn. It is defined in § 402(e)(4)(A) generally as payment from a qualifying trust "within one taxable year of the recipient of the balance to the credit of an employee" on account of the employee's death, disability (as defined), or separation from service or after the employee attains age 59½. Favorable income tax treatment of lump sum distributions after the employee attains age 59½ may be elected only once.[7]

Payment of benefits in installments or as an annuity allows their receipt to be spread over a longer period of time than if taken in a lump sum. The extent to which these options can be used to defer receipt is limited by the requirement that benefits to the employee's beneficiary be "incidental" to the primary purpose of distributing accumulated funds to the employee.[8] However, payment of equal monthly installments over as many as thirty years (commencing at a normal retirement age of 65) to an employee or his designated beneficiary, if the employee dies before the end of the period, satisfies the "incidental" test [9] and permits a substantial amount of deferral.

[2] Favorable Tax Characteristics of Plan Benefits

Employees and their beneficiaries should be aware of the important favorable tax characteristics of plan benefits representing employer contributions (and deductible employee contributions) [9a] and earnings thereon. These include:

(1) *Income Tax Deferral.* No income tax is payable on benefits until cash or property is distributed [10] to the employee or his beneficiaries. Even then, during the employee's life a "rollover" [11] of a lump sum distribution to an eligible retirement plan may allow deferral to continue for an additional period. The rollover technique generally is not available for amounts received after the employee's

---

prior year is the exclusion allowance. Amounts transferred to an annuity contract by reason of a rollover contribution are not deemed employer contributions for the purposes of § 403(b). See § 403(b)(8).

7. § 402(e)(4)(B). See note 13 infra.

8. See Reg. § 1.401–1(b)(1).

9. See Rev.Rul. 72–241, 1972–1 CB 108.

9a. § 72(o) was added by § 311(b)(1) of the Economic Recovery Tax Act of 1981 to provide for voluntary deductible employee contributions. Under § 219(b)(2)(A), the maximum amount is limited to the lesser of 15% of the employee's taxable compensation from the employer or the employer's contribution to "the simplified employee pension and included in gross income (but not in excess of $15,000)," with a further limitation applicable to employees who are officers, shareholders, or owner-employees. See § 219(b)(2)(C).

10. § 402(a)(1). § 314(c)(1) of the Economic Recovery Tax Act of 1981 repealed the former provision which also taxed amounts "made available," even though not actually distributed. Under prior law, in determining whether or not an amount had been "made available," the doctrine of constructive receipt applied. See, e.g., Lee L. Blyler, 67 T.C. 878 (1977); note 14 infra.

11. "Rollover" is commonly used to describe the transfer to an eligible plan of money or property received in a distribution in order to defer tax thereon. See § 402(a)(5). The rollover may be to any one of three alternative individual retirement arrangements (IRAs)—a retirement account (§ 408(a)), a retirement annuity (§ 408(b)), or a retirement bond (§ 409). See § 408(d)(3). Thus, a variety of investment vehicles are available for this purpose.

death.[12]   However, if such amounts are payable in installments or as an annuity, the result is a further deferral of part of the tax during the period in which payments are made, similar to the deferral in annuity or installment payments during the employee's life.

Deferral also may be achieved if a qualified plan makes a lump sum distribution that includes securities of the employer corporation.   Any net unrealized appreciation thereon is excludible, under § 402(e)(4)(J), from the recipient's gross income.   As the section requires an appropriate adjustment of the basis of such securities, the end result is deferral of gain until the stock is sold by the recipient and such appreciation is realized.

(2) *Income-shifting.*   To whatever extent benefits are not paid until after the employee's death, taxable income will have been shifted from him to his beneficiaries, which may result in its being taxed at a lower rate.

(3) *Favorable income tax rates.*   For qualifying lump sum distributions, extremely favorable tax computation formulae may be elected.   In general, an amount reflecting pre-1974 employer contributions (including earnings thereon) is taxed as a capital gain.   The balance is eligible for a special averaging treatment sometimes referred to as the "ten pauper" rule.[13]

(4) *Gift and estate tax exemption.*   The employee's selection of a beneficiary to receive payments after his death is not considered a gift and, thus, is exempt from gift tax under § 2517.   Benefits not payable in a lump sum are exempt from estate tax, under § 2039(c), as long as the recipient is not the client's estate and the employee did not "constructively receive" the benefits before he died.[14]   Lump sum payments are similarly exempt from estate tax, under § 2039(f), if the recipient foregoes the special income tax treatment referred to above.[15]

---

12.   A spouse may roll over a lump sum received on the employee's death.   § 402(a)(7).

13.   The tax treatment is similar to that which would apply if part of the amount were divided for tax purposes among ten paupers. A "minimum distribution allowance" (§ 402(e)(1)(D)) is subtracted and the balance is then taxable as if it had been received over a ten-year period by an unmarried individual with no other income.   See § 402(e)(1)(C).   If the taxpayer so elects, the entire amount attributable to employer contributions (including that reflecting pre-1974 contributions) may be taxed under this special averaging treatment.   See § 402(e)(4)(L).   There is also a $5,000 exclusion from income under § 101(b).

14.   See, e.g., Northern Trust Co. v. United States, 389 F.2d 731, 68–1 USTC ¶ 12,509 (7th Cir. 1968); Reg. § 20.2039–2(b), Ex-

ample (4).   If there is a substantial restriction or limitation on the employee's right to withdraw the plan proceeds during his life, no constructive receipt will be deemed to have occurred.   See Rev.Rul. 77–34, 1977–1 CB 276; Rev.Rul. 80–158, 1980–1 CB 196.

15.   The election to forego the special income tax provisions is made by reporting the distribution as taxable income or by rolling over any portion of the distribution.   Reg. § 20.2039–4(d).   The election can be made on an amended return, but once made it is irrevocable.   Reg. § 20.2039–4(e).   However, if there are multiple recipients of a lump sum distribution, each can make the election separately, and the § 2039(c) exclusion will apply to so much of the distribution as is paid to recipients so electing.   Reg. § 20.2039–4(f).

Amounts representing employee contributions (and earnings thereon) do not qualify for exclusion from estate tax under § 2039(c) except to the extent such amounts represent deductible employee contributions.[15a] Under Reg. § 20.2039–2(c) the exclusion from the gross estate is based on the ratio between the "employer's contribution" on behalf of the employee and the "total contributions." Many plans allow the employee to withdraw his own contributions at any time. If the ratio test is applied as of the employee's death, it is possible that such a withdrawal prior to the employee's death could qualify the entire amount under the plan, including the portion attributable to earnings on the employee's contribution, for the § 2039(c) exclusion.

The favorable income tax computation formulae for lump sum distributions are not applied to earnings on employee contributions, although amounts representing contributions, which are made from the employee's after-tax income, are not subject to income tax.[16] Deferral and income-shifting are not accomplished with respect to non-deductible employee contributions, which are necessarily made from after-tax income of the employee. Deferral may be achieved with respect to earnings on employee contributions, however, under the general deferral rule described at (1).

ESTATE OF MAX SILVERMAN

United States Tax Court, 1974.
61 T.C. 605.

SCOTT, Judge: Respondent determined a deficiency in estate tax of petitioner in the amount of $4,193.85.

The issue for decision is whether the proceeds of two contracts, providing that upon their maturity date they were exchangeable for contracts providing for an annuity or annuities as selected by the owner from certain annuity options which had been purchased by a qualified pension trust established by the employer of Max Silverman (the decedent) for the benefit of decedent or the beneficiaries designated by him, but unconditionally assigned to decedent upon the termination of his employment prior to his attaining the specified retirement age without being exchanged for a selected annuity contract, are includable in decedent's gross estate or should be excluded under the provisions of section 2039(c), I.R.C. 1954.

* * *

Decedent was employed on July 30, 1942, and had been employed prior thereto by I. Schneierson & Sons, Inc., hereinafter referred to as Schneierson. Decedent continued in the employ of Schneierson until August of 1957 when he terminated his employment at the age of 61.

Schneierson entered into an agreement dated July 30, 1942, with certain of its employees and the Public National Bank & Trust Co. of New York as trustee (now Bankers Trust Co.) creating and establishing a pension trust, effective as of July 30, 1942.

* * *

15a.   See note 9a supra.   16.   See § 402(e)(4)(D).

Decedent as an employee of Schneierson was entitled to and did in fact become a participant in the pension trust agreement. The pension trust agreement was a noncontributing plan and decedent made no contributions to the plan.

Article 4 of the pension trust agreement provided for a pension trust committee of five members who were required to be employees of Schneierson. Decedent was not a member of this committee at any time nor was decedent a stockholder of Schneierson.

Article 5, section 8, of the pension trust agreement provided that as soon as practicable, but not later than 3 months after application by an eligible employee to become a participant in the pension trust plan, the Pension Trust Committee shall apply to a life insurance company or companies selected by it for contract or contracts for the benefit of such employee, which contracts shall provide for the benefits set forth in the pension plan. The application for contract and the contracts shall nominate and designate the trustee of the pension trust plan as the sole owner of the contracts, except that these contracts shall provide that the income payable after the retirement date shall be payable to the employee participant and shall provide for beneficiaries other than the trustee to receive settlement of any amount due in case of the employee participant's death.

Pursuant to the provisions of this section of the pension trust agreement, the Pension Trust Committee made application after decedent became eligible as a participant under the pension trust agreement for retirement annuity contracts for the benefit of decedent and thereafter five such annuity contracts were issued for the benefit of decedent.

Article 8 of the pension trust agreement provided that the normal retirement date in respect of any participant shall be the anniversary date of the contract obtained for his benefit nearest to his 65th birthday. Article 8 further provided that if the participant remained employed by the company after his normal retirement age, he would nevertheless begin receiving his annuity at the anniversary date of the policy as if he had retired.
* * *

* * *

Upon the termination of decedent's employment by Schneierson, the Pension Trust Committee instructed the trustee to deliver five annuity contracts to decedent. On November 19, 1957, the trustee assigned each of the five contracts to decedent. The contracts assigned to decedent were issued by the Equitable Life Insurance Co. of Iowa (hereinafter referred to as Equitable). Decedent prior to his death surrendered three of these contracts to Equitable and received the cash surrender value of each contract so surrendered. The remaining two contracts issued by Equitable for the benefit of decedent were policy No. A 44389 issued on July 30, 1942, and policy No. A 68865 issued on July 29, 1950. Each of these contracts provided for its maturity on July 30, 1961. Each contract provided that if decedent were living on the July 30, 1961, maturity date and the policy was in full force and effect, he would be paid a monthly lifetime annuity with a 120 months certain unless one of the options for a life annuity with a longer period certain or a joint and survivor annuity were selected. The option also provided for beginning the annuity at an earlier or later date but in no event later than the anniversary date of the contract nearest the annuitant's 70th birthday.

* * *

No premiums were paid on these contracts after July 31, 1956. Because of nonpayment of the annual premium due July 30, 1957, both contracts were left in force as of that date on the reduced paid-up annuity basis with the cash surrender value at the date of lapse accumulating with interest.

* * *

Decedent left both contracts with Equitable, and as a result thereof interest was accumulated on the cash surrender value at the time premiums ceased to be paid for decedent's life. Decedent named his wife, Blanche S. Silverman, as the beneficiary under each of these Equitable contracts. During his life decedent made a loan on policy No. A 68865, and $2,407.22 of the loan remained unpaid at his death. On March 2, 1964, decedent deposited policy No. A 44389 as collateral for a loan of $10,000 which he made from the Manufacturers Hanover Trust Co. Although decedent's death occurred over 5 years after the maturity date stated in the policies and over 2½ months after the anniversary date nearest his 70th birthday, decedent had not surrendered the policies for supplemental policies specifying the annuity elected and at his death was receiving no annuity under either of these contracts.

Schneierson's plan, contained in the pension trust agreement in effect at the date of termination of decedent's employment, was terminated with approval of the Commissioner of Internal Revenue on February 10, 1958.

The assignment to decedent on November 19, 1957, of each of the contracts obtained for his benefit recited that for a valuable consideration the trustee "hereby sells, assigns, transfers and sets over * * * its right, title, and interest in and to said policy, subject to all the terms and conditions in said policy." The assignment further provided that it was made pursuant to the provisions of the pension trust established by Schneierson.

After decedent's death, the proceeds of policy No. A 44389 which totaled $45,849.26 and the proceeds of policy No. A 68865 which totaled $54,725.12, after giving effect to a loan made by decedent during his lifetime of $2,407.22, were paid to Blanche S. Silverman, the widow of decedent, in accordance with the designation of her as beneficiary of the policies.

On the estate tax return no amount was included because of the receipt by Blanche S. Silverman of the proceeds of the two Equitable policies.

Under item 5 of Schedule F of the estate tax return, the following appeared:

> Equitable Life Insurance Co. of Iowa—two policies issued in name of decedent (policies #A68865 and A44389) payable on death to Blanche S. Silverman. Policies were issued in connection with a qualified non-contributory employees Trust. Policies were distributed to decedent as an employee on his separation from service. The entire proceeds of $100,574.38 are excludable under Section 2039(c) of the Internal Revenue Code.

Respondent in his notice of deficiency increased the taxable estate as reported by the $100,574.38 with the explanation that "It is determined that the proceeds of two insurance policies in the amount of $100,574.38 are includable in the decedent's gross estate and that such amount is not excludable within the purview of Section 2039(c) of the Internal Revenue Code of 1954 as claimed on the estate tax return."

Initially, we point out that it is absolutely clear from the facts in this case that the proceeds of the two annuity contracts are includable in decedent's gross estate under the provisions of section 2033 unless excluded therefrom by some other provision of the Code. That section provides that the value of the gross estate shall include the value of all property to the extent of the interest of the decedent therein at the date of his death. In this case decedent at the date of his death was the absolute owner of the annuity contracts.

Petitioner does not deny that except for the provisions of section 2039(c), the value of the annuity contracts would be includable in decedent's gross estate under section 2033. Petitioner states that a literal reading of section 2039(c) permits of no conclusion except that the proceeds of the two Equitable contracts are excludable from decedent's gross estate.

Petitioner states that it is clear that the payments of the proceeds of these contracts were payments received by Blanche S. Silverman under a contract purchased by an employee trust which formed part of a pension plan which at the time of decedent's separation from employment met the requirements of section 401(a). Petitioner states that since facts to support this contention are stipulated, the entire proceeds of the contracts are excludable under section 2039(c).

Respondent's contention is that Blanche S. Silverman did not recieve the proceeds under contracts purchased by Schneierson's pension trust but under contracts in effect purchased by decedent. Respondent contends that when the contracts were assigned to decedent in lieu of a cash payment upon the termination of decedent's employment, decedent himself constructively received payment under the employees' pension plan and procured the annuity contracts. Respondent argues that therefore the beneficiary received the payments under contracts in effect acquired by decedent.

Respondent relies primarily on the case of Northern Trust Co. v. United States, 389 F.2d 731 (C.A.7, 1968). In that case the court held that certain annuity contracts did not fall within the provisions of section 2039(c) since the decedent in that case had constructively received his share of the proceeds under the plan prior to his death. The facts in that case showed that in 1951 decedent's employer, a corporation, in anticipation of dissolution, purchased annuity contracts with funds forming part of a qualified employee's pension trust which had been in effect since 1942 and then assigned these annuity contracts to the decedent, an employee participant. The facts showed that decedent was one of three trustees of the plan and at the direction of a trustee other than decedent the corporate trustee assigned to the decedent, who was then 77 years of age, the contract procured for him. The facts further showed that even though the decedent in that case had rights to obtain annuities or to obtain the cash surrender value of the contracts, he never exercised any of these rights and the entire cash surrender value at the date of his death was received by the beneficiaries he designated. The United States Court of Appeals for the Seventh Circuit there stated (p. 735):

> We agree with the District Court that the decedent in fact had an option to select the manner in which his interest in the plans would be distributed. The exclusion of § 2039(c) is not applicable. The cash surrender value of the annuity contracts were properly includable in decedent's gross estate as property owned by him at the date of his death. The decedent had unfettered control of his share of the plan assets. * * *

Petitioner points to certain factual distinctions in the Northern Trust Co. case and the instant case and argues that the facts in the instant case more nearly resemble the facts in Estate of Harold S. Brooks, 50 T. C. 585 (1968), and First Trust Co. of Saint Paul v. United States, 321 F.Supp. 1025 (D.Minn.1970).

In our view, as respondent contends, the facts in the cases of Estate of Harold S. Brooks, supra, and First Trust Co. of Saint Paul v. United States, supra, are distinguishable from the facts in the instant case, and these distinctions are such that those cases in no way support petitioner's position in the instant case. We further agree with respondent that here, as in the *Northern Trust Co.* case, there is no showing and no basis for assuming that the Pension Trust Committee would not honor the decedent's election as to whether he received cash or annuity contracts. There is no evidence in this case to indicate whether the committee, in fact, consulted with decedent and, if it did, what options decedent requested. However, in the absence of evidence, we must assume that the Pension Trust Committee honored whatever request decedent made as to the methods of distribution to him of his interest in the pension trust when he terminated his employment with Schneierson. We, therefore, agree with respondent that there is no substantive distinction in the *Northern Trust Co.* case and the instant case.

However, the facts in this case are such that we need not decide whether, when decedent was assigned his complete interest in the pension trust by being assigned absolute right in the contracts which the trustee had procured for his benefit, he had any form of constructive receipt of his interest in the plan. When a person is granted an option to take cash or property of a value equal to that cash as was the situation here at the time the policies were assigned to decedent, the actual receipt by that person of the property is clear. However, there remains a question whether under such circumstances the person may be said to have constructively received the cash he might have elected to take but did not and used it to purchase the property. In our view under the facts present in this case, the proceeds of the two annuity contracts received by decedent's widow are not excludable from decedent's gross estate under section 2039(c) for reasons other than those which might involve questions of constructive receipt. Therefore, we will not further consider the applicability of the doctrine of constructive receipt as set forth in the case of Northern Trust Co. v. United States, supra, to the facts in this case.

Section 2039(c) provides for the exclusion from the gross estate of "the value of an annuity or other payment" receivable by any beneficiary other than the executor "under—(1) an employees' trust (or under a contract purchased by an employees' trust) forming a part of a pension * * * plan" which at the time of decedent's separation from employment or the time of termination of the plan, if earlier, meets the requirements of section 401(a). Decedent's beneficiary here did not receive an annuity as that term is ordinarily used but the question still remains whether she received an "other payment * * * under an employees' trust (or under a contract purchased by an employees' trust) forming a part of a pension * * * plan." It is clear that decedent's beneficiary received nothing under an employees' trust other than via the contracts, since long prior to his death decedent had been given absolute and unconditional ownership of all his interest in the employees' trust. Our question, therefore, comes to whether decedent's beneficiary received a payment "under a contract purchased by an employees' trust" within the meaning of section 2039(c)(1). In our view she did not. The contract which had been purchased by the employees' trust which formed a part of a pension plan was a contract for an annuity which would be paid to decedent commencing on his 65th birthday whether or not he had actually retired from employment by Schneierson. The contract further provided for options which might have been selected by the owner of the contract for annuities to begin on the anniversary date of the policy nearest to the 70th birthday of the annuitant. However, the pension trust plan of Schneierson was absolutely clear that the Pension Trust Committee was required to have the annuity under the plan start when the annuitant reached age 65, even though the annuitant might still be employed by Schneierson. The owner of the policy under the plan was the trustee, but the trustee was required upon instructions from the committee to elect the option chosen by the committee, which option was required by the plan to be an annuity for life beginning at age 65. In our view the statute as written carrying the parenthetical statement "(or under a contract purchased by an employees' trust)" immediately preceding the words "forming a part of a pension * * * plan," logically interpreted, means a contract which would meet the requirements for an annuity payment in conformity with the provisions of the pension plan. Once the contract here involved was assigned to decedent absolutely, the restrictions contained in the pension plan that payment of an annuity to decedent would in all events commence at age 65 (thus eliminating any right of the owner of the contract to the cash surrender value) were effectively eliminated, thereby causing the contract as assigned not to be one conforming to the requirements of the pension plan. It would follow that the contract then ceased to be any part of a pension plan. The plan permitted the Pension Trust Committee initially to apply only for contracts for the benefit of the participant which *shall provide for the benefits set forth in the plan.*

In our view, in order for a payment to be exempt from estate tax under the provisions of section 2039(c), it must be a payment made under a plan which meets the requirements of section 401(a). The only portion of section 2039(c) which could cause the payments here involved to be excluded from estate tax is the provision of section 2039(c)(1). The portion of section 2039(c) following subparagraphs (1), (2), (3), and (4) thereof states:

> If such amounts payable after the death of the decedent under a plan described in paragraph (1) * * * , are attributable to any extent to payments or contributions made by the decedent, no exclusion shall be allowed for that part of the value of such amounts in the proportion that the total payments or contributions made by the decedent bears to the total payments or contributions made.
> * * *

In our view, this provision, though dealing with a problem not here involved of contributions by both employer and employee, is a clear indication that the exclusion applies only to payments made under the plan which is exempt under section 401(a). In this case the payments were not made under the plan since the contracts, after they were assigned absolutely to the decedent, were never surrendered as by their terms they should have been for annuity contracts so that decedent could obtain an annuity in accordance with the plan.

While the legislative history of section 2039(c), as originally enacted, is not helpful in determining the intent of the parenthetical provision "(or under a contract purchased by an employees' trust)," the report of the Senate Finance Committee with respect to the addition of subparagraph (3) to section 2039(c) by the Technical Amendments Act of 1958 contains an inference that the section applies only to payments received under a qualified plan. The report of the Senate Finance Committee, in explaining this amendment, states as follows:

Estate-tax exclusion

> Subsection (e) of section 24 of the bill is a committee amendment to section 2039(c) of the 1954 Code, relating to the exclusion of certain annuities from the gross estate. Section 2039(c) presently provides an exclusion from the gross estate for the value of an annuity or other payments receivable by a beneficiary (other than the executor) under certain plans qualified under section 401(a). * * *

S.Rept.No.1983, 85th Cong., 2d Sess. (1958), 1958–3 C.B. 1074. In our view this statement of the Senate Finance Committee is in effect an interpretation of the provisions of section 2039(c) to mean that only payments received under a qualified plan are to be excluded. In our view if a contract containing no restrictions that would cause it to comply generally with the restrictions contained in the pension plan is assigned to a participant in a plan, the exclusion was not intended to apply if the rights of the participant in the contract were so absolute that the contract was clearly includable in his gross estate under section 2033 as is the situation here. The interpretation which we have given to section 2039(c) is in accord with the interpretation given to that section by the United States Court of Appeals for the Second Circuit to which an appeal in this case would lie in Commissioner v. Estate of Albright, 356 F. 2d 319 (C.A.2, 1966), reversing 42 T.C. 643 (1964). The portion of section 2039(c) involved in the *Albright* case was the provision that "no exclusion shall be allowed for that portion of the value of such amount [amounts payable after death of the decedent under plans described in section 2039(c)(1), (2), (3), and (4)] in proportion that the total payment or contribution made by the decedent bears to the total payments or contributions made." * * *

* * *

This reasoning of the Second Circuit, that section 2039(c), insofar as it provides for apportionment, is applicable only in situations where the amount received by the beneficiary is attributable to contributions by both the decedent and his employer, requires section 2039(c) to be read as being limited in its applicability to payments which would not have been includable in the decedent's gross estate except for the provisions of section 2039(a) or (b).

While the factual situation involved in the *Albright* case differs from that in the instant case, the appeals court in that case refused to interpret the words of the section in a manner which it considered to defeat the overall purpose of the provisions of section 2039 even though a literal reading of the words of the section was susceptible of such an interpretation.

Based on our interpretation of section 2039(c) and considering the rationale of the Second Circuit in Commissioner v. Estate of Albright, supra, we conclude that the payments received by decedent's beneficiary under the two contracts here involved are not excludable from decedent's gross estate.

Reviewed by the Court.

Decision will be entered for the respondent.

———

TANNENWALD, J., concurring: I agree with the result reached by the majority simply because, as Judge Hall puts it, the facts herein show that the "decedent strayed materially from the plan's payment provisions" and hence section 2039(c) should not apply. I see no need in this case to engage, as both the majority and Judge Hall's opinions do, in an expansive analysis of what might be the situation in other circumstances or the applicability or nonapplicability to section 2039(c) of the principle of constructive receipt which infuses the treatment of qualified employee annuities for income tax purposes. The reach of that principle in the field of taxation is murky at best. A similar description can be ascribed to the language of the opinions in *Northern Trust, Albright*, and *Brooks*. In this latter connection, it is enough, for the purposes of this case, to note that those cases are all distinguishable on their facts. While I am not rigidly averse to "biting the bullet," I see no need to do it where, as is the situation herein, the facts do not demand such a course of action and to do so may cause us to foreordain, or at least foreshadow, the results of future cases.

RAUM, J., agrees with this concurring opinion.

———

HALL, J., concurring: While I concur in the results reached by the majority, I cannot subscribe to some of the language in the opinion. In my view, the annuity proceeds are includable in decedent's gross estate solely because decedent, by his inaction when he reached normal retirement date, avoided the clear intent and requirement of his retirement plan that the annuities were then to go into pay status, and thereby effectively converted them into savings accounts to be held at interest which accumulated for his benefit. By doing so, he removed them from the statutory category of "payment receivable * * * under a contract purchased by an employees' trust * * * part of a pension * * * plan" and precluded the availability of a section 2039(c) exclusion to his estate.

* * *

Respondent, paying little heed to the statutory purpose, points out that in 1957 the Pension Trust Committee had the right, instead of furnishing decedent with the annuity contracts in question at the time of decedent's termination from employment, to cash in the contracts and pay cash to decedent. Respondent observes further that after decedent had received the contracts, he could have surrendered them for cash, even though he did not. Respondent contends that the existence of such unexercised rights removes the contracts in question from the protection of section 2039(c) and exposes their proceeds to the estate tax.

In my view, this contention should be firmly rejected as inconsistent not only with the statutory language but with the beneficent purpose of the tax law providing special tax benefits for qualified plans, and as effectively negating section 2039(c). Qualified retirement plans frequently and customarily include optional provisions permitting payment of benefits in the form of cash in a lump sum on separation from service. The Code not only contemplates such payments but expressly provides them with favorable tax treatment. Sec. 402(a)(2). In the absence of any clear indication in the Code or regulations that the mere provision in a plan for the possibility of such payments at the time of retirement, whether exercisable at the option of the trustee, plan administrator or the participant, was intended to preclude the applicability of section 2039(c) in cases where no such option was in fact exercised, we ought to have little patience with any such contention. By the same token, respondent's argument that section 2039(c) is inapplicable if an annuity contract distributed to a participant may be surrendered for cash exceeds the statutory language and intent. If there had in fact been such a surrender, of course the resulting cash would be includable. But where an asset is in terms excludable from the gross estate, the mere fact that it could have been (but was not) exchanged for another asset (cash) not so excludable is no warrant for overriding the clear statutory language. This point derives added force from the fact that retirement annuities not yet in pay status are, indeed, customarily so exchangable.

In the light of industry practice, little would be left of section 2039(c) were respondent's contentions to be accepted. Respondent's position is particularly puzzling since he makes no such contentions of "constructive receipt" in the highly analogous income tax area. Section 1.402(a)–1(a)(2) of the Income Tax Regulations provides, in part, that if a qualified trust purchases an annuity contract for an employee and distributes it to the employee in a year for which the trust is exempt, the contract containing a cash surrender value which may be available to the employee by surrendering the contract, such cash surrender value will not be considered income to the employee unless and until the contract is surrendered. Estate of

George E. Russell, 47 T.C. 8, 10–11 (1966), approved this regulation. See Estate of Harry Snider, 39 T.C. 341 (1962); Estate of Harry Snider, 31 T.C. 1064 (1959); Rev.Rul. 65–267, 1965–2 C.B. 141; Rev.Rul. 55–298, 1955–1 C.B. 394 Rev.Rul. 68–482, 1968–2 C.B. 186, notes the rationale for such a position; it holds that the cash value of a section 403(b) annuity contract is not considered made available to an employee, merely because he can receive the cash value by surrendering the contract and forfeiting his rights thereunder, because the employee suffers a significant penalty in that normally the cash value of an annuity is insufficient to purchase a new annuity contract of comparable or greater value to the employee. Income is not constructively received if the taxpayer's control of its receipt is subject to substantial limitations or restrictions. Sec. 1.451–2, Income Tax Regs.

Here decedent has an annuity which is not only guaranteed in advance, but was probably purchased at a lower rate than he could obtain it because of absence of commission or expense.

Nor is respondent's reliance on Northern Trust Co. v. United States, 389 F.2d 731 (C.A. 7, 1968), well founded. In that case, the court included in a decedent's estate annuities which had been purchased at age 77 to go into pay status over 17 years later, at age 95. Clearly enough, any such extreme postponement of commencement of pay status leaves no doubt that the annuities in question were being used for the simple accumulation of an estate rather than for a bona fide pension. No pension plan providing for a normal retirement age of 95 would be likely to qualify, for the benefits thereunder would in no meaningful sense be benefits under a true "pension plan." Sec. 1.401–1(b)(1)(i), Income Tax Regs.; Rev.Rul. 72–241, 1972–1 C.B. 108; Rev.Rul. 72–240, 1972–1 C.B. 108. The assets in question were therefore not receivable under "an employees' trust (or under a contract purchased by an employees' trust) forming part of a *pension * * * plan* which * * * met the requirements of section 401(a) [emphasis added]." Had the *Northern Trust* plan called for a routine postponement of pay status to age 95, it would not apparently have qualified. And assuming the terms of the plan called for a more normal retirement age and an earlier pay status, if the decedent took it on himself with the individual trustees' cooperation to achieve such a postponement, the amount would have ceased to be received "under" a trust forming part of the qualified pension plan. It would instead have been received under the decedent's own arrangement, essentially an arrangement for a death-time transfer of wealth in lieu of a pension. Section 2039(c) therefore would not apply. While agreeing entirely with the result in *Northern Trust*, I must respectfully disagree with so much of its reasoning as finds the mere availability of a right of cash surrender at the option of a nonadverse committee disqualifying under section 2039(c). Cf. sec. 72(h).

The reason I agree with the majority conclusion is that on the facts of the present case decedent did not follow the qualified plan, which called for pay status to commence at age 65. Once decedent strayed materially from the plan's payment provisions, he converted the payment from one "under" a qualified employee trust into one under his own personal plan, which he implicitly arranged with the insurance company to substitute for the qualified plan. Having taken himself out from the scope of section 2039(c), he could no longer rely on its protective power.

*   *   *

* * * What decedent thereafter held was in effect a mere savings arrangement, under which the cash surrender value of his retirement contracts was held for him at interest, an arrangement quite foreign to the wording and intent of the qualified plan. In fact, had the plan contained a provision authorizing the mere indefinite retention and accumulation at interest until death of the amount standing in decedent's account at the time of termination, the plan probably would not have continued to qualify. See Rev. Rul. 56–656, 1956–2 C.B. 280; cf. sec. 20.2039–2(b), example 4, Estate Tax Regs. To hold otherwise would permit the conversion, by mere inaction, of a bona fide retirement annuity, subject to income tax under the rules of section 72, into a tax-free savings account, the interest on which would accumulate tax free until death, and which then would also escape estate tax under section 2039(c). In order to confine the generous provisions of the Code to the true pension to which they were intended to apply (without imposing extra-statutory, judge-made restrictions thereon which would be a trap for the unwary but bona fide pensioner) I would construe section 2039(c) to be unavailable to annuities the commencement of pay status of which had been prolonged beyond the contemplation of the plan, by express or implied special arrangement with the annuity carrier after receipt of the annuity contract.

[3] General Planning Considerations for Benefits Under Qualified Plans

In order to make optimum use of this impressive array of tax advantanges, the client needs sound advice in choosing the pay-out method (including the possible use of a rollover), as well as the designation of beneficiaries to receive amounts payable after his death.

Often, lump sum distribution is undesirable for either income or estate tax reasons, or both. From an income tax standpoint, the advantage of the special computation formulae for lump sums may be outweighed by the greater deferral possible with installment payments. And from an estate tax standpoint, a lump sum distribution destroys an otherwise available exclusion for so much of the benefit as is not attributable to employer and deductible employee contributions, unless the recipient foregoes use of the special income tax treatment.[17]

If distribution is made in installments, it then becomes important to take potential estate tax consequences into account. Distribution to the executor or to any recipient obligated to use the proceeds to pay estate obligations will destroy the exemption and should be avoided.[18] Because the benefit is already free from estate tax, distribution to the client's spouse likewise is often undesirable, as it does not produce any estate tax marital deduction.[19] If the death benefit is payable to beneficiaries other than the spouse, other assets may be used to qualify as a marital deduction gift to her.

17. See §§ 2039(c), 2039(f).

18. See Reg. § 20.2039–2(b)(4), referring to Reg. § 20.2042–1(b).

19. Section 2056(a) requires that a qualifying gift be includible in the gross estate.

Often the client's revocable trust [20] is the logical choice to receive the death benefit, whether the distribution is made in installments or in a lump sum. The funds can then be made available to the client's spouse as a beneficiary of the trust without adding assets to the spouse's taxable estate that do not generate a marital deduction in the client's estate. The death benefit can serve as a source of liquidity if the trustee has authority to make loans to the client's estate or purchase assets from it. The trust may also offer greater income tax flexibility. Drafting and planning considerations for a trust that may receive a death benefit under a qualified plan include a prohibition against allocation to the marital share,[21] characterization of the death benefit for trust accounting purposes, and the effect of a § 2039(f) election on the client's dispositive arrangements.[22]

[4] Planning Considerations for Benefits Under Qualified Stock Bonus and Employee Stock Ownership Plans

Qualified stock bonus plans provide benefits distributable in stock of the employer. Such plans resemble profit-sharing plans except that contributions by the employer need not be made solely from profits.[23] Employee stock ownership plans (ESOPs) invest primarily in employer securities and are stock bonus plans either exclusively or in combination with a qualified pension plan.[24] The distinctive characteristic of these plans for the plan beneficiary is that the net unrealized appreciation is not taxable when employer securities are distributed.[25]

Although the treatment of net unrealized appreciation provides favorable opportunities for deferral of tax, the lack of diversification of this investment may be a disadvantage for the employee and his beneficiaries. Fluctuations in the price of the employer's stock may have a major impact on the net worth of the employee. If there is no ready market for the stock, as in the case of a closely held corporation, it may be difficult to shift the investment into other assets.

¶ 21.03 HR 10 (KEOGH) PLANS

An HR 10 (Keogh) plan is a qualified pension or profit-sharing plan that covers self-employed individuals.[26] Additional rules are applicable to such plans, including lower limits on amounts that may be contributed.[27] The limits might in effect be expanded if the client borrows from the plan at a relatively high but reasonably justifiable interest rate. Such a loan may

---

20. A testamentary trust can be used if local law permits such a distribution and does not make the distribution available to creditors of the estate.

21. See § 2056(b)(2).

22. Application of the "ten pauper" rule, supra note 13, may decrease the income taxes on the distribution, but the resulting inclusion of the distribution in the client's gross estate will increase both a formula marital deduction bequest and the estate taxes payable, thus depleting the residue in favor of the client's spouse. A trustee receiving a lump-sum distribution may face a serious fiduciary dilemma if the spouse is not also the primary beneficiary of the residue.

23. See Reg. § 1.401–1(b)(1)(iii).

24. See § 409A(a) for the statutory definition.

25. See § 402(e)(4)(J). An appropriate adjustment of basis is required. Id.

26. See §§ 401(c), 401(d).

27. See § 401(e).

provide the plan with a higher return than other available investments, and if the interest exceeds the return the client can expect to realize from his own investment of the funds, the additional interest in effect represents an additional contribution to the plan. Whether such a practice would adversely affect the qualifications of the plan or the client's interest deduction has not been determined.

Keogh plans were developed to allow individual owners and partners in unincorporated business and professional firms to participate in pension and profit-sharing plans. If a client is individually eligible or is a member of an eligible partnership, careful consideration should be given to the estate-planning benefits that may result. Such eligibility requires that the individual derive "earned income," as defined in § 401(c)(2)(A).

As in pension and profit-sharing plans that do not include self-employed individuals, and hence need not satisfy the additional requirements for HR 10 plans, there are defined benefit [28] plans and defined contribution [29] plans. Under the former, the plan is designed to provide retirement benefits in accordance with a pre-determined formula. Under the latter, the plan provides an individual account for each participant, with benefits based on the amounts contributed plus income earned thereon and other relevant additions and deductions.

¶ 21.04 NONQUALIFIED DEFERRED COMPENSATION AND SURVIVORSHIP PLANS

Nonqualified deferred compensation and survivorship plans do not offer as impressive an array of tax advantages as is available under qualified plans. However, the former do permit much more flexibility, as there is no need to comply with specific requirements other than avoidance of constructive receipt.[30] Deferred compensation, as its name implies, permits deferral by the employee. As with benefits under qualified plans, income represented by payments made after the employee's death will have been shifted from him to his beneficiaries. However, unlike qualified plans, the corollary of deferred taxation to the recipient is deferred deductibility by the employer.[31]

An employee's performance of services in return for payment at a future date is equivalent to a loan by him to his employer. Unless the employer is willing to take this into account and increase the future payments to compensate the employee for the loan, the arrangement, in effect, gives the employer interest-free use of funds due the employee. In that case, the

28. § 401(j).

29. § 401(e).

30. Reg. § 1.451–2(a); Rev.Rul. 60–31, 1960–1 CB 174, modified in other respects by Rev.Rul. 70–435, 1970–2 CB 100. To avoid constructive receipt, the employer's promise should be unsecured and unfunded and should not be represented by notes. If the employer becomes insolvent, the employee may lose all or part of the amounts deferred. See, e.g., In re Penn Central

Trans. Co., 484 F.2d 1300 (3d Cir. 1973), cert. denied 415 U.S. 951, (1974), in which certain salaried employees with approximately $10 million in deferred compensation benefits were awarded approximately 25 percent of the deferred amounts in a compromise settlement with the bankruptcy trustee.

31. § 404(a)(5) (deferred compensation plans); § 83(h) (property subject to restriction that is transferred in connection with the performance of services).

cost of the deferral to the employee in lost investment opportunities may be more than it is worth in income tax savings.

No estate tax exclusion is available for deferred compensation. To whatever extent it is unpaid at the client's death, the value of any contractually required payments is likely to be included in his gross estate either under § 2033 [32] or § 2039. [33]

A death benefit payment can be excluded from the client's gross estate if he is willing to forego any post-employment benefits (other than any benefits under a qualified plan) [34] for himself. [35] One form of such an arrangement involves a death benefit equal to twice [36] the employee's annual compensation at death payable to named beneficiaries, often over a period of years. No taxable gift arises on the execution of the death benefit contract, due to the contingent and uncertain nature of the beneficiaries' interests. However, Revenue Ruling 81–31 [37] held that such an arrangement results in a taxable gift in the quarter in which the employee dies, when the beneficiaries' rights vest and the value of the death benefit becomes ascertainable.

Death benefit and other non-qualifying deferred compensation arrangements are of special consequence in the context of a closely held business, where the parties have the greatest flexibility in designing arrangements to suit their circumstances and where some of the concerns that are important in dealing with an independent employer may be less pressing. For example, a controlling shareholder may find it easier to give up retirement benefits that might jeopardize the estate tax exclusion and rely on a death benefit that is contingent on continued employment until death. [38] However,

32. Inclusion under § 2033 has been held to require an "enforceable vested" right to have the amounts in question paid. See Estate of William E. Barr, 40 T.C. 227 (1963), acq. in result 1978–1 CB 1.

33. § 2039 requires by its terms that an annuity or "other payment" be payable to the employee and to the survivor as well. Thus, if the employer makes payments to the employee under one plan and to his widow or other survivors under another, the question is whether the two plans are to be integrated so as to require inclusion in the employee's estate of the value of the survivor's payments under § 2039 or whether they are to be treated as separate. Compare Estate of J. William Bahen v. United States, 305 F.2d 827, 62–2 USTC ¶ 12,091 (Ct.Cl.1962) (includible), with Estate of William V. Schelberg v. Commissioner, 612 F.2d 25, 79–2 USTC ¶ 13,321 (2d Cir. 1979) (not integrated and not includible), and Estate of Firmin D. Fusz, 46 T.C. 214 (1966), acq. 1967–2 CB 2 (same). See generally, Hagendorf, "Death Bargains for Executive Compensation—Gift and Estate Tax Consequences of Executive Compensation Techniques," 36 N.Y.U.Inst. on Fed.Tax. 243 (1978). Sometimes inclusion may be based on § 2038 if the decedent, either alone or in conjunction with the employer, had

the power to modify the beneficiaries' rights to post-death payments. See Estate of Murray J. Siegel, 74 T.C. 613 (1980).

34. A qualified plan cannot be aggregated with a non-qualifying arrangement in determining whether the employee had a right to receive an "other payment" that might make the death benefit includible in the employee's gross estate under § 2039. Rev.Rul. 76–380, 1976–2 CB 270.

35. Id.

36. This choice for the size of the death benefit may reflect a rule of thumb under the 1939 Code. The regulations allowed a corporate income tax deduction for salary continuations for a "limited period." It was held that the limitation related to the amount of the payment rather than the period of the pay-out, and that two years was a "limited period." See I. Putnam, Inc., 15 T.C. 86 (1950), acq. 1950–2 CB 4; Rev.Rul. 54–625, 1954–2 CB 85.

37. IRB 1981–4, 30, 3 CCH E & GT ¶ 12.440z.

38. Without such a contingency the implementation of the death benefit arrangement would likely result in a taxable gift. Id.

the "family flavor" in the context of a closely held business may subject the arrangement to close scrutiny.[39]

The future of non-qualified survivorship benefits as an estate planning tool is presently somewhat clouded. While there has been some movement toward liberalizing the availability of the estate tax exclusion, at least outside the context of closely held businesses,[40] the challenges to the income and transfer tax benefits of such arrangements, as represented by Revenue Ruling 81–31[41] and the *MSD*[42] case, will, if sustained, seriously undermine their effectiveness, although they may still be useful for income tax planning.

ESTATE OF EDWARD A. TULLY v. UNITED STATES

United States Court of Claims, 1976.
528 F.2d 1401, 76–1 USTC ¶ 13,120.

KUNZIG, Judge.

The single issue presented in this estate tax case is the includability in decedent Edward A. Tully, Sr.'s gross estate of death benefits paid directly to Tully's widow by his employer.

* * *

The facts in this case are uncontested. Before his death, Tully was employed by Tully and DiNapoli, Inc. (T & D), a company owned 50% by decedent and 50% by Vincent P. DiNapoli. On July 1, 1959, Tully, DiNapoli and T & D entered into a contract whereby T & D promised to pay death benefits to the Tully and DiNapoli widows. Later, in October 1963, the same parties amended the 1959 agreement to limit the maximum amount of death payments to $104,000. On March 7, 1964, Tully died. T & D paid his widow the $104,000 called for in the contract.

Because the death benefits were paid directly by T & D to the widow, plaintiffs did not include this sum in Tully's gross estate when they filed the estate tax return. On audit, the Internal Revenue Service (IRS) concluded that the $104,000 was part of Tully's gross estate and assessed an estate tax deficiency. Plaintiffs paid the deficiency, filed a refund claim and by timely petition filed in this court, brought the present action after the IRS disallowed their claim.

In essence, plaintiffs say section 2038(a)(1)[43] is inapplicable because Tully never transferred an interest in the death benefits, either at the time

39. See, e.g., MSD, Inc. v. United States, 434 F.Supp. 85, 1977–1 USTC ¶ 9361 (N.D. Ohio 1977), aff'd per curiam, 1979–2 USTC ¶ 9712 (6th Cir. 1979), where the corporation was denied deductions under §§ 162 and 404(a) for payments to a shareholder's widow under a death benefit arrangement, even though the court found the arrangement to be a type of transaction which would have been negotiated on an arm's length basis, where the taxpayer did not prove the arrangement was intended to benefit the corporation.

40. See Estate of William V. Schelberg v. Commissioner, note 33 supra, in which the Second Circuit questioned the correctness

of *Bahen*, the leading case on the integration of separate plans to satisfy the requirements of § 2039.

41. See note 37 supra.

42. See note 39 supra.

43. "The value of the gross estate shall include the value of all property * * * *to the extent of any interest* therein of which the decedent has at any time *made a transfer* * * * *where the enjoyment thereof was subject at the date of his death to any change through the exercise of a power* (in whatever capacity exercisable) by the decedent alone or by the decedent in conjunc-

of their creation or thereafter, and even if he had, he kept no power to "alter, amend, revoke or terminate" the interest.   Further, plaintiffs assert, decedent had no "interest" in the death benefits at the time of his death within the meaning of estate tax section 2033.   Defendant takes an opposing viewpoint.   It contends that Tully made a transfer of his interest in the benefits prior to his death, but kept a power to "alter, amend, revoke or terminate" such transfer until the time of his death.   Defendant claims this power requires addition of the benefits to Tully's gross estate under section 2038(a)(1).   Alternatively, the Government argues, Tully still had sufficient "interest" in the benefits at the time of his death to force the $104,000 into his gross estate under section 2033.

The Government relies only on sections 2038(a)(1) and 2033, and no others, in its argument that the death benefits at issue here are includable in Tully's gross estate.

Defendant's contentions, specifically its argument that sections 2038(a)(1) and 2033 must be treated as virtually identical, suggest at the outset that we consider the basic philosophy of estate tax law.   As enacted by Congress, the primary purpose of the estate tax is to tax "the transfer of property at death."   C. Lowndes & R. Kramer, Federal Estate and Gift Taxes § 2.2 (3d Ed. 1974).   If sufficient incidents of ownership in an item of property are given away before death, no tax will be imposed.   Since all estate tax statutes are direct [sic] at taxing property transferred at death, it can become easy to confuse their operation or to apply them in an overlapping fashion.

Within this context, the estate tax sections involved in the instant case, 2038(a)(1) and 2033, both impose a tax on property transferred at death.   However, they are directed at two different situations.   Section 2038(a)(1) is specific in its terms.   It taxes property which an individual has given away while retaining enough "strings" to change or revoke the gift.   Section 2033 [44] is more general in its approach, and taxes property which has never really been given away at all.

Certain of defendant's arguments misconstrue this basic difference between section 2038(a)(1) and section 2033.   By suggesting that the same "controls" over property which might represent a section 2038(a)(1) "power" can also be viewed as a section 2033 "interest," the Government attempts to turn section 2033 into an estate tax "catch all."   This was not the intent of Congress in enacting section 2033.   Congress has provided a "catch all" in the income tax statutes.[45]   It has not done so in the estate tax area. [Citations omitted.]   Therefore, defendant's efforts to treat the two sections as virtually identical by the "catch all" method are misplaced.

In accordance with this analysis, our inquiry takes two avenues.   First, did Tully transfer the death benefits but keep a power to change or revoke

---

tion with any other person (without regard to when or from what source the decedent acquired such power), *to alter, amend, revoke, or terminate.* * * * " Int. Rev.Code of 1954, § 2038(a)(1). (Emphasis added).

44. Section 2033 applies to "interests" in property, but interest is not defined in the statute.

45. Int.Rev.Code of 1954, § 61 provides: " * * *   [G]ross income means all income from whatever source derived. * * * "

them until the time of his death? If so, section 2038(a)(1) applies. Second, did Tully have an "interest" in the benefits at his death? If he had an "interest," section 2033 applies.

We find that Tully effectively transferred his interests in the death benefits before his death, determine that he did not keep any significant powers to "alter, amend, revoke or terminate" the transfer and conclude that he had no "interest" in the benefits at the time of his death. We, therefore, hold that the death benefits at issue here were not includable in Tully's gross estate.

I. Section 2038(a)(1):

Defendant argues that Tully transferred an interest in the death benefits at some point prior to his death and kept a section 2038(a)(1) power to "alter, amend, revoke or terminate" the enjoyment of the benefits after the transfer until his death. Plaintiffs counter that there was no "transfer" in the 1959 contract or thereafter because decedent never had any interest in the benefits which he could transfer. Even if a transfer is found, plaintiffs claim Tully did not keep a section 2038(a)(1) "power" after such transfer.

Contrary to plaintiffs' position, Tully did transfer an interest in the death benefits to his wife by executing the 1959 contract. In one of the three death benefit plans at issue in Estate of Bogley v. United States, 514 F.2d 1027, 206 Ct.Cl. 695 (1975), the decedent (an employee, officer, director and 34% shareholder) entered into an enforceable contract with his employer. In consideration of decedent's past and future services, the employer promised to pay decedent's *widow* or the estate two years' salary after his death. We found that where decedent was married at the time of the execution of the contract he " * * * did make a transfer of his interest to his wife during his lifetime by making the contract with [the employer]." *Bogley*, supra, 514 F.2d at 1039, 206 Ct.Cl. at 715. In the instant case, the basic facts are nearly identical. The 1959 agreement looked to Tully's past and future services to T & D for consideration. The benefits here were also payable to the "widow" and decedent was married at the time of the 1959 contract. Tully in substance, if not in form, made a gift of a part of his future earnings to his wife.

However, within the meaning of section 2038(a)(1), Tully did not keep a power to "alter, amend, revoke or terminate" the death benefit transfer after the 1959 contract. There was no express reservation of such power in either the 1959 or 1963 contracts and no indication in the record of any other express agreements in which Tully obtained a section 2038(a)(1) power.

The Government implies that Tully's 50% stock ownership of T & D gave him unfettered power to change the death benefit plan to suit his own tastes. The facts do not bear this out. To the contrary, Tully's every movement could have been blocked by the other 50% shareholder. Tully did not have individual control of T & D and could not by himself, alter the terms of the death benefit, agreement.[46] As stated by the court in Harris

---

46. In effect, defendant asks us to hold that corporate control constitutes a section 2038(a)(1) "power." In United States v. Byrum, 408 U.S. 125, 92 S.Ct. 2382, 33 L.Ed.2d 283 (1972) (Justices White, Bren- nan, and Blackmun dissenting), the Supreme Court rejected the Government's argument that the corporate control could provide a section 2036 right to alter beneficial enjoyment of trusts. The Court spe-

v. United States, 29 Am.Fed.Tax R.2d 1558 (C.D.Cal.1972), section 2038(a)(1) powers must be *demonstrable*, *real*, *apparent* and *evident*, not speculative. *See also* Hinze v. United States, 29 Am.Fed.Tax R.2d 1553 (C.D.Cal.1972). We agree with this test and find Tully did not have a section 2038(a)(1) power to "alter, amend, revoke or terminate" through his 50% stock ownership in T & D at the time of his death.

Moreover, the death benefits are not includable in Tully's gross estate despite the fact that Tully *might* have altered, amended, revoked or terminated them in conjunction with T & D and DiNapoli. A power to "alter, amend, revoke or terminate" expressly exercisable in conjunction with others falls within section 2038(a)(1), but "power" as used in this section does not extend to *powers of persuasion*. If section 2038(a)(1) reached the possibility that Tully might convince T & D and DiNapoli to change the death benefit plan, it would apply to *speculative powers*. Section 2038(a)(1) cannot be so construed.[47] *Harris*, supra; *Hinze*, supra. In addition, if section 2038(a)(1) applies to situations where an employee *might* convince an employer to change a death benefit program, it would sweep all employee death benefit plans into the gross estates of employees. It would always be at least possible for an employee to convince the employer that it would be to their mutual benefit to modify the death benefit plan. In light of the numerous cases where employee death benefit plans similar to the instant plan were held not includable in the employee's gross estate,[48] we find that Congress did not intend the "in conjunction" language of section 2038(a)(1) to extend to the mere possibility of bilateral contract modification. Therefore, merely because Tully might have changed the benefit plan "in conjunction" with T & D and DiNapoli, the death benefits are not forced into Tully's gross estate.

Tully also did not obtain a section 2038(a)(1) "power" from the remote possibility that he could have altered the amount of death benefits payable to his widow by changing his compensation scheme. The death benefits here were to be paid based on decedent's annual salary. From this, defendant reasons that up until the time of his death, Tully could have accepted lesser compensation or terminated his employment in order to alter or revoke the death benefits.[49] In practical terms, we reject this *possibility*.

cifically noted the vagaries and uncertainty which a corporate control test would produce in the estate tax area. Id., at 138, n. 13, 92 S.Ct. 2382.

Since we find that Tully did not have *control* of T & D, we need not reach the equally complex question of whether corporate control might give rise to a section 2038(a)(1) "power."

47. There is no evidence in the record that the 1963 modification resulted from a demonstrable, real, apparent and evident power by Tully to coerce DiNapoli and T & D to effect the change. At best, it appears that the parties were mutually convinced that the clarification was desirable.

48. *See e.g.,* Estate of Kramer v. United States, 406 F.2d 1363, 186 Ct.Cl. 684 (1969);

Hinze, supra; *Harris*, supra; Molter v. United States, 146 F.Supp. 497 (E.D.N.Y. 1956); Estate of Barr v. Commissioner, 40 T.C. 227 (1963).

49. Defendant does not argue that the failure to set a specific dollar amount on the death benefits gave Tully a section 2038(a)(1) "power." Instead it contends this represents a section 2033 "interest" held by decedent until his death. Such position is misplaced. Section 2033 is not a "catch all," but taxes property over which the owner has kept so much control that he has never really transferred it. In this context, the only control that Tully *might* have had over the death benefits by virtue of the failure to set a specific dollar figure was an ability to change or terminate the payments. This is a section 2038(a)(1) "power." Having

This is not a factor which rises to the level of a section 2038(a)(1) "power." An employee might accept lesser compensation or terminate his employment for a myriad of reasons, but to conclude that a motive for such action would be the death benefit plan itself is not only speculative but ridiculous. And we have already made clear that a section 2038(a)(1) "power" cannot be speculative, but must be *demonstrable, real, apparent* and *evident. Harris*, supra; *Hinze*, supra. In addition, modification of Tully's employment contract would have required the cooperation of T & D or a breach by Tully. Neither of these two events constitutes a section 2038(a)(1) "power." Further, it is a common practice to "peg" employee death benefit plans to the employee's salary. To our knowledge, no court has ever held that such practice subjects death benefits to inclusion in the employee's gross estate. On the contrary, in Estate of Whitworth v. Commissioner, 22 CCH Tax Ct.Mem. 177 (1963), the court concluded that although the decedent could have terminated his widow's benefits by leaving his employ or by breaching his employment contract, the death benefits at issue were *not* includable in his estate as a section 2038(a)(1) revocable transfer. Due to the practicalities of death benefit contracts and using the rationale of the *Whitworth* case, we hold that no section 2038(a)(1) power was created by the remote possibility that Tully might have changed the amount of death benefits prior to his death.

Finally, Tully did not retain a section 2038(a)(1) "power" to revoke or terminate the transfer to his wife by virtue of the *possibility* that he could have divorced her. The contract called for T & D to make the death benefit payments to Tully's *widow*. It might be argued that Tully could have divorced his wife to terminate her interest in the death benefits,[50] but again such an argument ignores practicalities, reduces the term "power" to the speculative realm, and is not in accord with prior cases. In reality, a man might divorce his wife, but to assume that he would fight through an entire divorce process merely to alter employee death benefits approaches the absurd. Further, in various cases, death benefits payable to the "widow", Estate of Porter v. Commissioner, 442 F.2d 915 (1st cir. 1971), or "wife", Estate of Kramer v. United States, 406 F.2d 1363, 186 Ct.Cl. 684 (1969), were not thereby held includable in the gross estate.[51] The possibility of divorce in the instant situation is so *de minimis* and so speculative rather than *demonstrative, real, apparent* and *evident* that it cannot rise to the level of a section 2038(a)(1) "power." *Harris*, supra; *Hinze*, supra. Thus the use of "widow" in the death benefit contract did not give Tully a real power to revoke or terminate the death benefit transfer to his wife.

---

once given away the benefits, he could not have obtained any part of the benefits to spend for his own use or any one else's use and, therefore, did not have a section 2033 "interest."

50. Again, the Government fails to make such argument in the section 2038(a)(1) context. Rather it contends that this possibility left Tully with a section 2033 "interest" in the benefits until his death. Since the possibility of divorce might represent

a section 2038(a)(1) "power", we consider it in this context despite defendant's failure so to argue.

51. In *Kramer*, the death benefits were payable to "wife, Carrie Kramer." Using the same argument, since Kramer could have divorced his wife, the Government would *appear* in the instant case to be disputing the *Kramer* section 2038(a)(1) rationale. Yet the Government did not so argue.

In short, in the 1959 contract, Tully transferred certain interests to his wife by obtaining T & D's promise to pay death benefits. While it may be argued that Tully kept a certain *de minimis* association with the death benefit plan, such association never rose to the dignity of a power to "alter, amend, revoke or terminate" the transfer. In *Kramer*, supra, we held that a substantially similar plan did not create section 2038(a)(1) powers. The facts here are not significantly different. Therefore, section 2038(a)(1) does not operate to compel inclusion of the death benefits in decedent's gross estate.

II. Section 2033:

Nor does section 2033 require addition of the benefits to Tully's gross estate. The Government argues that corporate control, "pegging" the benefits to Tully's salary, and naming "widow" as beneficiary constituted section 2033 "interests" kept by Tully until his death. We found above that these facts did not give rise to a section 2038(a)(1) "power." We also determine that they did not create a section 2033 "interest."

Having found that Tully transferred the death benefits to his wife and that he could not reach them for his own use, he could not have kept a section 2033 "interest." The *de minimis* associations Tully may have still had with the benefits are not strong enough to force a conclusion that decedent never transferred his interest in the benefits to his wife.

Defendant would use section 2033 as a "catch all." The simple answer to this is that section 2033 is not a "catch all," * * * but applies to situations where decedent kept so much control over an item of property that in substance he still owns the property. "Interest" as used in section 2033 connotes a stronger control than "power" as used in section 2038(a)(1). If controls over property cannot rise to the dignity of section 2038(a)(1) "powers" they equally cannot create section 2033 "interests." In the instant case, having failed to establish that corporate stock ownership, "pegging" the benefits to Tully's salary and naming the "widow" as beneficiary created section 2038(a)(1) "powers," defendant equally fails to demonstrate that the same facts create section 2033 "interests."

In summary, we have considered an employee plan in which the employee transferred death benefits to his wife, but kept until his death certain tangential associations with the plan. These *de minimis* associations did not rise to the level of section 2038(a)(1) "powers" to "alter, amend, revoke or terminate" the transfer, and did not constitute "interests" sufficient to force the conclusion that section 2033 applies. Therefore, the death benefits at issue here were not includable in Tully's gross estate.

* * *

¶ 21.05 INDIVIDUAL RETIREMENT ARRANGEMENTS (IRAs)

Individual Retirement Arrangements (Individual Retirement Accounts,[52] Retirement Annuities,[53] and Retirement Bonds [54]) are widely used

---

52. § 408(a).   54. § 409.

53. § 408(b).

to provide a combination of income and wealth-transfer tax advantages for individuals who do not derive "earned income" from a trade or business so as to qualify for an HR 10 (Keogh) plan.   The classic example is the individual employee whose employer has not established a pension or profit-sharing plan.   Deductible contributions for an individual may not exceed $2,000 per year or 100 percent of his earned income, whichever is less.[55] But even these modest amounts, augmented by the tax-free accumulation of earnings on the account, mount up over a working lifetime.   And more impressive sums may be in IRAs if they are used for a rollover of lump sum distributions from a qualified plan,[56] to which no dollar limit applies.

IRAs generally offer the same tax advantages as qualified pension and profit-sharing plans for employees.   They allow the individual to deduct currently amounts set aside for his retirement that will not be included in income until withdrawn by him or paid to his beneficiaries after his death. However, the favorable tax computation formulae for certain lump sum distributions under qualified plans [57] may not be elected for IRAs.

¶ 21.06   EMPLOYEE BENEFITS AND INDIVIDUAL RETIREMENT ARRANGEMENTS (IRAs) IN COMMUNITY PROPERTY STATES

The federal tax treatment of employee benefits and Individual Retirement Arrangements (IRAs) in community-property states generally tracks that which is applied in common-law states.[58]   The major problems from an estate-planning perspective are to determine the extent of the non-employee spouse's community interest in employee benefits and to determine whether recognition of such an interest under state law is preempted by federal legislation.   In McCarty v. McCarty,[59] the Supreme Court held that military retired pay may not be treated as a divorcing couple's "quasi-community property" subject to division under California law.   The Court noted that Congress has expressly authorized federal recognition of court-ordered divisions of Civil Service retirement benefits on divorce and has provided, as a matter of federal law, that an ex-spouse is entitled to a pro rata share of Foreign Service retirement benefits.[60]   McCarty, however, relied on considerations peculiarly applicable to military retired pay and may have more limited implications for other kinds of employee benefits than a prior decision, Hisquierdo v. Hisquierdo,[61] in which the Supreme Court held that provisions of the Railroad Retirement Act [62] preempted state community-

---

55.   § 219(b)(1).   For a married individual, the annual dollar limit for an arrangement for himself and his wife may be as much as $2,250.   § 219(c)(1).   Certain divorced or separated individuals, for whom a spousal IRA was established at least 5 years before a decree of divorce or separate maintenance was entered, may deduct contributions not exceeding the lesser of (1) $1,125 or (2) compensation plus alimony includible under § 71(a)(1).   § 219(b)(4).

56.   § 402(a)(5).

57.   See note 13 supra.

58.   See, for example, § 402(e)(4)(G) (lump sum distribution);   § 408(g) (IRAs); Prop. Reg.   § 1.402(e)–2(e)(2);   Reg. § 1.408–1(e).

59.   101 S.Ct. 2728 (1981).

60.   Id. at 2740.

61.   439 U.S. 572, 99 S.Ct. 802, 59 L.Ed.2d 1 (1979).

62.   45 U.S.C. §§ 231 et seq.; § 231m.

property laws, which would otherwise have given an interest in retirement benefits under the Act to the non-employee spouse, and that an award of other property in lieu of that interest also contravened such provisions. Similar language in the Employees' Retirement Income Security Act (ERISA), which governs employee benefits under qualified plans, could be held to have a similar preclusive effect.[63]

Until there is a definitive determination by the Supreme Court, the reasonable assumption is that most state community-property laws will apply in determining rights to such benefits.[64] Most states have used a variation of the "time rule" for division of interests. The result is to give the non-employee spouse an interest proportionate to the years the employee worked for a given employer while he was married compared to his total period of employment.[65] Another method for division of interests is the "contribution rule," where the respective interests are measured by the contributions made by the employee while single and while married.[66] The community interest under either rule may be limited to that earned while living or domiciled in a community-property state while married.[67]

The California courts sometimes treat the non-employee spouse's interest in retirement benefits as subject to termination upon the death of either spouse. This is known as the terminable interest rule and is sometimes referred to as the Benson-Waite doctrine, a name derived from the two cases most responsible for its formation.[68] Its continued viability after In re Marriage of Brown [69] is questionable, as *Brown* repudiated part of the reasoning of *Benson*.[70]

---

63. The Supreme Court specifically reserved this question. 439 U.S. at 590, n.24, 99 S.Ct. at 813, n.24, 59 L.Ed.2d at 76, n.24. Its denial of certiorari in Johns v. Retirement Fund Trust, note 64 infra, is consistent with the view that Hisquierdo should not apply to ERISA. See also W. Reppy, "Learning to Live with *Hisquierdo*," 6 Comm.Prop.J. 5, 18 (Winter 1979).

64. See, e.g., Johns v. Retirement Fund Trust, 85 Cal.App.3d 511, 149 Cal.Rptr. 551 (1978), cert. denied 444 U.S. 1028 (1980).

65. See, for example, In re Marriage of Adams, 64 Cal.App.3d 181, 134 Cal.Rptr. 298 (2d Dist. 1976); Ramsey v. Ramsey, 96 Idaho 672, 535 P.2d 53 (1975); Swope v. Mitchell, 324 So.2d 461, 462–3 (La.App.1975); LeClert v. LeClert, 80 N.M. 235, 453 P.2d 755 (1969); Taggart v. Taggart, 552 S.W.2d 422 (Tex.1977).

66. See, for example, Gettman v. Los Angeles Dept. of Water and Power, 87 Cal.App. 862, 197 P.2d 817 (1948); Sims v. Sims, 358 So.2d 919, 923 n.5 (La.1978); T. L. James & Co. v. Montgomery, 332 So.2d 834 (La.1976), on rehearing at 852 (1976).

67. See, for example, Ramsey v. Ramsey, note 65 supra; Swope v. Mitchell, note 65

supra; Gaulding v. Gaulding, 503 S.W.2d 617 (Tex.Civ.App.1973). See also, Roebuck v. Roebuck, 87 N.M. 96, 529 P.2d 762 (1974).

68. Benson v. City of Los Angeles, 60 Cal.2d 355, 33 Cal.Rptr. 257, 384 P.2d 649 (1963), and Waite v. Waite, 6 Cal.3d 461, 99 Cal.Rptr. 325, 492 P.2d 13 (1972) disapproved on other grounds, In re Marriage of Brown, 15 Cal.3d 838, 126 Cal.Rptr. 633, 544 P.2d 561 (1976).

69. 15 Cal.3d 838, 126 Cal.Rptr. 633, 544 P.2d 561 (1976).

70. 15 Cal.3d at 849 n.11, 126 Cal.Rptr. at 640 n.11, 544 P.2d at 568 n.11. See Reppy, "Community and Separate Interests in Pensions and Social Security Benefits After Marriage of Brown and ERISA." 25 U.C.L.A. L.Rev. 417 (1978). However, the rule was applied in In re Marriage of Andreen, 76 Cal.App.3d 667, 143 Cal.Rptr. 94 (1978). The rule has been much criticized. See, e.g., Comment, "The Community Property Status of the Pension and the Widow's Death Benefits," 37 So. Cal.L.Rev. 594 (1964).

Application of the terminable interest rule means that the non-employee spouse is not entitled to any minimum share of post-death benefits if she is the survivor [71] and cannot dispose of a share if she dies first. [72]   Dissolution of the community by divorce does not terminate the non-employee's interest, but it is limited to the joint lives. [73]   The effect of dissolution of the marriage is to give the spouse an interest as tenant in common in undivided community property [74] unless a division is agreed upon or decreed by the court granting such dissolution.

Two of the more common methods for settlement of community property interests after division has been made are the "when, as, and if" method and the lump-sum (present value) method.   The "when, as, and if" method ties payment of the wife's interest to the husband's receipt or possible receipt of the benefits. [75]   The lump-sum method reduces the wife's interest into a present value amount which is payable either at once or in installments. [76]

The estate and gift tax exclusions for certain employee benefits transferred during life or owned at death also expressly apply to the interest of the non-employee spouse, if the non-employee spouse predeceases the employee. [77]

71. The non-employee spouse does not have a right to share in benefits payable after the employee dies.   In re Marriage of Peterson, 41 Cal.App.3d 642, 115 Cal.Rptr. 184 (1974), disapproved on other grounds, In re Marriage of Brown, note 68 supra.   In In re Marriage of Peterson, the court described the rule as unfair but felt bound by prior holdings.   41 Cal.App.3d at 656, 115 Cal.Rptr. at 194.   An ex-wife has no rights in widow's benefits.   Benson v. City of Los Angeles, note 68 supra.

72. Waite v. Waite, note 68 supra.

73. Waite v. Waite, note 68 supra; Benson v. City of Los Angeles, note 68 supra.

74. In re Marriage of Brown, note 68 supra. See also Yeats v. Estate of Yeats, 90 Wash.2d 201, 580 P.2d 617 (1978).

75. See, e.g., Sims v. Sims, note 66 supra, at 922; Swope v. Mitchell, note 65 supra; LeClert v. LeClert, note 65 supra; Cearley v. Cearley, 544 S.W.2d 661 (Tex.1976); Wilder v. Wilder, 85 Wash.2d 364, 534 P.2d 1355 (1975).

76. See, e.g., Everson v. Everson, 24 Ariz.App. 239, 537 P.2d 624 (1975); Copeland v. Copeland, 91 N.M. 409, 575 P.2d 99 (1978); Freeman v. Freeman, 497 S.W.2d 97 (Tex.Civ.App.1973); DeRevere v. DeRevere, 5 Wash.App. 741, 491 P.2d 249 (1971).

77. § 2039(d) (estate tax); § 2517(c) (gift tax).   See also Rev.Rul. 75–408, 1975–2 CB 366 (only one-half of the value of survivor benefits attributable to community contributions by decedent-employee are included in decedent's gross estate).

*

INDEX

References are to Pages